KAGAN COOPERATIVE LEARNING

Dr. Spencer Kagan
Miguel Kagan

© 2009 **Kagan Publishing**

Kagan Publishing
981 Calle Amanecer
San Clemente, CA 92673
1 (800) 933-2667
Fax: (949) 545-6301
www.KaganOnline.com

ISBN: 978-1-879097-10-0

Table of Contents
At a Glance

Kagan Cooperative Learning • Dr. Spencer Kagan & Miguel Kagan
Kagan Publishing • 1 (800) 933-2667 • www.KaganOnline.com

iii

Table of Contents

▶ Chapter 1

Frequent Questions

▶ Chapter 2

Why Do We Need Cooperative Learning?

▶ Chapter 3

What Does the Research Say?

Chapter 4
Why Does Cooperative Learning Work?

Chapter 5
Seven Keys for Success

Chapter 6
Key 1. Structures

Chapter 7
Key 2. Teams

Kagan Cooperative Learning • Dr. Spencer Kagan & Miguel Kagan
Kagan Publishing • 1 (800) 933-2667 • www.KaganOnline.com

v

Chapter 8
Key 3. Management

Chapter 9
Key 4. Classbuilding

Chapter 10
Key 5. Teambuilding

Chapter 11
Key 6. Social Skills

Kagan Cooperative Learning • Dr. Spencer Kagan & Miguel Kagan
Kagan Publishing • 1 (800) 933-2667 • www.KaganOnline.com

Table of Blacklines

Table of Structures

Kagan Cooperative Learning • Dr. Spencer Kagan & Miguel Kagan
Kagan Publishing • 1 (800) 933-2667 • www.KaganOnline.com

ix

Table of Structures continued

x

Kagan Cooperative Learning • Dr. Spencer Kagan & Miguel Kagan
Kagan Publishing • 1 (800) 933-2667 • www.KaganOnline.com

Kagan Cooperative Learning • Dr. Spencer Kagan & Miguel Kagan
Kagan Publishing • 1 (800) 933-2667 • www.KaganOnline.com

xi

Structure Functions

This dot chart illustrates recommended uses for the structures featured in this book. The structures here represent a subset of the over 200 Kagan Structures.

KEY ★ Highly Recommended • Recommended

Structures	pg.	Classbuilding	Teambuilding	Social Skills	Communication Skills	Decision-Making	Knowledgebuilding	Procedure Learning	Processing Info	Thinking Skills	Presenting Info
			Interpersonal				*Academic*				
AllWrite Consensus	6.33		★	★	★	•	★		•	★	
AllWrite RoundRobin	6.33		★	★	•		★		•	★	
Carousel Feedback	6.25			★	•		•		•	★	•
Fan-N-Pick	6.25		★	★			★	•		★	
Find Someone Who	6.26	★		★			★	•			
Find-the-Fiction	6.26		★	★	•	★	★			★	
Flashcard Game	6.27		•	★			★				
Inside-Outside Circle	6.27	★		★			★		•	★	
Jot Thoughts	6.28		★	★			•		•	★	
Match Mine	6.28		•	★	★		★	•		★	
Mix-Freeze-Group	6.29	★		★			★			•	
Mix-Pair-Share	6.29	★		★	•		•		★	★	
Numbered Heads Together	6.30		•	★	•	•	★	★	★	★	•
One Stray	6.30	•		★			•	•	•	•	★
Pairs Compare	6.31		★	★	•		★			★	
Pass-N-Praise	6.34		•	★	•				•	•	
Poems for Two Voices	6.31			★	•	•	★				•
Quiz-Quiz-Trade	6.32	★		★	•		★	★	•	•	
RallyCoach	6.32			★	•		•	★		•	
RallyRobin	6.33			★	•		★	•	★	★	
RallyTable	6.34			★	•		★	•		★	
RoundRobin	6.33		★	★	•		★	•	★	★	★
RoundTable	6.34		★	★	•		★	•	•	★	
RoundTable Consensus	6.34		★	★	★	•	★	•	★	★	
Showdown	6.35			★			★				
Simultaneous RoundTable	6.34		★	★	•		★	•	•	•	
Spend-A-Buck	6.35			★	•	★				•	
StandUp–HandUp–PairUp	6.36	★		★	•		★	•	★	★	
Stir-the-Class	6.30	★		★	•	•	★	★	★	★	•
Talking Chips	6.36		★	★	★		•			★	
Team Stand-N-Share	6.37			★	•				•		★
Telephone	6.37		•	★	★		★	★		•	•
Think-Write-RoundRobin	6.33		★	★	•		★	★	★	★	
Three-Step Interview	6.38		★	★	★		•	•		★	•
Timed Pair Share	6.38			★	★		•	•	★	★	•
Traveling Heads Together	6.30			★	•	•	★	★	★	★	

Kagan Cooperative Learning • Dr. Spencer Kagan & Miguel Kagan
Kagan Publishing • 1 (800) 933-2667 • www.KaganOnline.com

Table of Cooperative Learning Classic Methods

Jigsaw Designs

Learning Together

Cooperative Investigations

Mastery Designs

Kagan Cooperative Learning • Dr. Spencer Kagan & Miguel Kagan
Kagan Publishing • 1 (800) 933-2667 • www.KaganOnline.com

xiii

Preface

What's New?

Everything! For those of you who have read a prior edition of this book, you will find everything changed. Our last major revision was a few decades ago. Since then, we have learned so much experimenting with and training teachers in cooperative learning that we had to completely revise this book. You will also find new structures and the steps of old structures revised and improved. You will find updated research and rationale.

We have new data showing the power of cooperative learning; we have a new understanding of why cooperative learning works, based on the explosion of new findings about the brain. As teachers, we are the only profession that has as its mission to daily change brains. New discoveries about the brain have direct applications to what we do on a moment-to-moment basis in our classrooms. You will find this new edition replete with Brain Links.

The organization of the book is transformed; no longer are structures nested under domains—we outgrew that as we discovered the structures were far more versatile than we originally thought. Rather, you will find the structures all neatly organized in one place, easy to find and use. To fit in all the new content, we had to drop some of the old. What we dropped is what teachers have not been using; what we added are theory and methods that teachers are finding most useful.

Back in 1980, I was begging schools to give me permission to conduct an experiment: to allow students to work together. Some were gracious enough to say yes. But they were cautious: "Try it in spelling." They knew I couldn't mess up their spelling curriculum too much! In those days, teachers were admonishing students to "Keep your eyes on your own paper." Looking at someone else's paper was considered cheating. Today, we are admonishing students to "Keep your eyes on your partner's paper." Looking at someone else's paper is the first step toward tutoring. Traditional methods set students one against another in competitive battles for the teacher's approval and for the best grades. Cooperative methods set students on the same side, encouraging, tutoring, and liking each other. Social and ethnic relations are transformed while achievement soars.

We are proud to offer the most comprehensive and useful book on cooperative learning ever written. We are certain it will help you take your next steps in making your classroom more engaging, and more successful. Applying the methods in this book, your students will learn more academically, like school and class more, feel more accepted and supported by their peers, acquire essential employability skills for fuller participation in the 21st century work world, and be prepared to live more fulfilling lives. These are boastful claims. But they are offered humbly. We present in this new edition data that backs up those claims and humbles us. We are proud to be part of a process that is transforming education. We thank you for joining us in this process!

Appreciations

In 1980, when I first wrote this appreciation, I expressed thanks to one principal, Roger Skinner, who opened his school to me. As I write now, I am overwhelmed. It is almost thirty years later and many districts have completed multi-year cooperative learning implementation with plans, providing every teacher in the district with training and coaching in a variety of cooperative learning structures. There are teachers, trainers, superintendents, staff developers, teacher training organizations, and publishing companies in many parts of the world helping spread the word about the power of structures. I am no longer a lone psychologist trying to convince schools to try this new thing called cooperative learning; I am part of a worldwide movement. I am no longer begging for permission to research the effects of cooperative learning; we now have teachers, schools, and districts sending us data, telling us remarkable success stories of dramatic gains in academics and social relations, along with dramatic decreases in discipline problems.

Even with our large staff at Kagan Publishing & Professional Development and our expansive team of trainers, we have a hard time keeping up with the demand for trainings, publications, and products. It seems to have gone so quickly. And it went beyond my best dreams!

Attempting to fully express here my appreciation to all those who have contributed to this book, and who are continuing to contribute to this positive transformation of education, would take a book in itself. I beg forgiveness for not writing that book. Instead, I want to mention my gratitude to just a few individuals without whom this book and the cooperative learning movement would be far less. Miguel Kagan, my co-author and son, is an inspiration and a powerhouse. We have bounced ideas off each other, and there is not a page in the book that has not been improved in the process. It is a great and humbling moment when a father can say he trusts his son's judgment more than his own. Miguel was not only the mastermind behind the design of the book, but also took primary responsibility for writing substantial portions. His ideas and drive for excellence are an inspiration. Laurie Kagan, my wife, who heads our professional development, has had a major impact on both my training and on this book. She has a deep understanding of cooperative learning theory, but always has an eye on what will best serve teachers. She has transformed my workshops. As a participant recently remarked, "I saw Spencer fifteen years ago, and now I saw him train today. Laurie, you did a good job with him." Time and again, Laurie has forced me to ask the simple question, "What will best serve teachers?" Time and again in response, I have simplified and refined. As we wrote this book, Laurie's input has caused us to rework it to make the book practical and useful—to better serve teachers.

Not only is this book about teamwork, but it truly required teamwork to make this revision a reality. Miguel Kagan directed the design and the production of the book and cover. Becky Herrington worked tirelessly, managing all aspects of book production including the art, design, and freelance coordination. Erin Kant made the pages come alive with whimsical new illustrations. Celso Rodriguez drew illustrations for a previous version that we just had to keep. The following designers all contributed their creative skills and time to the current version: Di Anne Epperson, Alex Core, and Jeremie Rujanawech. Jill Headon provided editorial assistance with the manuscript and references. Kim Fields copyedited the final version. Cristina Haley created the indices. The cooperative efforts of these fine individuals resulted in a much better book than any of us could have done alone!

We would also like to thank the Kagan team of trainers. They are truly committed ambassadors of cooperation and active engagement who share the Kagan Structures, philosophy, and methods with teachers, schools, and districts around the globe. Speaking of around the globe, we'd also like to thank our international partners who bring Kagan Cooperative Learning to their respective countries by translating our work into their respective languages and/or training educators in their regions: Dook Kopmels and his associates at RPCZ in the Netherlands, Elaine Brownlow and her staff at Hawker Brownlow Education in Australia, Gavin Clowes of Teacher2Teacher in the United Kingdom, Jette Stenlev and Forlag Malling Beck of Denmark, Mike Thiruman of the Singapore Teachers' Union who has coordinated long-term teacher training programs in Singapore, the Önkonet group in Hungary, Timothy Publishing House in Korea, and Edizioni Lavoro in Italy. We are deeply appreciative to the many hosts around the globe too numerous to name who have invited us to share the Kagan approach to teaching and learning.

Thank you for sharing our vision with teachers around the world. Together we work to make the world a more cooperative and harmonious place to live.

▶ **Spencer Kagan**
Director of Kagan Publishing

▶ **Miguel Kagan**
Director of Kagan Publications

Dedication

We dedicate this book to the teachers of the future and their students. Our hope is for those kindergarten students of today who eventually will become teachers. We hope they will experience such a broad range of cooperative learning structures throughout their schooling that when they become teachers and prepare their first lesson, they will no more dream of trying to teach primarily through teacher talk than they would dream of going back to the 20th century.

Frequent Questions

I t has been over twenty-five years since I wrote the first version of this chapter. At that time, overwhelming empirical evidence favoring cooperative learning had been collected and most educators had stopped asking

if cooperative learning worked—they were asking *how* to make cooperative learning work. Nevertheless, many were still skeptical or resistant. The questions educators were posing were of three types: practical, philosophical, and veiled resistance. *Practical*: How often should cooperative learning be used? *Philosophical*: Would the shift to cooperative learning prepare students for a competitive world? *Veiled Resistance*: Won't cooperative learning create management problems?

Admittedly, the shift to cooperative learning is a radical shift, so the intelligent educator should be asking many questions.

Each year our company provides cooperative learning workshops to tens of thousands of teachers in many countries. When we poll our trainers to find which questions are most frequently asked today, remarkably, in various forms many of the same questions are asked today as were asked twenty-five years ago. So there remains the need to respond. In addition to the old questions, however, new questions are being asked. Differentiated Instruction and Multiple Intelligences have emerged, and educators want to know how cooperative learning aligns with those approaches. There is intense pressure to boost test scores, so today some of the most frequently asked questions focus on testing, evaluation, assessment, and grading.

Thus we begin this new edition of *Cooperative Learning* with answers to questions new and old. The questions remain a mix of practical and philosophical concerns, as well as questions springing from resistance to making the radical shift into cooperative learning. Admittedly, the shift to cooperative learning is a radical shift, so the intelligent educator should be asking many questions.

Kagan Cooperative Learning · Dr. Spencer Kagan & Miguel Kagan
Kagan Publishing · 1 (800) 933-2667 · www.KaganOnline.com

1.1

From Traditional to Cooperative Learning

From...		To...
"A good class is a quiet class."	➡	"Learning involves healthy noise."
"Keep your eyes on your paper."	➡	"Help your partner solve it."
"Sit quietly."	➡	"Get up and look what others did."
"Talking is cheating."	➡	"Verbalize to learn."

This chapter is not designed to be read straight through. Rather it was written and organized to help you easily find responses to the questions that interest or concern you. Most responses include references to other chapters that address the issue in greater detail. We hope you find our answers helpful in your ongoing reflection process.

The Questions at a Glance

Boosting Achievement

1. There is pressure to boost achievement. How does cooperative learning align with direct instruction and the need to boost test scores?

2. There is a lot of pressure to cover the curriculum. How can I cover the curriculum if I allow time for student discussions, teambuilding, classbuilding, and even silly sport energizers?

3. In our school, we can only use innovations with a scientific research base. Does cooperative learning have a scientific research base?

Lesson Planning

4. Doesn't preparation of cooperative learning lessons take too long? If I have to plan complex cooperative lessons, I will have to spend my days teaching and my nights planning.

5. Where does cooperative learning fit into my lesson plan?

6. How often should I use cooperative learning?

Management

7. My classroom furniture cannot be rearranged. How can I possibly do cooperative learning?

8. With students all interacting at once, won't noise escalate? Will my class get out of control?

9. Do students sit in teams all class period?

10. What do I do with students who are frequently absent or frequently pulled out?

Grading, Rewards

11. How do we grade group work?

12. Some people advocate elimination of rewards because they erode intrinsic motivation, yet your cooperative learning structures include praising and celebrations. How can this be reconciled?

Difficult Students

13. Some students refuse to work with others or can't work with others. What should I do with them?

14. Some of my students are window watchers. They don't like school. They don't even work alone. How can I get them to work in teams?

The Questions at a Glance (continued)

Different Learners

15 Kindergarten students are egocentric. Can cooperative learning work with kindergarten students?

16 I teach gifted students (or have some gifted students in my class). Is cooperative learning appropriate for gifted students?

17 I have special education students in my regular classroom. What do I do with them during cooperative learning?

Multiple Intelligences, Differentiated Instruction

18 Doesn't frequent use of cooperative learning counter the need for differentiated instruction? If I have some students in my class several grade levels above others, how does it make sense to have them on the same team and doing the same work?

19 Doesn't frequent use of cooperative learning counter multiple intelligences theory? Some students are interpersonal/social; others are not. Shouldn't we teach students using their strengths? Shouldn't we teach different students differently?

Possible Adverse Effects

20 If I call on a student, I hear that student's answer. I can check for understanding and offer correction if necessary. If students are all talking in pairs or teams at once, how can I check for understanding and offer corrective feedback? Won't wrong answers be shared?

21 Are high achievers slowed down because they are stuck working with low achievers? Aren't we just using high achievers to help the low achievers?

22 Don't group projects really mean extra work for some and a free ride for others?

23 Students don't know the curriculum nearly as well as the teacher. Isn't cooperative learning the blind leading the blind?

24 If a group has to make a decision or one presentation, doesn't that mean students have to become conformist or give up their individuality?

25 Aren't cooperative learning structures too rigid? Are they behaviorist manipulations? What about the need for students to construct knowledge?

26 Isn't it wrong to teach using cooperative learning when we must prepare students for a competitive world?

27 What will happen to students who become dependent on cooperative learning when they enter higher education where cooperative learning is not used? Isn't cooperative learning too childish for my high school students? Shouldn't I prepare them for the rigors of the predominantly lecture-based university system?

Why Cooperative Learning? Why Kagan?

28 I use direct instruction and it works very well. Why should I shift to cooperative learning?

29 Aren't there different ways to do cooperative learning? What's so special about Kagan Cooperative Learning?

How Do I Get Started, Convince Others?

30 Since I have been using Kagan Structures, my whole attitude toward teaching has changed. Students are achieving more and liking school more. I used to look forward to retirement, but now I look forward to teaching. Every teacher should know about and use these methods. How can I convince others to use cooperative learning?

31 I have seen the evidence, and I'm committed to trying cooperative learning structures. How do I get started?

Boosting Achievement

1 There is pressure to boost achievement. How does cooperative learning align with direct instruction and the need to boost test scores?

There are two false assumptions embedded in this question! The assumptions among too many educators are 1) we need more direct instruction if we are to boost test scores; and 2) cooperative learning is somehow antithetical to direct instruction.

To correct the misconception that more direct instruction will boost achievement and test scores, we need only look at the hard data. In their summary of various meta-analyses of nearly a thousand research studies, Marzano and associates[1] found dramatic increases in achievement to the extent teachers used cooperative learning. We present and analyze this and other achievement data in *Chapter 3: What Does the Research Say?*

To correct the idea that cooperative learning is antithetical to direct instruction, we need only look at how cooperative learning structures are actually used by experienced teachers. The most frequent use of cooperative learning structures is to have students reflect on or review ideas presented in direct instruction or to practice skills presented in direct instruction. For example, the teacher has used direct instruction to define and give examples of literary techniques. Following the direct instruction, the teacher may have students pair up to do a RallyRobin, taking turns pointing out and naming literary techniques in a poem they are analyzing. Or the teacher may use Sage-N-Scribe or one of the other mastery structures to have students coach each other as they recognize or produce literary techniques. Cooperative learning complements rather than replaces direct instruction; it is used to cement learning that occurs via direct instruction.

When learning depends on expert presentation of information or skills, cooperative learning without direct instruction can be the blind leading the blind. However, direct instruction with no cooperative learning can be information in one ear and out the other!

2 There is a lot of pressure to cover the curriculum. How can I cover the curriculum if I allow time for student discussions, teambuilding, classbuilding, and even silly sport energizers?

If we want to cover as much curriculum as possible, we need to stand in front of our class, talk fast, and allow no interruptions, student questions, or student discussion. We will cover the most curriculum possible that way, but students will understand, enjoy, and retain little.

The goal of covering the curriculum is noble only if it includes teaching with understanding and appreciation. And if we want our students to understand and appreciate our curriculum, we need to stop talking on a regular basis and let them talk. It is through student discourse and the interaction of different ideas that students construct meaning. Often it is through peer tutoring and coaching that skills are cemented.

Actually, we retain a great deal more of what we say than what we hear; there is an inverse relation between teacher talk and student learning!

But there is more to the story. In today's world, information is fast outdated. It is estimated that the half-life of knowledge for a graduating engineer or psychologist is less than five years.[2] That is, half the information they acquire in school will be outdated within five years! The implication of this is profound: If we are to provide our students with skills for success, we must imbue a love of learning. If they are to be successful, our students must become lifelong learners. If they get 100% on our tests, but hate the subject matter and do not leave our class hungry to learn more, we have failed them! The classbuilding, teambuilding, and energizers create a positive class climate conducive to that fundamental goal: creating a love of learning.

The energizers serve another function. Have you ever been in a lecture and found your mind wandering while the presenter kept talking? We can only take in so much before we need to process what has been said. We can only sit so long before we become exhausted from inhibiting our impulses to move. By inclusion of frequent processing time, brain-breaks, and energizers, a good teacher keeps the energy in the room high and minds focused. What is better: 1) Presenting the curriculum 100% of the time with little student energy and enthusiasm and their minds half focused? Or, 2) Presenting the curriculum 80% of the time with high student energy and focused alertness? Retention for content, as well as a love for learning, is increased by teambuilding, classbuilding, frequent brain breaks, and energizers.

3 In our school, we can only use innovations with a scientific research base. Does cooperative learning have a scientific research base?

YES! Cooperative learning has perhaps the strongest empirical research base of any educational innovation. Over 1,000 studies demonstrate the positive effects of cooperative learning on academic achievement, social/emotional development, cognitive development, liking for school and class, as well as a host of other positive outcomes. See *Chapter 3: What Does Research Show?*

Lesson Planning

4 Doesn't preparation of cooperative learning lessons take too long? If I have to plan complex cooperative lessons, I will have to spend my days teaching and my nights preparing.

Years ago, when cooperative learning was in its infancy, we advocated complex cooperative learning lessons. It was basically a replacement model: "Stop doing traditional lessons and do cooperative learning lessons instead." At that time, it made sense to advocate complex cooperative learning lesson designs because we had a strong research base supporting their use. What we discovered, however, is that teachers did not have time to spend their days teaching and their nights rewriting their curriculum. It is time-consuming to create Jigsaw worksheets or prepare complex cooperative learning lessons. Initial enthusiasm waned, and teachers dropped cooperative learning. It was a harsh realization: What was proven by research was of little value because it was not consistently implemented.

It was at that point that I made a radical departure from the way cooperative learning was trained. It was the beginning of Kagan Cooperative Learning. All other trainers persisted in training teachers in complex cooperative learning lessons and ways to design cooperative learning lessons. Instead, I began telling teachers not to do cooperative learning lessons! My pet phrase was, "Don't do cooperative learning lessons; make cooperative learning part of every lesson." Instead of training teachers how to do a two-week Co-op Co-op or a two-day Jigsaw, I began training teachers how to do a two-minute Timed Pair Share or a one-minute RallyRobin. Rather than telling teachers to throw out their traditional lessons, I was giving them ways to make existing lessons more interactive and engaging.

We still believe in the power of complex cooperative learning lessons (see *Chapter 17: Classic Cooperative Learning*) and feel there is an important role for cooperative learning lesson planning (see *Chapter 14: Planning Cooperative Lessons*). Complex, well-designed cooperative learning lessons provide wonderful learning experiences for students that cannot be obtained if we use only the simple structures. But good cooperative learning does not require complex lesson designs, lesson planning, or special preparation of materials. Once a teacher knows and uses the simple structures, every lesson becomes a cooperative learning lesson. An additional benefit of starting with the simple structures is that later, when one does a complex cooperative learning lesson, the simple structures are used as part of those lessons, greatly enhancing outcomes.

the teacher might have students do a RallyCoach to practice and perfect the skill. For closure, the teacher might have students do a Team Statement about what they learned.

Now this sounds like a lot of lesson planning. In fact, the teacher experienced with cooperative learning structures could have done that lesson with little or no lesson planning. The teacher had done Timed Pair Share so often that it was second nature to stop and use it during the set. The teacher knew RallyCoach was a better way to practice and perfect a skill than having students do solo worksheet work. The teacher experienced with the power of a Team Statement naturally gravitated toward that structure for closure. The teacher's lesson little resembled what the lesson would have been prior to learning the structures. Without any lesson planning—by simply using structures—the lesson was transformed into an actively engaging cooperative learning lesson.

What we are describing is not the starting point in the use of structures; it is where we end up. At first, the teacher might just include an occasional Timed Pair Share. Later, more structures are added, and in the process, otherwise mundane lessons become increasingly powerful cooperative learning lessons.

5 **Where does cooperative learning fit into my lesson plan?**

6 **How often should I use cooperative learning?**

Teachers using cooperative learning structures do not redesign their lessons, but their lessons get redesigned! How is that possible? In our approach, we do not emphasize cooperative learning lessons; we make cooperative learning part of every lesson by using structures. For example, during the Set for a lesson, a teacher might use a Timed Pair Share to assess prior knowledge or to have students verbalize what they would like to learn. After some initial input, the teacher might have students do a RallyRobin to review the key points. After modeling a skill,

There is no one answer to this question. As we train teachers in cooperative learning structures, they gradually increase their repertoire of structures. At first, a teacher may use only an occasional RallyRobin or Timed Pair Share. Seeing the benefits of these simple structures— students are more engaged, like class more, retain more—the teacher begins to use them more often. Later, once these structures become part of the teacher's repertoire, the teacher begins adding additional structures. So we recommend staying within your comfort zone, beginning with simple structures and using them only on an occasional basis. As you and your students become more comfortable with the structures, you will want to use more structures and use them more often. Teachers experienced with the structures use them on an average every ten minutes, but sometimes the interaction may be as brief as a one-minute RallyRobin or a half-minute Instant Star.

During demonstration lessons with fixed furniture, often I have found it easiest to first have students form pairs and then for the pairs to pair up to form teams of four, gathering as best they can to face each other. When possible, I try to have students sit in groups of four so all four students have easy access to each other (sitting in a circle, not a line), with no student with her/his back to the front of the room.

Management

7

My classroom furniture cannot be rearranged. How can I possibly do cooperative learning?

8

With students all interacting at once, won't noise escalate? Will my class get out of control?

Teachers can do successful cooperative learning, working around furniture that is bolted to the floor! Probably my most challenging experience in releasing the power of cooperative learning was in India. In some classrooms, there were over seventy students per class in rooms much smaller than what is common in Europe or the USA! There was no space at all for a teacher to move among the students; the classrooms were literally packed with students. Nevertheless, we could form groups of four and do most of the structures. And the students loved it! In labs, we often do cooperative learning by simply having students move their lab stools to gather around ends of lab tables. Many kindergarten teachers take advantage of a rug area. Each student may have her/his carpet patch. Although the students are on the floor, they know who is their face partner and who is their shoulder partner. When there is a will, there is a way! For room arrangement ideas, see *Chapter 8: Management*.

Years ago I worked extensively in Chaparral Middle School in Diamond Bar, California. Chaparral went on to win the coveted Golden Bell Award as a model middle school for the state, in part based on their excellent use of cooperative learning. I mention this here because the classrooms at Chaparral were open—many had walls only shoulder high with openings to other classrooms. So we had to develop ways of doing "quiet cooperative learning." We detail how to deal with noise level in *Chapter 8: Management*. By having students formulate their own plans to use quiet inner voices (a voice that cannot be heard by a neighboring team), reflect on how well they are using inner voices, hold up quiet teams as a model, assign a Quiet Captain for each team, teach students and have them develop silent cheers, and so on, it is possible to have very quiet but enthusiastic cooperative learning.

The issue of control is key to successful cooperative learning. Many teachers fear by allowing students to talk and interact, they might lose control of their classrooms. In cooperative learning, we release a great deal of energy. We are allowing students to do what they most want to do: talk, interact, and move. In the cooperative learning classroom, we must always be able to stop the release of energy and/or direct it in a productive way. That is why we provide a whole chapter on management that deals with noise, questions, and other management issues.

The social skills program associated with cooperative learning also eliminates many management and discipline problems. For example, students learn how to keep on task, appreciate rather than put-down ideas of others that differ from their own, and deal in positive ways with a teammate who is bossy, aggressive, or shy. See *Chapter 11: Social Skills*.

9 Do students sit in teams all class period?

We advocate stable, well-formed teams. When students enter class, they sit with their teammates. There are many advantages to carefully selected, stable teams. See *Chapter 7: Teams*. The advantages include heterogeneous achievement levels maximize tutoring; integrating teams improves race relations; carefully assigning special needs students assures their needs are met; and separating students with behavioral issues minimizes problems. Further, stable heterogeneous teams make classroom management far easier: with a high achiever on each team, the teacher has a student aide for every three students. If students are in stable teams, it is easy to shift between direct instruction, teamwork, and pair work. Without any interruption, at any moment the teacher can say, "Make sure everyone on your team knows...." Also, for pair work, if students are in teams of four it is easy to say, "Turn to your face partner" or "Turn to your shoulder partner." Students in stable teams bond, becoming more supportive of each other; they learn how to learn together. So the answer to this question is yes: We recommend students sit in their teams all class period.

Even with well-established base teams, students often do not sit in teams all class period. We recommend frequent use of classbuilding structures in which students leave their teams to work with classmates. Further, occasional breakouts to learning centers, sponge activity tables, anchor activities, random teams, and interest teams all create additional learning opportunities.

Most teachers who experience Kagan Cooperative Learning immediately understand the power of stable teams and jump right in to rearrange the furniture and carefully assign students to stable, heterogeneous teams from the start. Some teachers take a few weeks to make the transition. They leave students in rows or in whatever seating configuration they are now using, easing into cooperative learning by first doing classbuilding activities and using simple structures— with random pairs, or by having students either turn to the person in the row next to them or having every other student spin around to work with the person behind them.

10 What do I do with students who are frequently absent or frequently pulled out?

When assigning students to teams, we spread around the most frequently absent or pulled-out students so our teams of four generally don't become less than teams of three. Sometimes, though, if many students are pulled out frequently, we form teams of four with two students who frequently leave and two students who stay. When the students leave, the remaining pair teams up with another remaining pair to form a team of four. These and many other options for team formation are covered in *Chapter 7: Teams*.

Cooperative learning gives us several management techniques that help us deal with the frequently absent student. We set a norm that teammates will explain what has been missed to the returning absentee. Further, we set up homework buddies so absent students know who to call to get their assignments or to get help with homework.

Grading, Rewards

11 **How do we grade group work?**

We don't. I have argued repeatedly that cooperative learning is for learning, not for grading.[3,4,5] Although others in the field of cooperative learning have argued that it is legitimate to give individual grades based on group projects, we disagree. For example, David and Roger Johnson[6] advocate the use of group grades based on group projects. They give as a template a course in which 400 of the 1,000 points possible in a course are based on group projects. This to us seems blatantly unfair because two students with exactly the same ability and motivation, one assigned to work with weak teammates and the other who happens to have strong teammates, may receive different course grades. There are many other reasons we feel grades should be based only on individual work. This is not to say that students should not receive feedback on the work they do in groups. Feedback from the teacher, teammates, classmates, and self-evaluation is very productive. But course grades should be a reflection of what a student does, not partially a reflection of what other students do or don't do. See *Chapter 16: Assessment & Grading*.

We don't grade group work! I have argued repeatedly that cooperative learning is for learning, not for grading.

12 **Some people advocate elimination of rewards because they erode intrinsic motivation, yet your cooperative learning structures include praising and celebrations. How can this be reconciled?**

Not all rewards and not all ways of giving rewards erode intrinsic motivation. Imagine for a moment you love scrapbooking. Just as you are proudly completing a page, a friend walks by and says, "That's beautiful." Are you now less motivated to scrapbook? Of course not! You know you scrapbook for the pleasure of it, and the praise did not make scrapbooking less pleasurable—it actually made it more pleasurable and you felt even more competent at scrapbooking. You will eagerly continue to scrapbook not for praise, but because you find scrapbooking intrinsically motivating. On the other hand, if someone hired you, telling you they would pay you $20 for each scrapbook page you completed, and you began making pages under those conditions, after a while you might say to yourself, "I am doing these pages for the money." Your intrinsic motivation would be eroded—you knew you did scrapbook pages for a fee, not for pleasure. If the fee were then taken away, you would be less motivated to scrapbook.

What is the difference in the two scenarios? In the first scenario you received an unexpected intangible reward (praise); in the second scenario you received an expected tangible reward ($20). Research clearly supports different outcomes for those different types of rewards: Whereas expected tangible rewards (tokens, prizes) often erode intrinsic motivation, unexpected, intangible rewards (praise) usually enhance intrinsic motivation. In designing the Kagan

Structures, we have been careful not to offer tangible rewards for doing tasks; we include praise and celebrations, which enhance rather than erode motivation.[7]

We have intentionally designed many of the cooperative learning structures to include praise and celebrations because of the numerous positive benefits they hold for our students and our class. Not only do students feel more competent when they receive positive feedback, we harness powerful social forces when students praise each other and celebrate successes. Think about the last time you were complimented. How did you feel about yourself? How did you feel about the person who gave you the compliment? We boost students' self-esteem and liking for others by including praise and celebrations in our team learning structures. We create a more positive learning environment; students feel more secure, arc more likely to participate, and more willing to take risks. We develop in students the habit of mind of looking for good in others. We transform classroom norms. Instead of being ridiculed as a know-it-all or worse, students are appreciated for their knowledge and skills.

Brain Link

Recent brain research corroborates the argument for inclusion of frequent praise and celebrations in the classroom. James McGaugh,[8] perhaps the world's leading expert in memory research, elaborates the principle of retrograde memory enhancement. What he and his co-workers have established is that emotion is a signal to the brain, "This is worth remembering!" Thus when we teach in ways that generate emotion in our students, our lessons are better remembered. If they praise each other after solving a problem, the solution is better cemented into memory. We deal with the issue of rewards and motivation in depth. See *Chapter 16: Motivation Without Rewards & Competition.*

Difficult Students

13

Some students refuse to work with others or can't work with others. What should I do with them?

There are a host of behaviors students can bring to cooperative learning that create challenges. Some students refuse to work with others, some are rejected, some are hostile, others are bossy, yet others are shy or have special behavioral, cognitive, and/or emotional needs. We dedicate a whole section of the Social Skills chapter to troubleshooting the most frequently encountered social skills problems and offer specific ways to deal with each. See *Chapter 11: Social Skills.*

With regard to the "Refusenik," the student who refuses to work with others, our answer is pretty simple: You cannot make a student cooperate, but you certainly can make it attractive for that student to cooperate. And if you make it attractive enough, sooner or later the reluctant and even the openly obstinate student will eventually join in to work with others. There are many ways you can make cooperation attractive for the reluctant or resistant student. Give a choice between working alone or in groups and provide tasks that can be finished much more quickly and accurately in groups, and couple that with an attractive activity that can be done only when the task is done. Provide encouraging gambits for teammates to use such as, "We could really use your help" or "We really appreciate your contribution." Begin with tasks well within the capacity of the hesitant student. Choose tasks that align with a special interest or ability of the reluctant student.

14

Some of my students are window watchers. They don't like school. They don't even work alone. How can I get them to work in teams?

Different Learners

15

Kindergarten students are egocentric. Can cooperative learning work with kindergarten students?

We are not talking about the student who is hesitant to work with others; we are talking about the student who is hesitant to work! We are in the realm of motivation theory.

Some students are far more motivated to work as an important member of a team than to work alone. Almost all students are motivated by peer approval, and they see performance for the team as a way to gain that approval. This may be why we have quite a few students who blossom when we shift to cooperative learning.

In general, motivation is enhanced as tasks are made more interesting and relevant, and we prefer that approach to using extrinsic rewards to try to bribe students to do meaningless or boring tasks. Thus, if students are not motivated, the first place we look is at the tasks we are asking them to perform. Can assignments be made more developmentally appropriate—not too easy, not too hard? Students respond well to a challenge if they think it is within their capacity and if they see meaning or relevance in the task. If we are trying to motivate students to master a skill, we need also to make sure they see the skill mastery as empowering them to obtain their own goals. Too often we try to teach a skill before sharing the relevance of the skill.

Motivation is enhanced also by use of the structures. The structures are engaging and carefully designed to create equal participation and individual accountability in the context of mutual support. There is a world to be said about motivation theory. See *Chapter 16: Motivation Without Rewards & Competition*.

Early work by Jean Piaget, the famous Swiss psychologist, concluded that students could not take the role of another or experience genuine empathy until well beyond kindergarten. Later work proved students develop earlier; students are quite capable of empathy and of understanding the thoughts and feelings of others well before kindergarten. Many kindergarten teachers use cooperative learning every day with great success. One of our most important missions with our earliest learners is to foster positive socialization. Cooperative learning is an excellent vehicle for that learning because it emphasizes basic social skills (taking turns, expressing appreciation, requesting rather than grabbing) as well as skills necessary for academic success (listening, following directions, staying on task). Many structures are used successfully with early learners. Much of this book can be applied to the kindergarten classroom. We recommend also books that provide management hints and lessons to ensure success with Kagan Cooperative Learning structures at the kindergarten level.[9,10,11]

16

I teach gifted students (or have some gifted students in my class). Is cooperative learning appropriate for gifted students?

If you ask the teachers of gifted students in what areas their students are doing well, there is no question: academics. If you ask them in what areas some gifted students are struggling, there is also a definitive answer: social skills. Many gifted students are excelling academically yet struggling socially.

So when we ask if cooperative learning is appropriate for gifted students, our answer is that for many gifted students cooperative learning is *the most appropriate* approach possible. Why? Gifted students will do well academically no matter which approach to instruction we take. The question is, will they also do well socially? Cooperative learning improves the range of social skills, including listening, taking the perspective of others, leadership, problem solving, conflict resolution, and helping. Acquisition of these social and leadership skills will determine if gifted students will be well-rounded and whether they will assume leadership roles in their work and in their community.

Cooperative learning is also very powerful in developing higher-level thinking skills. One of the most powerful tools we have for developing higher-level thinking is the heterogeneous team. As students with different points of view interact, they challenge each other's assumptions and bring different data to the argument. This pushes each student to a higher-level synthesis than if they worked alone. Those who advocate higher-level thinking converge on the call for cooperative learning.[12]

There is another question that is often asked: Should gifted students be in separate programs, or should they be integrated into regular classrooms? There is a great deal that can be said on both sides of this argument. The question of whether cooperative learning is good for gifted students, though, is a separate question than the question of whether we should have special, separate programs for the gifted. Cooperative learning is important for gifted students whether or not they are in separate programs. Most major recognized special programs for gifted students recognize the need for and include cooperative learning.[13]

17

I have special education students in my regular classroom. What do I do with them during cooperative learning?

Gains for special education students in cooperative learning have been well documented.[14,15] Students not only improve academically, often quite dramatically, they also improve in self-esteem. Another outcome is that the attitudes of other students toward students with special needs improve as well. Special needs students are better liked when they are included as part of a team than when they are just another individual in the class. It is dramatically different for a student to be integrated into a classroom than to be integrated into a team—especially if the teammates have been coached in what to say and do to help the student feel welcomed and to meet special needs.

Multiple Intelligences, Differentiated Instruction

18

Doesn't frequent use of cooperative learning counter the need for differentiated instruction? If I have some students in my class several grade levels above others, how does it make sense to have them on the same team and doing the same work?

As we have moved toward full inclusion and away from tracking, we have moved to greater heterogeneity within our classrooms. This is one of the greatest challenges any teacher faces, and the response has been a great clamoring for differentiated instruction. How do I teach in the Zone of Proximal Development for all my students? Given vastly different achievement levels, how can I make my curriculum developmentally appropriate for every student?

It turns out that almost all Kagan Structures can be adjusted for differentiated instruction. See *Chapter 6: Structures*. For example, while we teach with Quiz-Quiz-Trade, the teacher may color-code the question cards and have students with a green card (low difficulty) trade only with others with green cards; students with orange cards (medium difficulty) trade with others with orange cards; and students with red cards (high difficulty) trade with others with red cards. Or to take another example, during RallyCoach some pairs might be working on one set of problems, and other pairs another set of problems. In fact with 15 pairs in the classroom, there can be as many as 15 levels of differentiation!

19

Doesn't frequent use of cooperative learning counter multiple intelligences theory? Some students are interpersonal/social; others are not. Shouldn't we teach students using their strengths? Shouldn't we teach different students differently?

We believe strongly that we should teach students by matching our instruction to their strengths. Matching is one of the three visions of Multiple Intelligences theory.[16] If matching were our only goal, and we had to teach just one way to match as many students as possible, we would gravitate to cooperative learning. Why?

The preferred learning style of most students is to work cooperatively rather than competitively or individualistically.[17] The cooperative structures do include an interpersonal, social component, but most engage and develop a range of intelligences. By using a variety of structures, we match students' many ways to be smart.

But there is much more to MI theory than matching. The second vision in MI theory is Stretching. That is, we want to develop the non-dominant intelligences of each student. When we teach using any cooperative learning structure, we match the dominant intelligence of some students, but we also provide stretching for others. For example, if we use Draw It! (a structure in which students draw the curriculum concepts), we create a match for students who are strong in the visual/spatial intelligence; but at the same time we provide a stretch for students who are weak in the visual/spatial intelligence. By having all students work part of the time in cooperative teams, we ensure that those students weak in the interpersonal/social intelligence learn interpersonal/social skills. They become better prepared with employability, parenting, and relationship skills. They get a stretch, developing character virtues and aspects of their emotional intelligence.

The third vision of MI theory is Celebrating. By teaching using a wide range of structures that engage the full spectrum of intelligences, students come to appreciate their own unique pattern of intelligence and that of others. A student who has trouble with Logic Line-Ups might excel with Team Word Webbing. As students experience success by using their strengths, they get a boost in self-esteem and are better appreciated by teammates. By teaching with a wide range of structures, we allow students and their teammates to appreciate the unique gifts each person brings to the team.

When we teach using any cooperative learning structure, we match the dominant intelligence of some students, but develop a non-dominant intelligence for others.

Possible Adverse Effects

20

If I call on a student, I hear that student's answer. I can check for understanding and offer correction if necessary. If students are all talking in pairs or teams at once, how can I check for understanding and offer corrective feedback? Won't wrong answers be shared?

In the traditional classroom, the teacher calls on students one at a time and has the luxury of hearing everything students say; the teacher can respond to or correct every misconception that is verbalized. In the cooperative learning classroom, the teacher gives up that luxury. It turns out, however, that by giving up the ability to hear everything, we can offer more rather than less corrective feedback, and we can offer it where it is most needed!

How? In the traditional classroom, the students most likely to have misconceptions are most likely to leave class with their misconceptions uncorrected! Let's take two examples:

> **Example 1:** The teacher asks a question. Students who think they know the answer raise their hands to be called on. They answer and the teacher offers correction if necessary. In this common scenario, who do not raise their hands and do not receive correction? It is the students who are most likely to need help, who are least likely to verbalize their thinking. Thus, those who most need it are least likely to receive corrective feedback!

> **Example 2:** A teacher presents a skill or information, then asks, "Does anyone have any questions?" For fear of embarrassment or for lack of engagement, the students who most need to ask questions are those least likely to ask. Those without understanding or with misconceptions leave class without receiving clarification and without having their misconceptions corrected.

If instead, we have students interacting in pairs and give each partner a minute to verbalize, we can walk around and listen in to a number of pairs, hearing the ideas of a much more representative sample of our class. We hear misconceptions that would never be verbalized in the traditional classroom. We may choose to give corrective feedback in the moment or to the whole class after the pair interaction. In either case, we have a more realistic assessment of the understanding level of our students. Because all students are verbalizing their thinking, not just the high achievers, those most in need of a correction opportunity are most likely to receive the help, either from their partner or from the teacher.

Wrong answers will be shared in teams. Because the answers are verbalized in the cooperative learning classroom, there is a much greater probability of correction, either by a teammate or by the teacher. To increase the probability of correction, we set up a norm within teams: If you ever hear an answer you are not sure is correct, everything stops and you check a resource: another pair, the book, the Internet, and/or the teacher. In cooperative learning, we actually want wrong answers to be shared—only if they are shared can they be corrected!

21 Are high achievers slowed down because they are stuck working with low achievers? Aren't we just using high achievers to help the low achievers?

This question has been around as long as cooperative learning. The answer is no. The empirical evidence offers a clear, unambiguous answer: High achievers do as well or better in cooperative learning classrooms as they do in traditional classrooms. This is counter-intuitive. The high achievers do in fact spend time tutoring lower-achieving students. Why then would they not achieve less? It turns out that doing one more worksheet problem will make little difference in the achievement level of high achievers, but they do benefit from explaining to others. Every teacher knows: as we teach we learn. Further, the high achievers experience heightened motivation to achieve because being a high achiever in a cooperative learning classroom is associated with high status ("He helps our team." "We want her on our team.") rather than the low status and social ostracism that often accompanies high achievement in the traditional classroom ("He is a geek." "She is a brown-noser.")

When we ask, "What do students gain from cooperative learning?" suddenly the benefits for high achievers come into sharp focus. Cooperative learning offers our high achievers the opportunity to develop important social skills, and the full spectrum of their intelligences. As they work in cooperative teams, they learn social skills such as leadership skills, teamwork skills, listening, validating others, respecting points of view different from their own, and conflict resolution skills. As they experience a range of structures that integrate higher-level thinking and activate the full spectrum of intelligences, students acquire skills they wouldn't otherwise. Cooperative learning is enrichment for all students.

When the parent of a high achieving student raises the issue of whether cooperative learning is appropriate for their student, I like to ask, "What would you like your student to do when they grow up?" Almost invariably the response is doctor, lawyer, corporate president, or some other high-paying, high-status job. My follow-up question is, "What do you think is the single best predictor of success in that position?" After they give their answer, I refer to the seminal books, *Emotional Intelligence*[18] and *Social Intelligence*[19] by Daniel Goleman. Goleman has synthesized an enormous amount of data demonstrating that success in the job world, as well as life success, depends more on emotional and social intelligence than on IQ or academic success. Social skills acquired via cooperative learning will determine the job and life success of many of our highest achieving students.

22 Don't group projects really mean extra work for some and a free ride for others?

Group projects are a prescription for an inequitable distribution of the workload. Cooperative projects are not. With group projects, the teacher assigns a task to a group and leaves it to the group to determine how to structure how they will work together. In many groups, some take over, and others contribute little or even nothing. In contrast, cooperative projects are carefully structured. Cooperative projects limit the resources, assign roles, and distribute jobs so everyone is held responsible and accountable for their own contribution. See *Chapter 13: Cooperative Projects & Presentations*.

23 Students don't know the curriculum nearly as well as the teacher. Isn't cooperative learning the blind leading the blind?

If cooperative learning were students working together with no input or direction from the teacher, it would be the blind leading the blind. But that is not cooperative learning; that is unstructured group work coupled with an abdication of responsibility on the part of the teacher. We are very careful to distinguish group work from cooperative learning. Telling students to work together without structuring how they work together almost invariably leads to some students doing the work while others take a free ride. It also leads to off-task behavior, poor production of and dissemination of information, management, and discipline problems. We are very careful to structure how students work together so they remain focused and equitably share the work. Further, we do not leave to chance the presentation of key concepts and information. We strongly believe in the importance of teacher input and modeling. Most often the cooperative learning structures are designed to process and practice information and skills presented and modeled by the teacher.

if some members prefer different locations. There are times a workplace team has to decide on one method to make a product or one set of office procedures, even if some members prefer different methods or different procedures. Through cooperative learning, students learn conflict resolution skills and acquire a give-and-take orientation that is essential for harmonious and productive relations.

This does not mean, however, that students work only in teams. Just as students need to learn to work well with others, they need to learn to work well on their own. Thus, to prepare students fully, the classroom needs a healthy mix of teamwork and independent work. Students need room to fully express their individuality and to create products for which they alone are responsible. Cooperative learning corrects the imbalance present in schooling today by adding collaborative skills to the curriculum.

24 If a group has to make a decision or one presentation, doesn't that mean students have to become conformist or give up their individuality?

Cooperative learning in important ways parallels real life. There are times the family has to decide on a single vacation destination, even

25 Aren't cooperative learning structures too rigid? Are they behaviorist manipulations? What about the need for students to construct knowledge?

Cooperative learning structures are highly structured: they are step-by-step sequences designed to structure the interaction of students with each other and with the curriculum. It is not, however, easy to apply one label to the cooperative learning structures; they encompass a wide range of ways for students to interact. At the behaviorist end of the spectrum are structures like the Flashcard Game—students receive peer praise after each correct answer and the game is structured so students have repeated trials on missed items. At the constructionist end of the spectrum are structures like Team Statements. Through Team Statements, students construct knowledge: First they generate and share their individual definitions of a concept, explore the differences among their concepts, and finally construct one definition that they can all endorse more strongly than their original individual definition. Notice, although Team Statements is highly structured, through the structure students construct their own meaning. Thus it is not possible to lump all cooperative learning structures into one group and apply one label to the group. Some structures help students master high-consensus, right-wrong content; others are designed to promote divergent thinking, encouraging each student to express her/his unique point of view. Some structures are designed to have students acquire knowledge or skills; other structures are designed to have students construct knowledge. Some structures are designed to promote very specific communication skills; other structures are designed to promote positive interaction among teammates across a very wide range of content areas.

Some educators equate constructivist education with unstructured group interaction. If that is your definition of constructivism, then Kagan Structures are not constructivist. We have a different definition of constructivism that aligns with the cognitive construction of knowledge. Construction is an active process of building in the mind new ideas and concepts. Simply spoon-feeding knowledge and giving answers is not construction. To the extent possible, we want students to discover principles themselves. We want them to argue, negotiate, debate—sometimes reaching consensus, and sometimes agreeing to disagree. But that is not to say we simply put a group together and say figure it out yourself. That predictably leads to lack of individual accountability, unequal participation, and less engagement by all students. When we fail to structure the interaction of our students, we violate the principles of effective cooperative learning critical for learning.

For example, let's take a student discussion. Language is among the strongest tools we have for cognitive growth. We ask students the provocative question: "Why do you think the chemicals reacted the way they did?" For one class, we pick one student in the class to answer.

For the second class we don't structure the interaction. We simply say, "Discuss it in your team." For the third class, we use RoundRobin so each teammate takes a turn talking. In class one, there is very little construction of knowledge. In the second class, we're better off because now at least one student in the team is formulating and expressing ideas. However, since the discussion is unstructured, one student may choose to do most or even all the talking. In the third class, everyone must formulate their ideas and express them during the RoundRobin. Students listen to the responses of their teammates. Students may hear multiple perspectives and may be more open to alternative explanations than if they hear a single response. Structuring the discussion helps facilitate the construction of knowledge by every student.

Take another example with hands-on manipulatives, another powerful tool for understanding and growth. Through manipulation of concrete representations of the curriculum, students build an understanding of the nature of the content. But if only one student in class or one student on the team gets his or her hands on the manipulatives, then are we really successful helping all students construct meaning?

As teachers, we want to encourage students to build their own understanding of the curriculum. But that doesn't mean we abdicate our role as facilitators of the construction of knowledge. We are the engineers of students' learning experiences, and our use of structures and the basic principles of cooperative learning are powerful tools to ensure that all students engage in the process of constructing knowledge.

26 Isn't it wrong to teach using cooperative learning when we must prepare students for a competitive world?

If we were advocating exclusive use of cooperative learning, we would leave students very ill prepared. Students need to know how to work independently, and they need to know how to compete. We don't, however, advocate cooperative learning as the only way to teach. We feel cooperative learning should be a big part of the instructional diet, not the whole diet. What we are doing with structures is making it easy to include cooperative learning.

Why is it important to include cooperative learning? Students in cooperative learning classrooms outperform those in individualistic and competitive classrooms. Including cooperative learning is preparation for the real world: Three out of four new jobs include working on a team at least part of the time. In the United States, the two largest studies of employability skills, one by the American Society of Training and Development[20] and one by the Secretary's commission on Achieving Necessary Sills (SCANS)[21], both emphasize the importance of group effectiveness skills (teamwork skills, interpersonal skills, communication skills). For example, the SCANS report concluded:

> *"the emphasis on teamwork in more and more workplaces means that instructional approaches must also emphasize learning collaboratively not just individually. For all types and levels of schooling and training, the field's emerging research findings challenge what we teach and how we teach it."* [22]

We live in an interdependent world in which, somewhat paradoxically, the ability to compete depends on the ability to cooperate. Take a look at today's computer.

In different parts of the world, teams coordinate their efforts with other teams in their own plant to coordinate their efforts with teams in plants across the globe. As we move increasingly into a high-tech global economy, the workplace becomes more complex. No one working alone can compete. The ability to compete depends on the ability to cooperate—to communicate with others, coordinate efforts, resolve conflicts, and create a common vision. If students work only alone and/or only in competition with others, they will not acquire the cooperative skills that will allow them to participate well in the workplace of tomorrow. The traditional classroom in which sharing is defined as cheating is out of sync with the workplace our students will enter.

Employability surveys indicate employers seek one set of skills above all others: The ability to communicate well with and work well with others.[23] See ***Chapter 2: Why Do We Need Cooperative Learning?*** Where will students get those skills if they do not regularly work with others?

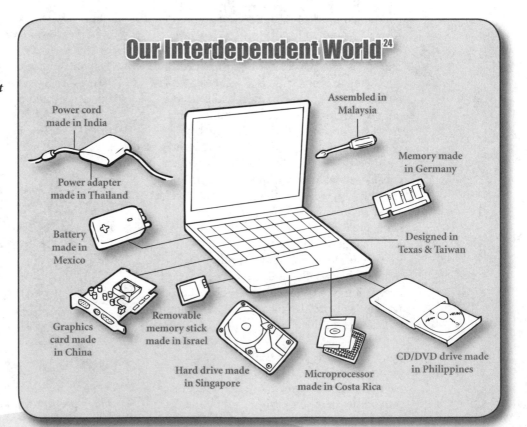

Our Interdependent World[24]

Power cord made in India

Power adapter made in Thailand

Battery made in Mexico

Graphics card made in China

Removable memory stick made in Israel

Hard drive made in Singapore

Assembled in Malaysia

Memory made in Germany

Designed in Texas & Taiwan

CD/DVD drive made in Philippines

Microprocessor made in Costa Rica

27 **What will happen to students who become dependent on cooperative learning when they enter higher education where cooperative learning is not used? Isn't cooperative learning too childish for my high school students? Shouldn't I prepare them for the rigors of the predominantly lecture-based university system?**

For a number of reasons, students coming from classrooms that include cooperative learning are better prepared for higher education, even if the higher education system does not include cooperative learning. First, the research is clear: students taught with cooperative learning achieve more. See *Chapter 3: What Does the Research Say?* Students achieving at a higher level are better able enter and to thrive in the college or university of their choice. Additionally, students who have experienced cooperative learning on a regular basis are more likely to form study groups, and those college and university students who form study groups have a distinct advantage over those who try to go it on their own. Further, it is a fallacy that higher education is entirely lecture-based. Large lecture courses have regularly scheduled discussion sessions. Graduate courses are generally small with a high degree of interaction. Students experienced in cooperative learning are much more likely to participate and benefit from those discussion sessions and graduate courses.

Finally, regular use of cooperative learning creates adaptive habits of mind that better prepare students to excel in a lecture-based system. Let's contrast two classrooms, one in which the teacher lectures without frequent use of cooperative learning and one in which the teacher uses structures to process the lecture. Let's say each teacher will deliver a half-hour of lecture content. The first teacher does not know about the power of stop structures—quick interaction structures, such as Timed Pair Share and RallyRobin, to punctuate lectures. The teacher therefore delivers the half-hour straight. After about ten minutes the minds of some students begin to wander. They cannot hold more than about ten minutes of content in their minds, and the rest of the lecture is like pouring more water into a glass that is already full. Now let's look at what happens in the classroom of the teacher who knows the power of stop structures. After about ten minutes the teacher stops and says to the students, "Do a RallyRobin with your face partner: What were the most important points I just covered?" A minute later the teacher continues the lecture. After another ten minutes the teacher stops and says, "Do a Timed Pair Share with your shoulder partner: To you, what is the most meaningful part of the lecture so far?" After another two minutes the teacher continues the lecture.

What has happened to the students in the two classrooms? In the traditional classroom, students have acquired the habit of tuning out during lectures. In the cooperative classroom, the students have acquired the habit of mind of actively reviewing, evaluating, and processing information as it is presented. This habit of ongoing active cognitive engagement serves students well when they enter a lecture-based university system.

Why Cooperative Learning? Why Kagan?

28 **I use direct instruction and it works very well. Why should I shift to cooperative learning?**

There are many intelligent, well-organized, energetic, humorous teachers who can maintain active cognitive engagement for many students during lengthy direct instruction. They are so good at presenting that their students retain a very high proportion of the content and test well. Even if you are one of those teachers, we recommend you include cooperative learning structures. Why? As we indicated, students need to know how to cooperate if they are to thrive in the job world. Beyond that, there is a very rich, embedded curriculum students acquire when cooperative learning structures are used—a curriculum that cannot be acquired by exclusive use of direct instruction.

When students use Paraphrase Passport, they learn how to listen well and develop their empathy skills. When students do a Team Statement, they learn how to synthesize divergent ideas into a meaningful whole and how to resolve conflicts. When students do Logic Line-Ups, they engage and develop a specific thinking skill in the right hemisphere of their brains. When students do Kinesthetic Symbols, they engage the motor cortex and learn alternative ways to symbolize and remember the content. When students do a StandUp–HandUp–PairUp and then a Timed Pair Share, they learn to, literally, "think on their feet" and acquire diversity skills—listening with respect to different points of view. With each structure we use, new skills are acquired. Any one way to teach is good for some types of learning and not others. The more ways we teach, the more learning opportunities we afford our students.

29

Aren't there different ways to do cooperative learning? What's so special about Kagan Cooperative Learning?

There are many approaches to cooperative learning. See *Chapter 17: Classic Cooperative Learning*. What primarily distinguishes Kagan Cooperative Learning from the other approaches is the emphasis on simple structures that can be used as part of any lesson. As we have indicated, the other approaches to cooperative learning emphasize ways to design cooperative learning lessons. In the Kagan model we say, "Don't do cooperative learning lessons; make cooperative learning part of every lesson."

There are many advantages to this approach. Because the approach relies on simple structures, takes no special materials, no special preparation, and no change in lesson design or lesson content, cooperative learning becomes integrated into every lesson. This is quite in contrast to methods that would have teachers throw out their traditional lessons, design new cooperative learning lessons, and do those lessons on an occasional basis. With the Kagan approach, there is consistent, sustained implementation because teachers and students find the structures easy to use, fun, and successful. Because the Kagan approach is an integrated approach, the structures are used as part of every lesson so students are actively engaged much more of the time, multiplying the benefits of cooperative learning.

How Do I Get Started, Convince Others?

30

Since I have been using Kagan Structures, my whole attitude toward teaching has changed. Students are achieving more and liking school more. I used to look forward to retirement, but now I look forward to teaching. Every teacher should know about and use these methods. How can I convince others to use cooperative learning?

After experiencing the power of Kagan Structures first-hand at our workshops, teachers regularly have a teaching epiphany. They immediately see the power of Kagan Structures. They ask, "Why didn't we learn about this sooner?" or "How can I share Kagan in my school?" Structures make the teaching and learning experience much more fun—not just for students, but for teachers as well. Many teachers who are regularly using structures are appalled to walk by classrooms in which students are all quietly sitting in rows facing forward—some listening to the teacher, but many bored, tuned-out.

It is our experience that you cannot convince teachers of the power of cooperative learning structures by talking about the structures or your positive experiences with the structures. To become convinced, teachers need to experience the structures. It usually does not work to invite reluctant teachers in to see structures at work in your own classroom. The resistant teacher says, "But that would never work with my students."

Thus we have advocated two ways of convincing teachers: 1) have them experience the structures in a workshop and have them derive the rationale from their own experience; and 2) do demonstration lessons in their own classroom, with their own students, working on their own regular academic content. When teachers see how engaged their own students can be, and how well they retain the content because they have processed the content using interactive structures, they become convinced.

The other thing that has been very helpful in melting resistance is to emphasize there is no need to change everything. Ask the resistant teacher to simply try an occasional RallyRobin. Let the teacher and his/her students become comfortable with one new, simple structure. Work within the comfort level of the teacher so resistance melts. It is when we ask more of a teacher than they are comfortable doing that we meet resistance. After all, how difficult is it to stop talking, ask students to find a partner, and have students take turns talking?

31 **I have seen the evidence, and I'm committed to trying cooperative learning structures. How do I get started?**

Actually, you have gotten started! You are reading this book. In this book you will find a world of resources—the theory and the practical strategies to get you started using Kagan

Structures. We recommend you start with very simple structures like RoundRobin, RallyRobin, and Timed Pair Share. Take an easy structure and use it one time. Ask yourself afterwards how it went, and how you could make it go even better. Use that same structure again. Gradually you and your students will become more comfortable with the structure, until it becomes just part of the way you teach. When you are really comfortable with one structure, begin using a second structure. Always stay within your comfort zone and that of your students.

To minimize resistance among your students, when you introduce any new structure, begin with very easy, fun content. For example, if the structure is a RoundRobin, have students do a RoundRobin describing fun things to do after school. If you are a high school math teacher, don't make the first RoundRobin naming prime numbers! If students think they might not succeed, they will avoid failure by putting down the task. "This is stupid" is code for, "I am afraid to fail in front of my peers." It is much less threatening for students to say, "This is a stupid task" than to say, "I am afraid." Make sure the students know they will be successful, and resistance melts.

We recommend you take a Kagan workshop. This may sound like a sales pitch. It is. As much as we have tried to convey the power of structures through writing this book, we know there is no substitute for experiencing the structures and being guided by an expert trainer. It is very difficult to offer to our students what we have not experienced. The structures feel very different from the inside than they look like from the outside, and to really understand what we are offering our students when we use structures, we need to experience them ourselves. The Kagan workshops provide tips and guidance that go beyond anything that can be conveyed in writing.

Get support. Find at least one other teacher who is using the structures so you can share and problem solve together. Make use of the Kagan online discussion board. If you have a question about how to use a structure, want suggestions for content for your class, or if you simply want to share, post your question or idea on Kagan's discussion board.[25] You will receive responses within a day or two. We are here to help you get answers to your questions and to support your work in cooperative learning.

References

[1] Marzano, R., D. Pickering & J. Pollock. *Classroom Instruction that Works. Research-Based Strategies for Increasing Student Achievement.* Alexandria, VA: ASCD, 2001.

[2] Machlup, F. *Knowledge Production and Distribution in the United States.* Princeton, NJ: Princeton University Press, 1962.

[3] Kagan, S. "Group Grades Miss the Mark." *Educational Leadership,* 1995, 52(8): 68–71.

[4] Kagan, S. "Avoiding the Group-Grades Trap." *Learning,* 1996, 24(4): 56–58.

[5] Kagan, S. "Group Grades Miss the Mark." *Cooperative Learning and College Teaching,* 1995, 6(1): 5–8.

[6] Johnson, D. & R. Johnson. *Assessing Students in Groups.* Thousands Oaks, CA: Sage Publications, 2004.

[7] Kagan, S. *In Praise of Praise.* San Clemente, CA: Kagan Publishing, Kagan Online Magazine, Spring 2007. http://www.KaganOnline.com

[8] McGaugh, J. *Memory and Emotion: The Making of Lasting Memories.* New York, NY: Columbia University Press, 2003.

[9] Curran, L. *Lessons for Little Ones: Mathematics.* San Clemente, CA: Kagan Publishing, 1998.

[10] Curran, L. *Lessons for Little Ones: Language Arts.* San Clemente, CA: Kagan Publishing, 2000.

[11] Candler, L. *Cooperative Learning and Wee Science.* San Clemente, CA: Kagan Publishing, 1995.

[12] Davidson, N. & T. Worsham. *Enhancing Thinking Through Cooperative Learning.* New York, NY: Teachers College Press, 1992.

[13] Kagan, S. "Cooperative Leaning and the Gifted: Separating Two Questions." *Cooperative Learning,* 1994, 14(4): 26–28.

[14] Putnam, J. *Cooperative Learning and Strategies for Inclusion: Celebrating Diversity in the Classroom.* Baltimore, MD: Paul H. Brookes Publishing, 1998.

[15] Putnam, J. *Cooperative Learning in Diverse Classrooms.* Saddle River, NJ: Prentice Hall, 1997.

[16] Kagan, S. & M. Kagan. *Multiple Intelligences: The Complete MI Book.* San Clemente, CA: Kagan Publishing, 1998.

[17] Johnson, D. & R. Johnson. "Students' Perceptions of and Preferences for Cooperative and Competitive Learning Experiences." *Perceptual and Motor Skills,* 1979, 42: 989–990.

[18] Goleman, D. *Emotional Intelligence: Why It Can Matter More Than IQ.* New York, NY: Bantam Books, 1995.

[19] Goleman, D. *Social Intelligence: The New Science of Human Relationships.* New York, NY: Bantam Books, 2006.

[20] Carnevale, A., L. Gainer & A. Meltzer. *Workplace Basics: The Essential Skills Employers Want.* San Francisico, CA: Jossey-Bass, 1990.

[21] Secretary's Commission on Achieving Necessary Skills. *What Work Requires of Schools: A SCANS Report for America 2000.* Washington, DC: U.S. Department of Labor, 1991.

[22] Secretary's Commission on Achieving Necessary Skills. *What Work Requires of Schools: A SCANS Report for America 2000.* Washington, DC: U.S. Department of Labor, 1991.

[23] National Association of Colleges and Employers. *Job Outlook 2007: Employers Rate the Importance of Specific Qualities and Skills.* http://www.jobweb.com

[24] Friedman, T. *The World Is Flat: A Brief History of the Globalized World in the Twenty-first Century.* London, England: Allen Lane, 2005.

[25] Discussion Board. San Clemente, CA: Kagan Publishing. http://www.KaganOnline.com

CHAPTER 2

Why Do We Need Cooperative Learning?

I t is not an exaggeration to say we face four major crises in our society that we as educators must address. Each of these crises is best addressed by frequent use of cooperative learning in our classrooms. In this chapter, we will describe and explain the four crises in some depth; in the chapter that follows we will describe the research that supports the claim that cooperative learning provides our best response to each of the crises.

We are facing four interrelated crises in education, each of which is becoming more intense. Cooperative learning provides our best response to these four crises.

The Four Crises

We are facing four interrelated crises in education, each of which is becoming more intense because of changes in economics, urbanization, migration, differential birth rates, culture, socialization, and technology. What are these major challenges? The table below summarizes the four crises.

It may seem overblown, or even a bit apocalyptic, to say we are at the intersection of four intensifying crises in education. Nevertheless, a calm evaluation of the evidence supports the conclusion that education is facing crisis-magnitude challenges. Let's examine the four crises.

The Four Crises

1 The Achievement Crisis
Academic performance in the United States is failing compared to other leading nations.

2 The Achievement Gap Crisis
Academic outcomes are inequitable for different races and socioeconomic classes.

3 The Race Relations Crisis
Racial tensions and discrimination create roadblocks to social harmony and justice.

4 The Social Skills Crisis
Students increasingly lack essential character virtues and social skills.

Kagan Cooperative Learning • Dr. Spencer Kagan & Miguel Kagan
Kagan Publishing • 1 (800) 933-2667 • www.KaganOnline.com

2.1

Crisis 1

Achievement

A Nation At Risk

In 1983, the U.S. Department of Education created a National Commission on Excellence in Eduation tasked with discovering and reporting on the quality of education in America. Their findings were unequivocal:

> **Our nation is at risk.** Our once unchallenged preeminence in commerce, industry, science, and technological innovation is being overtaken by competitors throughout the world. This report is concerned with only one of the many causes and dimensions of the problem, but it is the one that undergirds American prosperity, security, and civility. We report to the American people that while we can take justifiable pride in what our schools and colleges have historically accomplished and contributed to the **United States and the well-being of its people, the educational foundations of our society are presently being eroded by a rising tide of mediocrity that threatens our very future as a nation and a people.** What was unimaginable a generation ago has begun to occur—others are matching and surpassing our educational attainments.

If an unfriendly foreign power had attempted to impose on America the mediocre educational performance that exists today, we might well have viewed it as an act of war. As it stands, we have allowed this to happen to ourselves. We have even squandered the gains in student achievement made in the wake of the Sputnik challenge. Moreover, we have dismantled essential support systems that helped make those gains possible. **We have, in effect, been committing an act of unthinking, unilateral educational disarmament.**[1]

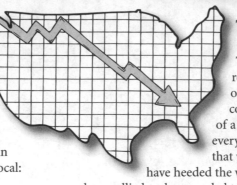

The Rising Tide of Mediocrity

The *A Nation at Risk* report is decades old. Surely we as a country, "inheritors of a past that gives us every reason to believe that we will succeed,"[2] have heeded the warning shots and have rallied and responded to the impending threat. Or have we?

The Trends in International Mathematics and Science Study (TIMMS) is a barometer of how U.S. students compare to students in other countries on math and science tests. Data has been collected in 1995, 1999, 2003, and 2007 (not reported as of this writing). The table below compares U.S. eighth graders to their international peers.

The United States is one of the world's wealthiest nations, among the highest in per capita Gross National Income (GNI).[4] We are presently considered the world's superpower. However, never once have U.S. eighth graders been ranked in the top ten in both math and science, much less first. Countries outperforming the United States academically include Singapore, Hong Kong, Japan, Chinese Taipei, Belgium–Flemish, Netherlands, Estonia, Latvia, Lithuania, Russian Federation, England, Hungary, Malaysia, and Slovak Republic.

How Do Our Students Rank Internationally?[3]

	Mathematics	Science
	U.S. Students 8th Grade International Rank (Score)	
1995	28th (500)	17th (534)
1999	19th (502)	18th (515)
2003	15th (504)	9th (527)

The TIMMS report examines math and science. How about other content areas? The Organization for Economic Cooperation and Development (OECD) conducts international comparisons of the academic achievement of fifteen-year-old students in the twenty-nine OECD countries. In 2000 and 2003, students in the United States scored near the bottom in both math and problem solving, and performed at a mediocre level in reading and science.

Most disturbing of these results is the very low performance of U.S. youth in problem solving. Given the advance of technology and the ever increasing change rate, problem solving is perhaps the most predictive of future success—and that is where the United States scores lowest!

Academic achievement in the United States is lagging behind other advanced and even less-advanced countries. Part of the problem is the achievement gap: We are failing to provide equal educational outcomes for all our students. The achievement gap between the highest and lowest performing students in the United States is among the greatest of all OECD member countries.[6] For example, in problem solving, the average African American and Hispanic American scores were worse than all but two OECD countries. Because minority populations represent a disproportionate share of the lowest-achieving students and are the fastest growing segment of the student population, the overall achievement of the United States compared to other countries will drop further unless we are able to successfully address the achievement gap and obtain more equitable educational outcomes. Crisis 1 is a lack of academic excellence; Crisis 2 is a lack of educational equity. As we will see in *Chapter 3*, Cooperative Learning is a powerful way to address both of these crises.

Crisis 2
Achievement Gap
The Race Achievement Gap

A racial school achievement gap exists in the United States Black, Hispanic, and Native American students score substantially below Euro-American and Asian-American students in all academic content areas at all grades. For example, while 39 percent of White fourth-grade students scored at proficient level or higher in reading, only 12 percent of Black and 14 percent of Hispanics did. Forty-two percent of White fourth graders scored proficient or above in math, compared with just 10 percent of Black and 15 percent of Hispanic students.[7] The graphs show average scores for 13-year-olds in reading and math. They show that every year, for decades, there is a sizeable gap between White students and their Black and Hispanic peers.

The Economic Achievement Gap

The achievement gap is partially a consequence of economic disparities. Black and Hispanic children in general come from poorer families who have less education, fewer educational resources, and often attend more disadvantaged schools. When we compare students of different

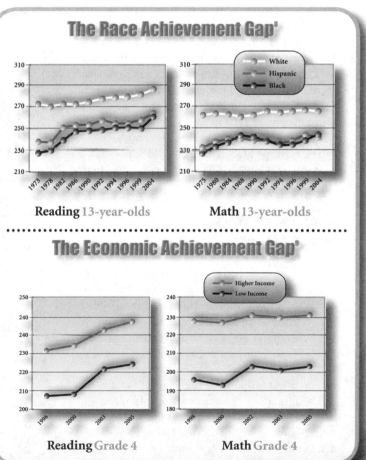

The Race Achievement Gap[8]

White
Hispanic
Black

Reading 13-year-olds   **Math** 13-year-olds

The Economic Achievement Gap[9]

Higher Income
Low Income

Reading Grade 4   **Math** Grade 4

Kagan Cooperative Learning • Dr. Spencer Kagan & Miguel Kagan
Kagan Publishing • 1 (800) 933-2667 • www.KaganOnline.com

2.3

economic classes (free and reduced lunch v. not), we find an achievement gap that goes a long way toward explaining the race achievement gap.

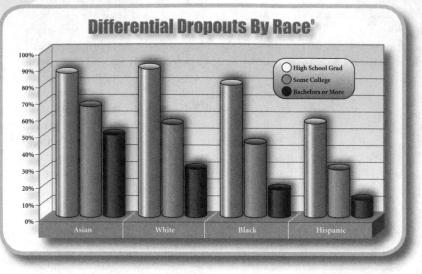

Differential Dropouts By Race[9]

Legend: High School Grad, Some College, Bachelors or More

Categories: Asian, White, Black, Hispanic

Differential Dropouts

In part because of their poor performance and alienation in traditional schools, and in part for social and economic reasons, Black, Hispanic, and Native American students drop out of school earlier and at much higher rates than do Euro-American and Asian-American students. Whereas only 10% of Euro- and Asian-American students fail to graduate from high school, twenty percent of black students and almost half of our Hispanic students drop out. More important for participation in the 21st century economy are rates of college graduation. Only 15% of Black students and 10% of Hispanic students graduate from college.[10]

The Crisis is Worse than it Appears!

The achievement gap graphs show a serious problem, yet still badly underestimate the extent of the crisis. Because there is a differential drop-out rate, beyond middle school it is impossible to get accurate comparison figures for achievement levels. Students who drop out are those who generally score lowest on standardized tests. Without testing dropouts, the achievement of Black and Hispanic students is artificially inflated. Imagine if we tested students at the beginning of year, then again at the end of the year. However, for the second test our lowest achieving students were absent. What would happen to our average scores? Our classroom would appear as if it were performing much

better than reality. When we factor in differential drop-out, the achievement gap problem is substantially worse than it appears.

Less Employment for Dropouts

The importance of education for participation in our modern economy has increased dramatically: In 1970, education was not a prerequisite for employment: The unemployment rate for high school dropouts was 4.6% compared to an unemployment rate of 1.3% for college grads. By 2005, education level had become a major determinant of employability: The unemployment rate for those without a high school diploma was 9.0%, compared to only 2.3% for college grads.[10] Education is becoming increasingly important.

On a Collision Course?

We are moving simultaneously toward a greater need for higher education and a population in which higher education will be less common. We are on a collision course: the need for a more educated workforce is about to bump squarely into the reality of a less educated workforce.

Lower Earnings for Less Education

Inability to hold and educate minority students relegates them to a lower income. Students who drop out of high school earn about one-third as much as those who graduate from college.[11]

Our education system, by failing to successfully close the gap, is perpetuating a class-based society. Minority students are learning less, and thus earning less.

Learning Predicts Earning[11]

Categories: No HS Degree, HS Grad., Some College, Bachelors, Advanced Degree

Crisis 3
Race Relations
Racism Throughout History

The history of our country is rife with examples of racism. From Native American genocide, to slavery, to lynching, to the "separate but inferior" Jim Crow era, to school segregation, to voting disenfranchisement, to exploitation of migrant farm workers—we are yoked with a long standing history of racial inequity and hostility. While we as a society have made great strides forward, most commendably in civil rights, we still have a formidable challenge before us.

Recent Racial Tensions

True integration and equality in our schools, and in society at large, are still unfulfilled promises. In addition to unequal educational attainment and consequently a race-stratified socioeconomic structure, there are more telling signs of racial tension and violence that plague America today. As Hispanic immigration into the United States rises in the new millennium, so too does racial antipathy and hostility. Illegal immigration is a critical political issue dividing our country. Race riots and hate crimes unravel the threads that hold our patchwork quilt together. Gangs, most formed along racial or ethnic lines, are responsible for the majority of delinquent acts by adolescents. Gangs commit the most serious youth violence. The terrorist attacks of September 11 introduced a new type of racial fear and discrimination. If united we stand and divided we fall, then dysfunctional race relations may prove to be the biggest threat to the social fabric of our democratic society.

Mandated Desegregation

Our courts have mandated desegregation, but they have not provided resources or training so that our schools can create integration. We have court-mandated desegregation, but within our classrooms and schools students self-segregate themselves along race lines.

We could write a book, and indeed many have been written, on the abominations of racism in the United States. But that is not our goal here. The point is merely to state a fact: Race relations have been and remain a serious problem for our country; a problem that instead of being ameliorated in schools is oftentimes exacerbated. Case in point: progressive racism.

Progressive School Racism

Schools generally have not adopted effective practices to create positive race relations. The problem of poor race relations among students is progressive. Each school year, students choose fewer friends outside their own ethnic or cultural group.[12] In the early years of elementary school, children play and work easily in mixed-racial groups, but by the end of elementary school, they begin to segregate themselves along race lines. Racial divisions and tensions increase through middle school, culminating in high school students isolated from those in other racial groups. In most high schools, one need only look at cafeteria seating patterns. Blacks at some tables; Whites at others; Hispanics at yet others. Few tables are integrated. Self-segregation and racial tension is the norm among American youth.

Infamous Race Cases

Years of Riots

In Watts in 1965, a California Highway Patrol pulled over a Black motorist who was driving erratically. A mob formed and escalated into a fatal and costly riot. The riot occurred during a decade of heavy rioting across the nation that affected Rochester, New York City, San Francisco, Cleveland, Detroit, Newark, Washington D.C., and Chicago.

White Supremacy

Justice has finally been served on unresolved hate-crimes:

- White supremacist Byron De La Beckwith was convicted in 1994 for the 1963 hate crime and murder of NAACP field secretary Medgar Evers.
- Former KKK imperial wizard Sam Bowers was convicted in 1998 for the 1966 hate crime and firebombing of an NAACP leader.
- Klansmen were convicted in 2001 and 2002 for the hate-crime and first-degree murder during the 1963 Birmingham church firebombing that resulted in the deaths of four Black schoolgirls.

More Rioting

The Los Angeles race riot in 1992 was sparked when a predominantly white jury acquitted four police officers for beating Black motorist Rodney King. The riot resulted in looting, assault, arson, and murder.

The O. J. Verdict

When the O. J. Simpson double-murder trial ended with an acquittal in 1995, 49% of Whites thought the verdict was wrong whereas 10% of Blacks thought the verdict was wrong.

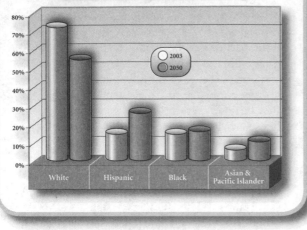

Population Projections[12]
Moving Toward Increased Diversity

○ 2003
● 2050

White | Hispanic | Black | Asian & Pacific Islander

The Need for Diversity Skills

The population of the United States is shifting radically and swiftly. In less than 50 years, we will have reached a remarkable turning point: Hispanics, Blacks, Asians and Pacific Islanders will comprise a majority of the U.S. population! Immigration and differential birth rates insure the trend will continue. Our students will live and work within an increasingly heterogeneous population. The increasing heterogeneity within our population increases the demand for students who can work well with others who have different value systems, customs, motivational systems, learning styles, and ways of thinking. Thus diversity skills are increasingly at a premium in the workplace and in our society as a whole. It is hard to imagine that our students can acquire diversity skills if they do not work some of the time in diverse, heterogeneous cooperative learning teams.

Crisis 4
Social Skills

There is an increasing demand for positive social skills, yet we are becoming morally bankrupt as a nation. In the workplace where teamwork, communication skills, and interpersonal skills reign supreme, we are awakening rudely to the reality that students lack the skills they need to succeed. Violence and aggressive behaviors are supplanting the pro-social values we once took for granted. As we preview this mismatch between needs and reality, we realize we are at peril.

There is an increasing demand for positive social skills, yet we are becoming morally bankrupt as a nation.

To explore the social skills crisis, we first present the increasing demand for social skills. Next, we document the declining supply of social skills and character virtues among our nation's youth. Finally, we explain why today's students lack the basic kindness, politeness, responsibility, and respect that once defined the youth of our country.

Increasing Demand for Social Skills
EQ Outweighs IQ

Emotional intelligence (often dubbed EQ for Emotion Quotient) includes self-awareness, self-control, and self-motivation, as well as empathy and relationship skills. EQ predicts life success better than IQ does.[14] Individuals who possess a high EQ are happier and more successful in their relationships, as well as in their jobs. These skills have been described in depth in different frameworks using different terms, including emotional intelligence, character virtues, interpersonal skills, teamwork skills, leadership skills, employability skills, and life skills. They include traditional values and behaviors like honesty, integrity, respect, kindness, teamwork, responsibility, and citizenship. Increasingly, personal and social skills are no longer being

Embracing Diversity

We must learn to live together as brothers, or we are going to perish together as fools.
—Martin Luther King, Jr.

The wave of the future is not the conquest of the world by a single dogmatic creed but the liberation of the diverse energies of free nations and free men.
—John F. Kennedy

I do not want my house to be walled in on all sides and my windows to be stifled. I want all the cultures of all lands to be blown about my house as freely as possible. But I refuse to be blown off my feet by any.
—Mohandas K. Gandhi

We have become not a melting pot but a beautiful mosaic. Different people, different beliefs, different yearnings, different hopes, different dreams.
—Jimmy Carter

developed at home, nor developed in the traditional schoolplace, and our population is suffering the consequences.

Employability Skills

In large national surveys, employers are asked to rank skills in terms of importance. Good grades do not top their lists. It is not even computer skills that are most in demand. What do employers most seek? The most frequently mentioned skills are ability to work well with others, interpersonal skills, and traditional virtues like honesty, integrity, initiative, and a strong work ethic.[15]

What Employers Seek[15]
In Order of Importance

1. Communication skills (verbal and written)
2. Honesty/integrity
3. Interpersonal skills (relates well to others)
4. Motivation/initiative
5. Strong work ethic
6. Teamwork skills (works well with others)
7. Analytical skills
8. Flexibility/adaptability
9. Computer skills
10. Detail-oriented
11. Leadership skills
12. Organizational skills
13. Self-confidence
14. Friendly/outgoing personality
15. Tactfulness
16. Well-mannered/polite
17. Creativity
18. GPA (3.0 or better)
19. Entrepreneurial skills/risk-taker
20. Sense of humor

The demand on schools by employers to foster interpersonal skills is a world-wide phenomena. Large representative surveys from a number of countries reveal employers state the most important employability skills are ability to work well with others, communication skills, and teamwork skills. For example, the National Training Organizations of England found that skills shortages in ability to work with customers, teamwork skills, and communication skills were greater than shortages in numeracy and literacy.[16] The Conference Board of Canada states the skills most needed to "participate and progress in today's dynamic world of work" are of three types: fundamental skills, personal management skills, and teamwork skills.[17] In the United States, the two largest studies of employability skills, one by the American Society of Training and Development,[18] and one by the Secretary's Commission on Achieving Necessary Skills (SCANS),[19] both emphasize the importance of group effectiveness skills (teamwork skills, interpersonal skills), developmental skills (self-esteem, motivation and goal-setting, career planning), and communication skills. The SCANS report concluded, "the emphasis on teamwork in more and more workplaces means that instructional approaches must also emphasize learning collaboratively not just individually."[20]

Teams in the Workplace[21]

Size of Organization	% with Some Employees in Teams
100–499	71%
500–999	75%
1,000–2,499	84%
2,500–9,999	83%
10,000+	86%
All Sizes	73%

Teams in the Workplace

Teamwork is increasingly the norm; teams are most common in larger organizations, which employ the majority of our graduates.[21] Organizations are turning to teams due to an accelerating change rate and increased interdependence in the workplace, coupled with findings that teams are more efficient and productive.

Change Rate and Increased Interdependence. Employers could once teach an employee a set of skills they would use for years or even for an entire career. Employers today are coping with a fast-paced, competitive, changing environment that puts a premium on innovation, problem solving, and flexibility. This change rate creates greater interdependence. No one person can have all the knowledge and skills. No single person builds a computer. No person working alone can build even a component of a computer. In successful corporations, teams are coordinating their efforts with other teams—and the teams are often located in different countries. Because complexity will continue to increase, we can predict increasing use of teams in the workplace. The traditional classroom, in which students work alone, is out of step with the need to prepare our students for teamwork they will encounter in the work world.

Kagan Cooperative Learning • Dr. Spencer Kagan & Miguel Kagan
Kagan Publishing • 1 (800) 933-2667 • www.KaganOnline.com

2.7

Teams Are More Efficient, Productive.

Teams are simply more successful in the workplace than independent work. Self-directed workplace teams are scoring dramatic improvements in service, efficiency, morale, and profits.[22] *Business Week* recently reported that self-directed work teams are, on average, 30–50% more productive than their conventional counterparts. Organizations attribute major improvements in productivity to the advantages of self-directed work teams.[23]

Self-Directed Workplace Teams Increase Efficiency[22]

▶ **AT&T**
Increased the quality of its operator service by 12 percent.

▶ **Federal Express**
Cut service errors by 13 percent.

▶ **Johnson & Johnson**
Achieved inventory reductions of $6 million.

▶ **Shenandoah Life Insurance**
Cut staffing needs, saving $200,000 per year, while handling a 33 percent greater volume of work.

▶ **3M's Hutchinson Facility**
Increased production gains by 300 percent.

Managers Turning to Teams[23]

A survey of more than 500 organizations offered several reasons why senior line managers chose to revolutionize their approach to work. Results of adopting self-directed work teams include:

- Improved quality, productivity, and service
- Greater flexibility
- Reduced operation costs
- Faster response to technological change
- Fewer, simpler job classifications
- Better response to workers' values
- Increased employee commitment to the organization
- Ability to attract and retain the best people
- A more skilled workforce

Decline of Social Skills and Character Virtues

While forces are converging to increase the demand for character and social skills, our social character is deteriorating. Any teacher who has been in the profession for a couple of decades proclaims that students today are radically different from students a generation ago. An alarming percentage of students have lost the fundamental values of respect, honesty, kindness, and lawfulness. The decline of character and emotional intelligence is not just an impression among those of us who have been educators for a number of years; shocking statistics substantiate the radical transformation of the nation's youth. See boxes, The Decline of Character and Increase in Violence and Aggression.

Why Are Social Skills on the Decline?

How has this come about? Why are we seeing a generation of students who do not share the basic positive social values and behaviors we once took for granted? To understand the radical transformation of social character that has occurred in the last century, we need first to examine economic changes that have driven rapid urbanization, which in turn has had an irreversible impact on family structure and socialization practices.

Urbanization

At the beginning of the last century, about one-third of all employed people were either farmers or farm laborers. Today the proportion is a fraction of 1%! The trend is projected to continue: "Farmers and ranchers" is the job category with the largest numerical projected decrease in employment

The Decline of Character

What do high school students report doing within the last 12 months?[24]

81% lied to a parent about something significant
62% lied to a teacher about something significant
33% copied an Internet document to turn in as a school assignment
60% cheated during a test at school
28% stole something from a store
42% believe that "A person has to lie or cheat sometimes in order to succeed."
yet…
92% state "I am satisfied with my own ethics and character."

Increase in Violence and Aggression

Violent crimes, as defined by the FBI, include murder, forcible rape, robbery, and aggravated assault. The rate of youth arrests for violent crimes quadrupled between 1965 and 1994, from 58 to 231 per 100,000 youth under age 18. The increase has been fairly constant over time.[25]

- In 1950, among youth of 14–17 years, less than one-half of one percent was arrested; by 1990, the figure had climbed to over 13%.[26]
- 160,000 students skip school each day because they fear bullies.[27]
- More than 1 in 3 students report they do not feel safe at school.[28]
- 83% of girls and 60% of boys have been sexually harassed at school—touched, pinched, or grabbed in a sexual way.[29]
- 47% of high school students report they stole from a store in the past 12 months.[30]

projected for the future.[31] The dramatic migration from farm to urban jobs is depicted in the graph, How Do We Work Today? On the farm, everyone worked together for a common goal. Cooperation and helpfulness were not just valued; they were a necessity. Large, extended families were at a premium. Grandparents helped take care of the children, freeing parents for work. Grandparents transmitted traditional norms and values. They modeled caring and kindness. They were there for the children. Children felt secure. There was always a watchful eye.

With mechanization came transformations in the job market. As families moved from the farms to cities, everything changed. Family size shrank, the extended family disappeared, families were no longer part of stable communities, and the two-

How Do We Work Today?[32]

● 1910
○ 2000

(Categories: Professional, Technical, Kindred; Service Workers; Clerical, Kindred; Managers, Officials, Proprietors; Farmers; Farm Laborers)

parent income became the norm. All of these factors combined to create a socialization void. Students were spending an increasing proportion of their time unsupervised.

Urbanization Breeds Violence. Violent crimes (rape, sexual assault, robbery, aggravated assault, and simple assault) and theft against teachers occur about twice as often by urban compared to rural students. Twice as many urban compared to rural teachers (10% v. 5%) are threatened with injury by students.[33] With urbanization, there is a disappearance of traditional positive socialization influences. Rural students were almost always under the watchful eye of an older caregiver or caring member of the community. Urban students are often unsupervised. I am reminded of a story told to me by an older

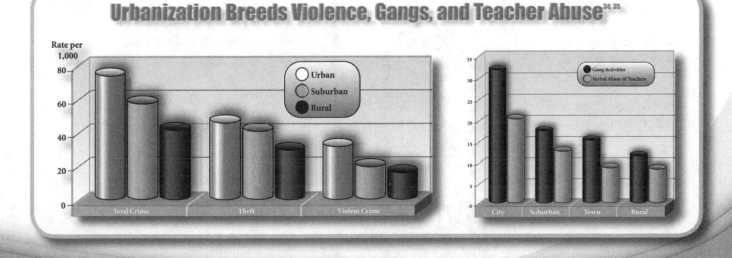

Urbanization Breeds Violence, Gangs, and Teacher Abuse[34,35]

Rate per 1,000

○ Urban
○ Suburban
● Rural

(Categories: Total Crime, Theft, Violent Crime)

● Gang Activities
○ Verbal Abuse of Teachers

(Categories: City, Suburban, Town, Rural)

gentleman in one of my workshops. He grew up in a rural community. One day he and two other boys were fooling around, throwing rocks at an old abandoned mill on the outskirts of town. One of the rocks broke a window. The boys were frightened and ran straight home. By the time he got home, his mother had received two phone calls about the broken window, and one visit. She was waiting for his return!

Family Size

With the exodus from farms, family size shrunk (additional children were more mouths to feed, not more helping hands). Families had to move to seek jobs, and a mobile family had to be a small family. Family size has continued to shrink to this day. As late as 1970, one of every five households had five or more people; by 1995, only one of every 10 households had five or more people.[36] In that same time frame, among families with children, the percentage of families who had four or more children shrank from 18% to 6%.[37] As children have fewer siblings, they have fewer opportunities to learn care-giving skills, cooperation, and conflict resolution skills. They are more likely to become self-centered.

Family Mobility

The longer a family lives in one place, the more the neighbors come to know and care for their children. Most families today do not have time to put down those kinds of roots: Half of the U.S. population changes its residence every five years![38] Over two-thirds of those moves are outside the county. Of the 33 million people in California, half were born in another state and a quarter were born outside the United States! As mobility increases, community and extended family ties decrease. Instead of a daily living presence, grandparents become an occasional phone call at best.

Fewer Domestic Workers

There is another important shift in the employment picture that bears on the decrease in supply of social skills among the nation's youth. At the turn of the century, it was the norm for many families to have a full-time maid to help in the care for and socialization of children.[39] Today it is the exceptional family that can afford a full-time maid.

Part-Time Mothers

As our economy shifted, the full-time care-giving mother became mostly a thing of the past. The year 1970 was the tipping point. In that year, exactly half of school-aged children had a full-time care-giving mother; fathers were the sole bread-earner. Each year after 1970, full-time care-giving mothers became more and more of an exception. By the year 2001, only one in four school-aged children had a mother who was not working outside the home, and 78% of those working, worked full-time.[40] Norms shifted. Traditionally, following a birth, a mother stayed home to become a full-time caregiver. Now most women return to work. In 1976, only 31% of women in the labor force had a child within the last year; by 2004, the percentage had climbed to 55%.[41] In 1950, of married working mothers, only 11% had a child under six years of age; by 1995, the figure was 64%!

Divorce Rate

The number of adults caring for our children shrank more as the divorce rate climbed dramatically. At the turn of the century, divorce was almost unheard of. Even by the middle of the century, most all marriages were for life: Of couples married in the 1940s, only 14% divorced.[43] Today, over 50% of marriages end in divorce.

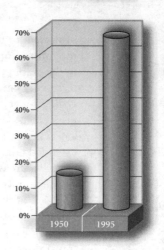

Working Mothers[42]
Working Mothers with Children Under Six

70%
60%
50%
40%
30%
20%
10%
0%
1950   1995

Increasingly, the full-time care-giving mother has become a thing of the past.

Climbing Divorce Rate[43]

60%
50%
50%
40%
30%
20%
10%
0%
1900   1950   2000

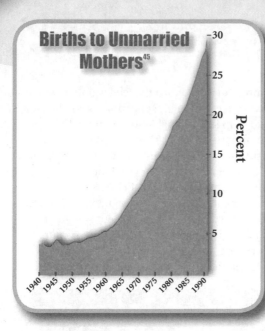

Births to Unmarried Mothers[45]

Never-Married Mothers

Many mothers today are never married. Between 1970 and 1992, the proportion of babies born outside of marriage leaped from 11% to 30%.[44]

The institutions that once secured goodwill are eroding. It is incumbent upon us as educators to guard against the dying of the light.

Single-Parent Families

The consequence of the combination of the climbing divorce rate and climbing rate of never-married mothers has been a radical change in the care-giving landscape for school-aged children. In 1970, 13% of school age children were living with one parent; by the year 2000, the number had climbed to 31%![46] The age of the latchkey child was upon us. For a huge number of children, gone is the day when mother was waiting to welcome them home from school with milk and cookies and a chat about how school went; children come home to an empty house. When their single mother or father do come home, it is a tired parent, who alone has to make the meals, clean the house, and attempt to attend to their child's needs. Further, for many single parents, it is not just one child: 46% of single-mother households contain more than one child.[47] Nearly 60% of children born in 1983, before reaching age 18, will have lived with only one parent.[48]

The Disappearance of Traditional Families[50]

The Traditional Family is Disappearing

If we define the traditional family as a working father, housewife mother, and two or more children, we have to say the traditional family is primarily a thing of the past. In 1955, it was the norm (60%); twenty-five years later, it was uncommon (11%); and by 1985, it was rare (7%).[50] What is most remarkable is the rapidity of this transition.

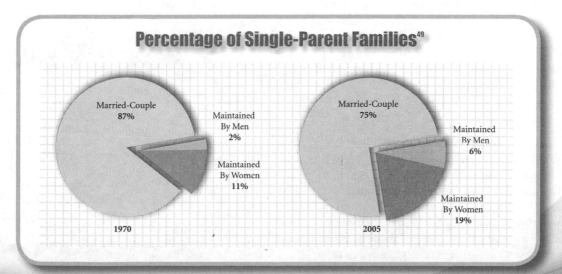

Percentage of Single-Parent Families[49]

1970: Married-Couple 87%, Maintained By Men 2%, Maintained By Women 11%

2005: Married-Couple 75%, Maintained By Men 6%, Maintained By Women 19%

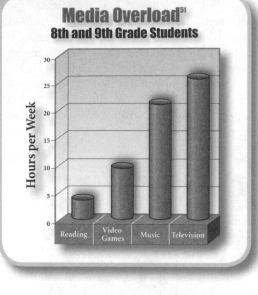

Media Overload[51]
8th and 9th Grade Students

Hours per Week

Reading · Video Games · Music · Television

Negative Media and Peer Influences

Without intending, we have created an abandoned generation. Too frequently, no one is watching our children, modeling what is right, steering them away from what is wrong. In the absence of the traditional family structure, our children are getting their morals and beliefs from the media and peers. All too often, neither are positive alternative socialization agents.

The Prevalence of the Media

As teachers, we would like to think we have more influence on our students than video games, music, and TV. But in terms of sheer hours per week, during a school week, the media wins, hands down. In fact, when we factor in summer months, when there is no school and media time increases, media has about twice as much time per year to socialize our youth than does class time! To answer the question of why today's youth are so much less cooperative than youth of the past, we need to examine the content and influence of media, especially the TV.

Television
Excessive Television Viewing

Children today spend 1,680 minutes a week watching television; they spend 40 minutes a week in meaningful conversation with a parent.[52] Of the total time watching TV and conversing with a parent, 97.7% of the time is spent watching TV and 2.4% of the time is spent in conversation with a parent! On any given Saturday at 10:00 A.M., 60% of all American children are watching television.[53] As family members orient toward the television, they turn away from each other. Opportunities are lost for children to learn valuable social interaction and communication skills. Television is a very poor substitute for caring family interaction. Overall, the TV programs children watch do not promote positive values. Only 10% of children's viewing time is spent watching TV designed for children. The other 90% of the time is spent watching programs designed for adults.[54] And, of course, that content is not designed to develop positive character and a cooperative social orientation.

Buying In

A fortune goes into television advertising, all designed to communicate a fundamental message: If you would like to feel more popular, potent, powerful, or successful, what you need to do is buy something. If you want to feel better about yourself, purchase a product. If you want to be more like this or that popular hero, buy this product. Character is no longer something you forge through meaningful interactions. Apparently, it is something you buy.

Television Violence

The amount of violence on television is alarming and is increasing. The average American child sees 200,000 violent acts on TV by age 18.

In 2002, depictions of violence were 41% more frequent during the 8:00 P.M. family hour, and 134.4% more frequent during the 9:00 P.M. hour than in 1998.[55] Sixty percent of all TV programs contain violence; 4% have an anti-violence theme. When violence does occur, over one-third of the time it goes unpunished.[56] What message are we giving our youth?

Is TV Violent?[58, 59]

- By the end of grade school, average U.S. child views: 8,000 TV murders 100,000 violent acts

- During 1980s, nightly TV violence tripled

- Average day of TV contains scenes with violent acts:

Assaults without guns	389	Pushing, dragging	272
Gunplay	362	Threat with weapon	262
Isolated punches	273		

There is now enough data to definitively conclude that viewing violence on television increases the likelihood that a child will be aggressive or violent.

> Well over 1,000 studies… point overwhelmingly to a causal connection between media violence and aggressive behavior in some children. The conclusion of the public health community, based on over 30 years of research, is that viewing entertainment violence can lead to increases in aggressive attitudes, values, and behavior, particularly in children.[57]

TV Time is Wasted Time

Sitting and watching a television program often is dead time. We "zone out." Our minds go to rest. "Watching television is neurologically analogous to staring at a blank wall."[60] Television time is passive time, often wasted time. It is quite in contrast to how we use our minds during social interaction, puzzle solving, interacting with nature, sports, creative hobbies, or play. As children spend more time watching television, they spend less time in active pursuits. The result: less physical, cognitive, and social development.

Video Games

The industry that started with Pong in 1972 has become a multi-billion dollar worldwide industry. Seventy-nine percent of all American children now play computer or video games on a regular basis. Eighty-four percent of all teens, and 92% of teenage boys, play regularly.[61] Children between the ages of seven and seventeen play for an average of eight hours a week. Many of the games on the market are appropriate for young players; they are fun and provide practice in problem solving, fine motor skills, logic, and strategizing.

Video games, however, like television compete for time and more often than not promote aggressive, anti-social behaviors. The more time spent playing electronic games, the lower the school performance; teens that play violent games do worse in school than teens who don't.[62] Children report their favorite video games are violent games.[63] Eighty-nine percent report their parents never limit time spent playing video games.[64]

Violent Video Games[66]

Based on 35 research studies, we know violent video games result in more violence and less helping.

- **Aggressive Behavior:** High video-game violence is definitely associated with heightened aggression.

- **Prosocial Behavior:** Violent video games cause at least a temporary decrease in prosocial behaviors (helping).

- **Aggressive Cognition:** Violent video games increased aggressive thoughts.

Violent Video Games Cause Aggression

The unsupervised generation plays violent games without parental supervision or knowledge. "Only 2% say their parents routinely check ratings. Only 1% report their parents have ever prevented them from buying games because of the ratings. Eighteen percent of boys report their parents would be upset if they knew what games they were playing."[65]

Violent games result in more arguments and fights, and less caring and helping behavior. A meta-analysis of the results of playing violent video games involved 35 research studies and 3,033 participants.[66] Results are summarized in the box, Violent Video Games.

Music Videos and Lyrics

MTV is very popular with today's youth and contains a heavy dose of violent rap videos. Watching violent music videos increases aggression: researchers were able to reduce aggressive behavior in an inpatient ward by simply removing MTV.[67] Males randomly assigned to view violent rap music videos became more accepting of the use of violence in dealing with interpersonal problems.[68] Males and females exposed to violent rap music videos became more accepting of teen dating violence.[69]

Today's youth is tuned in to music a remarkable amount of the time. The iPod has replaced the more cumbersome boom box. The result is not only to isolate individuals more, but also to make music more accessible any place, any time. And what are students listening to? Popular lyrics often promote antisocial values. Five studies demonstrate that listening to violent lyrics increases aggressive thoughts and hostile feelings, which in the short-run can prime individuals for aggressive action and in the long-run can foster the development of an aggressive personality.[70]

> "Music is the shorthand of emotion."
> —Leo Tolstoy

What Happens When Students Can't Fill the Void?

The need to feel cared for is necessary for survival. Primates and human infants that are fed but not cuddled wither and die. Students who are outcasts turn violent—toward others or toward themselves. A common thread among students who commit violent acts at school is that their schoolmates have rejected them. A common thread among students who commit suicide is that they do not feel included, cared for, or loved. An indirect measure of the socialization void is the suicide rate among school-aged students. From 1979 to 1998, the suicide rate among adolescents 10 to 14 years of age increased over 100%. More teenagers die from suicide than from cancer, heart disease, AIDS, birth defects, stroke, pneumonia, influenza, and chronic lung disease combined.[71] Students need to belong. Students need to fit in. The traditional classroom structure premised on competition and individualism does little to foster inclusion and belonging, whereas students in cooperative learning are valued team members.

Peer Influences

Needing to belong, but often finding themselves unsupervised by older family members, students turn to each other. Whereas students once developed their values primarily within the family context, today they develop their values within their peer groups. To the average student today, it is more important whether their peers will approve of their behavior than if their parents approve.

In the extreme case, the gang becomes the substitute family. Among gang members, the term almost universally used to refer to the gang leader is "father." A robust finding of gang literature is that students join gains to belong. Comradeship, belonging, and protection are among the key attractions to gangs. Unsupervised and undirected peers hardly offer the type of guidance and modeling necessary for pro-social development. Children, especially those with anti-social values, cannot successfully "bring each other up." Peer norms evolve to fill the short-run needs of students; they are not tempered by values forged by long-run life experiences. As we will see in *Chapter 3*, cooperative learning represents our most powerful antidote to the myriad forces that have combined to erode the positive social orientation of our nation's youth.

In Sum: Why are Social Skills on the Decline?

A variety of forces have combined to create a socialization void. Students are reared differently today than throughout history and across cultures—they no longer spend most of their time under the watchful eye of a caring, concerned elder:

- Parents work at a distance
- Grandparents live at a distance
- Single parents are busy and tired
- There are fewer older siblings
- Neighbors do not know them
- Community members feel no responsibility to give guidance

No one is consistently providing correction opportunities, helping children forge positive values and virtues. But students need a value system—rights and wrongs to guide their behavior. Lacking the traditional sources of guidance, today's youth is overly influenced by commercial pop culture and succumbs to peer pressures. Discipline and virtue are replaced by immediate gratification, lack of impulse control, competition, and aggression.

Additional Support for Cooperative Learning

Although we have placed our emphasis in this chapter on four crises, there are many additional possible responses to: "Why do our students need cooperative learning?"

1 The change rate is accelerating. Lifelong learning is required to stay on top of the fast-paced workplace. Students taught with cooperative learning have a more enjoyable learning experience and are more motivated to continue learning beyond school, especially from and with others.

2 People are living longer. Thus many of our students will have the responsibility for caring for elders. Students taught with cooperative learning become more helpful, caring and better prepared to serve our aging population.

3 To be successful in life, to persist in the face of challenge, one needs a high self-esteem. Students taught with cooperative learning have a higher self-esteem.

4 Learning is soon forgotten if it is not personally relevant and meaningful. Students taught with cooperative learning construct meaning and make learning more relevant.

5 Increasingly employers are using teams in the workplace. Students taught with cooperative learning are more prepared for the workplace.

6 Many of our classrooms struggle with discipline problems. Students taught with cooperative learning are less disruptive and spend more time on task.

7 Students today are accustomed to a very high stimulus level. A teacher's lecture alone cannot compete with the stimulus provided by MTV, DVDs, iPods, and video games. Students taught with cooperative learning are far more active; their classroom is far more stimulating than a teacher-centered classroom. Thus cooperative learning is a good match for the needs of today's students.

8 Our students need experienced teachers who are motivated to teach. Stress level is high and retention rates are low among today's teachers. Teachers using cooperative learning find teaching less stressful and find renewed desire and energy to teach. Many report they were facing burnout until they discovered cooperative learning and now look forward to, and take joy in, teaching.

Chapter Summary

We are facing severe, intensifying crises in education. If we do not change, we will be less able to compete in the new global economy. Without positive change, more of the population will be relegated to lower achievement or dropout out the educational system. We will be faced with a more polarized rather than pluralistic society. Without change, we face a breakdown in race relations, both in our classrooms and in the society as a whole. Students will be unprepared with the social skills and teamwork skills necessary to successfully participate in the work world of the 21st century.

We can allow social character to evolve in ways discrepant with our projected needs, or, as educators, we can have a direct positive impact, changing our teaching practices in ways that prepare our students for the interdependent world they face. The question is not whether schools will impact on social development, but what direction that impact will take. At present, schools contribute heavily toward socializing our future generation toward a less caring and more competitive social orientation. As educators, we can make a different choice. We can restructure our classrooms so that students experience situations in which it is adaptive to help. Students need a diet that includes cooperation, not just competition and isolation.

As educators, we have not taken responsibility for the socialization we are providing for our students. Today's students work primarily in isolation or in competition, contributing to the socialization void. Competitive and individualistic classroom structures, at present, remain an unquestioned given. But in fact, they are not a given; they are something we create each day. And as we do so, we create negative race relations, poor achievement (especially for non-white students) and a social character ill-equipped to meet the demands of an increasingly interdependent social and economic world.

As we will see in the next chapter, frequent inclusion of cooperative learning is a responsible response to each of the four major educational crises we face. We need to include cooperative learning experiences in our classrooms because many traditional family socialization practices are now absent, so students come to school without an established caring and cooperative social orientation.

Additionally, we need cooperative learning if we are to preserve democracy. Exclusive use of autocratic, teacher-dominated classroom structures leaves students unprepared for participation in a democratic society. Democracy is not nurtured by a system that fosters racial cleavages, educates only an elite group, models autocratic decision making, and expects passive obedience among pupils.

Cooperative, interdependent educational experiences in our classrooms are necessary if we hope to make possible the democratic ideal of informed and equal participation. Cooperative learning is necessary if we hope to maintain traditional values, including respect, kindness, and the ability to enter and maintain positive social relations.

Chapter Questions

▶ Questions for Review

1. What are the four major crises education in America faces?
2. How does the United States compare academically to other countries?
3. How would you define the achievement gap?
4. What is meant by progressive racism in school?
5. What factors have lead to the "abandoned generation"?

▶ Questions for Thinking and Discussion

1. Are the problems presented in this chapter exaggerated to push an agenda, or do we really face crisis-magnitude challenges?
2. Of the four challenges, which do you think is most pressing to address and why?
3. If you look into your crystal ball, do you see conditions getting better or worse in the next 5 years? 10 years? 50 years?
4. What is another argument you could make that favors the widespread implementation of cooperative learning in schools?
5. Pick one crisis and describe ways cooperative learning could abate the problem.

References

[1] The National Commission on Excellence in Education. *A Nation at Risk: The Imperative for Educational Reform.* Washington, DC: U.S. Government Printing Office, 1983.

[2] The National Commission on Excellence in Education. *A Nation at Risk: The Imperative for Educational Reform.* Washington, DC: U.S. Government Printing Office, 1983.

[3] Gonzales, P., J. Guzmán, L. Partelow, E. Pahlke, L. Jocelyn, D. Kastberg & T. Williams. *Highlights From the Trends in International Mathematics and Science Study (TIMSS) 2003 (NCES 2005-005).* Washington, DC: U.S. Department of Education, National Center for Education Statistics, 2004.

[4] The World Bank. *World Development Indicators 2006.* Washington, DC: The World Bank Group, 2006. http://www.worldbank.org

[5] Organization for Economic Cooperation and Development. *Education at a Glance 2007: OCED Indicators.* Paris, France: Organisation for Economic Cooperation and Development, 2007. http://www.oecd.org/dataoecd/4/55/39313286.pdf

[6] Kirsch, I., H. Braun, K. Yamamoto & A. Sum. *America's Perfect Storm: Three Forces Changing Our Nation's Future.* Princeton, NJ: Educational Testing Service, 2007.

[7] U.S. Department of Education, Institute of Education Sciences, National Center for Education Statistics. *National Assessment of Educational Progress.* Washington, DC: U.S. Department of Education, 2003.

[8] U.S. Department of Education, Institute of Education Sciences, National Center for Education Statistics. *National Assessment of Educational Progress.* Washington, DC: U.S. Department of Education, 2003.

[9] Stoops, N. *Educational Attainment in the United States: 2003.* Washington, DC: Current Population Reports, U.S. Census Bureau, 2004. http://www.census.gov/prod/2004pubs/p20-550.pdf

[10] U.S. Department of Labor, Bureau of Labor Statistics. *Charting the U.S. Labor Market in 2005.* Washington DC: U. S. Department of Labor, 2005. http://www.bls.gov/cps/labor2005/home.htm

[11] U.S. Census Bureau. *Current Population Survey, Annual Social and Economic Supplement, 2003.* Washington DC: U. S. Consensus Bureau, 2003.

[12] Kagan, S., G. Zahn, K. Widaman, J. Schwarzwald & G. Tyrrell. "Classroom Structural Bias: Impact of Cooperative and Competitive Classroom Structures on Cooperative and Competitive Individuals and Groups." In R. Slavin, S. Sharan, S. Kagan, R. Hertz-Lazarowitz, C. Webb & R. Schmuck (eds.) *Learning to Cooperate, Cooperating to Learn.* New York, NY: Plenum, 1985.

[13] Day, J. *National Population Projections.* U.S. Census Bureau, Population Division and Housing and Household Economic Statistics Division. Washington DC: U. S. Consensus Bureau, 2001. http://www.census.gov/population/www/pop-profile/natproj.html

[14] Goleman, D. *Emotional Intelligence.* New York, NY: Bantam Books, 1995.

[15] National Association of Colleges and Employees. *Job Outlook 2004.* Bethlehem, PA: National Association of Colleges and Employees, 2004. www.naceweb.org

[16] NTO National Council. *NTO National Council Skills Survey, 1999.* London: Learning Skills Council, 1999. http://lsc.gov.uk

[17] Conference Board of Canada. *Employability Skills 2000+.* Ottawa, Ontario: Conference Board of Canada, 2000. http://www.conferenceboard.ca/education/learning-tools/employablility-skills.htm

[18] Carnevale, A., L. Gainer & A. Meltzer. *Workplace Basics: The Essential Skills Employers Want.* San Francisico, CA: Jossey-Bass, 1990.

19 Secretary's Commission on Achieving Necessary Skills. *What Work Requires of Schools: A SCANS Report for America 2000.* Washington, DC: U.S. Department of Labor, 1991.

20 Secretary's Commission on Achieving Necessary Skills. *What Work Requires of Schools: A SCANS Report for America 2000.* Washington, DC: U.S. Department of Labor, 1991.

21 Based on 1,194 responses. *Training Magazine.* October, 1994.

22 The HR Management Toolkit. *Volunteer Burnaby and the Self-Directed Work Team Model.* Ottawa, Ontario: HR Council for the Voluntary & Non-profit Sector, 2002. http://www.hrcouncil.ca

23 The HR Management Toolkit. *Volunteer Burnaby and the Self-Directed Work Team Model.* Ottawa, Ontario: HR Council for the Voluntary & Non-profit Sector, 2002. http://www.hrcouncil.ca

24 Josephson Institute of Ethics. *2006 Josephson Institute Report Card on the Ethics of American Youth: Part One—Integrity.* Los Angeles, CA: Josephson Institute of Ethics, 2006. http://www.josephsoninstitute.org

25 U.S. Department of Health and Human Services, Office of the Assistant Secretary for Planning and Evaluation. *Trends in the Well-Being of America's Children & Youth, 1997 Edition.* Washington, DC: U.S. Department of Health and Human Services, 1997. http://aspe.hhs.gov/hsp/97trends/sd1-6.htm

26 U.S. Department of Education, Office of Educational Research and Improvement. *Youth Indicators 1993: Trends in Well Being of American Youth.* Washington, DC: U.S. Department of Education, 1993.

27 Peterson, K. *"When School Hurts: Continued Violence has Schools, States Taking a Hard Look at Bullying."* USA Today, April 10, 2001, D06.

28 Josephson Institute of Ethics. *2001 Report Card on the Ethics of American Youth.* Los Angeles, CA: Josephson Institute of Ethics, 2001.

29 *American Educational Research Association Journal.* Washington, DC: American Educational Research Association, 1996.

30 Josephson Institute of Ethics. *1998 Report Card on the Ethics of American Youth.* Los Angeles, CA: Josephson Institute of Ethics, 1998. http://www.josephsoninstitute.org/98-Survey/98survey.htm

31 U.S. Bureau of Labor Statistics. "Tomorrow's Jobs." *Occupational Outlook Handbook.* Washington, DC: U.S. Bureau of Labor Statistics, 2006. http://www.bls.gov/oco/pdf/oco2003.pdf

32 Wyatt, I. & D. Hecker. "Occupational Changes During the 20th Century." *Monthly Labor Review.* Washington, DC: U.S. Bureau of Labor Statistics, 2006, 35–57. http://www.bls.gov/opub/mlr/2006/03/art3full.pdf

33 Dinkes, R., E. Cataldi, G. Kena & K. Baum. *Indicators of School Crime and Safety: 2006.* Washington, DC: U.S. Departments of Education and Justice. Publication No. NCES 2007–003/NCJ 214262, 2007. http://nces.ed.gov/pubs2007/2007003.pdf

34 DeVoe, J., K. Peter, P. Kaufman, S. Ruddy, A. Miller, M. Planty, T. Snyder & M. Rand. *Indicators of School Crime and Safety: 2003.* Washington, DC: U.S. Departments of Education and Justice. Publication No. NCES 2004–004/NCJ 201257, 2004. http://nces.ed.gov/pubs2004/2004004.pdf

35 DeVoe, J., K. Peter, P. Kaufman, S. Ruddy, A. Miller, M. Planty, T. Snyder & M. Rand. *Indicators of School Crime and Safety: 2003.* Washington, DC: U.S. Departments of Education and Justice. Publication No. NCES 2004–004/NCJ 201257. http://nces.ed.gov/pubs2004/2004004.pdf

36 Bryson, K. *Family Composition Changing, Census Report Shows.* Washington, DC: United States Department of Commerce News, U.S. Census Bureau, 1996. http://www.census.gov/Press-Release/cb96-195.html

37 U.S. Department of Health and Human Services, Office of the Assistant Secretary for Planning and Evaluation. *Trends in the Well-Being of America's Children & Youth, 1997 Edition.* Washington, DC: U.S. Department of Health and Human Services, 1997. http://aspe.hhs.gov/hsp/97trends/sd1-6.htm

38 Berkner, B. & C. Faber. *United States Census 2000. Geographical Mobility 1995–2000.* U.S. Department of Commerce, 2003.

39 Wyatt, I. & D. Hecker. "Occupational Changes During the 20th Century." *Monthly Labor Review.* Washington, DC: U.S. Bureau of Labor Statistics, 2006, 35–57. http://www.bls.gov/opub/mlr/2006/03/art3full.pdf

40 Maternal and Child Health Bureau. *Child Health USA 2002: Population Characteristics.* Washington, DC: U.S. Department of Health and Human Services, 2002. http://mchb.hrsa.gov/chusa02/main_pages/page_14.htm

41 Dye, J. "Fertility of American Women: June 2004." *Current Population Reports,* Washington, DC: U.S. Census Bureau, 2005. http://www.census.gov/prod/2005pubs/p20–555.pdf

42 Hodges, M.W. *Family Income Report.* The Grandfather Economic Report, 2007. http://mwhodges.home.att.net/family_a.htm

43 Gallagher, M. *The Abolition of Marriage: How We Destroy Lasting Love.* Washington, DC: Regnery Publishing, Inc., 2007.

44 Gallagher, M. *The Abolition of Marriage: How We Destroy Lasting Love.* Washington, DC: Regnery Publishing, Inc., 2007.

45 U.S. Census Bureau, Bureau of Health Statistics. *The 2008 Statistical Abstract of the United States.* Washington, DC: U.S. Census Bureau http://www.census.gov/compendia/statab/

46 PWP, International. *Facts About Single Parent Families.* Boca Raton, FL: Parents Without Partners, 2002. http://www.parentswithoutpartners.org/Support1.htm

47 Gallagher, M. *The Abolition of Marriage: How We Destroy Lasting Love.* Washington, DC: Regnery Publishing, Inc., 2007.

48 Boldt, W. "All One System." *Journal of Extension,* 1986, 24(3). http://www.joe.org/joe/1986fall/rb1.html

49 Bureau of Labor Statistics. *Charting the U.S. Labor Market in 2005.* Washington, DC: U.S. Department of Labor, Bureau of Labor Statistics, 2005. http://www.bls.gov/cps/labor2005/home.htm

50 Hodgkinson, H. All One System: *Demographics of Education, Kindergarten Through Graduate School.* Washington DC: The Institute for Educational Leadership, Inc., 1985.

51 Roberts, D., P. Christenson & D. Gentile. "The Effects of Violent Music on Children and Adolescents." In Gentile, D. (ed.) *Media Violence and Children.* Westport, CT: Praeger, 2003. http://www.psychology.iastate.edu/~dgentile/106027_08.pdf

52 Koplewicz, H. & A. Gurian. *TV: Facts and Tips Every Parent Should Know.* New York, NY: NYU Child Study Center, 2004. http://www.aboutourkids.org

53 Comstock, G. & E. Scharrer. *Television: What's On, Who's Watching, and What It Means.* San Diego, CA: Academic Press, 1999.

54 Oesterreich, L. *Getting Along: Taming the TV.* Ames, IA: Iowa State University, 1996.

55 Parents Television Council. *TV Bloodbath: Violence on Prime Time Broadcast TV.* Los Angeles. Parents Television Council, 2006. http://www.parentstv.org/PTC/publications/reports/stateindustryviolence/exsummary.asp

56 Kaufman, R. *Filling Their Minds with Death: TV Violence and Children.* 2004. http://www.turnoffyourtv.com/healtheducation/violencechildren/violencechildren.html

[57] Congressional Public Health Summit. *Joint Statement on the Impact of Entertainment Violence on Children.* 2000. http://www.aap.org/advocacy/releases/jstmtevc.htm

[58] American Academy of Pediatrics.

[59] Center for Media and Public Affairs, June 1992.

[60] Moore, W. *Television: Opiate of the Masses.* Family Resource, 2001. http://www.familyresource.com/lifestyles/mental-environment/television-opiate-of-the-masses

[61] Walsh, D. *Interactive violence and children: Testimony submitted to the Committee on Commerce, Science, and Transportation.* United States Senate, 2000. http://www.mediafamily.org/press/senateviolence.shtml

[62] Walsh, D. *Interactive violence and children: Testimony submitted to the Committee on Commerce, Science, and Transportation.* United States Senate, 2000. http://www.mediafamily.org/press/senateviolence.shtml

[63] Buchman, D. & J. Funk. "Video and Computer Games in the '90s: Children's Time Commitment and Game Preference." *Children Today,* 1996, 24: 12–16.

[64] Walsh, D. *Interactive violence and children: Testimony submitted to the Committee on Commerce, Science, and Transportation.* United States Senate, 2000. http://www.mediafamily.org/press/senateviolence.shtml

[65] Walsh, D. *Interactive violence and children: Testimony submitted to the Committee on Commerce, Science, and Transportation.* United States Senate, 2000. http://www.mediafamily.org/press/senateviolence.shtml

[66] Anderson, C. & B. Bushman. "Effects of Violent Video Games on Aggressive Behavior, Aggressive Cognition, Aggressive Affect, Physiological Arousal, and Prosocial Behavior: A Meta-Analytic Review of the Scientific Literature." *Psychological Science,* 2001, 12(5): 353–359.

[67] Waite, B., M. Hillbrand & H. Foster. "Reduction of Aggressive Behavior After Removal of Music Television." *Hospital and Community Psychiatry,* 1992, 43: 173–175.

[68] Johnson, J., L. Jackson & L. Gatto. "Violent Attitudes and Deferred Academic Aspirations: Deleterious Effects of Exposure to Rap Music." *Basic and Applied Social Psychology,* 1995,16: 27–41.

[69] Johnson, J., M. Adams, L. Ashburn & W. Reed. "Differential Gender Effects on African American Adolescents' Acceptance of Teen Dating Violence." *Sex Roles,* 1995, 33: 597–605.

[70] Anderson, C., N. Carnagey & J. Eubanks. "Exposure to Violent Media: The Effects of Songs with Violent Lyrics on Aggressive Thoughts and Feelings." *Journal of Personality and Social Psychology,* 2003, 84(5): 960–971.

[71] National Youth Violence Prevention Resource Center. *Youth Suicide Fact Sheet.* Atlanta, GA: National Youth Violence Prevention Resource Center, 2007. http://www.safeyouth.org/scripts/facts/suicide.asp

What Does the Research Say?

In this new millennium, despite being faced with challenges of formidable proportions, we stand at a very exciting time in the history of education. Until recently, teachers had to rely on what they *thought* were sound instructional practices. That's not

Cooperative learning is the most extensively researched educational innovation of all time. And the results are clear.

to say there wasn't good teaching because indeed there was. But today we can say with great confidence: We *know* what works. We know how to help students achieve more academically. We know how to close the gap between majority and minority achievement. We know how to improve race relations. We also know how to foster social and emotional skills. As an educational and scientific community, we have amassed a tremendous amount of research. The numbers have been crunched and results are in: Cooperative learning is the single most effective educational innovation to simultaneously address the many challenges and crises we face in our schools and in our society.

As unabashed advocates of cooperative learning, perhaps it may reek of hubris to say that we have the answers to all that ails education—that we have the panacea. But we do not make this bold claim willy-nilly. As a psychology professor for the University of California, I conducted large-scale studies of cooperative learning and the results were staggering. We found unprecedented positive outcomes. Hundreds of research studies corroborated our findings. The results of the ground-breaking research supporting the use of cooperative learning was presented in *Learning to Cooperate, Cooperating to Learn*,[1] the seminal book on cooperative learning research co-edited by myself and other leaders in the field of cooperative learning. In that book, hundreds of empirical research studies were described, establishing cooperative learning as the most researched and most strongly supported educational innovation at the time.

My research and experience left me fully convinced that cooperative learning was the most effective way to achieve a broad range of desired educational objectives. I was confronted with a decision: Do I stay at the university and conduct more research on the positive impact of cooperative learning? Or do I move on and focus my efforts on helping teachers, schools, and districts use what we know works very well? Although leaving the university was a difficult decision, I knew which path would make the most positive difference.

After leaving the research field what seems like a lifetime ago, I moved on to develop and train cooperative learning methods. The empirical research, however, has continued to amass, proving cooperative learning boosts achievement and reduces the achievement gap. Cooperative learning remains at the fore of research-based instruction. In an extensive review of research on educational innovations, Ellis and Fouts concluded: "Of all the educational innovations we have reviewed for this book, cooperative learning has the best, largest empirical base."[2] There are new and different types of research supporting cooperative learning, and now specifically Kagan Cooperative Learning. In addition to the early empirical research conducted by social scientists to test the effectiveness of cooperative learning, case study success stories by teachers, schools, and districts are pouring in.

"Of all the educational innovations we have reviewed for this book, cooperative learning has the best, largest empirical base."
—Ellis & Fouts

In this chapter, we will overview the empirical research conducted on cooperative learning. Then, we will turn to exciting new research on Kagan Cooperative Learning. Cooperative learning is the solution to many problems and challenges we face as a nation. With cooperative learning, we have great hope for the future. Don't take our word for it. Let the facts speak for themselves!

Experimental Research on Cooperative Learning

Hundreds of lab and field research studies demonstrate that cooperative learning has a positive impact on classroom climate, student self-esteem, empathy, internal locus of control, role-taking abilities, time on task, attendance, acceptance of mainstreamed students, and liking for school and learning. Before summarizing those findings, let's examine how cooperative learning addresses the four major crises we described in *Chapter 2*.

Crisis 1
Excellence: Enhanced Academic Achievement
Literally hundreds of studies demonstrate cooperative learning boosts achievement more than traditional methods. Cooperative learning outperforms competitive and individualistic

Cooperative Learning Solutions to the Four Crises

1 **The Achievement Crisis**
Hundreds of research studies demonstrate cooperative learning boosts achievement at all grades and in all academic content areas.

2 **The Achievement Gap Crisis**
Cooperative learning promotes academic gains, especially for minority and low achieving students, lowering the achievement gap and increasing educational equity.

3 **The Race Relations Crisis**
Cooperative learning improves mixed-race interaction, creates more cross-race friendship, and replaces racism with understanding and empathy.

4 **The Social Skills Crisis**
Cooperative learning improves the development of personal and social skills, largely missing in society, yet desperately sought in the 21st Century workplace.

learning structures across all age levels, subject areas, and almost all tasks. In identifying research-based instructional strategies for boosting achievement, Robert Marzano[3] summarized the results of various meta-analyses of cooperative learning. A meta-analysis combines many research studies to determine an average effect. Across hundreds of research studies, compared with strategies in which students compete with each other or work individually, cooperative learning has an effect size of .78. That is an average of a 28 percentile gain for students in the cooperative learning classrooms. To state it in classroom terms, if a student scoring 50 in a traditional classroom were placed in a cooperative classroom, on average the student would be scoring 78! The number of studies along with the size and consistency of the findings make cooperative learning one of the best approaches to boosting achievement.

> *"Of all classroom grouping strategies, cooperative learning may be the most flexible and powerful."*
> —Marzano, Pickering & Pollock

Cooperative Learning Boosts Academic Achievement

These studies summarize hundreds of research studies finding positive achievement results using cooperative learning:

- Hall[4]
- Johnson, Maruyama, Johnson, Nelson & Skon[5]
- Lipsey & Wilson[6]
- Marzano, Pickering & Pollock[7]
- Slavin[8]
- Slavin, Sharan, Kagan, Hertz-Lazarowitz, Webb & Schmuck[9]
- Schereens & Bosker[10]
- Walberg[11]

Crisis 2
Equity: Closing the Achievement Gap

That cooperative learning boosts achievement, however, does not necessarily mean it is a good solution to the achievement gap crisis. If it boosted achievement of all students equally, the gap would remain. The question is: Does cooperative learning narrow the achievement score gap between majority and minority students? Does it provide more equitable educational outcomes?

Four controlled experimental studies, which examined the gains of minority and majority students in traditional and cooperative classrooms, found that in cooperative learning classes, minority students *gained* far more than majority students, closing the achievement gap.[12] It is important to note that in each of these studies, the dramatic achievement gains of non-white students in cooperative learning classrooms are not bought at the expense of white students—the white students also gained more in the cooperative learning classrooms than they did the traditional classrooms.

For example, the graph in the box below represents the results of a twelve-week pretest-post test study of gains in standardized junior high English grammar proficiency among black and white students in inner-city school classrooms. Notice black students gained dramatically in the cooperative learning treatment. Notice also, white students gained more in cooperative learning than with traditional instruction. Cooperative learning produced both excellence (everyone gains more) and equity (it closes the achievement gap).

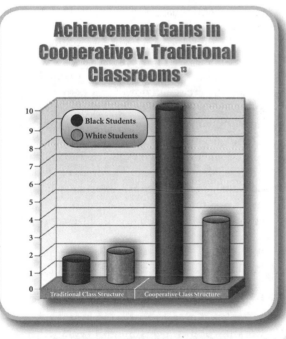

Achievement Gains in Cooperative v. Traditional Classrooms[13]

- Black Students
- White Students

Traditional Class Structure · Cooperative Class Structure

We have found similar dramatic results in our own research. In the case studies presented in the last section of this chapter, we examine a Kagan Cooperative Learning school whose achievement gap is reduced to nearly half of that of its state and district peers (see Case Study 3). Foster

Road Elementary School, through its extensive use of Kagan Cooperative Learning, reduced the school achievement gap between minority and majority students from 53% down to 10%. To take a second example, in its very first year using Kagan Cooperative Learning, Berkley Elementary School (see Case Study 4) reduced the black-white achievement gap from the state and district average of 45% to 25%!

Some resist cooperative learning, fearing that the gains of low achievers will be bought at the expense of the high achievers. Research suggests the opposite: High achievers achieve more in cooperative learning than if they were working independently. As they teach, they learn. They expand their understanding and cement their learning as they explain to others. With elevated status, high achievers are more motivated to learn. Studies of cross-age peer tutors find that tutors who are sent to lower grades to work with low achieving students gain almost as much as tutees in both academics and liking for school —both groups show substantial gains compared to students who do not engage in the tutoring process. Meta-analyses of hundreds of studies on tutoring produce consistent results: both tutors and tutees gain in academic achievement, attitudes toward learning, and self-esteem.[14,15]

Everyone learns more with cooperative learning, but there is a dramatic catch-up effect. Low achievers watch and learn as their more able peers think aloud and model how to solve a problem. Low achievers get to hear the inner workings of their peers' minds in comprehensible terms. They receive frequent and immediate feedback as they solve problems and express ideas.

Whatever the reasons, the dramatic gains of low achieving students in cooperative learning is our best hope of successfully responding to two crises that face education: the need to reduce the school achievement gap and to boost achievement.

Crisis 3
Improving Race Relations

Another consistent finding of cooperative learning research has been improved ethnic relations among students. The race relations data from my own research[16] was dramatic. Working in desegregated schools with about equal numbers of black, white, and Hispanic students, we found in traditional classrooms, with each passing year, there was increased segregation of students along race lines. Entering school, students were essentially color blind. Students didn't base friendship on skin color. However, we identified progressive racism. By grades 2–4, we identified more friendliness toward members of the same racial group. By fifth and sixth grade, the small racial cleavage became an enormous chasm: Being of the same race was almost a prerequisite for high levels of friendship. Our data confirmed a phenomenon many teachers take for granted. As students get older, they self-segregate into same-race cliques, groups, and gangs. Racial prejudice, mistrust, and self-segregation is well documented.

Students in cooperative learning groups behaved very differently. Same-ethnicity dropped as a significant predictor of friendship in the cooperative classroom. In the cooperative classes, race was no longer the basis for choosing friendships. Having worked together cooperatively in mixed-race teams, Martin Luther King Jr.'s dream was realized—students began choosing their friends more on the content of their character than the color of their skin.

Emerging From Racial Tension

Lincoln Elementary School in Long Beach, CA, serves a student population that is shifting from predominantly African American to predominantly Latino. Principal Bob Williams recalls before cooperative learning when the two groups—and others—struggled with interaction. According to Principal Williams: "After implementing Kagan Cooperative Learning, we don't see that at all. Our students generally like each other because they work together so much in the classroom. There is very little polarization of groups today." [17]

A massive set of research studies on race relations has found similar results. Johnson and Johnson[18] cite 177 studies that have been conducted since the 1940s that find that compared to competitive and individualistic structures, cooperative experiences promote greater interpersonal attraction. Specifically, they identify 53 studies that compare the relative effect of cooperative versus competitive interactions on interpersonal cross-ethnic relations and conclude, "Cooperative experiences promoted significantly better relationships between white and minority individuals than did competition (effect size =.54)."

Slavin[19] reviews the research conducted on cooperative learning and intergroup relations. The studies find that cooperative learning promotes more positive ethnic attitudes, gains in cross-racial friendships (both casual and close), and produces fewer negative ratings based on race.

Compared to students in traditional classrooms, students grades 2–8 had a 37.9 percent increase of listing a student from a different race as a friend.[20] That's a powerful effect, but what makes it even more telling is that these were the results of a follow-up study conducted in the year after students had been assigned to cooperative groups. Ziegler[21] also found improved racial relations held up ten weeks later. Cooperative learning, when used for short-term research studies that last sometimes but a few weeks for a selected subject, has been shown to have a significantly positive residual effect on race relations that lasts well beyond the duration of the study.

Without cooperative learning we have merely desegregation—students self-segregate. With cooperative learning we achieve true integration.

African-American, Anglo-American, Hispanic, and Asian-American students come from different backgrounds, cultures, and often live in different neighborhoods with different family structures and economic realities. When schooling is competitive or students have little interaction with their classmates, who are they most likely to band with at recess and after school? It is only natural for them to be attracted to those who are most like themselves. There are strong biological and sociological forces that oppose harmonious integration in school and in our society. But with cooperative learning in classrooms, students interact freely on equal-status footing, making true integration a reality in our schools.

> *"We are caught in a network of mutuality. We are tied in a single garment of destiny. What affects one directly, affects us all indirectly."*
> —Martin Luther King, Jr.

In cooperative learning, students work in mixed-race teams. Teambuilding activities help teammates get to know and like each other. They debate issues. They discuss each other's ideas. They come to understand and empathize with their teammates regardless of race. Teammates break down the superficial stereotypes and get to know each other as individuals. Racial tension gives way to teamwork and friendship.

Crisis 4
Filling the Socialization Void

The socialization crisis described in the previous chapter can be summarized in a sentence: Personal and interpersonal skills are becoming increasingly vital in our society, but are disappearing due to major societal changes. Cooperative learning counters that trend.

Understanding, Empathy, Cooperativeness. Cooperative leaning is more effective than non-cooperative alternatives for developing understanding, role-taking, compassion, and empathy. Research shows that cooperative experiences are more effective for developing the ability to understand the cognitive and emotional perspectives of others.[22] This is easy to understand. When students work independently, there is little interaction and few opportunities to truly get to know and understand how classmates think and how they feel about issues. Open discourse is part and parcel to cooperative learning and many cooperative learning structures. For example, Same-Different, Paraphrase Passport, and Match Mine are explicitly designed to promote perspective-taking skills. Ability to understand the needs and perspectives of others is the basis for tolerance, empathy, and moral development.

In competitive situations, students easily develop and maintain negative stereotypes and labels for their classmates. In contrast, in the cooperative classroom, students work together and get to know each other for their individual nuances. They develop a more accurate and differentiated view of others.[23] It is tough to maintain negative attitudes, stereotypes, and perceptions of others in face of so much evidence to the contrary.

It almost goes without saying that students who cooperate in the classroom become more cooperative. Research supports this statement with multiple studies finding cooperative learning leads to more helpfulness, kindness, and cooperativeness. No studies find more cooperativeness resulting from non-cooperative settings.[24]

Liking and Being Liked. Cooperative learning places students on the same team, increases interpersonal contact, includes shared goals, and promotes sharing, helping, and praising. Studies indicate that cooperative learning increases interpersonal attraction. Students list more students as friends and fewer students who they don't want to work with. More students feel liked by classmates.[25] Research on acceptance of academically and emotionally handicapped students demonstrates cooperative learning promotes more acceptance, liking, and lower rates of rejection of mainstreamed students with handicaps.[26]

Cooperative learning provides in the school a surrogate, stable community in which prosocial values and skills are nurtured and developed.

Additional Positive Outcomes

Cooperative learning also builds communication skills, develops self-esteem and internal locus of control, increases student motivation, reduces discipline problems, and promotes cognitive development.

"Perhaps the most important psychological outcome of cooperative learning methods is their effect on student self-esteem."
—Robert Slavin

Communication and Language Acquisition Skills

Communication among teammates is a hallmark of cooperative learning. In the traditional classroom, students work alone and are required to keep quiet unless prompted. Only the teacher or a single student may speak at once. In cooperative learning settings, students use language to ask and answer questions, ask for and offer help, explain ideas, express opinions, argue, debate, and negotiate. The sheer volume of student communication is dramatically increased: Language is being practiced all over the room at once in each team. Communication is functional and listening is active. Many cooperative structures (for example, Timed-Pair-Share, Three Step Interview) are designed to maximize oral communication development and ensure each student has the opportunity to talk and listen.

As English is a second language for many of our students, we need methods to promote language acquisition. Research demonstrates students learning a new language are more willing to participate and persevere in a cooperative versus competitive setting.[27] Cooperative learning discussion groups in college significantly reduce communication apprehension.[28] Cooperative learning is particularly effective for developing language skills for native and ESL students.[29]

Self-Esteem, Internal Locus of Control

Having a high self-esteem has been related to having fewer prejudices,[30] fewer emotional problems,[31] being less socially awkward,[32] less susceptible to peer and social pressures,[33] more likely to persevere in the face of adversity,[34] and to genuinely liking others.[35] Meta-analysis reveals cooperative experiences are linked with higher self-esteem.[36]

Several studies find students in cooperative learning classrooms are more motivated and possess an internal locus of control—they attribute their success in the classroom to their own efforts.[37] Cooperative learning gives students the perception that they have a chance to succeed (they receive more tutoring and peer support), and this expectation of success contributes to actual success, which in turn further raises expectations.

Increased Motivation

Studies on a variety of measures of motivation and liking for class find students prefer cooperative learning over alternative ways to learn. A study across student groups and geographic regions found students in various ethnic groups share a common preference for cooperative learning. Fifth-grade students from urban and suburban schools chose cooperative learning (73%) over individual work (15%), and competitive work (22%).[38] Research finds cooperative learning results[39] in:

- Increased Time On Task
- Liking for Class
- Increased Motivation
- Increased Attendance

Fewer Discipline Problems

Perhaps because they are more engaged and like class more, students in cooperative classrooms are less often disruptive.[40] Cooperative learning results in:

- Fewer Suspensions
- Fewer Expulsions

Cognitive Development
Higher-Level Thinking

Extensive theory and research supports the conclusion that cooperative learning promotes higher-level thinking. The many different ways cooperative learning promotes higher-level thinking are summarized in a classic book, *Enhancing Thinking Through Cooperative Learning*.[41] Scores of empirical research studies demonstrate cooperative learning enhances the quality of reasoning, the developmental level of thinking, metacognition, quality of problem solving, creativity, and social perspective taking.[42] Let's take a peek at a few of the studies.

Cognitive and Moral Development.

When students interact, they provide each other new information and new ways of thinking about information. In the process, they are pushed to a higher-level cognitive framework—they come to a point at which the new information cannot be assimilated into their old conceptual system, so they must accommodate. That is, they move up to more differentiated thinking. Numerous studies demonstrate this process occurs with the understanding of the world (Piaget's conservation tasks) and with moral reasoning (Kohlberg's stages of moral development). With no direct teaching of conservation or moral reasoning, students at lower levels move to higher levels by interacting with others.

Part of why social interaction drives advances in level of cognition is that during interaction, students are presented with information discrepant with their own, motivating them to rethink their solutions. In an interesting demonstration of this, students who could not correctly solve conservation tasks were presented with erroneous information that conflicted with their initial view. These students advanced significantly, and sometimes dramatically in a post test.[43] For example, some students who scored 0 out of 18 on the pretest scored between 16 and 18 out of 18 on the post test after receiving the erroneous interpretation. What happened? The discrepant view forced them to rethink their initial view, and in the process, they came up with the correct solution. As students interact, they push each other to higher levels of thinking!

Reasoning Strategies.

First grade students were given a random ordered list of 12 words to memorize (three each of toys, animals, fruits, and clothing), were instructed to put the words in an order easy to memorize, and memorize the words. Eight of the nine cooperative groups discovered and used the four-category system; only one subject in the competitive and individualistic conditions did.[44] Most interesting is that the most intelligent and gifted students used higher-quality reasoning strategies following the cooperative interactions than following working competitively or on their own. The implications are that these gains are not merely the higher level students transmitting strategies to the lower level students. Rather, out of the interaction of ideas emerged solutions beyond what anyone working alone could do— an excellent example of synergy.

Research on Kagan Structures

Case Studies

Professional development on Kagan Structures is our primary focus as an educational organization. Through our various teacher workshops, institutes, academies, school and district improvement plans, administrator trainings, and in-class coaching, we help schools and districts achieve greater success through the implementation of cooperative learning structures. With increased federal pressure to both track and increase student achievement, schools and districts are documenting and sharing their success with us. Following are some success stories they have shared.

> ### Case Study 1
> ### Catalina Ventura School[45, 46]
> #### Scott Heusman, Principal & Don Moenich, Title I
>
> Catalina Ventura is a K–8 elementary school with over 1,300 students. Catalina Ventura is located in Phoenix, Arizona, and is part of the Alhambra Elementary School District. Catalina is an inner-city school with a high poverty rate. During the past several years, teachers at Catalina have been extensively trained in using Kagan Structures in their classrooms. Students' scores on standardized tests have soared while using Kagan Structures.
>
> A remarkable aspect of the Catalina experience is they have posted dramatic gains while experiencing a demographic shift that would predict exactly the opposite! During the year of the study, free and reduced lunch count progressed from 55% to 74%. As poverty increased, test scores have significantly risen! From Year 1 to Year 2, testing data from the District Assessment Plan in the area of reading, writing, and math showed marked improvements in 23 of 26 areas when looking at percentages of students that mastered a skill. Some grade levels showed as much as 25% growth in students, who demonstrated mastery. The graphs are a few highlights of test data.
>
>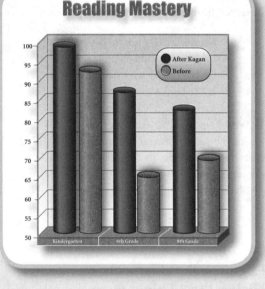
>
> This growth is attributed to Catalina Ventura's outstanding leadership, staff development, and the implementation of highly successful Kagan teaching strategies.

Case Study 1 continued

Catalina teachers began using Kagan Structures in their classroom to get students actively involved in learning and to make learning fun. Since then, teachers have worked diligently to increase the number of Kagan Structures used in their classroom. As a result, test scores have significantly improved. Additionally, the social skill training and benefits that accompany the implementation of cooperative structures are great. Teachers report that their students are better listeners, more patient with classmates, and genuinely care about the learning of other classmates after using cooperative structures in their classroom.

—**Don Moenich, Title I**
Catalina Ventura School

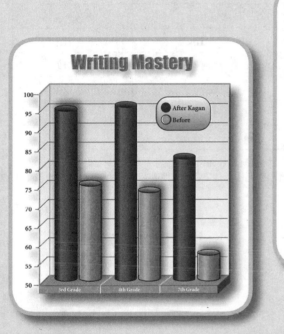

"Without a doubt, teachers love Kagan Structures, students have fun and learn more as they participate in the structures, and standardized test scores have dramatically improved as teachers have become more confident with using these structures. Many thanks to you and your team for providing such a blessing to our school."

—**Scott Heusman, Principal**
Catalina Ventura School

▶ Case Study 2

Anderson County Schools[47]

Steve Burkich, Assistant Superintendent

Anderson County Schools in Lawrenceburg, Kentucky, is a district comprised of six schools and over 270 teachers. Anderson County had no systematic Kagan implementation or professional development prior to 2002, and therefore the following data serves well as a "before" and "after" snapshot of academic achievement as measured by the CTBS test. One of the elementary schools was labeled by the state of Kentucky as a "School in Decline" as determined by state-based CAT assessments. The Kagan professional development involved principals in a three day training on effective teaching strategies; all teachers grades P–12 in 12 hours of Kagan Teaching Strategies; a team of teachers and administrators evaluating Kagan Teaching Strategies; and teams of teachers and administrators attending Kagan Summer Academies. The use of Kagan Structures has resulted in dramatic gains across the board. The graph and table compare 2002 "before Kagan" and 2004 "after Kagan" test data for elementary schools in the district.

"Kagan has had a very positive impact on our test scores."

—Steve Burkich, Assistant Superintendent
Anderson County Schools

Comparison of Test Data Prior to and After Kagan

	2002 Test Data	2004 Test Data
CTBS	88.71	96.75
Reading	83.89	92.74
Writing	71.06	71.61
Math	71.02	82.35
Science	82.29	97.65
Social Studies	81.92	96.52
Arts & Humanities	54.58	69.60
Practical Living	80.61	102.12

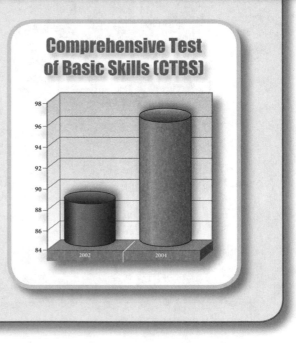

Comprehensive Test of Basic Skills (CTBS)

▶ Case Study 3

Foster Road Elementary School[48,49]

Dr. Jean Maddox, Principal

Foster Road Elementary is a Pre-Kindergarten to 5th Grade school and is part of the Norwalk-La Mirada Unified School District. It is a community center school located approximately 18 miles southeast of metropolitan Los Angeles. It is a unique school setting that includes preschool, regular education, and a large population of special education students. Spanish is spoken as the primary language in many of the homes. 82% of the students are Hispanic, 9% white, 4% African American, 3% Asian, and 1% Filipino. 68% of the students participate in free and reduced school breakfast and lunch programs.

All the teachers at Foster Road have been trained in and use Kagan Structures. In 2004, Foster Road Elementary had the highest growth points in their district. They exceeded California's Academic Performance Index (API) target by 485%. Since the inception of the Public Schools Accountability Act, Foster Road's gains have surpassed the state's target by large margins (see graph below). Principal Dr. Jean Maddox attributes much of their success to their implementation of Kagan Structures.

In a recent report—Multiple Year Growth in API, Elementary Schools in Norwalk-La Mirada USD—Foster Road is identified as the #1 API elementary growth school. Including Foster Road, there are 18 elementary schools in the district. When we compare Foster Road's 299 point growth to the rest of the district's 180 point average, we see Foster Road's growth is 65% higher. The chart compares the API growth point difference.

One of the most interesting and exciting things to note about the consequence of implementing Kagan Structures is that Foster Road successfully closed the Achievement Gap between traditionally high and low achieving students and schools.

If we compare Foster Road in 1999 and 2006 to the three highest-scoring elementary schools in the district, we see a wonderful trend. By transforming its approach to instruction, Foster Road dramatically reduced the chasm that separates the highest and lowest achieving schools within the district.

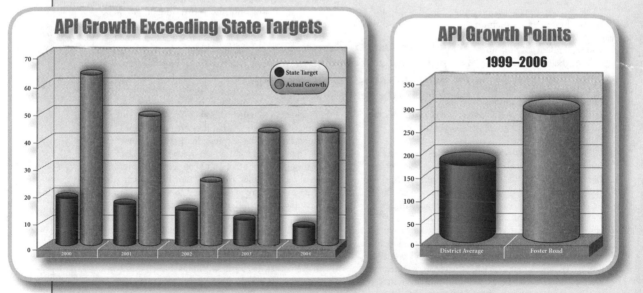

"We received the results of our state testing, and my school had the highest growth points in our district. We made it to #1. It is all because of Kagan Structures and Strategies. Thank you for all your help and training."
—**Dr. Jean Maddox, Principal**
Foster Road Elementary

Case Study 3 *continued*

On the chart at the right, the gray line represents Foster Road's API score in 1999 and 2006. The black line represents the average of the three highest schools in the district. In 1999, the highest schools scored 235 points higher. By 2006, the gap was down to 78 points. The difference between schools was reduced from 53% to a mere 10%!

Closing the API Gap

A Principal's Reflections on Implementing Kagan Structures

"The structures have transformed our school in many ways. Most of the teachers were positive from the start, learning the structures and having a practical framework to guide their instruction. Because the teachers were all practicing the same structures—they were all on the same page discussing the strategies, trying them with their students and with themselves—they became much closer, supporting each other, and willing to share with one another.

"The structures make lessons much smoother. Most of the teachers use the structures many times a day. When you walk in the classrooms, you see students pairing up sharing their thoughts. It gives teachers a structure to put their content in, and gives teachers more options in delivering their lesson in a more meaningful way to students. Lessons just go more smoothly.

We at Foster Road have become a completely different culture now, there is so much more caring and sharing going on, thanks to the Kagan Structures.

"Since we have been using structures, we have come a long way with our instruction. There have been some big changes in our students, as well as with our staff. We have documented dramatic improvements in academic achievement. But the students themselves are different. Before we began with structures, there were tons of discipline problems. Classrooms were often boring; students were not engaged, even teachers lacked focus with their instruction. Students would get off task and act up. They were not sure what the teacher wanted. We had some teachers even yelling at students and were sending students to the office all the time. Now, there is a big difference in teachers teaching and students actively engaged. People who visit our campus always compliment us on the wonderful atmosphere we've created. We have had zero suspensions for the last three years! Teachers model the structures and students know

just what they are to do. Students stay on task; they are more engaged. They just aren't disruptive. Well planned instruction and teachers working together are producing great gains in our school. When we have visitors, they comment, 'We just don't see any disruptive behavior; students are working.'

"Another way students have changed is the depth of their thinking. Before, if a teacher asked a question, maybe a student would answer, or the answers were not as in depth and only one or two students would be held accountable. Now, the teacher asks a question and then has the students interact using a structure. They have a rich discussion and together develop greater meaning on what's going on. The students are much more critical in their thinking, and the teachers stretch their thinking. You see students making connections to what they are reading and learning about as they express themselves at a deeper level. They are understanding more, willing to share their thoughts with others, and you see them thinking more about what they are doing. Our English Language Learner students are making more connections and understanding the material being presented in class.

"Something else to mention is social skills. Because the structures involve listening, taking turns, wait time, and sharing ideas, the students have become more polite with each other. They will say things to each other on the playground like, 'Let's take turns' or will paraphrase each other, saying 'What I heard you say is….,' 'My partner and I feel that...,' 'I have something I could add ….,' 'It's your turn now.'"

"Structures have transformed our school."
—Dr. Jean Maddox, Principal
Foster Road Elementary

Case Study 4
Berkley Elementary School
Randy Borland, Principal

Berkley Elementary school is a K–5 charter school in the Polk County School District in Auburndale, Florida. Berkley designated itself as a "Kagan School," and provided training in Kagan instructional strategies for all of its teachers. Florida grades schools to measure schools' academic performance. Each school is assigned an A to F letter grade, based on their performance on the Florida Comprehensive Assessment Test (FCAT), the percent of eligible students who took the test, and whether or not students made progress in reading and math. Berkley has risen to and has maintained an A grade.[50]

Berkley outperforms their district and Florida state norms on assessment measures. Not only is there a higher percent of students proficient overall, but the achievement gap between black and white students is dramatically reduced. Take a look at the reading and math achievement graphs comparing Berkley to its district and state neighbors. The graphs show the achievement scores of black and white students.

White students outperform white students in the state and in the district. Black students outperform black students in the state and district too. Also of interest, in both math and reading, black students from Berkley outperform white students from other schools in the district.

Without emphasis on closing the achievement gap per se, Berkley teachers are successful at closing the gap. The achievement gap is approximately 45% for schools in the state and district. The gap is reduced to approximately 25% for the Kagan school.

Principal Randy Borland points to Kagan as the major contributing factor explaining their success.

Florida Comprehensive Assessment Test
(FCAT) 2004–05, Grades 3–5

Reading Proficiency

Percent of Students Scoring 3 and Above

● Black
○ White

State · District · Kagan School

Math Proficiency

● Black
○ White

State · District · Kagan School

"We opened as a Title I school, with 61% free and reduced lunch. We were very diversified. We were just like any other school. We had our problems, kids adjusting, cliques, the fighting, the hierarchy you see in some classrooms and grade levels. But it's all disappeared. Completely. And it did it in the first year we implemented Kagan.

The kids love it. It's fun to them. The teachers like it because it's friendly and easy to implement a structure. It's very content friendly. It's just so different from traditional teaching that we've used in the last 200 years. It's just different."
—Randy Borland, Principal
Berkley Elementary School

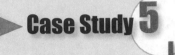

► **Case Study 5**

Lincoln Elementary School
Robert Williams, Principal

Lincoln Elementary School in Long Beach, California, had not met Annual Yearly Progress for a number of years prior to 2000; they had been placed on Program Improvement as dictated by Title I and No Child Left Behind legislation. Then they began Kagan training. Training consisted of workshops at the school and a retreat at which all teachers learned the Kagan Structures. That year and the following year they made AYP and were taken off Program Improvement status.

Lincoln Elementary School raised its Academic Performance Indcx (API) by 71 points whereas the state targeted just a 10-point growth. Lincoln outpaced their target by over 600 percent! What's impressive about Lincoln's gains is they are the second largest gains in a very large district that has taken the national stage for its ability to demonstrate the greatest overall performance and improvement in student achievement while reducing achievement gaps. Long Beach Unified

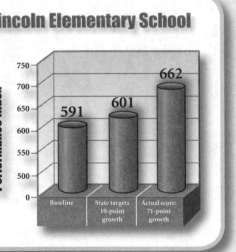

School district is the 3rd largest school district in California. Tens of thousands of pieces of information on student performance collected by an independent team of national experts show that Long Beach is outperforming America's large school systems. Their low-income African-American and Hispanic students outperformed their peers in similar urban districts in reading and math at all levels.[51] Principal Robert Williams credits the dramatic gains at Lincoln to the Kagan Structures and their ability to engage all students. Teachers learned to integrate the structures into their moment-to-moment teaching. Initially, he said, teachers would "do Kagan." With practice, they transitioned into using Kagan Structures to more efficiently deliver any content. In his words, "The teachers internalized Kagan Structures so they became part of how they taught." Principal Williams also cites the importance of PIES. Teachers learned to check their activities to make sure the PIES principles were in place. (See *Chapter 12: Basic Principles [PIES]* for more information about PIES.)

"We believe our achievement in posting the second biggest elementary API increase in our district is a reflection of the way we have improved our teachers' academic and pedagogical expertise in equal measure. We have focused on student participation in their own learning process by implementing the cooperative learning structures developed by Dr. Spencer Kagan. By combining our curriculum with Dr. Kagan's Structures, teachers actively involve at least 50 percent of all students at any time. This is a far cry from classrooms where the only person active is either the teacher or the one student whom he/she has asked a question."

—Robert Williams, Principal
Lincoln Elementary School

Positive Outcomes of Kagan Structures

Numerous studies have focused on the effect of Kagan Structures on achievement, attitude, and engagement. The chart below summarizes some recent studies on Kagan Structures, finding positive results across grade levels and subjects areas.

Positive Results with Kagan Structures

Research Study	Structures	Summary of Results
High School Journalism *Howard*[52]	• Quiz-Quiz-Trade • Timed Pair Share	• Achievement: 22% increase in pretest to post test score with Kagan Structures. 12% average gain prior to Kagan Structures • Attitude: Favorable results on attitudinal study
College Math 99 *Murie*[53]	• Inside-Outside Circle • One Stray • RallyCoach • RallyRobin • RallyTable • Showdown	• Achievement: Math section taught with Kagan Structures outscored eight other sections taught with traditional strategies by 20–79% compared to 59% average • Other: Increased engagement and student communication
Adult Computer Numeric Control Math *Major & Robinette*[54]	Various Kagan Structures	• 20% increase in test scores with Kagan Structures • Increased engagement in the class and enthusiasm for the content
High School Chemistry *Mele*[55]	• Numbered Heads Together • Pairs Compare • Pairs Check • RallyRobin • RallyTable • RoundRobin • RoundTable • Timed Pair Share	• Class averages increased from approximately 75% to 83% • Active engagement, excitement, teamwork, and positive relations
6th Grade Social Studies *Dotson*[56]	• Think-Pair-Share • RallyTable • Numbered Heads Together • Showdown • Teammates Consult • 4S Brainstorming	• Higher curriculum-based assessment scores (85.47%) with Kagan Structures. 76.92% for control group • Achievement gains for all student groups, including mentally impaired, students with learning disabilities, at-risk, and gifted students
5th Grade Math *Cline*[57]	• RallyCoach • RallyTable • Timed Pair Share	• Class taught with Kagan Structures scored higher on tests and quizzes than control class (88.5% vs. 79.2%)

Chapter Summary

If the research found only the impressive gains in academic achievement, it would be enough to justify the widespread use of cooperative learning. If it found only the reduction in the achievement gap, it would be enough. If it found only improvement in cross-race relations, it would be enough. If it found only improved interpersonal skills, it would be enough.

Research by scientists and educators converge on the same finding: Cooperative learning shows marked improvement in all those outcome areas and more. The question is not: Is cooperative learning a research-based innovation? The question is: Why would any serious educator or educational system overlook what is the most promising and proven innovation ever studied? What does the research say? Cooperative learning is a positive, proven response to the most pressing crises facing our world today.

Chapter Questions

▶ Questions for Review

1. Is cooperative learning scientifically research-based? Why or why not?
2. Name at least three positive outcomes of cooperative learning.
3. Without intervention, what is the default racial interaction patterns among schoolchildren?
4. A high self-esteem is correlated with many positive benefits. Name at least three.
5. What is the difference between experimental and case study research?

▶ Questions for Thinking and Discussion

1. What type of evidence do you personally find more compelling: experimental research conducted by social scientists or actual case studies and statements made by educators? Why?
2. How might you respond to a parent who opposed cooperative learning because he didn't want his daughter wasting her time working with lower achievers?
3. What are some of the changes we would see in society if children were exposed to mixed-race teams throughout their schooling?
4. What would you value most for your own child: 1) academic success or 2) ability to work successfully with others?
5. If you were going to conduct a research study on cooperative learning, how would you design your research?

References

[1] Slavin, R., S. Sharan, S. Kagan, R. Hertz-Lazarowitz, C. Webb & R. Schmuck (eds.). *Learning to Cooperate, Cooperating to Learn.* New York, NY: Plenum, 1985.

[2] Ellis, A. & J. Fouts. *Research on Educational Innovations.* Princeton Junction, NJ: Eye on Education, 1993.

[3] Marzano, R., D. Pickering & J. Pollock. *Classroom Instruction That Works: Research-Based Strategies for Increasing Student Achievement.* Alexandria, VA: Association for Supervision and Curriculum Development, 2001.

[4] Hall, L. "The Effects of Cooperative Learning on Achievement: A Meta-Analysis." *Dissertation Abstracts International,* 1989, 50: 343A.

[5] Johnson, D., G. Maruyama, R. Johnson, D. Nelson & L. Skon. "Effects of Cooperative, Competitive, and Individualistic Goal Structures on Achievement: A Meta-Analysis." *Psychological Bulletin,* 1981, 89(1): 47–62.

[6] Lipsey, M. & D. Wilson. "The Efficacy of Psychological, Educational, and Behavioral Treatment." *American Psychologist,* 1993, 48(12), 1181-1209.

[7] Marzano, R., D. Pickering & J. Pollock. *Classroom Instruction That Works: Research Based Strategies for Increasing Student Achievement.* Alexandria, VA: Association for Supervision and Curriculum Development, 2001.

[8] Slavin, R. *Cooperative Learning.* New York, NY: Longman, 1983.

[9] Slavin, R., S. Sharan, S. Kagan, R. Hertz-Lazarowitz, C. Webb & R. Schmuck (eds.). *Learning to Cooperate, Cooperating to Learn.* New York, NY: Plenum, 1985.

[10] Scheerens, J. & R. Bosker. *The Foundations of Educational Effectiveness.* New York, NY: Pergamon, 1997.

[11] Walberg, H. "Productive Teaching." In Waxman, H. & H. Walberg (eds.). *New Directions for Teaching Practice and Research.* Berkley, CA: McCutchen Publishing Corporation, 1999.

[12] Aronson, E., N. Blaney, C. Stephan, J. Sikes & M. Snapp. *The Jigsaw Classroom.* Beverly Hills, CA: Sage Publications, 1978.

[13] Slavin, R. & E. Oickle. "Effects of Cooperative Learning Teams on Student Achievement and Race Relations: Treatment by Race Interaction." *Sociology of Education,* 1981, 54: 174–180.

[14] Cohen, P., J. Kulik & C. Kulik. "Educational Outcomes of Tutoring: A Meta-Analysis of Findings." *American Educational Research Journal,* 1982, 19(2): 237–248.

[15] Cohen, P. & J. Kulik. "Synthesis of Research on the Effects of Tutoring." *Educational Leadership,* 1981, 39(3): 226–227.

[16] Kagan, S., G. Zahn, K. Widaman, J. Schwarzwald & G. Tyrrell. "Classroom Structural Bias: Impact of Cooperative and Competitive Classroom Structures on Cooperative and Competitive Individuals and Groups." In Slavin, R., Sharan, S., Kagan, S., Hertz-Lazarowitz, R., Webb, C. & R. Schmuck (eds.). *Learning to Cooperate, Cooperating to Learn.* New York, NY: Plenum, 1985.

[17] Sapp, J. *Teaching Tolerance.* Montgomery, AL: Southern Poverty Law Center, 2006.

[18] Johnson, D. & R. Johnson. *Cooperation and Competition: Theory and Research.* Edina, MN: Interaction Books, 1989.

[19] Slavin, R. *Cooperative Learning Theory, Research, and Practice (2nd ed.).* Boston, MA: Allyn & Bacon, 1995.

[20] Slavin, R. "Effects of Biracial Learning Teams on Cross-Racial Friendships." *Journal of Educational Psychology,* 1979, 71: 381–387.

[21] Ziegler, S. "The Effectiveness of Cooperative Learning Teams for Increasing Cross-Ethnic Friendship: Additional Evidence." *Human Organization,* 1981, 40: 264–268.

[22] Johnson, D. & R. Johnson. *Cooperation and Competition: Theory and Research.* Edina, MN: Interaction Books, 1989.

[23] Johnson, D. & R. Johnson. *Cooperation and Competition: Theory and Research.* Edina, MN: Interaction Books, 1989.

[24] Slavin, R. *Cooperative Learning.* New York, NY: Longman, 1983.

Slavin, R. "When Does Cooperative Learning Increase Student Achievement?" *Psychological Bulletin,* 1983, 94: 429–445.

[25] Slavin, R. *Cooperative Learning Theory, Research, and Practice (2nd ed.).* Boston, MA: Allyn & Bacon, 1995.

[26] Johnson, D. & R. Johnson. *Cooperation and Competition: Theory and Research.* Edina, MN: Interaction Books, 1989.

[27] Bennet, R. *Cooperative Learning with a Computer in a Native Language Class.* Humboldt, CA: Humboldt State University, 1987.

[28] Kim, E., J. Kim & M. Rhee. "Effects of Cooperative Learning Sessions on Communication Apprehension, Academic Achievement, and Class Satisfaction Among College Students." *Paper presented at the annual meeting of the International Communication Association, New Orleans Sheraton.* New Orleans, LA. May 2004. http://www.allacademic.com/meta/p113092_index.html

[29] Lotan, R. & J. Benton. "Finding Out About Complex Instruction: Teaching Math and Science in Heterogeneous Classrooms." In Davidson, N. (ed.). *Cooperative Learning in Mathematics: A Handbook for Teachers.* Menlo Park, CA: Addison-Wesley, 1990.

[30] Stephan, W. & D. Rosenfield. "Effects of Desegregation on Racial Attitudes." *Journal of Educational Psychology,* 1978, 70: 670–679.

[31] Fitts, W. *The Self-Concept and Psychopathology.* Nashville, TN: Counselor Recording and Tests, 1972.

[32] Rosenberg, M. *Society and the Adolescent Self-Image.* Princeton, NJ: Princeton University Press, 1965.

[33] Wells, L. & G. Marwell. *Self-Esteem: Its Conceptualization and Measurement.* Beverly Hills, CA: Sage Publications, 1976.

[34] Shamir, B. "Protestant Work Ethic, Work Involvement, and the Psychological Impact of Unemployment." *Journal of Occupational Behavior,* 1986, 7(1): 25–28.

[35] Baron, P. "Self-Esteem, Ingratiation, and Evaluation of Unknown Others." *Journal of Personality and Social Psychology,* 1974, 21: 495–497.

[36] Johnson, D. & R. Johnson. *Cooperation and Competition: Theory and Research.* Edina, MN: Interaction Books, 1989.

[37] Slavin, R. *Cooperative Learning Theory, Research, and Practice (2nd ed.).* Boston, MA: Allyn & Bacon, 1995.

[38] Johnson, L. "Elementary School Students' Learning Preferences and the Classroom Learning Environment: Implications for Educational Practice and Policy." *Journal of Negro Education,* Summer, 2006.

[39] Slavin, R. *Cooperative Learning Theory, Research, and Practice (2nd ed.).* Boston, MA: Allyn & Bacon, 1995.

[40] Slavin, R. *Cooperative Learning Theory, Research, and Practice (2nd ed.).* Boston, MA: Allyn & Bacon, 1995.

[41] Davidson, N. & T. Worsham (eds.). *Enhancing Thinking Through Cooperative Learning.* New York, NY: Teachers College Press, 1992.

[42] Johnson, D. & R. Johnson. *Cooperation and Competition: Theory and Research.* Edina, MN: Interaction Books, 1989.

43 Ames, G. & F. Murray. "When Two Wrongs Make a Right: Promoting Cognitive Change by Social Conflict." *Developmental Psychology,* 1982, 18: 894–897.

44 Johnson, D., L. Skon & R. Johnson. "Effects of Cooperative, Competitive, and Individualist Conditions on Children's Problem Solving Performance." *American Educational Research Journal,* 1980, 17(1): 83–94.

Skon, L., D. Johnson & R. Johnson. "Cooperative Peer Interaction Versus Individual Competition and Individualist Efforts: Effects on the Acquisition of Cognitive Reasoning Strategies." *Journal of Educational Psychology,* 1981, 73(1): 83–92.

45 Moenich, D. "Kagan Structures Increase Achievement at Catalina Ventura School." *Kagan Online Magazine.* San Clemente, CA: Kagan Publishing, Fall 2000.

46 Heusman, S. & D. Moenich. "Achievement Still on the Rise at Catalina Ventura School." *Kagan Online Magazine.* San Clemente, CA: Kagan Publishing, Summer 2003.

47 Burkich, S. "Anderson County Teachers Excel with Kagan." *Kagan Online Magazine.* San Clemente, CA: Kagan Publishing, Spring 2006.

48 Kagan M. "Closing the School Achievement Gap." *Kagan Online Magazine.* San Clemente, CA: Kagan Publishing, Summer 2007.

49 Maddox, J. "Foster Road Elementary Is on the Road to Success with Kagan Structures." *Kagan Online Magazine.* San Clemente, CA: Kagan Publishing, Winter 2005.

50 Florida Department of Education, 2007. www.fldoe.org

51 Steinhauser, C. *LBUSD Is Among the Best —Again.* LongBeach, CA: Long Beach Press—Telegram, 2007.

52 Howard, B. "Cooperative Learning Structures Improve Performance and Attitudes of High School Journalism Students." *Kagan Online Magazine.* San Clemente, CA: Kagan Publishing, Spring 2006.

53 Murie, C. "Effects of Communication on Student Learning." *Kagan Online Magazine.* San Clemente, CA: Kagan Publishing, Summer 2004.

54 Major, E. & J. Robinette. "Kagan Stuctures Add Power to Corporate Classes." *Kagan Online Magazine.* San Clemente, CA: Kagan Publishing, Fall 2004.

55 Mele, J. "Kagan Cooperative Learning Creates Explosive Results in High School Chemistry." *Kagan Online Magazine.* San Clemente, CA: Kagan Publishing, Summer 2001.

56 Dotson, J. "Cooperative Learning Structures Can Increase Student Acheivement." *Kagan Online Magazine.* San Clemente, CA: Kagan Publishing, Winter 2001.

57 Cline, L. "Impacts of Kagan Cooperative Learning Structures on Fifth-Graders' Mathematical Achievement." *Kagan Online Magazine.* San Clemente, CA: Kagan Publishing, Fall 2007.

CHAPTER 4

Why Does Cooperative Learning Work?

When we turn the chairs around in our classrooms and have students work together on a regular basis, we radically transform classroom dynamics. Students who otherwise would not be motivated become engaged. Students

Because so many positive changes are made in the cooperative classroom, it is perhaps impossible to uncover their relative impact on social and academic gains. Different theoretical frameworks help explain why cooperative learning works.

have the opportunity to do what most students most want to do—interact in positive ways with their peers. Students hold each other on task and regularly receive encouragement, tutoring, and praise. They feel included. Students become part of a community of learners; they experience joy in working and learning together. They see the teacher as someone who coaches and assists them, someone on their side, not someone who stands back and evaluates them. Students who work in teams feel better about themselves—not only because their need for inclusion is met, but also because they are more successful academically. And, of course, learning becomes more fun—for the students, and for the teacher.

There are so many positive dimensions of cooperative learning that it is impossible to determine how much each contributes to the academic and social gains that result. Certainly they contribute in different ways and different amounts in different classes and for each individual student.

Some schools and districts turn to cooperative learning because they are seeking to boost achievement. Others want to improve race relations. Others include cooperative learning as part of their character development program or their violence prevention program. Yet others wish to prepare students for the workplace of the future—a workplace in which teamwork skills and communication skills will be at a premium. And cooperative learning works. It produces all of these positive outcomes.

Cooperative learning is an educator's dream: It gives us an incredible amount of leverage. When we place a lever in the right place, we

Kagan Cooperative Learning • Dr. Spencer Kagan & Miguel Kagan
Kagan Publishing • 1 (800) 933-2667 • www.KaganOnline.com

4.1

obtain a mechanical advantage and can lift a large load with little effort. Cooperative learning is like that. It is the properly placed lever in any classroom. With relatively little effort, by placing cooperative learning structures in place, a wide range of positive outcomes result. Why is cooperative learning so powerful along so many dimensions? Let's explore eight theoretical frameworks to glean insights as to why cooperative learning results in so many positive outcomes.

8 Theories Supporting Cooperative Learning

1. Cooperative Learning Theory
2. Classic Learning Theory
3. Social Learning Theories
4. Brain-Based Learning Theory
5. Motivation Theories
6. Individual Differences Theories
7. Expectation Theory
8. The Power of the Situation

PIES Principles
Transforming Instruction Transforms Outcomes

P Positive Interdependence
Positive interdependence creates mutual support among students, creates peer norms favoring achievement, and increases the frequency and quality of peer tutoring.

I Individual Accountability
Individual accountability dramatically increases student participation and motivation to achieve.

E Equal Participation
Students who otherwise would not participate or who would participate very little become engaged when we equalize participation.

S Simultaneous Interaction
The amount of participation per student and our efficiency in teaching and managing the classroom are increased enormously when we use simultaneous rather than sequential structures.

1. Cooperative Learning Theory

The most important tool we have for understanding the positive impact of cooperative learning is the four basic principles, symbolized by the acronym PIES. The PIES principles go a long way in explaining the academic and social gains that flow from cooperative learning, see PIES Principles box.

Each principle contributes to the success of cooperative learning in a different way. These PIES principles are overviewed briefly in *Chapter 5: Seven Keys for Success* and they are explored in depth in *Chapter 12: Basic Principles (PIES)*, so we will not spend more time on them here. Instead we will examine the remaining seven frameworks.

2. Classic Learning Theory

Let's focus on four dimensions of classic learning theory: Reinforcement, Correction Opportunities, Practice Opportunities, and Transference.

Reinforcement

When behavior is followed by a reward, it is more likely to be repeated. The power of a reward to influence behavior depends on how *immediately* it follows the behavior, how *frequently* it is given, and the *desirability* of the reward. For example, if I tell you that you will get \$1 in ten years from now if you read this chapter, it would not motivate you much, if at all. If, however, I tell you that you will get $100 immediately after reading each paragraph of this chapter, you will put all else aside and read the whole chapter. I changed from delayed reinforcement to immediate reinforcement, from one-time reinforcement to frequent reinforcement, and from a mildly desirable reward to a highly desirable reward.

Cooperative learning dramatically increases the *immediacy* of rewards, the *frequency* of rewards, and the *desirability* of rewards for achievement. Let's contrast the traditional classroom with a cooperative classroom.

Traditional Classroom

In the traditional classroom, the teacher asks students to complete a worksheet, either in class or for homework. The teacher then collects the worksheets, grades them, and passes them back to the students.

Delayed Reinforcement. The reward for doing the worksheet (a mark or positive comment) comes following a long delay—after the teacher has had time to grade the papers. At best students receive their papers the next day, often it is not until after the weekend. In fact, this delay is so great, the mark or comment has no rewarding properties! The power of a reward decreases with the square of time. That is, any delay makes a reward far less powerful, and a delay of a full day makes the reward almost useless with regard to classic reinforcement properties.

Infrequent Reinforcement. Students get only one reward following each worksheet.

Weak Reward. For many students, a teacher's mark is a relatively weak reward. Many students today are not motivated by grades or marks from the teacher.

Cooperative Classroom

In the cooperative classroom, the teacher has students work in pairs using RallyCoach, Sage-N-Scribe, or Pairs Check. In RallyCoach, one student does a problem and the partner watches, coaches, and praises. Then the students switch roles.

Immediate Reinforcement. Immediately following completion of each problem, students receive praise from their peer; the reward occurs in seconds, not a day or so later.

Frequent Reinforcement. Students receive a reward following each problem, not following each worksheet.

Powerful Rewards. Today's youth live in a peer-based culture. Praise from a peer is more desirable than praise from a teacher. In RallyCoach and the other Kagan Structures, we work with peers to show how to give praise that is particularly desirable so it has very strong rewarding properties. Rather than a tired old "good job" each time a partner successfully finishes a problem, the partner gives surprising and delightful praise.

Two Additional Advantages

There are two additional advantages to the cooperative classroom with regard to reinforcement.

Process-Based Rewards. In the traditional classroom, rewards are given primarily for outcomes. The teacher does not have time to watch each student as they do each problem, so the traditional approach is to provide outcome-based rewards—marks on completed assignments. In contrast, with cooperative structures, students are encouraged to reward the effort and thinking of teammates *while they* do problems and *while they* come up with ideas that contribute to group discussions. Rewards are formative rather than summative; process-based rather than solely outcome-based. Process-based rewards increase attention to tasks and motivation to complete tasks.

Equal Reward Opportunity. Yet another dimension along which the cooperative and traditional classrooms differ is the equality of reward opportunity. In the traditional classroom, when teachers ask questions of the class and call on volunteers to answer, what often results is a subset of the students who frequently raise their hands, and another subset of the students who seldom or never raise their hand to risk a response.

Volunteer participation in a heterogeneous class creates a subgroup of students who participate very often and another subgroup who participate seldom or even never. Thus, teacher and peer recognition and appreciation—powerful rewards—are distributed very unequally.

In the traditional classroom, we end up calling on and praising most those who least need the practice and praise. We end up praising least those who most need the praise and encouragement. So there is far greater reward opportunity for the high compared to the low achievers.

Reinforcement in Traditional and Cooperative Classrooms

Reward Property	Traditional Classroom	Cooperative Classroom
Immediacy	Delayed	Immediate
Frequency	Infrequent	Frequent
Strength	Weak	Strong
Type	Outcome-Based	Process and Outcome-Based
Equality	Unequal	More equal

Correction Opportunities

When does a student find out if they are solving problems correctly? Do they find out only after practicing a series of problems incorrectly, or do they get back on track as soon as they go wrong? Cooperative Learning transforms the dynamics of correction opportunities similar to how it transforms the dynamics of reinforcement. In cooperative learning, correction is immediate, frequent, more equal, peer-based, and supportive rather than evaluative.

Immediate, Process-Oriented Corrections. In the traditional classroom, students work alone and turn in their papers for the teacher to grade. Students do not get their marked papers returned until after a substantial delay. This means that a student can practice the whole worksheet wrong, think they are doing well, expect a good mark, and feel devastated when they get back a poor grade. The traditional mode is summative, outcome-oriented—only *after* doing problems do students find out if they are doing them correctly. In contrast, cooperative learning structures provide formative feedback. They are process-oriented—students get feedback *while* they are doing problems. Because correction opportunities occur while students are doing each problem, practicing wrong and forming misconceptions and bad habits are much less likely. This immediate, process-oriented, formative feedback is present in many structures for knowledge building, procedure learning, and processing information such as RallyCoach, Pairs Check, Sage-N-Scribe, Numbered Heads Together, Showdown, RoundTable Consensus, and Listen Right!

Frequent Corrections. In the traditional approach, students receive corrections following each worksheet. With cooperative structures, students receive corrective feedback with every problem.

Equality of Correction Opportunities. Low achievers in the traditional classroom are likely to have ideas that are never subject to correction—they simply don't raise their hands to be called on. Because they don't verbalize their thinking, their false concepts are not open to corrective feedback. These students are likely to leave class with their ideas uncorrected. In contrast, in the cooperative learning classroom, all students verbalize their ideas. We establish

4.4

Kagan Cooperative Learning • **Dr. Spencer Kagan & Miguel Kagan**
Kagan Publishing • 1 (800) 933-2667 • www.KaganOnline.com

a correction norm: Students know that if they are not certain of the correctness of a peer's response, everything stops and they are to consult an authoritative source (text, Internet, peers who know, or teacher). Thus the probability of all students receiving corrective feedback is dramatically increased.

Comprehensible and Supportive Peer-Based Correction.
Many students are more open to feedback from a peer than feedback from the teacher. Sometimes peers can explain to a fellow student in ways the student can better understand.

When students receive corrections from the teacher on a worksheet after completing the worksheet, they perceive the feedback as evaluative rather than helpful. The corrections are seen as *grading,* not an attempt to teach or help the student. In contrast, peer feedback during cooperative learning is seen as *support*. The worksheet is seen as an opportunity to improve learning—not a tool for evaluation.

When students receive grades after completing a task, the tendency is to ask, "Did I get my A?" or "Did I pass?" The bottom-line focus is not on learning, but on the grade. When students receive feedback during the task from a teammate who is helping them succeed, they feel supported rather than evaluated; the focus is on learning. We become a community of learners.

Many students are more open to feedback from a peer than feedback from the teacher.

Practice Opportunities
During oral responses in the traditional classroom, students respond one at a time to the teacher's questions. This allows very limited practice per pupil. The teacher talks twice for each time a student talks, first asking the question and then providing feedback (praise, a correction opportunity, filling in missing information, or modeling an alternative way to respond). Because the teacher talks twice for each time a student

talks, the teacher talks about 60% of the time. This results in extraordinarily low participation rates for individual students—See Box: Less than one Minute per Hour! For an in-depth discussion of the pitfalls of calling on students one-at-a-time, see the Simultaneous Interaction principle in *Chapter 12: Basic Principles (PIES)*.

Less than One Minute per Hour!

When a teacher has students respond one at time to questions in a class of thirty, students receive less than one minute per hour of active participation. Why? Over half the time is taken by the teacher asking questions and providing feedback—the teacher talks twice for each time each student talks, first to ask the question and then to provide feedback. This leaves less than half an hour for student participation. But because students participate one at a time, we must divide less than thirty minutes among the thirty students, leaving less than one minute each!

In contrast, using any of the pair response structures, rather than one minute per hour, students verbalize almost 30 minutes. For example, the teacher asks a question and then in pairs students do a RallyRobin or a Timed Pair Share. In these pair response structures, half the class is verbalizing their responses at any one moment, not just one student. In the case of oral language production, students receive fifteen times more practice recalling their ideas, articulating answers, and clarifying their own thinking. This fifteen times more practice contributes greatly to the success of cooperative learning.

In the same amount of time a teacher can call on and respond to two students, each giving one response, using RallyRobin the teacher could have every student give several responses!

Transference

How likely is it that learning will be applied? Will students use what they have learned in class, outside of class? The answer depends on transference. We want students to learn skills in the classroom they will apply in work and life situations. For example, we would like students to learn social skills they will later use during casual social interactions, with significant others, with their children, and in workplace teams. The social skills include listening with respect to opinions that differ from one's own, caring, sharing, helping, and communicating clearly. How likely it is that a skill learned in one situation will be applied (transferred) to another depends on variables described by transference theory. The amount of transference depends on the similarity of the situation of acquisition and the situation of later performance. In the traditional classroom students are seated in rows and work alone. This structure is very unlike work in workplace teams, and very unlike other social interaction situations. Thus in the traditional classroom, even if we teach about the importance of social skills, there is very little probability those skills will be transferred to actual social interaction situations. In contrast, cooperative teams are social interaction situations, so the situation of acquisition is more similar to the situations in which students will apply the skills they learn.

This line of reasoning extends beyond social skills. Increasingly, today's youth will work in teams. Over 75% of all new jobs in the United States involve at least partial time working in teams, and that percent is increasing![1]

No one person can build an airplane or design a computer. The increasing complexity of workplace tasks pushes us ever more into interdependence in the workplace. Science, math, and even writing are now team endeavors. Thus, if we want students to transfer the skills they learn in school to the situations they will encounter in their lives, we need to create structures where they frequently work in teams.

Cooperative learning works well in part because it reduces the transference gap. When cooperative learning is in place, students are learning skills like those they will need in life—and they are learning them in situations like those they will encounter in life.

> *"I hear and I forget. I see and I remember. I do and I understand."*
> —Confucius

3. Social Learning Theories

There are two quite different social learning theories, and each of them goes a long way toward explaining why cooperative learning works. We will examine each in turn.

Social Learning Theory 1: The Power of Modeling

Learning is not merely a function of the rewards and punishments we receive.

Albert Bandura articulated a social learning theory that focuses on the importance of observational learning.[2] We watch others. If they are successful, we do as they do. Monkey see, monkey do. Anyone who has watched a child imitate an older sibling or an adult understands the power of this form of social learning. Any parent who to their own surprise finds themselves acting toward their children the way they were treated by their own parents (even if they did not like that treatment and swore never to treat their own kids that way) knows the power of social learning. Any teacher who has tried unsuccessfully to give verbal instructions to a complex procedure, but was successful when they demonstrated the procedure, knows the power of modeling. Students immediately "get it" when the procedure is shown, whereas many miss it when the procedure is described. We observe and imitate others. Who do we imitate? Social learning theory has demonstrated that we are more likely to model powerful, successful, and admired others, especially those with whom we feel a link or bond, or with whom we can identify.

The Power of Modeling

Learning would be exceedingly laborious, not to mention hazardous, if people had to rely solely on the effects of their own actions to inform them what to do. Fortunately, most human behavior is learned observationally through modeling: from observing others one forms an idea of how new behaviors are performed, and on later occasions this coded information serves as a guide for action.[3]

—Albert Bandura

When we observe someone carrying out an action, the same neurons in our brains fire as if we were carrying out the action. We actually practice as we observe. The discovery of mirror neurons[4] explains the power of observational learning!

Why is observational learning and modeling so important in explaining the gains of cooperative learning? When we form cooperative learning, we intentionally seat the low achiever next to and across from higher achieving students within the team. See *Chapter 7: Teams*. Proximity, however, is just the beginning. Social learning theory demonstrates we more often emulate successful individuals, so that increases the probability the low achievers will emulate the higher achievers. Further, social learning theory demonstrates that we more often emulate those with whom we can identify. Teambuilding activities are designed to have students identify themselves as part of the same team, and promotes teammate bonds that increase the probability of modeling. Finally, many of the structures, such as Team-Pair-Solo, Telephone, Circle-the-Sage, and RallyCoach, explicitly call for students to model for others. In short, cooperative learning harnesses one of the most powerful forces for learning—modeling.

Social Learning Theory 2: The Power of Mediation

Lev Semenovich Vygotsky offers another social learning theory, based primarily on mediation rather than imitation. We learn by being taught. As obvious as it is, this is among the most powerful explanations of the gains of cooperative learning.

Vygotsky provides an extremely important way to conceptualize learning. His theory makes it clear that successful learning occurs when instruction is within the Zone of Proximal Development. It is incumbent, then, for all educators to understand the concept of Zone of Proximal Development. It is most easily understood with an illustration. In the illustration below, Zone of Proximal Development, the gray line represents task difficulty. The farther right we go along the line, the more difficult the task. At the far left are very simple tasks; at the far right are very difficult tasks. Each learner has an area at the left where tasks are so easy they could do them alone. Teaching in this area is useless because the student already knows how to do these simple tasks. As we move to the right, though, we reach an area where the student cannot do the tasks alone, but could do them with coaching, help, or teaching. In Vygotsky's theory, teaching, tutoring, and coaching is called mediation. Mediation in the Zone of Proximal Development, of course, is very useful. Moving yet farther to the right, we reach an area where the tasks are so difficult that the student cannot master them, even with instruction. Here again teaching is useless because the student is simply not ready to learn tasks that difficult. For example, I could not solve problems of special relativity no matter how much coaching you gave me—I simply do

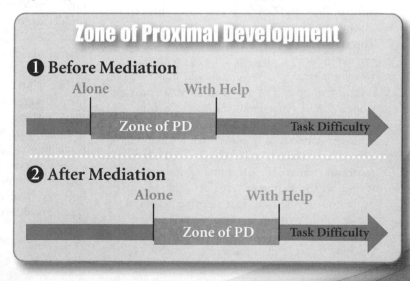

Zone of Proximal Development

❶ Before Mediation

Alone   With Help

Zone of PD   Task Difficulty

❷ After Mediation

Alone   With Help

Zone of PD   Task Difficulty

not have the prerequisite knowledge and skills. Vygotsky calls the area in the middle, the area where teaching is useful, the Zone of Proximal Development. It is where students can next learn, and to be useful all teaching should be in the Zone of Proximal Development.

Vygotsky's Theory provides a very important definition of learning. The second line of the illustration represents student learning after mediation. The student can do problems alone that previously he/she could do only with help. Note: There are also problems the student can do with help that previously were beyond the student's Zone of Proximal Development. Learning then is simply advancing the Zone of Proximal Development.

> *"What children can do together today, they can do alone tomorrow."*
> —Lev Vygotsky

Vygotsky Explains Cooperative Learning Gains

What does Vygotsky's theory have to do with why cooperative learning works? Many cooperative learning structures provide exactly the kind of mediation that advances the Zone of Proximal Development. Let's examine two examples: direct instruction and worksheet work.

Example 1: Direct Instruction— The Teacher's Dilemma

Every time we present to a heterogeneous class, we face a dilemma. Do we present to the highest achievers and lose the low achievers? Or do we present to the lowest achievers and fail to stimulate the high achievers? In whose Zone of Proximal Development do we teach? Cooperative learning provides a solution. Through cooperative learning, far more students can get input in their own Zone of Proximal Development. How? We present our material toward the top half of the class. Then, we provide students in heterogeneous teams ample time to make sure all their teammates understand. Students automatically adjust their level of help to their teammates' level of need. They are motivated to have their teammates understand. If they see the teammates are not "getting it," they explain in another way. Peer tutoring occurs in the Zone of Proximal Development. Teaching one-on-one, there is the luxury of adjusting our teaching to the level of the learner. Teaching to the whole class, the more heterogeneous the class,

the greater the dilemma we face: At any one time we teach in the Zone of Proximal Development of only some students.

Example 2: Worksheet Work

Traditional Worksheet Work. In the traditional approach, students are given direct instruction and then students practice independently, answering problems or completing a worksheet. Because classrooms are heterogeneous with regard to skill level, any worksheet is likely to be too easy for some students (below their Zone of Proximal Development) and too difficult for others (above their Zone of Proximal Development). Further, in the traditional classroom, because students are expected to work alone, those for whom the worksheet is too difficult to do alone do not receive the coaching (mediation) that would help them learn. They struggle, practice wrong, and sometimes "fake it" to avoid embarrassment, pretending to understand when they don't. Students may think they understand when they do not, and turn in a paper expecting a good grade, but receive a poor grade. They could have benefited from mediation, but do not receive it because the traditional approach provides help only if students request it.

Cooperative Worksheet Work.

Cooperative learning provides more mediation. For example, let's examine Team-Pair-Solo. Students are in heterogeneous teams, with one high achiever, one high-middle achiever, one low-middle achiever, and one low achiever on each team. (See *Chapter 7: Teams.*) In the first step of Team-Pair-Solo, the teams are given a problem that is beyond the ability of the lower achieving students, but the team members are instructed that they have two jobs: 1) to solve the problem; and, more importantly, 2) to make sure everyone on their team knows how to solve that type of problem.

Team-Pair-Solo

Students are instructed in how best to coach. For example, they learn that telling an answer is poor coaching; but showing how to get an answer is good coaching. After the team has successfully completed some problems, and is sure all teammates can solve that type of problem, they break into two pairs and the partners each in turn do a problem like the one that was solved as a team. Finally, students perform similar problems alone, applying what they learned first as a team and then during pair work. Students, who initially could not do the problems alone, now can. They have advanced their Zone of Proximal Development due to the coaching (mediation) embedded in the structure. Other structures, such as RallyCoach, Pairs Check, Sage-N-Scribe, Showdown, and Numbered Heads Together, also provide ample opportunities for coaching. Students are motivated to help their teammates succeed, so they adjust their input to the learning needs of their teammates, teaching them in their Zone of Proximal Development. Thus a far greater percent of students receive input in the Zone of Proximal Development when cooperative learning structures are implemented than during the traditional approach. Vygotsky's theory provides a very strong theoretical foundation for cooperative learning.[5]

The Power of Social Learning

Every function in the child's cultural development appears twice: first, on the social level, and later, on the individual level; first, between people (interpsychological) and then inside the child (intrapsychological). This applies equally to voluntary attention, to logical memory, and to the formation of concepts. All the higher functions originate as actual relationships between individuals.[6]
—**Lev Semenovich Vygotsky**

4. Brain-Based Learning Theory

Brain science is now advanced to the point that we can with say with certainty that some ways of teaching align how the brain best learns and others do not. When we teach the way the brain best learns, teaching is easier and more enjoyable, students attend with more interest; they retain more, and like class, the teacher, and learning more. Teaching the way the brain best learns is like swimming with rather than against the current.

There are a number of ways cooperative learning compared to traditional teaching better aligns classrooms with how brains best learn. Every major expert in brain-based learning calls for cooperative learning. A full discussion of all the ways cooperative learning is brain-friendly is beyond the scope of this chapter. We will, however, touch on five of the most important principles of brain-based instruction and how they link to cooperative learning: safety, nourishment, social interaction, emotion, and information processing.

Safety

In the center of the limbic system of the brain are two almond-shaped structures, the left and right amygdales. Among other functions, the amygdales function as threat sensors. When there is a threat in the environment, the amygdales fire at an accelerated rate, which sets off a cascade of reactions including the release of stress hormones including Cortisol and ACTH. Stress hormones interfere with hippocampus functioning so we do not lay down new memories efficiently. Our body tenses in preparation for fight or flight. Blood lactate increases and we feel anxious. In that state, we have constricted cognition and perception. Anyone taking a very important exam who has felt too anxious to think clearly has experienced the effect of those threat sensors firing.

Active brain imaging demonstrates the right amygdala fires more when we view an angry or frightened face; the left amygdala fires more when we hear a threatening sound or tone of voice. The amygdales fire more when we see the face of a stranger than a friend; more when we see the face of a person from an out-group than part of our in-group. Whenever the amygdales fire, we move further from the state of relaxed alertness, the optimal state for learning.

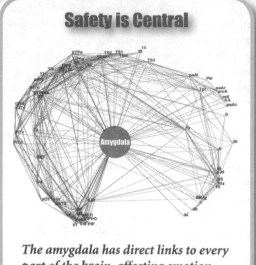

Safety is Central

The amygdala has direct links to every part of the brain, affecting emotion, cognition, perception, memory, and performance.[7]

What does all this have to do with cooperative learning? Cooperative learning converts strangers to friends, out-group members to in-group members. Students are more relaxed because they feel accepted and perceive there are no threats in the environment. Positive interdependence creates mutual support and trust. Teambuilding and classbuilding activities are designed to help students feel known, accepted, and included. If a student does not know the answer, teammates encourage and help the student. This is in contrast to the traditional classroom where, when a student begins to falter, the other students wildly wave their hands, glad for the opportunity to be called on and have a chance to get the right answer. In the traditional classroom, students are set against each other. Competition results in students hoping others do not do well so they can shine in comparison. In the cooperative classroom, students experience themselves on the same side, receiving mutual encouragement and support. This leads to fewer stress hormones and more of

Cooperative learning includes social interaction over content, and literally the brains in a cooperative learning classroom are more engaged.

a state of relaxed alertness, the optimal state for thinking and learning.

Nourishment

The brain comprises only two percent of our body weight yet consumes up to a quarter of the oxygen and glucose in our body. It takes a great deal of energy to keep the 100 billion neurons firing optimally. Each neuron has on the average 2,000 dendrite connections, and each connection is firing about 200 times a second. The brain is a busy place: 100 billion networked computers, each neuron connected to every other neuron in the brain within a few synapses.

Why is this important for cooperative learning? Brains function well only if there is an ample supply of oxygen and glucose. We all know that only a few minutes of oxygen deprivation results in loss of brain function and a few more minutes leads to permanent brain damage—the brain is that dependent on a constant flow of nutrients. Oxygen and glucose in the brain are increased when breathing rate/volume and heart rate/volume are increased—both of which result from movement. Cooperative learning classrooms include movement on a regular basis via classbuilding and teambuilding activities. Stroll-Pair-Share, just one Kagan Structure that makes physical movement an integral part of learning, has partners walk or "stroll" as they discuss. Cooperative structures encourage movement so brains are better nourished, more alert, and more receptive to learning.

Social Interaction

Brains are more engaged during social interaction than when listening to a lecture or viewing a visual presentation. See box, Social Interaction Activates the Brain on the following page. From birth, brains naturally attend far more to people than to inanimate objects. Cooperative learning includes social interaction over content, and so literally the brains in a cooperative learning classroom are more engaged. This greater engagement leads to greater retention.

Social Interaction Activates the Brain

PET Scans reveal the brain is more engaged during social interaction over content than during solo learning activities.[8]

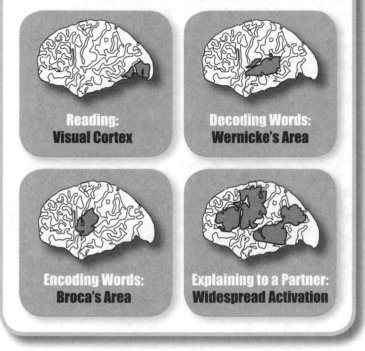

Reading:
Visual Cortex

Decoding Words:
Wernicke's Area

Encoding Words:
Broca's Area

Explaining to a Partner:
Widespread Activation

Emotion

Anything followed by emotion is better remembered. This principle, called retrograde memory enhancement,[9] is well established. If content is associated with emotion, the neurons in the brain fire at a higher rate, signaling the hippocampus "this is worth remembering." We may have a hard time remembering a telephone number, but no trouble remembering our first kiss! Cooperative learning creates genuine social interactions, which in turn generates emotions. Because cooperative learning is more emotion-laden learning than independent learning, content is better retained.

Information Processing

The brain attends to, processes, and retains certain kinds of information far more effortlessly than other information. The brain remembers multi-modal content better; records episodes effortlessly; attends more readily to novel stimuli; and craves predictability. These principles help explain why cooperative learning produces positive results—cooperative learning provides multi-modal, episodic learning experiences.

Multi-Modal Content. If we present our content with a picture as well as words, there are links to the visual and the auditory cortices as well as dendrite connections between them. Literally that content is placed in more areas in the brain, so there are more associative links to the content and it is more easily recalled. Cooperative learning is inherently multi-modal because we look at the facial expressions, body language, and gestures of those with whom we interact (visual cortex); we decode their words (Wernicke's area) and tone of voice (amygdala); we encode our own thoughts into words (Broca's area); we evaluate what they say and assimilate and accommodate their information and conceptual framework (pre-frontal cortex). Further, many cooperative learning structures involve movement so the pre-motor and motor cortices are involved as well. Because so many parts of the brain are engaged, cooperative learning content is more fully processed and retained.

Episodic Memory. The brain has a number of distinct memory systems. For example, we process and store isolated bits of information with our semantic memory system, but we store events with our episodic memory system. The episodic memory system is the most brain-friendly; the brain is exquisitely designed to remember episodes. We effortlessly remember what we had for dinner last night and where we were. In contrast, we have difficulty remembering a list of states and capitals. The brain is not designed to store and recall isolated, unrelated bits of information. Structures are brain-friendly because they are episodes and the brain's most natural way to remember is via episodes. RallyRobin, Timed Pair Share, Sage-N-Scribe or any other structure are events that take place at a time and in a place for a specified duration. What happens during those events is therefore more easily remembered; it is stored more effortlessly in the episodic memory system.

Timed Pair Share

Kagan Cooperative Learning • Dr. Spencer Kagan & Miguel Kagan
Kagan Publishing • 1 (800) 933-2667 • www.KaganOnline.com

 4.11

Novelty. We are walking in the woods. We hear a branch crack. We get a rush of adrenaline and immediately turn, alert, focusing our attention in the direction of the noise. We are wired to attend to novel stimuli—to check it out, determine if it is a threat or an opportunity. Our brains become more alert and focused in the face of novel stimuli. The teacher who teaches the same way every day presents no novelty so students in that class are less alert and less attentive.

How does this relate to cooperative learning? First, one of the greatest sources of novel stimuli is interaction with another person. The unexpected alerts the attention system. Greater attention in turn produces greater retention. Solo activities produce few unexpected events compared to cooperative learning activities. We can never fully predict what another person will say or do. Thus the brain is much more attentive during interaction, and this enhanced engagement leads to more processing, deeper understanding, and greater retention.

The use of a range of structures in itself provides novelty. After a RallyRobin, the teacher gives some input via Teacher Talk. Following that the teacher has students StandUp-Hand Up-PairUp, and do a Timed Pair Share. The students are constantly alert and attentive as they work first with this person, attend to the teacher, and next work with a different partner. As the teacher uses a sequence of structures within the lesson, the novel stimuli associated with the changes in structures makes students more alert and attentive, increasing engagement and retention.

Predictability. About twice a second, the brain is making predictions. As long as the world acts the way we expect, the brain remains relative quiescent. When our predictions are contradicted, the brain goes into full gear to process and resolve the contradiction. For a deeper understanding of this process, we recommend the revolutionary work of Jeff Hawkins.[10] The struggle to construct a meaningful, predictable world is rooted in our need to feel safe and secure. Contradicted expectations are a form of novelty and evoke

processing and enhance retention, but we are constantly struggling to make our world predictable, to know what is coming next. When we do not know what is coming, when our world is not predictable, we feel insecure. If a teacher has no routines and students never know what is coming next, the classroom feels chaotic and the students become insecure, anxious. Anxiety interferes with learning.

Balancing Routine & Novelty

Too Much Routine
Monotony → Boredom

Balanced
Relaxed Alertness

Too Much Novelty
Chaos → Anxiety

Best of Both Worlds. The balance scales above symbolize the relationship between amount of novelty and amount of predictability. Too much predictability with no novelty, and we feel bored. Too much novelty with no predictability, and we feel anxious. The optimal state for learning is relaxed alertness.

We want our students to feel safe and relaxed—to feel like they are living in a predictable world. On the other hand, we want our students to be alert, attentive, stimulated, and wide awake. How can we resolve this apparent paradox of wanting both novelty and predictability in our classrooms? Cooperative learning structures provide a unique solution: Structures are predictable sequences, meeting the need for a predictable environment. When we are in a RoundRobin or a Timed Pair Share, we know just what is going to happen next. The structures are routines that create the security of a predictable world. At the same time, structures create novelty: The variety of structures within a lesson and interaction over novel content within the structures create novelty. Students are relaxed, working within a predictable sequence, but they are fully alert because of the novelty provided by the structures. Thus use of a range of structures resolves the paradox: We create the best of both worlds— novel stimuli within a predictable world.

5. Motivation Theories

What do we strive for? What motivates us? There are numerous theories of motivation. Each of the theories helps explain why cooperative learning produces such positive results. We will overview briefly four motivation theories: Maslow's Hierarchy of Needs, Csikszentmihalyl's Flow Theory, Seligman's optimism Helplessness Theory, and Hunter's ASK IF I model.

Maslow's Hierarchy of Needs

Abraham Maslow postulated that we attempt to fill our deficiencies before we attempt to meet our need to grow. At a crude level, this is obvious: When we are starving, we seek food, not the opportunity to master calculus or read another Shakespeare play. But Maslow's theory is very refined,[11] describing a differentiated hierarchy of needs. We focus on filling needs lower in the hierarchy before we are freed to focus on the higher needs.

Maslow's Hierarchy of Needs[11]

▶ **Self-Actualization**
To obtain knowledge, beauty, fulfillment, and transcendence….

▶ **Belongingness/Love**
Feel included, accepted, cared for….

▶ **Esteem**
Feel competent, to achieve, to obtain recognition….

▶ **Safety/Security**
Escape danger; avoid embarrassment….

▶ **Physiological**
Hunger; Comfortable Temperature….

How does Maslow's Hierarchy explain the positive outcomes of cooperative learning? If students do not feel safe and included, their energy is directed to meeting those deficiency needs and is not free to meet the need to know and understand. We see this on a daily basis, especially in middle school where the need for peer acceptance is so intense. Students are so busy worrying about their status among peers that they have a difficult time concentrating on studies. When we put cooperative learning in place, the need for safety is satisfied through the social norms (no put downs; disagreeing politely). The need for inclusion is satisfied through teambuilding and classbuilding (I am included, part of the team). With the needs for safety and security satisfied, the students have more free energy to move up the hierarchy, striving for esteem and knowledge.

Co-op Co-op

The hierarchy of needs explains what otherwise would be a puzzling event. In 1973, I began developing Co-op Co-op to use in my undergraduate psychology courses at the University of California–Riverside.[12] Co-op Co-op is a project/presentation structure in which each student on a team works on one "mini-topic" (one part of the team project) and then the mini-topics are synthesized to create a team presentation to the whole class. (See *Chapter 17: Classic Cooperative Learning*.) In the early version of Co-op Co-op, students received a grade based in part on the quality of their group presentation to the class. Co-op Co-op was a favorite among undergraduate students: They created elaborate, interesting, and informative presentations—presentations that obviously took a great deal of time and effort to prepare. Although the method worked very well, I did not like the inherent unfairness of group grades—students who performed at exactly the same level would receive different grades, depending on the performance of their teammates.

Given my desire to avoid the unfairness inherent in group grades (see *Chapter 15: Assessment and Grading*), I decided to modify Co-op Co-op. Students would receive feedback rather than grades on their presentations; their course grade would be based only on their individual performance. But I was worried. I knew that in the busy life of an undergraduate, it would be logical to put little or even no effort into a presentation that would not affect the course grade. With some trepidation, however, I decided to go ahead with the plan to have the team presentations ungraded. The big surprise came when the presentations were made: The presentations were as good or better than when they were graded! It turned out that a grade was not needed to motivate students; Maslow's hierarchy explains what was motivating the students. They were motivated by the drive for esteem—the opportunity to be of value to their classmates, to receive approval and recognition, to be competent, to feel of worth.

Csikszentmihalyl's Flow

Mihaly Csikszentmihalyl provides an explanation of the conditions necessary for optimum motivation and performance.[13] Sometimes we work at our peak: We are productive, but it occurs without anxiety or struggle. During peak performance, time seems to disappear.

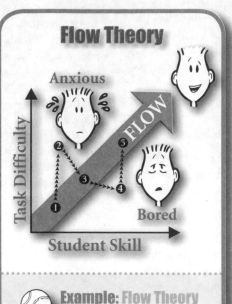

Flow Theory

Anxious

FLOW

Task Difficulty

Student Skill

Bored

Example: Flow Theory and Tennis Lessons

Flow occurs when task difficulty matches skill. For example, you go to a pro to learn tennis for the first time. The numbers below correspond to the numbers on the Flow diagram above.

1 Your skill level is very low but the pro recognizes that and so hits you easy lobs. You feel great because you are being successful. In fact, you feel you could do this all day. You are in the flow.

2 Now, the pro sees you doing great, and she increases task difficulty. In fact, she increases task difficulty beyond your ability. As you miss ball after ball, you begin to feel anxious. You are definitely not in the flow. In fact you are considering throwing down your racquet and leaving.

3 Your pro is sensitive and sees you are anxious and frustrated. So she decreases task difficulty. You are once again in the groove, hitting again, feeling great. Why did you re-enter the flow—because task difficulty matches skill.

4 But as your skill increases, the pro continues to lob you easy ones. Now how are you feeling? You are no longer in the flow. In fact, you are feeling bored. Tennis isn't a very exciting game; you begin to toy with the idea of taking up golf! Why did you leave the flow? Because task difficulty no longer matches skill.

5 What does the pro have to do to get you back in the flow? Given your increased skill, the pro needs to hit you more challenging shots.

In fact, in these peak moments, all thoughts of anything other than our task disappear. When is it that we are in this kind of flow? Flow occurs when there is an optimal relation between our skill level and task difficulty.

The art of keeping students motivated and excited about learning is the art of matching task difficulty to skill level.

How does flow theory help explain the positive outcomes of cooperative learning? What we see in the tennis example (box: Flow Theory) is that motivation remains high as long as task difficulty matches skill level. When students are working in a cooperative group, the norm is to ask for help if needed and offer help if requested. This translates into an ongoing adjustment of task difficulty. If a student bumps into a roadblock while doing problems, the student asks for help. The help makes the task more manageable, so the student is much more likely to re-enter the flow state and remain motivated. There is also added challenge for the high achiever. Basic instructions during cooperative learning are that you always have two jobs: 1) Make sure you can solve the problems; 2) Make sure everyone on the team can also. The high achiever has the challenges of tutoring, modeling, coaching, explaining, encouraging, and praising their lower achieving teammates—often a challenging set of tasks/skills. Thus, rather than rushing through a worksheet and feeling bored (task too easy for skill), the high achiever must meet the challenges associated with monitoring teammates and offering help as needed. Thus all students are more likely to remain in the flow zone, increasing motivation.

The amount of reward may be great or little; that is not what is important to motivation.

Seligman's Optimism/ Helplessness

Martin Seligman and associates have demonstrated that whether we feel motivated or apathetic, helpless or optimistic, is not a function of how many rewards we receive, but rather the contingency of those rewards.[14] That is, our motivation depends on whether we feel that what we do makes a difference. If the probability of reward is the same whether or not I try, there is no reason to try. The amount of reward may be great or little; that is not what is important to motivation. In a deprived environment, I get no rewards no matter what I do, so there is no reason try. In situations in which my efforts make no difference, I become depressed, and may even give up the will to live.[15] In contrast, in situations in which my efforts determine my rewards, I become motivated.

The three illustrations in the box on the page depict how the relationship between effort and rewards affects our perceptions. First illustration: If I get rewarded when I try, I am motivated to try. I feel my efforts make a difference. Middle illustration: If I get a reward regardless of whether or not I try, I become apathetic. I don't care about trying because I may be rewarded anyway. Last illustration: If my efforts don't increase the probability of reward, I enter the state of helplessness. I feel my efforts don't make a difference, and I give up trying.

How does this well-established theory of optimism/helplessness help explain the positive effects of cooperative learning? The most powerful reward for most students is positive attention/approval from peers. In the traditional classroom, academic achievement is often associated with negative peer responses:

The student who always has a hand up, always can add to someone else's answer, and always gets the high score is labeled "geek" or "brown-nose." Thus, for many students, there is little or no motivation to perform their very best academically; and some even fake dumb to avoid negative peer responses. In contrast, there is high motivation to perform well academically in the cooperative learning classroom: The student who does well helps the team, and helping the team is associated with the most powerful reward for students—positive peer attention. In cooperative learning, students see that effort and academic achievement is the road to success and peer approval. In the traditional classroom, achievement is not linked to peer approval so there is less motivation to achieve.

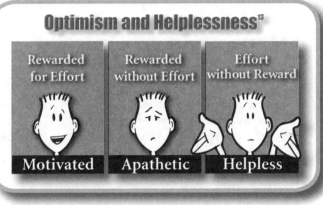

Optimism and Helplessness[13]

Rewarded for Effort — Motivated

Rewarded without Effort — Apathetic

Effort without Reward — Helpless

Hunter's ASK IF I

Madelyn Hunter's comprehensive approach to instruction[16] distinguishes six principles of motivation that can be symbolized by the acronym ASK IF I: Anxiety, Success, Knowledge of results, Interest, Feeling tone, and Intrinsic motivation. Each of these principles helps explain why cooperative learning produces positive results.

Anxiety. When anxiety is too high, motivation to continue the task drops. This is similar to the flow concept. As we have explored in the discussion of brain-based learning, teambuilding, classbuilding, and mutual support all decrease anxiety.

Success. No one is motivated to continue a task if they do not obtain, or at least think it is possible to obtain, success. Students perceive they are more likely to succeed via cooperative learning because of the tutoring and teamwork, so they are more motivated.

Knowledge of Results. If we don't know if we are successful or not, we are less likely to remain motivated. We want feedback. Cooperative learning provides immediate rather than delayed feedback, with feedback following each problem, not following each worksheet.

Interest. Interesting tasks motivate us. Creating interest can occur in a number of ways, including a contrary-to-expectations demonstration, a link to personal interests, and understanding how the skill will be useful in one's life. Cooperative learning tasks stimulate interest in part because they are an opportunity for most students to do what they most want to do—interact with their peers. Interest is generated also because of divergent points of view interacting. Also, cooperative learning projects are intrinsically interesting.

Feeling Tone. When there is a positive feeling tone, we are more motivated to remain engaged in a task. No one wants to remain in a work environment in which there are put-downs and a negative feeling tone. Because of the praise, encouragement, validations, and celebrations built into many of the cooperative learning structures, a positive feeling tone is created, enhancing motivation.

Intrinsic Motivation. Intrinsic motivation exists when a student performs a learning task because the student enjoys the task and enjoys learning; extrinsic motivation exists to the extent the student performs the task because the student expects a reward for task completion. In one case, the reward is intrinsic to the task; in the other case, the reward is extrinsic—something tacked on to motivate performance. In some cases extrinsic rewards undermine motivation; the student becomes hooked on extrinsic rewards and will be less motivated when extrinsic rewards are taken away.[17] Cooperative learning tasks are far more intrinsically motivating for most students than are solo learning tasks. Why? Because students find it enjoyable to work with others, interact, feel part of a team, experience

the pleasure of working together to reach a common goal.

The "ASK IF I" conditions are all present in cooperative learning, translating to enhanced motivation. This enhanced motivation takes the form of greater persistence in the face of difficulty, more time on task, and heightened engagement—all of which result in higher achievement.

6. Individual Differences Theories

There are many individual difference theories. Students differ in their cognitive styles, multiple intelligences, learning styles, and personality styles. Because students have different minds and learn in different ways, any one way of teaching biases outcomes in favor of some students and against others. Differentiated instruction provides different learners access to the curriculum.[18, 19]

In differentiated classrooms, teachers begin where students are, not the front of a curriculum guide. They accept and build upon the premise that learners differ in important ways. Thus, they also accept and act on the premise that teachers must be ready to engage students in instruction through different learning modalities, by appealing to different interests, and by using varied rates of instruction along with varied degrees of complexity.[20]

Two general approaches to differentiated instruction can be distinguished: Teaching different students in different ways v. Teaching all students in many ways. These two approaches are not mutually exclusive—we can teach all students in many ways and also assess them and attempt to meet their individual needs by teaching them differently, depending on the assessment. Any attempt to assess students and teach them in different ways is fraught with huge potential pitfalls. For example, if we assess students and find that Johnny is weak in the verbal/linguistic but strong in the visual/spatial intelligence, we might be tempted to tailor instruction for Johnny to minimize verbal/linguistic input and maximize visual/spatial input. If we did, we would fail to develop the very intelligence Johnny is most in need of developing. We have argued elsewhere, as forcefully as we know how, that the better course is to teach all students in many ways rather than to track them into groups that receive different types of instruction.[21]

If we are committed to teaching in many ways so that all students receive their preferred mode of instruction some of the time, we must begin with the question: How do students learn differently? Four major dimensions can be distinguished (See Individual Difference Dimensions table below.)

Individual Difference Dimensions

Dimension		Definition
Multiple Intelligences	→	The type of stimuli we are attracted to and skilled with.
Cognitive Styles	→	How we think.
Learning Styles	→	How we learn.
Personality Styes	→	How we relate.

We ignore these intelligence and style dimensions at the risk of failing to serve all of our students well. Students with different intelligences are attracted to and skilled with different types of information. A student weak in the verbal/linguistic intelligence but strong in the visual/spatial intelligence doesn't enjoy or understand the content much when the content is presented exclusively via lecture, but likes and understands the content better when the content is presented in a diagram. An interpersonal student, who finds traditional solo worksheet work boring, lights up and does well when processing the exact same worksheet through RallyCoach.

Not only do learners differ in their intelligences, they differ in their learning styles. Dr. Ned Herrmann provides an excellent example of the need to relate to different learning styles. Dr. Herrmann was teaching an unstructured course at General Electric's Management Development Institute.

"On this particular occasion, we started the workshop at 8:30. At the 10:00 AM coffee break, one of the key staff managers came up to me and said, *'Ned, if I don't find out in the first five minutes after we reconvene what this workshop is all about, where it's going, and where it will end up, I will be leaving after lunch, and I will be taking with me all four of the people who work with me and anybody else who is as uncomfortable as I am at this minute!'"*

Dr. Herrmann quickly drew up a "Workshop Road Map" to share right after the break. As he shared the road map,

"...I noticed at least five or six people looking visibly relieved. Expressions of hostility softened into expressions of understanding, acceptance, and comfort."[22]

Dr. Herrmann discovered that not all students have the same learning style. Some are inductive learners: They are happy to be thrown into the content without a roadmap, to be given many examples without being given a general principle—they prefer to create their own roadmap, create their own meaning, and derive their own principles from the content. Others are deductive learners: They want the roadmap up front. Deductive learners do not feel comfortable without knowing from the outset just where the lesson is going and what principles the content and the examples support.

There are many theories of intelligences, cognitive styles, learning styles, and personality styles. There have been intriguing attempts to explore their interrelations and to integrate these various dimensions.[23] Exploration of all the style dimensions and how cooperative learning responds to the needs of every type of learner would take us far beyond the scope of this book. As examples, we will examine just two of the many individual difference theories: Howard Gardner's Multiple Intelligences and the Dunn Learning Styles. We will show how when the teacher uses a range of cooperative learning methods, different learners each receive instruction in the way they best learn.

Multiple Intelligences

Different cooperative learning structures respond to the needs of students strong in different intelligences. A sample of structures to engage and develop each of the intelligences is provided in the table below. Details of those structures and how they engage and develop the different intelligences is provided in our book on multiple intelligences.[24]

Learning Styles

The most extensively researched learning style model is that of Rita and Kenneth Dunn. They define learning style as the way in which each learner begins to concentrate on, process,

and retain information. They emphasize that because students differ in their learning style, the same teaching method will be effective for some students and ineffective for others.[25] Some students prefer to work alone; others prefer to work with a partner or in a small group. This alone is a strong rationale for including cooperative learning in the mix of instructional strategies and may explain why inclusion of cooperative learning boosts achievement—it is the way many students prefer to learn.

The Dunn and Dunn model, however, is quite comprehensive and provides additional reasons why inclusion of cooperative learning improves outcomes for many students. In the Dunn and

Structures Engage and Develop Multiple Intelligences

Verbal/Linguistic
- Debate
- Dialogues
- Discussion
- Team Interview
- Talking Chips

Bodily/Kinesthetic
- Formations
- Kinesthetic Symbols
- Line-Ups
- Take Off, Touch Down
- Team Charades

Logical/Mathematical
- Blind Sequencing
- Find My Rule
- Jigsaw Problem Solving
- Who Am I?

Naturalist
- Categorizing
- Look-Write-Discuss
- Observe-Draw-RallyRobin
- Same-Different

Visual/Spatial
- Draw It!
- Formations
- Guided Imagery
- Mind Mapping
- Same-Different
- Visualization

Interpersonal/Social
- Jigsaw
- Numbered Heads Together
- Paraphrase Passport
- Pairs Check
- Pairs Compare
- Stir-the-Class
- Team Statements
- Three-Step Interview

Musical/Rhythmic
- Lyrical Lessons
- Poems for Two Voices
- Songs for Two Voices
- Team Chants

Intrapersonal/Introspective
- Agreement Circles
- Corners
- Proactive Prioritizing
- Timed Pair Share

Kagan Cooperative Learning • Dr. Spencer Kagan & Miguel Kagan
Kagan Publishing • 1 (800) 933-2667 • www.KaganOnline.com

Dunn model, there are five basic stimuli with 26 elements:

1. **Environmental:** sound; light; temperature; seating-design
2. **Emotional:** motivation; persistence; responsibility; conformity structure
3. **Sociological:** learning alone; with peers; team; adult
4. **Physiological:** perceptual: auditory, visual, tactile, kinesthetic; time-of-day, energy level, mobility
5. **Psychological:** global v. analytic; hemisphericity; impulsive v. reflective

The use of a range of cooperative learning structures relates to a number of the elements in four dimensions of the Dunn's model (see table below). Inclusion of a range of cooperative learning structures ensures that the needs of more learners are met. In the table, a few of the many possible structures are listed to illustrate how different structures meet the needs of different learning styles.

As we overview how the different cooperative learning methods respond to the needs of different learners, we can say with certainty that the teacher who uses a wide range of cooperative learning methods provides a greater number of students greater access to the curriculum through their preferred styles and intelligences. This explains in part why cooperative learning boosts achievement. In short: ***The more ways we teach, the more students we reach.***

Learning Styles Served by Cooperative Structures

Emotional	**Motivation**	Students from some cultures are motivated to work hard for the group, but not for individual achievement, so cooperative learning is culturally compatible for some cultural groups.
	Persistence	Cooperative learning teaches students how to encourage each other in the face of difficulty, motivating persistence. Tutoring and support also motivate persistence.
	Responsibility	In some structures, students are responsible not just for their own outcomes, but also for their contribution to the team as well as the team's contribution to the class: Co-op Co-op
	Conformity	**Conformity:** Team Consensus **Non-conformity:** Debate
	Structure	**High structure:** RallyRobin **Low structure:** Team Projects
Sociological	**Preferred Interaction Style**	**Alone:** Many structures include think time and solo write **Pairs:** Pairs Compare, Pairs Check, Timed Pair Share **Teams:** The defining characteristic of cooperative learning **Classmates:** Classbuilding structures: Corners, Circle-the-Sage **Adult:** Some structures include interaction with the teacher: Choral Practice, Show Me!, Numbered Heads Together. Structures free the teacher for more quality interaction time with individual students.
Physiological	**Perceptual**	**Auditory:** Listen Right!, Telephone **Visual:** Mind Mapping, Same-Different… **Tactile:** Team projects with manipulatives **Kinesthetic:** Kinesthetic Symbols, Formations
	Energy Level	**High Energy:** Team Charades **Low Energy:** Draw-What-I-Write
	Mobility	**Movement:** Mix-Music-Meet **Seat Work:** RoundRobin
Psychological	**Global v. Analytic**	**Global:** Formations **Analytic:** Same-Different
	Inductive v. Deductive	**Inductive:** Find My Rule **Deductive:** Logic Line-Ups
	Hemisphericity	**Right Hemisphere:** Team Mind-Mapping **Left Hemisphere:** Sequencing
	Impulsive v. Reflective	**Impulsive:** RallyRobin **Reflective:** Timed Pair Share

Kagan Cooperative Learning • Dr. Spencer Kagan & Miguel Kagan
Kagan Publishing • 1 (800) 933-2667 • www.KaganOnline.com

4.19

7. Expectation Theory

In a classic study on the impact of expectations on performance, Robert Rosenthal and Leonore Jacobson gave an intelligence test to all of the students at an elementary school.[26] They told the teachers that in addition to an IQ test, they were administering "The Harvard Test of Inflected Acquisition"—a test that revealed which students were the "academic spurters" who could be expected to "bloom" or "spurt" in their academics the next year. In fact, there is no such test. The researchers simply wanted to test the effects of manipulating teacher expectations.

Researchers randomly selected twenty percent of the students from each class list—without any regard to their intelligence test results—and told their teachers that their testing had revealed those students were the ones who would make rapid, above-average intellectual progress that year. At the end of the year, the researchers came back and re-tested the IQ of all the students.

The results: Students labeled "bloomers" gained significantly more IQ points than the unlabeled group. The effect was more pronounced among the youngest students. For example, among the first grade students, those randomly labeled "bloomers" gained 15 IQ points more than their non-selected classmates, and nearly half of first- and second-grade "spurters" showed an IQ increase of 20 points or more!

Further, the teachers' subjective assessments, such as reading grades, showed similar differences and the teachers indicated that these "special" students were better behaved, more intellectually curious, had greater chances for future success, and friendlier than their non-special counterparts.

These results have been replicated many times and hold across hundreds of studies in school, lab, clinic, and everyday settings.[27] Studies have revealed the power of expectations—for Air Force Academy students taking Algebra, and for members of a bowling team—no matter the group, *what we expect is what we get.*

> *"If you think you can do a thing or think you can't do a thing, you're right."*
> —Henry Ford

Why are our prophecies self-fulfilling? Expectations are communicated in a number of ways, and in turn affect motivation and performance. Teachers who expect less of students give them less challenging work. Their nonverbal communication is different. We can't help but communicate our expectations. Those expectations are communicated not just to the student, but to the student's peers, who in turn treat the student differently. Most importantly, the student's self-image is transformed; we live up to or down to our image. The student who believes he/she "can" puts in the extra effort when faced with a challenge; the student who believes he/she "can't" gives up with less effort.

How do expectancy effects help explain the positive outcomes of cooperative learning? One of the most often cited research outcomes of cooperative learning is that the lowest achievers

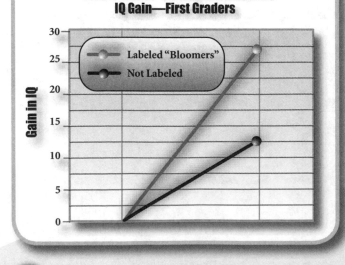

The Power of Expectations
IQ Gain—First Graders

Gain in IQ

- Labeled "Bloomers"
- Not Labeled

Kagan Cooperative Learning • Dr. Spencer Kagan & Miguel Kagan
Kagan Publishing • 1 (800) 933-2667 • www.KaganOnline.com

blossom. When this is communicated to teachers, their expectations are changed. This in turn promotes achievement for those students. Cooperative learning is based on the premise that all students can do well if they get proper encouragement and support. We teach students to encourage each other with gambits like, "You can do it!" To the extent these expectations are internalized, they change their self-image and students begin to live up to their own higher expectations. The praising, celebrations, and "we can do it" attitudes inherent in cooperative learning all support transformed, higher expectations. Raised self-expectations in turn promote achievement.

8. The Power of the Situation

A central finding of social psychology research is the power of the situation. We behave as we do to a great extent based on situational variables. This discovery runs counter to the common tendency to attribute behavior to personality variables. When we see someone cooperate or compete, we tend to attribute the behavior to their personality: "He is a cooperative person; she is competitive." Social psychology research, however, reveals that across many situations, among most individuals, behavior is more a function of situation than personality.

Let us offer three of many possible examples, one theoretical and two empirical.

Rich Lady with Bucket of Gold Coins

For the theoretical example, let's ask ourselves how people would behave in two different situations.

Situation 1: Competition

A very rich lady enters a crowded room with a bucket of gold coins. She announces: "I have decided to distribute my wealth." She explains the rules: I will stand on the stage and toss out all the gold coins in this bucket. You will have three minutes. All the coins you have collected at the end of the three minutes will be yours to keep. She then tosses the coins.

Situation 2: Cooperation

The same rich lady enters the same crowded room with the same bucket of gold coins. She announces to the same group of people: "I have decided to distribute my wealth." She explains the rules: I will stand on the stage and toss out all the gold coins in this bucket. Then the bucket will be placed on the stage. You will have three minutes. All the coins your group has managed to return to the bucket at the end of the three minutes will be divided equally among you and will be yours to keep. She then tosses the coins.

The results: In Situation 1, there is frenzied competition: People are shoving each other and even grabbing coins from each other. In Situation 2, there is frenzied cooperation: People are handing the coins to others who are running to get them into the bucket.

What is important to note is that the number of coins and the time were the same. The personality of the people in the room did not change. Their personal histories, the way they were raised as children, was the same. What changed? People respond to situations. Why did one situation produce intense competition and the other intense cooperation? In Situation 1, there was negative interdependence (if one person got a coin, the other did not). In Situation 2, there was positive interdependence (one person getting a coin in the bucket helped everyone).

We behave as we do to a great extent based on situations we are in. Each cooperative learning structure presents different situational variables to produce specific, positive behaviors.

Stanford Prison Experiment

In a classic social psychology study, Stanford psychology professor Philip Zimbardo took normal young men and randomly assigned them to be prisoners or guards in what became known as the Stanford Prison Experiment.[28] The participants were given tests to ensure they had no psychological problems, medical disabilities, or history of crime or drug abuse. They were an average, healthy, intelligent, middle-class group of young men. One group was rounded up by Palo Alto police and dropped off at a new jail—in the basement of the Stanford psychology department. Strip searched, sprayed for lice, and locked up with chains around their ankles, the "prisoners" were part of an experiment to test people's reactions to power dynamics in social situations. The other college students, the "guards," were given complete authority to dictate 24-hour-a-day rules.

The result: Guards were soon humiliating the prisoners and invented sadistic methods in an effort to break the will of their prisoners, including making them urinate and defecate in buckets they were not allowed to empty. They escalated their abuse of prisoners at night when they thought no researchers were watching, inventing ever more pornographic and degrading abuse. The treatment was disturbing enough that one prisoner began suffering from acute emotional disturbance, disorganized thinking, uncontrollable crying, and rage. Details of this classic experiment can be viewed in an online slide show.[29]

The Power of Roles

In a few days, the role dominated the person. They became guards and prisoners. These guys [the guards] were all peaceniks. They became like Nazis. It shows how easy it is for good people to become perpetrators of evil.[30]

—**Philip Zimbardo**

The Milgram Experiment

Stanley Milgram, in a much more controlled set of experiments, demonstrated beyond doubt the power of situational variables.[31] The experiment was performed in many ways in many settings across the world, always with similar results. Subjects of the experiment were introduced to an experimenter in a white coat and a co-subject. The experimenter explained that the experiment tested the role of punishment in learning, and that one would be the "teacher" and one would be the "learner." It was made to appear that the subject and co-subject were randomly assigned to the teacher and learner roles. In actuality, the co-subject was a paid actor; the experiment was rigged so the individual who answered the ad always became the teacher.

The co-subject was taken to a room where he was strapped in a chair to prevent movement and an electrode was placed on his arm. Next, the teacher was taken to an adjoining room containing a shock generator with switches the teacher could turn to administer shocks. The switches were labeled: Slight Shock, Moderate Shock, Strong Shock, Very Strong Shock, Intense Shock, Extreme Intensity Shock, Danger: Severe Shock. The two switches after this last designation were marked XXX.

The teacher was instructed to read a list of two word pairs and ask the learner to read them back. If the learner answered correctly, the teacher was to move on to the next word. If the answer was incorrect, the teacher was to administer a shock to the learner.

The teacher was instructed to increase the intensity of the shock each time the learner missed a word in the list, beginning at 15 volts. As shock levels were increased, the learner, (paid actor), emitted increasing cries of pain and distress; at 75 volts, he grunts; at 120 volts, he complains loudly; at 150, he demands to be released from the experiment. The actor complains of a weak heart. As the voltage increases, his protests become more vehement and emotional. At 285 volts, his response is an agonized scream. Soon thereafter, he makes no sound at all.

At times, the worried teachers questioned the experimenter, asking who was responsible for any harmful effects resulting from shocking the learner at such a high level. The experimenter assumed full responsibility and stated it was essential that the experiment continue. Most teachers expressed discomfort, both verbally and nonverbally.

The Power of Situational Variables

I observed a mature and initially poised businessman enter the laboratory smiling and confident. Within 20 minutes, he was reduced to a twitching, stuttering wreck, who was rapidly approaching nervous collapse. He constantly pulled on his ear lobe, and twisted his hands. At one point, he pushed his fist into his forehead and muttered, "Oh God, let's stop it." And yet he continued to respond to every word of the experimenter and obeyed to the end.[31]
—Stanley Milgram

The results: Findings revealed 65% of all of the teachers punished the learners to the maximum 450 volts, and no subject stopped before reaching 300 volts! Milgram's obedience experiment was replicated many times by many researchers in many countries over a 25-year period from 1961 to 1985. Compelling transcripts of the interaction between the "teachers" and the experimenter can be accessed on the Web.[32] The results of these experiments are quite similar worldwide, with some tendency for greater obedience in Europe and non-USA countries. In one study conducted in Germany, over 85% of the subjects administered an electric shock labeled "lethal." Males and females were equally obedient, but females showed more signs of distress. Most subjects were obedient even when the experiment was set up so the learner refused to be shocked and the teacher had to force the learner's hand onto the shock plate—even when the learner complained of heart problems before and during the experiment and begged for the experiment to stop.

Talking Chips

The Power of Situational Variables.

Obedience in these experiments was directly a function of many situational variables. By manipulating situational variables, obedience could be as high as 37 of 40 participants willing to administer the highest shock level. Situational variables determined level of obedience:

Fewer shocks were administered if…
…The experimenter was farther away from the teacher.
…The experimenter communicated by phone.
…The experimenter didn't wear a white coat.
…The "learner" was in the same room.
…Other "teachers" were present and refused to administer shocks.
…The "teacher," as opposed to someone else, had to pull the shock lever.

The Power of Situations Explain Cooperative Learning

How do these sets of findings help explain the positive impact of cooperative learning? The answer can be formulated in a few words: *Cooperative learning structures are situations!* Although the most dramatic examples of the power of situations are illustrated by the power of situations to cause people to treat each inhumanely, the power of situations extends to the opposite: If we align situational variables correctly, they cause people to be helpful, cooperative, considerate, and kind.

Years ago I was experimenting with ways to equalize participation in groups. I cut out one-inch cardboard squares and gave each member of four-member groups ten squares of their own color: red, blue, green, and yellow. I gave the participants in this experiment a discussion topic and told them that each time they talked, they had to put in one of their "talking chips." In many groups the pattern was something like this: red, blue, red, blue, red, blue, green occasionally, and yellow never. I then changed the situation. I gave participants only one chip each and told them they had to put in their chip each time they talked. Further, they could not collect their chips and talk again until all chips had been used. The pattern changed immediately: everyone participated. What changed? The situation.

4S Brainstorming

The use of cooperative learning structures in the classroom works to produce positive results because it is the application of the most important finding of social psychology: Behavior is determined to a large extent by situational variables. Each cooperative learning structure presents different situational variables designed to produce specific positive behaviors. Paraphrase Passport creates listening; 4S Brainstorming creates idea generation; Sum-the-Ranks creates collaborative decision making; Circle-the-Sage creates transmission and evaluation of knowledge; RallyRobin generates an oral list; Timed Pair Share promotes in-depth disclosure. The list goes on and on. Each time we use an established cooperative learning structure, we are releasing the power of situations to promote thinking, learning, and collaboration.

of cooperative learning flow from all of the following variables:

- Immediate and frequent reinforcement
- Powerful and desirable rewards
- Supportive, peer-based feedback
- Feedback during performance
- Increased time on task
- Frequent practice recalling and verbalizing
- Peer praise, tutoring, observational learning, and modeling
- Instruction in the Zone of Proximal Development
- Greater opportunities to construct meaning
- Reduced transference gap
- Equal student participation
- Greater brain nourishment
- Reduced stress
- Multi-modal input
- Creation of episodic memories
- Balance of novelty and predictability
- Instruction oriented to the needs of individual learners
- Higher expectations
- Improved self-esteem and self-image
- Cultural compatibility
- Increased student choice
- Enhanced motivation
- Greater engagement and retention
- Interaction of different points of view
- Shift in teacher attitudes and behaviors
- Releasing the power of situations

Why Does Cooperative Learning Work?

It is impossible to single out just one explanation of why cooperative learning works so well on so many dimensions. Cooperative learning is a teacher's dream but a researcher's nightmare. When students interact in a positive way on a consistent basis, many variables are affected. This review indicates that the positive benefits

If we seek a single explanation of why cooperative learning works, we are destined to be frustrated. When we consider the many ways cooperative learning works to produce so many powerful positive outcomes, we stand back in awe. Cooperative learning works in different ways to produce positive results for students of different ages, cultures, and learning styles. It is rare that we educators are given such a gift. We are grateful that these relatively simple instructional strategies release so many powerful repetitive forces to consistently produce a wide range of positive outcomes.

Chapter Questions

▶ **Questions for Review**

1. What is reinforcement? How does cooperative learning change reinforcement in the classroom?
2. What is the difference between the two components of the social learning theory presented: modeling and mediation?
3. Name three principles of brain-based learning. Describe the interface of cooperative learning and the three principles.
4. Define the Zone of Proximal Development. How does cooperative learning promote learning in the "zone"?
5. Define Flow. How does cooperative learning encourage "flow"?
6. What is episodic memory? How does cooperative learning promote the development of episodic memories? How does this boost retention?

Questions for Thinking and Discussion

1. Of all the reasons why cooperative learning works, which do you think best explains the success of cooperative learning? Defend your choice.
2. Why do you think students who are traditionally the lowest achievers show the greatest gains in cooperative learning?
3. Students have different styles and intelligences. Do you think cooperative learning is appropriate for all students or just for some? Explain.
4. How can a cooperative learning structure alter situational variables to positively influence student achievement? Provide a specific example.
5. Which approach to differentiation do you prefer: Teaching different students in different ways or teaching all students in many ways? Why?

References

[1] The HR Management Toolkit. *Volunteer Burnaby and the Self-Directed Work Team Model.* The HR Managment Toolkit, Hot Topics. 2002. http://www.hrcouncil.ca

[2] Bandura, A. *Social Foundations of Thought and Action.* Englewood Cliffs, NJ: Prentice-Hall, 1986.

[3] Bandura, A. *Social Learning Theory.* New York, NY: General Learning Press, 1977.

[4] Rizzolatti, G. & L. Craighero. "The Mirror Neuron System." *Annual Review of Neuroscience,* 2004, 27: 169–192.

Rizzolatti, G., L. Fogassi & V. Gallese. "Neurophysiological Mechanisms Underlying the Understanding and Imitation of Action." *Nature Reviews Neuroscience,* 2001, 2: 661–670.

Rizzolatti, G. & L. Craighero. "Mirror Neuron: A Neurological Approach to Empathy." In Changeux, J., A. Damasio, W. Singer & Y. Christen (eds.) *Neurobiology of Human Values.* Berlin, Germany: Springer-Verlag, 2005.

Kagan Cooperative Learning • Dr. Spencer Kagan & Miguel Kagan
Kagan Publishing • 1 (800) 933-2667 • www.KaganOnline.com

4.25

[5] Doolittle, P. "Vygotsky's Zone of Proximal Development as a Theoretical Foundation for Cooperative Learning." *Journal on Excellence in College Teaching,* 1997, 8(1): 83–103.

[6] Vygotsky, L. *Mind in Society: The Development of Higher Psychological Processes.* Cambridge, MA: Harvard University Press, 1978.

[7] Young, M., J. Scannell, A. Burns & C. Blakemore. "Analysis of Connectivity: Neural Systems in the Cerebral Cortex." *Reviews in the Neurosciences,* 1994, 5(3): 227–250.

[8] Carter, R. *Mapping the Mind.* Los Angeles, CA: University of California Press, 1998.

[9] McGaugh, J. *Memory and Emotion.* New York, NY: Columbia University Press, 2003.

[10] Hawkins, J. & S. Blakeslee. *On Intelligence.* New York, NY: Times Books, 2004.

[11] Maslow, A. *Motivation and Personality.* New York, NY: Harper, 1954.

Maslow, A. & R. Lowery (eds.) *Toward a Psychology of Being, (3rd ed.).* New York, NY: Wiley & Sons, 1998.

[12] Kagan, S. "Co-op Co-op: A Flexible Cooperative Learning Technique." In Slavin, R., S. Sharan, S. Kagan, R. Hertz-Lazarowitz, C. Webb & R. Schmuck (eds.). *Learning to Cooperate, Cooperating to Learn.* New York, NY: Plenum, 1985.

[13] Csikszentmihalyl, M. *Flow: The Psychology of Optimal Experience.* New York: NY: Harper & Row, 1990.

[14] Peterson, C., F. Steven & M. Seligman. *Learned Helplessness: A Theory for the Age of Personal Control.* New York, NY: Oxford University Press, 1995.

Seligman, M. *Learned Optimism.* New York, NY: Knopf, 1990.

[15] Seligman, M. *Helplessness.* San Francisco, CA: W.H. Freeman, 1975.

[16] Hunter, M. *Mastery Teaching: Increasing Instructional Effectiveness in Elementary and Secondary Schools.* Thousand Oaks, CA: Corwin Press, 2004.

[17] Kohn, A. *Punished by Rewards: The Trouble with Gold Stars, Incentive Plans, A's, Praise, and Other Bribes.* New York, NY: Houghton Mifflin, 1993.

[18] Gregory, G. & C. Chapman. *Differentiated Instructional Strategies: One Size Doesn't Fit All.* Thousand Oaks, CA: Corwin Press, Inc., 2002.

[19] Tomlinson, C. *The Differentiated Classroom: Responding to the Needs of All Learners.* Alexandria, VA: Association for Supervision and Curriculum Development, 1999.

[20] Tomlinson, C. *The Differentiated Classroom: Responding to the Needs of All Learners.* Alexandria, VA: Association for Supervision and Curriculum Development, 1999.

[21] Kagan, S. & M. Kagan. *Multiple Intelligences: The Complete MI Book.* San Clemente, CA: Kagan Publishing, 1998.

[22] Herrmann, N. *The Creative Brain.* Lake Lure, NC: BrainTools, 1995.

[23] Butler, K. *The Styles Integration Chart. Levels of Thinking, Learning Styles, and Multiple Intelligences: Learning Styles and Modality Preferences.* Columbia, CT: The Learner's Dimension, 1995.

Silver, H., R. Strong & M. Perini. "Integrating Learning Styles and Multiple Intelligences." *Educational Leadership,* September 1997, 22–27.

[24] Kagan, S. & M. Kagan. *Multiple Intelligences: The Complete MI Book.* San Clemente, CA: Kagan Publishing, 1998.

[25] Dunn, R. *Synthesis of the Dunn and Dunn Learning-Style Model Research: Analysis from a Neuropsychological Perspective.* Queens, NY: St. Johns University, 2001.

Dunn, R. & K. Dunn. *Teaching Elementary Students Through Their Individual Learning Styles: Practical Approaches for Grades 3–6.* Boston, MA: Allyn & Bacon, 2001.

Dunn, R. & K. Dunn. *Teaching Students Through Their Individual Learning Styles: A Practical Approach.* Reston, VA: Reston Publishing Division of Prentice-Hall, 1978.

[26] Rosenthal, R. & L. Jacobson. *Pygmalion in the Classroom.* New York, NY: Rinehart and Winston, 1968.

[27] Rosenthal, R. & D. Rubin. "Interpersonal Expectancy Effects: The First 345 Studies." *Behavioral and Brain Sciences,* 1978, 3: 377–341.

[28] Zimbardo, P. "A Situationist Perspective on the Psychology of Evil: Understanding How Good People are Transformed into Perpetrators." In Miller, A. (ed.). *The Social Psychology of Good and Evil.* New York, NY: Guilford Press, 2004.

Zimbardo, P., C. Maslach & C. Haney. "Reflections on the Stanford Prison Experiment: Genesis, Transformations, Consequences." In Blass, T. (ed.). *Obedience to Authority: Current Perspectives on the Milgram Paradigm.* Mahwah, NJ: Erlbaum, 2000.

[29] Zimbardo, P. *Stanford Prison Experiment: A Simulation Study of the Psychology of Imprisonment Conducted at Stanford University.* Stanford, CA: Stanford University, 1971. http:www.prisonexp.org

[30] Alexander, M. *Thirty Years Later, Stanford Prison Experiment Lives On.* Stanford Report, August 22, 2001. http://news-service.stanford.edu/news/2001/august22/prison2-822.html

[31] Milgram, S. *Obedience to Authority: An Experimental View.* New York, NY: HarperCollins, 2004.

Milgram, S., J. Sabini & M. Silver. *The Individual in a Social World: Essays and Experiments (2nd ed.).* New York, NY: McGraw-Hill, 1992.

Milgram, S. "Behavioral Study of Obedience." *Journal of Abnormal and Social Psychology,* 1963, 67: 371–378.

[32] Milgram, S. "The Perils of Obedience." *Harper's Magazine,* 1974.

Seven Keys for Success

For over a quarter of a century, I have been training teachers in cooperative learning. Countless hours of observation, experimentation, analysis, and abundant teacher feedback have led to a simple conclusion: there are seven keys to success. When a teacher neglects one of these keys elements, success is not assured. When all seven are in place, cooperative learning is successful.

Underlying the diversity which is cooperative learning are seven simple concepts. Competence in the following seven key concepts defines a teacher's ability to successfully implement cooperative learning.

Cooperative learning is different. What distinguishes cooperative learning from traditional classrooms is the inclusion of cooperative student-to-student interaction over subject matter as an integral part of the learning process. In contrast, the traditional classroom consists primarily of teacher-fronted lessons, independent work, and competition. Student practice is almost always independent— independent problem solving or worksheet work. Often, student interaction is discouraged: "Keep your eyes on your own paper." "No talking." And there is often a competitive component to the traditional classroom as when students vie for the teacher's attention by answering teacher review questions. Cooperative learning is characterized by frequent student cooperation.

Cooperative learning is also different from group work. In group work, students are put together and asked to work together to learn, to complete a group project, or to do a group presentation. Like cooperative learning, the social organization of group work is cooperative. Cooperation is the goal. But as anyone that has worked in a unstructured group can attest, often that's not what happens. Some students may do most or all the work. Some students do little or none. Some students work independently. What is the main difference between group work and cooperative learning? Group work lacks structure. Effective cooperative learning carefully structures the interaction to ensure students work together well.

Because cooperative learning is different from both traditional classrooms and group work, cooperative learning presents new challenges and requires new skills for teachers and students. Teachers need cooperative instructional strategies to ensure all students participate, are held accountable for their contributions and learnings, are maximally engaged, and work together toward shared team goals. Students need to learn to trust each other, how to work together, and how to resolve conflicts and make team decisions. From years of research, use, and refinement, we have identified seven key concepts that make cooperative learning work very well. A teacher with these seven keys in her/his pocket is well prepared to meet the new challenges cooperative learning presents and to unlock the doors to successful cooperative learning.

The Seven Keys Concepts

The table below summarizes the seven keys to successful cooperative learning and the teacher skills associated with each. For a teacher new to cooperative learning, this list may appear daunting. It includes many new skills to master. To be sure, not all keys are necessary all of the time for successful use of cooperative learning. In fact, a teacher very easily could learn a few cooperative learning structures (Key 1) and integrate them in the classroom with great success, without knowledge or mastery of any of the other keys.

We encourage teachers new to cooperative learning to start by trying some simple structures

in their classrooms. Once they see the excitement, engagement, and achievement that structures create, teachers get hooked. Teachers new to structures want to make this new way of teaching and learning a regular part of the way they teach. They want to make a serious commitment to implementing powerful cooperative learning and to maximizing its effectiveness. That's where the seven keys come in: The seven keys are for the teacher wishing to become a master cooperative learning teacher—to harvest the full basket of benefits cooperative learning has to offer, to maximize success.

In this chapter, we will briefly introduce each key concept. Each key is subsequently addressed in complete detail in its own dedicated chapter. Let's look at the first and most important key: Structures.

Key 1. Structures

KEY 1

What Is a Structure? A Structure Organizes Classroom Instruction.

Simply put, a structure is the way the teacher organizes the interaction in the classroom at any moment. The structure describes the relationship of the teacher, the students, and the learning content—how interactions are structured. Take lecturing for example. Lecturing is a structure, but not a cooperative learning structure. It describes what the teacher is doing: orally delivering the content. It describes what students are doing: listening. And it describes how the content is processed: auditorily, in a transmission mode delivered from teacher to student. At any moment, there is always a structure in the classroom. A structure

The Seven Keys	
Key 1. Structures	How to use cooperative learning instructional strategies
Key 2. Teams	How and when to form and re-form the various types of teams
Key 3. Management	How to manage the cooperative classroom
Key 4. Classbuilding	How to create a caring, cooperative community of learners
Key 5. Teambuilding	How to develop powerful learning teams
Key 6. Social Skills	How to develop students' ability to cooperate
Key 7. Basic Principles (PIES)	How to use the proven principles of cooperative learning

is simply the way the interaction among teachers, students, and content is organized. Dr. Kagan developed the concept of structures in the '70s and his cooperative structures have revolutionized instruction. Kagan Structures are carefully designed to promote achievement, engagement, thinking skills, and social skills. Kagan Structures are used world-wide by tens of thousands of teachers.

Numbered Heads Together, Showdown, RallyCoach, and Timed Pair Share are a few of the Kagan Cooperative Learning Structures. They are all instructional strategies that describe the relationship of the teacher, the students, and the content. What makes them cooperative learning structures is they all have student-to-student interaction as an integral part of the learning process and implement the basic principles of cooperative learning. In Numbered Heads Together, after students write their own responses to the teacher's question, students put their heads together to improve their answers. In RallyCoach, partners take turns coaching each other as they solve problems.

Cooperative learning structures are content-free, repeatable instruction sequences that organize the interaction of students to implement the basic principles of cooperative learning.

A Structure Is Content-free and Repeatable.
Structures can be used repeatedly. Each time a structure is used with new content, it creates a new learning experience. Returning to our lecturing example, a teacher could lecture about the moral of *The Three Little Pigs* or a teacher could lecture about quantum physics. The sophistication of the content is markedly different, but the lecturing process is remarkably similar. Structures can be used to deliver an infinite range of content. Each time new content is used with a structure, it creates a new learning experience—a new activity.

Like lecturing, cooperative learning structures are content-free. That is, cooperative learning structures can hold a range of content. Let's take the cooperative structure, RoundRobin. In RoundRobin, each student on the team says

something in turn. We may have students do a RoundRobin naming objects that have a right angle, naming possible endings for a story, or stating opinions on a social issue. Each time we use RoundRobin with different content, we create a different activity.

The quality of being "content-free" is what makes cooperative learning structures so powerful. Once a teacher learns how to lecture, she/he can use a lecture to deliver any content and to create a new learning experience. The same is true with cooperative structures. Once a teacher masters a cooperative learning structure, she/he finds it easy to create a range of successful cooperative learning activities.

A Cooperative Learning Structure Implements PIES.
We will just mention here, and discuss in greater detail later, cooperative learning structures are carefully deigned to implement the basic principles of cooperative learning—PIES. Some instructional strategies that include student-to-student interaction do not qualify as true cooperative learning. Why not? They lack PIES, proven principles that ensure positive academic and social outcomes. It is the implementation of PIES that distinguishes cooperative learning from group work. But more about that later.

How Many Structures Are There?
Kagan and practitioners of Kagan Structures continue to develop new structures and variations on structures. There are currently over 200 Kagan Structures. *Chapter 6* presents dozens of Cooperative Learning Structures.

Why So Many Structures?
When we open the door to student-to-student interaction in the classroom, we open a world of new and exciting teaching and learning possibilities. Each structure is designed to achieve different educational objectives. Some are designed for teambuilding; others for classbuilding. Some help students master basic knowledge and skills; others help develop thinking skills. For example, Find My Rule develops inductive reasoning while Logic Line-Ups enhances deductive reasoning.

Kagan Cooperative Learning • Dr. Spencer Kagan & Miguel Kagan
Kagan Publishing • 1(800) 933-2667 • www.KaganOnline.com

5.3

Some structures are designed for very specific objectives; others are useful for a range of outcomes. It is not necessary to know and use all the different Cooperative Learning Structures to be very successful at cooperative learning. Because each structure performs at least one function better than any other structure, knowledge of each structure is essential if a teacher is to be as efficient as possible in reaching the full range of learning objectives. Lesson planning with cooperative structures is the art of selecting an appropriate structure to reach a given teaching objective.

> *"A snowflake is fragile, but look what they can do together."*
> —Unknown

With So Many Structures, Where Do I Start?

Start small. Introduce a RallyRobin. Get comfortable using it at different points in your lesson (set, checking for understanding, closure). Use it with different content. When you and your students feel comfortable, introduce a new structure. Before you know it, you'll be fluent in a range of structures, making learning more fun and engaging than ever before! Structures are examined in detail in *Chapter 6: Structures*.

Key 2. Teams

What Is a Team?

A group may be of any size, and does not necessarily have an identity or endure over time. Cooperative learning teams, in contrast, have a strong, positive team identity, ideally consist of four members, and endure over time. Teammates know and accept each other, and provide mutual support. Ability to establish a variety of types of cooperative learning teams is the second key competency of a cooperative learning teacher.

What Are the Different Types of Cooperative Teams?

There are four different basic types of cooperative learning teams: 1) heterogeneous, 2) homogeneous, 3) random, and 4) student-selected.

Heterogeneous Teams. Heterogeneous teams are mixed teams. The heterogeneous team is a mirror of the classroom. To the extent possible, it includes high, middle, and low achievers, boys and girls, and an ethnic and linguistic diversity. Heterogeneity of achievement levels maximizes positive peer tutoring, and serves as an aid to classroom management. With a high achiever on each team, introduction and acquisition of new material becomes easier. Mixed ethnicity dramatically improves ethnic relations among students. The rationale for heterogeneity is simple: If all students on a team had exactly the same skills and knowledge, they would have nothing to learn from each other. To a degree, the greater the team heterogeneity, the greater the learning potential.

Homogeneous Teams. Homogeneous teams are formed based on a shared student characteristic. Homogeneous teams may be created based on students' ability level as when ability groups are used when differentiating instruction or curriculum. Another use of homogeneous teams is the use of language teams. In bilingual and multilingual classrooms in which some students are not fluent in English, creating occasional homogeneous primary language teams enables non-fluent students access to the curriculum in their primary language.

Teams can also be formed based on shared interests. Students interested in researching and presenting their findings on the animals of the rain forest form one team. Students who want to explore and present the flora and fauna of the rain forest form another team. Interest teams have the benefit of allowing students the freedom to pursue their own interests. Accelerated learning and presentations can result from students' innate inquisitiveness.

Random Teams. Random teams are teams formed by the luck of the draw. For example, each student could be handed a number corresponding to the number of teams in the classroom. They all stand up and mix in the classroom, repeatedly trading number slips until the teacher calls, "Freeze." The number they have when they freeze is their new team number. They go to the table marked with their team number and meet their new teammates. As the name suggests, random teams are governed entirely by chance. Random teams can be used to great effect to create excitement and promote classbuilding.

Lack of planning also can be a disadvantage. The luck of the draw can put the four lowest achievers together on a team! Long-term random teams are usually not advisable. Unless you have a very homogeneous class, random teams generally cannot stay together very long without substantial differences in achievement among teams.

least one relatively high achiever on each team, improving tutoring. Heterogeneous teams equalize team status avoiding "winner" and "loser" teams. Heterogeneous teams improve cross-race and cross-gender relationships. Mixed ability, race, and sex teams balance teams' aggregate ability level. This equalizing factor also makes management easier and results in more equitable team processes and products. Well-balanced teams can stay together for a long time. With enduring teams, students can form a strong team identity and have the opportunity to learn together.

The Four Types of Teams

Heterogeneous	Mixed ability, sex, ethnicity
Homogeneous	Similar ability, or same sex, language, ethnicity
Random Teams	Randomly formed teams
Student-Selected Teams	Student created teams

Student-Selected Teams. Occasionally, students are allowed to select their own teams. Student-selected teams can be used at the beginning of the school year, on an occasional basis for fun or variety, or for practice or review. Sometimes it is nice to simply allow those students who want to work together to work together. When allowed, students will often choose to work with their friends. Friends share familiarity, regard each other with affection, and trust each other. This closeness can promote a positive classroom environment. It can promote productivity as friends often find working together enjoyable. And it can facilitate team decision making as friends often share similar interests and perspectives.

There are potential pitfalls of student-selected teams. Friends often share interests beyond the classroom content, which can easily lead to off-task behavior. Student-selected teams can result in high- and low-status teams. Less-popular students can be left out or be the last students selected for teams. In *Chapter 7: Teams*, we offer solutions to these potential pitfalls of student-selected teams.

What Type of Teams Should I Use?

With four different types of teams to use, you may be asking, "Which type of teams should I use?" The answer for the experienced cooperative learning teacher is: all of them. We recommend heterogeneous teams as the stable, cooperative learning base teams, but all types of teams have a place in the cooperative classroom. Heterogeneous teams ensure at

An exception to this preference for heterogeneous base teams is in classrooms in which there are numerous non-fluent language speakers. In this case, we recommend that English language learning students have a same-language buddy on the same team to provide each other support. For difficult content, nonnative speakers can form homogeneous language teams. This facilitates content acquisition by reducing the language barrier to the challenging content.

Homogeneous ability teams, random teams, and student-selected teams are recommended for occasional use. We will examine the different uses for the different types of teams more in *Chapter 7*.

How Do I Form Teams?

There are a variety of methods to form and re-form the various types of cooperative teams. In *Chapter 7*, we explore teamformation methods in detail.

How Long Should Teams Last?

If random teams are used as base teams, the teams must be changed frequently because the luck of the draw could result in "loser teams"—the four lowest achievers in the class could end up on the same team. If the teacher carefully designs teams, they can stay together for a long time and students can learn how to learn together. Students can stay together in their heterogeneous base teams longer if there are frequent opportunities to work with classmates beyond immediate teammates. Classbuilding, silly sports and goofy games, and the occasional temporary use of other team compositions break the monotony of always sitting and working with the same teammates.

We suggest changing teams after about six weeks. Changing teams too frequently does not allow students to get to know their teammates well, to bond as a team, and form a team identity. However, even if they are functioning well, we recommend changing teams after about six weeks. This creates variety and excitement and enables students to transfer their new social and academic skills to new situations.

How Many Students Should Be on Each Team?

Teams of four are ideal. They allow pair work, which doubles active participation, and open twice as many lines of communication compared to teams of three. Teams larger than four offer less per-student participation, and they are harder to manage. Teams of three offer fewer lines of communication, eliminate valuable pair work opportunities, and can degenerate into a pair and an outsider. Teams are examined in detail in *Chapter 7: Teams*.

Key 3. Management
What Management Strategies Will I Need to Manage the Cooperative Classroom?
Efficient management of a classroom of teams involves quite a number of teacher skills not necessary in the traditional classroom. Some of the new skills include:

Managing Noise. Because cooperative learning encourages student-to-student interaction, noise can be a problem if not managed well. We need to establish and maintain an effective quiet signal to quickly get students to stop interacting and focus on us. We also need procedures for monitoring noise and for keeping noise levels from escalating.

Room Arrangement and Seating. The cooperative classroom is arranged with students seated in teams. Students are close enough to discuss any topic with any teammate and so all teammates can easily put both hands on a common piece of paper. But seats are also arranged so students can comfortably orient forward toward the teacher and blackboard.

Managing Materials.
Teams share materials, so the teacher needs to create team tubs or team packs with team materials. There are numerous timesaving ways to collect and distribute work and materials from teams.

Giving Directions. Assigning teamwork can be more complicated than independent work. Different teammates may have different roles and responsibilities. We need good direction-giving methods, including extensive use of teacher and student modeling, to ensure teams know their goal and every teammember knows their role in the team task.

Solving Team Problems. There are a host of potential problems when we put students together on teams, especially if cooperative learning has not been a regular part of students' prior school experience. We need to put preventative procedures in place and have management procedures for dealing effectively with interpersonal conflicts when they arise.

In *Chapter 8: Management*, we cover effective management strategies and tips for the cooperative classroom.

Key 4. Classbuilding
What Is Classbuilding?
Classbuilding is the process by which a room full of individuals, with different backgrounds and experiences, become a caring community of active learners. Classbuilding creates a lively and fun environment where students are cared about by others. Classbuilding creates an "our class" feeling where students feel they belong and enjoy learning together.

Why Do Classbuilding?
To many educators, the rationale for creating a caring, cooperative classroom is self-evident. Many welcome the opportunity to create a social context in which character virtues, such as respect, caring, kindness, and cooperation,

can thrive. However, there are serious educators among us who ask, "What does having fun have to do with classroom learning?" And even some who proclaim, "If you want to have fun, go to a party." Brain research indicates that reducing perceived threat in the classroom optimizes the atmosphere for productive learning. See the box on the next page, Classbuilding and Teambuilding Are Brain-Friendly.

How Do I Do Classbuilding?

The easiest way to do classbuilding is through classbuilding structures and activities. Classbuilding activities are whole-class inclusion activities; students interact with their classmates in positive ways. In classbuilding activities, students are out of their seats and working with classmates, usually classmates who are not also teammates. We explore Classbuilding structures in **Chapter 9**. The book, *Classbuilding*,[1] is the best available resource for classbuilding structures and activities.

Another way to establish a positive classroom tone is by restructuring the classroom democratically and empowering students. Class meetings accomplish both goals. In **Chapter 9**, we explore class meetings and other methods to restructure the classroom so students feel ownership and a sense of belonging.

Is Classbuilding Time Off Academics?

Think of classbuilding as an investment. We invest some class time to create a positive learning environment so that learning time is more productive. But not all classbuilding time is necessarily time off the academic curriculum. All of the classbuilding structures can be used to have students interact with classmates in positive ways while still focusing on the learning objectives. For example, we can use Quiz-Quiz-Trade as a classbuilder where students get to interact with their classmates, but the structure also promotes academic learning since classmates quiz each other on academic content. The twin goals of interacting with classmates in a positive way and mastering academic curriculum are accomplished simultaneously.

Key 5.
Teambuilding
What Is the Difference Between Teambuilding and Classbuilding?

Classbuilding promotes a safe and supportive class environment. It enables students to get to know and trust classmates. Teambuilding does for the team what classbuilding does for the class. Through teambuilding, teammates get acquainted, create a team identity, promote mutual support, value individual differences, and develop synergistic relationships.

Is Teambuilding Necessary If Classbuilding Is Used?

In the cooperative classroom, teamwork is the norm. It is at the team level where the rubber meets the road. The majority of cooperative interactions are with teammates. If students don't like their teammates or don't want to work with them, we can expect management problems and poor achievement. How willing is a student to ask for help or offer tutoring to a student they don't like? If teammates know, like, and trust their teammates, they will not only work together well, but they will go the extra mile to ensure that their teammates understand the content and how to solve the problems. Teambuilding creates a genuine liking, trust, and caring among students on the same team.

How Does Teambuilding Work?

Research in psychology has established a link between propinquity (physical proximity) and friendship. The findings suggest people who are close often become friends. This phenomenon helps explains why neighbors often become friends; why dorm room living arrangements predict friendship patterns; and even why couples fall in love, and may fall out of love when there is too great

Closeness Promotes Friendship

Closeness
↓
Interaction
↓
Familiarity
↓
Discovered Similarity
↓
Liking

of geographical distance between them. The explanation is common-sensical: proximity breeds interaction, which in turn produces familiarity and discovery of similarity. If we are in frequent contact, we are more likely to interact. If we interact, we are more likely to discover shared interests. We are attracted (even sometimes romantically attracted) to people with whom we are close, interact, and share interests.

Seating teammates in close physical proximity can promote interaction and liking, but merely altering the seating arrangement in our classroom is not enough to fully promote the kind of familiarity and liking that unleash powerful team dynamics. We want teammates to be genuinely concerned with the contribution and success of all members. We want teams that generate a synergistic power as students bounce ideas off each other and build on each other's ideas. We want teams in which students can argue their point, politely disagree, and reach consensus. We want teams where everyone gets a chance to be a leader and a follower.

Teambuilding is a catalyst that speeds the interaction process and discovery of shared goals and interests, strengthening the bonds between teammates.

How Do I Create Powerful Learning Teams?

Teambuilding structures and teambuilding activities are our most powerful ally to create strong teams in the classroom. The book, *Teambuilding*,[2] is the best resource for teambuilding structures and activities. Teambuilding is examined in detail in *Chapter 10: Teambuilding*.

Key 6. Social Skills
Which Social Skills Do Students Need for Cooperative Learning?

There is a spectrum of social skills required to be a good teammember. You have to know how to help when help is requested. But you also don't want to be a know-it-all. You need to know how to be a good leader. But you don't want to become too bossy. You can't be too shy to participate, but not too loud or assertive to overwhelm your teammates. You have to know how to motivate your teammates when they are down. You have to listen to teammates to understand their perspectives. You have to know how to accept rejection gracefully when your idea is not selected. You have to know how to

---

Classbuilding and Teambuilding Are Brain-Friendly

Brain research reveals that teambuilding and classbuilding align our teaching with how the brain best learns. Teambuilding and classbuilding actually change brain chemistry in ways that make students more likely to focus on and retain academic content.

In the center of the brain are almond-shaped structures called amygdalae. The right amygdala and left amygdala are constantly responding to potential threats in the environment. If someone displays anger or makes a threatening facial expression, the right amygdala shows heightened activity and sends signals that set off a cascade of defense alarm reactions in the brain and body. If someone speaks in a threatening tone, the left amygdala goes into action, setting off the defense alarm reactions. The fight or flight defense alarm reactions include release of cortisol and ACTH, increased heart and respiratory rates, constricted blood vessels, increased blood lactate, and the experience of stress and anxiety. Chronic stress leaves blood vessels chronically constricted, a condition we call hypertension, one of the leading causes of premature death. The stress hormones that are released when the amygdala fires constrict both perception and cognition in ways that make focusing and learning less likely. In fact, chronic release of the stress hormones can actually damage the hippocampus in ways that permanently impair memory.[3]

What does all this have to do with teambuilding and classbuilding? It turns out that when people are shown pictures of strangers, their amygdala fires more than when they are shown pictures of people they know. Even if a person believes they have no prejudice at all, their amygdala fires more if they are shown a picture of someone with a different race or ethnicity than their own. We are biologically prepared to become more defensive when faced with out-group members. What teambuilding and classbuilding do is convert out-group members to in-group members, converting strangers into friends. And when that happens, we radically change brain chemistry, aligning it with how the brain best learns.

We have all had the experience of being too anxious to concentrate. When we leave out teambuilding and classbuilding, anxiety levels among some students are heightened enough to interfere with learning. When students are sitting with, and being asked to work with, others whom their brain perceives as a potential threat, they simply cannot concentrate well on the content. The optimum brain state for learning is relaxed alertness. When we include teambuilding and classbuilding, we transform brain chemistry to create greater relaxed alertness. A classroom free of threat, where students know and trust each other, is a safe environment that aligns brain chemistry with how brains best learn.

take turns, politely disagree, resolve conflicts, and reach consensus. These are just some of the many skills necessary to be a good teammate. Parenthetically, these are also life skills critical for success in the workplace, for family life, and for positive social relations.

Social Skills and Character Virtues

Students require a variety of social skills to be successful in cooperative learning and in life. These are the very skills students practice daily in the cooperative classroom.

- Active listening
- Appreciating others
- Asking for help
- Building on others' ideas
- Caring
- Conflict resolution skills
- Consensus seeking
- Cooperation
- Diversity skills

- Encouraging others
- Helping
- Leadership skills
- Patience
- Perspective-taking
- Respect
- Responsibility
- Sharing

How Do I Promote Social Skills?

The need for instruction in social skills depends in part on the characteristics and background of your students, and in part on the type of cooperative learning you do. If cooperative learning is limited to highly structured interactions, little cooperative skill development is necessary. On the other hand, when students move to complex cooperative projects, they need, among other skills, to learn how to listen to each other, resolve conflicts, set and revise agendas, keep on task, and encourage and appreciate each other.

Many of these social skills are naturally acquired in the process of working together. There are five powerful strategies to help nurture the development of social skills in the cooperative classroom: 1) structures and structuring; 2) roles and gambits; 3) modeling; 4) reinforcement; and 5) reflection and planning. Social skill development is examined in detail in *Chapter 11: Social Skills*.

Key 7. Basic Principles (PIES)
What Are the PIES Principles?

There are four basic principles fundamental to cooperative learning symbolized by the acronym PIES: Positive Interdependence, Individual Accountability, Equal Participation and Simultaneous Interaction. The basic principles of cooperative learning are derived from theories of cooperation, proven cooperative learning practice, and research on cooperative learning. When these four principles are in place, all students cooperate, take responsibility for their own learning, pull for their teammates, become actively engaged in the learning process, participate often and about equally, and, not surprisingly, accelerate their rate of academic achievement.

These four basic principles are the essence of cooperative learning. PIES distinguish cooperative learning from other forms of learning and are fundamental to the success of cooperative learning. Let's examine each principle briefly.

Positive Interdependence

Positive interdependence embodies two distinct concepts: 1) positive and 2) interdependence.

Positive Correlation.

If two students have a positive correlation of outcomes, the success of one student is linked to the success of the other. Picture two mountain climbers tethered together. If one gets a good grip, he/she can better pull up the other. When student outcomes are positively correlated, students see themselves on the same side and encourage and help each other. If, for example, I know that your doing well will help me, I want you to do well, so I will encourage and help you. When all students in a team or class know their outcomes are linked, a powerful force for achievement is released. Peer norms shift in favor of achievement, and students become a helpful community of learners, supporting each other's learning. *A positive correlation among outcomes creates a cooperative classroom.*

The opposite of a positive correlation among outcomes is a *negative correlation*. If gains are negatively correlated, the success of one student decreases another's chances of success. If we set up a negative correlation among student outcomes, students will not encourage or help each other. For example, when we grade on the curve, students know there are a limited number of top grades. They know that if a classmate gets a top grade, it decreases their chances of success. They do not encourage or help their classmates and may actually hope for the failure of others. A negative correlation can also occur as a result of the instructional strategies we use. For example, if the teacher uses a traditional call-on-one-student-at-a-time strategy to have students answer teacher-posed questions, the teacher has inadvertently set the students against each other. If a student wants to be called upon, the student hopes classmates do not get called on. Further, if a classmate is called upon, others hope the student will give the wrong answer. The failure of one is the only way the others have a chance to get what they want—to be called upon and win approval from the teacher and recognition from peers. *A negative correlation among outcomes creates a competitive classroom.*

There is a third way gains can be related: no correlation. If students work independently, and the individual gains of one student are not related to the gains of others, there is a lack of correlation. Whereas a positive correlation creates cooperation and a negative correlation generates competition, a lack of correlation generates an individualistic orientation—each student is concerned with her/his own outcomes and may be relatively indifferent to the outcomes of others. *No correlation among outcomes creates an individualistic classroom.*

Interdependence. Picture two boys who want to build a skateboard. One has a board and the other has wheels. Only if they work together can they reach their goal. Interdependence means students are mutually dependent on one another. They have to rely on their teammates. If it is impossible to achieve a goal or be successful at

a task without the help of others, then there is strong interdependence. The strongest form of interdependence occurs when a contribution by every teammate is necessary for the success of the team—everyone has to do her/his part. When students are interdependent, they are motivated to encourage and help each other; they know their success depends on the success of their teammates. Perceived interdependence creates bonding within teams and within a class. Each student knows, I cannot do it alone, but we can do it together. Thus, interdependence creates cooperation and strong peer norms in favor of achievement.

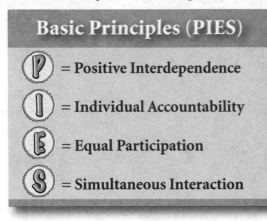

Basic Principles (PIES)

P = **Positive Interdependence**

I = **Individual Accountability**

E = **Equal Participation**

S = **Simultaneous Interaction**

Positive Interdependence Produces Cooperation.

Both components of positive interdependence create cooperation and boost achievement. If there is a positive correlation between my outcome and yours, I will tutor and encourage you to do well—Your gain is my gain. If we are interdependent, neither of us can do the task alone, but if we can do it if we work together, then we will work together. By putting positive interdependence in place, we create a caring, cooperative community and increase achievement in the process.

Individual Accountability

Cooperative learning methods, which do not make each teammate accountable for his/her own achievement or contribution, do not consistently produce achievement gains.[4] If evaluation is not based on individual performance, it is possible for a freerider and/or a workhorse to develop. The freerider benefits from the team score or project, but actually did little or no work. The workhorse does more than his/her share. If I am on a team that will have one score or one group product and there is no accountability for who does what, I am likely to do quite different things, depending on my motivation and achievement level. If I am a very bright, motivated student,

I may decide the best way to ensure continued high marks is to do it all myself. If I am a low achieving, unmotivated student, I may decide the road to success is to let the bright, motivated student do what he or she does well—in fact, do it all. To this end, I might loaf or even play dumb or helpless.

If there is individual accountability, everything changes. Individual accountability is created when the individual student is held accountable for some public display. For example, in Numbered Heads Together, each student must write their best answer on their own and show it to their teammates before they put their heads together to tutor and coach each other. Further, on each round, one student on each team is randomly selected to share the team's answer with the class and teacher. Thus all students are individually accountable; each round they must perform in front of their teammates, and on any round they may have to perform on their own in front of the teacher and the class.

In cooperative learning, students work in teams to learn. But that does not mean students can hide behind teammates. If we are to have gains for all students, each student must be regularly held individually accountable for his/her own contributions and learning.

Equal Participation

If students are actively participating, they are processing the content, and are engaged and learning. If they do not participate, learning is not guaranteed. This simple fact goes a long way in explaining the achievement disparity among students, perhaps even the achievement gap crisis we face as a nation.

The traditional classroom structure is the perfect example of unequal participation. The teacher asks a question and then volunteers raise their hands, competing for the opportunity to respond. Who responds? The high achievers. Classroom interaction is often a conversation between the teacher and the higher achievers, the students who least need to participate.

Who doesn't respond? The low achievers. The shy students. The cultural and language minority students. The students with special needs. The students who most need to be included in the learning process are allowed to voluntarily opt out of participating and learning. They hide.

Equal participation is the principle of cooperative learning that reverses this epidemic. Equal participation means participation is not voluntary. Everyone must participate about equally. Instead of calling on one student to respond to a question, the teacher simply states, "A Partners, tell your B Partner what you think." For the next question, "B Partners, please share your response with your A Partner." By virtue of the structure, every student must participate. No one slips through the cracks when we structure for equal participation.

Research on cooperative learning finds the strongest gains in cooperative learning are for the lowest achieving students. Equal participation operates in tandem with individual accountability to reduce achievement disparity. Students are held individually accountable to participate about equally in front of peers and/or the teacher. Students who would otherwise tune out because of lack of involvement are brought into the mix thanks to equal participation. Everyone must participate. Everyone learns. When equal participation is put in place, cooperative learning closes the achievement gap.

Simultaneous Interaction

In cooperative learning, not only are students participating about equally, they are participating frequently. Why? Because many students participate at once. Simultaneous interaction is a major advantage for cooperative learning over traditional teaching. In the traditional classroom structure, one person at a time speaks (usually the teacher), or occasionally a student, as the teacher calls on him/her. This is a sequential structure: Each person participates in turn, one after the other in sequence.

A little mathematics reveals that sequential structures are disastrous because they leave very little time per pupil for active participation. Let's examine the mathematics of sequential structures—it goes a long way toward explaining the failure of traditional teaching methods.

In the largest study of schooling ever conducted, John Goodlad[5] demonstrated that teachers on the average do almost 80% of the talking in a classroom. Because some time is taken for management, less than 20% of the time is left for student talk.

At first glance, it does not seem disastrous that out of every 50 minutes, the students will be allowed about 10 minutes for active participation. But because the 10 minutes are spent in a sequential structure, as one student after another is called upon, the active participation time per pupil is 10 minutes divided by 30—or an average of just a third of a minute per student! No wonder that the dominant emotion of many students in the traditional classroom setting is boredom. Students are allowed to express themselves on the average of only 20 seconds a class period. They must listen to others, mostly the teacher, for the remaining 49 minutes and 40 seconds!

Contrast that outcome with what happens when we restructure the classroom using the simultaneity principle. Although in the cooperative classroom the teacher would never take 40 out of the 50 minutes to speak, for purposes of comparison, let's take the same ten minutes of time for student talk. If we abandon the sequential structure of the classroom and adopt a simultaneous structure, say a Timed Pair Share, then active participation is not occurring by just one student at a time. During Timed Pair Share, at any one time half the class is talking. Thus, during the ten minutes, the average speaking time per pupil is not just 20 seconds, but rather a full five minutes. This amounts to 15 times as much student language production over subject matter. Further, the other five minutes is also far more active than in the traditional classroom, because students are far more involved when one person is speaking directly to them than when they are looking at the back of the head of a student responding to the teacher.

Thus the ability to apply the simultaneity principle is a key to maximizing positive outcomes in cooperative learning. Essentially, when all else is equal, pair work is better than teamwork, teamwork is better that whole-class work, and smaller teams are better than larger teams.

There are seven keys to successful cooperative learning. Each key unlocks another door to success.

If Structures Implement PIES, Why Learn PIES?

As stated earlier, a teacher can be successful with cooperative learning by using cooperative learning structures in part because the structures implement PIES. Why, then, bother learning the PIES principles? A working knowledge of the PIES principles is essential for experienced teachers wishing to modify the structures, create cooperative interactions on the fly, evaluate the effectiveness of lessons, or design new cooperative learning projects or activities. The PIES principles are examined in detail in *Chapter 12: Basic Principles (PIES)*.

Chapter Summary

With a whole new approach for teaching and learning come a host of challenges. When the classroom is devoid of interaction, students may be more tractable, but is our goal as teachers to develop obedient little soldiers? Or do we want to produce a citizenry of critical and creative independent thinkers? If not in the classroom, where will students learn the skills of working together? Leading others? Thriving in diversity?

When we master the seven keys and become more confident practitioners of cooperative learning, the new challenges fade away. What remains is a powerful new way to engage every student in the learning process—a way to boost achievement, reduce discipline problems, and to deliver a rich embedded curriculum of social skills, character virtues, and thinking skills.

Chapter Questions

▶ Questions for Review

1. What are the seven keys to cooperative learning?
2. What type of social skills do students need to work together?
3. What are the four basic principles to cooperative learning?
4. What are the four types of teams?
5. What is a cooperative learning structure?

▶ Questions for Thinking and Discussion

1. What excites you about cooperative learning? What concerns you?
2. If you could master only one of the seven keys, which key would you want to master? Why?
3. What are the similarities and differences between teambuilding and classbuilding?
4. In a democracy, the classroom should be structured democratically. Do you agree or disagree? Why?
5. How are teamwork skills important life skills?

References

[1] Kagan, M., L. Kagan & S. Kagan. *Cooperative Learning Structures for Classbuilding.* San Clemente, CA: Kagan Publishing, 1995.

[2] Kagan, L., M. Kagan & S. Kagan. *Cooperative Learning Structures for Teambuilding.* San Clemente, CA: Kagan Publishing, 1997.

[3] Jensen, E. *Teaching With the Brain In Mind.* Alexandria, VA: Association for Supervision and Curriculum Development, 1998.

[4] Slavin, R. "When Does Cooperative Learning Increase Student Achievement?" *Psychological Bulletin,* 1983, 94: 429–445.

[5] Goodlad, J. *A Place Called School.* New York, NY: McGraw-Hill Book Company, 1984.

CHAPTER 6

Key 1
Structures

> Structures redefine teaching. Teaching is not what the teacher says, but rather providing students learning experiences. Structures maximize student interaction with each other and engagement with the academic content.

Structures are a revolutionary educational innovation.

Traditionally, we have thought of good teaching as the design and delivery of a good lesson. Structures lead us to re-evaluate. The best example I have of why "the design and delivery of a good lesson" is an inadequate definition of good teaching occurred years ago when I was a university professor:

I was returning to my office after my lecture when I saw a professor from my department walking back from his own lecture. He was beaming, obviously feeling very good about something. When I asked him, he proudly said, "I think I just delivered the best lecture of my life." He then paused. After a few more steps, he added, "It's too bad. I think there were only two or three students who understood it."

Good teaching for him was the design and delivery of a good lesson. What was left out of the formula was what students had learned. It is common for professors to focus on what they deliver; after all, their job is to "profess." Good teaching is far different. Teaching goes beyond the words that come out of the teacher's mouth, it reaches out to students and asks, What is learned? Good teaching is student-centered, focusing on learning not teaching.

> "If teaching were the same as telling, we'd all be so smart we could hardly stand it."
> —Mark Twain

Structures redefine teaching. Teaching is not what the teacher says, but rather creating student learning experiences. Cooperative structures maximize student interaction with each other and with the academic content. There is tremendous power in having students learn from their experiences rather than from our words. There is far more engagement and retention of meaningful experiences; the content is processed in episodic memory, not just in semantic memory. Learning in context more mirrors the natural acquisition of knowledge than mere passive transfusion of information.

Where lectures and teacher talk are strictly visual and auditory, structures are experiential. Structures open up a world of possibilities for multimodal actions and interactions. With fun and active learning adventures, we are more likely to reach more students with different intelligences and learning styles; we lose far fewer students to boredom and disengagement.

What Is a Structure?

The previous chapter offered a three-part definition of a cooperative learning structure. We will quickly review the definition and extend it with a metaphor.

A Cooperative Learning Structure ...

1 Organizes Classroom Instruction. A structure is an instructional strategy that describes how the teachers and students interact with the curriculum.

2 Is Content-free and Repeatable. Structures are used to explore the curriculum, but are not tied to any specific curriculum. They can be used repeatedly with different curriculum, creating new learning experiences.

3 Implements the Basic Principles of Cooperative Learning (PIES). Cooperative Learning Structures have PIES built in. The inclusion of PIES is what makes cooperative learning truly effective. We will cover PIES in great detail in *Chapter 12: Basic Principles (PIES)*.

Structures are Teaching Tools

Structures are tools in a teacher's toolbox. Without many tools, a builder is ill-equipped to build a house. Without many structures, a teacher is ill-equipped to construct a wide range of cooperative learning experiences for students. Just like each tool has an intended use, each structure is good for building some types of learning, but no single structure works for all types of learners and learning objectives. We wouldn't use a hammer to cut wood. A hammer pounds nails. A saw cuts wood. Jot Thoughts is used to generate ideas. Sum-the-Ranks is used to make team decisions. When we have a range of structures at our disposal, we have many tools in our teaching toolbox. Structures empower us to build a variety of learning experiences and to do so efficiently, selecting the best tool for the learning objective at hand.

Structures: A New, Better Way to Teach and Learn

According to our analogy, any instructional strategy is really a tool. However, structures are qualitatively different from the tools many teachers currently have and use. Dare I say, better?

Teachers A, B, and C

To distinguish structures form other instructional strategies, let's take three imaginary teachers. Each of them has a different style of teaching:
- Teacher A: **Traditional Instruction**
- Teacher B: **Group Work**
- Teacher C: **Structures**

We'll see how these three teaching styles play out for two of the most common classroom practices: 1) Question and Answer, and 2) Guided Practice.

Question and Answer

As teachers, we ask questions of our class to check for understanding, to create active engagement, and to review content. Depending on our teaching style, we handle questions differently.

Teacher A: Traditional Instruction. Teacher A asks a question of the class, allows those who want to answer to raise their hands, calls on one of the volunteers to answer, then responds to the answer.

Teacher B: Group Work. Instead of calling on one student, Teacher B often says something like, "Talk it over in your groups" or "Turn to a partner and discuss it."

Teacher C: Structures. Teacher C chooses from a variety of student interaction structures. For example, Teacher C may use RallyRobin to have partners take turns generating an oral list. Or Teacher C may use Numbered Heads Together for review, to have students share and improve their answers with teammates, then have individuals from teams share with the class.

Guided Practice

The three styles also play out differently during practice time. After modeling a skill, we want students to practice that skill by applying it to different problems, often on a worksheet of some type.

Teacher A: Traditional Instruction.

Teacher A passes out individual worksheets and has students practice the skill alone, turning in their papers afterwards for feedback. During worksheet work, the teacher admonishes the students: "Keep your eyes on your own paper."

Eyes on your own paper

McPherson, John. *For Whom the Late Bell Tolls.* © Kagan Publishing

Teacher B: Group Work.
Teacher B has the students in small groups or pairs and tells them to "Help each other," or "Solve the problems as a group."

Teacher C: Structures.
Teacher C has many structures to choose from. For example, Teacher C may use Sage-N-Scribe: One student, the Sage, states how to solve the problem, step-by-step, while the other student, the Scribe, records the steps and the answer. The Scribe coaches the Sage if necessary and offers praise. Students rotate roles following each problem so the Scribe becomes the Sage.

> *"Competition has been shown to be useful up to a certain point and no further, but cooperation, which is the thing we must strive for today, begins where competition leaves off."*
> —Franklin D. Roosevelt

What's the Big Difference?

There is a dramatic difference in how students experience school and in their educational outcomes. The students in the cooperative learning class (Teacher C) learn more (especially the low-achievers who have the most to learn), are more actively engaged, enjoy school more, and develop a wide range of personal and social skills. See *Chapter 3* for a review of the research, and *Chapter 4* for theoretical explanations of why cooperative learning consistently outperforms other instructional strategies on virtually all measures of school success. Let's see the difference on a number of important variables.

Traditional Instruction—Teacher A

Achievement. Traditional instruction results in the achievement gap. Minority students achieve at lower rates than their majority peers.

Social Skills. Students who leave Teacher A's classroom have not worked with others on a regular basis, so they have not had the opportunity to develop their social skills, interpersonal intelligence or character virtues such as caring, understanding, turn taking, leadership, and respect. Students may actually learn to hope for the failure of others: If a student misses a question during Q&A time or does poorly on a worksheet, it gives the other students an opportunity to shine by comparison.

Required Participation. If a teacher calls only on volunteers to answer the questions, predictably there will emerge a group of students who almost always raise their hands and another subset of the class who seldom or never do. Teacher A ends up calling most on those who least need the practice and least on those who most need the practice! Volunteer participation in a heterogeneous group almost always results in very unequal participation.

Engagement. Traditional Q&A is terribly inefficient for promoting engagement. Only one student is active at a time. We'll elaborate on this later when we describe how structures optimize engagement.

Group Work—Teacher B

Group work is easy. Basically, the teacher tells students to work together, using statements like, "Talk it over with your partner," "Discuss it in your groups," or "Solve it as a team." Group work takes no special planning or materials, so is easy to implement and therefore quite attractive. But beware of group work!

Achievement. Group work, unlike cooperative learning, does not consistently produce academic gains for all students. If we're not careful, students in group work may learn even less than in Teacher A's class. Often during group work, a few students in each group do most or even all of the talking or problem solving. Those left out learn little or even nothing!

Social Skills. Students are working in small teams, which is the ideal breeding ground for social skills. However, without structure, students are often not ready to work effectively in teams. Since there is nothing to equalize participation among group mates, resentments often build up. The high achiever feels, "I had to do it all." The low achiever feels, "My ideas weren't included; I wasn't respected."

Required Participation. Unfortunately, what typically happens during group work is that one or a few students take over while others do little. Teachers using group work complain about the "hogs and logs." Some students become "free riders" allowing their more skilled or more motivated teammates to do most or even all of the work. We have all experienced the group project that was really a project completed by some of the members of the group. All of us have been in groups where one or two people did most or all of the talking. Even in a pair, one person may do all the talking, or take over the worksheet and do most or all the problems. The weaker students, those who most need the practice, do the least. Group work does not ensure individual accountability. In Teacher A's class, all students are held accountable for doing their own worksheet work. In Teacher B's class, students may hide behind the work of group mates and choose not to participate at all.

Engagement. There is much more engagement in Group Work than in Traditional Instruction. When teacher A asks a question of the class, at any moment only one student is responding. When Teacher B asks a question for groups to discuss, at any moment one person in each group is responding: However, thanks to the "hogs and logs" problem, engagement by all is not assured.

	Teacher A Traditional Instruction	**Teacher B** Group Work	**Teacher C** Structures
Achievement Gains	Not By All	Not By All	By All
Social Skills	By None	Not By All	By All
Required Participation	Q&A: Not By All	Not By All	By All
	Guided Practice: Yes	Not By All	By All
Active Engagement	Q&A: Few	By Some	By All
	Guided Practice: By All	By Some	By All

Teacher A, B, C Comparison

Structures—Teacher C

Achievement. Students achieve more academically. The gains are greatest for those who traditionally score the lowest, closing the achievement disparity.

Social Skills. The structures describe students' interaction pattern. In RallyTable, students take turns writing ideas. In Sage-N-Scribe, students take turns solving problems. Students acquire the social skills prescribed by the structure: turn-taking, patient waiting, helping, and praising. Lack of structure invites chaos. Structure promotes order.

Required Participation. Every student has a part to play in every structure. Participation by all is "built into" each structure. Hiding is not an option.

Engagement. In every team or pair, all students are actively engaged.

Cooperative Lessons, Structures, and the Replacement Cycle

Structures were born of cooperative learning theory and research. However, they are very different from their cooperative learning predecessors. Traditional forms of cooperative learning were cooperative lessons. A teacher planned out the cooperative lesson in advance.

One of the great pitfalls of educational reform is the replacement cycle. If educational innovations last only a few years, they don't really add up.

The form of the lesson was quite different, depending on the type of cooperative learning lesson: a Jigsaw lesson, a Complex Instruction lesson, a Learning Together lesson, a STAD lesson, or a Group Investigation lesson. However, all lesson-based approaches take considerable planning and usually take at least a full class period to implement, sometimes several days or even weeks. The problem with lesson-based approaches is not that they don't work. They do. There is plenty of research demonstrating that cooperative learning lessons consistently produce gains. The problem with complex lessons is that they have a half-life.

As trainers, if we teach teachers how to do complex cooperative learning lessons, we are disappointed when we check back with them later. When we come back in a few months or a year, very often the teachers we have trained are not doing cooperative learning lessons. When asked, among the most common responses are, "It was too hard to spend my day teaching and my night planning lessons," or "Our curriculum changed and I did not have time to rewrite all those Jigsaw lessons." Or "All the scoring and recognition was just too time-consuming." Because lessons are one-time events, we might walk into a classroom where the teacher has just been trained in cooperative learning and find the students all in rows, not interacting at all. When asked, the teacher says, "Oh, you should have been here on Tuesday. We did our cooperative learning lesson on Tuesday." We walk away saddened, knowing that which we don't do daily doesn't really add up.

The Replacement Cycle

One of the great pitfalls of educational reform is the replacement cycle. There is hardly a teacher who has been in education for more than five years who has not seen a good innovation come and go. Teachers make snide comments about "This year's new thing." A school or district decides to focus on, let's say, multiple intelligences. They offer readings and trainings and discussion groups and perhaps even coaching. The big push is to engage and develop the range of intelligences among students. Teachers design and implement creative multiple intelligences lessons. After a few years, the decision is made to move on to, let's say, brain-based learning. The school or district offers readings and trainings and discussion groups and perhaps even coaching on how to create brain based lessons. Teachers shift their focus and begin designing lessons to implement the principles of brain-based learning. Because lesson planning and implementation takes time and effort, there is not enough time to design and implement both brain-based learning lessons and multiple intelligences lessons, so the multiple intelligences lessons get dropped in favor of the brain-based lessons. After a few of these replacement cycles, experienced teachers get jaded. When the next new educational innovation is presented, they give it little or no effort, saying, "This too will pass."

The Replacement Cycle
A Tragedy for Students and Teachers

Schools and districts put their hopes, energy, and funds into instructional innovations, but in the process, abandon big investments they have made in prior innovations. This year's new thing replaces last year's new thing. That is, after a year or two, the school moves on from Multiple Intelligences, replacing it with Brain-Based Instruction, and then replacing that with Differentiated Instruction, and so on. The result: Students get a smattering of each innovation, which is soon replaced by the next innovation. The process is subtractive rather than additive. Students do not get the full benefit of any innovation. Teachers lose too: They become weary, knowing "This too will pass." What is the solution? Structures. Structures better deliver any innovation while delivering a rich, embedded curriculum.

This is tragic. It is tragic for teachers who get turned off to the whole process of educational innovation. It is tragic for students who do not reap the benefits of powerful positive educational innovations. If the multiple intelligences cycle hit when a student was, say, in third through sixth grade and then faded, would the student have engaged and developed her multiple intelligences as fully as if engaging multiple intelligences were part of every lesson for the student's entire educational career? If educational innovations last only a few years, they don't really add up for students.

Structures Break the Replacement Cycle

The structural approach was designed in part as an explicit attempt to break the replacement cycle. Prior to structures, cooperative learning was becoming another victim of the replacement cycle. When I analyzed why something so positive was being replaced, I realized the problem was the lesson-based approach to educational innovation. Early approaches to cooperative learning were cooperative learning lessons. After a few years, teachers who had been trained in cooperative learning moved on to accommodate their school or district's new instructional or curricular focus. Planning one more cooperative learning lesson is a burden in an overcrowded day. There was not enough time to plan and implement the complex cooperative learning lessons and next year's new thing. Cooperative learning got dropped.

Educational innovation is inevitable. There will always be new innovations to implement. Therefore, lesson-based innovation has a half-life: It is destined to be replaced by new innovations that demand new types of lessons.

In response to that realization, I created an alternative to the lesson-based approach. I began training teachers in simple structures that could be used as part of any lesson. Instead of training teachers in a two week Co-op Co-op or a two day Jigsaw lesson design, I began training teachers in a two-minute Timed Pair Share or a one-minute

Becoming Fluent with Structures

Learning structures is like learning a second language. When you first learn a language, you have to think a lot about the vocabulary and conjugations. When you reach fluency, you no longer think about the language, you think about what you want to say. When you first learn a structure, you have to think a lot about the steps. When you reach fluency in the structure, you no longer think about the steps, you think about what you want to teach.

RallyRobin. The simple structures were carefully designed to implement the proven principles of cooperative learning, but they could be used as part of any lesson. I began telling teachers, "Don't do cooperative learning lessons; make cooperative learning part of every lesson." I was explicitly attempting to break the replacement cycle. I wanted to make sure that when next year's innovation came along, teachers could still include cooperative learning as part of any lesson. Teachers could add structures to their teaching toolboxes, and use those tools to teach whatever needed to be taught—and more effectively! Structures are not one more lesson to teach—they are a better way to teach any lesson!

Make Cooperative Learning Part of Any Lesson

A cooperative learning lesson may take the entire period or span multiple periods. Some cooperative learning structures are completed in the matter of minutes. We may not have the time to implement a cooperative lesson when there are competing lessons to teach. But regardless of what we teach and how things change, we will be more effective if we teach using cooperative learning structures. Don't teach separate cooperative learning lessons! Integrate cooperative learning. Use structures to make cooperative learning part of every lesson!

The emphasis on simple cooperative structures is a shift in faith. Lesson-based approaches put their faith in the lesson; the structural approach puts its faith in the teacher. What we are striving for is automaticity or unconscious competence in a range of structures. What do we mean by that? When we repeat an action many times, the brain encodes the action in a program that can be run without thinking. For example, when you first learned to drive, you had to do a great deal of thinking about when to stop, how to turn lanes, and so on. It was exhausting. Now you can drive and have a conversation and listen to the radio at the same time. What has happened? Anything we do repeatedly enough is transferred to the cerebellum, freeing the prefrontal cortex for new learning or thinking.

Thanks in part to our mirror neurons, we learn many behaviors by simply observing others. For example, when you first became a teacher and first stood before a class, it was automatic to ask the class a question and wait for students to raise their hands to answer. You did not plan on doing that, you had observed that enough times that you did it without thinking. Most of us imprinted on a Teacher A style because that is how we were taught.

Four Steps to Unconscious Competence

What we are striving for in the structural approach is making the simple structures as automatic as it once was to ask a question of the class, have the students raise their hands, and call on one. The great thing is that once we get to the point that using the structures becomes automatic, we reap the benefits of cooperative learning without any special lesson planning or preparation of special materials. The process of making structures automatic can be symbolized as a four-step staircase. (See illustration above.)

When we have never heard of a structure, we are at the level of *Unconscious Incompetence.* That is, we don't know how to do the structure, and we don't know that we don't know how. We are completely unaware that we are incompetent in the structure because we are completely unaware the structure exists. If right now I mention a structure that is new to you, say Carousel Mind Map, if you had never heard of that structure before, you have just moved up a step on the staircase. You are now at the level of *Conscious Incompetence*. That is, you are now aware that there is something you don't know how to do. If you go to a workshop and Carousel Mind Map is demonstrated, you move up to the third step: *Conscious Competence*. You are now able to go back to your class and do the structure. Because

Unconscious Competence
Conscious Competence
Conscious Incompetence
Unconscious Incompetence

it is the first time you do that structure, you will have to give it a lot of thought. You will have to be conscious of each step as you do the structure. Even the very simple structures like Timed Pair Share take a lot of thought the first time you do them: How will I form pairs? How long will I have each student talk? How will I time it? How will I say who goes first? After the first person talks, will I have the second person compliment their thinking? If so, how? After you do a structure some twenty or thirty times, you move up to the last step of the staircase: *Unconscious Competence*. It is like learning to drive. All those decisions have been made often enough; you no longer have to think about them. They run off automatically. When you get to Unconscious Competence, you no longer think about how you will teach, you think only about what you are teaching and you are free to enjoy your students as they learn.

When we become versed in the Structural Approach, we are fluent in a range of structures. When this happens, we not only have tools today to boost achievement and engagement, we have tools for a lifetime, regardless of what comes down the innovation pipeline.

Structures Optimize Engagement

Structures increase active engagement in the classroom, but more importantly—for every student! How? Going back to our earlier teacher comparison, Teacher A, who uses traditional instructional methods, fails to promote active engagement. During Q&A, Teacher A calls on students one at a time. The teacher asks a question, some students raise their hands, the teacher calls on one, that student answers, and then the teacher responds to the answer with praise or a correction. Notice that the teacher talks twice for each time a student talks, first to ask the question and then to respond to the answer. Analysis reveals teachers talk about 60% of the time in this structure. The result is that to give each student one minute to express her/his idea, it takes over two minutes. Thus, in a class of 30, to give each student a minute of active engagement during Q&A, Teacher A would have to spend over an hour! If the teacher went for a straight hour of Q&A, how would the students

Active Engagement or Insanity? Let's Ask Einstein

In 1984, the largest study of schooling ever conducted[1] to that date revealed:
- Only 5% to 10% of classes had "reasonably intense" student involvement with learning.
- 70% of instruction was the teacher talking and the students listening passively.

In 2007, a study of 2,500 classrooms[2] revealed things had not improved:
- 91.2% of fifth-graders' classroom time was spent listening to teacher or working alone.

> **Insanity:**
> *Doing the same thing over and over again, expecting different results.*
> —Albert Einstein

spend their time? One minute per hour of active engagement—the rest of the hour listening to the teacher or looking at the back of the head of a student responding to the teacher!

Naturally, no teacher would spend a full hour on Q&A. But actually Teacher A does! The teacher doesn't spend that hour in one sitting, but rather breaks it up. The teacher may spend five minutes of Q&A at the beginning of class, and another five minutes later in the class period. The next day the teacher may spend another ten minutes of Q&A. At some point, even though it is broken up over time, Teacher A has devoted an hour of valuable class time to Q&A. How has each student spent her/his time? Each student spent about one minute of the hour expressing his/her ideas and opinions, actively engaged. The rest of the hour they were passive, listening to the teacher or to their classmates. The traditional Q&A structure is a prescription for boredom. Disengaged students often become discipline problems. In Teacher A's classroom, often we have their bodies, but we don't have their minds.

In contrast, Teacher C uses structures to create engagement. For example, instead of calling on students one at a time, Teacher C chooses a pair interaction structure such as Timed Pair Share. In each pair, one student shares for a minute and then the other student shares for a minute. In a little over two minutes (it took some time to ask the question), every student in the class has had their minute of active engagement. Whereas Teacher A took an hour to give each student their minute, Teacher C did it in slightly more than two minutes!

> *"School was so boring today that I actually finished the day dumber than when I woke up."*
> —High School Senior

Teacher C uses Timed Pair Share repeatedly on different days with different content. At some point, the students in Teacher C's classroom have spent an hour in Timed Pair Share. How have the students spent their time?—During almost half the hour they expressed their ideas and opinions. Note, also that the other 30 minutes is far more active than if they had been in teacher A's class—it is far more engaging to listen to someone talking right to you compared to listening to a student across the room talking to the teacher.

How does Teacher C produce thirty times as much active engagement? The students in Teacher C's class are taking turns (Equal Participation) and half the classroom is talking at once instead of one at a time (Simultaneous Interaction). Because the PIES principles are built in to structures, structures optimize classroom engagement.

Traditional Instruction is still prevalent worldwide. Teachers transmit; students receive. That students are passive recipients of knowledge so much of the time is tragic for many reasons.

Mrs. Mortleman made sure that everyone participated in class.

DAN, I SEE YOUR HAND IS UP.

McPherson, John. *For Whom the Late Bell Tolls.* © Kagan Publishing

6.8

Kagan Cooperative Learning • Dr. Spencer Kagan & Miguel Kagan
Kagan Publishing • 1 (800) 933-2667 • www.KaganOnline.com

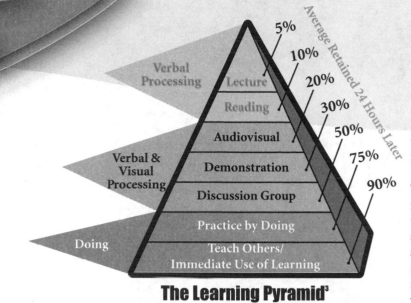

The Learning Pyramid within:

- 5% — Lecture
- 10% — Reading
- 20% — Audiovisual
- 30% — Demonstration
- 50% — Discussion Group
- 75% — Practice by Doing
- 90% — Teach Others/ Immediate Use of Learning

Verbal Processing

Verbal & Visual Processing

Doing

Average Retained 24 Hours Later

The Learning Pyramid[3]

The more passive students are, the less they like school. The classroom without active engagement is a joyless class. Students who attend joyless classrooms do not want to continue learning beyond their required education. The change rate is accelerating; increasingly success depends on becoming a lifelong learner. We can't afford to have our students turned off to education by classrooms devoid of active engagement.

Engagement is not a metaphor. It is a state of activation of the brain. In *Chapter 1: Why Does Cooperative Learning Work?* we showed active brain images that reveal students' brains are only slightly engaged when listening to a teacher compared to when students are explaining their ideas to each other. If we were only narrowly concerned with boosting achievement, we would demand active engagement. The Learning Pyramid above is a summary of research conducted by the National Training Laboratories,[3] illustrates how much more effective "doing" is for retention.

Structures Deliver a Rich, Embedded Curriculum

Traditionally, educators have made a firm distinction between curriculum and instruction. Curriculum is what we teach; instruction is how we teach. This distinction is institutionalized in our schools of education, our districts, and in

educational conferences. During teacher training, courses are given on curriculum and separate courses on instruction. At major educational conferences, participants can attend sessions on curriculum and different sessions on instruction. In schools and districts, some specialists hold the title of curriculum specialists while others are instructional coaches.

The development of the structural approach forces us to reevaluate this long-standing, unquestioned dichotomy. When we teach with structures, the distinction between curriculum and instruction becomes a false distinction! *Every time we change how we teach, we change what we teach.* There is a curriculum embedded in how we teach. Further, the curriculum embedded in how we teach may be the very most important curriculum we can deliver!

Let's say we have our students do a Three-Step Interview on a current event. After reading an article, students are interviewed on their current event by a partner, and finally each student shares what they learned in the interview with the team. The goal is academic—but by virtue of the interaction sequence, students develop their communication skills because students have to listen to their partner well and represent their partner's ideas to the team. Three-Step Interview also develops personal and social skills, including listening, understanding, and responsibility. Embedded in every structure is a rich curriculum students acquire. In addition to the academic curriculum, structures deliver a second curriculum—the curriculum embedded in the structure.

Making the Impossible Possible

Quite a lot is being asked of us as teachers. Teachers are asked to achieve high academic standards with a very diverse group of learners. But that's not all. Teachers are expected to help students learn social skills, thinking skills, communication skills, make wise decisions, be creative, develop their multiple intelligences, acquire interpersonal skills, and become persons of character. The list is overwhelming. How can we possibly do all that? There are not enough hours in the day or days in the year to teach that many lessons. True! That's the wonderful thing about using structures. So much of what we want students to learn and acquire is embedded in structures. With structures, every day we have students practice leadership, thinking, creativity, social skills, and character virtues *while* they are focusing on and mastering the academic curriculum. A long parade of positive outcomes is the by-product of the positive, structured interaction process inherent in structures. Which will add up more: Separate infrequent lessons on social skills or daily practice using social skills? Separate infrequent lessons on thinking skills, or daily practice engaging and developing the range of thinking skills? The curriculum embedded in structures empowers us to meet the challenge of delivering the broad curriculum today's students need.

How Do I Select the Appropriate Structure?

Many Objectives, Many Student Differences, Many Structures

We have developed over 200 cooperative learning structures, and surely we will continue to develop more. The reason: The human mind and education is multifaceted. If education had but one goal, and all students learned the same way and had the same minds, perhaps we could get away with one or two structures. But as educators, we know that there are many things we want and need to teach our students. We want students to acquire knowledge, skills, develop multiple intelligences, think critically and creatively, and acquire social and emotional skills—to name a few important goals. No single tool will suffice.

Multiple intelligences theory, learning styles theory, brain-based learning, and differentiated instruction have elevated awareness within the educational community that students are unique individuals with designer brains. There are sound teaching principles, but no single universal methodology will be equally successful with all students. No one tool can build everything.

Thus, it is imperative that we as teachers have a wide range of sound instructional practices from which to choose as we engineer various types of learning experiences for our students. We need

a whole toolbox if we are to be successful. To take a simple example, let's contrast RallyRobin and Timed Pair Share. If I want students to generate as many adjectives as possible to describe a character, RallyRobin works far better than does Timed Pair Share. Why? If I do a Timed Pair Share, the first student generates an oral list and then the second student says, "You named all of mine; I can't think of any more." With RallyRobin, the students take turns each adding to the list. If, in contrast, I want the students to state which adjective best describes the character and give reasons why they choose that adjective, Timed Pair Share is the better structure. Timed Pair Share allows one in-depth explanation of thinking whereas RallyRobin is better for many briefer responses.

If education had but one goal, and all students learned the same way and had the same minds, perhaps we could get away with one or two structures.

Structures Have a Domain of Usefulness

We call this idea—the range of usefulness of a structure—the "domain of usefulness."

Back to our tool analogy: Some tools have very specific uses, and some work well for many uses. We must be careful not to exceed the domain of usefulness of a structure. Just as we wouldn't use a hammer for sawing, we wouldn't want to use a high-consensus structure to develop divergent thinking.

Specific-Use Structures. Measuring tapes perform one specific function very well—they measure. Some structures have a relatively limited utility, too. Logic Line-Ups was developed to have students practice deductive reasoning. Find My Rule was developed to have students practice inductive reasoning. Sum-the-Ranks was developed to allow teams and classrooms to make decisions collaboratively, without falling into the win-lose pitfall associated with voting. Talking Chips was developed to solve the problem of one or two students dominating a team discussion. Paraphrase Passport was created to solve the problem of team discussions in which everyone is talking but no one listening. Different structures are better suited for reaching different learning objectives.

Multi-Use Structures.
Some structures are like many bladed Swiss army knives that can be used for a variety of jobs. For example, we can use a Three-Step Interview for teambuilding when we first form teams. It is also great for book reports, current events, and science reports. Many structures, because they are content-free, are very flexible. We can use academic content with a RoundRobin, "What was the most important thing you learned from the experiment?" But we can also plug classbuilding content into the structure: "Convince your teammates why your theme for the class party should be chosen."

Selecting the Right Tool for the Job
The list of structures is long—there are many tools from which to choose. How do you pick the right one for the job? Selecting the appropriate structures for the desired outcome is part of the art of teaching with structures. In previous editions of this book, we categorized structures by domain of usefulness, and structures were listed in one category. This was very helpful because teachers could look in the Mastery Structures chapter to find some of the best structures for content mastery.

However, many structures fit into multiple categories, and the attempt to pigeonhole them into a single category is misguided. We now have what we feel is a much better solution than nesting structures under a single domain. In this book, we present selected structures

alphabetically at the end of this chapter. However, to retain the practicality of categorizing structures by their function, we have provided a dot chart. It is easy to see at a glance which structures are particularly good for producing which learning outcomes.

We have found it useful to divide the domains of usefulness of structures into ten categories, five to develop interpersonal skills and relations and five to develop academic skills. See box, Structure Functions. The dot chart on page 6.24 illustrates which structures are best for the different functions.

Before presenting the steps of a range of structures, we briefly describe each of the ten functions, give examples of how structures are designed to help us reach each, and share the history of structures—how they came about.

Structure Functions

Interpersonal Functions
1. **Classbuilding**
2. **Teambuilding**
3. **Social Skills**
4. **Communication Skills**
5. **Decision-Making**

Academic Functions
6. **Knowledgebuilding**
7. **Procedure Learning**
8. **Processing Information**
9. **Thinking Skills**
10. **Presenting Information**

---

1. Structures for Classbuilding

▶ **Critical Attributes:** Students get up from their seats and interact with others in the class who are not their teammates.

▶ **Functions:** Classmates know, accept, and like each other. They feel a sense of belonging and inclusion. The class becomes "our class."

▶ **Sample Structures:** Corners • Find Someone Who • Inside-Outside Circle • Line-Ups • Mix-Pair-Share • Similarity Groups • StandUp–HandUp–PairUp • Stir-the-Class • Who Am I?

Structure Functions
Interpersonal Functions
1. Classbuilding

If students come to class each day and work only with their teammates, positive relations among classmates are not assured. Many of the early cooperative learning methods emphasized between-team competition. Although students bonded with their teammates, they did not feel on the same side with their classmates. They could get through the entire year without even knowing some of their classmates, let alone liking or caring for them.

In the early days of cooperative learning, to improve relations among classmates, practitioners developed "Whole Group Inclusion Activities." These activities were one-time events such as having each student randomly draw the name of another student from a hat, interview that student, then present that student to the rest of the class. At cooperative learning trainings, these whole group inclusion activities were modeled.

As I looked at this process, it bothered me that participants in a workshop would spend a half hour experiencing an activity that would empower them to do a half-hour activity in their class. I saw the need for structures. Because structures are content-free, once you learn a structure, you can design an infinite number of activities.

Corners

As I began to design structures to bring classmates together, I did not like calling them "Whole Group Inclusion Structures." It was simply too much of a mouthful, so I coined the term "Classbuilding." Although you won't find *classbuilding* in the dictionary yet, it has become common language among educators. Classbuilding structures create positive relations among classmates—just as teambuilding structures create positive relations among teammates.

Let's take an example: Corners. In Corners, the teacher posts three or four alternatives in the corners of the room. For example, the corners could be labeled with the four seasons. The teacher asks students to think about which is their favorite season, write it on a slip of paper, then go to that corner. First students talk with others in their corners, using a Timed Pair Share or a RoundRobin, sharing why they made the choice they did, and then they listen to and paraphrase those from different corners who made different choices. Students come to know their classmates, respect differences, and come to celebrate diversity: Our class is richer because we had ideas from each corner rather than all being the same. Knowing one's classmates and gaining mutual respect are among the aims of classbuilding.

The great thing about classbuilding structures like Corners is that they can be used regularly for academic content. One of my favorite examples is the teacher who wanted to have students write with better lead sentences for their creative stories. She posted different lead sentences from classic literature in each corner such as, "It was a dark and stormy night." She then asked students to read each of the four sentences, and decide which book they would most like to read. As students shared why they had gone to the different corners, they were deriving the elements of a good lead sentence. After listing and reviewing these elements, students wrote far better lead sentences for their own stories. Although the primary intent of the activity was academic, because Corners was used, an embedded curriculum was delivered. Students were understanding and respecting different points of view and getting to better know and appreciate their classmates.

Classbuilding is one of the seven keys for successful cooperative learning. For a book on Classbuilding structures with hundreds of classbuilding content ideas, see *Classbuilding*.[4] For an in-depth discussion of classbuilding and tons of classbuilding activities, see **Chapter 9: Classbuilding**.

2. Teambuilding

Those of us first developing cooperative learning discovered early on that you could not jump right into academic content without first establishing positive relations among students.

You can't jump right into academic content without first establishing positive relations among students.

We discovered this was especially true if we created heterogeneous teams. We get the most out of cooperative learning when we create mixed ability teams; it maximizes the opportunity for tutoring, makes sure there are not winning and losing teams, and side-steps the behavior

2. Structures for Teambuilding

▶ **Critical Attributes:** Students interact with their teammates in an enjoyable and successful way.

▶ **Functions:** Teammates know, accept, and like each other more. They feel a sense of team identity, mutual support, belonging, and inclusion. Teammates bond.

▶ **Sample Structures:** Blind Sequencing • Find-the-Fiction • Match Mine • Pairs Compare • RoundRobin • RoundTable • Same-Different • Team Formations • Team Interview • Team Line-Ups • Team Projects • Team Statements • Three-Step Interview

and management problems that occur if low achieving or disruptive students are all on one team. But when you form heterogeneous teams, you have placed students on a team with those they would least likely choose on their own. The high achiever looks across the team table at the low achiever, and asks himself/herself (or, if rude, blurts out) "Do I really have to work with him?" The low achiever is doing something similar: "I got stuck with that nerd!" If at that moment we rush into academic content, having students work together to create something or to solve a problem together, the most likely outcome is failure.

> *"Education has for its object the formation of character."*
> —Herbert Spencer

So, when we first form teams, the first thing we do is teambuilding. Any activity that results in teammates liking each other more and wanting to work together is teambuilding. One of the best forms of teambuilding is to have students experience success as a team. Activities, however, must be carefully structured. If we give a problem to a team and do not structure their interaction, the high achiever will likely take over. Even if they are successful, the activity will not serve the aims of teambuilding unless each members feels she/he had a contribution to the success. Group work often undermines the sense of team unity because of the unequal participation that most often results.

Team Interview

Thus, structures play an essential role in teambuilding. Structures are carefully designed to produce positive interdependence and equal participation so everyone contributes and the contribution of each is necessary for success. An example of one of the many structures we use

for teambuilding is a Team Interview. Each student in turn is interviewed by her/his teammates. If we have students interview each other on fun content ("What would you do if you had a million dollars?" "Describe your favorite desert." "Describe a TV episode that made you laugh." "What do you most like to do after school?"), the team enjoys the interaction, and begins to pull together.

Teambuilding is one of the seven keys for successful cooperative learning. For a book on Teambuilding structures with hundreds of teambuilding ideas, see *Teambuilding.*[5] For an in-depth discussion of teambuilding and tons of teambuilding activities, see *Chapter 10: Teambuilding*.

3. Social Skills

One of the first discoveries we made when developing cooperative learning was that students did not know how to cooperate. In retrospect, it should not have been a surprise. After all, for years students had been sitting in rows and were told not to talk, not to pass notes, and not to look at their neighbor's paper. Helping was defined as cheating!

When we turned the chairs around and told students to work together, often it was not pretty. At the young ages, students had not learned the difference between making a polite request and grabbing. At the older ages, they had not learned the difference between respectfully disagreeing and putting each other down. Rather than, "I can understand how you believe that, and what I believe is…." we would hear, "Stupid, can't you see that…."

Cooperative learning did not create social skills problems; it unmasked the fact that there was a hole in the traditional curriculum. Because students in Teacher A's class never work together, they do not acquire social skills. However, the teacher is unaware of this missing piece of curriculum because the students never work together! It is like failing to discover a student cannot spell because we never ask her to write! Students in traditional classrooms do not acquire basic social skills.

Early in the development of cooperative learning, various lesson-based approaches to social skill development were adopted, and are

Kagan Cooperative Learning • Dr. Spencer Kagan & Miguel Kagan
Kagan Publishing • 1 (800) 933-2667 • www.KaganOnline.com

6.13

3. Structures for Social Skills

▶ **Critical Attributes:** Students interact with others in ways that help them acquire social skills, character virtues, and emotional intelligence.

▶ **Functions:** Students become more polite and cooperative. They are able to resolve conflicts and understand and acceptpoints of view different from their own. Students are more respectful and responsible, and better able to control their impulses.

▶ **Sample Structures**
- **Turn Taking:** RoundRobin/RallyRobin • RoundTable/ RallyTable • Team Interview • Talking Chips • Timed Pair Share
- **Helping, Teaching, Tutoring:** Circle-the-Sage • Flashcard Game • Inside-Outside Circle • Jigsaw • Numbered Heads Together • RallyCoach • Sages Share • Team-Pair-Solo
- **Praising, Celebrating:** Gambit Chips • Pairs Check • Pass-N-Praise • Praise Passport
- **Fairness, Reaching Consensus:** AllWrite Consensus • Proactive Prioritizing • Placemat Consensus • Spend-A-Buck • Sum-the-Ranks • Team Statements
- **Listening, Understanding, Respect:** Agree-Disagree Line-Ups • Corners • Paraphrase Passport • RallyInterview • Similarity Groups • Team Statements • Timed Pair Share

fosters tolerance and celebration of diversity; Agree-Disagree Line-Ups foster both integrity and respect. The ways structures deliver a differentiated character curriculum has been detailed in a prior publication.[6] There are different character virtues embedded in each structure. We need our students to go beyond just learning about the virtues; we need them to *acquire* the virtues. Structures foster acquisition, not just learning.

Many structures develop a variety of social skills. Some structures are designed explicitly to develop or have students practice specific skills. For example, Turn Toss and Timed RoundRobin were both designed to equalize participation—one by non-sequential turn taking and the other by equalizing time. Many structures improve social skills because they include helping, turn taking, consensus seeking, praising, and celebrating.

Social skills development is one of the seven keys for successful cooperative learning. For an in-depth discussion of ways to develop social skills, and which social skills and character virtues are developed by each structure, see *Chapter 11: Social Skills*.

4. Communication Skills

Because of the shift to teams in the workplace and the shift to a service-based and information-based economy (see *Chapter 2: Why Do We Need Cooperative Learning?*), increasingly, communications skills are employability skills. For success in the 21st century workplace, our students need to understand others and communicate well.

Effective communicators are able to impart and interchange their thoughts, ideas, or information. Communication includes speaking, listening, reading, and writing. But communication also encompasses the ability to encode and decode

still emphasized by other schools of cooperative learning. Very often the lesson-based approaches include some variation of a skill-of-the-week, or a skill-of-the-lesson. For example, the skill may be disagreeing politely, listening, or participating equally. The skill is modeled; what the skill looks like, sounds like, and feels like is posted. Students plan how they will use the skill during the lesson, and afterward process how well they did in practicing the skill. Although this curricular approach to social skills has its value, in the structural approach, we emphasize social skills as an embedded curriculum.

Circle-the-Sage

Any structure that has students practice a social skill increases the probability students will acquire that skill. For example, a simple RoundRobin has students practice taking turns; a RallyInterview has students practice listening; and a Team Statement has students seeking consensus. Different structures foster different virtues. Through Circle-the-Sage, students acquire leadership skills; Paraphrase Passport fosters respect and understanding; Corners

ideas and information in body language, signs, and symbols.

Most structures by their interactive nature are highly communicative. But some we classify as *communication builders*— they are designed with the specific intent of having students practice and acquire communication skills. Match Mine is a great example of a structure that hones communication skills. Students are seated in pairs facing each other. Each student has an identical set of game pieces and game boards.

Match Mine

fostering communication skills, many structures improve communication skills because they include listening, speaking, reading, and writing.

Numerous structures are *communication regulators*. Talking Chips, Turn Toss, and RoundRobin are all examples of structures that equalize communication, giving every student a chance to use and develop language skills. Timed RoundRobin and Timed Pair Share give each student an equal amount of time. Through the use of turns and time, structures ensure that all students have the forum to sharpen their budding language skills.

5. Decision-Making

There has been an overreliance on voting for decision-making. Although our democracy is based in part on a majority rule voting system, there are serious problems with exclusive reliance on voting for decision-making. Voting polarizes. Voting promotes advocacy, but puts no premium on listening to the other side and seeking win-win solutions that will meet the needs of all. Voting results in winners and losers, and the losers are not likely to fully endorse a solution they voted against.

Where voting really breaks down is in very small groups. Let's say a team of four is trying to decide on a topic of study. Two students really want one topic, one student does not want that topic, and the fourth student doesn't care. The two advocates convince the apathetic student to go along with them, and declare "majority rule." We now have one outcast on the team who will give only minimal support to the project or who might even attempt to undermine the group efforts.

---

4. Structures for Communication Skills

▶ **Critical Attributes:** Students interact with others in ways that foster acquisition of communication skills.

▶ **Functions:** Students improve their ability to accurately send and decode oral, written, and non-verbal messages.

▶ **Sample Structures**
• **Communication Builders:** Draw-What-I-Write • Formations • Kinesthetic Symbols • Match Mine • RoundRobin • Same-Different
• **Communication Regulators:** Gambit Chips • Talking Chips • Timed Pair Share • Timed RoundRobin • Turn Toss

---

A barrier is set up so students can't see each other's game pieces or game boards. One student is designated the "Sender" and the other is the "Receiver." The Sender arranges her game pieces on her game board. The pair's challenge is to have the Receiver match the Sender's arrangement using only oral communication skills. To succeed, students must speak with precision, use academic vocabulary, check for understanding, ask for clarification, and take the perspective of another.

Different structures develop different communication channels. For example, Draw-What-I-Write improves the ability to write without ambiguity; Team Charades improves the ability to communicate non-verbally. Although some structures like Match Mine, Paraphrase Passport, Draw-What-I-Write, and Same-Different were designed explicitly for the purpose of

---

5. Structures for Decision-Making

▶ **Critical Attributes:** Students verbalize and show respect for all points of view, then make a decision that seeks consensus.

▶ **Functions:** Teams and classes learn to seek win-win solutions that meet the needs of all students. Students hone their consensus-seeking and conflict resolution skills, and become more cohesive.

▶ **Sample Structures:** AllWrite Consensus • Consensus Seeking • Fist to Five • Numbered Heads Together • Placemat Consensus • Proactive Prioritizing • Pros-N-Cons • RoundTable Consensus • Spend-A-Buck • Sum-the-Ranks • Team Statements

---

In contrast to voting, some structures promote more thoughtful and fair decision-making. For example, when students use Sum-the-Ranks, after a full discussion in which all points of view are aired and respected, each student ranks all alternatives from highest to lowest and the ranks are summed. What results is a team decision that represents the weight of the opinions on the team, without creating winners or losers.

Numerous structures promote examining ideas and issues from multiple perspectives, and foster consensus-seeking skills. In AllWrite Consensus, teammates come to consensus before each writes his/her answer. In Proactive Prioritizing, teammates present their positions and negotiate to prioritize outcomes. In Pros-N-Cons, partners examine all the evidence in favor and against an issue prior to making an informed decision.

Academic Functions
6. Knowledgebuilding

Every curriculum area has important associated facts and information. There is hardly a subject area without a vocabulary list we require students to master. Math facts, history dates, the symbols for elements, types of literary techniques, and spelling words are but a few of the myriad knowledge sets we teach. When we talk about knowlegebuilding, we are talking about declarative knowledge.[7] It is the "stuff to know" that students can immediately recall without stepping through procedures or solving a problem. For example, when we ask "What is 2 x 5?" we expect students to be able to answer "10" without counting on their fingers. We want them to know the answer.

Brain research makes it clear that facts and information are processed and recalled in a very different way than skills and procedures. Facts engage semantic memory pathways; whereas "how-to" skills activate procedural memory. How to gracefully steer and break a car is processed in a very different part of the brain than remembering the speed limit in a school zone or how long you can park

"You do not really understand something unless you can explain it to your grandmother."
—Albert Einstein

6. Structures for Knowledgebuilding

▶ **Critical Attributes:** Students interact in highly structured ways to acquire facts and information.

▶ **Functions:** Students build their information base—their ability to immediately recall important facts and information, including math facts, spelling words, states and capitals, or parts of a cell.

▶ **Sample Structures:** Choral Response • Fact-or-Fiction • Find Someone Who • Find-the-Fiction • Flashcard Game • Inside-Outside Circle • Mix-Freeze-Group • Numbered Heads Together • Pairs Check • Quiz-Quiz-Trade • RallyCoach • Sage-N-Scribe • Sages Share • Send-A-Problem • Showdown • Team Test-Taking • Trade-A-Problem • Whisper It!

next to a green curb. The speed limit and parking rules are knowledge retrieved from the temporal lobe; the steering and braking skills are under the command of the cerebellum.

Very different structures are efficient in having students master knowledge in contrast to skills. Knowledgebuilding structures incorporate a variety of learning principles such as associating new with prior knowledge, reducing anxiety, repetition, graduated tasks, and incorporating multi-sensory stimulation. A very simple structure that can be used for knowledgebuilding is RallyRobin. We use it to have students recall items that belong to a category (prime numbers, words that start with S, things that happened in the '60s). Another structure useful for knowledgebuilding is the Flashcard Game. Students set aside those items they have mastered, working only on those they miss. The game provides immediate reinforcement of success and immediate correction opportunities and coaching. The task is graduated into progressively more difficult rounds so that students are always working within their comfort level. Further, students are encouraged to use a variety of associations and multi-sensory stimuli to link the new information to prior, familiar information.

7. Procedure Learning

Just as every content area has an associated set of knowledge we want students to master, it also has a set of skills or procedures. We want students to "know by heart" the answer to 2 x 5, but we want them to be able to "figure out" the answer to 13 x 24. That is, we teach both knowledge

7. Structures for Procedure Learning

▶ **Critical Attributes:** Students interact to acquire and practice skills and procedures.

▶ **Functions:** Students develop all types of academic skills, including ability to perform math algorithms, read maps, type, defend a point of view, and edit.

▶ **Sample Structures:** Fan-N-Pick • Jigsaw Problem Solving • Mix-Pair-RallyCoach • Numbered Heads Together • One Stray • Pairs Check • Picking Stickies • RallyCoach • RallyRead • RallyQuiz • RoundRobin/RoundTable • Rotating Role RoundRobin/RoundTable • Sage-N-Scribe • SeeOne-DoOne-TeachOne • Team Projects

and academic skills, or procedural knowledge.[8] Procedures involve knowing which algorithm to apply and being able to apply it accurately, correctly punctuating a paragraph, reading with comprehension, applying the laws of physics to a specific problem, and locating a city on the globe using longitude and latitude.

Different structures are designed to facilitate the learning of different types of procedures. For example, RallyCoach and Sage-N-Scribe work extremely well to have students practice basic academic procedures such as long division, apply grammar skills, or draw the structural diagram of a molecule. Repeated practice with corrective feedback cements procedural learning. With more complicated procedures, such as building a circuit or operating a device, modeling and processing are paramount. Team-Pair-Solo enables the team to pool their knowledge and skills to try the new procedure. After success as a team, they break into pairs and the pair completes the procedure. And finally, after much support and modeling, students are ready to perform the skill independently.

8. Processing Information

During a lecture, we have a choice. We can lecture straight through or we can occasionally stop and have students process the information they have just received. Frequent processing distinguishes successful from unsuccessful teachers. Why? Working memory can only hold a limited amount of information; more information beyond about ten minutes is like pouring more water into a glass that is already full. However, if the teacher stops and has students interact over the content, students tag the information for storage in long-term memory so recall is greatly enhanced. After processing, students clear working memory so they are much better able to take in and retain additional information.

There are many simple structures excellent for processing. Some teachers call these "Stop Structures" because the teacher stops talking and has students interact, often for a brief time. Structures for processing include RoundRobin, RallyRobin, Listen Right! and Timed Pair Share. The teacher simply stops talking, asks a question, and has students in teams or pairs interact to process the content just presented.

9. Thinking Skills

Because of the accelerating change rate, we cannot predict with certainty the knowledge or skills our students will most need as they work and live in our fast-evolving work world. We can say with certainty, however, that the thinking skills they acquire will be of value. Ability to categorize, analyze, evaluate, summarize, deduce, and induce are among the many thinking skills fostered by different structures.[9]

Brain science has established that various types of thinking are located in different areas of the brain, and it is not the case that "higher level" thinking is based on "lower level"

8. Structures for Processing Information

▶ **Critical Attributes:** Students interact, talking about or reviewing information that has been presented.

▶ **Functions:** Students remember dramatically more of what they say or do than what they hear. Processing structures tag information for storage in long-term memory and clear working memory to receive new information.

▶ **Sample Structures:** Instant Star • Journal Reflections • Listen Right! • Listen-Sketch-Draft • Listen Up! • Mix-Pair-Share • Popcorn • RallyRobin • RoundRobin • Share-N-Switch • Show Me! • StandUp–HandUp–PairUp • Stroll-Pair-Share • Think-Pair-Share • Three-Step Interview • Timed Pair Interview • Timed Pair Share • Traveling Star

Kagan Cooperative Learning • Dr. Spencer Kagan & Miguel Kagan
Kagan Publishing • 1(800) 933-2667 • www.KaganOnline.com

6.17

9. Structures for Thinking Skills

▷ **Critical Attributes:** Students interact in ways that engage and develop different types of thinking.

▷ **Functions:** Thinking is a skill developed by practice; students learn to think by thinking. Different structures develop different types of thinking.

▷ **Sample Structures**

Critical Thinking
- **Analyzing:** Match Mine • Same-Different
- **Categorizing:** Similarity Groups • Find-A-Frame
  • Team Word-Webbing • Team Mind-Mapping
- **Deducing:** Think-Pair-Share • Inside-Outside Circle
  • Numbered Heads Together
- **Evaluating:** Find-the-Fiction • Fact-or-Fiction
  • Spend-A-Buck • Sum-the-Ranks • Proactive Prioritizing
- **Inducing:** Find My Rule • Think-Pair-Share
- **Perspective-Taking:** Match Mine • Same-Different
  • Sage-N-Scribe • Paraphrase Passport
- **Predicting:** Corners • Inside-Outside Circle
  • RoundRobin • Numbered Heads Together
- **Problem-Solving:** Jigsaw Problem Solving
  • RallyCoach • Team Projects
- **Summarizing:** Telephone • Three-Step Interview

Creative Thinking
- **Brainstorming:** 4S Brainstorming • Jot Thoughts
  • GiveOne–GetOne
- **Symbolizing:** Draw It! • Formations
  Think-Draw-RoundRobin • Kinesthetic Symbols
- **Questioning:** Fan-N-Pick • Team Interview • Who Am I?
- **Synthesizing:** RoundRobin • Team Projects
  • Team Statements

Timed Pair Share

We use critical thinking as we reflect on existing ideas and information to reach conclusions, better understand the material, make sense of the world, or make judgment calls. In contrast, creative thinking, as the name implies, involves creative processes. We use creative thinking as we generate ideas, innovate, or combine elements to develop novel solutions.

We want both critical and creative thinking to become habits of mind in our students. In the classroom, we regularly use different structures to inculcate different types of thinking skills. For example, one of the many thinking skills we would like students to acquire is the ability to categorize. If we take a lesson-based approach to fostering categorizing skills, we design a special lesson or lessons to teach students how to categorize information. If we take a structural approach to fostering categorizing skills, we present our regular academic content, but have students use a variety of structures that foster categorizing skills such as Similarity Groups, Corners, Team Mind-Mapping, Team Word-Webbing, and Pairs Compare. As students engage in these structures, they practice different forms of categorizing. Because these structures can be used with any content, we use them all school year so students acquire the habit of mind of categorizing information. Lessons are one-time events, but any skill that is not repeatedly practiced does not become a habit of mind. Changing how we teach actually results in better acquisition of categorizing skills, or any thinking skill, than does changing what we teach.

thinking.[10] Because we actually exercise and develop different parts of the brain when we engage in different types of thinking, different cooperative learning structures promote brain development. To be very concrete, we actually develop parts of the brain in the right hemisphere when students do the deductive reasoning embedded in Logic Line-Ups! A mixed diet of structures that engage different types of thinking skills more fully develop students' brains.

There are many ways we can think about thinking, and many ways to classify thinking skills. Many teachers gravitate to the simple critical thinking skills versus creative thinking skills distinction. Critical thinking refers to mental processes like analysis and evaluation.

6.18

Kagan Cooperative Learning • Dr. Spencer Kagan & Miguel Kagan
Kagan Publishing • 1 (800) 933-2667 • www.KaganOnline.com

10. Structures for Presenting Information

▶ **Critical Attributes:** Students interact simultaneously to share ideas or projects.

▶ **Functions:** Presentation structures allow efficient sharing of ideas, solutions, or projects.

▶ **Sample Structures**
- **Team to Class:** Carousel Feedback • Carousel Review • Team Presentations • Team Stand-N-Share • Team Statements
- **Team to Team:** One Stray • Roving Reporter • Number Group Presentation (Focus Group, Interview) • Teams Compare • Team-2-Team
- **Team to Teacher:** Numbered Heads Together • Teams Post
- **Students to Teacher:** Answer Back • Choral Practice • Team Show Me! • Dot-the-Wall • Echoing • Popcorn • Show Me! • TakeOff–TouchDown • Whip
- **Student to Teammates:** Instant Star • Jigsaw • Pairs Compare Partners • RoundRobin • Sages Share • Share-N-Switch • Sharing Secrets • Team Interview • Telephone • Think-Pair-Share • Three-Step Interview • Timed Pair Share
- **Student to Classmate:** Circle-the-Sage • GiveOne–GetOne • Inside-Outside Circle • Opinion Sages • Roam-the-Room • StandUp–HandUp–PairUp • Stroll Pair Share

When students do Paraphrase Passport and Debate, students learn to shift perspective; when they do Logic Line-Ups, they learn deductive reasoning; Find My Rule has students practice inductive reasoning. Three-Step Interview requires summarizing; 4S Brainstorming requires generating ideas; Team-Pair-Solo engages application level thinking; Agreement Circles develops evaluative thinking. The use of a range of structures delivers a differentiated thinking skills curriculum because each structure fosters different kinds of thinking.

Carousel Feedback

10. Presenting Information

In the cooperative learning classroom, there are a variety of times we want students to share information. For example, we ask a question and want every student to respond so we do a quick RoundRobin—students take turns sharing within their teams. Or perhaps we have teams generate ideas, and we want teams to share their ideas with the class. We may use Teams Post and have one rep from each team record the team's ideas on a designated area of the board.

After generating ideas or creating projects, we usually want students to share what they have created with other teams or with the class. A wide range of formal and informal presentation structures allow efficient sharing. We place an emphasis on simultaneous sharing. That is, instead of having one representative from each team sharing with the class, we might have a representative from each team rotate to another team to share. If sharing takes three minutes, after three minutes all the teams have shared instead of just one. If we have eight teams and have them share one after another to the whole class, it would take 24 minutes plus time for transitions, or half the class period. In that same amount of time, we could have teams each present to a partner team, receive feedback, revise the presentation, and present the improved presentation to a second partner team.

For informal sharing, simple structures like One Stray fit the bill. For formal team presentations, we move up to more complex structures like Number Group Presentations.

An entire chapter is devoted to projects and presentations and the structures that make them effective and efficient, see *Chapter 13: Cooperative Projects and Presentations*.

The History and Future of Structures
Looking Back

During workshop breaks, I am frequently asked, "How did you develop the structures?" It is a tough question to answer because each structure has a unique history.

The first structures I developed were variations of assessment techniques I had developed as a researcher to test the cooperativeness of students. Together with my co-workers, I had developed quite a number of behavioral tests to assess the cooperativeness of students in various parts of the world. RoundTable, for example, was a variation of one of these research instruments.

Kagan Cooperative Learning • Dr. Spencer Kagan & Miguel Kagan
Kagan Publishing • 1 (800) 933-2667 • www.KaganOnline.com

6.19

Others structures were adapted from watching what excellent teachers did. Some were created by the teachers I was working with. Some were derivations from basic principles. Others were developed spontaneously as I taught workshops. Yet others appeared, literally, in a dream! Most have been tweaked and modified over the years, as we have discovered more efficient and powerful ways to have students interact.

Video Analysis: Numbered Heads Together.

At the time I was coining the word "structures" to describe the simple content-free instructional strategies I was developing, I was analyzing what worked and what did not work as we trained teachers and student teachers. Roger Skinner, the principal at Chapparal Middle School in Diamond Bar, California, had graciously opened up his school for me to study. I had trained his teachers in some cooperative learning methods and was visiting classes to observe what teachers were doing.

Roger said to me, "You have to see the classroom of Russ Frank. Russ is a madman. I don't know what he is doing, but the kids love him and they are learning." Sylvia Andreatta and I went to Russ' class. Sylvia, a student teacher supervisor at UC–Riverside, was taking videos so we could analyze what we were observing and share it with student teachers. When we entered Russ' class, it was like no other class we had ever seen. Students were seated in teams and Russ was at the overhead, teaching a language arts lesson. Russ would project a sentence on the overhead and ask a question about the sentence. There would be an animated buzz of interaction within teams. Russ would then touch his ear and one student would jump up from each team. Russ would call on a student and if that student answered

correctly, the team would earn a point. Russ had a frenetic pace and had all sorts of signals, and if one team missed, another could challenge. The classroom was controlled chaos, and the students loved it. At the time, I couldn't understand what was going on. All I could see was Russ giving all sorts of nonverbal signals to which the students responded, with kids jumping out of their chairs, yelling answers, and earning points.

A few days later Sylvia said to me, "You have to look at the video of Russ' class! He really has something." As we ran and re-ran the video, it was clear to me that underlying the chaos in Russ' room was a structure. To make this structure something any teacher could do, my job was to adapt and transform the unique 'Russ-only language arts performance' into a content-free, repeatable sequence of steps any teacher could use to better deliver any curriculum. Russ was asking a question, having the students interact, and then giving a signal to indicate which student in each team had a right to respond. If that student was the first to jump up, be called on, and respond correctly, the student earned a point for a team. If not, another team would have the opportunity to

I called it Numbered Heads Together to convey the idea that each student had a number and that all the students on the team put their heads together to come up with their best answer.

win the point. Later when I sat at my computer, I gave this simple sequence a name; I called it Numbered Heads Together to convey the idea that each student had a number and that all the students on the team put their heads together to come up with their best answer. Numbered Heads Together was one of the first cooperative learning structures I began training. I cut out the between-team competition and the yelling out of answers, but kept the basic underlying structure.

Teacher Innovation: Simultaneous Numbered Heads.

As I trained teachers in Numbered Heads Together, they came up with variations and improvements. Becky Nehan of Coachella Valley Unified School District, CA, developed a tremendous improvement for the structure by having more than one student at a time respond. Rather than calling on just one team, Becky would have a representative from each team go to the blackboard to write his/her answer, correct answers earning a point for their team. Becky's variation multiplied by eight the active participation among students and the number of students who were held accountable for giving an answer. I loved it. A teacher who had never met Russ was collaborating with him, building off his ideas to help develop methods that would benefit any teacher. I gave Becky's innovation the name "Simultaneous Numbered Heads Together."

Soon teachers flooded me with additional ways students could respond when their number was called, including slates, response cards, thumbs up/down. The structural approach was becoming richer and more varied. There were structures and variations on structures.

Applying Basic Principles: Improving Numbered Heads Together. My co-workers and I developed and modified many structures by simply applying the four basic principles: Positive Interdependence, Individual Accountability, Equal Participation, and Simultaneous Interaction (PIES). For example, recently we modified Numbered Heads Together, inserting a new step, individual write, after the teacher asks a question. Why did we insert a step? To increase individual accountability.

Some structures have literally appeared as dreams. When you think structures all day, your mind does not stop thinking structures while you sleep!

Without having to respond on his/her own, a student could get away without thinking about the answer at all, just waiting to be told the answer by teammates during the heads together time. Adding an individual write strengthens individual accountability. Over the years, we have modified existing structures and created new structures to implement the PIES principles. Two of the four PIES principles, Positive Interdependence and Individual Accountability, are common to almost all approaches to cooperative learning. I developed the other two principles; they are unique to the Kagan approach. Whereas others call for "face-to-face" interaction, the Kagan approach calls for equal participation and simultaneous interaction. Implementing the "E" and "S" of PIES strengthens structures dramatically. Students can be "face-to-face" while one does most or even all the talking; asking "How Equal?" pushes

us to design structures in which no student is left behind. "Face-to-face" does not inform us about the quality of a structure nearly as much as does Simultaneous Interaction. Simultaneous Interaction focuses us on exactly what percent of our class is overtly active at any one moment—it is quantitative rather than just qualitative. Unlike "Face-to-face," the "S" of PIES informs us that pair work doubles the active engagement compared to square work, and that with regard to increasing engagement, teams of four are better than teams of 5 or 6. Testing structures against the PIES principles elevates our endeavor—it gives us a yardstick with which to measure the quality of a structure.

Applying Basic Principles: Paired Heads Together. Paired Heads Together is a new structure I recommend over Numbered Heads Together for most learning tasks. I developed Paired Heads Together to apply the simultaneity principle. In Paired Heads Together, the teacher asks a question, students write their answer on their own, and then turn to their shoulder partner to share and discuss their answers. They then turn to their face partners to share their answer one on one. Why would I recommend Paired Heads Together over the tried and true Numbered Heads Together? Because the simultaneity principle reveals Paired Heads Together doubles the overt active participation—twice as many students are sharing their answers at any one moment during the heads together time, and half the class are sharing their answer in the final step, not just one student in the class.

How Salt Melts Snow: Circle-the-Sage. Some structures have been created on the fly. On the way to the workshop I was giving in Maine, we drove slowly behind a truck salting the snowy roads. We could not pass. With plenty of time to think about it, I became curious about how salt melts snow, so I asked my workshop host. When I asked her, she was at a loss for an answer. During the workshop that day, without pre-thought, I asked the workshop participants, "How many of you know how salting the roads is a catalyst for the snow to melt?" About ten people raised their hands. Without knowing what I was going to do next, I said, "Please stand up." I then asked for people to leave their teams and gather around the experts, each teammate from each team gathering around a different "sage." After the sages shared, I had the teammates return to their team to

Kagan Cooperative Learning • Dr. Spencer Kagan & Miguel Kagan
Kagan Publishing • 1 (800) 933-2667 • www.KaganOnline.com

6.21

compare notes. We all got an unexpected bonus: There are two different ways to salt the roads, so when teammates compared notes, even many of the "experts" learned something they did not know. Circle-the-Sage is now used on a regular basis by many teachers to have students teach each other how to solve a problem or to share special information they have gathered.

Late for a Workshop: Sages Share. One structure came into existence through rather inglorious means. I got caught in traffic one morning driving to a workshop in Los Angeles. It was about the tenth meeting of a year-long training for trainers. In spite of having left in plenty of time to set up the workshop, because of the traffic, I arrived after all the participants, just in time to stand in front of them to start the workshop. Without a thought about what I was about to do, I asked the participants to each take out about eight or so small slips of paper. I then asked them to do a RoundRobin each naming structures they had tried with students, writing the name of the structure on a slip of paper and placing the paper in the center of the table. After a number of rounds, the tables were full of slips of paper with structure names. I then asked each person to initial all the structures they had tried. Next, I had the teammates do a RoundRobin each in turn asking questions about a structure they had not initialed, with those who had initialed them, the "Sages," answering. Although I had initiated the structure as filler to keep the participants occupied while I unpacked my briefcase, the structure worked so well, it became an integral part of our trainings. Sages Share is good for recall and review of information from a chapter, procedures from a lab, or vocabulary definitions. It can be used also by having the homework problems each on a separate slip of paper, so those who get the problem right can initial the slip and become sages to share with the others.

Solving Two Puzzles: Three-Step Interview. Early in my work developing cooperative learning structures, I focused on fostering participation and language development among students limited in English fluency. I saw that students were much more fluent talking with a partner than when asked to share with a team or with the whole class. So I began having students do Pair Interviews: In pairs, each student interviewed the other on various topics. I was pleased with the increased fluency and engagement that resulted, but puzzled over two problems: 1) How could I hold the students accountable for having listened and having understood? 2) How could the other teammates benefit from the information shared in the Pair Interview? As I puzzled over these problems, I felt I was struck by an electric bolt when the solution hit me: After Partner A interviewed B, and B interviewed A, I could have students in the team do a RoundRobin, each briefly sharing what they had learned in the interview. Three-Step Interview was born: Students were held accountable for listening, and everyone benefited from the interview!

A Dream: Stir-the-Class. Some structures have literally appeared as dreams. When you think structures all day, your mind does not stop thinking structures while you sleep! One morning, I awoke with a clear picture of students in a classroom standing in teams around the class. The teacher asked a question. The students put their heads together to formulate their best response. The teacher then called a student number and how many teams to rotate: *"Student three, rotate two teams clockwise."* The student with that number in each team responded and then shared her/his answer with the new group, receiving praise.

I was excited about the structure because it combined mastery, movement, and classbuilding. In fact, I was so excited, I wanted to try it with students right away. Unfortunately, I was committed to being at home for the next four days. So I did the next best thing. I called my wife Laurie who was in North Carolina, training teachers. I described the structure to her and asked her to share it with the teachers she was working with. Four days later when I flew from California to North Carolina, Laurie and four teachers met me at the airport. They had all tried the structure and had glowing reports of how much their students enjoyed it and how well it worked to promote mastery. In fact, they had put their heads together to give the structure its name: Stir-the-Class.

Looking Forward

As we try to look beyond the road just ahead, beyond the work in progress, we get more expansive. In a relatively short time, we have come so very far in the development of structures. It gives us courage to dream. Some thrilling images come to mind:

• Structures become used so frequently in all classrooms that the next generation of teachers find it as natural to use a wide range of structures in their classrooms as the past generation found it to rely almost exclusively on traditional Teacher A instruction.

• Student teachers are trained in a wide range of structures during pre-service training so each is prepared to give their very first class using a range of structures, efficiently delivering their academic content plus a rich, embedded curriculum.

• Schools all adopt some form of SAM club meetings—Structure-A-Month Club meetings—at which teachers work together as a community of learners, learning at least one new structure a month.

• Schools all adopt some form of peer and expert coaching on structures so teachers become a community of learners.

• All students are fully engaged in every lesson in every class through a range of structures, and all students show marked gains in achievement and social skills.

• All students learn to value the uniqueness and the contributions of every other student. Interpersonal and racial tensions give way to productive teamwork and diversity skills.

• The widespread use of structures brings about a general transformation of social character— each person approaches each other not as someone to best, but as a valuable resource to know, understand, value, and team up with.

We have seen dramatic improvements in race relations among students in desegregated classrooms and schools using structures. Is it too much to dream that one day, people of all nations will not see each other as "us and them" but rather as "we"? If on a daily basis we make that transformation in our classrooms, when we send our students out into the world, we will be that much closer to our shared goal of a peaceful and mutually supportive humanity.

Selected Structures Step-by-Step

We've covered quite a bit about structures so far, but the most important part is yet to come—the structures themselves! Here, we provide a step-by-step reference guide for using some of the most powerful and frequently used cooperative learning structures. When we began revising this book, we planned to include a comprehensive resource including all the Kagan Structures. However, as we completed writing this book, we realized that if we included all the theory as well as all the structures, the book size would be larger than a telephone book! So we decided to present the structures in a companion book entirely dedicated to the structures and how best to use them. But we couldn't leave them out of this book altogether! So we made a compromise: In this book, we offer a quick reference to numerous favorite cooperative learning structures. See *Kagan Structures*[11] for a comprehensive presentation of all the cooperative learning structures.

Structure Functions

This dot chart illustrates recommended uses for the structures featured in this book. The structures here represent a subset of the over 200 Kagan Structures.

KEY ★ Highly Recommended · Recommended

Structures	pg.	Classbuilding	Teambuilding	Social Skills	Communication Skills	Decision-Making	Knowledgebuilding	Procedure Learning	Processing Info	Thinking Skills	Presenting Info
				Interpersonal					Academic		
AllWrite Consensus	6.33		★	★	★	•	★		•	★	
AllWrite RoundRobin	6.33		★	★			★	•	•	★	
Carousel Feedback	6.25			★	•		•		•	★	•
Fan-N-Pick	6.25		★	★	•		★	•		★	
Find Someone Who	6.26	★		★			★	•			
Find-the-Fiction	6.26		★	★	•	★	★			★	
Flashcard Game	6.27		•	★			★				
Inside-Outside Circle	6.27	★		★			★		•	★	
Jot Thoughts	6.28		★	★			•		•	★	
Match Mine	6.28		•	★	★		★	•		★	
Mix-Freeze-Group	6.29	★		★			★			•	
Mix-Pair-Share	6.29	★		★	•		•		★	★	
Numbered Heads Together	6.30		•	★	•	•	★	★	★	★	•
One Stray	6.30	•		★			•	•	•	•	★
Pairs Compare	6.31		★	★	•		★			★	
Pass-N-Praise	6.34		•	★	•				•	•	
Poems for Two Voices	6.31			★	•	•	★				•
Quiz-Quiz-Trade	6.32	★		★	•		★	★	•	•	
RallyCoach	6.32			★	•		•	★		•	
RallyRobin	6.33			★	•		★		★	★	
RallyTable	6.34			★	•		★	•		★	
RoundRobin	6.33		★	★	•		★	•	★	★	★
RoundTable	6.34		★	★	•		★	•	•	★	
RoundTable Consensus	6.34		★	★	★	•	★	•	★	★	
Showdown	6.35			★			★				
Simultaneous RoundTable	6.34		★	★	•		★	•	•	•	
Spend-A-Buck	6.35			★	•	★				•	
StandUp–HandUp–PairUp	6.36	★		★	•		★	•	★	★	
Stir-the-Class	6.30	★		★	•	•	★	★	★	★	•
Talking Chips	6.36		★	★	★		•			★	
Team Stand-N-Share	6.37			★	•		•		•		★
Telephone	6.37		•	★	★		★	★		•	•
Think-Write-RoundRobin	6.33		★	★	•		★	★	★	★	
Three-Step Interview	6.38		★	★	★		•	•		★	•
Timed Pair Share	6.38			★	★		•	•	★	★	•
Traveling Heads Together	6.30			★	•	•	★	★	★	★	

(handwritten) S = Stop Structure (this means no prep)   ★ requires prep

Kagan Cooperative Learning · Dr. Spencer Kagan & Miguel Kagan
Kagan Publishing · 1 (800) 933-2667 · www.KaganOnline.com

Carousel Feedback

Teams rotate from project to project to leave feedback for other teams.

Setup: Teams spread out team projects around the room. Each project has feedback form attached.

1 Teams stand in front of their assigned projects.

2 Teams rotate clockwise to the next project.

3 For a specified time, teams discuss their reactions to the other team's project, with no writing.

4 Student #1 records feedback on feedback form. Students are encouraged to include positive comments.

5 Teacher calls time.

6 Teams rotate, observe, discuss, and give feedback on next project. A new recorder is selected each round.

7 Teams continue until each team rotates back to its own project, or until Teacher calls time.

8 Teams review the feedback they received from the other teams.

Fan-N-Pick

Teammates play a card game to respond to questions. Roles rotate with each new question.

Setup: Each team receives a set of question cards.

1 Student #1 holds question cards in a fan and says, "Pick a card, any card!"

2 Student #2 picks a card, reads the question aloud, and allows five seconds of think time.

3 Student #3 answers the question.

4 Student #4 responds to the answer:
• For right/wrong answers, Student #4 checks and then either praises or tutors.
• For questions that have no right or wrong answer, Student #4 does not check for correctness, but praises and then paraphrases the thinking that went into the answer.

5 Students rotate roles, one person clockwise for each new round.

Modifications: Fan-N-Pick can be played in pairs. Student #1 fans; Student #2 picks and reads; Student #1 answers; Student #2 tutors or praises; students switch roles.

Find Someone Who

Students circulate through the classroom, forming and reforming pairs, trying to "find someone who" knows an answer, then they become "someone who knows."

Setup: The teacher prepares a worksheet or questions for students.

1. Students mix in the class, keeping a hand raised until they find a partner that is not a teammate.

2. In pairs, Partner A asks a question from the worksheet; Partner B responds. Partner A records the answer on his or her own worksheet and expresses appreciation.

3. Partner B checks and initials the answer.

4. Partner B asks a question; Partner A responds. Partner B records the answer on his or her own worksheet and expresses appreciation.

5. Partner A checks and initials the answer.

6. Partners shake hands, part, and raise a hand as they search for a new partner.

7. Students repeat Steps 1–6 until their worksheets are complete.

8. When their worksheets are complete, students sit down; seated students may be approached by others as a resource.

9. In teams, students compare answers; if there is disagreement or uncertainty, they raise four hands to ask a team question.

Find-the-Fiction

Students write three statements and read them to teammates. Teammates try to "find" which of the three statements is the "fiction."

1. Teammates each write three statements: two true, one false, attempting to trick their teammates.

2. One student on each team stands, and reads his/her statements to teammates.

3. Without consulting teammates, each student writes down his/her own best guess which statement is false.

4. Teammates RoundRobin and defend their "best guess." (Note: Teacher may or may not ask teams to attempt to reach consensus.)

5. Teammates announce their guess(es).

6. The standing student announces the false statement.

7. Students celebrate: The standing student congratulates teammates who guessed correctly. Teammates who were fooled congratulate the standing student.

8. The next teammate stands to share. The process is repeated.

Variations

Class Find-the-Fiction. Find-the-Fiction may be played with the whole class. The teacher or a student may attempt to outwit the whole class.

Fact-or-Fiction. Fact-or-Fiction is a variation of Find-the-Fiction, also used on an occasional basis to spice up a review. In Fact-or-Fiction, students state either a true or false statement and it is up to teammates to decide if the statement is either a fact or fiction. Fact-or-Fiction is easier for young students because they only need to deal with one statement at a time.

Flashcard Game

Partners proceed through three rounds as they quiz each other with flashcards, mastering the content to win cards.

Setup: Students each have their own set of flashcards.

1 In pairs, the Tutee gives his/her flashcards to the Tutor.

2 **Round 1: Maximum Cues**
The Tutor shows the question on the first card, reads the question, and shows and reads the answer written on the back of the card. The Tutor then turns the card back over and again reads the question on the front of the card asking the Tutee to answer from memory.

3 The Tutee answers. If correct, Tutee wins the card back and receives a surprising, delightful praise from the Tutor. If wrong, the Tutor shows the Tutee the answer side of the card and coaches. The card is then returned to stack to try again later.

4 When the Tutee wins all cards, partners switch roles. When the new Tutee wins all her/his cards, partners advance to Round 2.

5 **Round 2: Few Cues**
The process is repeated, except the Tutor shows only the question on the front of each card, and asks the Tutee to answer from memory.

6 **Round 3: No Cues**
The process is repeated, except the Tutor quizzes Tutee on each question without showing the Tutee the flashcards.

Hints: For young students, limit each round to no more than five cards. If a student has won all cards, he/she can add bonus cards.

Inside-Outside Circle

Students rotate in concentric circles to face new partners for sharing, quizzing, or problem solving.

Setup: The teacher prepares questions, or provides a question card for each student.

1 Students form pairs. One student from each pair moves to form one large circle in the class facing outward.

2 Remaining students find and face their partners (class now stands in two concentric circles).

3 Inside circle students ask a question from their question card; outside circle students answer. Inside circle students praise or coach. (Alternative: The teacher asks a question and indicates inside or outside student to answer to their partner.)

4 Partners switch roles: Outside circle students ask, listen, then praise or coach.

5 Partners trade question cards.

6 Inside circle students rotate clockwise to a new partner. (The teacher may call rotation numbers: "Rotate Three Ahead." The class may do a "choral count" as they rotate.)

Note: When played with cards, steps 3–6 are Quiz-Quiz-Trade.

Variation
Inside-Outside Line. Students stand in two straight lines facing each other. One line rotates, and the other remains in place. Rotating students rotate to a new partner and rotate to the back of their line when they pass the last student in the fixed line.

Jot Thoughts

Teammates "cover the table," writing ideas on slips of paper.

Setup: Students each have multiple slips of paper (e.g., pre-cut sticky notes, cut-up bond paper).

1 Teacher names a topic, sets a time limit, and provides think time (e.g., In three minutes, how many questions can you write that have the answer 17? What are ways we could reduce poverty?).

2 Students write and announce as many ideas as they can in the allotted time, one idea per slip of paper.

3 Each slip of paper is placed in the center of the table; students attempt to "cover the table" (no slips are to overlap).

✱ *Each student must contribute at least two ideas (shoulder partners check).*
[This adds the Individual Accountability piece.]

Match Mine

Partners on opposite sides of a barrier communicate with precision, attempting to match the other's arrangement of game pieces on a game board.

Setup: Partners sit on opposite sides of a barrier with identical game boards and game pieces. One is designated to be the Sender, the other the Receiver.

1 Sender arranges game pieces on game board while Receiver waits quietly.

2 Sender gives the Receiver directions to match the Sender's arrangement of game pieces on the game board.

3 When finished, partners set game boards side by side to check for accuracy.

4 Receiver praises Sender, and they develop improvement strategies.

5 Roles are switched, and the game is played again.

Hints: Teacher instructs students in communication skills: asking for clarification, checking for understanding, giving unambiguous directions.

Mix-Freeze-Group

The classroom is bursting with energy as students rapidly "Mix" around the room, "Freeze" in their tracks, and frantically "Group" to avoid falling into the lost and found.

Setup: Students stand. An area of the room is designated as the "Lost and Found."

1 Students "mix" around the room.

2 Teacher calls, "Freeze," and students freeze.

3 Teacher asks a question to which the answer is a number or which corresponds to a key with a number. Teacher gives think time. (Examples: How many planets are there in our solar system? What direction is Washington, DC, from California? Key: North = 2, South = 3, East = 4, West = 5)

4 Teacher calls, "Show Me," and students show their answer with fingers on their chests.

5 Students group according to the number, and kneel down.

6 Students in their groups discuss a question provided by the teacher. Can you name the planets in order? How far do you think Washington, DC, is from Los Angeles?

7 Students not in groups go to the "Lost and Found."

Optional: Once students know the game, students in Lost and Found may be the ones to generate and ask the next question. After they ask the question, they rush to join a group.

---

* Class Builder ← fun questions / content questions (handwritten)

Mix-Pair-Share

Class Builder (handwritten)

The class "mixes" until the teacher calls, "pair." Students find a new partner to discuss or answer the teacher's question.

Setup: Teacher prepares questions to ask students.

1 Students mix around the room. *Silently ♪♪ while music plays* (handwritten)

2 Teacher calls "Pair." *♪♪ stop music first* (handwritten)

3 Students pair up with the person closest to them and give a high five. Students who haven't found a partner raise their hands to find each other. *Class job* (handwritten)

4 Teacher asks a question and gives think time. *(3-5 seconds)* (handwritten)

5 Students share with their partners using:
pick one ← • Timed Pair Share *open ended* (handwritten)
• RallyRobin *-list of answers* (handwritten)

Optional: Students may practice greetings or affirmations during Step 1.

Hint: For oral lists (name animals that live in the rain forest), use RallyRobin. For longer in-depth responses (how do you think we can save the rain forest?), use Timed Pair Share.

Numbered Heads Together

Teammates put their "heads together" to reach consensus on the team's answer. Everyone keeps on their toes because their number may be called to share the team's answer.

Setup: Teacher prepares questions or problems to ask teams.

1 Students number off.

2 Teacher poses a problem and gives think time. (Example: "How are rainbows formed? Think about your best answer.")

3 Students privately write their answers.

4 Students stand up and "put their heads together," showing answers, discussing, and teaching each other.

5 Students sit down when everyone knows the answer or has something to share.

6 Teacher calls a number. Students with that number answer simultaneously using:
- AnswerBoard Share
- Choral Practice
- Finger Responses
- Chalkboard Responses
- Response Cards
- Manipulatives

7 Classmates applaud students who responded.

Variations
Paired Heads Together. Students are in shoulder partner pairs. After teacher asks a question, pairs huddle to improve the answers they have each written. Teacher then calls for either A or B to share their best answer with their face partner.

Traveling Heads Together. Traveling Heads starts the same as Numbered Heads, but when the teacher calls a number, the students with that number on each team stand, then "travel" to a new team to share their answers. For fun, seated students beckon for a standing student to join their team.

Stir-the-Class. Teams stand around the outside of the class with spaces between teams. Teammates stand shoulder-to-shoulder. The teacher poses a question, then students write their own answers on an AnswerBoard or slip of paper. Teammates huddle to reach consensus, then unhuddle when done. The teacher selects a number and tells students with that number how many teams to rotate forward to share their answer.

One Stray

One teammate "strays" from her team to a new team to share or gather information.

1 A number is randomly called and that student from each team stands up. The remaining three teammates remain seated but raise their hands.

2 Teacher calls, "Stray."

3 Standing students stray to a team that has their hands up.

4 Teams lower their hands when a new member joins them.

5 Students work in their new teams to share or gather information.

Optional: Students return to their original teams to share what they learned when they strayed.

Random Teams: Three rounds of One Stray can be used to form random teams: A different number is called each round, and students may not join a team where a teammate is seated.

Pairs Compare

Pairs generate a list of possible ideas or answers. Pairs pair and compare their answers with another pair. Finally pairs work as a team to create additional answers or ideas.

1 Teacher provides a question that has multiple possible responses and provides think time.

2 RallyTable: Shoulder partners RallyTable answers. They "keep it a secret" from the other pair.

3 Teacher calls time.

4 Pairs Compare: Pairs pair to RoundRobin their answers. For each answer, the face partner in the other pair adds the answer to that pair's list, or checks it off if they already had it.

5 Team Challenge: As a team, students generate new answers, taking turns within pairs recording answers on their pair lists.

Poems for Two Voices

Partners create and present a poem they recite using one voice, the other voice, or both.

1 The teacher assigns each pair a poem topic.

2 Partners work together to write their poem.

3 Partners label each line of their poem, A, B, or AB, representing who will read each line.

4 Pairs rehearse their poems.

5 Pairs recite their poems to another pair or to the class.

Note: Students may progress through three stages:
1. Teacher provides poem and AB scripting.
2. Teacher provides poem, and students provide AB scripting.
3. Students create or select poem and script it.

Quiz-Quiz-Trade

Students quiz a partner, get quizzed by a partner, and then trade cards to repeat the process with a new partner.

Setup: The teacher prepares a set of question cards for the class, or each student creates a question card.

1 The teacher tells students to "Stand up, put a hand up, and pair up."

2 Partner A quizzes B.

3 Partner B answers.

4 Partner A praises or coaches.

5 Partners switch roles.

6 Partners trade cards and thank each other.

7 Repeat steps 1–6 a number of times.

RallyCoach

Partners take turns, one solving a problem while the other coaches.

Setup: Each pair needs one set of high-consensus problems and one pencil.

1 Partner A solves the first problem.

2 Partner B watches and listens, checks, coaches if necessary, and praises.

3 Partner B solves the next problem.

4 Partner A watches and listens, checks, coaches if necessary, and praises.

5 Partners repeat taking turns solving successive problems.

Note: RallyCoach may be used with worksheet problems, oral problems provided by the teacher, and with manipulatives.

Variation
Pairs Check. After solving two problems, pairs check their answers with the other pair in their team.

RoundRobin & RallyRobin

Students take turns responding orally. In RoundRobin, students take turns in their teams. In RallyRobin, partners take turns.

1 Teacher poses a problem to which there are multiple possible responses or solutions, and provides think time.

2 Students take turns stating responses or solutions.

RoundRobin

RallyRobin

Variations

AllWrite RoundRobin

During RoundRobin, students each record each answer on their own paper.

AllWrite Consensus

During RoundRobin, after reaching consensus, students each record each answer on their own paper.

Think-Write-RoundRobin. Students think about their response, then independently write it down before the RoundRobin.

Single RoundRobin. The team does just one round of sharing, each teammate getting one turn.

Timed RoundRobin

Each student shares in turn for a specified time.

RoundTable & RallyTable

Students take turns generating written responses, solving problems, or making a contribution to a project. In RoundTable, students take turns in their teams. In RallyTable, partners take turns.

1 The teacher provides a task to which there are multiple possible responses, and provides think time.

2 Students take turns passing a paper and pencil or a team project, each writing one answer or making a contribution.

Variations
Pass-N-Praise
Students praise the contribution of the person passing the paper to them.

RoundTable Consensus
Students must reach consensus before recording each answer.

RoundTable

RallyTable

Simultaneous RoundTable

In teams, students each write a response on their own piece of paper. Students then pass their papers clockwise so each teammate can add to the prior responses.

Setup: Each team of four needs four papers and four pencils.

1 The teacher assigns a topic or question and provides think time.

2 All four students respond, simultaneously writing, drawing, or building something with manipulatives.

3 The teacher signals time, or students place thumbs up when done with the problem.

4 Students pass papers or projects one person clockwise.

5 Students continue, adding to what was already completed.

6 Continue, starting at Step 3.

Optional
Pass-N-Praise. Students are instructed not to release their paper until they receive a praiser that makes them feel good.

Variation
Simultaneous RallyTable
In pairs, students each have a paper with a label or topic. For example, one paper may say Pro and the other Con. Or one paper may be labeled Mammals and the other Reptiles. Students add a response to the paper they have, then trade with their partner to add a response to the other paper. They continue adding responses and trading papers until time is up.

Showdown

When the Showdown Captain calls, "Showdown!" teammates all display their own answers. Teammates either celebrate or tutor, and then celebrate.

Setup: Teams each have a set of question cards stacked facedown in the center of the table.

1 The teacher selects one student on each team to be the Showdown Captain for the first round.

2 The Showdown Captain draws the top card, reads the question, and provides think time.

3 Working alone, all students, including the Showdown Captain, write their answers.

4 When finished, teammates signal they're ready.

5 The Showdown Captain calls, "Showdown."

6 Teammates show and discuss their answers.

7 The Showdown Captain leads the checking.

8 If correct, the team celebrates; if not, teammates tutor, then celebrate.

9 The person on the left of the Showdown Captain becomes the Showdown Captain for the next round.

Modifications: Rather than cards, students can play Showdown with oral questions from the teacher, or from questions on a handout or questions displayed by a projector.

Spend-A-Buck

To make a team decision, teammates use funny money and "spend a buck" to vote on their top picks. The option with the most bucks is deemed the team decision.

Setup: Each person needs 10 play dollars. Options to be voted on are each written on separate cards or slips of paper.

1 Alternative option cards are laid out on team tables.

2 Students put a dollar on each alternative.

3 Students spend remaining dollars any way they want.

4 Teams count the results to determine the team decision.

Note: To break ties, losing items are set aside, and students repeat Steps 1–4 with remaining items.

Hint: Prior to voting, give students time to make proactive statements, saying why they favor the options they chose.

No Music → 1 time

StandUp–HandUp–PairUp

Students stand up, put their hands up, and quickly find a partner with whom to share or discuss.

1 Teacher says, when I say (go,) you will "stand up, hand up, and pair up!" Teacher pauses, then says, "Go!"

2 Students stand up and keep one hand high in the air until they find the (closest) partner who's not a teammate. Students do a "high five" and put their hands down. *(can do "air" high five)*

3 Teacher may ask a (question) or give an assignment, and provides think time.

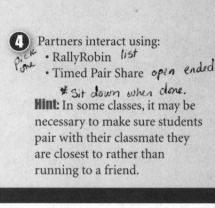

4 Partners interact using:
Pick one
- RallyRobin *list*
- Timed Pair Share *open ended*

★ Sit down when done.

Hint: In some classes, it may be necessary to make sure students pair with their classmate they are closest to rather than running to a friend.

Talking Chips

Teammates place Talking Chips in the center of the table to make sure everyone contributes to the team discussion.

Setup: Teams have talking chips (maximum: two chips each).

1 The teacher provides a discussion topic and provides think time.

2 Any student begins the discussion, placing one of his/her chips in the center of the table.

3 Any student with a chip continues discussing, using his/her chip.

4 When all chips are used, teammates each collect their chips and continue the discussion using their talking chips.

Modifications: Students may be given just one chip each, or two chips. Students with no chips left must wait until teammates have used all their chips before they all collect their chip(s) and continue the discussion.

Kagan Cooperative Learning • **Dr. Spencer Kagan & Miguel Kagan**
Kagan Publishing • **1 (800) 933-2667** • **www.KaganOnline.com**

Team Stand-N-Share

Teams check off or add each idea as it is shared by other teams, sitting down to show every teams' ideas have been shared.

Setup: Teams generate a list of items to share.

1 All students stand near their teammates.

2 The teacher calls on a standing student holding the team list.

3 Selected student states one idea from the team list.

4 The student in each team, who is holding the team list, either adds the item to the list, or if it is already listed, checks it off.

5 Students pass their team lists one teammate clockwise.

6 Steps 2–5 are repeated.

7 Teams sit when all their items are shared. While seated, they add each new item using RoundTable. When all teams are seated, all items have been shared and Team Stand-N-Share is complete.

Variations
Pair Stand-N-Share. Pairs generate ideas, and then play as a pair.

Individual Stand-N-Share. Each student plays with her/his own list of ideas.

Telephone

One student per team leaves the room during instruction. When students return, teammates provide instruction on the information missed.

1 One student from each team ("the Learner") is selected to leave the room.

2 Remaining students ("the Teachers") receive instruction.

3 The Teachers plan how best to instruct the Learner, making sure each Teacher has a part in the teaching. The Teachers decide how they will check for understanding.

4 Learners return to their teams.

5 Teachers each teach their part of the content, with teammates augmenting as necessary. They then check for understanding.

6 The Learners may take a practice test.

Use everyday

Three-Step Interview

Students interview their partner and then each share with teammates what they learned.

1 Teacher provides the interview topic, states the duration of the interview, and provides think time.

2 In pairs, Student A interviews Student B.

3 Pairs switch roles: Student B interviews Student A.

4 RoundRobin: Pairs pair up to form groups of four. Each student, in turn, shares with the team what he/she learned in the interview.

Use everyday!

Timed Pair Share

In pairs, students share with a partner for a predetermined time while the partner listens. Then partners switch roles.

1 The teacher announces a topic ①, states how long ② each student will share, and provides think time ③.

2 In pairs, Partner A shares; Partner B listens. *(and asks questions if A finishes early)*

3 Partner B responds with a positive gambit. *Teacher led*

4 Partners switch roles.

Hint: The teacher provides positive response gambits to use in Step 3:

Copycat response gambits
- "Thanks for sharing!"
- "You are interesting to listen to!"

Complete the sentence gambits
- "One thing I learned listening to you was…."
- "I enjoyed listening to you because…."
- "Your most interesting idea was…."

Chapter Summary

Cooperative Learning Structures are step-by-step instructional strategies. Structures differ in many ways from other forms of cooperative learning, but they share principles that have been shown to make cooperative learning more successful than traditional instruction and unstructured group work.

As we use structures to deliver the regular academic curriculum, our students excel academically. Simultaneously, they also learn teamwork and leadership skills; engage and develop their multiple intelligences; and engage and develop a range of social skills, thinking skills, and character virtues. Structures deliver an exceedingly rich, embedded curriculum. There are many structures to reach the many different learners we encounter in the classroom today. Different structures help us reach different learning objectives. The variety of structures allows us to wisely select the most appropriate structure for our desired learning outcome.

Because structures are content-free, they may be used over and over to create an infinite number of activities. Teachers versed in a wide range of structures are empowered to create a full spectrum of active learning experiences.

Chapter Questions

▶ Questions for Review

1. Structures were compared with two other ways to teach. What are they?
2. What does it mean to say a structure is content-free? Pick a structure and give some examples of how it is content-free.
3. How do structures differ from group work?
4. Define the Replacement Cycle. How do structures break the cycle?
5. What are the four steps to success with structures?
6. What is the Embedded Curriculum, and how does it relate to structures?
7. Name and describe at least six of the ten functions of structures.

▶ Questions for Thinking and Discussion

1. Define a structure in your own words.
2. Which structures are automatic for you? Which structure would you most like to achieve a level of automaticity with? Why?
3. Do you think selected structures will become so prevalent that all teachers will know and use them?
4. Pick one structure and describe how it can be used for at least three different purposes.
5. Prioritize the ten functions of structures, based on outcomes for students you value, from most to least.

References

[1] Goodlad, J. *A Place Called School.* New York, NY: McGraw-Hill Book Company, 1984.

[2] Pianta, R., J. Belsky, R. Houts & F. Morrison. "Opportunities to Learn in America's Elementary Classrooms." *Science,* 2007, 315: 1975–1976.

[3] NTL Institute for Applied Behavioral Science. *The Learning Pyramid.* Alexandria, VA: 2006. http://www.ntl.org

[4] Kagan, M., L. Kagan & S. Kagan. *Cooperative Learning Structures for Classbuilding.* San Clemente, CA: Kagan Publishing, 1995.

[5] Kagan, L., M. Kagan & S. Kagan. *Cooperative Learning Structures for Teambuilding.* San Clemente, CA: Kagan Publishing, 1997.

[6] Kagan, S. "Teaching for Character and Community." *Educational Leadership,* 2001, 59(2): 50–55.

[7,8] Marzano, R.F. *A different kind of classroom: Teaching with dimensions of learning.* Alexandria, VA: Association for Supervision and Curriculum Development, 1992.

[9] Kagan, S. "Kagan Structures for Thinking Skills." *Kagan Online Magazine.* San Clemente, CA: Kagan Publishing, Fall 2003.

[10] Kagan, S. "Rethinking Thinking: Does Bloom's Taxonomy Align with Brain Science?" *Kagan Online Magazine.* San Clemente, CA: Kagan Publishing, 2005.

[11] Kagan, S., M. Kagan & L. Kagan. *Kagan Structures.* San Clemente, CA: Kagan Publishing, 2010.

Resources

McPherson, J. *For Whom the Late Bell Tolls.* San Clemente, CA: Kagan Publishing, 2005.

CHAPTER 7

Key 2
Teams

W hen you peek into a cooperative learning classroom, the first thing you notice is the seating arrangement. Students are seated in teams. Student teams are a defining characteristic of cooperative learning; they are the "cooperative" in cooperative learning. Teams promote strong bonds between students, facilitate interaction over curriculum, and improve learning. Teams are one of the seven keys to successful cooperative learning. In this chapter, we'll cover when and how to use the various types of cooperative teams as well as techniques for forming and reforming teams.

Working cooperatively in teams is a wonderful experience for students and provides opportunities for students to develop social and life skills that will serve them well throughout life.

The Basic Cooperative Learning Team

The Four Student Team

To the extent possible, students are seated in teams of four. Why? Much of the rationale for cooperative learning is based on the benefits of active participation. As we add students to teams beyond four per team, fewer and fewer students are engaged at any one moment, and our classroom becomes less and less efficient.

In a class of 30, when one student is called on and responds, 1/30th of the class is actively participating. It would take 30 minutes to give everyone one minute to verbalize her/his ideas. If we divide the class into two large groups of 15 and allow one person at a time to talk within each group, during the discussion time we double the amount of active participation—1/15th of the class is talking. In only 15 minutes, we give each student one minute. As the group size is made smaller, the percentages get better. Groups of four allow 1/4 of the class to produce language at any one time—from the perspective of active participation, teams of four are twice as good as groups of eight.

Kagan Cooperative Learning · Dr. Spencer Kagan & Miguel Kagan
Kagan Publishing · 1 (800) 933-2667 · www.KaganOnline.com

7.1

If students talk one at a time, it takes only four minutes for each to get one minute, not the 30 minutes it would take in the whole-class structure.

Given this rationale, why not move to groups of three or even pairs? Why stick with teams of four? There are four reasons.

1. Teams of Four Allow Pair Work.
Many structures such as RallyCoach and Timed Pair Share call for pair work. Many structures such as Three-Step Interview and Pairs Compare include pair work as part of the teamwork process. Pair work maximizes simultaneous interaction. Groups of three don't divide evenly into pairs.

2. Teams of Four Avoid Odd Man Out.
The social psychology of a group of three is often a pair and an outsider. Two people hit it off well and talk to each other often. Result: one is left out. In triads, it is easier for one student to "drop out" or be excluded than in a team of four.

3. Teams of Four Optimize Cognitive and Linguistic Mismatch.
Compared to a group of three, a group of four doubles the probability of an optimum cognitive and linguistic mismatch. The Piagetian cognitive development work, as well as research in the area of linguistic development, indicates that we learn well from someone only somewhat different from our own level of development—someone who can provide stimulation in our Zone of Proximal Development. In a group of three, there are three possible pairs or lines of communication; in a group of four, there are six. (See box, Teams of Four Double the Lines of Communication.) Various structures take advantage of these many possible pairings.

4. Teams of Four Increase Variety.
In teams of four, the teacher can sometimes call for students to work as a team of four. Sometimes they work with their shoulder partner. Sometimes they work with their face partner. The flexible arrangements within a team of four create variety, which enhances interest.

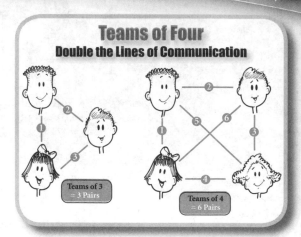

Teams of Four
Double the Lines of Communication

Teams of 3 = 3 Pairs

Teams of 4 = 6 Pairs

How to Handle Extra Students.
The class will only break evenly into teams of four a quarter of the time. The other three-quarters of the time, you will have one, two, or three extra students. When your class does not divide evenly by four, use the Extra Student Guidelines. (See box.)

With one student left over, place that student as a fifth member on a team with a student who is frequently absent, or where he or she would best learn or help others. With two students left over, steal a student from one of the teams of four to create two teams of three. The two teams of three should sit next to each other. During teamwork they may work as two triad teams, but they can break evenly into three pairs for pair activities. With three students left over, keep those three as a team.

> **Extra Student Guidelines**
> ....
> ▶ **1 Extra Student**
> 1 team of 5
> ▶ **2 Extra Students**
> 2 teams of 3
> ▶ **3 Extra Students**
> 1 team of 3

Dealing with Absences.
If two or more students from a single team are absent on the same day, teams can be adjusted for the day to accommodate the absences. See the Absent Teammates Guidelines box for how to deal with absences on the same team.

> **Absent Teammates Guidelines**
> ....
> ▶ **1 Teammate Absent**
> No change necessary.
> ▶ **2 Teammates Absent**
> Pull a student from a team of 5 or 4 to work with that team.
> ▶ **3 Teammates Absent**
> Move remaining student to the smallest team.

Seating Arrangement. Usually teammates have their individual desks pushed together to form a team table. This allows students to interact easily and work together on their various team tasks. The guidelines and many possible seating arrangements are covered in depth in *Chapter 8: Management.*

The Heterogeneous Base Team

Heterogeneous teams are recommended for stable base teams. The heterogeneous team is mixed in achievement level, sex, and ethnicity. When possible, the base team is a microcosm of the classroom's diversity. Heterogeneous teams maximize the potential for cross-ability tutoring, positive race relations, improved cross-sex relations, and efficient classroom management. Although there is good theoretical rationale for using a variety of teamformation methods, it is important to note almost all of the empirical studies showing academic achievement gains are based on heterogeneous teams. Heterogeneous teams are research-based.

> ### Team Assignment Tips
> • When first announcing team assignments, name tags are placed on the team tables, indicating where students are to sit. Rather than a sequential reading by the teacher of each student's name and team assignment, the teacher simply places the name tags at each seat and then tells students to find their seats.
>
> • Numbered mobiles above each team table make good signs for students and for teachers. As a teambuilder, teams create their own team mobile with their individual names and team name.

Team Duration

As a general guideline, we suggest changing base teams after six weeks. If teams are changed too frequently, students don't get the opportunity to bond fully as a team and to create a strong team identity. Teammates who know and trust each other work very well together. There is a short adjustment period when forming new teams. Changing teams too frequently introduces too many adjustment periods and creates a bit of uncertainty.

> *"Nothing truly valuable can be achieved except by the disinterested cooperation of many individuals."*
> —Albert Einstein

So why change teams at all? There are three important reasons to change teams, even if they are functioning well. The first reason is to offer students the opportunity to transfer their teamwork skills to a new social context. Students who are exposed to multiple groupings are better prepared to thrive in diversity. They leave the classroom more prepared to work as an effective team member or leader in any team. Working cooperatively in teams is a wonderful experience for students and provides contextual opportunities for students to develop social and life skills that will transfer to many social situations throughout life.

The second reason to change teams is team dynamics. Even with heterogeneous teams, there may be a team that does not work well together. For some reason, the chemistry just isn't right. When we change teams every six weeks, over the course of the school year, students are members of six or seven teams, allowing plenty of exposure to diversity and various team dynamics.

The third reason to change teams is, to put it bluntly, to share the burden. No matter how much we work on social skills, some students may be bossy, inclined to put others down, or unable to understand points of view different from their own. If we never changed teams, the only team experience the other three teammates would have would be with a "difficult" teammate. Further, having the difficult teammate work in a variety of teams increases the probability that student will acquire much-needed teamwork skills.

The Various Types of Teams. The basic cooperative learning team is a heterogeneous team of four that stays together for approximately six weeks. If we use heterogeneous teams exclusively, however, the high achievers would never interact (missing important academic stimulation) and the low achievers would never be on the same team (missing leadership opportunities). To reap the full potential of cooperative learning, we use more than one type of team.

We will examine here the four main types of teams and their associated teamformation methods. Let's start with the most common type of team—Heterogeneous teams.

Team Type 1
Heterogeneous Teams

A number of researchers and theorists have identified heterogeneous student teams as a defining characteristic of cooperative learning. Heterogeneous teams are mixed ability, mixed sex, and mixed race. We put a high, two middle, and a low achieving student on each team; we put males and females on each team and to the extent possible, each team is ethnically diverse. In general, heterogeneous teams are preferred because they 1) increase opportunities for peer tutoring and support, 2) improve cross-race and cross-sex relations and integration, and 3) make classroom management easier—having a high achiever on each team can be like having one teacher aide for every three students. Non-heterogeneous teams can be formed in a variety of ways, including self-selection (allowing students to group themselves by friendships or interests) and random selection (students draw a number from 1 to 8 and sit down at the table with the corresponding number). Self-selection runs a strong risk of promoting or reinforcing status hierarchies in the classroom ("in-" and "out-groups"); random selection runs the risk of creating "loser" teams (the four lowest achievers or the four greatest behavior problems in the classroom may end up on the same team). Stable, heterogeneous, teacher-formed teams avoid these pitfalls and maximize the potential for achievement gains.

The Four Major Types of Teams

1	Heterogeneous Teams	Mixed ability, sex, race teams
2	Random Teams	Randomly formed teams
3	Student-Selected Teams	Students select own teams
4	Homogeneous Teams	Teams with a shared trait (ability, interest, language)

Heterogeneous Teams, Tracking, Labels, and Expectations

Using heterogeneous ability level teams in the classroom is the opposite of homogeneous ability grouping and tracking. Homogeneous ability groups and tracking are common educational practices that are fraught with problems. Ability grouping or streaming occurs when the teacher forms similar-ability level groups within the classroom such as reading groups. The teacher may have unbiased names for the groups such as the green group, blue group, and purple group, but students quickly identify the differences. They have their own names for the groups: the top group is the "eagles," the middle group is "seagulls," and the low group is the "droppings."

Tracking occurs at the class level, too. Students are placed in different tracks based on their ability level. It is most evident in high school. There's the advanced placement track. They're the students heading for fine universities. They're often given the best teachers, most challenging curriculum, and are expected to succeed. The middle group is comprised of the normal ability level students. They are state college and community college bound. The curriculum is not so challenging and the expectations are not so high. The remedial track, otherwise known as the dummies and dirtbags, don't have high hopes. The football coach gives them independent worksheet work ("busy work") in an attempt to mitigate the discipline problems.

Now this picture may be an offensive gross generality to some, but unfortunately there is quite a bit of truth to it. Separate is far from equal. Ability grouping and tracking are more responsible for perpetuating inequality than they are effective for addressing preexisting differences. Research has shown that labels and expectations become self-fulfilling prophecies.[1]

On a macro-level, heterogeneity is found to close the achievement gap between the races and socioeconomic classes. Studies found that racial integration could cut the gap in standardized test scores between blacks and whites by as much as one-half by bringing the bottom up rather than bringing the top down.[2,3] Recently, districts that have used economic integration—limiting the proportion of low-income students in a single school by integrating schools' socioeconomic composition—show very promising results with increased test scores and decreased dropout rates.[4,5]

We use heterogeneous groups in the classroom to equalize educational opportunities, resources, and expectations. Research demonstrates cooperative learning does not bring the high achievers down. Quite the opposite. It brings the low achievers up. Cooperative learning narrows the achievement gap. See *Chapter 3: What Does the Research Say?* Imagine a school in which students from different socioeconomic levels and ethnicities were put on heterogeneous teams from a very early age. They were all expected to succeed and given the best engaging instruction and the best-available curriculum. What would be the result at the end of their schooling process? Would there still be an ability-level discrepancy? Perhaps. But nowhere near the achievement gap crisis that our nation faces today.

When we form heterogeneous groups in the classroom, we must bear in mind the insidious nature of labels. We rank students to create balanced, heterogeneous teams. But students never see the ranks. We have high expectations for all students in the class, and we take great satisfaction in watching all our students living up to those expectations.

Unequal Numbers of Boys and Girls.

If there are more boys than girls or more girls than boys, usually the best strategy is not to share the scarce resources equally, assigning one boy or one girl to each team. One boy and three girls often amounts to the male receiving an inordinate amount of attention. One girl and three boys often results in the female being ignored by the three males. Solution: Assign students to teams of two boys and two girls until you run out of boys or girls; the remaining teams will have either all boys or all girls.

Ability Level Shoulder and Face Partners.

Some teachers report better luck if during initial team assignments they have students sit so that the high achiever is next to a middle achiever and across from a middle achiever; they place the low achiever kitty-corner to high achiever. Some high achievers initially have difficulty working with students far below their level. The graphic below illustrates a seating arrangement that minimizes interaction between the highest and lowest achievers on the team.

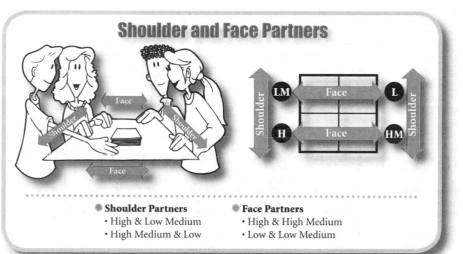

Shoulder and Face Partners

● **Shoulder Partners**
• High & Low Medium
• High Medium & Low

● **Face Partners**
• High & High Medium
• Low & Low Medium

Heterogeneous Teamformation Methods

There are many different ways to effectively form heterogeneous teams. Different teachers prefer different methods. Below, a variety of methods are presented, so you can select your favorite. Remember, heterogeneous base teams should be long-term, so you only have to form new teams approximately every six weeks.

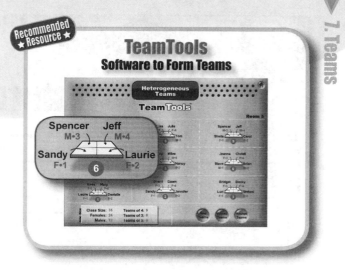

Recommended Resource

TeamTools
Software to Form Teams

TeamTools Software

TeamTools software makes teamformation easy. For each student, you enter: 1) name, 2) male or female, and 3) a numeric score from 0 to 100. The score can be a quiz score, class grade, assessment score, or any number that represents student ability. Next, you click a button and TeamTools takes your class info and recommends teams for you, showing student names around team desks (see sample above). If you like the recommended teams, you save, print, or display them for your class. If you're not happy with the suggested teams, you push a button to try again, or fine-tune the teams yourself by moving students around.

To form cooperative learning teams, TeamTools maximizes the teams of four. Extra students are assigned to either a team of five or one or two teams of three. TeamTools takes heterogeneous ability as the most important variable, and always creates balanced ability teams. Next, it tries to put two girls and two boys on each team, but when you run out of balanced sex teams, it creates same-sex teams so the solo boy or solo girl are not given too much or too little attention. Students are strategically placed on teams so shoulder partners and face partners are of the recommended ability and sex to increase tutoring and equalize interaction between boys and girls. It's really a time-saver and forms ideal teams for Kagan Structures. Of all the ways to form cooperative teams, TeamTools is our favorite.

Kagan Cooperative Learning • Dr. Spencer Kagan & Miguel Kagan
Kagan Publishing • 1 (800) 933-2667 • www.KaganOnline.com

7.5

Teamformation Cards

Instructions. Copy these student cards to form cooperative learning teams.

Sex _____	Score _____		Sex _____	Score _____
_____			_____	
Name			**Name**	
Prior Teams			Prior Teams	
○ ○ ○ ○ ○ ○			○ ○ ○ ○ ○ ○	

Sex _____	Score _____		Sex _____	Score _____
_____			_____	
Name			**Name**	
Prior Teams			Prior Teams	
○ ○ ○ ○ ○ ○			○ ○ ○ ○ ○ ○	

Sex _____	Score _____		Sex _____	Score _____
_____			_____	
Name			**Name**	
Prior Teams			Prior Teams	
○ ○ ○ ○ ○ ○			○ ○ ○ ○ ○ ○	

Sex _____	Score _____		Sex _____	Score _____
_____			_____	
Name			**Name**	
Prior Teams			Prior Teams	
○ ○ ○ ○ ○ ○			○ ○ ○ ○ ○ ○	

Sex _____	Score _____		Sex _____	Score _____
_____			_____	
Name			**Name**	
Prior Teams			Prior Teams	
○ ○ ○ ○ ○ ○			○ ○ ○ ○ ○ ○	

Kagan Cooperative Learning • Dr. Spencer Kagan & Miguel Kagan
Kagan Publishing • 1 (800) 933-2667 • www.KaganOnline.com

Card Sorting Method

Anita Kissinger (Director of Staff Development for Springfield, MO Public Schools) developed the Card Sorting Method for forming heterogeneous teams. See box for the steps of the Card Sorting Method.

Card Sorting Method

Step 1. **Make Cards.** Write students' names, sex, and test scores on Teamformation Cards (blackline provided on the previous page), one student per card.

· ·

Step 2. **Sort the Cards.** Divide the total number of students in the class by four to determine the number of teams. For example, if there are 29 students in the class divided by four, there will be 7 teams with 1 extra student. The cards are sorted by achievement level so that there are 7 in each of the four categories: High, High Medium, Low Medium, and Low. If your math resulted in extra students, use the Extra Student Guidelines (see box).

Extra Student Guidelines

▶ **1 Extra Student**
The High Medium OR Low Medium category will have 1 more student.

▶ **2 Extra Students**
The High Medium AND the Low Medium category will have 1 more student each.

▶ **3 Extra Students**
Three categories will have 1 more student.

· ·

Step 3. **Color-Code the Cards.** Color-code the cards by category using colored markers or colored sticker dots. Here's a possible color scheme:

H Blue = **High**
HM Green = **High Medium**
LM Yellow = **Low Medium**
L Red = **Low**

· ·

Step 4. **Form Teams.** Lay out the cards in rows by category as illustrated. Each team will have one student from each ability-level category.

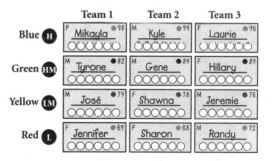

· ·

Forming New Teams. This card sorting method works well for forming new teams. Record students' team assignments at the bottom of the cards. Then, lay out the cards as in step 4. Check down each team column to see if students were already on the same team. If so, exchange a student for another student of the same ability level.

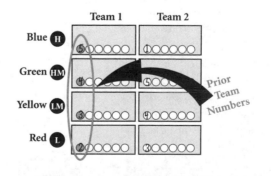

Teamformation Pocket Chart Method

A Teamformation Pocket Chart is available from Kagan Publishing to easily form and re-form heterogeneous teams. The nice thing about the pocket chart is how easy it is to adjust teams and to evaluate prior team assignments.

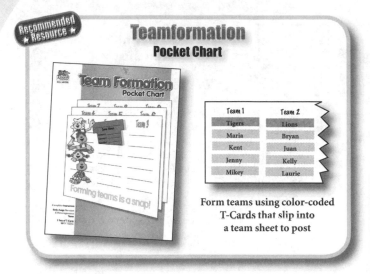

Recommended Resource

Form teams using color-coded T-Cards that slip into a team sheet to post

Achievement-Ranked List Method

In this method, the teacher ranks students on a list by achievement level. Then the teacher uses the list to select a high, two mediums, and a low for each team. Use the blackline, Forming Heterogeneous Teams (on the next page).

Step 1. Rank-Order Students. Produce a numbered list of students, from highest to lowest achiever. The list does not have to be perfect. To produce the list, use one of the following (in order of preference): pretest, recent past test, past grades, or best guess.

Step 2. Select First Team. Choose the top student on the list, the bottom student on the list, and two students from the middle of the list. Assign them to Team 1, unless they are:

- All one sex;
- All one ethnicity in a mixed ethnicity group;
- Worst enemies or best friends;
- Incompatible (e.g., all chatterboxes, all bossy, all introverts, all easily distractible)

To make switches, move up or down one student from the middle to readjust. Once you have selected the first team, check off the students' names on your list so you know not to select them again.

Step 3. Select Remaining Teams. Repeat the procedure to select the remaining teams of four.

Step 4. Assign "Extras." Assign one extra students to one team of five, two extra students to two teams of three, and three extra students to one team of three.

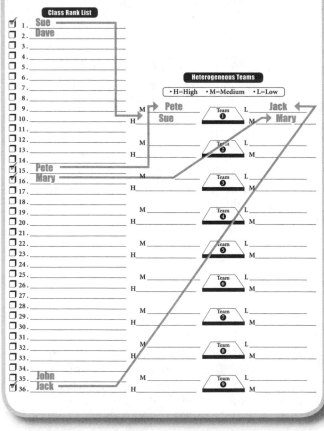

Forming Heterogeneous Teams

Achievement-Ranked List Method

Instructions

Step 1. Fill in your students' names in rank order by ability.

Class Rank List

☐ 1. _____
☐ 2. _____
☐ 3. _____
☐ 4. _____
☐ 5. _____
☐ 6. _____
☐ 7. _____
☐ 8. _____
☐ 9. _____
☐ 10. _____
☐ 11. _____
☐ 12. _____
☐ 13. _____
☐ 14. _____
☐ 15. _____
☐ 16. _____
☐ 17. _____
☐ 18. _____
☐ 19. _____
☐ 20. _____
☐ 21. _____
☐ 22. _____
☐ 23. _____
☐ 24. _____
☐ 25. _____
☐ 26. _____
☐ 27. _____
☐ 28. _____
☐ 29. _____
☐ 30. _____
☐ 31. _____
☐ 32. _____
☐ 33. _____
☐ 34. _____
☐ 35. _____
☐ 36. _____

Step 2. Select a High, Low, and two Mediums to assign the first team. Check off the students' names from your list.

Step 3. Assign the rest of the teams to teams of four.

Step 4. Assign extra students using the following guidelines:
- **1 Extra Student**—1 team of 5.
- **2 Extra Students**—2 teams of 3.
- **3 Extra Students**—1 team of 3.

Heterogeneous Teams

• H=High   • M=Medium   • L=Low

M _____ Team **1** L _____
H _____   M _____

M _____ Team **2** L _____
H _____   M _____

M _____ Team **3** L _____
H _____   M _____

M _____ Team **4** L _____
H _____   M _____

M _____ Team **5** L _____
H _____   M _____

M _____ Team **6** L _____
H _____   M _____

M _____ Team **7** L _____
H _____   M _____

M _____ Team **8** L _____
H _____   M _____

M _____ Team **9** L _____
H _____   M _____

Kagan Cooperative Learning • Dr. Spencer Kagan & Miguel Kagan
Kagan Publishing • 1 (800) 933-2667 • www.KaganOnline.com

7.9

The Sticky Note Method

First, divide your class into four equal parts: High, High Medium, Low Medium, and Low. Next, write student names on color-coded sticky notes. All the Highs are one color, all the High Mediums another color, and so on. When forming teams, simply select four sticky notes, one of each color. If the team doesn't feel right, it is easy to un-stick the notes and form a new team assignment. Some teachers even stick their sticky notes on a classroom schematic so it doubles as a seating arrangement chart.

The Spreadsheet Method

A spreadsheet application such as Excel can be very helpful in team formation and for keeping track of previous team assignments to use when forming new teams. This method requires a basic working knowledge of spreadsheets. Here's how it works: Create a "Students" column with students rank-ordered by achievement. The next column is students' "Ability Level." The rank list is divided into four equal parts and students are labeled as High, High Medium, Low Medium, and Low. Now, move student rows in your spreadsheet to represent your team selection, ensuring you have a high, two middle, and a low on each team. There are two ways to move students around in your spreadsheet while keeping the rest of your data intact. Either create a second spreadsheet and copy and paste rows

so students from the same team are one below another, or using your original spreadsheet, insert a row where you wish to move a student, then move the student to that empty row (if you try to drag a row on top of existing data, you will overwrite that data).

Once you're happy with your selection, add the team numbers in the third column, "Assignment 1." By recording your team assignments, when it comes time to form new teams, you can see if students have worked on the same team. A nice thing about spreadsheets is you can sort on any column to easily manipulate your list.

Pairs Pair Method

Dr. Julie High, author of *Second Language Learning Through Cooperative Learning*,[6] developed Pairs Pair. Students are divided into four groups; High, High Medium, Low Medium, and Low. Students are not told the groups are based on ability level. The High and Low groups meet on one side of the room, and the two middle groups meet on the other. The students then form pairs (High and Low on one side of the room and High Medium-Low Medium on the other). Next the pairs pair. Thus the students have selected heterogeneous teams. Julie is a very experienced cooperative learning teacher and trainer, and she reports that Pairs Pair has produced the best functioning teams in her classroom. Pairs Pair is good for classrooms in which there is not a big ability-level gap between students. It is not recommended for classrooms in which students would recognize they are initially grouped by their ability level.

The Spreadsheet Method

Forming Teams with Spreadsheets

	Students	Ability	Assignment 1	Assignment 2
1	**Students**	**Ability**	**Assignment 1**	**Assignment 2**
2	Larry	High	1	8
3	Terry	High	2	7
4	Peter	High	3	6
5	Esther	High	4	5

Team Leader Method

The following is a version of a method developed by Richard Shetley (Alta Loma Junior High School, Alta Loma, CA). This is an easy, fair way to have students select their own heterogeneous teams, and it provides some students the most powerful peer inclusion experience of their life!

Step 1. Select Team Leaders. Select the highest achieving 7 or 8 students as team leaders, one per team.

Step 2. Leadership Meeting. Meet with the leaders as a group. Explain to them that the success of the team approach depends on mixed ability-level teams. Have them decide which of the lowest ability students will be on each team. Explain to them what they are to do the next day.

Step 3. Leaders Choose Teammates. The next day in class, announce that there will be student teams and announce the team leaders. Ask the team leaders to choose someone to be on their team. As per agreement, the team leaders each go up to one of the low ability students and say something like, "I want you to be on my team."

Be prepared. Many of the low ability students have never been selected by their peers for anything. They are used to being the leftovers. There may be tears or at least moist eyes.

Step 4. High-Low Pair Choose Middle. The leader and his/her first selection sit down together and decide on a second choice from the pool of remaining middle ability-level students. Students are informed that they cannot choose teams all of one sex. The teacher maintains the option to make final decisions and adjustments if necessary.

Step 5. High-Low-Middle Triad Choose Last Teammate. The three members choose the remaining teammate.

Team Type 2
Random Teams

As the name suggests, random teams are truly random. There is no rhyme or reason why students are placed on the same team. The team is formed completely by chance. The teacher could pull four names out of a hat and put those four students together as a team. The four highest achievers could be on the same team. The four lowest achievers could be on the same team. Best friends could be on the same team. Sworn enemies could be on the same team.

Random teams add excitement and suspense to the classroom. Who will I get to work with today?

Why in the world would a teacher want to form random teams? Because random teams are fun. Students like the opportunity to work with classmates beyond their immediate teammates. Random teams may be very short-lived as in the case of a five-minute classbuilding activity, or for a temporary breakout to discuss an issue with new teammates, or to practice a skill or procedure. Or the random teams may last long-term, but meet only briefly once a week to work on a project. Random teams add excitement and suspense to the classroom. Who will I get to work with today?

However, random teams are not recommended for long-term stable base teams. They are not balanced by ability level, so teams will finish at different rates. And they are not controlled for student characteristics, so the two class chatterboxes could be put together and easily get off task.

Random Teamformation Methods

Early in the development of cooperative learning methods, we relied on intrusive and time-consuming methods for forming random teams. With time and with the development of structures, we became more sophisticated and found ways to form random teams without special manipulatives or taking time from academics. Let's look first at some of the early, formal random teamformation methods. Then we'll turn to methods embedded in structures that can be used while teaching any content, without stealing time from the content.

Traditional Methods

Counting Off

Early in cooperative learning, Counting Off was the most frequently used random teamformation method, but it soon lost favor as it took time during class. To use the method, you first divide the number of students in the class by four to know how many teams you will have. For example, if you have 35 students, you know you will have eight teams of four with three left over to make one team of three, so there will be nine teams in the class. Next you have students count off by nine, telling them to either write down their number or to remember it. To count off, the first student says "1," the student behind her says "2," and so on until the students reach "9." The student after "9" each time says "1." In our example, because there are 35 students, the last student would say "8." (If there were 36 students, our class would divide evenly by four and there would be four teams of nine, so the last student would say "9.") When all students have a number, they are told to find and stand with the others with their number. In our example, there will be four 1's, four 2's, and so on, with three 9's. Once students are standing with their number, we instruct them to sit down as a team. The three 9's would be a team of three. If the count-off resulted in two teams of three, we have the two teams of three sit together so that during pair work, they are three pairs and no one is left out. If the count-off resulted in three teams of three, we would probably break up one of those teams and fill in the other two teams to become a team of four and a team of five.

Number Cards

The teacher creates a deck of number cards. First, the teacher divides the number of students in the class by four to determine how many teams there will be. For example, if the teacher has 32 students in her class, she divides by four to find she will have eight teams. The teacher then creates a deck of number cards with four 1's, four 2's, and so on, up to four 8's. As students enter class, the teacher stands by the door and hands each a card from the shuffled deck. Team tables are numbered and a student receiving a 4, for example, goes to table 4 to sit. This method works well and does not take time from academics. One caution: once students know how the method works, if the teacher does not prevent it, the students will trade cards so they can sit with their friends.

Playing Cards

Playing cards work exactly like Number Cards, but they have two big advantages. First, the teacher does not have to make up the deck, but rather uses a store-bought deck of playing cards. Second, the cards have a built-in role assignment. Typically, the heart is the Praiser; the club is the Taskmaster; the spade is the Materials Monitor; and the diamond is the Recorder. Of course, different roles can be assigned to the four suits, depending on the project or task.

Fun, Teambulding Methods

Two random teamformation methods have built-in teambuilding. Puzzled People has students solve a mini jigsaw puzzle to find their teammates; Animal Sounds has students find their new teammates with their eyes closed!

Puzzled People

A picture is torn into four parts, and each student gets one part. Like a jigsaw puzzle, students move about the room to find their teammates with matching pieces of the puzzle. Once all the puzzles are solved, students sit down as a team.

Step 1. Prepare Pictures. The teacher selects one picture for each team in the class. If there are eight teams, the teacher selects eight pictures. Tearing full-page pictures (related to the theme of the lesson) out of old magazines, works well.

Step 2. Tear Pictures. The teacher distributes the pictures to students and has one student tear the picture into four jagged parts. That student keeps one part and gives the three other parts to three other students.

Step 3. Mix and Trade. Have students mill around the room, repeatedly trading picture pieces with other students.

Step 4. Solve Puzzle. Call, "Stop!" and then let students solve the puzzles by grouping with the others who hold pieces of the same picture.

Step 5. Sit as a Team. Tell students to sit down as a team with their new teammates.

Variations. Puzzled People can use academic content. For language arts, the four pieces can be four sentences in a content-related statement, or four lines of a proverb or poem. For social studies, the four pieces can be pieces of a map.

Animal Sounds

Animal Sounds is a raucous, fun way to form teams. Students are each given a card with the name of an animal or picture of the animal. There are four cards for each animal. Students mix through the room trading cards with each other until the teacher calls, "Stop." To their surprise, the teacher says: "look at your card. Now close your eyes. With your eyes closed, you must find your teammates by making the sound of your animal!" The classroom is transformed into a wild zoo as students team up. The Animal Sounds blackline (on page 7.15) is provided for your entertainment and that of your students!

Structures with Built-In Random Teamformation

A number of structures have built-in random teamformation methods. The advantage of this approach is that random teams can be formed with no special preparation, no special materials, and without taking time away from academic content. In effect, we form random teams during our lesson, without missing a beat.

Traveling Heads Together

Traveling Heads Together is a variation of Numbered Heads Together (see *Chapter 6*). After students have put their heads together to formulate their best answer to the teacher's question, the teacher calls a number, say "3," and Student #3 in each team stands. Next, the teacher tells the seated students to wildly beckon for a new Student #3. All the Student #3s travel to a new team to share their best answer.

To form random teams while playing Traveling Heads Together, the teacher simply calls a different number on three consecutive rounds, instructing the students that when they travel, they cannot sit down at a team where a teammate from their original team is seated. After three rounds, all students have all new teammates, and we can have them work together as a team for the remainder of the class period.

Stir-the-Class

Stir-the-Class is just like Traveling Heads Together except student teams begin by standing as a team around the perimeter of the room (see *Chapter 6*). Random teams are formed after three rounds of Stir-the-Class if the teacher has the first student rotate one ahead, the next student rotate two ahead, and the third student rotate three ahead.

One Stray

Three rounds of One Stray, with the straying student remaining at the team they joined, forms random teams exactly like three rounds of Traveling Heads Together. Again, students need to know they cannot stray to a team where an original teammate is seated.

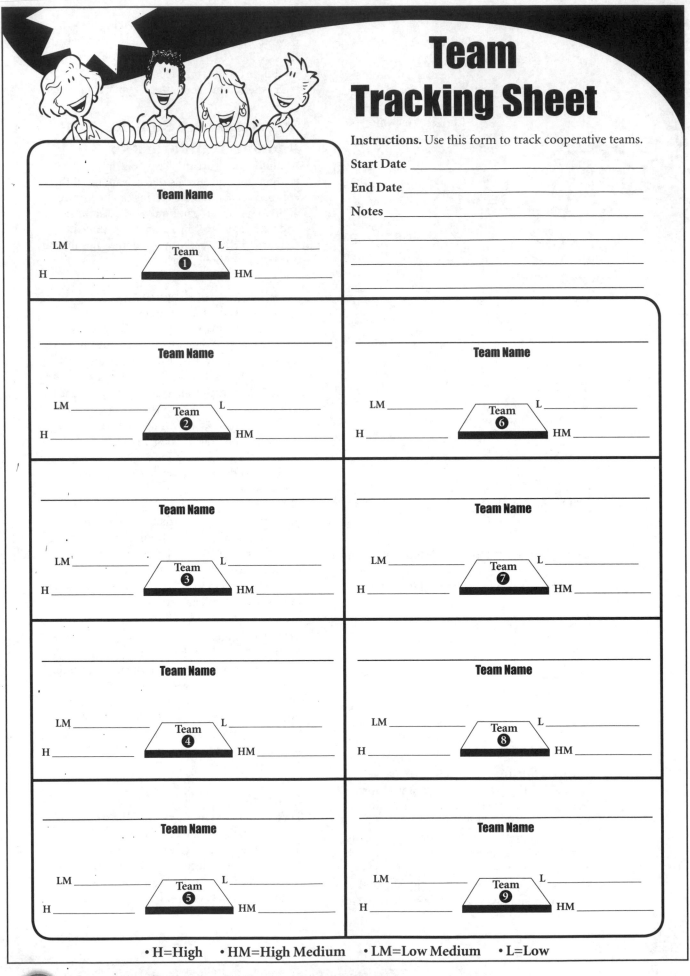

Team
Tracking Sheet

Instructions. Use this form to track cooperative teams.

Start Date _____

End Date _____

Notes _____

_____

_____

_____

Team Name

LM _____ Team **1** L _____

H _____ HM _____

Team Name

LM _____ Team **2** L _____

H _____ HM _____

Team Name

LM _____ Team **6** L _____

H _____ HM _____

Team Name

LM _____ Team **3** L _____

H _____ HM _____

Team Name

LM _____ Team **7** L _____

H _____ HM _____

Team Name

LM _____ Team **4** L _____

H _____ HM _____

Team Name

LM _____ Team **8** L _____

H _____ HM _____

Team Name

LM _____ Team **5** L _____

H _____ HM _____

Team Name

LM _____ Team **9** L _____

H _____ HM _____

• H=High   • HM=High Medium   • LM=Low Medium   • L=Low

Kagan Cooperative Learning • Dr. Spencer Kagan & Miguel Kagan
Kagan Publishing • 1 (800) 933-2667 • www.KaganOnline.com

Animal Sounds

Instructions. Make four copies of this blackline. There are ten animals—enough for up to ten teams. Only use as many animals as you have teams. Cut apart the animal cards and give every student one card. Students mix and trade cards until you call, "Stop." Then, they close their eyes and make the sounds of their animal to find their teammates.

Lion

Cow

Cat

Monkey

Sheep

Pig

Donkey

Dog

Bird

Horse

Mix-Freeze-Group

In Mix-Freeze-Group, students each have a number from one to four and are mixing in the classroom until the teacher calls, "Freeze." The teacher then gives two directives: what size group to form and who should be in the group. For example, to form random groups of three the teacher might say, "Form groups of three, everyone with a different number." To form a random group of four, the teacher might call out, "Form groups of four, even numbers together and odd numbers together." Depending on the number of students in the class, groups will not always work out evenly. To handle the "leftovers," the teacher creates an area in the class called the "lost and found." Students who did not find a group go to the lost and found. When forming random teams of four, we assign the students in the lost and found to teams in the usual way—one left over: one team of five; two left over: two teams of three that sit next to each other; three left over: one team of three.

Find Your Number

In teams, students each have a number. This allows the teacher to easily assign roles ("for this task, Student #3 will be the beaker cleaner") or to use the Selector Spinner or SelectorTools (see *Chapter 8*) to call on a student to respond. Given that students have their numbers, it becomes easy to form random teams on the fly. We simply say,

When I say, "Go," everyone will stand up, put a hand up high using your fingers to show your number, and form groups of four, everyone with the same number. Once you have formed your group, put your hands down so those who are still looking can easily find each other.

Once students are standing in groups of four, we have them sit down as a group to work as a random team.

Inside-Outside Circle

During Inside-Outside Circle, students stand in two concentric circles around the room with the inside circle facing in and the outside circle facing out, so each student is facing a partner. See *Chapter 6: Structures*. Inside-Outside Circle is used to have students respond to teacher questions or question cards, but we can use the structure to move smoothly from Inside-Outside Circle into random teams. To include a built-in team builder, we have students do a Three-Step Interview, but the first two steps of the interview happen while the students are standing in the circle, and the last step happens once they sit down as a team. Does this all sound confusing? It becomes very simple if you follow these steps:

Step 1. Fun Interview. While students are standing in the Inside-Outside Circle, they do a Pair Interview with their face partner, each interviewing the other on a fun topic like dream vacation, favorite food, or ideal profession. (The Pair Interview is the first two steps of a Three-Step Interview.)

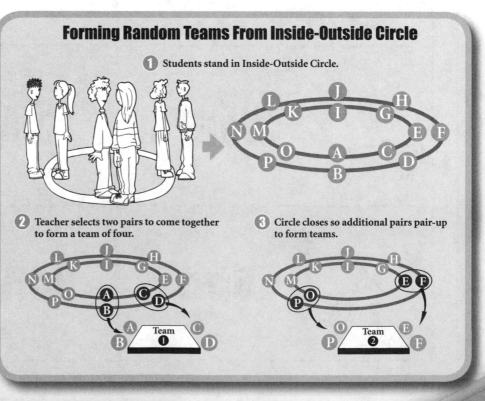

Forming Random Teams From Inside-Outside Circle

1. Students stand in Inside-Outside Circle.

2. Teacher selects two pairs to come together to form a team of four.

3. Circle closes so additional pairs pair-up to form teams.

Step 2. Pairs Selected. The teacher selects two adjacent pairs to team up to form a team of four and sit down as a team.

Step 3. Pairs Pair. A gap is created when the first team leaves the circle. Pairs from each side walk toward each other to close the gap. When they meet, they leave to sit down as a team. The process is repeated to form additional teams. (See graphic on page 7.16). If there is an extra pair, steal a person from one of the groups of four to form two groups of three and have them sit next to each other.

Step 4. Timed RoundRobin. When students are seated as a team, they do a Timed RoundRobin, each introducing their partner by sharing what they learned in the Pair Interview. For example, "My new friend, Steve, would spend his dream vacation...." (The RoundRobin is the third step of the Three-Step Interview.) We don't tell students in advance that we will be moving from Inside-Outside Circle to random teams. Thus it comes as a surprise when pairs pair to form a group of four, and as another surprise when students are asked to take turns introducing their partner. Occasional unexpected events in our class create stimulation.

Team Type 3
Student-Selected Teams

On an occasional basis, students are allowed to form their own teams. When given the opportunity, students usually select partners and teammates that they know and like. This familiarity can be a big plus for team dynamics. Students having similar interests facilitates team decision making. Students have already bonded, so less time for teambuilding is required.

Students enjoy the control and feeling trusted to occasionally select their own teams. The enjoyment of friendships spill over into the academic realm, making learning more fun and productive. Allowing friends to work together at times can bring new energy to academics.

Student-Selected Teamformation Methods
Free-Choice Method

If the teacher does not have academic information to form balanced heterogeneous teams at the beginning of the year, the teacher may use student-selected teams. Students are happily surprised to learn they can sit anywhere they want and with whom they want, as long as they form groups of four. The teacher announces that these free-choice teams are temporary (only for the first week or two), so students get adjusted to working in teams and class is fun as well as productive.

During this free-choice team period, the teacher pays careful attention to friendship patterns and makes notes for future reference. Who chooses to work together? Who isn't chosen by anyone? Who works together well? Which students are a management problem and should never be put on the same team? Use the Team Dynamics Observation Form (on the next page) to record your observations. For the confident cooperative learning teacher, this student-selected trial period can set a positive class tone and provide valuable insight to student dynamics.

Team Captains

The teacher selects a Team Captain for each team. If there are to be eight teams, for example, eight Team Captains are selected. The eight captains each go to a different team table. The rest of the class stands up around the perimeter of the room. Each captain takes a turn selecting a new teammate. When selected, students join their captain at their new team table. Team Captains can consult with their newly-selected teammates for their next teammate. When all students are selected, the teams are already sitting at their team table, ready to get started. This approach must be used very cautiously. The last students to be chosen may feel like "leftovers."

Numbered Choice

Numbered Choice turns the tables around, allowing students to decide for themselves which team they want to be on. Each student picks a number out of a hat corresponding to the number of students in the class. The class

Team Dynamics
Observation Form

Instructions. Use this form to record your observations of student interaction patterns.

Perfect Partners
Students who work well together

Student _____ Student _____
Reason _____
_____

Student _____ Student _____
Reason _____
_____

Student _____ Student _____
Reason _____
_____

Problem Partners
Students to avoid putting on the same team

Student _____ Student _____
Reason _____
_____

Student _____ Student _____
Reason _____
_____

Student _____ Student _____
Reason _____
_____

Student Observations
Individual student observations to consider when forming teams

Student _____
Observations _____
_____

Student _____
Observations _____
_____

Student _____
Observations _____
_____

Kagan Cooperative Learning • Dr. Spencer Kagan & Miguel Kagan
Kagan Publishing • 1 (800) 933-2667 • www.KaganOnline.com

forms a circle around the classroom. The student who selected number one sits at any team table. The student who selected number two can sit at the same table or any other table. This process continues until all students have made their selection.

StandUp–HandUp–PairUp, Pairs Pair

Students put a hand up and stand up in the classroom. They find a partner they want to work with, put their hands down, and stand shoulder-to-shoulder. If students are seeking just a partner, their job is done. They sit down with their new partner. But if they are forming a team, the pairs pair up with another pair to form a team of four.

Potential Pitfalls and Solutions

Off-Task Behavior. Friends share interests beyond academics and can get off task. To avoid off-task behavior, the teacher makes it very clear in advance that teams will only get one warning for off-task behavior. If the off-task behavior persists, they will be split up. Students find working with their friends rewarding and will make an effort to keep focused.

Last To Be Picked. No one likes to be the last picked for a team. It can be a blow to an already fragile self image. If left to their own devices, low achievers, "loners," and "losers" will be the last to be picked or may form a "loser" team by default. To avoid this problem, the teacher identifies the students least likely to be selected by other students and selects them to be Team Captains. The Numbered Choice method is also an effective solution as students decide for themselves which teams they'd like to work on.

Team Type 4

Homogeneous Teams

Homogeneous means "the same or similar." Students on homogeneous teams share the same or similar characteristics along one dimension. Students can be of the same ability level. Students can share similar interests. Or, same language teams can be formed to facilitate content acquisition for the bilingual or multilingual classroom.

> ## How to Form Homogenous Ability Teams
>
> The easiest way to form homogeneous ability teams is using an achievement ranked list. The bottom four students are Team One. The next four are Team Two, and so on. Unlike forming heterogeneous teams, sex and ethnicity are not taken into consideration. However, for management purposes, it is still advisable to keep best friends and worst enemies from being on the same team.

Homogeneous Ability Teams

There are some advantages of allowing like-ability students to work together occasionally. In the heterogeneous team, we have the highest achiever and the lowest achiever sit across from each other. They are not face or shoulder partners and therefore have fewer interactions with each other than with other teammates. The rationale is that there might be too big of an ability level discrepancy. Students learn best when they work with someone at a higher level, but not so high that they don't communicate well. If the discrepancy is too large, the lower achiever can't keep up, and tunes out to avoid failure. Students at a slightly higher level offer stimulation in the Zone of Proximal Development. They challenge students to reach beyond their current achievement level. If the assistance is above or below the students' zone, growth is limited. Homogeneous ability teams put students at approximately the same level together, so there is challenge at the appropriate level of difficulty. One caution with homogeneous teams, however: Growth is limited if students are too similar with regard to achievement. There is no challenge to take the next step forward.

Differentiated Instruction. Another plus of occasional use of homogeneous ability teams is facilitating differentiated instruction. With differentiated instruction, the teacher makes modifications of the curriculum or instruction to make the content more accessible. Differentiating instruction for a whole team at about the same ability level is much more manageable than trying to differentiate instruction for every student. There is a caution here too: There is a fine line between differentiation and within-class tracking. For this reason, homogeneous teams are only recommended on an occasional basis. And when used, the teacher operates under the motto: What's good for the best, is good for the rest. Modifications and adaptations are made only if the task has proven too challenging, not before.

A Two-Way Win. If we have students only work in heterogeneous ability teams, then students miss out on opportunities to learn to be leaders and good teammates.

When all the high achievers are put on the same team, the team cannot function well if they all act as leaders. It's the classic case of too many generals and not enough soldiers. High achievers learn important life skills such as listening, reaching consensus, and making compromises. High achievers who are accustomed to being the team leaders learn to become team players.

The converse is true for low-ability students put together on the same team. Students who have been followers are now given an opportunity to step up. They learn leadership skills: how to communicate a message, and how to be assertive.

When the school year is done, will we be happy to know we have produced some good leaders and some good followers? No. We want all students to learn the important skills associated with each position. In life and in the workplace, our students will definitely find themselves in different roles at different times, and it is our job in education to prepare every student for the full spectrum of situations they will encounter.

Indeed, the occasional homogeneous ability team has advantages. But the advantages are bought at the expense of some major disadvantages, so we recommend homogeneous teams on an occasional basis only. How occasional is up to each teacher, but five to ten percent of the time is a good rule of thumb.

Homogeneous Interest Teams

Students turn on to the curriculum when they are given choice and allowed to explore what interests them. Homogeneous interest teams can be used when writing research papers, doing a team project, or for a team presentation. Students with the same interests form a team to investigate their selected topic.

Interest teams usually revolve around a class theme, so the class is exploring different aspects of the same theme. For example, if the class is studying states, different teams may select different states as their focus. If the class is studying an historical event, such as the Civil War, teams could focus on different key historical persons such as Lincoln, Grant, Sherman, Lee, Jackson, Tubman, and Douglass. If the class just read a story, each team may select a different literary element to explore: the setting, plot, characters, conflict, moral, and resolution. The class theme can be broad: If the class is exploring the theme of discovery, one team can research inventions, another land discovery, and another medical breakthroughs.

Interest teams can be used on a more regular basis than homogeneous ability teams without fostering negative stereotypes (We are the dummy team!). Students on interest teams share similar interests, but the teams will likely be mixed with regard to race, sex, and ability.

Forming Interest Teams
Corners and the Predetermined Selection

Corners is a great way to get students into their interest teams. The teacher posts options in the four corners of the classroom. If the class is studying animals, the teacher may post mammals, amphibians, reptiles, and birds in the four corners. Students first write down the number of the corner that most interests them, then go to that corner to form a team with other students in the same corner. The alternatives don't have to be four. The teacher can do Sides, and students choose between two alternatives. Or the teacher could post multiple alternatives. Note: In Corners, the teacher chooses the topics in advance and allows students to select from predetermined alternatives.

Similarity Groups and the Open-Ended Selection

In Similarity Groups, students group by interests, but there are no predetermined options provided by the teacher. For example, if the class is studying mammals, students form teams based on different animals of interest. The students who want to study monkeys form a team. The students who want to study lions form a team. With Similarity Groups, students decide the topic of the interest team, not the teacher.

Avoiding Friendship Selection. The key to interest teams is for students to investigate what genuinely interests them. A potential problem is that when given the choice of teams, some students will invariably go to a team their friends are on regardless of their personal interests. To avoid this, have students write down their corner selection or topic of interest on a response board in large letters. After students go to their corners or form their similarity groups, have them hold up their response boards to verify they've followed their interest, not their friends.

Homogeneous Language Teams

Limited English Proficient students, with different levels of English language proficiency, need different kinds of input—lower level students need more context and less cognitively demanding materials. Therefore, at certain points in the instructional cycle, and especially when there is a large range of language abilities and demanding content, teams based on English language ability are desirable, and the homogeneity principle should override the heterogeneity principle.

Different Teams at Different Times
Teamformation and the Curricular Cycle

As teachers, we often follow a curricular cycle. First, we introduce a new, difficult concept or skill. Next, we offer guided practice on the skill, modeling and coaching, helping students work through their difficulties. Finally, when students have mastered the skill well enough, we have them practice the skill without mediation— we assign independent practice, either as homework or in class.

Teamformation interfaces with this curricular cycle. When we are first introducing a new, difficult concept, we want our students in heterogeneous teams. At this point in the cycle, if a student has a question, we want someone on the team who knows the answer or who can model and coach the skill. With a high achiever on each team, we have a greater probability of success. Later, once students have acquired the skill and need only to cement the skill with practice, we can afford to have students break out from their heterogeneous teams and work within random or student-selected teams. Random teams offer variety and an important meta-communication: We can work well with anyone.

Thus in some classrooms, students are in heterogeneous teams for the first part of the week as they learn and master new skills, and then break out into random teams for practice on Thursday before the Friday test.

Kagan Cooperative Learning · Dr. Spencer Kagan & Miguel Kagan
Kagan Publishing · 1 (800) 933-2667 · www.KaganOnline.com

7.21

The Pros and Cons of Different Types of Teams

Each type of team has positives and negatives. The chart below summarizes the advantages and drawbacks of the four types of teams. On the whole, heterogeneous teams are the most effective teaming technique. But for the best of all worlds, we encourage the use of occasional, random, homogeneous, and student-selected teams.

Parting Activities

Teams have been working together for six or so weeks. The teacher suddenly announces, "Tomorrow we will be forming new teams." The class is headed for trouble. Without closure, students are likely to spend the first couple of weeks in their new teams wishing they were in their old teams. Parting activities allow students to express their feelings and prepare emotionally for departing from the old team and joining a new team. Some favorite parting activities follow.

Team Pictures. Take a snapshot of teams before they part and post the photos, or have the teams paste them in the class scrapbook.

Team Statements. Have the teammates make a final Team Statement to the class as a team: "Together we learned...."

Teammate Introductions. Have teammates introduce each other to the class as exciting potential new teammates. "What you can really learn from Johnny is...." "One thing you will like about working with Susan is...."

The Pros and Cons of Different Types of Teams

Team Type	Positives (+)	Negatives (−)
① Heterogeneous	• Balanced • Maximum cross-race, cross-sex, and cross-ability contact • Maximizes tutoring • Management easier for equal ability level teams • High achiever on each team	• Requires teacher prep time • Requires ranking and labeling students • Limited contact between the high achievers • Limited leadership opportunities for low achievers
② Random	• Fair • Side-steps labels and ranking • No prior student knowledge necessary • Classbuilding and networking opportunities • Quick and easy • Novelty, variety, fun	• Could form "winner" and "loser" teams • Diversity not ensured • Teams with friends, potential for off-task behavior • Teams with enemies and conflicts
③ Homogeneous	• Leadership opportunities for low achievers • Interaction opportunities for high achievers • Opportunity for some high achievers to experience being a teammate, not leader • High esteem for top groups • Interest teams promote inquisitiveness	• Too-similar groups lack input in Zone of Proximal Development • Negative stereotypes • Poor self-esteem for low groups • Lack of equity • Difficult to manage class of teams at different ability levels
④ Student-Selected	• Novelty, variety, fun • Familiarity • Easy decision making and consensus	• Not balanced • High potential for off-task behavior

Parting Messages. Have students write a parting letter to each of their teammates. Emphasis is on "What I have learned from you," "What I have enjoyed about working with you," or "What I appreciate about you." More sophisticated students can also deal with regrets. (See Parting Messages blackline on the next page.) See the box below for a Simultaneous RoundTable activity for parting messages.

Parting Messages Activity
Simultaneous RoundTable

We all have many partings throughout life; school can be a place where we learn to part with dignity and grace.

1 Students each write their name at the top of a copy of the Parting Messages form. (Use colored paper when you copy the form.)

2 Students pass their Parting Message form to the person on their left within the team.

3 Each student writes a positive message to the person whose form they have.

4 Forms are passed and filled out until they return to the original sender.

Team Reunions

Michael L. Bettino (Rolling Hills High School, Palos Verdes Peninsula Unified School District, CA) has a class with the following ethnic makeup: eight Anglo American, four Persian, four Japanese, three Chinese, two Indian (from India), one French, one Canadian, and one South American student. They instituted Team Reunions as follows:

"After six weeks of heterogeneous groups in an 11th grade regular English III class (American Literature and Composition), it was time to

make new groups. I made the changes and found a certain amount of hostility to the new groups. A student asked if they could have a five minute 'Group Reunion.'

I let them do this—and then they returned to their new groups. Now the new groups are rolling along very smoothly.

A new Group Reunion will take place in two weeks and will be a regular part of the program."

The Team Reunion well might be used in any class to have an old team become an ongoing support group for students. As students discuss with their old teammates how things are going in their new teams, they might gain support as well as insights not otherwise possible.

Chapter Summary

Teamwork is a defining characteristic of cooperative learning. In the cooperative learning classroom, students sit in teams and work with teammates to master and deepen their thinking about the curriculum, create cooperative projects, and plan collaborative presentations.

The ideal team size is four students. Teams of four are large enough to unleash synergy; yet, teams of four are small enough to keep every student actively engaged. Teams of four offer many grouping options within the team—twice as many as teams of three. Importantly, teams of four break evenly into pairs for frequent pair work.

There are four major types of teams. We recommend students spend most of their time in *heterogeneous teams*. The heterogeneous team is a mirror of the diversity in the classroom containing males and females, students of different races, and students at all levels of achievement. Heterogeneous teams allow peer tutoring, increasing achievement, and allow positive interaction among students of all backgrounds, improving race relations.

Parting
Messages For...

Teammate Name _____

Instructions. Write a special message to your teammate in one box, then pass the form to the next teammate. After everyone has written a message, give the form to your teammate.

I appreciate you because... _____
_____
_____
_____
_____

From _____

I appreciate you because... _____
_____
_____
_____
_____

From _____

I appreciate you because... _____
_____
_____
_____
_____

From _____

I appreciate you because... _____
_____
_____
_____
_____

From _____

Kagan Cooperative Learning • Dr. Spencer Kagan & Miguel Kagan
Kagan Publishing • 1 (800) 933-2667 • www.KaganOnline.com

The second type of team: *random teams*. Random teams do not take student characteristics into account. Random teams add excitement to the classroom. We recommend random teams as an occasional break-out from heterogeneous teams. Students have the opportunity to work with classmates outside of their team. Because random teams are not balanced and do not maximize either achievement potential or potential to improve race relations, we recommend they be used only for short-term interactions.

The third type of team: *student-selected teams*. Occasional use of student-selected teams allows students to work with those they already know and like. Working with friends can make academics more pleasurable. Again, we recommend student-selected teams for short-term activities and projects.

The fourth type of team: *homogeneous teams*. Homogeneous teams place students with the same or similar characteristics on the same team. Students can be the same sex, at similar ability levels, speak the same language, or share similar interests. Homogeneous ability teams give students the opportunity to work with others at their academic level which allows us to differentiate the curriculum for teams. We must be careful not to overuse same-ability teams as they are a form of within-class tracking undermining motivation of lower achieving students. One form or homogeneous team, the interest team, allows students to choose what they wish to investigate and pursue common interests; they are brain-friendly and motivational.

We encourage using the many types of teams to group and regroup students. We want our students to thrive in diversity—to work productively with others like and unlike them, just as they will need to do to succeed in an increasingly diverse and interdependent world. While all types of teams are good for frequent break-out activities and projects, students should spend the majority of their time in heterogeneous teams. Heterogeneous teams are research-based; sidestep the damaging effects of tracking; reduce the achievement gap; promote diversity and bonding with others of different sexes, abilities, interests; reduce racial tensions; and contribute to a more harmonious and pluralistic society.

Chapter Questions

▶ Questions for Review

1. What are the four main types of cooperative teams?
2. Why are teams of four the best team size?
3. How would you describe the basic cooperative learning base team?
4. Heterogeneous teams are mixed along several dimensions. What are the dimensions?
5. How can you keep students from forming friendship teams when you want them to team up by interests?

▶ Questions for Thinking and Discussion

1. On a philosophical level, do you think heterogeneous teams or homogeneous teams are more appropriate for the classroom? Why?
2. What kind of class would benefit most from heterogeneous teams? When would random teams and interest teams be most useful?
3. What types of teams will you use in your classroom? How will you use them? For how long?
4. Do you think it is a good idea to allow students to form their own teams the first week of school? Why or why not?
5. How can we do differentiated instruction without creating within-class tracking?
6. If all classrooms used heterogeneous teams, we could drastically improve the race relations that plague our society. Do you agree or disagree? Explain.

References

[1] Oakes, J. *Keeping Track: How Schools Structure Inequality.* Birmingham, NY: Vail-Ballou Press, 1985.

[2] Kahlenberg, R. "Socioeconomic Integration: A Promising Alternative. Every Child Should Be Able to Enjoy the Benefits of Attending a Solidly Middle-Class School." *Principal—The New Diversity,* May 2000, 79(5): 12–19.

[3] Mahard, R. & R. Crain. "Research on Minority Achievement in Desegregated Schools." In Rossell, C. & W. Hawley (eds.). *The Consequences of School Desegregation.* Philadelphia, PA: Temple University Press, 1983.

[4] Rimer, S. "Cambridge Schools Try Integration by Income." *New York Times,* May 8, 2003.

[5] Finder, A. "As Test Scores Jump, Raleigh Credits Integration by Income." *New York Times,* September 25, 2005.

[6] High, J. *Second Language Learning Through Cooperative Learning.* San Clemente, CA: Kagan Publishing, 1993.

Resources

Aronson, E., N. Blane, C. Stephan, J. Sikes & M. Snapp. *The Jigsaw Classroom.* Beverly Hills, CA: Sage Publishing Company, 1978.

TeamTools™ Software. San Clemente, CA: Kagan Publishing. www.KaganOnline.com

Kagan, S., G. Zahn, W. Lawrence, F. Keith, J. Schwarzwald & G. Tyrrell. "Classroom Structural Bias: Impact of Cooperative and Competitive Classroom structures on Cooperative and Competitive Groups." In Slavin, R. et al. (eds.) *Learning to Cooperate, Cooperating to Learn.* New York, NY: Plenum Press, 1985.

Teamformation Pocket Chart. San Clemente, CA: Kagan Publishing. www.KaganOnline.com

Slavin, R. "How Student Learning Teams Can Integrate the Desegregated Classroom." *Integrated Education,* 1977, 15: 56–58.

Slavin, R. & E. Oickle. "Effects of Learning Teams on Student Achievement and Race Relations: Treatments by Race Interactions." *Sociology of Education,* 1981, 54: 174–180.

CHAPTER 8

Key 3
Management

Many teachers report that their management problems decrease dramatically once they switch to cooperative learning. The reason is that in the traditional classroom, there is a mismatch between the needs of the students and the structure of the classroom. We are social beings and our basic nature is active and interactive: Students want to "do" and talk. The traditional classroom demands that students be passive and isolated. Students are told to sit still and be quiet. Those who move and talk are considered management and discipline problems. Because students do not give up their basic needs without a struggle, in traditional classrooms, a great deal of energy is spent keeping students in their seats, quiet, and "not bothering their neighbors."

The cooperative classroom, in contrast, is better aligned with student needs. It is based on the assumption that learning occurs through doing and interacting. Students are encouraged to interact, move, and create. Students who move and interact are not viewed as management problems. They don't have to become a management problem to meet their needs. Feeling their basic needs met, students like the teacher and class more.

Nevertheless, successful cooperative learning requires a number of management skills that are not necessary in a traditional classroom. In the traditional classroom, students do little talking and interacting. Traditional classroom management is an extension of the noninteractive norm. Students are seated in rows facing the teacher, not each other. Rules are instituted that limit interaction: "Keep your hands to yourself," "No talking," "Keep your eyes on your own paper." In contrast, in the cooperative classroom, students are seated in teams and interaction is encouraged, so management involves very different skills. When we allow students to talk and to move, we are going with rather than against their basic needs, so we release a great

In the cooperative classroom, students are seated in teams and interaction is encouraged, so management involves very different skills.

deal of energy. Like a rocket that releases a great deal of energy, the energy must be released in a very controlled way. Without good management techniques in place, the classroom can blow up! Cooperative management is the control that channels energy to productive learning.

Among the cooperative management techniques we explore in this chapter are ways to efficiently manage noise, materials, attention, room arrangement, team seating, student energy, and what to do with teams that finish at different rates. The stronger our management techniques, the more we will reap the full benefits of cooperative learning.

In the cooperative classroom, students are given more freedom, but also assume greater responsibility. In the traditional classroom, the teacher is authoritarian. The teacher dictates the rules and the procedures; the teacher makes all the management decisions. Cooperative management is more democratic. Students are responsible for answering teammate questions, collecting team materials, generating classroom expectations, managing their own voice levels, communicating to the teacher via signals, and keeping on task after completing assignments. Through cooperative management, there is a shift: Students aren't passive and controlled by the teacher demands; they play an active role in learning, and also in managing their own cooperative behaviors. Students don't feel they are in the teacher's classroom; students are in "our class."

The Cooperative Management Style
Teacher's Role

Cooperative learning frees the teacher during teamwork time. The effective teacher uses this time for authentically assessing comprehension, observing and consulting, keeping the class on task, evaluating the lesson, and working with individual students or teams.

Authentically Assessing Understanding

Lack of comprehension can create management problems. Let's say we assign teams a task, but once they begin work, we discover they don't understand what they're supposed to do. Or, they don't know who is supposed to do what.

This is a recipe for management problems: off-task behavior and/or conflicts. To avoid these problems, after we assign team tasks, we circulate to observe teams and verify comprehension. If a team is befuddled, chances are they're not the only ones. At this point, we get everyone's attention and clarify instructions. It is much more efficient to prevent misunderstanding than to patch up after a misunderstanding has occurred.

Keeping Teams On Task

Visiting with teams helps keeps teams on task. Our physical proximity encourages students to stay focused and to not engage in off-task behavior. We can ask questions to focus teams on their task: "What's your next step?" "How do you plan to…?" "Who will…?"

Observing and Consulting

Once students are working well in their teams, it's not time for us to start grading papers. We continue to circulate to observe and consult with teams. Responsibility for the task and the learning remains with the students. Occasionally, if students are moving down a blind alley with no possibility of discovering and correcting their error on their own, we may intervene, but the intervention usually is to make students aware of a contradiction or of some additional resources. The responsibility for correcting or enhancing the work remains with the students. If a request from the students is made for an answer, we attempt to make students aware of their own resources, and provide an answer only if the students could not obtain one on their own. Ideally, we do not interrupt or interfere with the work of the students, but at the same time, we are seen as friendly and approachable rather than distant. This attitude is captured by the teacher, who finds in the students' work something interesting, and comments on that, perhaps even sharing a personal reaction to the work. But the reaction is shared as a person-to-person, not an authority-to-pupil, and the students know they, on their own, are responsible for the direction and quality of their work.

Evaluating Lesson Design

As we walk around checking on students' interaction, we gain insight into teamwork dynamics. This is a wonderful time to ask the PIES questions to check for the implementation of the principles:

P **Positive Interdependence.** Does the success of one produce a benefit for another? Is the task impossible to do without cooperation?

I **Individual Accountability.** Is a public performance by each student required?

E **Equal Participation.** Is the participation about equal?

S **Simultaneous Interaction.** Are many students overtly interacting or engaged at once?

If there's a problem with PIES, the lesson may be improved.

Working with Individuals or Teams

Once students have learned to work as teams, we are free to consult with teams or individuals who need help. We may organize pull-out programs for individuals with similar learning problems, so they may receive special tutoring as a group. In this way, cooperative learning facilitates differentiated instruction.

Positive Attention & Recognition
Positive Attention

One of the most powerful tools we have for shaping the behavior of our students is positive attention. Whatever we pay attention to, we will get more of. Yet, all too often, we highlight what students do wrong instead of what they do right. It's natural for us to focus on negative behaviors in the classroom on a reactive basis: "White Tigers, please get back to work!" Instead, focusing on positive behavior on a proactive basis is more effective and creates a more positive classroom tone: "I like the way Team Panthers are working so well together!" Positive attention paves the way to easy classroom management. Pay positive attention to what you want, and you will get more of it.

Focus on the negative, and you will get much more of it. Studies demonstrate that in traditional classrooms, if teachers pay attention to undesired behaviors, such as out-of-seat behavior or talking, the frequency of those behaviors increases. Students crave attention from their classmates and from the teacher. Even negative attention is rewarding for some students. If the teacher scolds students who get out of their seats without permission, other students will model themselves after the students who received the attention. The same principle holds in a cooperative classroom. If we give attention to the team that is too noisy or not on task, other teams will follow the lead of the team that has managed to win our attention.

Conversely, if we give attention and special recognition to students with model behavior, soon most or all teams will be on task. The power of positive attention is enhanced if the recognition is immediate and public. We do well to articulate to the whole class exactly why the model team is receiving positive attention. When all groups are working well, we give positive recognition to the whole class.

Managing Teams with Positive v. Negative Attention

Getting Teams' Attention	• **Positive:** "Thank you, Mavericks, for quieting down so quickly." • **Negative:** "Wiz Kids, you need to quiet down quicker."
Keeping Teams on Task	• **Positive:** "I really appreciate the way Team 3 is working so hard on their project." • **Negative:** "Team 1, stop horsing around and start working on your project."
Working Quietly	• **Positive:** "Great job using your 'Team Voices' today." • **Negative:** "Keep it down, Dream Team."
Cooperating	• **Positive:** "Class, look how Pedro and Tyrone are working together. That's cooperation!" • **Negative:** "If you two can't work together right now, I'm splitting you up."
Sharing	• **Positive:** "Veronica just offered to share her textbook with Matt. Awesome, Veronica!" • **Negative:** "Mariah, stop grabbing Phong's book, right now!"

Kagan Cooperative Learning • Dr. Spencer Kagan & Miguel Kagan
Kagan Publishing • 1 (800) 933-2667 • www.KaganOnline.com

8.3

To implement positive attention, we proactively look for positive behaviors and regularly make positive comments to the teams and class.

The Power of Positive Attention

I cannot emphasize enough the power of giving positive attention to positive behaviors. One day I was in the classroom of a teacher first trying Jigsaw. She had been part of my one-day workshop, and had also seen me demonstrate Jigsaw with another class at her middle school.

She had all of the elements right. The class would come to full attention when she raised her hand. The student experts were standing as they presented their parts to their groups. One team had a missing expert, and the teacher handled that well by using the Teams Consult piece she had learned in the workshop.

But something was terribly wrong. The noise level was high. Over in one group, the expert was using her new found authority to scold her teammates for being stupid. In another group, as soon as the teacher was looking another way, the expert stuffed some paper in his nose, which led to loud giggles and laughter. And the quiet signal was really not much help: The kids responded by quickly coming to attention, but right afterwards they would return to loud talking and off-task behaviors.

As I watched, I became increasingly uncomfortable. What was wrong? What could be done? I remembered the power of positive attention and walked over to the teacher and said, "I am going to sit down again, but in a moment I want you to walk over to the best group in the class, give the quiet signal, and draw everyone's attention to the group, praising them for their good work, saying exactly what you like about their behavior. Don't give points; just say clearly what you like."

She did. And we were both surprised by the power of the praise. For about ten minutes after the positive attention, all the teams were markedly more on task. When they began to slip, I asked her to use positive attention again, focusing on another team. This time teams stayed on task longer.

By the end of the class period, the class had turned around. We both saw Jigsaw working the way it should. The teacher was thrilled; she had a powerful tool for shaping her class.

Positive attention establishes norms for the classroom; students learn which behaviors are valued; they receive a very clear message as to how to behave in the new setting. Holding up as a model the groups which are behaving well is a clear way to give the message that we value certain behaviors. The students feel more secure when clear norms are established.

Positive attention brings out from the class more of the positive behaviors. When a student or team does something you wish more students or teams would do, either academically or socially, stop the class and point out the positive behavior to the whole class.

Giving positive attention has several additional positive outcomes beyond shaping the behavior of our class. We model behavior and an attitude we hope students will adopt, and students like teachers more who create a positive tone.

Some teachers are hesitant to praise individuals, teams, or the class for fear of eroding intrinsic motivation. The fear is that students will begin working for the praise, rather than for the intrinsic rewards in learning. Research suggests the opposite is true: verbal rewards and positive feedback positively impact on intrinsic motivation.[1] Rewards and praise are covered in detail in *Chapter 16: Motivation Without Rewards & Competition*.

Recognition

Recognition is another way to give positive attention in the classroom. Recognition is publicly celebrating an individual, team, or the whole class's success in a form other than teacher praise. Recognition can take a number of forms.

- **Class Newsletter.** The team is celebrated for their accomplishment in the class newsletter. The newsletter may be sent home for students to share their success with their parents.
- **Class Money or Points.** The teacher hands out class play money or points to a team and publicly praises them. "Thank you Dream Team for how quickly you put away your project and cleaned up. Two points go to the class goal." Points or money can be redeemed for rewards.
- **Awards.** Teams are given unique awards for projects or presentations. There's different categories, such as Most Creative, Best Whole-Team Participation, Most Thoughtful, and Best Presentation, so each team receives an award.
- **Positive Letter Home.** The teacher gives a student a positive note to take home and share with parents.

- **Team or Class Reward.** The team can have a reward like free time, first pick for the center, or first to be dismissed for lunch. The class reward can be a party, trip, game, or activity.
- **Public Applause or Bow.** A team stands, and the class claps for their accomplishment. Or the team stands and takes a theatrical bow.
- **Celebration Board.** A celebration board is posted in the classroom with a student or team's accomplishment written on the board. The teacher reads the celebration to the class at the beginning of the week, and the class applauds the celebration. The celebration stays up for the rest of the week.
- **Team or Class Cheers.** The team or class performs a chant, cheer, handshake, or movement to celebrate their success.

Positive verbal attention and recognition promote a positive class atmosphere and encourage teams to work hard and behave well. Students know their efforts are recognized.

Simultaneous Management

A simultaneous, rather than sequential, management style eliminates downtime when distributing materials, answering questions, and forming teams.

Answering Questions

The traditional, sequential approach to answering questions in a classroom is for the teacher to have all students wait while the question of one student is answered. Because questions are relevant to only a few students, the traditional approach means dead time for most students. This procedure operates against our ability to provide in-depth answers to those who ask questions: We know that to answer an individual's question at length means increased downtime for all of the other students.

Applying the principle of simultaneous management, we do not have teams waiting to work while one student gets his/her question answered. We let both things happen simultaneously. The rule is "Team Questions Only." If a student has a question, he/she must try first to get it answered within the team. If no one on the team knows the answer, the team members all raise their hands. "Four Hands Up" is a signal to us that the team has exhausted its resources and that they need to consult with us. The "Team Questions Only" rule re-orients students away from the teacher and toward each other. Students become more self-reliant and view each other as valuable resources.

When the "Team Questions Only" rule is in place, when four hands are raised in a team, the teacher acknowledges the team question but does not answer it until all the other teams are working. This allows for more in-depth answers and consulting with teams: We do not feel the pressure of the other teams waiting. This approach is an example of simultaneous management: A team question is being answered while other teams are working on their projects. The other teams are actively involved in a learning task while we consult with the team with the question. Simultaneous management sidesteps the problem of creating dead time for other teams, and avoids the pressure of other teams waiting, which allows in-depth answers.

Forming Teams

One of my favorite examples of the power of simultaneous management occurred one morning while I was observing teachers following an initial cooperative learning workshop.

Teachers were first forming teams. In the first class I observed, the teacher read the team assignments to the students as they sat in their seats. She read from the class list, in alphabetical order: "Susan Aragon, you will be on team 4; Peter Birtch, you will be on team 7...." When she got done reading the list, predictably, there were a number of questions. "What is my team number? Where do I sit?, etc."

Somewhat irritated, the teacher again read the list, admonishing the students to listen carefully. Nevertheless, there were again some questions when she finished reading the list the second time. She ended up physically escorting some of the students to their new seats. By the time she finally had the students in teams, about twelve minutes had elapsed!

Team Question

In my next visit of the day, the teacher was also first moving students from rows into teams. Her management style was simultaneous rather than sequential. She said, "Boys and girls, on your tables are some index cards, facedown. Don't turn them over until I say. When you turn them over, you will find four names on each card. You are to quietly collect your books, and move to the table with your name. We will see how quickly and quietly you can find your new team and sit down ready to learn about teambuilding." The students were in their new teams and ready to work in a little over two minutes!

The simultaneous management technique saves time and creates greater student self-reliance and a more positive class tone with less dead time.

One teacher had attempted to manage a cooperative classroom using a sequential structure (reading the names one at a time) while the other teacher used a simultaneous structure (everyone up and moving at once). The simultaneous management technique saves time and creates greater student self-reliance and a more positive class tone with less dead time.

Distributing Materials

Some teachers use a sequential approach to distributing materials. They walk around and hand out a worksheet to each team one at a time, in sequence. Other teachers say, "Material Monitors, get one yellow worksheet for your team from the materials table." They are using a simultaneous approach—all teams getting their materials simultaneously. The simultaneous approach saves time and has students assume more responsibility. For more on this topic, see the Managing Materials section on page 8.20.

Taking Roll

Calling on one student at a time to take roll steals learning time. A more effective approach is to have an "In" board where students put themselves "in" each day as they enter class, simply moving a clip or magnet, or making a check mark on a dry-erase board.

Sharing Answers

Many structures have simultaneous sharing built in. Instead of calling on students one at a time, we can have all students respond by holding up an AnswerBoard, signaling their response with a thumbs up or down, or showing fingers. Half the class can share at once using a RallyRobin or Timed Pair Share. A quarter of the class can share at once using a RoundRobin or Instant Star. Reducing downtime reduces opportunity to get off track.

Giving Directions

Instructing teams how to do a complex project involves a totally different set of management skills than those involved in telling students to each open a workbook to page 293 and do problems 1 through 40. One cooperative learning lesson may include a number of structures, each of which can have many steps.

We want to convey complex sets of instructions briefly in order to maximize time for student-student interaction. A well-managed cooperative learning lesson requires much less teacher talk than a poorly managed lesson, saving precious time for student interaction and learning. Giving directions to groups is an art. The following principles help.

Verbal and Written Directions

Some students are better auditory learners, and others are better visual learners. Thus, it is wise to talk through instructions and at the same time, post them on the overhead, whiteboard, chart paper, or worksheet.

Bite-Sized Bits

Give instructions a bit at a time; do not give more instructions at a time than all teams can perform without asking for clarification. If you give a long sequence of instructions, students will not complete the sequence without needing clarification.

Triggering

A teacher addresses her class: "Students you are going to stand up, put a hand up…." Before the teacher has finished her instructions, some students start pushing in their chairs and stand! The noise makes it difficult for the class to hear the rest of the directions. This management problem occurred because the teacher did not know the power of triggering. The teacher next door is at the same place in the lesson and says: "Students, when I say 'Go,' and not before, you are going to stand up, put a hand up, find a partner you have not worked with today, give them a high five, put your hands down, and then remain standing until I give the quiet signal. [Dramatic Pause] 'GO!'"

Because the teacher has triggered the response ("When I say 'Go'"), students wait to hear the whole string of instructions. Then on the signal, they get up in unison. Triggering student responses avoids management problems and creates a more positive class tone.

Selecting Students and Teams

In the cooperative classroom, students work frequently in teams of fours and in pairs. We often need to pick a student on each team or in each pair. For example, to start a RallyRobin, Timed Pair Share, or RoundRobin, students need to know who will go first or else they will lose valuable time discussing or arguing over it. We have developed a number of resources to make student selection random and fun. See the box below for recommended resources for student and team selection. The advantages of these resources over calling a number are that selection is more fair, creates more interest

Partner Picker

The Partner Picker is one of the spinners in SelectorTools software. Projected for the whole class, each spin randomly selects Partner A or Partner B.

for students, and sidesteps the problem of having to remember which numbers we have called. If we just call a number, students complain: "You always call number 3!" or "You never call number 2!" For turn taking in teams, once the starting number is established, we have students take turns either clockwise or counter-clockwise, changing occasionally for variety.

Often, students are in random pairs, so we can't use student numbers. In pairs, we prefer to use Partner A and B, so we do not confuse students with their team numbers. In pairs, you can use the Partner Picker spinner in SelectorTools that picks A or B. Another favorite is to use Who's Up? in SelectorTools that randomly displays cues that determine who will go first:

- The student standing closest to the back wall.
- The student with the longest hair.
- The student with the smaller hand.
- The student who is more colorfully dressed.
- The student with darker hair.

Each of us develop our own cues to use. We need to avoid cues like "Student who lives farthest from school," or "Student who has traveled farthest on a vacation." These cues call for a discussion, and steal time from the task at hand.

We regularly pick one team in the class to share or go first. SelectorTools has a Team Sequencer that creates a sequence for teams for presentations. Craft sticks with student or team names or names in a hat may be less attractive, but they work just fine for random selection.

Modeling

Too often we try to provide instructions by talk. A far more efficient approach is modeling. Students understand in a moment what to do if they have seen it done; they take a great deal of time to understand if they are only told. If possible, use "Show-Don't-Tell" instructions.

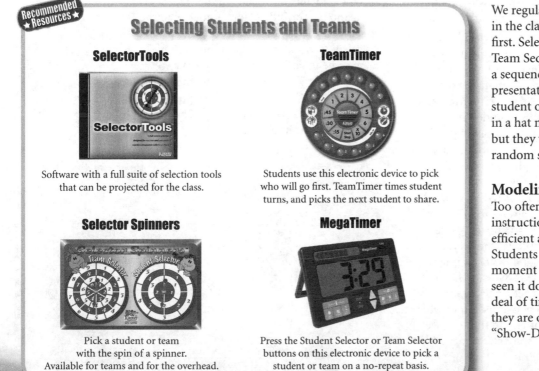

★ Recommended Resources ★

Selecting Students and Teams

SelectorTools

Software with a full suite of selection tools that can be projected for the class.

TeamTimer

Students use this electronic device to pick who will go first. TeamTimer times student turns, and picks the next student to share.

Selector Spinners

Pick a student or team with the spin of a spinner. Available for teams and for the overhead.

MegaTimer

Press the Student Selector or Team Selector buttons on this electronic device to pick a student or team on a no-repeat basis.

There are several ways to model: You can model the behavior yourself; you can pretend to be a member of a group and role-play the behavior with the group; you can work with a pair or group and then have them model for the class; or you can wait for the desired behavior to occur spontaneously and then ask the students to re-peat what they just did, so the whole class can see.

Checking for Understanding
After giving instructions, we need to check for understanding. The following are some structures and methods that work well for checking for understanding.

- **Choral Practice.** Students finish the teacher's sentence or respond in unison to a teacher question. Teacher: "The first thing we're going to do is...."
- **Simultaneous Sharing.** Use AnswerBoards for written responses or thumbs up or down for yes/no questions.
- **Showdown or Numbered Heads Together.** Students write their own answers, then compare them with teammates.
- **RoundTable or RoundRobin.** If directions involve a sequence of steps, each student in turn writes or says a step in order.

Structuring
Structuring is guiding the behavior of students within the steps of a structure. When students are about to rotate to a new partner in Inside-Outside Circle, we sometimes say, "Don't forget to use your authentic praisers with your new partner." In this way, we are structuring the behavior of our students, making it more likely they will remember to praise. Guided Imagery is another way to structure the experience of students. For example, during the think time of a Think-Pair-Share, we might say something like "I want you to imagine you were a settler and were about to go West in a covered wagon. What are all the things you would want to bring with you? Think about...." This structuring guides the thinking of students. While students are doing a Simultaneous RoundTable, we might say, "Be sure to read all the responses of your teammates each time you get a new paper before you add your response. Try to build off of what your teammates have written." In this way, we structure the behavior of students. Structuring can transform a lesson. See box, Structuring for Skill Acquisition.

Structuring for Skill Acquisition
Two Ways to Make a Team Mural

① Without Structuring
The teacher gives each team a piece of butcher paper, and lets students work as they please to make the mural.

Probable results: In many teams, each student takes out his/her colors and works alone on some corner of the mural. There is little if any cognitive or linguistic development, little interaction, and no development of conflict resolution skills.

② With Structuring
1. Give students time to discuss in teams the pros and cons of two murals. Mural one has an all-red rainbow, an all-blue flag, an all-yellow house, and an all-green tree. Mural two has a four-color rainbow, a tree with green leaves, a red apple, and a brown trunk.

2. Announce that a team mural is to be made with only four colors, each person is to use only one color, and the murals will be evaluated on how well they integrate the four colors.

3. Give teams time to plan their mural and who will do what. They must all agree on a team plan before they can take out their crayons.

Probable results: Equal participation, linguistic and cognitive development, and development of skills in the areas of planning, conflict resolution, and consensus seeking will occur.

Cooperative Management Signals
In the cooperative classroom, signals are not just from teacher to students, but also from students to teacher. Students actually help manage the class by signaling the teacher if the teacher is going too fast, or if they don't understand the content or instructions the teacher has given. A variety of visual signals promote smooth management. For example, instead of asking students if they are done or having to run around and check with groups, the teacher puts in place a visual signal for completed work, and at any moment, he/she knows how many students have finished a task.

Student Signals

Over My Head   **Slow Down**

Over My Head and Slow Down

Laurie Kagan developed two signals for students to communicate to the teacher that they don't understand or that the teacher is going too fast. The two Signals are the Over My Head signal and the Slow Down signal. If a student does not understand the teacher, the student waves an open hand, palm down, over her/his head, signaling the content is "Over My Head." If the teacher is going too fast for a student to keep up, the student places two hands, palms touching in front of her/him and then slowly moves the hands apart, signaling for the teacher to "Slow Down." By empowering the students with these signals, we receive important ongoing feedback that helps us adjust the pace and difficulty of the content.

I Need a Partner

In a number of classbuilding structures, students get out of their seats and pair up with different partners multiple times. Without a visual signal that a student needs a partner, it is difficult for students to distinguish who's available and who already has a partner. A simple visual signal is for students to put one hand up when looking for a partner. When they find their partner, they do a high-five and then they both put their hands down, indicating they have found a partner. A student looking for a partner can quickly locate and pair up with another student with a hand up.

We're Finished

Students and teams finish their assigned work at different rates. How do we know who's done and who's not? A simple visual signal. The visual signal for being done differs, depending on what students are working on. For example, in Numbered Heads Together, students put their heads together to compare and improve their answers. Instead of guessing when teams are done, the teacher may have teams standing during the heads together step and then sit down when finished. Similar signals to the teacher include turn your AnswerBoard over, put your pen down, and put your folded hands on the desk.

Response Boards. If you use response boards, use boards that have different colors on each side or use a different color tape to distinguish the two sides. When students are done, they turn over their boards, and the room literally changes color, giving us a clear picture of what percent of the class is finished.

Reading. If students are reading, when done they close their books or set them facedown on their desks so they don't lose their place.

Writing. If students are writing or solving problems, they put their pencils down.

Think Time

Think time is an important step in many structures. It improves the quality of student responses and encourages more students to participate. After asking a question, we may place an index finger to the side of our forehead. This is our pre-established "Think Time" signal. Students do the same to indicate they are thinking. Students indicate they are ready to respond by moving their hands down.

Structures

The class can create simple signals for frequently used cooperative learning structures such as Timed Pair Share and the RoundRobin family of structures.

Creating the Context for Cooperation
Procedures

A well-managed cooperative classroom uses procedures. Procedures are rehearsed classroom behavior patterns for repeated events. For example, the class is busily interacting in teams and the teacher wants to get students' attention. The teacher has a quiet signal procedure in place. She raises a hand, and students quickly raise their hands

Lost and Found

Often we have students get up from their seats and find a partner. A management tip that speeds the process is to establish a *"Lost and Found."* The Lost and Found is simply an area of the room to go to if most students have found a partner and you are still looking. Students easily pair up in the Lost and Found. If you have an odd number of students in your class, the last student can join a group of your choosing to become a triad.

Don't Wait for the Last Team!

As we see teams finishing a task, we don't wait for the last team to finish. It is inefficient management to have every team but one spinning gears, waiting for the slowest team. Instead, when about two-thirds of the teams are finished, we give the quiet signal and go on to the next step.

Unfinished Business!

Students can discuss a topic at any length. If most teams have finished but a team feels unfinished with a discussion, they can call *"Unfinished Business."* Unfinished business is a signal among teammates that they will come back to the topic later, rather than holding back the rest of the class.

and focus on the teacher. No time is wasted. We don't have to beg students to quiet down. Effective procedures save classroom time and reduce management problems. Students know what is expected of them, and they respond accordingly. Good procedures do not happen magically. To put in place and maintain effective procedures require a conscious effort on our part. This chapter covers a number of recommended cooperative learning procedures. Let's look first at how to establish and maintain procedures.

> *"People need to be reminded more often than they need to be instructed."*
> —Samuel Johnson

First Things First

Don't wait for classroom problems to arise to put procedures in place. We start with procedures the day students step into our classroom. We let students know this is how we're going to take roll in teams, dismiss teams, line up in teams, and clean up for the rest of the year. If we establish routines early on and are consistent in their use, students quickly learn this is the way the classroom works and act accordingly. The cooperative learning teacher may take a little extra time in the beginning of the year putting procedures in place. But this is not time lost. This is time invested. Once students know how to act and interact in the classroom, we are free to focus on teaching and learning, not on management and discipline.

Never Too Late

Ideally we would know all the potential management problems and put procedures in place to prevent those problems. And many veteran teachers come pretty close. But unanticipated management problems do arise. Repeated problems are a signal to us that a procedure needs to be put in place. For example, in Corners, when it is time for students to go to one of the four corners of the classroom representing their preference among four alternatives, some students don't take time thinking about the four options but simply go to the same corner as their best friends. The first step is to analyze the problem. Is there a problem with the procedure? In this case, students have free choice, but are not being held accountable for making a decision in advance. A simple procedure is for students to write down their corner choice in advance, so if necessary, their decision could be verified. If you have a repeated management problem, it's never too late to put in place a procedure to handle the problem, not only for the instance, but for the future.

Teach, Practice, and Reteach Procedures

Procedures are behavior sequences. The best ways to show students the new behavior sequence is for us to model it, or for us to work with a team to master the procedure and have the team model it. Seeing the procedure in action is much more vivid and understandable than trying to describe it. Since procedures are usually a series of behaviors, writing out the steps on a poster or filling out a step graphic organizer on the overhead can be helpful. The poster can be displayed while the class is mastering the procedure or the transparency can be reproduced for student reference.

Structures Are Management Tools

Many teachers report that since they began using cooperative learning structures regularly, management has been a dream. The students know what to do at each step of a structure, and the structures keep the students on task, fully engaged. Management is structuring the interaction of students in the classroom, and that is exactly what structures do. Structures are a form of management. Group work is unstructured interaction and often results in management problems. For example, if we simply tell students to review for a quiz without telling them how to review, the most probable outcome will be off-task behavior as students discuss or argue about what to do. If, on the other hand, we tell students to review for a quiz using Showdown, the Flashcard Game, or Fan-N-Pick, they know exactly what to do, and the steps of the structure keep them on task.

Once students are aware of the procedure, have them practice it several times. If it's a procedure for a team question, have a team practice signaling their team question. Have students practice lining up or going through their morning routine several times, giving them plenty of positive attention. Frequent, short practice sessions on different days are better than one long session. Distributing practice over time leads to greater retention. Practice the procedure until students have it wired. When students have mastered the procedure, it can be used successfully to mange behavior in context.

If students begin to slip in implementing a procedure, it's time to reteach the procedure. If it's taking too long to get students' attention, reteach and practice the quiet signal. If students are arguing about line-up sequence, reteach the line-up procedure. If taking roll is taking too long, reteach the roll-taking procedure. A simple refresher is usually all it takes to get students back on track.

Reinforce the Procedure

We have discussed the power of positive attention, but it's worth stating here: Compliments go a long way to maintaining procedures. Praise students for successful implementation of procedures. "I appreciate the way Team Einstein quickly put away their books and took out their AnswerBoards." As often as we can, we try to "Catch Students Being Good."

Cooperative Expectations

In the cooperative classroom, we set positive expectations rather than imposing "Class Rules." See if you can finish the two sentences below

Rules are made to be _____.
Expectations are something we _____.

Answers: "Rules are made to be *broken*." Rules are something imposed from the outside. They are authoritarian, top down. "Expectations are something we *live up to*." Expectations are like agreements between the teacher and the class, and among classmates. Expectations set a positive, cooperative tone.

Team Expectations
- Offer help to teammates
- Ask teammates for help when you need it
- Participate and make your contribution to the team
- Encourage others to participate and contribute
- Treat others with respect
- Listen respectfully to teammates

Possible Consequences
- Re-establish expectations
- Switch teams
- Work alone

Class expectations are helpful for classroom management. They establish clear behavioral expectations for students. Expectations should be established early on. It's best if students work with the teacher to derive their own expectations, rather than having expectations imposed on them.

In the cooperative classroom, rules such as, "No talking" are eliminated. Discussion is encouraged. Cooperative learning adds new expectations. The box on this page lists some typical expectations for teams, and consequences for those who do not live up to those expectations. On the following page is a Cooperative Class Expectations blackline you may share with your class.

Generating Class Expectations

When students participate in developing class and team expectations, they live up to the expectations far more than when expectations have been imposed on them. Here is a sample cooperative lesson to have students generate class and/or team expectations:

Step 1. Teacher Outlines Rationale for Expectations. The teacher explains to students why expectations are essential for smooth and safe functioning of the classroom. The teacher may offer examples, and even categories for expectations, to help lead teams to generating desired expectations.

Step 2. Teammates Brainstorm Expectations. Teams use Jot Thoughts to brainstorm class expectations. Each student has multiple slips of paper and a pen or pencil. They write a proposed expectation on a single slip of paper, place it in the center of the team table, and announce the expectation to teammates. Their goal is to cover the team table with class expectations.

Step 3. Teams Organize Expectations. When the teacher calls time, teams work together to review and organize their expectations. Duplicate expectations and ones teammates don't agree upon are eliminated; similar expectations are combined, and new expectations are created.

Step 4. Teams Share Expectations. Teams share their expectations with the class using Teams Post or Team Stand-N-Share.

Step 5. Class Processes Expectations. The class organizes and simplifies the expectations into an acceptable set of class expectations that everyone can agree with.

Step 6. Teacher Posts Expectations. As a final step, students create an expectations poster for the class and/or are given a handout.

Cooperative Class Expectations

As an important member of my class and team, I will...

1 Ask for and offer help.

2 Listen carefully and praise my classmates.

3 Share my ideas and work.

4 Give my best effort.

5 Be a good follower and a good leader.

Kagan Cooperative Learning • Dr. Spencer Kagan & Miguel Kagan
Kagan Publishing • 1 (800) 933-2667 • www.KaganOnline.com

Variations

Team Expectations. Each team generates their own class expectations and shares their expectations with the class. The class uses Sum-the-Ranks to select their favorite set of expectations to adopt as a class.

Add Consequences. The class can come up with fair consequences for failing to live up to class expectations.

Setting Up the Room

Seating in the cooperative learning classroom is arranged to accommodate student teams and frequent cooperative interaction. Good seating arrangement is conducive to teamwork; poor seating arrangement is an obstacle to teamwork and becomes a management problem. Different classrooms have different furniture, different space configurations, and different numbers of students, so the exact arrangement will vary. Below are a few basic guidelines when arranging the furniture for cooperative learning. Understandably, not all classrooms permit arrangements that fit all the guidelines; good cooperative learning can happen even if some, or even many, of the guidelines cannot be met.

Team Seating Arrangement
Guidelines

- Students are seated four per team.
- Students are physically close to all teammates.
- No backs to the teacher, and all students have an unobstructed view of the teacher at the board and screen.
- Every student has easy access to his or her seat.
- Team tables are far enough apart for easy movement within the class.
- Teams are close enough for team-to-team interaction.
- There is an open space somewhere in the class for classbuilding activities.

Team Seating with Different Classroom Furniture

Most classroom furniture lends itself well to cooperative learning. Sometimes it is necessary to work around existing furniture. Let's look at how to set up the classroom with a variety of furniture.

Individual Desks. The most common team setup is four individual desks pushed together to form a team table. Chairs with attached desks can be arranged so the desk tops form a common workspace. If chairs and desks are nailed down in rows, first choice would be a crowbar. If that's not an option, students are assigned to groups of four adjacent chair/desks. Depending on how far away they are, they may have to get out of their seats to interact.

Horseshoes. Often a horseshoe arrangement is preferable to having two students on one side and two on the other. In the horseshoe arrangement, the two students farthest to the back are seated side-by-side facing forward. The other two students are seated sideways. This allows an unobstructed view of the teacher or whiteboard for all students and better eye contact between teacher and students.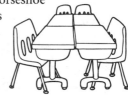

Team Desks. Team desks, such as large square or rectangular desks, have the advantage of a flat tabletop without the gaps created by individual student desks pushed together.

Long Tables. Long tables are preferred for workshops and work well in classrooms, too. Team members sit on each side of a table. This arrangement allows easy viewing of the front, equal and easy contact among teammates, and a comfortable workspace.

Carpet Patches. Carpet patches are common for primary classrooms where classroom space is used for centers or stations, rather than for individual desks. Students sit on their carpet patches just as they normally would. The difference is they are seated next to their teammates, two in front and two behind. When it is time to interact in teams, the two students in the front turn around and face their teammates.

Lab Tables. Lab tables are usually team-friendly. Students sit on one side of the lab table when it is time for instruction or pair lab work. When it is time for cooperative interaction, the pair turns around to unite with teammates.

Computer Labs. Computer labs are normally set up in rows of stations for one-to-one deployment, one student per computer. This is fantastic to maximize individual computer time, but does not take advantage of a powerful force for learning—interaction. For cooperative computer activities, pairs or teams move their chairs to gather around a shared computer. Pairs are seated right next to each other, and teammates are in the same row to facilitate forming pairs and teams. No special seating configurations are necessary for virtual cooperation via e-mail, discussion groups, online chats, and video conferencing. In fact, students can be in different parts of the world!

Lecture Halls and Amphitheaters.
Lecture halls are designed for professor-fronted lectures, not for participant cooperation.

Amphitheaters have basically the same layout, designed for people to observe the action on the stage, not to play a role in the action themselves. However, with a few modifications, lecture halls and amphitheaters can accommodate cooperative learning. To do so, teammates are seated in two adjacent rows. There are two teammates in the front row, and two teammates directly behind them. When it is time to team up, the two teammates in the front turn around and face their teammates behind them. Pair work is within shoulder partner pairs or front/back pairs. For ongoing teams, students remember their location and their team assignment.

If attendance is not mandatory in lectures, a consistent team seating arrangement cannot be assumed. The solution: Have students form groups of four as they file into the hall—two in front and two directly behind.

Interior Loops

One way to allow frequent and easy access to all students is to arrange team desks with an "interior loop," a path you can walk within the group of desks. If you only walk the perimeter, at every moment there are students far away. By more often walking the interior loop, more students are in proximity more of the time. Fred Jones describes the advantages of interior loops in his excellent book on classroom management.[2]

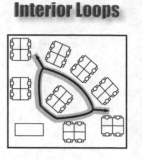

Interior Loops

An interior loop allows us easy access to all teams quickly.

Managing Attention

Managing noise during independent work is quite different than noise management in the cooperative class. When students work alone, we manage noise using a simple rule, "No talking!" If there is no talking, the teacher's voice is easy to hear, so we need only to begin speaking to get students' attention.

In cooperative learning, we encourage interaction. We need a quiet signal to quickly and effectively get students to refocus on the teacher.

The Quiet Signal

1. **Hand Up, Stop Talking, Stop Doing**
2. **Full Attention on the Teacher**
3. **Signal Others**

The Quiet Signal

Some teachers spend an enormous amount of time and energy trying to get their classrooms quiet and trying to get the attention of all their students. "May I get your attention, please?" "Quiet please!" are phrases oft repeated, with inadequate response. There is a simple solution: a quiet signal. The simplest one, and the one I like best, is a raised hand that signals to students to stop talking, stop doing, and to give their full attention to the teacher. The raised hand is a convenient quiet signal because we do not have to talk over the talk of the teams, and do not have to walk over to the light switch or find a bell. The hand quiet signal is more effective if students are instructed that when we raise a hand, they should raise a hand also, and signal other students to raise a hand, too. Thus, when we need the attention of the class, we simply raise a hand. This is quickly followed by vigilant students raising their hands, which leads to yet other students doing so. The raised hand of the teacher is like a pebble dropped in a pond: Quiet attention spreads from the teacher across the class like a ripple.

A bit of explanation to students may be helpful when the quiet signal is introduced. After the groups are formed, we explain that there is a natural tendency for a classroom of teams to become too noisy: As one team talks, a nearby team needs to talk a bit louder to be heard, which forces the first team to talk even louder. So noise levels can escalate. We tell students we do not want to shout over student talk to get the attention of the class, and the quiet signal solves this problem.

Immediate Attention

The Five Count. To emphasize that I expect full, alert attention in under five seconds, I tell students that if it ever takes over five seconds to get all hands quiet and all eyes on me, we will stop everything and practice the quiet signal. As a visual reminder of this, when giving a quiet signal, I count down with the fingers of my raised hand. Reinforce students' response with genuine appreciation (*"Thank you for that quick, full attention."*). Re-establish the signal if it loses effectiveness.

Quiet Signal Variations

Entire schools and school districts have adopted the hand up quiet signal. It works well in the school bus, cafeteria, gym, assembly room, or classroom. However, there are many possible signals to get students' attention. The best signals are fun and require a student response incompatible with continued talking and working. Here are a few alternatives:

Give Me Five. Teacher raises a hand with five fingers spread apart. The five fingers are to remind students of five rules:

1. **Eyes on the speaker**
2. **Quiet**
3. **Be still**
4. **Hands free (put things down)**
5. **Listen**

Some teachers instruct students that the five fingers symbolize two eyes on the teacher, two ears on the teacher, and one mouth closed!

Instrument Signals. At the sound of a pleasant bell, whistle, chime, piano key, or guitar strum, the students are to stop talking and give the teacher full attention.

The Quiet Signal
A Gift from the Cubs

I have been asked how I first developed the quiet signal. It turns out it was a gift from my past.

When I was doing my very first cooperative learning demonstration lesson—it was the first time I had ever taught an elementary class—I was a university professor applying the principles of cooperation to classrooms. As the students began to get involved in their cooperative learning task, the talk escalated. Soon each team was talking louder, trying to hear themselves above the rising noise. Without having planned it in advance, I told all the students, "When I raise my hand, that will be our 'Zero Noise Level Signal.' To make sure everyone sees the signal, when I raise my hand, you all do the same, until I lower my hand." It worked. Without knowing where the idea had come from, for several years I shared with many teachers the "Zero Noise Level Signal." It became popular. (Later I changed the name to "Quiet Signal" because talk in the cooperative classroom is not noise, but productive work.)

I never gave a second thought to where I had gotten the idea of a raised hand for a quiet signal, but several teachers asked. I told them I did not know. Then one day during lunch, without even knowing I was thinking about it, I had a very vivid memory of an early experience as a Cub Scout: When the troop leader wanted our attention, he had us all raise our hand and give the Cub Scout salute. Years later, without realizing it, in that moment during my first demonstration lesson, I had automatically turned to that early experience to help me manage my first elementary classroom.

Could it be that the extreme prevalence of the traditional classroom structure results from teachers unconsciously modeling themselves after the way they have been taught? If so, perhaps cooperative learning structures will become the way of the future as the students of today's cooperative learning classrooms become the teachers of tomorrow!

Lights. The teacher flips the lights off and on to get attention.

Music, Sound Effect, or Sound Bite. A snippet of music can do the trick. Try playing the first few lines of the song, "RESPECT." How about a cartoon sound effect? Many sound effects are readily available on the Internet. Students' favorite cartoon character saying, "Quiet" might be the ticket.

Clap or Snap a Rhythm. The teacher claps or snaps a rhythm, and the students respond by clapping a response rhythm in unison.

If You Hear Me, Clap Once! The teacher says, "If you hear me clap once," and then claps once. Some students clap. The teacher says, "If you hear me, clap twice!" Most students clap twice. The teacher then says, "If you hear me, clap three times!" All students clap three times and have full attention on the teacher.

Choral Response. Students all respond in unison to a teacher's prompt.

> Teacher: **One, two, three—eyes on me!**
> Students: **One, two—eyes on you!**

Too Elementary for High School?
On the Kagan Online Discussion Board, a high school teacher voiced her concern that the Quiet Signal just wouldn't work with her students. Dr. Vern Minor, Superintendent of Schools and Kagan trainer responds:

> *The bottom line is that kids will do whatever we ask them to do if we are consistent and it is important to us. Will kids raise their hands on the quiet signal? Absolutely…they already do when they want to ask a question. So, the question is not whether or not they will, but how the teacher approaches the task. If we model for them and the raising of the hand becomes a classroom routine/expectation, they will comply. It is like any other classroom rule…if you don't model and reinforce, it will not become routine.*

Dan Kuzma, veteran high school teacher and Kagan trainer, adds:

> *I call it the "attention signal" and say, one time only, "May I see your eyes please."*

Free Talk Time. A secondary teacher could not get his class to respond well to the quiet signal until he told them they were going to do "sophisticated time management." He used a timer and told the class each time he gave a quiet signal, he would count how long it took them to become quiet and to give him full attention. The number of seconds it took each time was posted, and times were summed each week. The total was time lost from a Friday ten-minute free talk period. Students began to manage themselves because they did not want to lose the free talk time.

Wait for the Last Hand Up!
If you get full attention from all but two or three inattentive or reluctant students, do not proceed. Wait for the last hand up! If you proceed without all students giving you the quiet signal, the message to the rest of the class is that they don't really have to raise their hands. Proceeding without all hands up is a prescription for erosion of compliance. We communicate our expectations by our behavior.

Managing Noise
The quiet signal is ideal for quickly getting students to focus on the teacher. But as a noise management method, it is inefficient. We want students to maintain acceptable voice levels for prolonged periods without having to interrupt the class. We need tools to keep noise to a productive hum.

How to Become a Puppet!
I walked into a class and saw the teacher giving the quiet signal every five minutes. She looked like a puppet with her hand tugged by an invisible string. What was happening? She was trying to manage noise level with the quiet signal. Students would get too loud, she would give the quiet signal, students would quiet down for a minute or so, and then noise would escalate again. The quiet signal manages attention, but does not work to manage noise level—unless, of course, you want to be a puppet!

Sound Level Training
Noise escalation can have a domino effect in the classroom: If your team is loud, my team will speak louder so we can hear each other. That will cause other teams in the class to speak louder, too. Noise escalation can be prevented if students know and use their appropriate voice levels during interaction time.

Voice Levels

Different voice levels are appropriate for different tasks. We teach students three voice levels:

1. **"No Talking."** Independent Work—No talking allowed
2. **"Partner Voices."** Pairs must be quiet enough not to be heard by the other pair on their team.
3. **"Team Voices."** Teams must be quiet enough not to be heard by neighboring teams.

We have students practice the three different voice levels. If necessary, we remind students of the voice level when assigning an activity, "RoundRobin what you did this weekend. Team voices." Some teachers use hand signals or color cues to signal voice level.

Some teachers also have students use a whisper voice level: whisper voice, six-inch voice, little voice, or tiny talk.

Choral Response

The teacher has a verbal cue that indicates to students they need to quiet down. Students chant a response in unison. For example:

Teacher: **"Quiet please."**
Students: **"Q–U–I–E–T … Shhhhhhhh."**

Noise Reduction Signal

There are times we want to remind students to keep their noise level down, but don't need absolute silence nor want to interfere with their projects or activity. A nonverbal noise reduction signal, such as horizontal palm slowly lowering, can be helpful to remind students to keep it down.

Stoplight Cards

The teacher places a green card on the desk of teams if their voice level is fine, a yellow card if they need to tone down a bit, or a red card if they need to become completely silent and count to ten before resuming interaction.

Background Music

To calm students and make quiet work more likely, we play soothing background music or sounds during team interaction times. Options include slow tempo music (50–60 beats per minute), calm classical music, and nature sounds such as ocean sounds.

Mechanical Noise Monitor

The Yacker Tracker is a commercial noise monitor. It looks like traffic light and allows us to set different acceptable sound levels in decibels. When the noise levels gets too high, the stoplight turns from green to flashing yellow. If the sound level reaches 20 decibels above the set level, the red light and audio cue come on. Students automatically quiet down when the buzz sounds.

Student Self-Monitoring

Students can become allies in monitoring noise by using a few simple strategies.

Quiet Captain. Each team has a Quiet Captain whose job is to remind students if they have become too loud. The Quiet Captain may use stoplight cards or a quiet meter: a dial with a "red zone" indicating the group needs to quiet down.

Class Noise Monitor. We can assign one student the role of Noise Monitor. When the Noise Monitor feels the classroom is too loud, he/she gives the class a simple signal such as ringing a bell or clapping a pattern. The class returns to their quiet voices. The Noise Monitor role gives younger students a sense of pride, and makes all students more conscious of classroom noise levels because the role is rotated daily.

Managing Noise

Music for the Mind

Music for the Mind is soothing background music to calm and focus students.

Yacker Tracker

A mechanical noise monitor lights up, based on sound level.

Sponge Ideas

Team	Individual
• Puzzles and games	• Journal writing
• Brainteasers	• Drawing
• Challenge problems	• Challenge problems
• Creative writing	• Silent reading
• Learning games	• Math games
• Brainstorm lists of….	• Listening center
• Top ten reasons….	• Creative play
• Task card	(clay, puppets,
• Draw a picture of the content	costumes, building)
• Write a song about the content	• Written report
• Use Question Dice to create	• Write review questions
thinking questions	
• Quiz a partner using flashcards	
• Explore content online	
• File folder games	

Team Noise Cue. If a neighboring team gets too loud or the class is too loud in general, teams can cue the class to quiet down and watch their noise level. The class decides on a simple cue that the entire team performs. For example, the team cue might be two snaps and a "sssshhhh!" in unison. Teams now have a polite way to let others know they are being too loud.

Managing Time

When teams work on an activity or project, they will finish at different times. Dead time is a waste of valuable classroom time and can be an invitation to discipline problems. We prepare a sponge activity for students or teams to turn to when they're done, or time the task so teams finish at about the same time.

Sponge Activities

A sponge activity soaks up students' extra time. It is a student or team self-directed activity that students turn to when they've finished their assigned task. Sponges are often used as a follow-up to a lesson to reinforce or extend student learning. But sponges can also be a fun reward for finishing quickly. Whenever students finish at different rates, we have a sponge ready for students to work on so there's no excuse for off-task behavior and always an answer to, "Teacher, we're done. What do we do next?"

Types of Sponges. The sponge activity may be for the entire team or for students to work on independently. Team sponges include a team challenge question or problem, a topic to discuss, or a content-related team task. Individual sponge activities include journal writing, drawing, or starting homework. The table on this page lists a number of sponges for teams and individuals.

Assigning Sponges. There are a number of ways to inform the class what to do if they finish early.

- **Announcement.** As we announce the team activity, we announce the sponge activity for teams that finish early.
- **Posted.** We write the sponge on the transparency or blackboard.
- **Sponge Center or Area.** Students or teams know to go to a sponge center or area. At the center, there is an activity on a clipboard, on the computer, in a bucket to select one, recorded Mission Impossible style, or students may be free to choose the sponge activity.
- **On the Assignment.** The sponge may be on the bottom, side, or back of a worksheet.

Sponge Structures. Once students know the structures well, many structures can be used as sponge activities. For example, we may say, "If you finish early, do a RoundTable Consensus to list the most important events in the story." Or, "Use Jot Thoughts to generate possible explanations of why the event occurred." Some of the many structures that we use as sponge activities include:

- Pairs Compare
- Talking Chips
- Team Interview
- Team Mind-Mapping
- Turn Toss

8.18

Kagan Cooperative Learning • Dr. Spencer Kagan & Miguel Kagan
Kagan Publishing • 1 (800) 933-2667 • www.KaganOnline.com

Quite a number of structures are game-like. We can use them to motivate students to finish their tasks. For example, we might say, "If you finish early, you can check out a Match Mine game board and play Match Mine with a partner." These are some structures that are game-like to use as a reward or to motivate students:

- Blind Sequencing
- Choose-A-Chip
- Fan-N-Pick
- Flashcard Game
- Logic Line-Ups
- Same-Different
- Showdown

Sponge Center. Tables in the back of the room or an area in the class can be designated as a "sponge center." That is, students know that if they finish their task early, they can go to the sponge center and either do the engaging games or activities at the center or check them out to do in their teams or independently. At the center, the teacher may have manipulatives and content-related questions ready to play. For example, Spin-N-Think can be played with any set of open-ended questions and Spin-N-Review can be played with any set of right-wrong questions. One thing that makes these games particularly attractive as sponge activities is that they can be played by 2 to 5 students. For example, two students finish early and are playing Spin-N-Think. They use the spinner to see who is called on to ask, answer, paraphrase, and praise each question. When a third student joins the group, that student becomes person three, and the same spinner picks among three rather than between two students.

Among the many manipulatives that make excellent sponge activities:

- Question Dice
- Learning Cubes
- Learning Chips
- Jigsaw Problem Solving
- Spin-N-Think
- Spin-N-Review
- Idea Spinner

Timed Activities

Many team tasks can be structured so that teams finish at the same time. For example, use a Timed Pair Share so that each partner has one minute to share (or any pre-assigned amount of time). All students finish sharing at the same time. Projects may also be timed, or broken into time increments for related tasks. For example, students have three minutes to come up with their kinesthetic hand signals, five minutes to practice them, and three minutes to prepare how they will teach them to the class. Additional tips and tools to avoid dead time:

- **Team Timers.** Teams keep their own stopwatch in their team tubs.
- **Time Captain.** The Time Captain is in charge of watching the clock and keeping teammates on task.
- **Class Timer.** A timer for the overhead projector, a software timer, or a large timer for the whole class keeps teams on time. Small timers with alarms work, but aren't as useful for student time management.

Managing Materials

In cooperative learning, teams share many materials. Simple procedures help us effectively manage team materials.

Team Tubs and Packs

Team tubs are material storage tubs that are usually placed in the center of the team table. Each team has their own tub. The tub can be anything from a decorated shoebox to a plastic tub with a lid. Team tubs are great timesavers because they allow teams to quickly access and store the materials they need for their team projects and activities. Transparent tubs allow students to quickly locate the materials they're looking for.

Team packs can be used instead of tubs. Team packs can be large pouches or shipping envelopes. One drawback of packs, though, is students may have to pour out the contents to get what they're looking for.

Suggested Team Tub Materials

• 4 Scissors

• 1 Roll of Transparent Tape

• 4 Dry-Erase Markers

• 1 Set of Crayons, Twist-Up Crayons, or Colored Pencils

• 2 Glue Sticks

• 1 Student Selector

• 1 Student Timer

• 1 Stress Ball

Restocking the Team Tub. Tape the list of materials on the inside lid or on the back side of the tub. After each project requiring materials from the team tub, the Materials Monitor is responsible for making sure the team tub is clean and all the materials are replaced and ready for the next activity.

Team Bins

In addition to or instead of a team tub, we can use a team bin. Bins are stored in a common classroom area and are retrieved by a teammate during cooperative work. They can contain larger items than the typical team tub.

Collecting and Distributing Work and Materials

Save time and keep students from getting restless by putting in place an effective procedure for passing out and picking up work and materials. One student per team—either the assigned Materials Monitor or a randomly selected student—is responsible for retrieving and passing out materials to teammates, as well as collecting teammates' work and taking it to the teacher. This technique avoids traffic jams and is much quicker than passing out and collecting materials one-at-a-time.

Managing Energy

One of the unspoken tasks of a good teacher is to orchestrate energy level in the classroom. The optimal state for learning is relaxed alertness: calm enough to concentrate, but alert and attentive. Often our students are either too alert or too relaxed. How can we keep our students in the zone of relaxed alertness?

Getting Them Up!

As students sit for any prolonged time, the supply of oxygen and glucose to the brain decreases, and they feel less and less alert. The solution: major muscle movement. Any time we have our students get up and move, their heart rates increase, and breathing rates and volume increase, so their blood is better oxygenated and there is a greater flow of blood to the brain. They wake up!

The following are some ways to quickly increase alertness (and ability to learn) in the classroom:
- StandUp–HandUp–PairUp
- Traveling Heads Together
- Traveling Star
- One Stray
- All *Classbuilding Structures*[4]
- All *Silly Sports and Goofy Games*[5]
- Energizing music

Bringing Them Down!

Students come bouncing in from recess, and they are too wound up to concentrate and way too energetic to start working together. How do we calm them down? Temporarily reducing external stimulation often does the trick. If we simply have students close their eyes and imagine they are in a calm quiet glade beside a gentle brook, in a minute or two they are closer to relaxed alertness and ready to take in new information and learn. Among the other easy ways to calm students:
- Timed Pair Share
- Sustained silent reading
- Journaling
- Drawing
- Solo problem solving or worksheet work
- Calming music

Student & Team Problems

Interpersonal problems will arise when using cooperative teams. Conflict is as inevitable in the cooperative classroom as it is in life. So should we shrink away from using instructional strategies that might result in the occasional disagreement? Of course not. Learning to prevent, manage, and resolve conflicts are important life skills. We implement preventative management procedures for reducing the likelihood of conflicts. With these procedures in place, student relations are more positive and problems are less frequent. However, there is still the occasional conflict or disagreement. Thus, we also implement management strategies for addressing conflicts once they arise. Let's look first at the strategies that make team problems less likely in the first place.

Preventing Team Problems

To prevent team problems, we avoid forming potentially problematic teams, and instead create a positive and cooperative classroom environment by frequent teambuilding, classbuilding, and ensuring positive interdependence is in place.

Team Formation. Team composition can play a role in student interaction patterns. Students who are a management problem on one team may pose no problem at all on a new team. Behavior and misbehavior is often a function of the individual and his/her social context.

Avoid putting best friends and worst enemies on the same base teams. Best friends often engage in off-task behavior or pair up, leaving the other two out. Worst enemies often refuse to cooperate, or worse yet, fight.

Teams with two males and two females are ideal. When forming teams, create as many two male/two female teams as possible. When you run out of boys or girls, create same-sex teams: all-boy or all-girl teams. Avoid teams with one boy or one girl, if possible. Teams with three boys and one girl tend to ignore the girl. On teams with three girls and one boy, the boy may receive an inordinate amount of attention and/or deference. For details on ways to form teams, see *Chapter 7: Teams*.

When we know our students well, we can often intuit which students will have problems being on the same team, and avoid potential problems by simply not teaming them together. However, we may discover surprising interpersonal dynamics arise when students are put together. Two high-achieving students compete for the control of their team. Two popular students compete for the attention of their teammates. Two low-status teammates compete for higher status. If team dynamics pose a management issue, a simple student exchange may be in order. One student on the problem team is exchanged with a student from another team.

Some students may be resistant to working in teams, regardless of who's on their teams. To overcome this resistance, the following will help.

Share Your Rationale for Using Teams.

If students are not accustomed to working in teams, some may resist working together. Share with students your rationale for doing teamwork in the classroom. Possible reasons include:

- Research shows students will learn more in teams than independently.
- Working together is more fun.
- Teamwork is preparation for the workplace, where work teams are common.
- Students will need the team skills and social skills to work with others from all walks of life.

Enumerating the benefits for students can melt resistance. Students often listen to the radio station WIIFM—What's In It For Me? Students are more willing to try teamwork if they know what's in it for them.

Teambuilding First.

When we create heterogeneous teams, we place students together with those they least likely would choose on their own. The high-achieving student may be reluctant to work with the low. The low may feel stuck with that "brainiac" or "nerd." We must overcome this resistance if cooperative learning is to be successful. How? Teambuilding. When teams are first formed, teambuilding is essential. Teambuilding activities are team-based bonding activities, often using fun, nonacademic content. The goal of teambuilding is for students to get to know each other, work together in a positive context, and establish a positive team identity. Without teambuilding, management and discipline problems are highly likely, especially for unstructured team tasks. When teams are having problems, ask yourself, "Do we need more teambuilding?"

"Two heads are better than one." —Anonymous

Classbuilding Too.

Classbuilding is another powerful set of tools that reduce management problems. Classbuilding creates a positive classroom atmosphere. Students get to know classmates, have fun interacting with them, and come to develop a genuine liking for one another. This friendly classroom environment promotes positive interactions so students are far less likely to become discipline problems. When you are having classroom discipline problems, ask yourself, "Am I doing enough Classbuilding?"

Check for Positive Interdependence.

Competition is synonymous with antagonism. Competing individuals, teams, organizations, and countries oppose one another, often to gain scarce rewards. Competition often breeds conflict, dislike, hostility, and aggression. Political opponents competing for office resort to mudslinging. Opposing athletic teams use excessive physical force and get into fights when they compete to win. Competing businesses sabotage their competitors to secure their position in the marketplace. Countries go to war over competing ideologies or for scarce resources. In contrast, cooperation breeds helping, liking, and collaboration. Political candidates on the same ticket work together. Sports teammates practice together, assist one another to win, and become good friends. Corporate partners share resources and strategies for their mutual benefit. Allied countries cooperate politically and economically.

These fundamental and universal outcomes of cooperation and competition apply to classroom management. To the extent students feel like they are on the same side, they will cooperate, they will work through disagreements, and they will not be management problems. If they feel like

---

Preventing Team Problems

▸ **Rationale for Teams**
Share with students the importance of acquiring teamwork skills.

▸ **Teamformation**
Create teams that are less likely to have problems.

▸ **Teambuilding**
Do ample teambuilding, especially when new teams are formed.

▸ **Classbuilding**
Create a caring class to promote positive student relations.

▸ **Positive Interdependence**
Ensure students see others on the same side, not as obstacles to their success.

they are in competition, they will butt heads; antagonism escalates to inappropriate classroom behavior. When the two dimensions of positive interdependence (my gain is your gain, and help is necessary) are in place, students are more caring, kind, and cooperative. Management problems disappear.

Dealing with Team Problems

Instituting preventative procedures reduces management and discipline problems dramatically, but does not eliminate all problems. For those problems, we need a different set of strategies. The strategies for managing team problems are sequenced below from least to most severe and are recommended to be used in this order. If a strategy does not resolve the problem, we take the next step.

Re-establish Expectations. If students are not living up to the class expectations, it is time to re-establish expectations. *Win-Win Discipline*[6] provides twenty moment-of-disruption structures and six follow-up structures. The structures are step-by-step responses to discipline problems. Re-establishing Expectations is a structure designed to reinforce knowledge, understanding, acceptance, and adherence to expectations. The eight steps of Re-establishing Expectations are as follows:

1. Express Caring
2. Establish Need
3. Check for Understanding
4. Explain Rationale for Expectation
5. Explore Obstacles
6. Explore Incentives
7. Elicit Commitment
8. Offer Support

By taking time to re-establish class expectations rather than jumping to punitive consequences, we establish buy-in and model a positive, cooperative approach to problem solving.

Work It Out. Often, the best solution for team problems is to give students time to work it out. A little disagreement between teammates can be a good learning experience, an experience from which students can acquire important conflict resolution skills. Here are some ways for teams to work out team problems:

- **Teammate Mediation.** If the problem is between two of the teammates, the other two can practice mediation skills.
- **Teacher Mediation.** The teacher gets involved to resolve the conflict.
- **Peer Mediation.** A classroom peer mediator resolves the conflict.
- **Conflict Resolution.** Through negotiation, the conflicting parties seek a peaceful, win-win solution.

Many conflicts can be resolved with a little effort. It is important first to try to resolve the problem, but it is not essential that every interpersonal problem be resolved. Students can learn that sometimes it is best to "agree to disagree." Coercing students to work together may be a losing battle. Doing so may be an obstacle to content learning for teammates and for the rest of the class. If teammate relationships become a persistent classroom disruption, we may need to move up a notch in our approach.

Form New Teams. If a student is very resistant to working on a team or if students refuse to work together, a team change may be in order. If it is near the end of the teams' time together, we consider forming all new teams. If it is in the beginning or the middle of the teams' term, we move as few students as possible to form new teams. We let students know honestly that we don't like disrupting teams, but in this case it is necessary, and we have confidence that these new teams will work out.

Separate the Problem Student. If a student has persistent trouble working with others, the student may need to work independently, either temporarily or permanently, depending on the severity of the problem. We have the student work at a separate independent desk and let him/her know that he/she may rejoin the team when he/she is ready to cooperate. Students usually find teamwork rewarding, and are quick to behave well to avoid the "time out" and return to their team. Repeated misbehavior can be reduced using a rule that states that any student who needs to work independently for a second time in the same day will remain there for the rest of the day. Whatever rules we select for required independent work, we let students know the rules in advance so that they know the consequences of their own actions.

Meta-Communication or Manipulation?

If a student is required to work alone, at that time we may assign all students a task that is easier to do as a group than alone. For example, complete all problems on a worksheet. Some teachers view this as manipulation—manipulating students to want to work on teams. Others view it as instructive meta-communication—informing students there are advantages to being able to work with others.

We can make the independent option available to the entire class by telling the class that if any student doesn't want to work with another student or refuses to participate with the team, he/she has the option of working independently. Students rarely choose to work alone.

Focus on Specific Skills. Students may simply lack the social skills required to work in cooperative learning teams. Student problems are a message to us: Some component of the social skills curriculum needs to be mastered. We address social skill development in detail in *Chapter 11: Social Skills.*

Discipline Strategies. If a student's disruptive behavior persists after the student is separated from teammates, it's safe to assume the problem is not a cooperative learning problem per se. At that point, discipline strategies are in order. For a comprehensive approach to classroom discipline that complements cooperative learning, see *Win-Win Discipline.*[6] Win-Win Discipline offers strategies for handling problems for the moment of disruption, but it goes beyond. Win-Win Discipline gets to the root of students' misbehavior and offers preventative procedures and life skills to eliminate students' needs to misbehave.

Strategies for Dealing with Team Problems

1. **Re-establish Expectations.** Review rationale and create buy-in.
2. **Work It Out.** Attempt to work out team conflicts.
3. **Form New Teams.** Adjust the teams or form new teams so problem students are not on the same team.
4. **Separate the Problem Student.** Send the student to a separate desk for a "time out."
5. **Focus on Specific Skills.** Social, emotional, and character development skills equip students with the essentials necessary to work together successfully.
6. **Discipline Strategies.** If students continue to be disruptive, use disciplinary strategies or actions to address the discipline problems.

Chapter Summary

Cooperative learning structures dramatically reduce management problems because students know exactly what to do, step-by-step, so they are far less likely to get off task. Additionally, with cooperative learning, we are going *with* rather than *against* student needs, allowing them to do what they most want to do—move and interact.

A special set of management skills is necessary for cooperative learning. By allowing students to interact, we release a great deal of energy, and this energy must be carefully controlled and directed toward learning. The techniques outlined in this chapter allow us to manage attention, and noise level, and arrange our rooms in ways to maximize good management.

Cooperative management, however, is more than a set of techniques. It is an attitude and orientation toward students. We give students a voice in establishing expectations. Through student signals, we empower students to help guide both the pace and the difficulty of the lesson. Cooperative management is democratic.

Management is critical. It frees us to teach and students to learn. The techniques outlined in this chapter are powerful tools for shaping group processes and classroom behaviors. I have seen some teachers and student teachers gain more from the cooperative learning management techniques than from any other aspect of cooperative learning—for the first time they gain a sense of control of their classroom.

Management, however, is not an end; it is a means. We use management techniques to set the proper environment for learning. A fully developed approach to classroom management—like good therapy—has as an aim to eliminate the need for itself. That is, in the well-managed classroom, students learn to manage themselves. As that goal is approached, the need for extrinsic rewards for desired behaviors vanishes. Students in a well-managed classroom find it intrinsically rewarding to take responsibility for their own learning and social development.

Chapter Questions

▶ Questions for Review

1. What are the three things students should do when they see the teacher's quiet signal?
2. What are two management strategies for addressing the issue of teams finishing at different rates? Describe them.
3. How should classroom seating be arranged for cooperative learning?
4. What is an Interior Loop?
5. Name two ways to increase students' energy and two ways to calm students.
6. Where are team materials kept?

▶ Questions for Thinking and Discussion

1. What are the top three management ideas you will implement from this chapter?
2. What additional cooperative learning management strategies do you think are important, but weren't covered in this chapter?
3. Would you say your current management style is simultaneous or sequential? Explain.
4. How can you implement class expectations so your students feel like they are generating the expectations, but you feel important expectations are addressed?
5. If a student said, "I don't want to work on this team," how would you respond?

References

[1] Kagan, S. "In Praise of Praise." *KaganOnline Magazine.* San Clemente, CA: Kagan Publishing, 2007. http://www.KaganOnline.com.

[2] Jones, T. *Tools for Teaching.* Santa Cruz, CA: Fred H. Jones & Associates, Inc., 2000.

[3] Kagan, S., P. Kyle & S. Scott. *Win-Win Discipline.* San Clemente, CA: Kagan Publishing, 2004.

[4] Kagan, M., L. Kagan & S. Kagan. *Classbuilding.* San Clemente, CA: Kagan Publishing, 2004.

[5] Kagan, S. *Silly Sports & Goofy Games.* San Clemente, CA: Kagan Publishing, 2000.

[6] Kagan, S., P. Kyle & S. Scott. *Win-Win Discipline.* San Clemente, CA: Kagan Publishing, 2004.

Resources

AnswerBoards. San Clemente, CA: Kagan Publishing. www.KaganOnline.com

Charles, C. *Elementary Classroom Management.* White Plains, NY: Longman, Inc., 1983.

Collis, M. & J. Dalton. *Becoming Responsible Learners: Strategies for Positive Classroom Management.* Devon Hills, Tasmania, Australia: Teamlinks, 1990.

Cummings, C. *Managing to Teach.* Edmond, WA: Teaching, Inc., 1989.

Emmer, E. *Classroom Management for Secondary Teachers.* Englewood Cliffs, NJ: Allyn & Bacon, 1984.

Evertson, C. *Classroom Management for Elementary Teachers.* Englewood Cliffs, NJ: Allyn & Bacon, 1984.

Kagan, S., P. Kyle & S. Scott. *Win-Win Discipline.* San Clemente, CA: Kagan Publishing, 2004.

Lamb, G. *Music For The Mind™ CDs.* San Clemente, CA: Kagan Publishing. http://www.KaganOnline.com

MegaTimer™. San Clemente, CA: Kagan Publishing. www.KaganOnline.com

Nelson, J. *Positive Discipline.* New York, NY: Ballantine Books, 1981.

Question Dice™. San Clemente, CA: Kagan Publishing. www.KaganOnline.com

Selector Spinners™. San Clemente, CA: Kagan Publishing. www.KaganOnline.com

SelectorTools™ Software. San Clemente, CA: Kagan Publishing. www.KaganOnline.com

Spin-N-Think™. San Clemente, CA: Kagan Publishing. www.KaganOnline.com

TeamTimer™. San Clemente, CA: Kagan Publishing. www.KaganOnline.com

TimerTools™ Software. San Clemente, CA: Kagan Publishing. www.KaganOnline.com

Yacker Tracker®. Timnath, CO: Learning Advantage.

CHAPTER 9

Key 4
Classbuilding

Classbuilding provides mutual support among all of the students in a class and creates a positive context for learning. Although students spend most of their time in teams in the cooperative classroom, it is important that students see themselves as part of a larger supportive group—the class—not just as members of one small team. There are a number of ways to improve class climate. The two primary approaches to classbuilding are Classbuilding Activities and Class Restructuring. Both approaches provide greater student empowerment and ownership and result in a feeling that this is "our class."

Cooperative learning works best in a caring classroom community. We create this caring and cooperative context through classbuilding.

Approach 1
Classbuilding Structures and Activities

Some Kagan Structures are particularly good for classbuilding. For a structure to be a "classbuilding" structure, students must interact with classmates. That means students are up out of their seats working with classmates beyond their immediate team. Getting up, moving about the classroom, and interacting with classmates is usually a fun time. We regularly do classbuilding with content that is non-academic. For example, the teacher may do a Mix-Pair-Share, having students pair up multiple times with different classmates. Each time they form a new pair, the teacher may ask a different fun discussion question like, "What was a fun thing you did this weekend?" Students light up when they get the opportunity to discuss their interests, get to know their classmates better, and have fun.

We sometimes refer to Classbuilding as "functional fun." It's fun, but with a purpose. In fact, we have five aims of doing classbuilding that we'll get to in a minute.

It's worth mentioning again here that structures are content-free. Structures that work well for classbuilding content work equally well for academic content. We can just as easily do a Mix-Pair-Share, discussing the merits of different presidential candidates. But even when we use serious academic content, there is still positive social interaction with classmates and an element of fun by virtue of the structure. When we plug different content into a structure (your weekend v. presidential candidates), we make a very different activity. We point this out because in this chapter you will find some favorite classbuilding structures and activities, but you can easily plug new content into the classbuilding structures to make literally thousands of classbuilding activities. We recommend you do classbuilding at least once a week, just for fun. Academic classbuilding can be done more frequently.

For a list of favorite classbuilding structures, see box: Selected Classbuilding Structures. In this chapter, you'll find numerous activity ideas for many of these structures. The book, *Cooperative Learning Structures for Classbuilding*[1] is the best available resource for classbuilding structures. It outlines some favorite classbuilding structures and provides many ideas for each structure, including ready-to-do classbuilding activities with blackline masters.

We will look first at the five aims of classbuilding and then examine classbuilding structures and activities organized using these five aims.

The Five Aims of Classbuilding
Picture the dream classroom. It's a place where students feel safe, comfortable, and like to be and learn. In the cooperative learning classroom, we use classbuilding to create this dream classroom. Even if we were never going to form teams, classbuilding would be well worth the effort. Classbuilding is especially important for productive cooperative learning. In the cooperative classroom, we want students to know and

Selelcted Classbuilding Structures

- Class Projects
- Corners
- Fact-or-Fiction
- Find Someone Who
- Find-the-Fiction
- Formations
- Inside-Outside Circle
- Line-Ups
- Linkages
- Mix-Freeze-Group
- RoundRobin
- Similarity Groups
- Value Lines

like their classmates. We want students to feel that this is not just any classroom. This is our classroom, and we all belong here. We want students to feel that their classmates are on their side. They're here to encourage and help, rather than to face off as competitors. We want students to feel free to express themselves and interact with all their classmates. These aims are summarized by the Five Aims of Classbuilding.

1. Getting Acquainted
All too often, students in the same class don't get to know each other. Sure, they may know other students' names and they may know them by their stereotypes, but do they really know each other as people? An essential part of classbuilding is for students to get to know each other. Interaction between classmates breaks down superficial barriers that divide classmates along lines of color and cliques. By simply taking some time for students to get to know each other, share their likes and dislikes, and interact on a friendly basis, we have power to transform the social orientation of our youth. Students discover that their classmates are just like them—real people with real feelings. They are more prepared to be empathetic and less capable of abusive behavior.

Five Aims of Classbuilding

1 Getting Acquainted
Getting to know classmates

2 Class Identity Building
Forming a class identity

3 Mutual Support
Feeling supported by classmates

4 Valuing Differences
Clarifying and respecting differing values

5 Developing Synergy
Building on classmates' contributions

When students feel they are known by others, we meet their basic needs to feel important, to be liked, and to belong. Students less often feel the weight of social isolation and social ostracism that causes students to withdraw, drop out, or lash out violently.

2. Class Identity

The goal of a class identity is for students to feel that their class is unique. This is not just any class. This is our class! Students feel they play an important role in the class and are proud members. To create this positive classroom identity, the class engages in a variety of projects to distinguish itself such as giving the class a name, designing a class logo, and coming up with a class song or chant. Class creations and accomplishments deepen this sense of class identity.

3. Mutual Support

Through mutual support activities, students come to feel they can depend on their classmates. Our class has gained a sense of mutual support when members feel the classroom is a caring community.

4. Valuing Differences

Students need to know that they are not only known by others in the classroom, but also that they are valued and appreciated. The norm in a strong class is that "We accept and appreciate those with values and characteristics different from our own." Through activities in which differences are understood and appreciated, we come to "celebrate diversity." Our class is richer because we have students taking different stances, and have multiple perspectives and insights to issues.

5. Developing Synergy

Synergy is the energy released through synthesis. All of us interacting produce and learn far more that the sum of what we all can produce and learn working alone. Students need to feel the power of synergy if they are to enter fully into the cooperative process.

As we will see in the next chapter, these five aims of classbuilding are parallel to the five aims of teambuilding, but at the team level. The team can be thought of as a microcosm of the class. We have the same goals for our teams as we do for our class as a whole.

1. Getting Acquainted

Structures and activities for students to get to know and like their classmates.

Find Someone Who

Find That Classmate. Find Someone Who is often used for academic content. For classbuilding, students go on a hunt for classmates with certain characteristics. For example, each student can submit one fact about themselves that classmates probably wouldn't know. Then, all the facts are compiled on a worksheet. For the hunt, every student has a worksheet and a pen. Students find a partner in the class, then they take turns asking each other one question, trying to match a classmate with a characteristic. If they find a match, they write the classmate's name next to the fact. After each asks a question, they shake hands and search for a new partner.

People Hunt. A variation of Find Someone Who is People Hunt. Students fill out a form that describes their characteristics such as favorite color, favorite school subject. (See blackline: People Hunt on the next page.) Then, students hunt for classmates who have matching characteristics. People Hunt is a fun way for students to get to know each other and discover shared interests and characteristics.

People Hunt is variation of the structure Find Someone Who. In Find Someone Who, students each receive a worksheet with questions or problems and repeatedly pair up with classmates to "find someone who" can answer a question or problem.

Similarity Groups

Student Characteristics. Similarity Groups is a great way for students to discover and share what they have in common with classmates. Here's how it works: The teacher announces a dimension such as favorite dessert or dream car. Everyone with the same answer forms a group. They then pair up within their groups to discuss why they chose what they did. The teacher can call on different groups to summarize their answers.

People Hunt

Instructions. Fill in your answers in the "Self" column. Then circulate throughout the class and find a partner. Attempt to find a match. If you do, write in your partner's name in the "Friend" column and discuss the match. Shake hands goodbye, then find a new partner to repeat the process. Your goal is to fill in the entire "Friend" column.

	Self	Friend
1. Favorite Color		
2. Favorite School Subject		
3. Favorite Ice Cream Flavor		
4. Favorite TV show		
5. Favorite Musician/Band		
6. Favorite Dessert		
7. Favorite Season		
8. Favorite Sport		
9. Favorite Hobby		
10. Dream Job		
11. Dream Car		
12. Dream Vacation		
13. Birthday Month		
14. Only, Oldest, Youngest, or Middle Child		
15. Eye Color		
16. (Fill In)		
17. (Fill In)		

Kagan Cooperative Learning • Dr. Spencer Kagan & Miguel Kagan
Kagan Publishing • 1 (800) 933-2667 • www.KaganOnline.com

Similarity Groups
Classbuilding Ideas

Form groups based on...
• **Animal to be for a day**
• **Most admired person**
• **Favorite food**
• **Favorite animal**
• **Dream vacation**
• **Dream job**
• **Tastiest dessert**

Classbuilding Content. Similarity Groups can be repeated many times, each time with a different dimension for students to form groups. See box: Similarity Groups Classbuilding Ideas.

Similarity Groups like Line-Ups and Class Bar Graphs can be followed by frequency graphs which provide a good visual description of the class.

Inside-Outside Circle
Who Are We? Students stand in two concentric circles. Students in the inside circle face out, and students in the outside circle face in so each student is facing a partner in the other circle. The teacher asks students a discussion question such as, "How did you get your name?" Students take turns responding to their partner. When done, the teacher tells them how many to rotate. They face a new partner and share information.

Getting-Acquainted Question Cards.
Another way to do Inside-Outside Circle is to use question cards. Have each student write two getting-to-know-you questions they'd like to share with classmates, one on each side of a slip of paper. For example, the question might be, "What is your most exciting memory?" Next, have them form inside-outside circles. Instead of asking a question, have them take turns reading and responding to their question cards. Before they rotate to face a new partner, make sure they trade cards and flip them over for a new question.

Class Project
Birthday Calendar. Have students do Line-Ups by their birthday. When they are in line, give the first student in the line the Class Birthday List sheet (see Blackline on the next page). Students write their name and birthday. When done, the sheet will have a sequenced list by birthday. This is perfect for creating the class Birthday Calendar (see blackline on page 9.7).

Each student's name is recorded on the class calendar. If a person's birthday falls on a non-school day, their name is recorded also on a school day, so each student's birthday can be celebrated.

Students are made to feel extra special on their birthday. Below are some ideas to make students feel appreciated on their special day.

Birthday Celebrations
Ideas for the Special Day

• The class sings "Happy Birthday."
• The class fills out a birthday card for the birthday child.
• The birthday child is interviewed by the class.
• The birthday child gets time to share something with the class.
• The birthday child gets to lead the class in a cooperative game.
• The birthday child gets to bring in and play a song for the class.

Formations
Class Bar Graphs. Students form a bar graph on some getting-acquainted topic such as number of blocks they live from school, times they have moved, or number of pets they have had. Later, they may make team or individual bar graphs of the data. The data may be posted, analyzed, and used as part of a math lesson.

Linkages
Student Preferences. Linkages is a visual and kinesthetic way to connect the entire class like the links in a chain. Students stand in a circle around the perimeter of the room. One student steps to the middle and states something about himself or herself, such as "I'm Susan, and I like chocolate ice cream." Any student in the class can link on by holding hands or linking arms and saying, "I'm Simon,

Class Birthday List

Instructions. Students line up by their birthday. They write their name, month, and birthday on the next open space when the list comes to them. When done, the list will be a sequenced list of birthdays ready for the Class Birthday Calendar.

Name	Month	Day
1.		
2.		
3.		
4.		
5,		
6.		
7.		
8.		
9.		
10.		
11.		
12.		
13.		
14.		
15.		
16.		
17.		
18.		

Name	Month	Day
19.		
20.		
21.		
22.		
23.		
24.		
25.		
26.		
27.		
28.		
29.		
30.		
31.		
32.		
33.		
34.		
35.		
36.		

Kagan Cooperative Learning • Dr. Spencer Kagan & Miguel Kagan
Kagan Publishing • 1 (800) 933-2667 • www.KaganOnline.com

Class Birthday Calendar

Month_____

Sunday	Monday	Tuesday	Wednesday	Thursday	Friday	Saturday

Kagan Cooperative Learning • Dr. Spencer Kagan & Miguel Kagan
Kagan Publishing • 1 (800) 933-2667 • www.KaganOnline.com

9.7

and I'm glad you like chocolate ice cream, Susan, because I do, too! And I like to go to the movies." A student who likes to go to the movies links on by saying, "I'm Carlos and I just love the movies too. I also like to go fishing." And so on.

When the last student links on, he or she completes the circle by walking around to link the first person while all classmates remain linked. When the students are in a circle, they might say, "We are (class name), and we are linked!" They then give the class cheer.

Fact-or-Fiction
Students state either a believable fiction or an unlikely fact about themselves. Classmates attempt to guess which it is.

Find-the-Fiction
Students say three statements about themselves. Two are facts; one is a fiction. Classmates try to guess the fiction.

Fact Bingo
Classmate BINGO. Each student receives a copy of the handout, Classmate BINGO (see blackline on page 9.10). Students try to get "Line BINGO" by finding a classmate for each cell of a horizontal or vertical line on the form. After one student gets Line BINGO, everyone tries to get "Blackout" by finding a classmate for every cell of the form. To play, students stand up, put a hand up, and pair up with a partner. They ask each other one question. For example, "Have you ever been out of the country?" If the partner answers affirmatively, the student has the partner write his/her name in the corresponding cell. If they find a match, students must also ask a follow-up question, because if they get Blackout, they lead the class in a getting-to-know-you activity. For example, "Mai has been out of the country. She went to Antarctica with her family on an expedition." It is important to emphasize that students may only ask each other one question each, otherwise they will try to fill out multiple cells with a single partner.

After partners each ask one question, they stick a hand up and find a nearby student with a hand up. The first person who gets five signatures in a row calls out, "Line BINGO," and draws a line through cells identified. The first person who gets all the signatures calls, "Blackout." After the student with Blackout leads the class in the getting-to-know-you activity, she/he may be awarded a prize.

If you want to use characteristics that are more specific to your class, cover up the text in each cell, copy the form, then fill in your own class characteristics.

RoundRobin
Gesture-Name-Game. Form circles of about ten students. One at a time, each student says his name, by breaking it into syllables, and adding a movement or gesture to go with each syllable. In unison, the group repeats the name and imitates the movements. Once students master first names, they add their last names.

All About Me. For homework or as a fun in-class activity, students fill out an All About Me form or poster. (See blackline: All About Me on page 9.11.) In class, students have their poster in hand and they stand up. The teacher calls out a number from two to four, and students form small groups with nearby classmates with that number of group members. The teacher then tells students to RoundRobin share some part of their Personal Profile. After students take turns sharing their profiles with classmates, the teacher calls out a new number and students must form groups with all new classmates. In their new groups, they can share another part of their form or poster.

Of course, students don't need a form or poster to share getting-acquainted information, but it allows students to express themselves visually and serves as a nice visual to display for classmates.

Class Line-Ups
Classbuilding Ideas

Line up based on…
- Height
- Shoe size
- Number of pockets
- Birthday
- Alphabetical order
- Length of hair
- Number of buttons
- Number of pets

Mix-Pair-Share
Getting to Know

You. The teacher plays upbeat music while students mix through the classroom. When the teacher stops the music, students pair up with the nearest classmate. The teacher asks a question and gives students a time allotment for each partner to take a turn answering. Any personal information works well to get to know each other better. Here's a few ideas:

- What I do with my best friend
- Family traditions
- What I did last weekend
- What I did yesterday after school
- One thing I really want is

2. Class Identity Building

Structures and activities for classmates to forge a unique class identity.

Class Name. It seems that teachers have universally settled on the naming convention, Mr. Kagan's 5th Grade Class (just change the name and the grade). This name suggests ownership. Who's class is it? What if a class has a name like the Brilliant Bunch or the Tremendous Troop?

Class Line-Ups
Student Characteristics. The teacher announces a dimension on which students can line up. For example, the teacher may say, "Line up in alphabetical order by your middle name." Students quickly and quietly form a single-file line. To quickly check the sequence, students do a sequenced Popcorn. Beginning at one end of the line, each student in turn shares his or her answer (their middle names in this example). If middle names are too embarrassing, to the left are some additional student characteristics Line-Ups ideas.

What do those names convey? In which class would students rather belong? We want a class name that suggests shared ownership, involves the whole class in the process, and is something we all like. Below is a fun lesson to come up with a class name.

Step 1. Teacher Shares Importance of Names. Tell students, "A name sets an individual or organization apart from others. It is how you are known to others, and it is often deep with meaning. People have names. Sports teams have names. Companies have names. We need a class name that screams this is our class."

Step 2. Teams Brainstorm Names. Using Jot Thoughts, teams brainstorm class names, announcing each name as they write it on a separate slip of paper and try to cover the table with possibilities.

Step 3. Students Select Favorite Name. Give students some think time to review all the names their team generated and to select their favorite class name. Then they do a RoundRobin, sharing their favorite name and why.

Step 4. Teams Select Top Name. Teams use Sum-the-Ranks to select a name to propose to the class. The names students identified as their favorites in the RoundRobin are placed on the team desk, and the other names are removed. With a different colored pen or marker, they write a number on each alternative corresponding to their rank for that name. So if there are four names to choose from, a student writes the number one on his top choice, two on his second choice, and so on. The ranks are summed, and the name with the lowest sum is the team choice.

Step 5. Teams Post Top Names. One team rep writes the selected name on a designated area of the board and announces the name to the class. It is important that the names are spread apart. Now, there are at most as many possible names as there are teams.

Step 6. Final Selection. Sum-the-Ranks is used again: Teams discuss and rank the alternatives. Once they have reached consensus on their final ranking, one team rep writes the team rank by each name on the board. The team rankings for each name are summed. The class name with the lowest sum is deemed the class name!

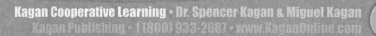

Classmate BINGO

Student Name _____

Instructions. Circulate throughout the class and find a partner. You may ask your partner if he or she is the person described in one cell below. If you are correct, have him or her sign that cell. Allow your partner a turn to ask you one question. Shake hands goodbye, then find a new partner to repeat the process. If you get five signatures in a row, call "Line BINGO." If you get all the signatures, call, "Blackout!"

B I N G O

Has been out of the country.	Favorite sport is a water sport.	Has a silly nickname.	Has a special family tradition.	Plays on a team.
Takes lessons.	Middle name starts with "S".	Is a member of a club.	Favorite food is...	Reads books for fun.
Has a hidden talent.	Can cook something delicious.	FREE SPACE	Is an artist.	Loves to play video games.
Loves to dance.	Is a social butterfly.	Keeps a diary or journal.	Is a collector.	Has done something adventurous.
Has lived somewhere far from here.	Plays an instrument.	Dreams of being famous.	Belongs to an online group or club.	Has many pets.

Kagan Cooperative Learning • Dr. Spencer Kagan & Miguel Kagan
Kagan Publishing • 1 (800) 933-2667 • www.KaganOnline.com

All About Me

Instructions. Fill out this page and get ready to share your info with your classmates.

Write and decorate your name here.

Personal Profile

- Birthday _____
- Family _____
- Pets _____
- Teams I'm on _____
- Clubs I'm in _____
- Classes I take _____
- One thing you probably wouldn't know about me_____
_____

Draw a picture of you doing your favorite thing here.

Hopes & Dreams

- When I grow up, _____
_____
_____
_____

- If I could be granted one wish, _____
_____
_____
_____

★ My Favorites ★

★ Color

★ Book ★ Subject ★ Game

★ Movie ★ Hobby ★ Food

Kagan Cooperative Learning · Dr. Spencer Kagan & Miguel Kagan
Kagan Publishing · 1 (800) 933-2667 · www.KaganOnline.com

9.11

Class Logo, Banner, Mural. Art has a tremendous capacity to visually depict meaning. Plus, it's a whole lot of fun for the class to do as a project. Once the class name has been decided, the class can come up with a class logo, banner, or mural.

Class Door. Students design and decorate their own door poster. First, cut a piece of poster paper to cover your classroom door. (Tip: Check with local printers to see if they have any remnant rolls they'd like to donate.) Next, divide the size of the door into the number of teams of four you have in the class. For example, if you have eight teams, then cut the door poster into eight parts. Each team receives their own piece of the door poster, and they may decorate it as they wish. The only rule is that they must have their team name and each teammates' name prominent on their part of the poster. You may have each student bring a photograph of him/herself to integrate into their team section of the door. Another way to do the class door is to decorate the class name. Students work in teams to submit a design proposal, pick a design as a class, then work in random teams to create a section of the door poster.

Class Song or Chant. Create a simple class song that your class can sing to celebrate a success, announce their presence, or just to focus everyone on the same thing at once. If your class is musically challenged, you can modify the good old Everywhere We Go chant:

> *Everywhere we go, people want to know,*
> *Who we are, so we tell them.*
> *We are the **Class Name**,*
> *The mighty, mighty **Class Name**.*

Pump up your class song or chant with some movements coordinated with the chant.

Student Wall. Students fill out a profile sheet and attach a picture to their profile. Their profile and their pictures are posted on the student wall. Students can browse the wall during free time.

Class Web Site. In this day and age, if you don't have a Web site, then do you really have an identity? The class Web site can be a fun project for the whole class. Make sure to collect ideas from students, but here are some possible elements for your class site:

- **Class Photo.** No site is complete without a class picture.
- **Photo Gallery.** Pictures of the class in action with student-written captions describing the pictures.
- **Newsletter.** Save a tree. Post your class newsletter online.
- **Links.** Students' favorite Web sites to visit.
- **Learning games.** Links to curriculum and grade-appropriate learning games.
- **Calendar.** Upcoming events and birthdays.
- **E-mail link.** A link to write the class an e-mail.
- **Honors and Awards.** Lists of students who made the honor roll, principal's list, had perfect attendance, or met another classroom goal.
- **Parents Corner.** Class policies, ideas for helping students at home, assignments and due dates, upcoming field trips.

Want to browse some sample class Web sites? Here's a tip to find a ton: Do an Internet search on "grade class." You'll find plenty of class Web sites to get some good ideas for your class.

Class Books. A class scrapbook or memory book is a great way to create a positive class identity. The scrapbook can have student work, team projects, and snapshots of past teammates. The class can create a book about a field trip—each team making a chapter and each teammate contributing a page to the team chapter. When done, we "publish" the class book by sending it to other classrooms, with some pages in the back for them to leave comments. Some other book possibilities: class cookbook, monster book, or shape books.

Classroom Signals. Foster belonging with your own unique language. Cultures have languages and dialects. Subcultures have lingo and jargon. Fraternities have secret handshakes. Use simple, nonverbal hand signals and gestures to communicate: Quiet please, I need help, I'm done, It's too hot in here, I need more time,

You're going too fast. See the Classroom Signals SmartCard[2] for an extensive description of ideas for classroom signals.

Class Mission Statement.

A mission statement is an organization's mission or purpose —its *raison d'être* (its reason for being). What is your class's mission? A clear, concise mission statement can help unify the class. Here's a mini-lesson using a series of structures—Mix-Pair-Share, Team Statements, RoundRobin, and Blackboard Share—to write a class mission statement.

> *"We must all hang together, or assuredly, we shall all hang separately."*
> —Benjamin Franklin

Mix-Pair-Share

Step 1. Mix. Students stand and mix in the class.

Step 2. Pair. When the teacher calls, "Pair," they pair with the nearest student.

Step 3. Share. The teacher asks a question, and gives think time. Partners are given 30 seconds each to respond (Timed Pair Share). Here are some questions to ask the pairs to share:

1. What do we value as a class?
2. What are our goals as a class?
3. How are we going to reach our goals?

Since students pair up with new partners each time, it is OK to repeat the same questions a few times.

Team Statements

Step 4. Students Write. Students independently write a class mission statement.

Step 5. Students Read Statements. In teams, students take turns reading their statements aloud (RoundRobin).

Step 6. Team Writes Mission Statement. Using the individual statements, the team writes one team mission statement for the class.

Teams Post

Step 7. Teams Share Statements. Each team posts their statement on the blackboard for all teams to see. Each team takes a turn reading their statements in unison.

Step 8. Class Discussion & Mission Statement. The teacher leads the class in discussing what they like from the team statements and works with the class to pen a class mission statement.

3. Mutual Support

Structures and activities for classmates to feel mutually supported by one another.

Hidden Helpers

Each student is assigned a secret pal. Their job is to do something nice for their secret pal each week without letting the secret pal discover who is their hidden helper. Guidelines are necessary, for example, gifts may be limited to compliments or favors, not material gifts. If material gifts are allowed, a dollar limit is necessary.

Ticket Agents

This exercise emphasizes looking for positive things in others' behavior. Every day, assign one or two students to hand out '"tickets" to those who are being very helpful, considerate, or cooperative during the day.

> *"One for all and all for one."*
> —Alexander Dumas, *The Three Musketeers*

Chain of Friendship

Ask the students to start noticing kind and helpful things that other students do at school. During the day, a child may come and tell the teacher about a good deed. That child will receive a colored "link" on which to write the good deed. The student announces the deed to the class as it is glued or stapled onto the chain. As the friendship chain grows, it is a visible measure of kind and helpful deeds.

Classroom Rules

Classroom rules can reinforce supportive behaviors and discourage negative behaviors. See *Chapter 8: Management* for more about cooperative class rules.

Class Party

Students have a great time while learning the importance of everyone's contribution. As a class, brainstorm a list of what makes a good party. Then have each student volunteer for one thing on the list. Have students reflect on the importance of their contributions. Ask them to discuss or write about what would happen if no one contributed to the party.

Who Am I?

Students brainstorm the names of familiar people or characters, often from books just read. Each name is written on a piece of construction paper. Each paper is punched with two holes in the upper corners and a string of about two feet of yarn is placed through the holes and tied to the corners. The paper is worn on the back of each class member so that they cannot see who they are. For older students, self-adhesive labels or name tags worn on the back work fine. Classmates then wander the room, attempting to find out who they are. They seek help from their classmates by asking up to three questions that can be answered with a "yes" or a "no."

Once students discover their secret identity, they wear their name tag on their chest. Then, they can circulate, giving hints to the classmates who have not yet discovered who they are.

As an aid to those who might not otherwise figure out their identity, a list of all the characters may be posted, and once students discover who they are, they place a check mark by that character.

Mix-Freeze-Group

Number Puzzles. Students "Mix" around the room until the teacher calls "Freeze." The teacher then poses a problem that has a number for an answer such as, "What is (teacher claps twice) plus (teacher claps three times)?" Students then rush to huddle and hold each other's hands in groups of five. Those who are left over go to a designated spot by the teacher, called "lost and found." Rule: You cannot go to lost and found twice in a row, so students must look to hold lost-and-found students first.

Service Learning Projects

Nothing says caring like service learning. Students can build bonds with classmates as they care for animals, other children, the elderly, the homeless, or beautify the environment. As a classbuilder, it's best to get the whole class working toward the same goal. See box: Service Learning Projects for ideas your class can choose from.

Service Learning Projects to Promote Caring

Help the Elderly
- Put on a performance at a retirement home.
- Read, shop, or help the elderly in the community.
- Spend time with the elderly at a home.

Care for Animals
- Volunteer to walk, groom, or care for animals at a local shelter.
- Work to match animals with caring families.
- Adopt and care for a classroom pet.

Help Other Children
- Read to or tutor younger children.
- Donate used books, clothes, and toys to less-fortunate children.
- Put on a performance at a children's hospital.

Beautify the Community
- Plant trees or a class garden.
- Pick up trash, paint over graffiti, or pull weeds.
- Hold a recycling drive and use the money for flowers, trees, or gardening supplies.

Help the Homeless
- Collect food, toiletries, or clothing for the homeless.
- Volunteer at a homeless shelter.

Silly Sports & Goofy Games

A rich array of mutual support activities is provided in the Helping Games section of *Silly Sports & Goofy Games*.[3]

4. Valuing Differences

Structures and activities for classmates to clarify their values and feel their values are accepted and respected.

Corners

Preferences. Corners works well for students to get to know and accept themselves and others more. Any individual difference dimension

can be the focus such as favorite season, desired profession, or even type of shoe you would like to be. Students go to the corner of the room representing their choice. For example, all the tennis shoe people go to one corner; the hiking boot people go to another. Students then share reasons for their choice with a partner in their corner. Finally, students may play a paraphrase game in which they must listen carefully to the reasons of the other groups (high heels, hiking boots, loafers) in order to be able to correctly paraphrase them. A typical Corners sequence follows.

Step 1. Announce Corners. Announce the corners, with a number in each corner and with visuals posted in each corner, if possible. Usually there are four corners, but sometimes three or more corners are appropriate, depending on the curriculum.

Step 2. Think & Write Time. Give students a bit of silent think time to clarify for themselves their preference. Have them write the number of their preferred corner on a slip of paper. (This way they will clarify their own values, not just go to the corner Johnny prefers.)

Step 3. Students Group in Corners. Students go to their corners and pair up to express the reasons for their preferences. They then form groups of four within the corner, and each share with the group the reasons their partner gave. The teacher calls on students from one corner to announce to the class reasons for that choice.

Step 4. Students Paraphrase. Students in pairs in the corners paraphrase the reason. This last sharing and paraphrasing is repeated for each corner.

Step 5. Teams Review. When students are back in their teams, they make sure everyone can name reasons supporting each choice.

Corners is also a useful structure to begin and end a lesson. For example, before a unit on the Civil War, I might ask the students who they would rather be (Soldier from the North, Plantation Owner, Abolitionist, or Southern General). Following the lesson, I might do Corners on students beliefs about which of four was the most important reason for the war. Students learn to see and appreciate multiple perspectives.

Agree-Disagree Line-Ups

Taking a Stance. A statement is announced, and students take a stand on an imaginary line that stretches from one end of the classroom to another. See box: Agree-Disagree Line-Ups.

Agree-Disagree Line-Ups
Sample Statements

Here are some Agree-Disagree statements on a variety of different classbuilding topics.

Student Empowerment
- I feel that my opinion counts in this classroom.
- The students are involved in making decisions in this class.
- We all have a voice in this class.

Understanding and Caring
- I feel that my classmates really try to understand my opinions.
- I feel like someone in this class really cares about me.
- I have people in this class that I can really trust.

Getting to Know You
- My classmates really know who I am as a person.
- Everyone in this class really knows and understands me.
- I really know everyone in this class well.

Class Rules
- Students should be allowed to have cell phones in class.
- There should be no dress code in our classroom.
- I agree with all our class rules.

Class Climate
- This is a fun class to be in.
- I feel safe to take risks in this classroom.
- I feel safe to ask for help in this classroom.
- I feel safe in this classroom to state my beliefs, even if they are different.

The strongest "agree" student in the class stands at one end of the line; the strongest "disagree" student stands at the other. The remaining students stand between, closer to one end or the other, depending on how much they agree or disagree with the statement.

Through Timed Pair Share, students listen carefully to those with a similar point of view (those standing next to them in the line). The line is then folded, and then they play Paraphrase Passport to make sure they listen to and understand a point of view different from their own.

5. Developing Synergy

Structures and activities for creating student interactions that produce outcomes better than the best student could produce alone.

Circle-the-Sage

An old tale illustrates the power of synergy and multiple perspectives. A group of blind men gather around an elephant. Each one touches a different part: the tusk, the trunk, the head, the ear, the foot, and the tail. They are asked to describe what they felt. They give such different answers that their disagreement turns violent. Each holds a different perspective and only part of the truth. Interaction creates a fuller picture.

Circle-the-Sage puts this synergy principle into action. Students who have expertise on a topic stand around the room. For example, we are about to do a unit on Mexico, and we ask students who have visited Mexico to stand. These "Sages" spread out. Then the seated members of each team each circle a different sage and learn from that sage. Finally, the teammates return to their teams and compare notes. Because each teammate now has a different body of knowledge to share, as they interact they get a fuller picture of Mexico. In the synthesis of divergent bodies of information, there is a higher-level understanding.

Circle-the-Sage is powerful with wide range of content. Because we have heterogeneous classes, we can do a pre-assessment on a topic and have those who score well become the sages. Further, we can create "Sages" by giving selected students different readings on a topic. An additional option is Opinion Sages. In this variation, students circle sages who have different opinions on a topic. When they return to their team, they first share the divergent opinions and then make a Team Statement representing the team's opinion.

Formations

Geometric Forms. The teacher draws a geometric figure such as two concentric circles, a square, or a triangle. Students form the figure with their bodies by holding hands. It is more challenging if they are not allowed to talk.

Objects. Laurie Kagan was teaching a unit on the Westward Movement. She had students become a covered wagon that actually traveled as the wheels rotated.

I like to have students become a happy face, sad face, and melting ice-cream cone. Other favorites are to have students spell words, make number sentences, and to act out the solar system, including the moon traveling around Earth, which is traveling around the sun.

Encourage Synergy

Play for students the credits of one of their favorite movies. Read the titles of all the individuals responsible for making the movie come to life. Tell students how some of their favorite things are the result of the cooperation of many people. If they learn to cooperate, they too can be involved in creating great projects.

Imaginary Machine. The teacher describes machines as having various parts and movements. One student plays the part of a crank by bending his arm at the elbow. Another student adds on by placing her hands on the waist of the first student and doing deep knee bends in time to the cranking motion. A third connects and moves her head in a circle, etc., until the whole class becomes a "Class Living Machine."

Class Projects and Presentations
Classbuilding Ideas

Design a...
- Poster
- Banner
- Bulletin board
- Brochure
- Catalog

Create, Practice, and Perform a...
- Dance
- Musical
- Song
- Instrumental performance
- Skit
- Play

Write and Film a ...
- TV show pilot
- Commercial
- Movie
- Documentary
- Exposé
- News broadcast

Plan and Have a...
- Pool party
- Holiday celebration
- Potluck meal

Conduct a...
- Survey
- Research project

Create a Class...
- Web site
- Storybook
- Magazine
- Newsletter
- Scrapbook
- Multimedia project
- Internet animation

Write a...
- Book
- Novel
- Skit/Play

Build a...
- Model
- Statue
- Structure
- Machine

Reflect on Cooperation. Reflection after Class Projects can reinforce cooperation and the importance of individual contribution. Use the blackline *A Piece of the Puzzle* (on the next page) to have students reflect on the collaborative process.

Approach 2
Class Restructuring
Class Meetings

How can we possibly prepare our students for full participation in a democracy by structuring our classroom autocratically? It is an amazing feature of our democratic educational system that we have settled so universally on an autocratic social organization of our classrooms. The teacher is the Congress (making the laws), the President (carrying them out), as well as the Judge, the Jury, and too often, the Executioner. Is it any wonder that teachers feel tired at the end of the day?

Functions of Class Meetings
1. Announcements
2. Mutual Support
3. Solve Problems
4. Improve Class
5. Plan Events

Class Projects
Class Plays, Skits, Performances. Class projects are the epitome of synergy. Through collaboration, students accomplish together what no single student could do alone. See box: *Class Projects and Presentations.* There is one essential ingredient for successful whole-class projects: Everyone needs a part or role to play.

If not all students are doing the same thing (like playing an instrument for the class song), the class projects should be broken into smaller elements integral to the the class goal. Individuals or teams take responsibility for the different pieces. For example, if the class project is a video, there will need to be scriptwriters, set designers, the audio-visual team, actors, directors, and editors, to name a few.

Regularly scheduled class meetings are one of the most powerful tools we have for teaching mutual respect, responsibility, caring, social awareness, cooperative attitudes, and democratic principles. The class meeting also can be a major source of support for the teacher as students actively strive to improve the class, find solutions to problems, and suggest consequences for behaviors.

Whenever a problem comes up that does not need to be solved immediately, it can be placed on the agenda for the next class meeting. This provides a cooling-off period in the heat of the moment and satisfies the students that something is being done about their problem. Often the problem is solved by the students before the class meeting, and when that item comes up on the agenda, students are asked to share their own creative solutions.

A Piece of the Puzzle

Instructions. Reflect on the class performance and your role in the performance.

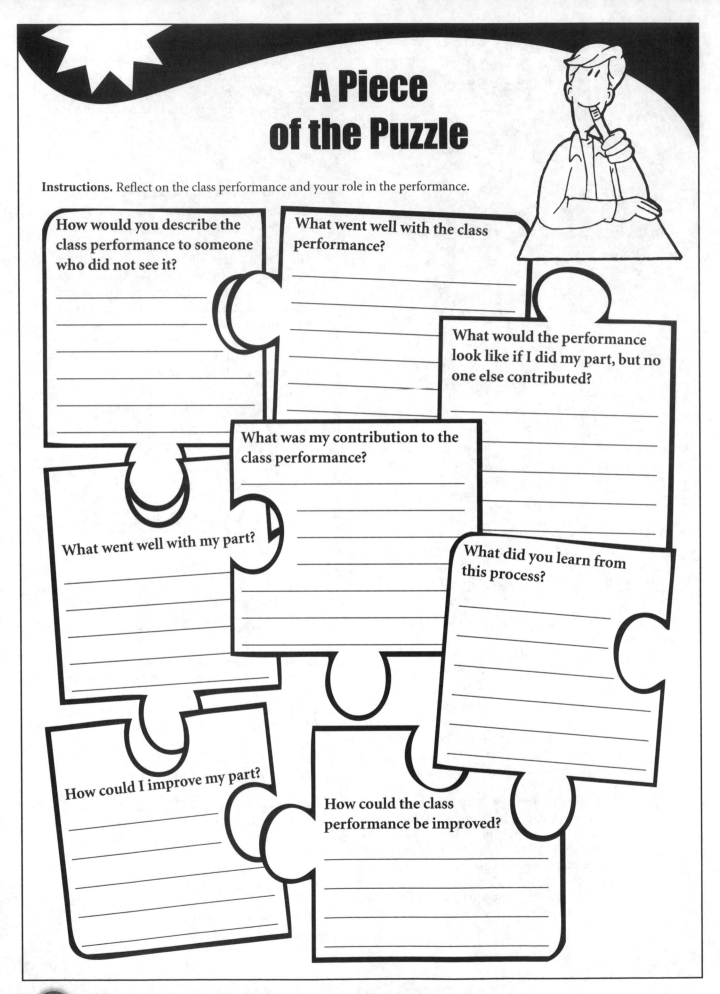

How would you describe the class performance to someone who did not see it?

What went well with the class performance?

What would the performance look like if I did my part, but no one else contributed?

What was my contribution to the class performance?

What went well with my part?

What did you learn from this process?

How could I improve my part?

How could the class performance be improved?

Kagan Cooperative Learning • Dr. Spencer Kagan & Miguel Kagan
Kagan Publishing • 1 (800) 933-2667 • www.KaganOnline.com

Class meetings are a time for creative problem solving. Tears came to more than a few eyes as a teacher at one of our summer institutes described how her students during a class meeting worked on the question of how a blind boy could participate in kickball. When the students hit on a solution, it was used for the remaining years of that child's elementary education.

Unexpected, creative, student-generated solutions to problems often occur at the class meetings because many heads are better than one, students are less tied to traditions, and because students are closer to many of the problems for which they ask help.

Function. Meetings are used to make announcements, plan events, solve problems, improve class functioning, and provide mutual support.

Structure. Regular meetings, rather than meetings just to put out fires, are preferable. When possible, time is allotted for each of the five major functions at each meeting. In this way, students know, for example, there will be some time for students to compliment or support each other at each meeting, setting a positive tone, and putting the problem solving in a larger positive perspective.

> *"Coming together, sharing together, working together, succeeding together."*
> —Unknown

Agenda. Usually the rule is that an item must be placed on the agenda prior to the meeting. Nothing is placed on the agenda unless the teacher feels comfortable with it, and no decision can be made unless the teacher agrees.

Student Planning. Students can be in charge of certain aspects of the meeting. For example, the class support committee, with a rotating membership, is in charge of finding creative ways to recognize and celebrate individual learning

gains and positive attitudes and behaviors among students. It can set a positive tone to both begin and end a class meeting with time for students to praise or compliment each other.

Schedule. It is best to begin with announcements and then to set a positive tone with compliments, both teacher and student generated. Problem solving might follow. Time is left for planning events and improving class procedures. Finally, it is a good idea to end with a mutual support activity such as a classbuilder, described in this chapter.

Student Input. While problem solving, we use a structure that ensures that each student's input can be seen by all the students. One such structure is a Team Discussion with a Simultaneous Blackboard Share; a member from each team can write on the board or chart paper as the team comes up with a possible solution.

Suggestion Box. A suggestion box empowers every student to have input. The suggestions can be reviewed by the teacher, or can be brought up at the class meeting.

Appreciations. The teacher can formally appreciate the efforts of individual students for their performance or contributions at the meeting. For exampe, "One thing I really appreciate in our class is how Frank takes time to give compliments. Yesterday I heard him give Pete a great compliment. He said...."

Students can also praise or appreciate classmates. Luci Bowers (Frank Jewett School, Bonny Eagle School District, W. Buxton, Maine) gift wrapped a shoe box. All week students deposit positive items in the Appreciation Box. During the Friday class meetings, there is time to "Read the Box." Students praise each other and provide inspirational quotes such as, "To have a friend is to be one."

Class Goals
If the success of each team contributes to a higher-level class goal, then all teams feel themselves to be on the same side—the success of one is success of all. This positive interdependence among teams can be created through the task structure—if each team project is one aspect

of a larger class project. It can be created also through the reward structure—if the points earned by each team are summed, and contribute to a class goal. The importance of setting class goals becomes clear when we visit a classroom in which there has been only team-level recognition and no class projects or class-level recognition. If students identify only at the team level, the classroom becomes a "civil war of teams"—each team rooting for the failure of the other teams. The climate changes radically if there are class goals: The success of each team contributes to a higher-level class goal, and students see themselves as classmates, and support each other.

Positive Class Tone
Silly Sports & Goofy Games

One of my favorite ways to have fun and establish a positive class tone is to do cooperative sports and games. Unlike traditional sports and games where the goal is to win, with Silly Sports, the goals is for everyone to have fun and for everyone to feel like a winner.

For example, in Ten Count, one of over 200 games in *Silly Sports and Goofy Games,*[4] the class shares the goal of trying to count to ten. Sounds simple, right? Give it a try: Any student starts off the count by saying, "One." Any other student can say, "Two" at any time. What makes the game tricky is that multiple students will call out the same number at the same time. Interesting strategies and group dynamics evolve as students try to solve this seemingly simple challenge.

Enhancing Class Climate

- Arts & Craft Projects
- Board Games
- Celebrations
- Class Garden
- Class Goals
- Class Pet
- Computer Games
- Dress-Up Days
- Field Trips
- Free Time
- Friendly Contests
- Game Show Review
- Guest Reader
- Guest Speaker
- Humor and Jokes
- Motivational Posters
- Movies & Videos
- Music Listening
- Music Playing
- Parties
- Plays, Skits & Acting
- Recognition Ceremonies
- Silly Sports & Goofy Games
- Sports
- Storytelling Time
- Student Art Gallery
- Writing

From Autocracy Toward Democracy

Autocracy is a political system governed by a single individual. In the traditional classroom, the teacher is the autocrat, making all the decisions for the class. Democracy, in its purest sense, is rule of the people through a numerical majority. The decision of the majority is the binding decision for the whole group. The United States is based on a form of democracy called representative democracy where we elect leaders to represent us.

We are not suggesting that the class be truly democratic. As such, students far outnumber the teacher, and recesses, PE, and art would likely replace academics. Nor can it be a representative democracy—the most popular student could conceivably be elected teacher, and that wouldn't work out too well either.

The teacher is a trained professional, and is ultimately responsible for decision making, especially as it pertains to the well-being of the students. We are recommending that students are empowered to make some decisions, and are free to have some input.

Within teams, true democracy can rule. Students can vote (although we prefer Spend-A-Buck and Sum-the-Ranks). In the class, we are not arguing for true democracy. We are, however, suggesting that the more we can empower our students to have input, make choices, and at times pursue their own interests, the happier and more productive our classrooms will be.

Enhancing the Class Climate

There are many ways teachers make the class a fun place to be, and a place where students want to come (see box: Enhancing Class Climate). The trick is to balance fun with academic learning. Sometimes we do fun things just for the sake of fun. Often, the fun activities can be integrated with classroom learning. For example, if students are learning about plants, a class garden is ideal for planting and growing seeds.

Class Empowerment

A basic drive of human nature is the desire to feel in control of our destiny. We need to feel like our opinions matter and that we have some control over our immediate circumstances. Students are no exception. If the teacher robs students of all control, they feel powerless, like puppets at the mercy of a force beyond themselves. They seek control in distracting ways. If instead, we allow students to have input, to make decisions, and to feel a sense of pride and ownership in the classroom, they are happier to be a part of our class and less likely to seek control in disruptive ways.

Student Input

Class Decisions. A vote often polarizes the class—some win and some lose. Thus, when the class is to make a decision, instead of a vote, it is usually better to use Consensus Seeking, Sum-the-Ranks, or Spend-A-Buck. In the long run, reaching consensus is far more positive than voting for making decisions. Consensus Seeking places a powerful value on minority rights. If we use consensus, we do not have a class decision until we are all comfortable with the decision. If we use voting, we might make a decision that nearly half the class hates. Consensus Seeking will work only if class members are flexible; they must realize that in the consensus process, the goal is not to get their very favorite outcome each time, but rather to get an outcome that everyone can live with.

Rewards and Celebrations. If there is a class goal, students can decide how to celebrate progress toward the goal. For example, teams can brainstorm and prioritize possible class celebrations (free-time music, snacks, class picnic, cooperative game). The teacher can determine which celebrations are acceptable.

Student Ownership of the Classroom

Student Bulletin Boards. A student bulletin board or collage allows students control over a portion of their environment. There can be a class decision as to how to use the space, and a provision that all students must contribute.

Room Arrangement. If students are asked how they would feel most comfortable and are given an opportunity to contribute to room arrangement, they get the feeling that this is "our class."

Student Jobs. A great way to give students ownership of the class is to share responsibilities for the classroom (e.g., the Zookeeper). The Student Jobs SmartCard[5] has many great classroom job ideas, their duties, and implementation ideas. Student jobs communicate to students that this is our class, and we each play an important role. Plus, this handy management technique saves teacher time and contributes to a cleaner, more harmonious class.

Student Government. Another way to empower students is to allow them to occupy positions of power. The President, Vice-President, Secretary, and Treasurer all have roles in the class. Short term-limits are highly recommended to allow many students the opportunity to hold elected positions.

Student Committees. Students can sign up for different classroom committees, each with a different role for contributing to how the class runs and what students do.

- **Party Planning Committee.** Help plan class parties.
- **Decorating Committee.** Make classroom decorations.
- **Art Committee.** Select the class art projects, helps display student art in class.
- **Budget Committee.** Determine how to spend class money.
- **Athletic Committee.** Choose sport or game to play.
- **Music Committee.** Choose free-time music.

In the Cooperative Class

In the Cooperative Class, we...
- **Work toward class goals.**
- **Make the class a fun place to be.**
- **Give students a voice.**
- **Have regular class meetings.**
- **Empower students.**
- **Give students jobs and roles.**
- **Share in the decision-making process.**
- **Give students choices.**
- **Move toward democracy.**
- **Involve students in problem solving.**

Learning Center Task Cards ✓

Learning Center Task Card

Instructions. Check off the center you selected for the day.
Check off _____ centers by the end of the week, and turn in your task card and work.

Student Name _____ **Date** _____

☐ _____

☐ _____

☐ _____

☐ _____

☐ _____

- -

Learning Center Task Card

Instructions. Check off the center you selected for the day.
Check off _____ centers by the end of the week, and turn in your task card and work.

Student Name _____ **Date** _____

☐ _____

☐ _____

☐ _____

☐ _____

☐ _____

Kagan Cooperative Learning • **Dr. Spencer Kagan & Miguel Kagan**
Kagan Publishing • 1 (800) 933-2667 • www.KaganOnline.com

How's Class Going?

Student Name _____

Instructions. Fill out the form to help your teacher help you.

Class Climate

The class class climate is (circle one):   **Excellent   Good   OK   Bad   Terrible**

Reason(s)_____
_____
_____

Idea for improvement _____
_____
_____

Teacher

One thing that helped me learn was _____
_____

One thing I didn't like was _____
_____

Idea for improvement _____
_____
_____

Curriculum

The most important thing I learned was_____
_____
_____

I liked learning about _____
_____

I am having a difficult time with _____
_____

Idea for improvement _____
_____
_____

How's Class Going?

Student Name _____

How I Feel About Class

Instructions. Mark the line to share how you feel about class.

1 I feel like I belong to this class.

No ├──────────────┼──────────────┤ Yes

2 I feel like the students in my class know me.

No ├──────────────┼──────────────┤ Yes

3 I like the students in this class.

No ├──────────────┼──────────────┤ Yes

4 Students in this class like me.

No ├──────────────┼──────────────┤ Yes

What I Like Most and Least About Class

Instructions. Write what you like most and least about today's class.

What I like most...

_____
_____
_____
_____

What I like least...

_____
_____
_____
_____

Kagan Cooperative Learning • Dr. Spencer Kagan & Miguel Kagan
Kagan Publishing • 1 (800) 933-2667 • www.KaganOnline.com

Chapter Summary

Student Choice

Choice of Centers. When using learning centers, individual students or whole teams can be given choices. For team choice: Each day a different team gets the first pick of a learning center. For student choice: Individual students have task cards, and it is up to them which learning center to work at, as long as they check off five centers on their task cards by the end of the week. Learning Center Task Card blackline masters are provided on page 9.22.

Choice of Activities. Many lessons have multiple activities to reinforce the same concept. For example, a lesson on the gold rush might include interviewing teammates in character, creating a mind map, answering review questions, and creating a team project. If the activities don't build on one another, the sequence is inconsequential. Allow students the choice: "Would you rather do a Team Interview or play Numbered Heads Together to answer review questions?"

Student Evaluations

Students can provide valuable input into the classroom environment and become coaches for their teachers. On a regular basis, students fill out a very simple questionnaire, which allows them to reflect on various aspects of classroom life: the class climate, the teacher, and the curriculum.

Two How's Class Going? forms are provided on pages 9.23 and 9.24. The first is for older students and the second for younger students. The teacher uses the answers to get students' perceptions of how things are going in the class with an eye toward improving conditions for students.

Because students are asked for their ideas for improvement, they take responsibility for the class climate and their own learning. The positive tone puts teachers and students all on the same side in an attempt to improve "our class."

Two quite different approaches to building classroom community are described in this chapter. The first approach is the use of classbuilding structures and activities to reach a range of classbuilding objectives: Students get to know their classmates better by sharing personal preferences, characteristics, and discussing personal issues. The class forges a unique identity through everyone's participation in identity-building activities. Students learn to care about and trust their classmates. Students clarify their own values, while classmates listen respectfully and validate each other's differences. And the class develops synergy: Through the contributions and collaboration of every class member, the class is capable of producing projects and presentations that surpass those that any single class member could do independently.

The second approach is restructuring the class. In this approach, we move from the traditional autocratic teaching style where the teacher makes all the decisions, toward a more democratic style where students have a voice. Students are empowered to have input. They are empowered to make classroom decisions. The teacher infuses fun into the class to make the tone more positive. The class becomes everyone's class, where everyone has a degree of control over their own environment and circumstances.

All of these wonderful changes in the classroom culture are a desirable end in themselves. If classbuilding had no spillover into academics, it would be worth doing. But the effort to build a safe and supportive learning environment does have a spillover effect—a tremendously positive one!

Classbuilding lowers the anxiety level in the class, elevates students' esteem level, and boosts motivation. Students feel safe asking for help, sharing how much they really know, presenting differing perspectives on contentious issues, and testing out fledgling knowledge or language skills. Classbuilding works to eliminate classroom fears: the fear of being ridiculed; the fear of not fitting in; the fear of failure.

The two approaches described in this chapter are different. But the outcome for both is the same: creating a cooperative, caring community of learners where everyone wants to be and learn.

Chapter Questions

▶ Questions for Review

1. What are the two main approaches to classbuilding?
2. Name and describe several classbuilding structures.
3. What are the five aims of classbuilding?
4. Describe two ways to empower students in the class.
5. What does a class meeting look like? Describe a class meeting.

▶ Questions for Thinking and Discussion

1. What impact does class climate have on student learning? Why?
2. What is the difference between a democracy and an autocracy? How do these political concepts apply to the classroom?
3. In your classroom experience, how often do you think classbuilding is appropriate?
4. Complete the following analogy: Classbuilding is like…. Describe your analogy.
5. If you were a researcher that wanted to study the impact of classbuilding, what study would you conduct?
6. Which classbuilding structures or activities have you used? How did they go? If you have not used any, which are you most excited about trying? Why?
7. Giving students choices and allowing them to have input in the arrangement and function of the classroom undermines the teacher's authority. Do you agree or disagree? Why?

References

[1] Kagan, M., L. Kagan & S. Kagan. *Classbuilding.* San Clemente, CA: Kagan Publishing, 1995.

[2] Kagan, M. *Classroom Management: Classroom Signals SmartCard.* San Clemente, CA: Kagan Publishing, 2004.

[3] Kagan, S. *Silly Sports & Goofy Games.* San Clemente, CA: Kagan Publishing, 2000.

[4] Kagan, S. *Silly Sports & Goofy Games.* San Clemente, CA: Kagan Publishing, 2000.

[5] Kagan, M. *Classroom Management: Student Jobs SmartCard.* San Clemente, CA: Kagan Publishing, 2004.

Resources

Co-operative College of Canada. *Co-operative Outlooks.* Saskatoon, Saskatchewan: Co-operative College of Canada, 1980.

Canfield, J. & H. Wells. *100 Ways to Enhance Self-Concept in the Classroom: A Handbook for Teachers and Parents.* Englewood Cliffs, NJ: Prentice Hall, 1976.

Chase, L. *The Other Side of the Report Card: A How-to-do-it Program for Affective Education.* Glenview, IL: Goodyear Books, 1975.

Gibbs, J. *Tribes: A Process for Peer Involvement.* Santa Rosa, CA: Center-Source Publications, 1987.

Glassman, M., E. Kisiow, L. Good, M. O'Connor, I. Alderson & S. Kutz. *Cooperation and Community Life.* Saskatoon, Saskatchewan: Cooperative College of Canada, 1980.

Graves, N. & T. Graves. *Getting There Together: A Sourcebook and Desktop Guide for Creating a Cooperative Classroom.* Santa Cruz, CA: Cooperative College of California, 1988.

Kagan, S. *Classbuilding SmartCard.* San Clemente, CA: Kagan Publishing, 1999.

Kagan, M. *Classroom Management: Class Meetings SmartCard.* San Clemente, CA: Kagan Publishing, 2005.

Kagan, M. *Classroom Management: Classroom Signals SmartCard.* San Clemente, CA: Kagan Publishing, 2004.

McCabe, M. & J. Rhoades. *The Nurturing Classroom: Developing Self-esteem, Thinking Skills, and Responsibility Through Simple Cooperation.* Willits, CA: ITA Publications, 1988.

Moorman, C. & D. Dishon. *Our Classroom: We Can Learn Together.* Englewood Cliffs, NJ: Prentice Hall, 1983.

Prutzman, P. *The Friendly Classroom for a Small Planet.* Wayne, NJ: Avery Publishing Group, Inc., 1978.

Raths, L., M. Harmin & S. Simon. *Values and Teaching: Working With Values.* Columbus, OH: Charles E. Merrill, 1966.

Saskatchewan Department of Co-operation and Co-operative Development. *Working Together, Learning Together.* Saskatoon, Saskatchewan: The Stewart Resources Center, 1983.

Schmuck, R. & P. Schmuck. *Group Processes in the Classroom.* Dubuque, IA: Wm. C. Brown Co., 1988.

Schniedwind, N. & E. Davidson. *Cooperative Learning, Cooperative Lives.* Dubuque, IA: Wm. C. Brown Co. Publishers, 1987.

Simon, S., L. Howe & H. Kirschenbaum. *Values Clarification: A Handbook of Practical Strategies for Teachers and Students.* New York, NY: Hart Publishing Co., Inc., 1972.

Spizman, R. *Bulletin Boards Plus.* Carthage, IL: Good Apple Inc., 1989.

Stanford, G. *Developing Effective Classroom Groups.* New York, NY: Hart Publishing, 1977.

Stanford, G. *Learning Discussion Skills Through Games.* New York, NY: Citation Press, 1969.

Vacha, E. *Improving Classroom Social Climate.* Orcutt, CA: Orcutt Union School District, 1979.

Vacha, E. *Project Class.* Orcutt, CA: Orcutt Union School District, 1982.

Wenc, C. *Cooperation: Learning Through Laughter.* Chicago, IL: The American Institute of Adlerian Studies, LTD., 1993.

Kagan Cooperative Learning · Dr. Spencer Kagan & Miguel Kagan
Kagan Publishing · 1 (800) 933-2667 · www.KaganOnline.com

9.27

CHAPTER 10

Key 5
Teambuilding

To create heterogeneous cooperative teams in the classroom, we seat students of different sexes, ability levels, and races at the same team table. Oftentimes, students find themselves sitting with the classmates they would least likely choose as teammates. How do we get this group of students with different backgrounds and experiences to work together as an effective team unit? The answer is teambuilding. Teambuilding is the process of converting a heterogeneous group into a cohesive team. It is the process by which different students come to know, trust, and respect their teammates.

Through teambuilding, students come to know, like, and respect their teammates. In the process, we convert a group of virtual strangers into a powerful learning team.

Teambuilding lays the groundwork for effective teamwork. Repeatedly, I have teachers tell me that when they take time off academic tasks for extensive teambuilding the result is greater, rather than less, academic achievement. This apparent paradox has a ready explanation: Teambuilding creates enthusiasm, trust, and mutual support, which, in the long run, lead to more efficient academic work. Wouldn't you rather ask or offer help to someone you know and like?

If there are racial or other tensions among students, teambuilding is a must. To go on with cooperative learning without dealing with interpersonal tensions is to run a race with sharp pebbles in your sneakers.

The Five Aims of Teambuilding

Creating powerful learning teams has many aims. There's the social component. We want students to know, like, and trust the students who they will be working with. And there's the task component. We want students to be able to work well together, take turns, share, communicate well, and make team decisions. There are five aims of teambuilding.

Five Aims of Teambuilding

1 **Getting Acquainted**
Getting to know teammates

2 **Team Identity**
Forming a team identity

3 **Mutual Support**
Feeling supported by teammates

4 **Valuing Differences**
Clarifying and respecting differing values

5 **Developing Synergy**
Building on teammates' contributions

1. Getting Acquainted

When students are first placed on the same team, they need to feel a sense of comfort with one another. When seated next to a stranger, we all feel a bit apprehensive. Getting acquainted activities help students get to know their teammates so they are no longer strangers and no longer feel anxiety. As teamwork progresses, students can get acquainted on a deeper level, resulting in familiarity, acceptance, and friendship.

2. Team Identity

A team forms an identity by defining itself in a unique way such as creating its own name, cheer, or solution to a problem. Successful completion of any team project can enhance the sense of team identity if the team is allowed to complete the project in its own unique way. When students are active in forging their team identity, they feel a solidarity with teammates and a belonging to the team.

3. Mutual Support

It is not enough for students to know each other and to feel they are part of a team. The team gains strength as the members feel they can count on each other for support. Any situation of positive interdependence creates the feeling of mutual support as students know they need each other, can depend on each other, and are on the same side.

4. Valuing Differences

Value clarification activities are designed to accomplish several goals. The activities clarify an individual's own values. The activities demonstrate that different individuals have different values and that there are no right or wrong values—that values of others are to be understood and respected. Students learn that the different values are to be accepted as enduring individual differences with which the team must work. Successful value clarification activities prepare students to live in harmony in a diverse society.

5. Developing Synergy

Synergy refers to the increased energy released when individuals are working in cooperation. Because of the synergetic effect, the group product can be better than the product of even the best individual working alone. The sum of the parts interacting is greater than the sum of the parts alone. There are various ways of generating synergy within teams. Synergy is released by tasks that encourage students to build on each other's ideas. Interaction causes stimulation and refinement of ideas.

Kagan Cooperative Learning • **Dr. Spencer Kagan & Miguel Kagan**
Kagan Publishing • 1 (800) 933-2667 • www.KaganOnline.com

Teambuilding Structures and Activities

If the Five Aims of Teambuilding are our destination, then think of teambuilding structures and activities as our vehicle. They are the "how" of teambuilding. They are how we achieve these varied aims.

Teambuilding Structures

Many Kagan Structures work particularly well for teambuilding. The criteria for a teambuilding structure is that it is team-based, involves the entire team, and furthers one of the five aims of teambuilding. The Selected Teambuilding Structures box below, lists some popular teambuilding structures.

Let's take Team Interview as an example. In Team Interview, each student on the team takes a turn being interviewed by teammates. Every teammate gets a turn to be interviewed and several turns interviewing teammates. It's a simple and wonderful structure for teambuilding. The topic of the interview could be "My Favorites." Students ask their teammates about their favorite hobbies, subjects, food... whatever they want to learn about their teammates. They get to know each other and may even discover some shared favorites. Using Team Interview in this fashion is purely for teambuilding. It accomplishes the first goal of teambuilding: Students get to know each other.

However, the same structure can be used for purely academic purposes, too. Students can interview each other in the role of literary characters or historical figures. Not all teambuilding is time off academic work. Using a range of cooperative learning structures, we can do content-related teambuilding activities that serve the dual purposes of uniting the team and providing an anticipatory set and/or distributed practice in a lesson. A teacher did a demo lesson on the rain forest, and she posted a list for students. It had food and items such as cocoa, coffee, bananas, chewing gum, tires, wood floor, diamonds, and medicine. Next, she had students do a RoundRobin in their teams. Student #1 picked one food or product on the list and stated why he/she believed it came from or didn't come from the rain forest. Each student stated his/her opinion in turn. After everyone shared, they discussed in their teams whether to place a "Yes" or "No" by the item representing whether or not it was a tropical product, or a "?" if they were unable to reach consensus. When time was up, students were very curious to learn which foods and products actually do come from the rain forest. RoundTable Consensus served as a set for the academic lesson, but was also an effective teambuilder. Students practiced taking turns, listening to differing opinions, making decisions as a team, and attempting to reach consensus.

Teambuilding structures are great for teambuilding whether the content is social or academic. In the Kagan Teambuilding Structures, the basic principles of cooperative learning are "built in." That ensures that as we use teambuilding structures, we are not only doing good teambuilding, but also good cooperative learning.

The book, *Cooperative Learning Structures for Teambuilding*[1] is the best available resource for teambuilding structures. It outlines favorite teambuilding structures for all grades and provides ready-to-do teambuilding activities with blackline masters.

When Teambuilding Is Essential

If the cooperative learning lesson is simple and fun, as with the Flashcard Game or Numbered Heads Together, the lesson itself is a form of teambuilding. Students help each other reach a common goal and in the process pull together. In fact, anytime students in a team are in a situation of positive interdependence, the result is a stronger sense of team identity: They feel "we are in it together."

If a lesson involves activities in which conflicts might arise (choosing a team name, or the topic or format for a project) it is important that a strong positive team identity is developed prior to the lesson. For unstructured cooperative work, making team decisions, working on projects, and preparing presentations, it is important that students can communicate well, feel like they're on the same side with the same goals, and know how to work together. Teambuilding helps accomplish these objectives.

Selelcted Teambuilding Structures

- 4S Brainstorming
- Blind Sequencing
- Find-the-Fiction
- Formations
- Line-Ups
- Match Mine
- Pairs Compare
- RoundRobin
- RoundTable
- Same-Different
- Team Interview
- Team Projects
- Team Statements
- Three-Step Interview

If there is racial tension in the classroom, or if there is a wide discrepancy among the achievement levels of students, then extensive teambuilding is necessary. Generally, primary students show little hesitancy toward working together. It is a sad comment on traditional classroom structures: More years in school result in poorer social relations and an increased need for teambuilding.

Teambuilding Activities

When we plug content into a teambuilding structure, we have a teambuilding activity. However, not all teambuilding is limited to the use of teambuilding structures. There is a wide range of team-based activities we can do to meet our five aims of teambuilding.

The structures and activities presented below are organized using these five aims of teambuilding.

It is a sad comment on traditional classrooms: More years in school result in poorer social relations and an increased need for teambuilding.

1. Getting Acquainted

Structures and activities for students to get to know and like their teammates.

RoundRobin

RoundRobin is one of the simplest, yet most flexible, teambuilding structures. In a Timed RoundRobin, each teammate takes a turn sharing for a preset amount of time. (See page 6.33.) For the objective of getting acquainted, each teammate individually prepares, then shares something about themselves. The following are topics students can share to get better acquainted.

RoundRobin

My Autobiography. Students create their autobiographies as a book. The book has a cover page with a cute title like, "The Life and Times of…." or "My Life by…." Each page has a photograph or student illustrations of important life milestones and brief text. For this activity, there is no need for students to write detailed descriptions because the goal of the book is for teammates to share their autobiographies orally. After students each share their autobiographies with teammates, the books can be combined into a team book or kept separately to use for classbuilding activities, sharing autobiographies with other classmates.

The "Me" Bag. Each student is given a brown lunch bag. Their goal is to pack five items in their bag that best describes them. The items can be magazine clippings, student drawings, photographs, clay models, or any physical objects to represent the student's hobbies, characteristics, or whatever he/she chooses to share about him/herself. Students decorate the outside of the bag. During a Timed RoundRobin, students pull the items out one-by-one and describe what each item represents.

Weekend Suitcase. This is a variation of the "Me" Bag. Here, students pack in a shoebox five items that represent the things students will need for an ideal weekend. For example, a student may pack a scarf because she loves to ski, or a miniature shovel because she plans to go to the beach. In turn, each student unpacks her/his suitcase and describes what the items are and why she/he packed them.

My Family. Family is an important part of who we are. Students create a simple family tree and share family customs, a day in the life of the _____ family, or a weekend with the _____ family.

Me Collage. Students create a collage about themselves to share with teammates. Encourage students to bring in old magazines that they subscribe to because personal magazines will have many relevant pictures to use.

Kagan Cooperative Learning • Dr. Spencer Kagan & Miguel Kagan
Kagan Publishing • 1 (800) 933-2667 • www.KaganOnline.com

Map of My Mind. Students create a mind map of themselves to share with teammates. For example, Brian writes: "Brian's Brain" in the center of his paper. Using colors, symbols, bridges, arrows, words, and drawings, Brian maps out his mind in preparation for sharing his thoughts, likes, hopes and dreams with teammates.

Me Puppets. (For young students.) Little ones create sock puppets of themselves. They share three important facts about themselves.

This Is My Friend.

(For primary students.) Teammates sit in a circle. One child introduces a person to the rest of the group by saying, "This is my friend John," raising his friend's hand as he does so. The friend introduces the person on the left, and around they go. The person who began is the last to be introduced, and at that point everyone is holding their hand up. They stand and applaud.

Dream Car. Students in turn name their dream car and one reason why.

Ideal Vacation. Students say how they would spend a one-week dream vacation, all expenses paid.

I Am … Students each introduce themselves to the group. They use "I Am …."

I Would Be … Students say who they would be if they had to be an animal with a tail, a type of bird, or a vehicle.

Quality Initials. Students can develop a rhythm to chant information that will help them remember their names. My favorite format is Quality Initials, which has four steps:

Step 1. Teammates Create New Names. Team members work together to create new names using their initials and adjectives (Spencer Kagan becomes Specially Kind Spencer Kagan).

Step 2. Teammates Use New Names in Chant. Teammates practice these as a chant, initials first, then names, in a RoundRobin

(Everyone would say "Specially Kind Spencer Kagan; Daringly Jovial David Johnson, Lovely Knowledgeable Laurie Kagan; Bountifully Smart Bob Slavin….").

Step 3. Add Rhythm. Rhythm is added as students chant the name and put it to a beat or a clap.

Step 4. Add Movements. Kinesthetic movements may be added, according to favorite hobbies. Students make jogging movements for Dave, swimming motions for Spencer, skiing movements for Laurie, and book reading movements for Bob.

Question Cards. Each team has a stack of getting acquainted questions. They place the question stack in the center of their team table facedown. Each student draws one question card and reads it aloud to teammates. The reader responds. Then, the teammate to the left responds. After all students have responded to the same question, the next student draws the next card for the next round of responses. The About Me Question Cards blackline on the following page has ready-to-use questions.

My Favorites. Students fill out the My Favorites form (blackline provided on page 10.7). Students use RoundRobin to take turns stating their favorites and describing why.

Recommended Resources

Teambuilder Cube & Chips

Both the Learning Cube and Learning Chips have fun questions for getting to know, respect, and like teammates.

About Me
Question Cards

Instructions. Cut out the following question cards. Shuffle them and place them facedown in the center of your team table. One teammate turns over the top question and reads it aloud. Each teammate takes a turn responding. Then, the next teammate turns over the next question, and everyone takes a turn responding again. Continue until your team has responded to all the questions.

1. About Me
What are three things that you are thankful for?

6. About Me
What makes you really angry and why?

2. About Me
What is your favorite thing to do and why?

7. About Me
Who is your hero and how are you alike or different?

3. About Me
What is your nickname and how did you get it? If you don't have one, what nickname would you like and why?

8. About Me
Complete the following sentence: One thing not many people know about me is…

4. About Me
Describe your best friend.

9. About Me
If you could have anything you wanted for your birthday, what would it be and why?

5. About Me
When are you happiest and why?

10. About Me
What do you really enjoy doing with your family?

Kagan Cooperative Learning • Dr. Spencer Kagan & Miguel Kagan
Kagan Publishing • 1 (800) 933-2667 • www.KaganOnline.com

My Favorites

Instructions. Fill out your favorites and take turns sharing your favorites with your teammates.

Activities

Sport to Play _____

Sport to Watch _____

Hobby _____

Holiday _____

Nature

Flower _____

Tree _____

Animal _____

Food

Restaurant _____

Food _____

Drink _____

Dessert _____

School

School Subject _____

Teacher _____

People

Friend _____

Person _____

Preferences

Color _____

Car _____

Job _____

Place to Be _____

Time of the Day _____

Season _____

Transportation _____

Entertainment

Book _____

Author _____

Song _____

Band _____

Movie _____

Cartoon _____

TV Program _____

Turn Toss

Name Learning. There are dozens of ways to have students learn names. Turn Toss is one of my favorites. Below are the steps of a Turn Toss activity for name learning.

Step 1. Teammates Learn Names. One team member wads up a piece of paper, catches the eye of another student, and tosses the paper to him or her, saying, "Hi, my name is Spencer, what's yours?" The student catches the paper ball, and then says, "Hi, my name is Shlomo, what's yours?" as he tosses the paper to yet a third student. This proceeds for several tosses by each student. Hint: Students are told to make gentle, underhand tosses.

Step 2. Teammates Greet Each Other Using Names. After all students have introduced themselves several times in Step 1, they begin using the names. Ask students to use a name first to get another student's attention, and then give a greeting or compliment. A student catches Spencer's eye, tosses him the paper ball and says, "Spencer, glad to meet you." That student then says, "Shlomo, happy to be on a team with you." Or "Laurie, what a pretty bow you are wearing."

Step 3. Teammates Ask Each Other Questions. In the third round, the students use the names to ask questions, such as, "Spencer, do you like school?" "Shlomo, how long have you been in this country?" and so on. A possible rule: If you don't like a question, answer a question you wish someone had asked.

Turn Toss regulates turn taking and can be used as an information exchange structure as students quiz each other, practice math facts, or share ideas. The rule in Turn Toss is no "toss backs." That is, you can't toss to the person who tossed to you.

Team Interview

Each teammate takes a turn standing and is interviewed by teammates for a predetermined time. Team Interview is a great structure for getting acquainted. Hint: After presenting the interview topic, have students write out questions they'd like to ask in advance of the interview. Below are some of the best getting acquainted topics.

Who Are You? Students interview each other, asking questions to get to know their teammate better. Questions can be about the student's family, their likes, dislikes, what they do on the weekends, and favorite subject and foods. (See blackline on page 10.9.) This is a great open forum for students to get to know each other better. Of course, students have the option to pass on any question deemed too personal.

Where Have You Been? Interviews about where students have traveled, and where they would like to travel.

What Will You Be? Interviews about career and life goals.

Who Would You Be? If you could be someone from a story, novel or movie, who would it be? Why?

Team Interviews are very useful in cooperative learning and may be used for getting acquainted, but also are used at various places in the cooperative learning lesson such as establishing an anticipatory set, checking for understanding, and processing content and feelings following a lesson.

Who Are You?

Instructions. Write questions below to ask your teammates to get to know them better. Compare your questions with your teammates before the interview begins to make sure you have good, unique questions to ask.

Your Favorites

1. _____
_____
2. _____
_____

Your Family

1. _____
_____
2. _____
_____

Your Hobbies

1. _____
_____
2. _____
_____

Your Dislikes

1. _____
_____
2. _____
_____

Your Hopes or Dreams

1. _____
_____
2. _____
_____

Kagan Cooperative Learning • Dr. Spencer Kagan & Miguel Kagan
Kagan Publishing • 1 (800) 933-2667 • www.KaganOnline.com

10.9

Three-Step Interview

Three-Step Interview is another excellent structure to help teammates get acquainted. (See page 6.38.)

In Three-Step-Interview, students interview each other in pairs within the team. After pairs have both interviewed each other, they reunite with their teammates. They share what they learned from their partner via a RoundRobin. Each student takes a turn sharing. Three-Step Interview promotes active listening because students are individually accountable for sharing their partner's information with the team.

Three Questions. The teacher and/or students select three important questions for students to ask each other. In pairs, students ask each other the three questions and record their partner's answer. Using questions such as:

1. What is your favorite free-time activity?
2. If you could switch places with anyone for a day, who would you switch places with?
3. How would describe your personality to someone who's never met you before?

What's in a Name? Students interview each other regarding their names. How did they get their name? Is there an interesting family history associated with their name? Do they like their name? What would they be called if they could have another name? Do they have a nickname? Have their feelings about their name or nickname ever changed? What interesting experiences have they had associated with their name?

Outside of School. Students interview each other about what they do outside of school:

- What do you do right after school?
- What do you do in the evenings?
- What do you do on the weekend?
- What do you do during summertime?
- What do you do during the holiday break?

Flashcard Game

The Flashcard Game is excellent for memorizing facts. Usually it is played for content learning. For teambuilding, students use flashcards to learn facts about their teammates.

Teammate Profile. In this fun activity, teammate information becomes the curriculum to memorize. Each team receives two Teammate Profile Flashcards handouts (see blackline on next page). They cut apart one handout to create four flashcards. Each teammate fills in his/her own personal information on one flashcard. When all four teammates have filled out their information, they do a quick RoundRobin sharing their own profiles. A teammate records the information on a blank flashcard on the other form. After the sharing and recording, they cut apart the second form so they have two sets of flashcards. Students then pair up with another student on their team, and use a set of the profile flashcards to quiz each other. They play the three rounds of the Flashcard Game (see page 6.27). As they quiz each other it sounds like, "What is Kyle's last name? What does he like to be called? What is his favorite hobby?"

Team Project
Uncommon Commonalities. Students list as many uncommon commonalities as they can. Uncommon commonalities are things that team members have in common that make them unlike other teams. If all team members like ice cream, that is a common commonality; if they all like escargot, that is an uncommon commonality.

Have students look for uncommon commonalities along a number of dimensions—Favorites (foods, subjects, sports, hobbies); Travel (places they have been, or have not been); Family (number of members, kind of house); Cars, Pets, etc.

The search for uncommon commonalities serves not only to help students get acquainted, but also serves to build a team identity: "We are the team where everyone loves pineapple/coconut ice cream. We all love butterflies."

My favorite format for having teams find their uncommon commonalities is to use Team Windows.

Teammate Profile Flashcards

Teammate Name _____

Instructions. Each teammate fills in a profile card. Take turns sharing your own profile. On another copy, fill out your teammates' profiles to quiz each other.

Teammate 1

First Name _____

Last Name _____

Likes To Be Called _____

Favorite Hobby _____

Favorite Subject _____

Can Help With _____

Could Use Help With _____

Likes the Compliment _____

Favorite Team Celebration _____

_____

Teammate 2

First Name _____

Last Name _____

Likes To Be Called _____

Favorite Hobby _____

Favorite Subject _____

Can Help With _____

Could Use Help With _____

Likes the Compliment _____

Favorite Team Celebration _____

_____

Teammate 3

First Name _____

Last Name _____

Likes To Be Called _____

Favorite Hobby _____

Favorite Subject _____

Can Help With _____

Could Use Help With _____

Likes the Compliment _____

Favorite Team Celebration _____

_____

Teammate 4

First Name _____

Last Name _____

Likes To Be Called _____

Favorite Hobby _____

Favorite Subject _____

Can Help With _____

Could Use Help With _____

Likes the Compliment _____

Favorite Team Celebration _____

_____

Team Windows. Windows are one of many ways to have student teams sort information. The steps of Windows are as follows.

Step 1. Student Draws a Rectangle. A
student draws a rectangle in the center of a paper and passes the paper to the person on his/her left.

Step 2. Corner is Connected. The next
student draws a line from a corner of the rectangle to the corresponding corner of the paper (see box) and passes the paper.

Steps 3–5. All Corners are Connected. The
process is continued until all four corners of the window are connected to all four corners of the paper.

Step 6. Sections are Numbered. The four
sections are numbered: 1, 2, 3, and 4.

Step 7. Students Record Commonalities.
Each student is the recorder for each section. For example, only Student #1 is allowed to record in section 1, Student #2 in section 2. Students record characteristics according to how many of them have the characteristic in common. For example, Student #1 suggests something all students might have in common such as "Do we all like chocolate ice cream?" If all students do, Student #4 writes, "chocolate ice cream" in section 4, if only two do, Student #2 records it in section 2. Next, Student #2 suggests a possible commonality and it is recorded in the appropriate window. Students use RoundRobin each in turn, suggesting a characteristic they might have in common. Students search for things they all have in common, especially uncommon commonalities —qualities that might make them distinct from other teams.

Step 8. Team Names are Created. Based on
their commonalities, a team name is created and recorded in the center segment of the window. For example, a team whose members all like pistachio ice cream and who would love to visit Spain might name themselves the Spanish Pistachios. Team Windows can be posted or clipped together to create a Team Windows book.

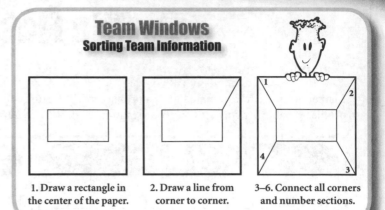

Team Windows
Sorting Team Information

1. Draw a rectangle in the center of the paper.

2. Draw a line from corner to corner.

3–6. Connect all corners and number sections.

Find-the-Fiction

To play Find-the-Fiction, students state two true facts and one fiction. See page 6.26. In turn they each stand and announce the three statements to their teammates, trying to fool them. Teammates come to consensus as to which one they believe is the fiction. If the teammates guess correctly the student stands, gives each teammate a pat on the back; if the teammates have been fooled, the teammate stands and turns around to receive a pat on the back from each teammate. Find-the-Fiction can be used with academic content on an occasional basis to spice up a review.

Life Facts. Teams play Find-the-Fiction with life facts. Each teammate writes three statements about themselves. Two are true, and one is a fiction. Teammates try to identify the fiction.

Fact-or-Fiction

Fact-or-Fiction is a variation Find-the-Fiction, also used on an occasional basis to spice up a review. In Fact-or-Fiction, students state either a true or false statement. It is up to teammates to decide if the statement is either a fact or fiction. Fact-or-Fiction is easier for young students because they need deal with only one statement at a time.

Life Fictions. Students tell either a believable fiction about themselves or reveal an unbelievable fact. It is up to their teammates to state whether they are hearing fact or fiction.

Individual Projects

Affirmative Passport. At the beginning of the school year, students make up a passport, including vital information about themselves such as date and place of birth, number of siblings, hobbies, favorite foods, likes, dislikes, places they have traveled to, times they have moved, taste in music, and a photo. These passports are available to share via RoundRobin, and for other students to browse through if they finish academic tasks early.

Teambuilding is the process of converting a heterogeneous group into a cohesive team. It is the process by which different students come to know, trust, and respect their teammmates.

2. Team Identity

Structures and activities for teammates to forge a unique team identity.

Who Are We?
Team Projects

1. Team Names. When teams are first formed, they are asked to make up a team mural that features their team name. Three simple rules for the group process are stated: 1) Each team member must have a say; 2) No decision can be reached unless everyone consents; 3) No member consents to the group decision if he or she has a serious objection. These rules set the tone for future group processes, which must include participation, consensus, and respect for individual rights.

The basis for the team name may be content (choosing the name of a planet during an astronomy unit), or may be personal preferences. Choosing team names can be facilitated by structure sequences. One sequence that works well is a RoundRobin to seek commonalities, coupled with Team Windows (see Team Windows box on page 10.12). Another sequence that works well is Jot Thoughts to generate possible names, followed by Sum-the-Ranks to choose the team name.

2. Team Hats. Paint stores sell inexpensive caps that are perfect for teams to decorate with the team colors. Alternatively, allow teams to make their own hats from assorted scrap material (styrofoam, corrugated cardboard, paper, newspaper, poster board, sequins, feathers, buttons) and fasteners (glue, staplers, tape, brads, clips).

Hats from one team are not necessarily identical, but they have at least one characteristic in common, distinguishing them from the hats of another team.

A fun twist: Tell students that they must connect the four team hats so they are all worn at once because four heads together are better than one, and we must practice putting our heads together!

3. Team Handshakes. Students develop a team handshake to celebrate team successes. The handshake can symbolize their team name or they can say or chant their name while doing the handshake. Below are three team handshakes to teach students.

Team Handshakes

Thumbs Up. One teammate puts a fist in the center of the table with a thumb up. Another teammate clenches a fist around the thumb and places his or her thumb up. The teammate on top keeps his or her thumb pointing up. The team lifts and drops their hands three times while they chant their team name three times and end with a positive expression: "Dolphins! Dolphins! Dolphins! Rule!" With the final superlative, they throw their hands in the air.

The Wave. Teammates interlock fingers on their right hands with the teammate on the right and interlock fingers on their left hands with the teammate on the left. One teammate starts the wave by rolling his or her hand, and the wave goes around the team multiple times while students chant a phrase.

Go Team. All teammates put a hand in the center of the team, stacking their hands palm down, one on top of another. They chant, "Goooooo Brainiacs (substitute team name)!"

---

4. Team Cheers. Team cheers are a great way for teammates to celebrate their successes. A simple, but effective team cheer is to have teams pick two adjectives and then repeat one three times and end with the other. For example, "Incredible…Incredible…Incredible…Great!" Cheers are also a great way for teammates to praise their teammates for a job well done. See the Team Cheers on the next page for great ideas for cheers teams can do together or one teammate can do for another. First we teach our class some of these cheers. We let them choose which ones they want to do in their teams.

Later we challenge them to modify these cheers and come up with their own. Team identity is enhanced any time a team creates a product unique to them that they are proud of.

5. Collage Cubes. Team collage cubes are made from an empty cardboard box, magazines (to cut out pictures and words) and colored paper. The box is covered with paper and then a collage of pictures and words that teammates paste on the cube to tell who they are. Starting with a shoe box, teams can create their own decorated team tub.

6. Team Scrapbooks. The team scrapbook is a place for teammates to record memories, draw pictures about team activities, and store rewards and team essays.

Additional Possibilities
7. **Team Banners**
8. **Team Logos**
9. **Team Mottoes**
10. **Team Monuments**
11. **Team Greetings**
12. **Team Colors**
13. **Team Puff-mobiles (made with drinking straws and beads for rolling)**
14. **Team Pipe Cleaner Inventions**
15. **Team Spaghetti Gum Drop Space Stations**
16. **Team Body Murals**
17. **Team T-Shirts**
18. **Team Murals**

Team Puzzles and Challenges
Team Projects

Team Word Finder. Students find words on a letter grid—large words are worth more points. See Team Word Finder blackline (on page 10.16).

Magic Number 11. In a circle, students hold out a clenched hand. They move their fists up and down three times while chanting "One, two, three." On the count of three, each student puts out a number of fingers. The team goal is to make their fingers add to 11. No talking is allowed. If teams finish early, they try another number. After each success, teammates give each other a pat on the back or do their team cheer and/or handshake.

Team Cheers

Instructions. Teach students these fun team cheers to celebrate class and team successes.

Alaska Hurray. Students (Eskimos) wrap their arms around themselves as if they are freezing cold and shiver out, "Brrrrrrr …," then they complete the cheer by saying, "… illiant," throwing their arms in the air.

Brain Kiss. Students kiss the fingers on their open right hands and transfer the kiss to their brains by tapping their foreheads with the kissed hand. They finish the kiss with a flair by throwing the kissed hand in the air.

Cheese Cheer. Students (chefs) hold a block of cheese in one hand and a cheese grater in the other. They slide the cheese against their graters five times while they say, "Grate, grate, grate, grate, grate job!"

Excellent. Students make an X in front of their chests with their arms twice as they say, "Excellent. Excellent."

Fantastic. Students squirt window cleaning agent in a circle on an imaginary pane of glass. They wipe the cleaner off in a circular motion with their open palms as they say, "Faaaaantastic!"

Fireworks. Students push their palms together in front of their chests and raise their palms above their heads, imitating a firework shooting into the sky, complete with a "whooooosh" sound. When the firework reaches its highest point of ascent, they clap their hands above their heads, snap their fingers, and wiggle their facedown fingers as they slowly lower their hands.

Golfer's Clap. Students (the golf gallery) clap just the index fingers of their hands together making a very quiet clap.

Ketchup Applause. Students (diners) hold an imaginary bottle of ketchup upside down in a closed right fist. With their left hand, they pat the bottom of the bottle to help the ketchup come out. Each pat makes a deep clapping sound.

Raise the Roof. Students (party people) place their hands in the air with their palms facing upward, and they pump the roof upward three times with a "whoooo, whoooo, whoooo" noise.

Rodeo Roundup. Students (cowpokes) twirl their lassos over their heads, cast it around an imaginary calf, and pull it in all the while saying, "Weeeeee, got it!"

Roller Coaster. Students place both hands in front of their chests, palms down. They make a roller coaster climbing noise, "Chhh, chhh, chhh" as their roller coaster hands climb the track skyward. When the roller coaster reaches the top, they quickly lower both hands down, then back up like a roller coaster descending and climbing back up again. During descent, some prefer to make a "weeee" sound as if riding the roller coaster, while others prefer a whooshing sound like the roller coaster makes.

Round of Applause. Students clap their hands, making a giant round circle in front of themselves.

Seal of Approval. Students (seals) clap their flippers in front of their chests while they bark out a seal-sounding, "Great, great, great, great."

Silent Applause. Students make a clapping motion, but stop just short of actually clapping.

Sparkles. Students wave their hands in front of them as they snap the fingers on both hands for about ten snaps.

Truck Driver. Students (truckers) put their hands on the steering wheel of their pretend big rigs. They reach their left hand up and pull the cord of their air horns and let out two throaty honking roars, "honk, honk!" Then they reach up with their right hand for their walkie talkies and speak into them, "Chhhsshhh. Good job, good buddy. Chhhsshhh."

Two Snaps and a Clap. Students snap the fingers on both hands twice and clap once.

Western Wahoo. Students (cowpokes) drum out the sound of horse hoofs on their desks. Then they take off their hats and wave them in the air with a "Yeeehaw!"

Team Spiral handshake

drjean.org for more cheers

Kagan Cooperative Learning • Dr. Spencer Kagan & Miguel Kagan
Kagan Publishing • 1 (800) 933-2667 • www.KaganOnline.com

10.15

Team Word Finder

Rules for Creating Words. Words are created from the letter grid below. To create a word, each letter must connect to the next letter by a side or corner. No letter box may be used twice for the same word.

Scoring Words. Each word is worth the square of the number of letters it contains. A 1-letter word is worth 1 point (1 x 1). A 4-letter word is worth 16 points (4 x 4).

Team Goal. Make as many points as possible in 4 minutes. Teammates take turns finding and recording each new word.

Team Word Finder

T	I	N	E	I
R	E	I	A	K
D	E	A	E	R
H	L	T	M	O
I	D	U	E	W

Kagan Cooperative Learning • Dr. Spencer Kagan & Miguel Kagan
Kagan Publishing • 1 (800) 933-2667 • www.KaganOnline.com

Team Sentences. Teammates build sentences using sentence chips. (See Team Sentences blackline on the next page).

Finding Rectangles. Have teams figure out how many rectangles there are in a three by three square. If they solve that one, let them work on a four by four square. (See Finding Rectangles blackline on page 10.19).

Team Shelters. Each team makes its own shelter from newspapers and masking tape. The shelter must be big enough for all members to keep dry in an imaginary rainstorm. Hint: Tent-like structures are relatively easy to make if poles are made from rolled-up newspapers.

Team Towers. Teams are told to make any kind of tower they wish from one piece of construction paper, scissors, and ten paper clips. All teams celebrate the uniqueness of each team tower. Assigning social roles can help: One person checks for agreement before any cuts are made, another does the cutting, another is the only one to touch the paper clips, and a fourth is the cheerleader responsible to make sure the team stops occasionally to celebrate its progress to that point.

Team Constructions. Remember how fun it was as a kid to build structures out of wooden blocks (unless you had that sibling bent on knocking your masterpiece down before you were done)? No one is too old for building those cool constructions.

And it's even more fun to do it as a team. Have students build and later describe, present, or write about their structure.

Possible Building Materials
- Craft sticks
- Legos®
- Lincoln Logs
- Foam blocks
- Wood blocks
- Playing cards
- Dominoes
- Toothpicks

Things to Build as a Team
- Space station
- Team clubhouse
- Tower
- Bridge
- Vehicle
- Free choice

Little Riddles. Teams create two-word rhymes and turn them into riddles. Some examples:

Riddle: What is an immobile large vehicle?
Answer: A "Stuck Truck."

Riddle: What is another name for a bee?
Answer: A "Nectar Collector."

Riddle: What do you call butter when you put it on toast?
Answer: "Bread Spread."

(See Little Riddles blackline on page 10.20.)

Team Sentences

Instructions. Cut out the word chips and spread them face-up in front of your team. Your goal as a team is to create and record sentences. First create a two-word sentence. Next, a three-word sentence. Then four words, and so on. Every teammate may contribute ideas, but only one teammate may touch the word chips for each new sentence. The person on the right of the Sentence Builder records the sentence.

the	is	a	an	the	but	and	to
yet	also	with	off	on	up
down	i	you	we	he	she	his
her	very	pretty	excellent
fast	clever	loud	fuzzy	cute
awesome	red	team	school
bike	car	shirt	shoes	friend
boy	girl	man	teacher	park
zoo	beach	is	was	has	skate
run	jump	fly	walk	see	go

Kagan Cooperative Learning • Dr. Spencer Kagan & Miguel Kagan
Kagan Publishing • 1 (800) 933-2667 • www.KaganOnline.com

Finding Rectangles

Instructions. How many rectangles can you find in the grids below? In your team, take turns finding each new rectangle. See if you can find them all!

3 x 3 Grid

4 x 4 Grid

Sponge Activity

Draw a 5 x 5 grid on the back of this sheet. As a team, find all the rectangles you can.

Little Riddles

Instructions. Little Riddles are questions whose answers are two-word rhymes.
For example: **Question:** What do you call a cooperative team member? **Answer:** Great Teammate.

Step 1.

Create Rhymes. To come up with two-word rhymes, each teammate takes a turn writing a noun in the first column. When you have your list of nouns, as a team come up with as many rhyming words as possible. Take turns writing the rhyming words in the second column.

Noun	Rhyming Words
1. _____	_____
	_____
2. _____	_____
	_____
	_____
3. _____	_____
	_____
4. _____	_____
	_____

Step 2.

Write Questions. Write your best two-word rhymes from above in the first column below, then come up with its riddle question. If your rhyme is Funny Money, the riddle might be, "What did the clown have in his wallet?"

Two-Word Rhyming Answer	Riddle
1. _____	_____
	_____
2. _____	_____
	_____
	_____
3. _____	_____
	_____
4. _____	_____
	_____

Famous Two-Word Rhymes and Their Meanings

Bed head — morning hairdo
Big rig — 18 wheeler
Big wig — important person
Boob tube — television
Chick flick — movie for women
Double trouble — mischievous pair
Funny money — counterfeit money
Hob nob — to socialize
Hodge podge — mishmash
Hoity toity — pretentious, snooty
Hocus pocus — magical incantation
Holy moly! — exclamation
Hot shot — a showoff
Itty bitty — small (also eensie weensie or teenie weenie)
Late great — former
Loosey goosey — freeform
Okey dokey — OK
Ooey gooey — slimy
Plain Jane — ordinary female
Rinky dink — cheap
Shock jock — outrageous radio host
Steer clear — avoid
Super duper — excellent
Tex-Mex — Texan/Mexican style
Wild child — undisciplined youth
Zoot suit — flashy suit of the '40s

Sponge Activity
Come up with as many Little Riddles as possible and submit them to your teacher for your class's Rhyme Time book.

RoundTable and RoundRobin

RoundTable and RoundRobin are extremely important cooperative learning structures. In essence, students take turns contributing to the group—in an oral form for RoundRobin and in a written form for RoundTable. For RoundTable, there is usually one piece of paper and one pen for the team. One student makes a contribution and then passes the paper and pen to the student on his or her left. The paper or pen literally goes around the table, thus the name: RoundTable. If the contributions are oral rather than written, it is called RoundRobin.

RoundTable can be used repeatedly in many subject areas, at a variety of places in the lesson plan. RoundTable can be used to create an anticipatory set for a lesson, to check for acquisition of information, or to liven up drill and practice. Below are some RoundTable teambuilding ideas.

Making Words. Teams make as many words as they can from a word or phrase. Team name, the school name, and the teacher's name are fun to use. Here are some other teambuilding words and phrases to use:

- Teamwork
- Our Team
- Teammates
- Cooperation
- Awesome Team

(See Making Words blackline on page 10.22.)

Alphabetical List. Teammates take turns writing a list of items for a specific topic or theme. The trick is the list is created in alphabetical order. For example, if the topic is foods, the first person writes Apple, second person Banana, next comes Candy. Here's some fun teambuilding topics:

- Foods
- Cartoons
- Movies
- Fun places to go
- Animal names
- Jobs

Change-A-Letter. Change one letter at a time in a core word and see what evolves (first person writes FUN, next writes FAN, next FAT, next SAT….).

Team Lists. Teammates take turns creating a list. The list can be on just about any topic: ice cream flavors, junk food snacks, cars, four-legged animals, equivalent fractions, synonyms….

Brainstorming

Any task that has many possible solutions may be set up for Brainstorming. Some possible topics: What are all the ways we could improve this school? This class? This world? What are all the ways we could solve the noise problem in this class? What are all the things we could put in a time capsule for the next generation of students your age?

Uses for a Belt. Teammates brainstorm and record all the ways they could use a belt if they were stranded on an island.

Send-A-Problem Paper Puzzles. Each team makes a picture or writes a message. They rip the paper with curved rips (by turning the paper as they rip) into about eight pieces. They send the pieces to the next team as a jigsaw puzzle to solve. When they are done, they send it to another team so the puzzles are sent around the room.

Pizza Parlor. Each team draws a Pizza Parlor menu complete with prices for mini, small, medium, large, and extra large pizzas. They make up problems to send to another group to solve. For example: The Jones family bought one extra large pizza with three toppings and paid with a $100 bill. What change should they receive?

Making Words

Instructions. As a team, see how many words you can make out of the letters in the phrase, **OUR TEAM IS AWESOME**. Everyone can come up with the words. Take turns recording the words on the list below.

1. _____
2. _____
3. _____
4. _____
5. _____
6. _____
7. _____
8. _____
9. _____
10. _____
11. _____
12. _____
13. _____
14. _____
15. _____
16. _____
17. _____
18. _____
19. _____
20. _____
21. _____
22. _____

23. _____
24. _____
25. _____
26. _____
27. _____
28. _____
29. _____
30. _____
31. _____
32. _____
33. _____
34. _____
35. _____
36. _____

37. _____
38. _____
39. _____
40. _____
41. _____
42. _____
43. _____
44. _____
45. _____
46. _____
47. _____
48. _____
49. _____
50. _____
51. _____
52. _____
53. _____
54. _____
55. _____
56. _____
57. _____
58. _____

Sponge Activity

Make words out of the phrase, **COOPERATIVE LEARNING**.

Kagan Cooperative Learning • Dr. Spencer Kagan & Miguel Kagan
Kagan Publishing • 1 (800) 933-2667 • www.KaganOnline.com

Same-Different

Same-Different is a barrier communication game in which pairs of students each look at a pair of pictures that are the same in some ways and different in others. For Teambuilding, students can make up Same-Different material for other teams to play. The process is easy: Two copies of any picture are made, and white-out is used to take out five different details on each copy. A black pen is then used to put in five different details on each copy. The resulting blackline masters contain twenty things that are different. The blackline masters are each copied on a different color paper to make a Same-Different game. Students have fun as a team making up the materials and then playing the game provided by another team. See Same-Different blacklines on the following pages.

"A rope of three strands is not easily parted."
—Malay proverb

3. Mutual Support

Structures and activities for teammates to feel mutual support—on the same side, encouraging and appreciating each other's efforts.

Many of these ideas are taken from *Silly Sports & Goofy Games*.[3]

Team Activities

Clapping Game. The clapping game is an all-time favorite. One teammate tries to find an object in the room the other teammates have selected. Clapping escalates as the teammate gets closer. Here's how it works.

Step 1. Teammate Steps Out. One person from each team steps out of the room.

Step 2. Teammates Pick Object. The remaining teammates agree on an object somewhere in the room that the teammate can touch. The object cannot be a person or on a person.

Step 3. Search Begins. Students outside return to their teams. They begin simultaneously searching for the object their teammates have chosen. The teammates clap louder and faster as their team member approaches the selected object.

Step 4. Teammates Cheer. When the team member touches the object, the team stands up, gives a cheer, and welcomes the searcher back to the team.

Blind Caterpillar. Teammates stand in a line, each with their hands on the shoulders of the person in front of them. The leader has his or her eyes open, and leads the others who keep their eyes closed. The leader talks to the teammates while leading them around the room, telling them where they are in the room and providing support. At intervals, the teacher calls "Switch!" and the person in front goes to the back. This activity produces feelings of trust. After each student has been a leader, teammates return to their seats and reflect on how they felt as the leader and as a follower. A variation has the leader with eyes closed and the three teammates with eyes open, leading from behind.

Blind Walk. One student closes his/her eyes while a teammate takes him/her on a tour of the room. The student "shows" them things in the room through the sense of touch—placing their hand on objects while describing the objects. After several minutes, students switch roles. Afterwards, teammates discuss how they felt giving and receiving care.

Care Lift. Two teams pair up. One student from one team lies down and closes his or her eyes. The remaining seven gather around to lift the student. One student carefully lifts the student's head, making sure it stays parallel with the body. Teammates take turns receiving the care lift. Team members gently lift the individual, rock him/her, and return him/her to the ground.

It is very important to emphasize that Care Lift is a very gentle exercise. The teammates are lifted so gently and gradually that they cannot tell when they have left the ground, how high they are, and when they are about to touch the ground again.

For safety, pillows may be used. Students can be on their knees around the person on the pillows and the Care Lift can be only one or two feet high. This variation is recommended for young participants; for them pillows are a must.

Same-Different

Picture 1

Instructions. Work in pairs. No peeking at your partner's picture. Find and record as many differences and similarities as you can between Picture 1 and Picture 2.

Same-Different

Picture 2

Instructions. Work in pairs. No peeking at your partner's picture. Find and record as many differences and similarities as you can between Picture 1 and Picture 2.

Square Balances. In teams of four, students experience mutual support by literally supporting each other during various balance activities. First, try the Blossoming Flower. Students form a circle, facing each other and holding hands. Students place their feet together. Keeping their bodies straight, they slowly lean backward on their heels, supporting each other. The group opens up like a blossoming flower. Next, try Back-to-Back: Students stand in a circle facing outward. They place their backs together and take small steps outward until they are all supporting each other. Before you set teams off to invent their own balances, you may like to lead them in Teepee: Students stand in a circle facing each other. They place their right hands in, palms touching above their heads. They slowly step back with their bodies, without bending at the waist, until they are all supporting each other.

Thank-You Cards

Greeting cards are a symbol of affection. We express our thoughts about and best wishes for others on the cards we exchange for every occasion: birthdays, anniversaries, holidays. No greeting card is more appropriate and more appreciated by a teammate than a simple thank-you card. Students use the Thank-You Card blackline (on the next page) or create their own cards to give to teammates. To ensure no student is left out, students may create a thank-you card for each teammate.

Team Formations

Letters, Shapes, Actions. There are many possible formations. Ask teams to shape letters or numbers by holding hands. They can become a common kitchen appliance, a silent jazz band with all the motions, or express a feeling.

> *"If two people have the same opinion, one is unnecessary... I don't want to talk, to communicate with someone who agrees with me; I want to communicate with you because you see it differently. I value that difference."*
> —Stephen Covey, *The 7 Habits of Highly Effective People*

4. Valuing Differences

Structures and activities for teammates to clarify their values, learn to understand and respect the values of others, and feel their own values are understood and respected.

Value Lines

Where Do I Stand? Students mark their position on a set of value lines indicating their preferences. (See blacklines: I Am, and I Prefer on page 10.28.) Later, students discuss their responses with their teams to discover and appreciate individual differences.

What Values Are Most Important?

Teammates rank what they value from most to least important. The values include the following: world peace, family security, happiness, excitement, helping others, inner harmony, salvation, wisdom, personal wealth, and health. In a second activity, teammates rank how they most want to be using adjectives: honest, loving, smart, adventurous, cooperative, independent, talented, attractive, successful, and creative. After working with the values, students share and celebrate their uniqueness as revealed by their differences. (See blacklines, What Do You Value? and How Do You Most Want to Be? on page 10.29.)

Team Projects

You Have to Have a Heart. Teams must make a crucial decision. They are to assign priority numbers to five patients on a waiting list for a heart transplant. A brief description of each prospective patient is included. (See blackline: You Have to Have a Heart on page 10.30.)

To reach the decision, first each student ranks the potential recipients. Next, students discuss their rankings and attempt to come to consensus.

Thank-You Card

Instructions. Write a thank-you message to your teammate on the lines provided. Cut along the dashed line and fold on the solid line ❶ first, then on solid line ❷. Give your teammate your token of appreciation.

Thank You

Thank You

❶ Fold Here First

Thank you for...

❷ Fold Here Second

I Am . . .

Instructions. Mark each line closest to the word that best describes you. Share your response with teammates and describe your answer.

Fast ←————————————→ Slow

Thinker ←————————————→ Doer

Listener ←————————————→ Talker

Leader ←————————————→ Follower

Morning Person ←————————————→ Night Person

Indoor Person ←————————————→ Outdoor Person

I Prefer . . .

Instructions. Mark each line closest to the word that best describes you. Share your response with teammates and describe your answer.

Adventure Movies ←————————————→ Comedies

Ice Cream ←————————————→ Cake

Airplanes ←————————————→ Boats

Sports Cars ←————————————→ Luxury Cars

Beaches ←————————————→ Mountains

Dogs ←————————————→ Cats

Kagan Cooperative Learning • Dr. Spencer Kagan & Miguel Kagan
Kagan Publishing • 1 (800) 933-2667 • www.KaganOnline.com

What Do You Value?

Instructions. Circle a number next to each value corresponding to how you rank-order these 10 values for yourself. 1 = value most; 10 = value least. After you have rank-ordered your list, take turns sharing your list with teammates and why you ranked the values as you did.

1.	World Peace	1	2	3	4	5	6	7	8	9	10
2.	Family Security	1	2	3	4	5	6	7	8	9	10
3.	Happiness	1	2	3	4	5	6	7	8	9	10
4.	Excitement	1	2	3	4	5	6	7	8	9	10
5.	Helping Others	1	2	3	4	5	6	7	8	9	10
6.	Inner Harmony	1	2	3	4	5	6	7	8	9	10
7.	Salvation	1	2	3	4	5	6	7	8	9	10
8.	Wisdom	1	2	3	4	5	6	7	8	9	10
9.	Personal Wealth	1	2	3	4	5	6	7	8	9	10
10.	Health	1	2	3	4	5	6	7	8	9	10

How Do You Most Want to Be?

Instructions. Circle a number next to each adjective to rank-order how you most want to be. 1 = most want to be; 10 = least want to be. After you have rank-ordered your list, take turns sharing your list with teammates and why you ranked the adjectives as you did.

1.	Honest	1	2	3	4	5	6	7	8	9	10
2.	Loving	1	2	3	4	5	6	7	8	9	10
3.	Smart	1	2	3	4	5	6	7	8	9	10
4.	Adventurous	1	2	3	4	5	6	7	8	9	10
5.	Cooperative	1	2	3	4	5	6	7	8	9	10
6.	Independent	1	2	3	4	5	6	7	8	9	10
7.	Talented	1	2	3	4	5	6	7	8	9	10
8.	Attractive	1	2	3	4	5	6	7	8	9	10
9.	Successful	1	2	3	4	5	6	7	8	9	10
10.	Creative	1	2	3	4	5	6	7	8	9	10

You Have to Have a Heart

Instructions. You are one of the members of the City Hospital Judicial Board and must make a crucial decision. Individually, you assign priority numbers to 5 patients on a waiting list for a heart transplant. Next, the Judicial Board (your team) meets to achieve consensus (1 = first in line; 5 = last in line).

Step 1.

Individual Ranking. Working alone, you make a priority ranking of the 5 patients waiting for a heart transplant.

Step 2.

Board Meeting. After you and the remainder of the Judicial Board (your teammates) have completed your own priority ranking, you have a meeting. You work together to finalize the priority ranking. The rule is before you can express your opinion, you must validate the thoughts or feelings of another member, even if they differ from your own.

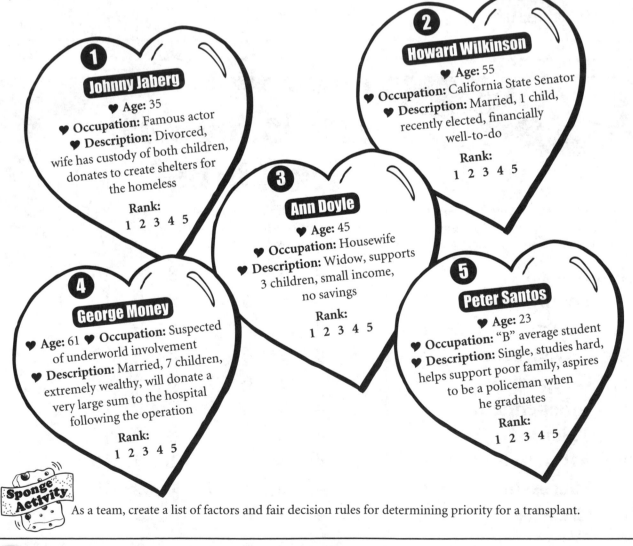

1 Johnny Jaberg
- **Age:** 35
- **Occupation:** Famous actor
- **Description:** Divorced, wife has custody of both children, donates to create shelters for the homeless

Rank: 1 2 3 4 5

2 Howard Wilkinson
- **Age:** 55
- **Occupation:** California State Senator
- **Description:** Married, 1 child, recently elected, financially well-to-do

Rank: 1 2 3 4 5

3 Ann Doyle
- **Age:** 45
- **Occupation:** Housewife
- **Description:** Widow, supports 3 children, small income, no savings

Rank: 1 2 3 4 5

4 George Money
- **Age:** 61 **Occupation:** Suspected of underworld involvement
- **Description:** Married, 7 children, extremely wealthy, will donate a very large sum to the hospital following the operation

Rank: 1 2 3 4 5

5 Peter Santos
- **Age:** 23
- **Occupation:** "B" average student
- **Description:** Single, studies hard, helps support poor family, aspires to be a policeman when he graduates

Rank: 1 2 3 4 5

Sponge Activity As a team, create a list of factors and fair decision rules for determining priority for a transplant.

Kagan Cooperative Learning • Dr. Spencer Kagan & Miguel Kagan
Kagan Publishing • 1 (800) 933-2667 • www.KaganOnline.com

Lost on the Moon
Scoring Guide

NASA Scientists' Rank

Item	Rank
Box of matches	1 2 3 4 5 6 7 8 9 10 11 12 13 14 ⑮
Food concentrate	1 2 3 ④ 5 6 7 8 9 10 11 12 13 14 15
50 feet of nylon rope	1 2 3 4 5 ⑥ 7 8 9 10 11 12 13 14 15
Parachute silk	1 2 3 4 5 6 7 ⑧ 9 10 11 12 13 14 15
Portable heating unit	1 2 3 4 5 6 7 8 9 10 11 12 ⑬ 14 15
Two .45 caliber pistols	1 2 3 4 5 6 7 8 9 10 ⑪ 12 13 14 15
Case of dehydrated milk	1 2 3 4 5 6 7 8 9 10 11 ⑫ 13 14 15
Two 100-pound tanks of oxygen	① 2 3 4 5 6 7 8 9 10 11 12 13 14 15
Stellar map (moon's constellation)	1 2 ③ 4 5 6 7 8 9 10 11 12 13 14 15
Life raft	1 2 3 4 5 6 7 8 ⑨ 10 11 12 13 14 15
Magnetic compass	1 2 3 4 5 6 7 8 9 10 11 12 13 ⑭ 15
5 gallons of water	1 ② 3 4 5 6 7 8 9 10 11 12 13 14 15
Signal flares	1 2 3 4 5 6 7 8 9 ⑩ 11 12 13 14 15
First-aid kit with injection needles	1 2 3 4 5 6 ⑦ 8 9 10 11 12 13 14 15
Solar-powered FM receiver-transmitter	1 2 3 4 ⑤ 6 7 8 9 10 11 12 13 14 15

Scoring

For each item, find the difference between your ranking and NASA's ranking number. Add these differences. The smaller your difference, the closer you are to the experts. Also do this for the team rankings. Compare accuracy of the individual predictions and group prediction.

Example	Your Ranking	NASA's Ranking	Difference
Box of matches	8	15	7
Food Concentrate	1	4	3

Explanation

These are the answers supplied by the NASA scientists. The answers are split into two groups—physical survival and traveling to the rendezvous.

The first two items are air and water, without which you cannot survive at all. After that comes the map for locating position and figuring out how to get to the rendezvous. Food comes next for strength on the trip. It is not as necessary for survival as air and water.

The FM receiver-transmitter is for keeping in touch with Earth. In a vacuum, without the ionosphere, radio transmission travels only in line of sight and would be limited on the moon to a destination of approximately ten miles. On Earth, powerful receivers could pick up messages, which would then be relayed to the mother ship. The next item would be the rope for lunar mountain climbing and traversing crevasses on the trip. The next item would be the first aid kit for injuries. Parachute silk would offer excellent protection from sunlight and heat buildup.

The life raft is a carry-all for supplies (the moon's gravity permits heavy loads to be carried), a shelter, and a possible stretcher for the injured. It also offers protection from micro-meteorite showers.

Flares cannot burn in a vacuum, but they, and the pistols, can be shot. Flares and guns would therefore be excellent propulsive devices for flying over obstructions. The milk is heavy and relatively less valuable.

On the moon, overheating is a problem, and it is not cold. Thus the heating unit is useless.

The magnetic compass is useless without a map of the moon's magnetic field.

The box of matches is the most useless item.

Kagan Cooperative Learning • Dr. Spencer Kagan & Miguel Kagan
Kagan Publishing • 1 (800) 933-2667 • www.KaganOnline.com

10.35

Team Statements

Team Statements is a structure explicitly designed to release the power of synergy. In Team Statements, teammates first make a statement working alone, next share and validate each individual statement, and then work together to synthesize into one Team Statement the best ideas contained in the individual statements. Team Statements is not stringing beads and creating one long run-on sentence; it is finding the place from which the individual statements sprang— discovering a more essential truth. Through Team Statements, students construct their conceptual knowledge. For example, if we have students do a Team Statement on "Democracy is…" they end up wrestling with and finding the essence of that concept and deepen their understanding of democracy. Team Statements are powerful on many topics. During Valentine's Day, students have small hearts on which they write their definition, "Love is…" and then a large team heart on which they put their Team Statement. We post the large heart with the small hearts around it. Usually the students like their Team Statement more than their own individual statement, demonstrating synergy.

My favorite example of this process came at the end of a five-day cooperative learning workshop. As one of the concluding events, I had teams do a Team Statement on "Cooperative Learning is…." One of the teams had a very simple Team Statement:

Cooperative Learning = Learning^4

When they read their statement, it was "Cooperative Learning equals learning to the fourth power." What is interesting is that no individual statement had anything like the final Team Statement. Through interaction, the team had come closer to what they felt was the essence of cooperative learning.

RoundTable Consensus

RoundTable Consensus

In RoundTable Consensus, students cannot write a response or make a contribution to the team project unless they all agree. This structure releases synergy because one student may have one idea; another student has a different idea and the structure requires that they reach consensus. In the process, they find something with which they all agree. Often the result is a higher-level synthesis, incorporating the best of everyone's input into a new, more differentiated idea. For teambuilding, use RoundTable Consensus to have teams build a team project or write a team story.

Pairs Compare

Pairs Compare is yet another structure that releases synergy. Using RallyTable in pairs, students create a list. The pairs then compare their lists. They add ideas the other pair generated to their own lists. The last step challenges the team to find new ideas—ideas that neither pair had come up with when working alone. Because each pair brought different ideas to the table, when those ideas interact it releases new energy and teams discover ideas neither pair alone could find. Through synthesis, there is a release of energy—the essence of synergy. For teambuilding, use Pairs Compare to have teams brainstorm on fun topics such as field trip ideas, dessert concoctions, or coolest superpowers.

Becoming A Teamplayer

World-class athletes, coaches, and managers tout the importance of teamwork.

Michael, if you can't pass, you can't play.
—Dean Smith, Coach to Michael Jordan in his freshman year at UNC–Chapel Hill

The strength of the team is each individual member...the strength of each member is the team.
—Phil Jackson, Chicago Bulls Coach

Individual commitment to a group effort—that is what makes a team work, a company work, a society work, a civilization work.
—Vince Lombardi, football Coach for the NFL

Gettin' good players is easy. Gettin' 'em to play together is the hard part.
—Casey Stengel, New York Yankees Manager during 5 straight world championships

Talent wins games, but teamwork and intelligence wins championships.
—Michael Jordan, basketball legend

"The way a team plays as a whole determines its success. You may have the greatest bunch of individual stars in the world, but if they don't play together, the club won't be worth a dime."
—Babe Ruth, baseball legend

When you're part of a team, you stand up for your teammates. Your loyalty is to them. You protect them through good and bad, because they'd do the same for you.
—Yogi Berra, baseball All Star, Coach, and Manager

The era of the rugged individual is giving way to the era of the team player. Everyone is needed, but no one is necessary.
—Bruce Coslet, Cincinnati Bengals Coach

Chapter Summary

Teambuilding is an investment. We invest a little classroom time for teambuilding structures and activities. Through teambuilding, students get to know, like, and respect their teammates. In the process, we convert a group of virtual strangers into a powerful learning team. Students from different social groups, races, sexes, abilities, and backgrounds come together as a team with a shared identity and with shared goals: to achieve and to help each other achieve.

Is it surprising to see students who would very unlikely choose each other as teammates be sad when it's time to form new teams? Not really when we think about it. Student teams meet some of students' most important needs: to feel known; to feel liked; to feel accepted; to feel a sense of belonging; to be successful. We feel a natural affinity to those who meet our needs, make us feel good about ourselves, and with whom we share intimate details and experiences. When students' deep-seated social needs are met, they are free to focus on academics. And that they do. They learn in a mutually supportive, cooperative team environment.

Teambuilding is an investment. Some people invest in stocks, bonds, commodities, or real estate in hopes of becoming rich. With teambuilding, we invest in our students. And that's never a poor investment!

? Chapter Questions

▶ Questions for Review

1. What are the five aims of teambuilding?
2. How often is teambuilding recommended?
3. What are some ways for students to get acquainted with their teammates?
4. How can we help students feel like they are part of the team?
5. Describe a synergy activity. How does it create synergy?

▶ Questions for Thinking and Discussion

1. Of the five aims of teambuilding, which one do you feel is most important?
2. Would you take time off academics to do purely fun teambuilding activities, or would you only integrate teambuilding into your academic lessons? Explain.
3. Do you feel teambuilding is 1) essential, 2) helpful, or 3) unnecessary? Describe your position.
4. Teambuilding has become a mainstay of the business world. What is happening in the work world to make teambuilding more frequent? More necessary?
5. If every teacher did teambuilding in heterogeneous teams, we would dramatically reduce the barriers that keep us divided as a nation. Do you agree or disagree? Why?
6. Different teambuilding activities reach different teambuilding aims. How can you schedule your teambuilding activities to ensure you are achieving all the goals of teambuilding?

References

[1] Kagan, L., M. Kagan & S. Kagan. *Cooperative Learning Structures for Teambuilding*. San Clemente, CA: Kagan Publishing, 1997.

[2] Kagan, S. *Silly Sports & Goofy Games*. San Clemente, CA: Kagan Publishing, 2000.

[3] Kagan, S. *Silly Sports & Goofy Games*. San Clemente, CA: Kagan Publishing, 2000.

Resources

Farnette, C., I. Forte & B. Loss. *I've Got Me and I'm Glad*. Nashville, TN: Incentive Publications, Inc., 1989.

Gregson, B. *Take Part Art*. Carthage, IL: Fearon Teacher Aids, 1991.

Johnson, D. & F. Johnson. *Joining Together: Group Theory and Group Skills*. Englewood Cliffs, NJ: Prentice Hall, 1975.

Macmillan, M. *Good Endings Make Good Beginnings*. Carthage, IL: Good Apple, Inc., 1989.

Schwartz, L. *Month to Month Me*. Santa Barbara, CA: The Learning Works, 1976.

Schwartz, L. *Think On Your Feet*. Santa Barbara, CA: The Learning Works, Inc., 1989.

Shaw, V. *Communitybuilding*. San Clemente, CA: Kagan Publishing, 1991.

Stanish, B. *The Ambidextrous Mind*. Carthage, IL: Good Apple, 1989.

Teambuilding Chips. San Clemente, CA: Kagan Publishing. www.KaganOnline.com

Teambuilder Cube. San Clemente, CA: Kagan Publishing. www.KaganOnline.com

Trend Enterprises. *Story Starters: We Need Friends*. St.Paul, MN: Trend Enterprises, 1990.

Trovato, C. *Teaching Kids to Care*. Cleveland, OH: Instructor Books, 1987.

Key 6
Social Skills

When cooperative learning teams fail, it is likely to be for one of two reasons. Either students do not want to work together or do not know how to work together. Cooperative learning teams have problems either because the students lack the will to work together or the skill to work together.

Today's youth often come to the classroom ill-prepared to be a good teammate. Cooperative learning empowers us to develop students' social skills that serve them in the classroom and beyond.

Will to Work Together

A lack of desire to work together, resistance to being part of a team, is usually overcome by teambuilding. When we first assign students to groups, we intentionally assign them to work with others they would be least likely to choose on their own. If students could group themselves, they would self-segregate themselves along the lines of race, achievement, interest, and gender. By assigning students to heterogeneous groups, we avoid having teams of high achievers and teams of low, teams of one race and teams of another. Through integrated teams, we improve cross-race relations, tutoring, and management.

But our good intentions may create strong resistance among some students —they would rather have other teammates. Some would even prefer to work alone. This is where teambuilding comes to the rescue. Having enjoyed the process of finding commonalities, coming up with a team name and handshake, building team shelters together, designing team T-Shirts, flying the team airplane, and supporting each other through a blind walk, resistance is usually overcome. At some point, the students "team." They feel a strong sense of belonging and identity; a desire to be with and work with their teammates. As we have described in *Chapter 10*, teambuilding works. We have witnessed the power of teambuilding in classrooms in many parts of the world. I have seen it overcome the resistance to working together even with members of different gangs. Teambuilding on an occasional basis throughout the time the team stays together renews and strengthens the will to work together.

Skill to Work Together

Having established the will to work together, teams begin a cooperative project. They want to work together and want to do well. We soon observe though, that the will to work together is no substitute for the skill to work together. In *Chapter 2: Why Do We Need Cooperative Learning?*, we examined in detail forces such as the disintegration of the family and violent teachings of the surrogate family, the media. Today's youth, without prior cooperative learning experiences, come to the classroom ill-prepared to be good teammates.

In one team, with all good intentions, Susie, the high achiever, tells everyone what to do. Resentment builds and the will to work together quickly erodes. In another team, Sam has decided not to participate. Sam's three teammates all want to include Sam, but they are not quite sure how to do it. They wish he would work as part of the team, but they don't know how to make that happen. In yet another team, a high achiever is telling a low achiever all the answers. "Write down eighty-eight for question seven." The high achiever wants to help, but does not know how. He never learned that telling an answer hurts a teammate; showing how to get an answer helps a teammate. He lacks coaching skills.

Students get too noisy; they put each other down; they get off task; they do not respect the ideas of others. Further, they don't know how to deal with difficult teammates who are dominant, shy, hostile, rejected, or who would simply rather work alone. The list of possible problems is long. For successful teamwork, a wide range of skills are helpful. See box: Social Skills Needed for and Developed by Cooperative Learning. The students lack these skills because nothing in

the traditional curriculum teaches cooperative skills. Students simply lack the skill to work together successfully. *Good teammates are made, not born.*

Problems as Social Skills Curriculum in Disguise

All of the social skills problems students experience are educational opportunities. Every social skill problem reflects an important piece of the social skills curriculum not yet acquired. The problems tell us what students need to learn.

Social Skills Needed for and Developed by Cooperative Learning

- Accepting a compliment
- Accepting decisions
- Active listening•
- Agreeing
- Apologizing
- Appreciating contributions
- Asking for help
- Asking questions
- Building on others' ideas
- Checking for understanding
- Clarifying ideas
- Coaching
- Coming to consensus
- Compassion
- Complimenting
- Compromising
- Contributing ideas
- Criticizing an idea, not a person
- Decision making
- Departing
- Disagreeing appropriately
- Elaborating
- Encouraging contributions
- Encouraging others
- Excusing oneself
- Expressing an opinion
- Following directions
- Forgiving
- Getting everyone's opinion
- Giving reasons
- Greeting others
- Helping
- Honesty
- Interviewing
- Introducing oneself
- Introducing others
- Leading
- Making friends
- Making sure everyone understands
- Negotiating
- Offering help
- Patience
- Praising
- Problem solving
- Providing clarification
- Quiet voices
- Redirecting a discussion
- Respecting differences
- Responsibility
- Sharing
- Staying on task
- Switching roles
- Summarizing progress
- Taking different perspectives
- Taking turns
- Tolerance
- Working together

If students are off-task, it is because they need to learn how to monitor their behavior, checking to see if it is on-task, and adjusting accordingly. Staying on task is a social skill. And like other skills, social skills need to be learned. In fact, all of the social skills problems in a classroom are simply an indicator that there is some part of the social skills curriculum yet to be mastered.

> *"I will pay more for the ability to deal with people than any other ability under the sun."*
> — John D. Rockefeller

Social Skills and the Embedded Curriculum

How do we help students develop social skills for successful cooperative learning and for success beyond school? There are resources for teaching social skills as its own curriculum. In this curricular approach, the teacher teaches lessons specifically on the social skills. However, for most teachers who find it challenging enough just to meet high academic standards, there is not enough time in the day or lessons in the year to teach all the important social skills as a separate curriculum.

> *"The most important single ingredient in the formula of success is knowing how to get along with people."*
> — Theodore Roosevelt

The alternative, and the approach we advocate and focus on in this chapter, is the natural acquisition of social skills by embedding social skills in daily instruction. By embedding social skills in how we teach and how students learn, students acquire the important social skills while they are doing their math, or science, or social studies with little or no time off the regular curriculum. With effective cooperative learning, students acquire a whole range of skills while they cooperatively interact every day with their teammates and classmates to master academic content. Social skills are honed through practice and use: Students watch teammates, model appropriate behaviors, practice their social skills, and receive instant feedback from their peers. A social skills curriculum is embedded in cooperative learning structures.

5 Strategies for Fostering Social Skills Development

Research reveals that even without any direct instruction of social skills, students in cooperative teams become more caring, helpful, and understanding of each other. Nevertheless, if we really wish to have our teams and classrooms run as efficiently as possible, we augment and accelerate this natural acquisition of social skills with five powerful strategies: 1) **Structures & Structuring**, 2) **Roles & Gambits**, 3) **Modeling**, 4) **Reinforcement**, and 5) **Reflection & Planning**. Let's examine each of these five strategies and how they can accelerate social skills development. After reviewing the five strategies, we will see how they can help solve some of the most common problems that occur in cooperative learning.

Five Strategies for Fostering Social Skills Development

1 Structures & Structuring
2 Roles & Gambits
3 Modeling
4 Reinforcement
5 Reflection & Planning

Strategy 1

Structures & Structuring
Structures

Many structures have social skills built into their steps. As teachers regularly use structures, students practice social skills in a natural context. Let's examine a simple example.

Students in two different classes have just finished reading a book. Teacher A checks for understanding by asking the class questions. Following each question, the teacher calls on students who have raised their hands. Teacher C asks the same questions, but following each question, the instructor has students interact with a partner using Timed Pair Share (students taking turns, each share for a minute their best response with their partner who just listens).

Although both instructors are delivering the same academic content, they are using different instructional strategies and delivering a different social skills curriculum. Embedded in Teacher C's instruction is a social skills curriculum not delivered in Teacher A's class. The students in Teacher C's room have practiced taking turns, cooperating, attentive listening, showing respect, and patient waiting. If the teachers use only their respective teaching strategies for the entire year, the students in Teacher C's class will leave class having developed a range of social skills.

There is no escaping it. Every choice of an instructional strategy is also a choice to deliver an embedded curriculum. There is a curriculum embedded in every instructional strategy. It is no accident that the structures develop the very social skills, communication skills, and teamwork skills that top the list of employability skills!

The structures are almost all cooperative and therefore help students develop a prosocial, cooperative orientation. But many structures are good for developing other social skills as well. For example, if students are working on the skill of Equal Participation, the structure of choice would be Talking Chips. For Praising, use Affirmation Chips. See table: Selected Structures for Promoting Social Skills.

Our greatest hope as teachers is that we can make a meaningful, positive difference for the students we teach. Cooperative learning makes a difference academically, but it has the very important added benefit of developing social skills and life skills. Schools that implement cooperative learning in the classroom report their students are more kind and caring, and they document fewer incidences of discipline referrals.

The cooperation and turn-taking embedded in many structures spills over to unstructured interactions. I have seen kindergarten students given the task of making a team picture. Without any special instructions from their teacher, each student worked for a little while and then passed the paper to a teammate to continue the work.

Selected Structures for Promoting Social Skills

Social Skills	Sample Structures
Turn Taking	• RoundRobin/RallyRobin • RoundTable/RallyTable • Team Interview • Talking Chips • Timed Pair Share
Helping, Teaching, Tutoring	• Numbered Heads Together • RallyCoach • Circle-the-Sage • Sages Share • Flashcard Game • Inside-Outside Circle • Jigsaw • Team-Pair-Solo
Praising	• Spin-N-Think • Pairs Check • Gambit Chips
Fairness	• Spend-A-Buck • Sum-the-Ranks
Listening and Understanding	• Paraphrase Passport • Agree-Disagree Line-Ups • Team Statements

These students had used RoundTable a great deal in previous cooperative work, and so had internalized the structure. When no structure was provided, they naturally assumed that RoundTable was a good way to do this project when working with others. Each structure teaches its own social skill or skills. Combined, frequent use of the structures is in essence a whole social skills curriculum covering the spectrum of skills from accepting a compliment to working together. See the Social Skills Chart on pages 11.6 and 11.7.

Structuring

Structuring is the myriad things we do to determine how an activity is carried out. We can structure learning tasks to promote the natural acquisition of social skills.

Structuring Within a Structure.

When using a structure or introducing a new structure to students, we can emphasize the social skills component of the structure by highlighting the embedded social skills. For example, "In Timed Pair Share, we will be practicing two important skills today, taking turns and active listening." The teacher models for students what the skills look like by doing the structure with another student or team, or using other students or teams to model the structure. The teacher reminds students of the desired skills, "Remember, Partner A, your job is to actively listen to your partner without interrupting for the first minute. Active listening means eye contact, nodding when you understand, facing your partner with an open stance, and trying to understand what your partner thinks and feels. After you listen, it will be your turn to share and Partner B will extend you the same courtesy." After students engage in the structure, the teacher reinforces successful use of the social skills. "I like the way Lupita is listening so carefully to Sammy. I even saw her jot down something Sammy said." Structuring for skill acquisition includes putting a spotlight on the skills you want students to practice and acquire.

Structuring for Accountability for a Social Skill.

One of the surest ways to structure for the acquisition of a skill is to hold students accountable for the skill. Many times it is possible to structure a cooperative learning task so that the acquisition of social skills is an integral part of the learning experience, or necessary for task completion. If students are held accountable for a specific social skill, they are more likely to use the skill. Let's return to our example of Timed Pair Share. If we want to hold students accountable for listening, after A shares, we give B a complete-this-sentence response gambit. We might say, "B's tell your partner…

"… two important things you learned from them as you listened."

"…one thing they shared that you found most interesting."

"…how their story made you feel, and why."

If we want to hold students accountable for giving compliments, during RoundRobin, the rule may be that you must compliment the teammate for one thing he/she shared before you may share.

We can let students know they will be held accountable for a target social skill after the task: "Listen to each other's ideas carefully because at the end of this activity, you will write two ideas you heard from someone else, sign it, and turn it in." Accountability holds students responsible to a partner, to teammates, or to the teacher for using the skill.

Equality and inequality are difficult concepts to grasp. Too often we operate under the false premise that Me > You, when in reality You = Me and We > I.

Structuring for Good Teamwork.

Students with limited team experience may not know what it means to be a good teammate. A little instruction on the skills of a good teammate, with frequent reminders and reinforcement, can go a long way. Use the Top 10 Tips to Be a Good Teammate blackline (see page 11.8) to share with students what it means to be a good teammate. Or have teams generate their own lists of qualities and create instructions for "How to be a good teammate."

> *"Power consists in one's capacity to link his will with the purpose of others, to lead by reason and a gift of cooperation."*
> —Woodrow Wilson

After direct instruction, use the "good teammate" qualities and terminology for reminders and reinforcement as students work together. As a reminder: "Remember, we want to be good helpers." For reinforcing good team behavior: "Thank you Serena for getting your team back on task. Now that's being a good teammate!"

Social Skills Chart

This dot chart, created by Laurie and Spencer Kagan, illustrates the social skills developed by different Kagan Structures. By using cooperative structures, we improve academics and simultaneously deliver a rich social skills curriculum.

Structures / Social Skills	Accepting a compliment	Accepting decisions	Active listening	Agreeing	Asking for help	Asking questions	Being honest/Honesty	Building on others' ideas	Checking for understanding	Clarifying ideas	Coming to consensus	Compassion	Compromise	Contributing your ideas	Criticizing an idea, not a person	Decision making	Departing	Disagreeing appropriately	Elaborating	Encouraging contributions
AllWrite Consensus		•	•		•	•		•		•	•	•	•	•		•		•	•	
AllWrite RoundRobin							•	•						•						•
Carousel Feedback			•							•				•	•			•		•
Fan-N-Pick	•		•			•								•						•
Find Someone Who			•	•	•									•			•			•
Find-the-Fiction	•	•	•	•						•		•		•				•		•
Flashcard Game	•		•	•																•
Inside-Outside Circle			•	•																•
Jot Thoughts			•					•						•						•
Match Mine	•		•						•					•						•
Mix-Freeze-Group																				•
Mix-Pair-Share						•												•		•
Numbered Heads Together		•	•	•	•	•				•	•	•				•		•		
One Stray																	•			
Pairs Compare			•	•				•		•	•			•		•		•		•
Pass-N-Praise	•		•											•						
Poems for Two Voices			•											•						•
Quiz-Quiz-Trade				•						•							•			•
RallyCoach			•																	•
RallyRobin	•			•																•
RallyTable																				•
RoundRobin							•													•
RoundTable								•												•
RoundTable Consensus		•	•	•		•	•	•	•	•	•	•	•	•	•	•		•	•	
Showdown				•														•		•
Simultaneous RoundTable								•												
Spend-A-Buck		•	•								•		•	•	•	•		•		•
StandUp–HandUp–PairUp								•										•		
Stir-the-Class			•	•	•	•				•	•	•				•	•	•		
Talking Chips			•				•	•						•				•		•
Team Stand-N-Share			•								•	•		•		•		•		•
Telephone			•						•	•				•		•	•			•
Think-Write-RoundRobin							•													•
Three-Step Interview			•	•	•							•		•						•
Timed Pair Share	•		•		•			•				•		•				•		•
Traveling Heads Together		•	•	•	•	•				•	•	•			•		•		•	

Kagan Cooperative Learning • Dr. Spencer Kagan & Miguel Kagan
Kagan Publishing • 1 (800) 933-2667 • www.KaganOnline.com

	Encouraging others	Expressing an opinion	Following directions	Getting everyone's opinion	Giving reasons	Greeting others	Leading	Making friends	Making sure everyone understands	Negotiating	Offering help/Coaching	Patience	Praising	Problem solving	Providing clarification	Quiet voices	Respecting differences	Responsibility	Sharing	Settling differences of opinion	Staying on task	Switching roles	Taking different perspectives	Taking turns	Tolerance	Working together
		•		•	•				•	•					•	•	•						•			•
		•										•												•		•
		•		•	•		•		•		•			•		•		•			•			•	•	•
	•	•						•	•	•	•	•		•	•		•	•	•			•		•	•	•
		•	•		•	•	•	•	•		•	•	•	•		•	•	•				•		•	•	•
		•		•				•	•	•	•		•	•		•	•				•		•	•	•	•
						•		•										•								•
	•	•			•		•				•					•								•	•	•
	•																•	•								•
	•		•				•	•	•		•			•	•	•	•	•				•		•	•	•
	•			•	•												•	•				•		•	•	•
		•		•	•		•				•	•		•	•	•	•	•						•	•	•
	•	•	•		•			•		•	•			•	•	•	•	•						•	•	•
													•					•						•	•	•
	•										•	•	•		•		•					•		•	•	•
				•	•						•	•		•	•	•	•	•		•		•		•	•	•
			•		•						•	•	•	•	•	•	•		•		•			•	•	•
																	•			•		•			•	•
					•					•					•	•	•	•		•		•			•	•
					•					•					•			•		•		•			•	•
											•					•		•							•	•
	•	•		•	•				•	•		•	•	•	•			•		•		•				•
	•											•			•					•						•
		•			•				•			•			•		•	•		•	•				•	•
	•				•		•									•		•						•		
					•																					
	•	•			•				•			•			•		•	•		•				•	•	•
		•							•								•	•		•						•
	•		•		•				•	•	•		•		•	•		•		•						•
	•	•			•						•			•		•	•		•		•		•		•	•
	•	•															•	•		•					•	•
	•	•	•		•					•	•		•		•	•		•				•		•		•

Top 10 Tips to Be a Good Teammate

1 **Be a Team Player.** Being a team player means cooperating and doing what's best for the team. Sometimes that means not getting your way. We work together to set and reach goals everyone can support.

2 **Ask for Help.** Everyone needs help sometimes. Ask for help when you need it. Don't be afraid to ask your teammates for help if you need it or don't understand something.

3 **Be a Good Helper.** If a teammate needs help, don't just give him or her the answer or do the task for him or her. A good helper teaches his or her teammate how to do it so the teammate can do it on their own next time.

4 **Keep the Team on Task.** If the team gets off task, a good teammate politely gets the team back on track. Say, "Come on team, let's focus on …."

5 **Compliment Teammates.** Compliments make us feel good about ourselves. We like people who give us compliments. Be generous with compliments toward teammates when they do a good job or contribute a good idea.

6 **Have a Positive Attitude.** Be positive and encourage teammates. A bad attitude drags your whole team down. Say things like "We can do it!" Everyone likes a winner, but no one likes a whiner.

7 **Watch Teammates.** Pay attention to your teammates. What can you learn from them? Are they being polite or rude? Copy their positive behaviors and avoid the negative.

8 **Listen to Teammates.** Listen to your teammates and try to understand what they have to say. Get everyone's opinion. Listening is a form of respect. Plus, you can learn a lot from different ideas. Echo your teammates to show them you listened, "I hear you say …."

9 **Piggyback on Each Other.** If a teammate has a good idea, build on it. Make it better. If you have a good idea, let your teammates add to it and make it better.

10 **Apologize.** Sometimes we get angry or act rude. Apologize for acting badly. Say, "I'm sorry for _____. What I will do next time is _____." Accept the apologies of your teammates.

Kagan Cooperative Learning • Dr. Spencer Kagan & Miguel Kagan
Kagan Publishing • 1 (800) 933-2667 • www.KaganOnline.com

Destructuring for Internalization

Clearly, our goal is for students to become so proficient with their social skills that we don't need to structure for them. We would like to reach a point where we do not have to assign structures and roles because our students know them so well that they automatically use them when appropriate. We will arrive at that destination much quicker through the use of structures and structuring than through unstructured group work and hoping that students discover and build cooperative skills.

We structure for the acquisition of social skills through structuring and structures, so all students experience a positive model of social interaction. However, as skills are acquired, we can destructure in a paced way for internalization of the social skills. If there is a high degree of structure and little interaction among students, fewer management and social relations problems arise among students, but there is also less opportunity for development of higher-level thinking skills, as well as internalization of social skills and roles. If we always structure every step of behavior, we rob students of learning opportunities.

As students become well versed with the social skills, we can systematically destructure learning tasks. In a paced way, we provide less and less structure, allowing the students to structure their interaction for themselves. Our goal is for students to internalize cooperative skills and to become cooperative, rather than just to behave cooperatively.

Roles & Gambits

Strategy 2

A cooperative learning role is an assigned action or task for a student to fulfill. Cooperative roles facilitate and enhance teamwork. Gatekeeper is an example of a role. When a student is assigned the role of Gatekeeper, his/her job is to equalize participation. If one student is dominating while another is not participating, the Gatekeeper skillfully closes the gate for the over-participator and opens the gate for the under-participator.

Gambits are what students say or do to fulfill their roles. For example, the Gatekeeper may politely say, "Sheila, thank you for sharing your opinion, let's hear what Phong thinks." There are verbal and nonverbal gambits to help students fulfill their roles.

Roles and gambits represent a powerful approach to developing social skills, especially in student interactions that have little structuring. As students fulfill their roles, they are practicing important social skills. Since roles are rotated, students get the opportunity to play many different cooperative roles, and are introduced to a range of important skills. Further, the roles that students play enhance teamwork and make cooperative learning more productive.

Roles

See box, Social Roles and Corresponding Social Skills and the blackline on page 11.11 for an overview of the dozen most common and important roles for cooperative learning.

Social Roles and Corresponding Social Skills

Cooperative Role	Social Skill
Encourager	Encouraging, Motivating
Praiser	Praising, Complimenting
Cheerleader	Celebrating Accomplishments
Gatekeeper	Equalizing Participation
Coach	Helping
Question Commander	Checking for Questions
Checker	Checking for Understanding
Focus Keeper	Staying on Task
Recorder	Recording Ideas
Reflector	Reflecting on Group Progress
Quiet Captain	Using Quiet Voices
Materials Monitor	Distributing Materials

Brief Overview of the Dozen Social Roles

1. Encourager

The Encourager "brings out" the reluctant student, and attempts to motivate the team if it gets bogged down. The Encourager goes to work before a student has spoken, with gambits such as, "Let's listen to Pete."

2. Praiser

In contrast to the Encourager, the Praiser goes to work after a student has spoken to show appreciation with gambits like "Great Idea."

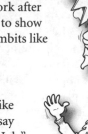

3. Cheerleader

The Cheerleader, unlike the Praiser, does not say things like "Fantastic Job." Rather he or she gets the team to show appreciation for the accomplishments of one teammate or the team as a whole. The cheerleader literally leads the group in a cheer with gambits such as, "Let's all give Pedro a pat on the back." "Let's do our team handshake!"

One of my favorite cheerleader gambits is to have students pick two positive adjectives or phrases and then chant the first phrase three times and the second one once. For example, students chant, "Smart! Smart! Smart! Brilliant!"

4. Gatekeeper

The Gatekeeper equalizes participation. If one student is talking too much and another very little, the Gatekeeper shuts the gate for one and opens it for another using gambits like "That is very interesting, Joe. Sally, what is your opinion?" "Bill, do you agree with the point that Pat just made?"

5. Coach

The Coach helps a student master academic content, but is very careful not to do the problems for the student. Coaches use gambits like "Remember rule two," and "Check over problem five again."

6. Question Commander

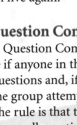

The Question Commander checks to see if anyone in the group has any questions and, if so, makes sure that the group attempts to answer them. The rule is that the team attempts to answer all questions first. If the team cannot, then the team has a "Team

Question," and the Question Commander uses a signal to let the teacher know that the team has exhausted its resources. My favorite signal for a team question is simply to have all four students on the team raise their hands. Alternatively, the Question Commander can have a red flag (slip of paper) to hold up.

7. Checker

The Checker makes sure everyone has mastered the material. The team knows that each person is on his/her own during the quiz or exam, so the team must check to see each person is prepared. The Checker leads the team in checking with gambits like "Let's do one problem each while the team watches to make sure we all have it." "Let's each do the next problem alone and see if we come up with the same answer."

Sometimes the teacher assigns other job definitions to the checker, so the checker may be asked to check for understanding, check for agreement, check for completeness, or check to see if the team is following a specific rule.

8. Focus Keeper

The Focus Keeper keeps the group focused on the task. It is important to distinguish positive and negative gambits for the Focus Keeper. Rather than saying, "Stop fooling around," they are to say things like "We have not done problem three yet."

9. Recorder

The Recorder may take notes, write down group decisions, and/or record answers. Sometimes, the role of the Recorder may be modified so that he or she is simply responsible for making sure things get recorded.

10. Reflector

The Reflector leads the group in looking back. The Reflector asks group reflection questions such as, "How well did we all stay on task? Did we keep our voices down? Did everyone participate?"

Kagan Cooperative Learning • Dr. Spencer Kagan & Miguel Kagan
Kagan Publishing • 1 (800) 933-2667 • www.KaganOnline.com

The Dozen
Cooperative Learning Roles

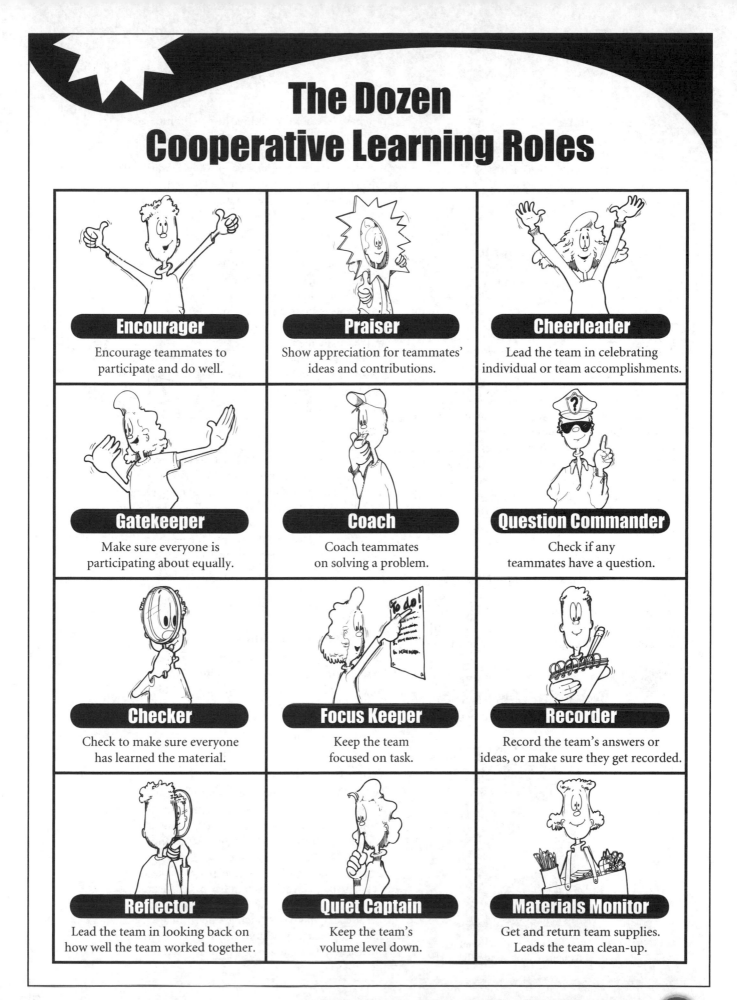

Encourager
Encourage teammates to participate and do well.

Praiser
Show appreciation for teammates' ideas and contributions.

Cheerleader
Lead the team in celebrating individual or team accomplishments.

Gatekeeper
Make sure everyone is participating about equally.

Coach
Coach teammates on solving a problem.

Question Commander
Check if any teammates have a question.

Checker
Check to make sure everyone has learned the material.

Focus Keeper
Keep the team focused on task.

Recorder
Record the team's answers or ideas, or make sure they get recorded.

Reflector
Lead the team in looking back on how well the team worked together.

Quiet Captain
Keep the team's volume level down.

Materials Monitor
Get and return team supplies. Leads the team clean-up.

11. Quiet Captain

The Quiet Captain keeps the team's volume level in check. If the team gets too loud, the Quiet Captain raises a "Quiet" card or tells the team, "We're getting too loud, let's use our team voices."

12. Materials Monitor

The Materials Monitor obtains and returns supplies and makes sure the team cleans up.

Activity Specific Roles

The dozen cooperative learning roles are the most common and important roles for cooperative learning. However, different types of activities may include very specific roles. If students are building a project, there may be a Cutter, a Measurer, a Colorist, and a Gluer. These specific roles are very helpful for ensuring a team project will be true cooperative learning as opposed to group work. We'll explore task roles in detail in *Chapter 13: Cooperative Projects & Presentations*.

Role Cards

Role cards can be made by simply folding a sheet of paper in half lengthwise. On one side of the role card, the name of the role is written so all can see; on the other side, there is room for gambits. Role Cards are also available for

The Role cards have a pop-up picture and role on the front, and things to do and say on the back.

purchase (see box). Whether they are homemade or commercial, sets of role cards have several benefits. They stack perfectly for easy storage; they can be turned inside out so twelve additional roles can be assigned; they can be laminated so students can write in their own gambits with a dry-erase marker and then easily wipe them clean when the role rotates.

Having a set of twelve role cards at their disposal is empowering for students. For example, if students are working on a project, you may ask them to take out all twelve role cards and discuss which of the roles they are already using, and which additional roles they might wish to adopt.

Role-of-the-Week

To introduce students to the various cooperative learning roles, assign a Role-of-the-Week. For example, to develop the social skill, Staying On Task, the Role-of-the-Week will be Focus Keeper. If the skill is Showing Appreciation, the role will be Praiser. The role rotates within the team each day so each student gets a turn practicing:

> Monday, the role is given to Student #1; Tuesday, Student #2; Wednesday, Student #3; and Thursday, Student #4.

When Not to Use Roles

Most Structures. Most simple cooperative learning structures, such as Numbered Heads Together, Three-Step Interview, RoundTable, and RoundRobin, do not need assigned roles. In fact, role assignment would detract from the effectiveness of these structures.

When to Use Roles

Team Projects. Whenever teams work on projects, roles are important. For example, without roles, given an interesting or challenging task, it is probable that the highest achieving students will "take over" and do the task for the team. It is the job of the Gatekeeper to make sure all participate. If each student has his or her role, such as Checker, Recorder, Focus Keeper, and Cheerleader, there is a much greater probability that all will participate and each will feel he or she has made a unique contribution to the project.

Team Discussions. Team discussions without assigned roles often consist of one or two students talking most or all of the time. As a remedy, you might assign one or more of the following roles: Gatekeeper (who makes sure all participate), Focus Keeper (who makes sure the team stays on the topic), Reflector (who makes sure the team occasionally reflects on its progress and on its use of any particular social skill that is the focus), Cheerleader (who makes sure the group stops to celebrate its accomplishments), and/or Encourager (who encourages participation by shy or reluctant students).

Gambits

Generate and Record Gambits

Students will not know how to fulfill their roles unless they have positive models of what to do and say. Students need to know the gambits for the role—what it "sounds like" and "looks like" to fill the role well.

Through gambit development, students learn how to solve social skill problems and how to fulfill roles. For example, if the skill is Staying on Task, the Role is Focus Keeper, and we might post the gambits that facilitate being a good Focus Keeper. Students learn that a good Focus Keeper does not say, "Stop talking about the big game." Rather, they learn to say, "The big game is really interesting, but if we are going to complete our project in time, we need to...." Students learn that one of the best gambits for a Focus Keeper is the art of redirection. Rather than saying, "We are off task," the Focus Keeper redirects the attention of the group, saying, "Problem three really looks interesting. Do you think the answer could be related to...?"

One of the most effective ways to develop gambits is to do a "Y-Chart." The Y-Chart has three sections: "Sounds Like," "Looks Like," and "Feels Like." For example, if the social skill is listening, the Y-Chart might look like the one pictured. Students and teacher work together to generate gambits for the three sections of the Y-Chart, and the chart is left posted for a few days to make the focus skill salient.

Social Skills Y-Chart

Listening

Feels Like
- Alert attention
- Receiving
- Caring

Sounds Like
- Do you mean...?
- I'm hearing you say....

Looks Like
- Nodding
- Eye Contact
- Open body language

One of the most effective ways to develop gambits is to use a Y-Chart.

We find it useful to use the Cooperative Learning Role Gambits blacklines (see pages 16.14 and 16.15) as we work with students to come up with the gambits for the various roles. We have students fill out the gambits in their teams. We can then make a class list by collecting and recording the best ideas from each team.

Students can generate very creative gambits. Here are a few student ideas:

- **Staying on Task.** "Drawing a happy face on one side of a slip of paper and a sad face on the other side, and keeping one or the other side of the paper turned up, depending on whether the team is on-task."

- **Keeping Quiet.** "Giving a 'thumbs-up' signal when the group is using quiet, inner voices, and a steady, soft knocking on the table when the group has gotten too noisy."

- **Encouraging Participation.** "Making slips of paper with question marks on them, and then handing one to any student who has not been participating. The Encourager who developed those gambit chips informed his group that they meant, 'What do you think?'"

Cooperative Learning Role Gambits

Instructions. Brainstorm ideas for what to do and what to say for each role.

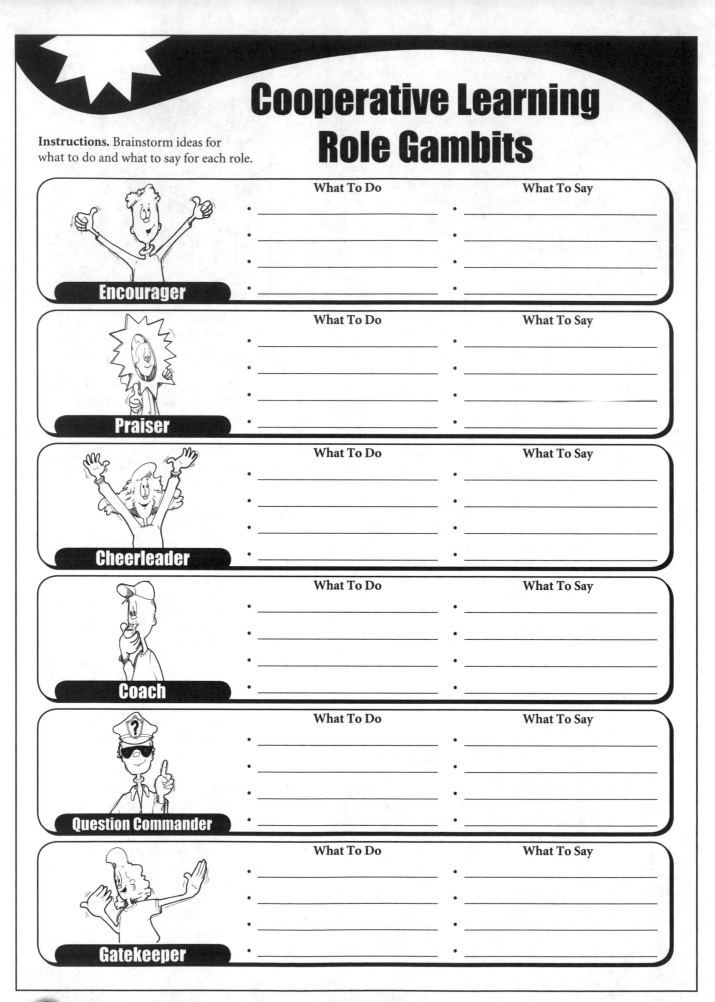

Encourager

What To Do
- _____
- _____
- _____
- _____

What To Say
- _____
- _____
- _____
- _____

Praiser

What To Do
- _____
- _____
- _____
- _____

What To Say
- _____
- _____
- _____
- _____

Cheerleader

What To Do
- _____
- _____
- _____
- _____

What To Say
- _____
- _____
- _____
- _____

Coach

What To Do
- _____
- _____
- _____
- _____

What To Say
- _____
- _____
- _____
- _____

Question Commander

What To Do
- _____
- _____
- _____
- _____

What To Say
- _____
- _____
- _____
- _____

Gatekeeper

What To Do
- _____
- _____
- _____
- _____

What To Say
- _____
- _____
- _____
- _____

Kagan Cooperative Learning • Dr. Spencer Kagan & Miguel Kagan
Kagan Publishing • 1 (800) 933-2667 • www.KaganOnline.com

Cooperative Learning Role Gambits

Instructions. Brainstorm ideas for what to do and what to say for each role.

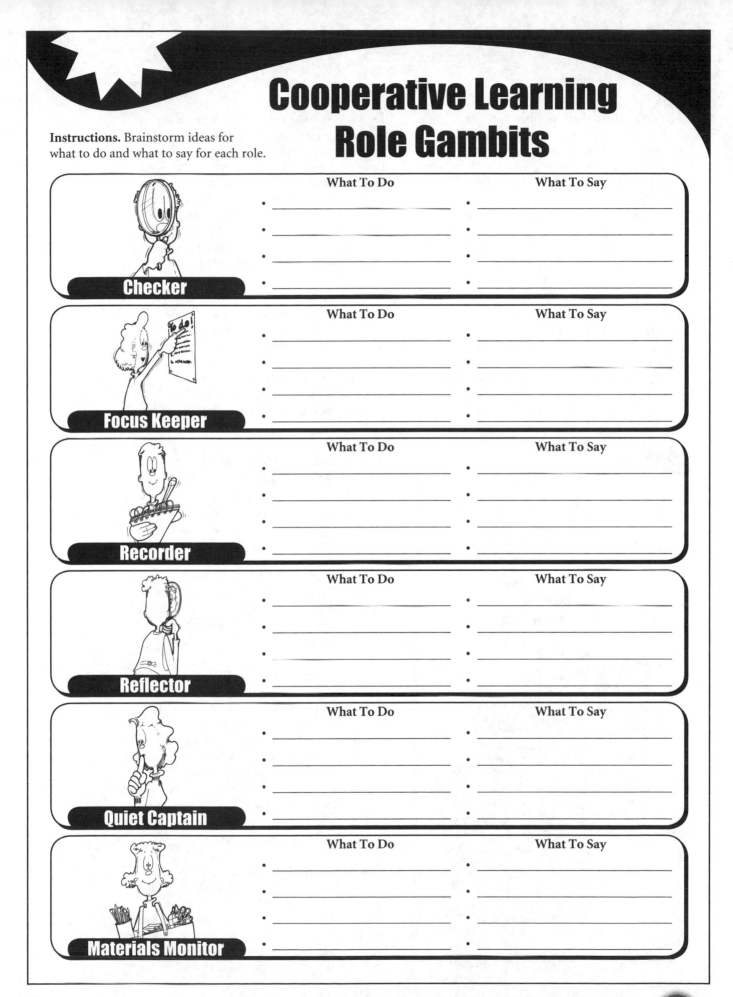

Checker

What To Do	What To Say
• _____	• _____
• _____	• _____
• _____	• _____
• _____	• _____

Focus Keeper

What To Do	What To Say
• _____	• _____
• _____	• _____
• _____	• _____
• _____	• _____

Recorder

What To Do	What To Say
• _____	• _____
• _____	• _____
• _____	• _____
• _____	• _____

Reflector

What To Do	What To Say
• _____	• _____
• _____	• _____
• _____	• _____
• _____	• _____

Quiet Captain

What To Do	What To Say
• _____	• _____
• _____	• _____
• _____	• _____
• _____	• _____

Materials Monitor

What To Do	What To Say
• _____	• _____
• _____	• _____
• _____	• _____
• _____	• _____

Making Gambits Visible

Once the gambits have been generated, it is helpful to have them available for students to see and use while they fulfill their roles. Here's a few top spots to make the gambits available to students:

- Back of role cards
- Poster in the class
- Bulletin board
- Transparency projected for the class to see
- Team sheets on desks

Gambit Structures

Gambits are central to two structures: Draw-A-Chip and Drop-A-Chip. The gambits that students generate can be recorded on chips for students to use during the two structures.

Learning Chips

Learning Chips are a set of 16 attractive, durable plastic chips with gambits. Most Learning Chips offer prompts for exploring the curriculum and for developing thinking, but some sets are specifically designed to facilitate social skill acquisition including:

- **Discussion Chips**
- **Interview Chips**
- **Paraphrase Chips**

Draw-A-Chip. The gambit chips are placed facedown on the team table for team discussions. Each time a teammate adds to the discussion, he or she draws a chip and must use the chip as part of his or her participation. If the chip says, "Paraphrase a teammate," he or she paraphrases. If the chip says, "Check for Understanding," he or she checks that all teammates understand. Learning Chips are attractive, pre-made gambit chips for teams. See box, Learning Chips.

Drop-A-Chip. The difference here is that students deal out gambit chips in advance. When they use their gambit chips, they drop them on a teammate. For example, if the chips are praisers, a student tells a teammate, "your idea rocks" as he drops the "you rock" chip on a teammate. Students try to use up their own gambits first, then use the gambit chips that are dropped on them.

Model and Practice Gambits

Teacher Models Gambits. We find it useful to model roles and gambits for the class. A strong strategy is to model the role correctly, then incorrectly, and have students in teams discuss the difference. For example, you might contrast weak versus strong Gatekeeper gambits, e.g., Weak: "John, you are talking too much; Susan, talk more." Strong: "That's interesting John; Susan, do you agree?" It is a good idea to finish modeling on a positive note, ending by modeling strong, positive gambits.

Team Models Gambits. Get one team "up on the role" by working with them while the other teams are busy on another task. The selected team then can model the role. For example, you might have one team member pretend not to know how to solve a problem, and have the "Coach" model how to help a student solve a problem without doing it for him. Choose one of the weakest teams to model for the class, and they will gain in status while they acquire the role at a level they might not otherwise.

Teacher Plays Dumb. Tell students, "I have been noticing that we have been getting off task while working on our projects, so 'Staying on Task' will be our next skill of the week. But I am not so sure what you would say or do in your teams if you saw someone off task. Put your heads together and discuss what you might say or do to get the team or a teammate back on track. What could we put on our Gambit Charts?"

Simulations. Have one student play the role of a problem student, and then have the teammates develop gambits to deal with the problem. Later have teams share their favorite gambits, or write them up for the Gambit Bank.

Unstructured Role-Plays. Role-play is a very natural mode of learning. It is a chance to play with behaviors, to try them on, and practice. Close observations of play reveal it is often practice of roles for later use. Unstructured role-play in the classroom is the same thing: the teacher provides students with a situation to role-play, allows them to experiment with possible solutions, and then to share and discuss their solutions with other teams.

For example, the teacher might say, "In your teams, role-play this situation and see if you can find a solution you like."

Sample Role-Play Situations

• Jennifer borrowed some crayons from her friend, Stacy. Jennifer accidentally broke one of the crayons. What should Jennifer do?
• Bill grabbed the ball away from John during recess. What should John do?
• Tom sees Pete hit Jim. What should Tom do?
• Sally and Monica find a wallet on the playground. It has money in it, but does not have the owner's name. What should they do?

To ensure positive solutions as students work with unstructured role-plays, it is helpful to orient them to basic principles for seeking solutions. Three positive guidelines for resolving moral dilemmas are:

• Win-Win: Seek solutions that have positive outcomes for all involved.
• Ask the question, "What would it look like if everyone acted that way?"
• Ask the question, "Have I treated others the way I would most like to be treated?"

As students work in unstructured role-plays, it is helpful if we occasionally stop the action to re-focus the students on the three positive guidelines and to point out helpful or cooperative behaviors for the other groups to see.

Structured Role-Plays. An effective technique for learning new behavior or changing old behavior is to practice the desired behavior in a context similar to the one in which it actually will be used. In China, teachers make extensive use of structured, teacher-written and directed role-plays to help students recognize and learn appropriate helping and cooperating behaviors. Through structured role-play, students practice proper responses to various situations such as returning a lost object, or asking permission to borrow something.

As a team role-plays the desired behavior, the other teams may be given observation forms to ensure that the behavior is being observed, and to give the group feedback.

Strategy 3 — Modeling

Modeling is a powerful way to communicate to students exactly what a social skill looks and sounds like. Modeling is brain-based learning. Whenever we watch a behavior, the mirror neurons in our brain fire as if we were performing that behavior. Without a word of instruction, we reshape brains by what we model and by the models we provide for students. When a student sees another student smile and congratulates her partner with a high 5, the same neurons fire in the brain of the student watching as if that student were smiling and giving a high 5! Students practice by watching and are primed to offer the same positive behavior. We can say to the class, "I want everyone one to be a good helper." But this really doesn't mean much to students who don't know what it means to be a good helper. If instead, we have a student role-play for the class what a good helper says and what a good helper does, students know exactly what a good helper is. Modeling is a powerful strategy for increasing the likelihood of positive social skills and also for decreasing the likelihood of negative behaviors. We want students to have an unequivocal visual image of positive social behavior. There are many ways to create this imagery for students.

Teacher Modeling. To model any skill for a team or for the whole class, we role-play the skill for the class. We may have another student or a team join us in the front of the class to model the behavior. Or we may join the team and have the class focus on the team.

Model Groups. If a desired behavior is not being used by most groups, we may wish to draw attention to a group that is using the skill well. We look for positive social skills. When we see a behavior we want more of, we stop the class and have the team or student repeat the behavior for everyone to see. Alternatively, we can work with one group or individual on the desired behavior until they are proficient, and then have them model for the whole class.

Student Model. Some students relish public attention. Select a student to model an appropriate behavior for the class. Here's a great tip: If you have a repeat offender, use him or her to model the opposite, appropriate behavior for the class. If a student is being too dominant, have him/her model effective turn taking. If a student is prone to blurting out answers, have him/her model for the class self-control or good helping. Once students have become a paradigm of good behavior for the class, they are less likely to misbehave. Shy students may not appreciate the attention, so we ask if the student is willing to volunteer.

Role-plays and Simulations. Role-plays, simulations, and skits are useful ways to model social skills.

Strategy 4

Reinforcement

Reinforcement is a term that comes to us from psychology, specifically from B.F. Skinner and his work in operant conditioning. A reinforcer is anything that strengthens the probability of a behavior. Here, our desired behavior is effective use of positive social skills. We can increase the use of social skills by giving positive attention whenever we see the skills being used.

In the cooperative classroom, we strive to create a positive learning environment. To that end, we use positive reinforcement liberally and negative reinforcement and punishment sparingly. Unpleasant experiences escalate the feeling of fear and threat, erode the positive environment, and lower students' receptiveness to learning. Laboratory studies with animals reveal, and subsequent research on humans confirms, that positive reinforcement is more effective and lasting than negative reinforcement and punishment.

Classroom Reinforcement and Punishment

Positive Reinforcement
Students Receive Something They Find Rewarding

▶ **Intrinsic Rewards**
  • Feeling of pride
  • Feeling of importance
  • Feeling of success
  • Feeling of competence
  • Feeling of caring or cooperation

▶ **Intangible Extrinsic Rewards**
  • Verbal praise
  • Positive attention
  • Motivating learning tasks
  • Free time, breaks
  • Social status

▶ **Tangible Extrinsic Rewards**
  • Stickers, gold stars
  • Toys, trinkets
  • Grades
  • Points
  • Tokens

Negative Reinforcement
Take Away Things Students Don't Like

  • Homework
  • Drill work
  • Boring lectures
  • Tests and quizzes

Punishment
Give Students Things They Don't Like

  • Warnings
  • Public embarrassment
  • Sense of powerlessness
  • Criticism and insults
  • Corporal punishment
  • Detention
  • Lost lunch, snack, recess
  • Busy work
  • Threats
  • Yelling

Notice, in the box (on page 11.18) we have broken positive reinforcement into three categories. Our goal is for students to be internally motivated to behave well. We want them to use their social skills because they feel good, or caring, or capable, or confident when they do. If students are not using their social skills, a little extrinsic reinforcement may be a gentle nudge in the right direction. We recommend trying the intangible rewards, such as praise and positive attention, before tangible rewards such as trinkets and gold stars. Why? The reasoning is simple: We don't want the reward to be the reason students behave well. Tangible rewards are seen more as bribes for good behaviors while the intangibles are more of a genuine appreciation. Genuine appreciation helps lead students toward internal motivation while bribes can lead students to attribute their good behavior to their desire to receive rewards, and thus when the tangible reward is gone, so too is the motivation to behave well.

Genuine verbal praise is a strong and effective extrinsic reinforcer for social skills development. Insincere flattery is phony and not recommended. Praise can be given in many forms:

Teacher Praise. The teacher can praise students, teams, or the entire class in a number of ways. The teacher can praise…

- **A student in private:** "I'm really proud of you Becky for…."
- **A student in front of team:** "Supreme Team, let's hear it for Bob for…."
- **A student in front of class:** "Everyone, listen to what Sudesh did…."
- **A team in front of class:** "The Incredibles did an excellent job of…."
- **The entire class:** "Class, I'm proud of you. You stayed focused and on task the whole period."

Student Praise. Peer-based reinforcement can be a strong force for developing social skills. Students want to be accepted and feel important. Think of the negative power of peer pressure. Student praise for good behavior is its positive counterpart. Students can praise each other…

- As part of the structure (e.g., RallyCoach).
- For use of a social skill ("Great job of staying on task, Peter.").

Frequent and Immediate Reinforcement

Two important principles regarding reinforcement apply to the class. To be most effective, reinforcement should be frequent and immediate. Frequent does not mean on a regular schedule or each and every time a student does something good. In fact, studies prove varying the schedule of reinforcement and the amount of reinforcement is most effective. Think of a slot machine. If you put in quarters, but never win, eventually you'll stop playing. If it's too infrequent, it's not rewarding enough. But if you win a small reward, then nothing, then a big one, then nothing, then a small one, and then jackpot—chances are you'll keep playing the game. Frequent rewards on a variable schedule are effective in the classroom too. The first time a student controls impulsivity, we may say simply, "Thanks for waiting patiently, Nick." The next time, we may not say anything. Then the next time, we are forthcoming with lavish praise.

Rewards also need to be immediate. Reinforcers lose their power when there is a delay between the behavior and the receipt of the reward. Brain research may help explain this phenomenon. Administration of adrenergic drugs and hormones can produce retrograde memory enhancement. That is, when subjects are emotionally aroused through drugs or through an emotionally charged stimulus, subjects remember the content better. The emotional charge is the brain's way of saying, "Remember this; this is important." Reinforcers should be administered immediately after the good use of a social skill. Many of the structures have built-in praise and celebration to arouse emotion and to cement academic and social learning.

The Exemplar Student or Team

Praising exemplar students and teams serves the dual purpose of modeling and reinforcement. The student or team receives praise and positive attention, but they also serve as a model for the rest of the class. When the teacher finds a team or a student using a desirable social skill, she holds it up as a model for the class. The teacher says, "Class, I would all like you to hear what I just heard. Johnny just used a wonderful gambit to paraphrase. He said, 'It seems to me you are saying….' I can tell that he's listening attentively.

Praise Can Be a Double-Edged Sword

When we hold up as a model an individual student or a team, we run the risk of inviting envy from the other students. We don't want to give up the power of holding up positive behavior as a model, but we don't want to invite envy. There are several solutions:

1. Don't use the same individual or team as a model too frequently.

2. Work with weaker individuals or teams to become models for the class.

3. Have the teams volunteer to show how the team as a whole or one of their teammates has used the skill.

4. Randomly pick a team and ask them how they have been using the skill.

Everyone turn to your partner and say, "It seems to me you are saying...." Notice, in our example, the teacher has students try on or practice the desired behavior. Modeling, reinforcement, and practice can all go hand-in-hand.

If we are focusing on a specific skill, we look for examples of that skill to hold up as a model for the rest of the class. If the skill is Staying on Task, we might get the attention of the class somewhere during the lesson and then say something like "I have been watching the Astronauts for a while, and I am really impressed with how well they have been staying on task. At one point, they started to talk about recess, but then got right back on task. Nice job, Astronauts!"

If the skill were Praising and Encouraging, we might say, "I just heard and saw a great praiser. Susan, would you please let the whole class hear what you just told Sally and show them the silent round of applause you just gave?" "Notice how Susan smiled and looked right at Sally as she told her what a great job she was doing." Reinforcing and focusing students on desired behavior creates positive class norms and produces more of the behavior modeled.

Strategy 5 — Reflection & Planning

Reflection and Planning are two related processes. Reflection is looking back; Planning is looking forward. Reflection and Planning as a package are among the most powerful of all strategies for fostering social skills because it

engages students in an ongoing self-improvement process. Students look back to see how well they have been using a social skill and then look forward, planning how they can improve. For example, if we want students to become better at staying on task, about a third of the way through a class period, we stop the action and have students reflect on how well they have been staying on task. Then we have them make a plan to improve that skill.

Reflection

During teamwork, students are usually so engrossed with using (or not using) their social skills that they are not consciously evaluating their team dynamics. Students may not focus on how well they are interacting themselves, nor on how well their teammates are behaving. Students may not let each other know that they are violating important teamwork norms. Or sometimes they do, but are not specific enough to inform teammates of the nature of the violation. Or the correction may be too quick and fleeting to have any lasting impression and therefore no impact on future misbehaviors. Reflection allows students to stop interacting and dedicate focused time and thought to their own and teammates' use of social skills to provide specific feedback to promote improvement. There are a variety of ways of promote reflection.

Reflection Questions. The teacher stops a team 10 minutes into a 30-minute team project to ask a reflection question designed to have students reflect on social skills. For example, "Have you and your teammates been encouraging each other?" Or, "How well are you using your roles?"

Notice, we do not wait until the end of the project to have our students reflect on the skill. If we did, some teams might discover too late that they had not used the skill for the entire project. Rather, the reflection time should come early in the lesson (about one-third of the way through) so that students have time to change their behavior and benefit from the reflection. See sample questions in the box, Teacher Reflection Questions on the next page.

Structures for Reflection. Any time students are going to interact, we consider structures. Many structures work well to promote reflection. Timed Pair Share is an excellent choice for any on-the-spot interactions in pairs. RoundRobin is a great choice too because it allows the entire team to hear every response. RoundRobin can be used to have each student respond to the reflection question: "Is your team doing a good job coaching a teammate who doesn't understand how to solve the problem, or are you just giving answers?" The interview structures, Three-Step Interview and Team Interview, work well to have students interview each other on the use of a skill. An interview question may be "What types of helping behavior did you witness?"

Teacher Reflection Questions

For Helping
- Did you give help when asked?
- Did you ask for help when you needed it?
- Do you think a teammate could have used help?

For Praising
- Did you praise a teammate for something?
- Did you receive any praise? How did it make you feel?
- What could you have praised a teammate for?

For Staying on Task
- Did your team get off task? On what?
- Did you or a teammate get the team back on task?
- How could you keep on task more?

Observations

Observing teams in action is an excellent source of information for later reflection. There are many formats for team observations and Observation Sheets can be used with any observation format. (See Social Skills Observation Sheets on the following pages.)

Team Self-Monitoring. One of the most effective ways of producing change is through self-evaluation. In family therapy, family members view themselves interacting on videotape and rate their own individual interactions. This technique leads to improved family dynamics. The same approach can be used in the classroom. To do this, set up a videocamera nearby on a tripod pointing at the team. If possible, capture the audio with a microphone. Record one team interacting for 10 minutes. Soon after, have the team watch their video and reflect on their interactions. If working on a specific skill, students may record its use or when it could have been used.

Although effective, videotaping may be unrealistic because of the time and resources required. Self-monitoring and evaluation forms may be the next best thing.

Teacher Observations. The teacher can observe teams and provide feedback on social skills. If a teacher stands by each team for one minute and records each instance of the use of a skill, after observing each team twice, we have a pretty good sample of how much the skill is being used and by which groups.

After observing each team, we may simply share an observation and leave. Teams take responsibility for what is to be done about it. For example, we may simply say, "One person in this group seems to be doing most of the talking. Take a moment to talk over how participation is unequal and decide what you need to do." Or, "Today during RoundTable Consensus, in some teams, I saw some Recorders begin to write before checking for consensus with all their teammates."

The Teammate Observer. One student on each team may be assigned the role of Observer. The Observer's job for the day, project, or activity is to focus on a specific social skill such as Encouragement. The Observer uses an observation form to record each instance of encouragement and its source so that good use of that skill is recognized among teammates.

Class Observers. Individuals are selected to watch for the good use of gambits and skills with the aim of fostering thoughtful reflection, based on the information they provide. Sometimes it is helpful to choose individuals who are low on a particular skill to observe that skill, providing them useful modeling experiences.

Team Observers. Occasionally, we may want teams as a whole to serve as observers for each other. A team may be asked to stand around another team in a fishbowl format, with observation sheets. When the team is finished with the learning activity, the observing team can give them input regarding the social skills under observation.

Skills
Observation Sheet

Instructions. Stand by each team, and observe their interaction for one minute. Do not interact with them. Record each use of the skill with a mark in the Number of Times Skill Observed column. Record things you heard, saw, or ideas for improvement in the Comments column to share with the class.

Featured Skill _____ **Date** _____

	Number of Times Skill Observed	Comments
Team 1		
Team 2		
Team 3		
Team 4		
Team 5		
Team 6		
Team 7		
Team 8		

Social Skills Observation Sheet

Instructions. Stand by each team, and observe their interaction for one minute. Do not interact with them. Record each use of a skill with a mark.

	Skill 1	Skill 2	Skill 3	Skill 4
Team 1				
Team 2				
Team 3				
Team 4				
Team 5				
Team 6				
Team 7				
Team 8				

Kagan Cooperative Learning • Dr. Spencer Kagan & Miguel Kagan
Kagan Publishing • 1 (800) 933-2667 • www.KaganOnline.com

How Did We Do?

Teacher Instructions. Students individually reflect on their use of social skills by coloring the happy face for "YES," or sad face for "NO." They then compare answers and discuss how to improve. The questions may be used individually to focus teams on one precessing question.

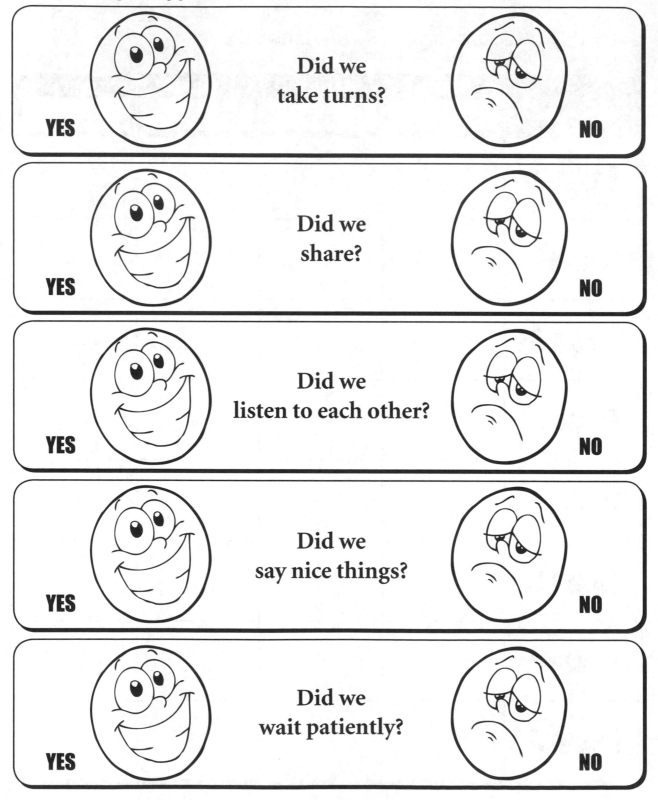

YES — Did we take turns? — NO

YES — Did we share? — NO

YES — Did we listen to each other? — NO

YES — Did we say nice things? — NO

YES — Did we wait patiently? — NO

Kagan Cooperative Learning • Dr. Spencer Kagan & Miguel Kagan
Kagan Publishing • 1 (800) 933-2667 • www.KaganOnline.com

How Are We Doing?

Student Name _____

Team Name _____ Date _____

Instructions. Reflect on your and your teammates' use of social skills as you worked together. Circle the number corresponding to how you feel about each statement.

① Strongly Disagree   ② Disagree   ③ Neither Agree nor Disagree   ④ Agree   ⑤ Strongly Agree

How did I do?

	Strongly Disagree ⟶ Strongly Agree				
I listened to my teammates.	1	2	3	4	5
I complimented my teammates.	1	2	3	4	5
I helped my teammates.	1	2	3	4	5
I stayed on task.	1	2	3	4	5

How did my teammates do?

	Strongly Disagree ⟶ Strongly Agree				
My teammates listened to me.	1	2	3	4	5
My teammates complimented me.	1	2	3	4	5
My teammates helped me.	1	2	3	4	5
My teammates stayed on task.	1	2	3	4	5

How could I improve?

_____

_____

_____

_____

_____

Reflection Form

Student Name _____ **Team Name** _____ **Date** _____

Instructions. Reflect on your and your teammates' use of social skills as you worked together. Circle "Yes" or "No" to answer each question. Then explain your answer.

Focus Questions

1. Is any teammate talking most of the time? Yes No

Explain your answer. _____

_____

2. Is your team staying on task? Yes No

Explain your answer. _____

_____

3. Are teammates listening to each other? Yes No

Explain your answer. _____

_____

4. Are teammates complimenting and encouraging each other? Yes No

Explain your answer. _____

_____

5. Do teammates ask each other for help when help is needed? Yes No

Explain your answer. _____

_____

6. If a teammate asks for help, is he/she being helped? Yes No

Explain your answer. _____

_____

7. Is there a positive tone in our team? Yes No

Explain your answer. _____

_____

8. Is any teammate being ignored? Yes No

Explain your answer. _____

_____

9. Is any teammate being overly shy or not contributing to the team? Yes No

Explain your answer. _____

_____

Summary Questions

1. On a scale of 1 to 10 (10 is best), how well is your team doing? 1 2 3 4 5 6 7 8 9 10

Describe your rating. _____

_____

_____

2. What is one thing you could do to make things go better? _____

_____

3. What is one thing your team could improve? _____

_____

Kagan Cooperative Learning • Dr. Spencer Kagan & Miguel Kagan
Kagan Publishing • 1 (800) 933-2667 • www.KaganOnline.com

Formal Reflection Forms

Reflection forms allow students to reflect on their own use of social skills. Each student independently fills out a reflection form. When done, the team does a RoundRobin with each student taking a turn explaining his or her answer. Another method for using reflection forms is to have the teams discuss each question, and come to consensus on an answer. To do this, the team uses RoundTable Consensus. The first teammate reads the first question. Then each teammate shares his/her answer in turn. Once the team reaches consensus on a team answer, the form is passed clockwise to the next teammate to read the next question. See the blacklines on the previous pages for reflection forms for various skills at various grade levels.

Reflection Review and Planning. A helpful process for teams before they begin working on their team project the following day or on a new project is for teams to review their notes about their group processes. For example, students may RoundRobin read their responses to the question, "What is one thing your team could improve?" If the general consensus is that the team needs to keep focused, the team makes a plan for staying on task. A quick review and planning session at the outset of a project helps teams focus on the skills they need to improve.

Troubleshooting in the Cooperative Classroom

What do I do when a student is off task? Too shy to participate? Hostile toward others? There are a number of social skills problems that may occur that derail cooperative learning. And what do I do when it is not a single student's lack of or inappropriate use of social skills, but rather it's an interpersonal conflict where two or more students are butting heads, or worse? Here, we examine tips and techniques for dealing with the eight most frequent social skills challenges.

Social Skills Challenges

The five strategies we have overviewed, when in place, prevent or resolve the most common social-skills related problems. Here we'll look at the eight most common cooperative learning social skills problems and how the five strategies help.

---

8 Most Common Social Skills Challenges

1 **The Refusenik.** Student who refuses teamwork or to cooperate

2 **The Outcast.** Student who is rejected or ignored by teammates

3 **The Shrinking Violet.** Student who is too shy to fully participate

4 **The Dominator.** Student who dominates team interaction

5 **The Bully.** Student who displays hostility toward teammates

6 **The Clown.** Student who seeks attention by clowning

7 **The Drifter.** Student who is off task or gets teammates off task

8 **The Saboteur.** Student who undermines teammates and projects

---

Although the five strategies are wonderful for promoting social skills development within the context of cooperative learning, if the social skills problems escalate into discipline problems, especially persistent discipline problems, then we recommend *Win-Win Discipline.*[1] Win-Win Discipline is based on the premise that misbehavior stems from unmet student needs. Win-Win Discipline is a comprehensive program designed to help students acquire the social skills and life skills students need so that they don't need to be disruptive to meet their needs.

The "Bully" Isn't Always a Bully!

For easy recognition, we label social skills challenges as character types—the Bully, the Shrinking Violet, the Sabotuer.... However, it is important to realize we are talking about behaviors, not people. Any of us might be dominant at one time and shy at another, a bully in some situations, but meek in another. As teachers, we need to avoid a labeling mindset and be cautious to not engender a labeling mindset of our students. A student at times may clown around, but that does not make them always a "Clown." We offer these stereotypes to easily find suggested strategies for dealing with students who are displaying challenging behavior. Thankfully, student behaviors are not fixed, and with the appropriate strategies in place, every student can behave responsibly and respectfully.

See *Win-Win Discipline* for a comprehensive approach to preventing discipline problems, handling disruptions in the moment they occur, and how to follow up with students.

The Refusenik

The Refusenik refuses to work with the team and prefers to work alone.

5 Social Skills Strategies

1 Structures & Structuring RoundTable, RoundRobin, Talking Chips, Three-Step Interview, Flashcard Game, and almost all structures encourage active involvement by all teammembers.

2 Roles & Gambits Encouragers learn how to "bring in" a student without getting into a power play. Demands ("You have to do more") are poor gambits. Polite requests ("Would you be willing to....") are strong gambits.

Weaker students who refuse to work with others can benefit from a buddy who encourages and coaches.

We may assign a special role to the Refusenik. For example, a student may be assigned to the role of Roving Reporter to check for bright ideas coming from various groups. Given special status, the student might warm up to participating.

3 Modeling We hold up as a model teams in which everyone is contributing.

4 Reinforcement We compliment the Refusenik for participating in teamwork. "Alex, it's nice to see you working so well with your team."

5 Reflection & Planning
• Is everyone participating?
• How can we be sure to include everyone?
• How encouraging have we been?
• What can we say to encourage a teammate to participate?

Key Teamwork Skills
• **Encouraging Participation**
• **Polite Requests**
• **Accepting Individual Differences**
• **Helping**

Challenge 1

The Refusenik

The Refusenik refuses to work with teammates. A student may refuse to work with others for a variety of reasons, including feelings of inadequacy, shyness, or prior negative experiences interacting with others. Masked fear of failure is often the cause. A student may fear not knowing how to perform well, and would not like to fail in front of others. It is much safer to say, "I don't want to work with anyone else," than to say, "I am afraid others will see my inadequacy."

Thus, often the solution is to provide initial tasks at which you are certain all students will be successful. Teambuilding is a great start. No one can fail when doing a RoundRobin naming favorite foods or TV programs. Easy academic tasks, within the capacity of all students, are a great transition into cooperative learning.

If a student is weak academically, another tactic is to work with them on the task independently first so they know they can be successful. Another possibility is to assign as a shoulder partner a sympathetic "buddy" who can support, encourage, and tutor.

Some Refuseniks, however, are very strong students. They have been very successful working alone and simply do not want the rug pulled out from under them. Why would I risk a brand new way of working and learning if I knew I could be very successful in the way I have been working? For these students, it is helpful to let them know working with others is a skill, and it is a skill they will need for success at almost every job, as well as in their family.

For some students, it is helpful to simply give them some time and space to get used to the idea of working with others. One day while watching Doug Wilkinson (Dana Point Elementary, Dana Point, CA) begin cooperative learning, I was surprised to see a young boy immediately pop out of his seat, walk over to Doug, and in a loud voice say, "I don't want to work with anyone else." Wisely, Doug replied, "That's OK, if you want to work alone, you can. There is a desk in the back you can use."

The boy worked alone for almost the full hour, and just as the hour was ending, he walked over and peeked at the work of the other students who were working in teams.

Within a few months, whenever Doug would call for cooperative work, the picture was quite different. The boy would walk over to Doug and in a quiet voice say, "I don't want to work with anyone." Doug would say that was OK, and the boy would begin working alone. Within about five minutes, he would join his group.

Doug reported that there had been a steady decline in how much time the boy worked alone and a steady increase in cooperative work. As a psychologist, I recognized a classic situation of desensitization. For whatever reason, prior to entering Doug's class, the boy had developed an aversion to working with others. And slowly, at his own pace, he was desensitizing himself to working with others, finding it rewarding.

The boy had learned the most important lesson possible that school year. And it was made possible because Doug wisely side-stepped the power play. If, when the boy had said he did not want to work with others, Doug had insisted, Doug and his pupil might have gotten stuck in a power play, each trying to control the other.

Although we feel it is wise to control teamformation, and ask students to sit with their teammates, cooperative learning should be an opportunity, rather than an assignment. If students are not ready for teamwork, that is fine. The modern think tank is a nice model for the classroom. Sometimes people work alone, sometimes in groups, and there are individual differences in how much time each person prefers team versus individual work.

One way of increasing the probability that all students will participate is to make the positive interdependence of the cooperative learning task more salient. If all students know that the gain of one is a gain for all, teammates will be more likely to encourage participation of all members. Further, if the Refusenik is a good student who does well on his or her own, when that student realizes that helping others will lead to gains for him/herself, the student will be more likely to participate.

Assigning attractive roles is another approach. For example, if the Refusenik is #3 on a team, we might say, "Today all the #3's will have a very special role. They will be in charge of carefully cutting out the materials we will use in building

our team space stations. Be very careful #3's, the success of your teams depends on you. Your teammates are counting on you." Later in the lesson, we might structure for encouragement or praise by saying, "Teammates, take a moment to let all the #3's know how much you appreciate the careful job they are doing."

Challenge 2

The Outcast

The Outcast is the student who is rejected by teammates. Some students begin the school year carrying heavy baggage from previous years. The rejected student may have been rejected before you began cooperative learning. As students first sit down in their teams, at one team there may

The Outcast

The Outcast is the student who is rejected or ignored by teammates.

5 Social Skills Strategies

1 **Structures & Structuring** RoundTable, RoundRobin, Team Interview, Jigsaw, RallyCoach, and almost all structures encourage inclusion of all students.

2 **Roles & Gambits** The Gatekeeper opens the gate for the Outcast's participation: "I would like to hear what you think, Stanford." The Gatekeeper may gracefully close the gate for one while opening it for another: "Bob, let's see if José agrees with you." Assign a high-status student the role of buddy to the outcasted student.

3 **Modeling** Model for students how to encourage participation and elicit everyone's opinions.

4 **Reinforcement** Pay positive attention to those teams who are including all students: "I really appreciate how every member of the Mars Team is involved."

5 **Reflection & Planning**
• What are we doing to make all students feel included?
• How can we make sure everyone is included?
• What can we say if we feel we are being ignored?

Key Teamwork Skills
• **Encouraging Participation**
• **Equal Participation**

be comments like, "Oh yuck!" and "Look who we got stuck with."

Students can be incredibly cruel. They do not realize the hurt they are causing by rejection. Often, students aren't trying to be hurtful, rather they're trying to fit in themselves. They need to stop and reflect on the effect they are having by rejecting others. One technique is to have students role-play receiving rejecting statements and then share with each other how they felt when they were rejected. This, of course, is done without specific reference to any person in the class. If we do this activity, we follow up by having students make and process the effect of accepting appreciative statements like "It's great to have you as a teammate!"

Sometimes teams don't actively reject a teammate, but for whatever reason, tend to ignore a teammate. In this case, students can share what it feels like to be ignored or to not fit in. These techniques lead to an enhanced empathy among students so they cannot reject or ignore a fellow student without sharing the pain. They know what it feels like to be on the receiving end. At that point, they will no longer want to reject a fellow student.

Another effective technique is to talk privately with one of the class leaders, preferably the most popular student in class and discuss the problem. Ask if he or she is willing to be a "super helper" or "big brother/sister" and "adopt" the rejected student. When an unpopular student becomes friends with a very popular student, the otherwise rejected student is almost always accepted by the other students.

Look also for special skills in the rejected student and then create a cooperative project to bring those skills to light. This approach can include giving the student some special reading or task in preparation for a team project, so the student will have a special contribution to make. Jigsaw and division of labor structures work well in this regard.

Challenge 3
The Shrinking Violet

The Shrinking Violet is a shy student. Shyness is common and can hinder social and academic development. Shy students, for fear of attention or social rejection, rarely risk participating in

front of the whole class, not voluntarily anyway. Frequently, they keep their ideas and opinions to themselves, which is unfortunate because many shy students are quite bright and could make valuable contributions.

The Shrinking Violet

The Shrinking Violet is the student who is too shy to fully participate in social situations.

5 Social Skills Strategies

1 **Structures & Structuring** Mix-Pair-Share, Talking Chips, Turn Toss, RoundRobin, Roundtable, Pairs Check, and Flashcard Game encourage everyone to participate.

2 **Roles & Gambits** The Encourager learns how to provide inclusion opportunities without putting a student on the spot. Weak gambit: "John, you haven't said a thing. What is your opinion?" Stronger gambit: "John, I would like to know what you think about that."

Have students practice "starter gambits"—gambits that begin a contribution. ("I have an idea…." "Let me add…." "What I think is….")

You may wish to assign the shy student the role of Observer, watching for a specific teammate behavior, with the job of reporting back to the group about that behavior.

You may wish to show empathy and encouragement. Let the student know you understand their difficulty and appreciate their contributions. "Sometimes I feel shy when I'm in an unfamiliar situation. But the more I practice and contribute, the more comfortable and confident I become."

3 **Modeling** Model for students the gambits to use if a student is not participating.

4 **Reinforcement** "Great job of contributing today, Sam."

5 **Reflection & Planning**
• Are we including everyone?
• Is everyone participating?
• How can we make everyone on the team feel comfortable?
• What can we do if someone is hesitant to share?

Key Teamwork Skills
• **Encouraging Participation**

Cooperative learning can help many students overcome what otherwise would become a limiting personality characteristic. The shy student finds it far easier to talk to a partner than to talk in a group of three, and infinitely more comfortable in pair work than when speaking in front of the whole class.

One of the most effective approaches with the shy student is to get the other three students to request, show interest in, and praise the contributions of the student. Teammates, when caring and motivated, can often "bring out" the shy student in remarkably short order.

As with the rejected student, if we engage a student leader to befriend the shy student, we have more than half the battle won.

Also, finding the special interests or talents of the shy student, and making one of those areas a project topic, is a powerful approach.

When forming groups, we find it helpful to include the shy student in a team with at least one other quiet or less dominant student. The shy student needs "room" to make an entry and does not do well in a group comprised solely of dominant teammates.

Challenge 4
The Dominator

The dominant student is often a well-intentioned, high-achieving student who does not realize the alienating effect of their controlling efforts. Sometimes, by sheer force of personality, a dominant student who is weak academically will get a team to go along with a poor approach to a problem or even a false answer, while a meeker student has a superior solution.

The dominant student needs to learn their stimulus value for others. It can be helpful to have students take turns playing the role of dominating the group, and then have students reflect on how it felt to be in that group. Finally, students discuss gambits for dealing with over-controlling behavior on the part of a teammate. It is also helpful if students recognize the good intentions that usually underlie the controlling behavior. This may increase the ability of teammates to label and deal with dominance gambits.

The Dominator

The Dominator controls the team with a forceful personality. The dominator hogs team time and may have an undue influence on team decision making.

5 Social Skills Strategies

1 **Structures & Structuring** Talking Chips with Timer, Timed Pair Share, Paraphrase Passport, Timed RoundTable, and Timed RoundRobin encourage equal participation.

2 **Roles & Gambits** Gatekeeper, Question Commander, Encourager. Have students practice gambits for including everyone. Poor: "John, you are doing all the talking." Stronger: "Susan, what do you think about what John has been telling us?"

Assign roles so that each person has a unique and important contribution to make to the task.

3 **Modeling** Have a team role-play for the class what a dominant student looks like and how to politely equalize participation.

4 **Reinforcement** Pay positive attention to groups in which there is equal participation. Appreciate the dominant student in private for sharing the floor with teammates. "Julie, I really liked the way you got everyone's opinion. That's great leadership."

5 **Reflection & Planning**
• How equal has our participation been so far today?
• How can we make it more equal?
• What can we say to the student who is being too bossy?
• How would you feel if you weren't allowed to participate?

Key Teamwork Skills
• **Equal Participation**
• **Taking Turns**
• **Getting Opinions of Others**

Challenge 5

The Bully

Often the Bully is either hostile toward others or uses hostile or bully behavior to dominate the group. Steven crumples up the team Mind-Map and throws it at Tyrell. Jane grabs the crayon out of Mai's hand. Peter calls Michelle an idiot. Before acquiring social skills, verbal and physical hostility among students, unfortunately, is common.

The first rule is that the classroom must be safe—physically and emotionally—for all students. If a student displays violent or abusive behavior toward other students or poses a threat to other students, the student must be immediately removed from the social situation. When a student is hostile to others he/she may be sent to an isolated desk, to a cool down area, or to the office if the offense warrants it.

Hostile and aggressive behavior is often attention-seeking behavior, so it is important that it not be rewarded with attention. The student is simply removed from team interaction quickly and quietly without interruption. For example, "Steven, five minutes time out please." After five minutes, the teacher walks up to Steven and asks if he's ready to apologize to teammates for his unacceptable behavior. If yes, then he apologizes to teammates and joins back in. If no, then the student is excused from teamwork for the activity, lesson, project, or day, depending on the student and the offense.

If the hostile behavior is less severe, and doesn't pose a threat (one student grabbing materials from another), then a warning or consequence reminder may be sufficient. When possible, we establish consequences in advance. We can then remind the student of the consequence: "If you do X, then Y will happen." There is no discussion, no negotiation, and no power play.

Some aggressive behavior occurs for lack of knowledge of alternatives, or the behavior is a reflection of negative peer norms. Students grab paper or materials because they have not practiced "Polite Requests." Students put each other down because putdowns have become an antisocial peer norm, and students sling them unthinkingly. For these cases, students need to know these behaviors are inappropriate and need practice using appropriate alternatives. For example, students may brainstorm put downs, then discuss how they would feel if the insult was directed to them. Then students list positive alternatives.

The Bully

The Bully is the student who displays aggressive behavior toward other students.

5 Social Skills Strategies

1 **Structures & Structuring** Structures that lavish a student with attention (Circle-the-Sage, Team Interview, Instant Star) meet the Bully's need for attention. Structures with praise (Drop-A-Chip) meet students' need for feeling liked and important. Structures that give leadership opportunities (Timed RoundRobin, Showdown) meet students' need for status or dominance. Structures with reflection components (Journal Reflections) allow Bullies time to think. High structuring is important to reduce aggressive behavior.

2 **Roles & Gambits** Praiser, Encourager, Cheerleader. Promote teamwork and getting along. Develop gambits for disagreeing politely, and for resolving conflicts.

3 **Modeling** Model for teams what to do when a student displays aggressive behavior toward teammates or classmates.

4 **Reinforcement** Praise the class for good teamwork. Compliment the Bully in private for good behavior. "I'm proud of you Billy. You've been getting along very well with your teammates."

5 **Reflection & Planning**
• Have we been showing respect and appreciation to each other?
• What can we do if there is a disagreement?
• What can we do if someone grabs something from us?
• What polite request gambits have you heard today?
• What can we say to the student who is being a bully?
• How would you feel if someone was being a bully to you?

Key Teamwork Skills

• **Praising**
• **Polite Requests**
• **Disagree Politely**
• **Conflict Resolution**

To have students take ownership of becoming more responsible, we may use Win-Win Discipline strategies for the moment-of-disruption. Two powerful strategies are "Make a Better Choice" and "Picture it Right."[2] In Make a Better Choice, the teacher empowers the student to reflect on the problem behavior and create a more positive response. To use Picture it Right, when a student acts irresponsibly, we ask the student to envision what appropriate behavior would look like, share it with the teacher, then attempt to align behavior to the vision.

Hostile and aggressive behavior is much more likely in situations in which there is low structuring and/or low motivation than if there is high structuring and high motivation. For example, hostile behavior will rarely occur during a quick-paced, exciting RoundTable. During an unstructured Team Discussion about an uninteresting topic, the probability of hostile or aggressive behavior increases dramatically. Therefore, if there is some likelihood of hostile behavior, high structuring is preferable.

If a student is hostile, very often we work with his/her three teammates to practice positive reinforcement. Teammates make positive statements and give attention to the student when the student is behaving well. They may say things like "I am really enjoying working with you today, Mike." Positive reinforcement may be applied with good success with full knowledge of all of the students, including the hostile student. In introducing the approach you might say something like "Mike, you have had some trouble controlling yourself. I want you to be clear about the positive effect it has on others when you do show control. So, I am going to ask your teammates to share with you how good they feel about working with you when you're respecting others."

Challenge 6
The Clown

The class clown, when placed on a team, may become the team clown. Clowning is usually an attempt to get attention. Since students receive far more positive peer attention in cooperative learning than in the traditional classroom, many class clowns end or reduce their clowning behavior when we put cooperative learning in place. Nevertheless, some persist, so we need to apply the five social skills strategies.

As we teach, we structure so that students get attention from us and from their peers. We can use simple techniques like using the student's name in an example, or making an extra effort as we circulate through the class to pause and comment on the work of a student needing special attention.

The Clown

The Clown craves attention and, in the process, may get the team off task.

5 Social Skills Strategies

1 Structures & Structuring
Use a variety of structures that give students individual peer attention like Instant Star, interview structures, Timed Pair Share, and Paraphrase Passport. Use structures that accept and validate individual differences like Corners, Agreement Circles, and Agree-Disagree Line-Ups.

2 Roles & Gambits
Keep the Clown on task with a Focus Keeper role. Develop appropriate gambits for getting the Clown back on task. Assign the Clown a busy job for which he/she will be accountable. Provide gambits to respond to a clown ("That is funny, but what we need to focus on is….").

3 Modeling Use on-task teams as positive models for the class. Model effective ways to respond to a clown.

4 Reinforcement Praise teams for staying focused on their task.

5 Reflection & Planning
• Did we stay on task?
• Did anyone get us off task? If so, how did we handle it?
• How could we respond even better in the future?
• Why is it important for us to stay focused on our work?
• When is it appropriate to clown around, and when not?

Key Teamwork Skills
• Self-Control
• Self-Validation
• Pride in One's work
• Impulse Control

We use structures that provide students plenty of attention and assign roles that give students special status and attention. When students receive plenty of attention as part of the regular classroom diet, they have less need to clown around in attempts to satisfy that "look at me" need.

Ultimately, we would like to have the Clown validate her/himself so she/he needs less validation from teacher and classmates. Of course, students don't suddenly become self-validating. The bridge to self-validation is acceptance and validation by others. When a student is frequently validated by others, the student begins to internalize that validation and the need for external validation gradually drops away. Many of the classbuilding structures that include acceptance and valuing of diversity help develop an internal sense of worth. For example, in Corners and Agree-Disagree Line-Ups, we listen with respect to all points of view. Paraphrase Passport is also excellent for conveying that each person is heard and understood.

Challenge 7
The Drifter

The Drifter is off task and often gets teammates off task too. Students may intentionally or unintentionally get their teammates off task for a variety of reasons, including lack of interest in the task, need to share personal information, need for attention from teammates, lack of impulse control, and/or lack of ability to sustain interest. For example, as a team is discussing their team science experiment, the Drifter may be more interested in talking about his weekend. If the team is brainstorming a list of possible solutions to the problem, the Drifter is too busy rearranging things on her desk to contribute. Do you know the Drifter? Maybe you have one or two in your class.

Cooperative learning goes a long way to getting the Drifter back on task. The two top reasons students get off task are 1) lack of interest in the content of the lesson, and 2) lack of engaging instructional strategies. Cooperative structures are the antidote to monotonous instruction. They make the learning process more engaging in part because they are more active and engage more intelligences and learning styles. When we are versed in a wide range of structures, there is more novelty in our classrooms. One minute students are working in teams, soon they are pairing up with someone else in the classroom, and before long they are drawing ideas in a Team Mind Map. Novel and varied tasks sustain interest.

The Drifter

The Drifter is easily sidetracked and may get the team off task.

5 Social Skills Strategies

1. **Structures & Structuring** Use a variety of structures to create novelty. Use structures frequently to allow for novelty and social interaction. Structure for Individual Accountability, holding students accountable for tasks. Structure for Simultaneous Interaction, making learning highly interactive.

2. **Roles & Gambits** Keep the Drifter on task with a team Focus Keeper. Have the Encourager encourage everyone to keep on task. Develop appropriate gambits for getting the Drifter back on task. Assign the Drifter a busy job such as Recorder.

3. **Modeling** Model effective use of the Focus Keeper role.

4. **Reinforcement** Praise teams and individuals for staying on task.

5. **Reflection & Planning**
   - Why is it important for the team that everyone stays on task?
   - Did we stay on task?
   - What got us off task?
   - When we got off task, what worked well to get us re-focused?
   - How can we keep on task more?

Key Teamwork Skills
- **Self-control**
- **Staying Focused**
- **Motivating Others**
- **Perseverance**

Cooperative learning is more engaging also because it makes the learning more social. People are social organisms. We hunger for human interaction. For proof, look no further than some of the most important technological breakthroughs in the modern era: cell phones, the Internet, instant messaging, e-mails—all modes of communication, connecting us to each other. When deprived of human interaction too long, we crave it. The Drifter's threshold for human interaction may be substantially lower, and therefore the Drifter seeks interaction by getting off task. In cooperative learning, students are seated in close physical proximity and frequently interact. This partially explains research that finds students in cooperative learning are more on task than in the traditional classroom.

We will have even less drifting in our classrooms if we structure learning tasks for the inclusion of two cooperative learning principles: Individual Accountability and Simultaneous Interaction. Individual Accountability holds students accountable for their participation. If the Drifter must represent the team by sharing the team's answer with the class, the Drifter is less likely to be sidetracked because his team is counting on him to represent them well. Simultaneous Interaction keeps all students engaged and reduces downtime to a minimum. Most structures have these two principles built in. But for unstructured cooperative interactions where off task behavior is more probable, ask the questions: How will my Drifters be held accountable? How will they be actively engaged?

Drifting increases in direct proportion to lack of interest in the academic task. We can make curriculum more motivating for our students as we:

- Show real-world applications
- Point out discrepancies
- Ask provocative questions
- Make a bang (science experiments, costumes)
- Point out the "cool" parts
- Link it to students' personal interests
- Evoke emotion
- Build a bridge between new and existing knowledge
- Express our own excitement about the content

Roles are helpful for keeping students on task. The first, and most obvious, is the Focus Keeper. With gambits like "Come on team, let's focus on….", the Focus Keeper gets the team to focus on the task at hand. A trick regarding roles is to give the Drifter the busiest role possible, so there is no time to get off task. You know the saying, "Idle hands are the Drifter's workshop." For example, if the team is generating a list, assign the Drifter the role of Recorder.

Challenge 8
The Saboteur

The Saboteur either subtly or overtly undermines the group. The overt Saboteur may make de-motivating statements ("That won't work.") or

The Saboteur

The Saboteur undermines the group by not doing his/her share, projecting a negative attitude, or making de-motivating and killer statements.

5 Social Skills Strategies

1. **Structures & Structuring** Teambuilding structures bring the team together. Instead of voting, which can polarize and isolate, use Consensus Seeking, Spend-A-Buck, and Sum-the-Ranks. Use Pass-N-Praise to promote a positive team norm.

2. **Roles & Gambits** Praiser, Encourager, Focus Keeper. "We can make this work if we all work together." "None of us can do it alone, but we can all do it together."

3. **Modeling** We hold up as a model teams in which everyone is contributing.

4. **Reinforcement** Teach teammates how to reinforce the Saboteur when she/he is positive. Reinforce teams that maintain a "can do" attitude.

5. **Reflection & Planning**
   - Did we make positive, encouraging statements?
   - When were we most positive? What got us down?
   - What are ways we can pick ourselves up when we get discouraged?
   - What can we do if someone puts down a teammate's idea?

Key Teamwork Skills
- **Positive Attitude**
- **Re-orienting the Focus**

killer statements ("That's stupid!"). The overt Saboteur is easier to deal with than the covert Saboteur who passively undermines by not doing his/her share, showing bored body language, or simply not working at all. The saboteur is not to be confused with the Refusenik. The Refusenik does not work with others; he or she would rather work alone. The Saboteur may actually enjoy his/her role in the team—undermining the team.

Why in the world would a student be motivated to undermine her/his own team? Often it is for revenge. For example, the team has a project to do. There has been a discussion of the topic for the project, and the idea of one student is not accepted because the other three prefer a different topic. Feeling rejected, the student may become a Saboteur. The student is motivated to show that the idea that was accepted over her own was not good and would not work. Alternatively, a student may become a Saboteur because he/she has been put on a team with others he/she does not want to work with. The Saboteur may want to prove that this new way of working together won't work.

Among our most powerful strategies for dealing with the Saboteur is creating buy-in when we first form teams and at the outset of tasks. An ounce of prevention is worth a pound of cure. When we first set up teams, we do plenty of teambuilding, ensuring that the teammates bond and want to be part of the team. When teams make decisions we do not use polarizing structures like voting because voting creates winners and losers. We use structures that seek consensus. We put in place a rule: We do not have a decision until we can all agree.

Roles, gambits, and modeling are all helpful. We can teach students what to do to keep the tone in groups positive; we can model how to respond to verbal and nonverbal put-downs and killer statements. When a student says, "This will never work," other students who have acquired appropriate gambits can reply, "It may seem like it won't work, but I am sure that if we all work together we can make it happen." Or, "If you think it won't work, you may be right, you may be wrong. But if we all think it will work and make it work, we can all be right!" To the student who says, "That idea is dumb," the others learn to say, "I respectfully disagree. I think it is a great idea—let me explain why." Re-orienting comments by teammates don't come about magically. We have students brainstorm and practice gambits that move the Saboteur from "can't do" to "can do."

Reflection and planning are helpful strategies as well. Students can reflect on how positive the tone and attitude was in their teams and what they all can do to make it even more positive.

Handling Interpersonal Conflicts

Conflicts are a reality for any class and are certain to occur from time to time in the cooperative class because students interact so much. There are, however, numerous positive forces operating to mitigate the likelihood of conflict in a well-run cooperative learning classroom. Because of teambuilding, classbuilding, social skill development, and positive interdependence, students' general orientation becomes more caring and cooperative, and less competitive and aggressive. Students are more communicative in the cooperative classroom and develop their communication skills so they are more capable of talking out and peacefully resolving conflicts. Nevertheless, conflicts will arise and the ability to resolve these conflicts are key skills for teachers and students.

Power Struggles and Decision Making

One of the most typical struggles in the classroom is the struggle for power and decision. One student wants the team report to be on starfish. The other wants it to be on dolphins. Neither is willing to budge. On another team, students argue whose idea is better for the team story. They butt heads. These power struggles can be easily resolved by using decision-making structures. Students need to know to seek consensus first, and if they can't come to consensus, they can use one of the following decision-making structures.

Consensus Seeking. Students talk over the alternatives seeking consensus. The guiding principle is to find an outcome that "everyone can live with." It may not be anyone's favorite outcome, but it is an outcome to which no one has strong objections. Students need to be "set" for consensus seeking with something like this:

> "When we seek consensus, we are not trying to get our way. We are looking for a decision we can all get behind, even if it is not our first choice. Consensus is a challenge for the group: Can we find something everyone can support?"

Sum-the-Ranks. The alternatives are spread out before the team. Each teammate writes a number corresponding to his or her rank of the alternative. For example, if there are three alternatives, the student would write "1" on his number one choice, "2" on his second choice, and "3" on his last choice. When all teammates have ranked the alternatives, the team sums the ranks. The alternative with the lowest sum wins.

Spend-A-Buck. Each student has ten dimes (chips, tokens). The rule is they must spend them on at least two alternatives. After students have spent their buck, the team sums the money and the one worth the most wins.

Conflicts over Materials

Materials are a frequent source of conflict, especially for the little ones doing unstructured team projects. Sherri and Mary both want the red marker. Rob and Bob both want to glue. Whatever should the team do? Here are some easy fixes.

Roles. Give each student a role. With the role, students have their own assigned task and materials. There is no confusion as to who gets what and gets to do what.

Turn Taking. Institute turn taking. If there are four markers, and each student wants red, they'll all get red—when it's their turn. Use an interval timer. Each minute, students rotate their materials clockwise.

Use a Timer. A timer works well with rules and turns. Students can rotate roles or switch materials when time is up so everyone gets a fair turn.

Right Revocation or Suspension. When all else fails, we may need to resort to suspending or even revoking access to the materials. When de-structuring the task and a conflict arises over materials, calmly tell the team, "I see we're having a difficult time deciding who gets to use the magnifying glass. Please resolve your conflict in your team. If I have to come back, you'll have to finish without it." This is not a hostile threat; it's a calm consequence. If the team continues to fight over the material in question, simply take it away, no negotiations, no questions asked. If the item is integral to the task, rights to use it may be suspended instead of revoked.

Team Conflict Resolution

We want students to become autonomous problem solvers. The responsibility for resolving nonphysical interpersonal conflicts resides with the team first. The teacher is brought in only after the team has tried unsuccessfully to resolve their own problem. For example, if a student is grabbing materials, the first step is for a teammate to make a polite request, "Jennifer, please don't grab the pen out of my hand." If the student continues to be rude, the next step is for the team to engage in conflict resolution

8 Modes of Conflict Resolution

To remember the 8 modes of conflict resolution, remember the acronym, **STOP HACC**.

Kagan Cooperative Learning • **Dr. Spencer Kagan & Miguel Kagan**
Kagan Publishing • 1 (800) 933-2667 • www.KaganOnline.com

or mediation. "I would like the team to mediate this conflict we're having." Positive peer influence is usually all it takes to resolve interpersonal squabbles. Students violating the appropriate code of team conduct need to hear how they are preventing the team from reaching the team's goal. If that still doesn't work, then the teacher may be called in for help.

Mediation. Students can be taught the skills of conflict resolution and how to be a conflict mediator. A team may need the teacher, another team, the class, or a student conflict mediator to help resolve the conflict. The teacher may ask other teams to brainstorm possible solutions. Student mediators usually have each person in the conflict, in turn, state what he or she wants, without interruption. Following their statement, the other person paraphrases. Once each feels they have been heard, they engage in problem solving, attempting to find a win-win solution—some way both of their needs can be met.

Conflict Resolution
Activities and Instruction

Conflict resolution and peacekeeping is a rich field. There are many excellent resources to help educators teach the skills of conflict resolution as a curriculum. In addition to mediation, conflict resolution activities include:

- **Role-play and Simulations.** Students act out situations of conflict and appropriate solutions.
- **Storytelling.** Students hear stories about conflict and how the conflicts are resolved.
- **Perspective Shifting.** Students practice taking the role of the other, and seeing the world through the eyes of the other.
- **Modes of Conflict Resolution.** Students learn about the many ways to resolve conflicts, so they are well prepared to handle conflicts once they arise. See the 8 Modes of Conflict Resolution on the previous page.

Chapter Summary

Students need a range of social skills for cooperative learning to run smoothly. To name a few, students need to know how to help, listen, share, participate, and respect differences. Many of these skills are not necessary for working independently in the traditional classroom. Perhaps that explains why students in cooperative classrooms are more cooperative and caring. They watch and practice effective use of social skills on a daily basis.

Through many and varied cooperative interactions, students acquire important people skills. Social skills are a curriculum embedded in structures. This social skills curriculum is delivered simultaneously with the academic curriculum, with little or no time taken away from the academic curriculum. Five strategies

facilitate the acquisition of social skills. These five strategies are also quite helpful in solving some of the most common problems that arise in groups. When problems arise in groups, it is a signal that some dimension of the social skills curriculum is not yet mastered. Cooperative learning offers the opportunity for students to acquire the skills they most need for success.

Through daily practice, students learn how to share resources. They learn how to include each other. They learn how to listen to each other. They learn to do their fair share. They learn to disagree politely. Cooperative learning delivers an essential curriculum—the social skills that will serve our students well throughout their lives and careers.

Chapter Questions

► Questions for Review

1. What are some important social skills for successful cooperative learning?
2. What are the "Will" and the "Skill" for cooperative learning?
3. List three reasons why students may be lacking the social skills necessary for effective cooperative learning.
4. What are the 5 Tools for developing social skills?
5. When should roles be used and when shouldn't they?
6. What is the difference between structures and structuring?

► Questions for Thinking and Discussion

1. Social skills are equally if not more important for students to master than the academic curriculum. Do you agree or disagree? Why?
2. How are social skills important for students in cooperative learning? In their family lives? In the workplace?
3. If you could develop just one social skill in every student whom you teach, what would be the skill and why?
4. Of the 5 Tools for developing social skills, which one do you think will be the most helpful for you? Why?
5. How have you used modeling? Has it been successful? What insights do you have that might be helpful for modeling social skills?
6. Which approach do you think would be more effective for developing students' social skills: direct instruction on social skills or teaching social skills as an embedded curriculum? Defend your answer.
7. Do you think using extrinsic rewards to develop social skills is being overly manipulative? Why or why not?

References

[1] Kagan, S., P. Kyle & S. Scott. *Win-Win Discipline.* San Clemente, CA: Kagan Publishing, 2004.

[2] Kagan, S., P. Kyle & S. Scott. *Win-Win Discipline.* San Clemente, CA: Kagan Publishing, 2004.

Resources

A.C. Nielsen and Company. *Nielsen Media Research.* A.C. Nielsen and Company, 2000.

American Family Research Council. *Parents Fight 'Time Famine' as Economic Pressures Increase.* American Family Research Council, 1990.

Andrini, B. *Cooperative Learning and Mathematics.* San Clemente, CA: Kagan Publishing, 1991.

Children Now. *Play Fair: Violence, Gender, and Race in Video Games.* Oakland, CA: Children Now, 2001.

Curran, L. *Lessons for Little Ones, Language Arts: Cooperative Learning Lessons.* San Clemente, CA: Kagan Publishing, 1990.

Federal Interagency Forum on Child and Family Statistics. *America's Children: Key National Indicators of Well Being Annual Report.* Federal Interagency Forum on Child and Family Statistics, 2002. http://www.Childstats.gov

Gwilliam, J., G. Hughes, D. Jenkins, W. Koczka & L. Nicholis. *Working Together, Learning Together: The Cooperatively Structured Classroom.* Regina, Saskatchewan: Department of Cooperation and Cooperative Development, Saskatchewan Co-operation and Co-operative Development, 1983.

Johnson, D. & R. Johnson. *Creative Conflict.* Edina, MN: Interaction Book Company, 1988.

Kagan, S. *The Role Card Kit.* San Clemente, CA: Kagan Publishing, 2004.

Kagan, S., P. Kyle & S. Scott. *Win-Win Discipline.* San Clemente, CA: Kagan Publishing, 2004.

Kreidler, W. *Creative Conflict Resolution.* Glenview, IL: Goodyear Books, Scott, Foresman & Co., 1984.

Lee, K., J. Oakes, J. Cohn, N. Webb & S. Farivar. *Helping Behaviors Handbook.* Los Angeles, CA: Unpublished Manuscript, Graduate School of Education, University of California–Los Angeles, 1985.

Learning Chips™. San Clemente, CA: Kagan Publishing. www.KaganOnline.com

Lewin, K. *Resolving Social Conflicts.* New York, NY: Harper & Row, 1948.

Sapon-Shevin, M. "Teaching Cooperation." In Cartledge, G. & J. Milburn (eds.). *Teaching Social Skills to Children.* New York, NY: Pergamon Press, 1986.

Senate Judiciary Committee. *Children, Violence, and the Media.* Senate Judiciary Committee, 1999.

Shaw, V. *Communitybuilding.* San Clemente, CA: Kagan Publishing, 1992.

Shure, M. *Problem Solving in the Preschool.* Philadelphia, PA: Hahnemann University, 1989.

Smith, S., K. Lachlan & R. Tamborini. "Popular Video Games: Quantifying the Presentation of Violence and Its Context." *Journal of Broadcasting and Electronic Media,* 2003, 47(1): 58–76.

Stone, J. *Cooperative Learning & Language Arts: A Multi-Structural Approach.* San Clemente, CA: Kagan Publishing, 1989.

TimerTools™ Software. San Clemente, CA: Kagan Publishing. www.KaganOnline.com

U.S. Department of Labor, Bureau of Labor Statistics. Various Years. http://stats.bls.gov

Webb, N. "Student Interaction and Learning in Small Groups: A Research Summary." In Slavin, R., S. Sharan, S. Kagan, R. Hertz-Larowitz, C. Webb, & R. Schmuck (eds.). *Learning to Cooperate, Cooperating to Learn.* New York, NY: Plenum, 1985.

CHAPTER 12

Key 7
Basic Principles
PIES

The PIES principles are what set cooperative learning apart from other approaches to instruction; the PIES principles are the lynchpin to successful cooperative learning.

Cooperative learning, when properly implemented, is a powerful instructional approach resulting in a spectrum of positive outcomes. Notice the caveat: *When properly implemented*. Research, theory, and years of implementation have led us to conclude that consistent success depends on four basic principles. When these basic principles are in place, cooperative learning consistently produces academic gains, improves race relations, develops social skills, educates for character, promotes self-esteem, enhances class climate, and fosters leadership and teamwork skills. When the four basic principles are not implemented, gains are not guaranteed.

The acronym PIES helps us remember the four basic principles:
- **P**ositive Interdependence
- **I**ndividual Accountability
- **E**qual Participation
- **S**imultaneous Interaction

sneak peek
- The PIES Critical Questions **12.2**
- A PIES Analysis **12.24**

The set of four basic principles, PIES, are unique to Kagan Cooperative Learning. Most approaches to cooperative learning recognize Positive Interdependence and Individual Accountability as basic principles, but each approach distinguishes different additional principles. Spencer Kagan developed the principles of Equal Participation and Simultaneous Interaction to help us ensure both equal and maximum engagement. We firmly believe the PIES principles are the lynchpin to successful cooperative learning. When all of the PIES principles are in place, we can be sure we will get academic and social gains. If any of the PIES principles are not implemented, we may or may not get gains. Once we understand PIES and how to implement the principles, we are prepared to unleash the full potential of cooperative learning. Applying PIES helps us understand why some instructional strategies successfully produce cooperation and achievement whereas others fail.

Understanding the principles and using structures that embody the principles empowers us to create classrooms where students work together, acquire social skills, care about each other, and achieve more. The PIES principles are so important, so foundational, that they should be an integral part of every educator's training. Knowing and applying the PIES principles determines to a large extent our effectiveness as teachers.

Group Work is NOT Cooperative Learning!

The PIES principles distinguish cooperative learning from group work. If any of the PIES principles are not present, we are merely doing group work. The PIES principles define true cooperative learning. Group work produces hit or miss results. True cooperative learning produces consistent gains for all learners.

The PIES Critical Questions

The PIES principles are best understood via five critical questions. By asking five simple questions, we determine if PIES are in place. The table below overviews the questions associated with each principle.

The PIES Critical Questions

Positive Interdependence
Question 1. Positive Correlation: *Are students on the same side?*
Question 2. Interdependence: *Does the task require working together?*

Individual Accountability
Question 3. *Is individual, public performance required?*

Equal Participation
Question 4. *Is participation approximately equal?*

Simultaneous Interaction
Question 5. *What percent of students are overtly interacting at once?*

Positive Interdependence
The "P" of PIES

Positive interdependence is the most well-established principle in the study of cooperation. When positive interdependence is in place, individuals are almost certain to cooperate. In the absence of positive interdependence, they may or may not cooperate. What do we mean by positive interdependence? Positive interdependence refers to two distinct conditions that promote cooperation:

1) a positive correlation of outcomes, and
2) interdependence.

Positive Correlation. The word *positive* in the term "positive interdependence" refers to "a positive correlation among outcomes." A positive correlation occurs when outcomes go up or down together, when they are positively linked. Picture two mountain climbers tethered together. One is above, and the other is below. If the one above gets a good foothold, she can support or pull up the one below. A gain for one is a benefit for the other. If the climber below slips, it puts a strain on the one above, or may even pull her down. Outcomes go up together or down together—they are positively correlated. The mountain climbers experience themselves as a team; they are on the same side working toward the same goal.

When there is a positive correlation among outcomes, participants almost certainly work together. They cooperate, help each other, and encourage each other. In class, if I know your success will somehow benefit me, naturally I hope you will do well and I will encourage, help, and tutor you. When there is a positive correlation among outcomes, we sense we're on the same side and encourage each other's successes: Your gain is a gain for me; my gain is a gain for you. It is the feeling we have when we are both working toward a common goal, building something together, or pooling the money we earn to use toward something we both want. Members of an athletic team cheer for and assist teammates in part because the success of one benefits all. We can test for a positive correlation by asking a very simple question: *Do students feel they are on the same side?*

The opposite of a positive correlation is a negative correlation. If your loss results in my gain, I will hope for your failure. This is the case in competitive classrooms that pit students against one another. For example, during Whole Class Q & A, after the teacher asks a question, students excitedly raise their hands. They compete to be called on, motivated by the opportunity to win teacher and peer attention and respect, validate their own thinking, or simply to be active and engaged. When a student is called on, those who were not selected lower their hands with a collective sigh of disappointment, "ahhhh." They were beat to the punch. But if the called-on student begins to falter, classmates' hands shoot back up, flailing wildly. Students are excited to see their classmate fail. Only if a classmate fails can they win what they wanted: to be called on. Their success depends on the failure of another. There is a negative correlation of outcomes. Classroom situations with negative interdependence develop an "against" social orientation. Students feel they are in competition with each other and see their classmates as obstacles to their success. They are on opposite sides, and therefore do not cooperate.

Positive Interdependence —A Natural State of Relations

Animal behavior provides wonderful and mysterious examples of positive interdependence where individuals cooperate for mutual benefit.

Sharing a Meal

- Wolves work together to bring down an animal much larger than any one of them.
- Sponges are a colony of individual cells that feed by coordinated beating of flagella: food is filtered out, and the water is expelled through vents.
- Vampire bats share blood meals in intimate exchanges with roost mates that have failed to find their own food.

Safety in Numbers

- Meerkats of the same den trade lookout duty to alert others of danger.
- When threatened, musk oxen form a circle around their young with their horns outward.
- Fish swim in schools to thwart predators.
- One or a few guppies sally forth from their school to approach a potential predator, or to gain information about potential danger.
- Colonial animals are less vulnerable to threats and better prepared to protect the young.

Keeping Healthy

- The Egyptian plover bird hops fearlessly into the open mouth of the Nile crocodile to remove parasites.
- Cleaning fish get a meal as they clean the teeth of larger fish. The cleaners swim inside the open mouths of larger fish, carefully eat the debris and parasites, and swim out unscathed.
- Impalas pick dangerous ticks from one another's backs.
- Monkeys and apes groom each other, picking ticks, fleas, and lice and eat them as a source of nutrition.

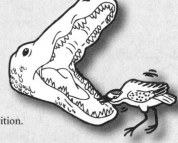

Symbiotic Relationships

- Bees pollinate flowers and agricultural crops while they collect precious nectar that provides their hives with food.
- The calvaria major plant nearly disappeared when the dodo bird became extinct because the bird germinated the seeds by scratching them in their gizzards.
- Fungi provide vital protection and moisture to algae; the algae nourish the fungi with photosynthetic nutrients that keep them alive.
- In perhaps the most complex symbiotic relationship known, leaf-cutter ants team up to fertilize mushroomlike fungus in vast underground gardens, and they protect the fungus against a devastating mold with antibiotics produced by a bacterium that lives in a patch on their skin. This interdependence involves four species.

Cooperation for mutual benefit is natural and pervasive.

To check for a positive correlation among outcomes, we ask a simple question:

Critical Question 1
Are students on the same side?

How Do Students Feel?
We are all on the same side.

If we can answer this question affirmatively, we have satisfied the first condition of positive interdependence.

Interdependence. The second condition of positive interdependence is interdependence. The word *interdependence* refers to how the task is structured. If a task is structured so no one of us can do it alone, but we can do it by working together, then we are interdependent. If I cannot do a task alone, but could do it with your help, what am I likely to do? Clearly, interdependence makes it more likely we will cooperate. If we are both really thirsty and want a soda that costs a dollar, but we each have only fifty cents, what are we likely to do? If there is buried treasure that neither of us alone could dig out, but we could obtain by working together, what are we likely to do? In the classroom, if we give each member of a team a different color and tell them they are allowed to draw with only their color, but that their team picture will be graded based on the integration of all of the colors, what are they likely to do? If we structure a learning task so that it cannot be done alone, but could be done if students work together, we have created interdependence and have dramatically increased the probability of cooperation.

It is important to note that a positive correlation does not always result in interdependence. For example, if we give a task to a team of students and tell them they will get a group grade, we create a positive correlation of outcomes. Their grades will rise or fall together. But if we have not carefully structured the task, a motivated or talented student might take over and do it all. While there is a positive correlation among outcomes and students experience themselves on the same side, we have not created interdependence. To create interdependence, we need to create a task where each person's contribution is necessary: The task requires working together.

To check for interdependence, we ask the second simple PIES question:

Critical Question 2
Does the task require working together?

How Do Students Feel?
We need each other to complete the task.

If we can answer this question affirmatively, we have satisfied the second condition of positive interdependence. There are varying degrees of interdependence as the table below describes. To ensure cooperation and achievement, we strive for the strongest form of interdependence.

Degrees of Interdependence

▶ **Weak Interdependence**
The contribution of each team member may contribute to the success of the team.

▶ **Intermediate Interdependence**
The contribution of each team member does contribute to the success of the team. But a team member could succeed on his/her own.

▶ **Strong Interdependence**
The contribution of each team member is necessary for the success of the team. The task is impossible without help—it requires working together.

Both Components Increase Cooperation. Both components of positive interdependence increase the probability of cooperation, but in different ways. A "positive correlation of outcomes" structures outcomes so students hope and work for positive outcomes for each other.

"Interdependence" structures the task so students need to work together. Teamwork is necessary to accomplish the task. When both conditions of positive interdependence are in place, students become helpful and encourage each other's academic success. Students feel teammates are on their side: Your knowledge and contributions benefit all of us. Peer norms shift to favor the achievement of all. A community of mutually supportive learners emerges.

The Two Components of Positive Interdependence

Component	Focus	Necessary Element
1 Positive Correlation	Outcome	A positive outcome for one benefits others.
2 Interdependence	Task	Cooperation is required for task completion.

Positive Interdependence Increases Cooperation

Positive interdependence increases cooperation in athletics, in the workplace, and in everyday life:
• The basketball player passes the ball so a teammate can shoot a basket, and their team is more likely to win.
• The author gives her paper to the editor, knowing the editor can catch errors the author could not.
• The workplace team pools knowledge and brainstorms solutions to come up with a better procedure or product.
• A husband and wife combine their money to buy a house neither alone could afford.

Creating Positive Interdependence

There are a number of ways we can create positive interdependence in the classroom. Some methods focus on creating a positive correlation of outcomes and others on creating interdependent tasks.

Positive Interdependence

• Two heads are better than one.
• None of us is as smart as all of us.
• We are in the same boat.
• We sink or swim together.

Creating A Positive Correlation: Structuring Outcomes

Team Goals. When teammates share an objective, they feel they are on the same side and help each other reach that objective. We can set up team goals by creating team products and team challenges. Team products include team reports, team collages, and team presentations. Team products create a shared destination. Teammates cooperate to arrive at their destination.

Team challenges also create a superordinate goal. Your mission as a team is to make sure everyone on the team gets an A on the test. The team's objective may be to read a combined eight books in a month. Or the goal may be to raise $100 for charity. The contribution of each helps all the team members reach their goal. They want everyone to succeed.

Shared goals are a central focus of teambuilding. Team solidarity is forged as teammates work together to accomplish a common goal.

Team Rewards. Team performance can be measured in various ways:
• A team score that is an average of individual scores.
• The sum of how many students reached a predetermined criterion.
• A randomly selected individual paper as the team score.
• The lowest score on the team as the team score.

Rewarding successful team performance can be motivating and set a positive tone. There are three powerful, simple forms of team rewards that we highly encourage: recognition, celebration, and praise. Teams find it's fun and rewarding to celebrate with a team handshake or cheer. Students find praise from the teacher or peers very rewarding. Recognition, such as having a team stand to take a bow in front of the class or featuring a team's project in the class newsletter, is a powerful team reward.

Pitfalls of Team Rewards
Extrinsic v. Intrinsic Motivation

Team rewards are to be used with great caution. They can be motivational, but they are also fraught with potential dangers. Extrinsic rewards, such as gold stars, toys, or perks, can erode intrinsic motivation. Under certain conditions, those who receive extrinsic rewards may attribute their motivation to the extrinsic rewards, rather than to the inherently interesting or challenging task. The same argument can be made for team rewards. If not used carefully, extrinsic team rewards may erode the intrinsically rewarding teamwork process. If the team product or goal is sufficiently intrinsically motivating, rewards may be superfluous and may actually undermine motivation. Genuine celebration and praise, in contrast, can increase intrinsic motivation.[1] See *Chapter 16: Motivation Without Rewards & Competition.*

Negative Interdependence Among Teams.
If we reward top teams based on their performance, we create positive interdependence within teams, yet we create negative interdependence among teams. Teams will not hope for other teams to succeed. The success of one team limits the chances of success for other teams. There are several solutions: All teams achieving a predetermined goal can be rewarded. Or better yet, team success can contribute to reaching class goals, thus creating a positive correlation of outcomes among teams. For example, all teams with an A average on the spelling test will contribute 1 point toward the 100-point class pizza party goal, or the points earned by each team are posted on a class graph or thermometer.

Group Grades.
Grades can be great motivators. Knowing this, some teachers use group grades, giving one grade to a team project and having that grade contribute to the grade of each individual. Although this does create a positive correlation among outcomes, there are so many problems with group grades that they should never be used. To give a student a grade, based on the ability or learning of another student, debases the grading system, fosters loafing, and creates rightful resentments—"I got a lower grade because Johnny did not do his work." For a detailed argument against the use of group grades, and for many better and fair ways to motivate students, see *Chapter 15: Assessment & Grading* and *Chapter 16: Motivation Without Rewards & Competition.*

Pooled Knowledge or Skill.
Positive interdependence is created by situations in which teammates pool knowledge or skills for mutual benefit. For example, in Numbered Heads Together, the teacher asks a question or poses a problem. After students write their own answers, they put their heads together to make sure everyone knows how to answer the question or solve the problem. If any teammate knows the answer or if the team can solve the problem by pooling their knowledge or skills, the success of each is a benefit to all. In some cases, the problem may be such that no one alone could solve it; only by pooling their knowledge or skills can teammates be successful.

Structures Create Positive Interdependence.
Many structures create positive interdependence by establishing shared goals and/or the need to pool knowledge or skills. Structures usually have a shared team goal so students cooperate for mutual benefit. For example, in Jot Thoughts, a team brainstorming structure, the team's goal is to generate as many creative ideas as possible in a limited time. As each teammate comes up with a creative idea, it is a boon to the team.

Many structures have built-in team celebrations and praising. For example, in Blind Sequencing, the team's goal is to sequence items. The catch is students cannot see their teammates' cards. If teammates sequence the cards correctly, they celebrate as a team.

Many structures allow students to pool their knowledge or skills to succeed as a team. For example, in Team-Pair-Solo students do a difficult type of problem first as a team, then in pairs, and finally solo. If anyone on the team knows how to do the problem, that skill gets transferred to the other teammates during the first step of Team-Pair-Solo.

T.E.A.M.
- ► **T**ogether
- ► **E**veryone
- ► **A**chieves
- ► **M**ore

12.6

Kagan Cooperative Learning • Dr. Spencer Kagan & Miguel Kagan
Kagan Publishing • 1 (800) 933-2667 • www.KaganOnline.com

Structures Create a Positive Correlation of Outcomes	
Method	**Sample Structure**
Team Goals	Jot Thoughts
Team Celebrations	Blind Sequencing
Pooled Knowledge or Skills	Team-Pair-Solo

Creating Interdependence: Structuring Tasks

Varied Knowledge or Skills. Team tasks that require varied knowledge or skills encourage cooperation. To take a musical example, a piano solo can be performed by an individual. A single individual has the knowledge and skills to perform the task independently. In contrast, the successful performance of an orchestra requires the cooperation of many individuals with specialized skills: wind, string, and percussion. Similarly, students cooperate if they bring unique knowledge or skills to the table. In Jigsaw, we explicitly provide each student with specialized knowledge and/or skills so the only access to success for each student is via the teaching of teammates. We structure for interdependence. Tasks that call for a range of knowledge or skills that no single individual possesses encourage mutual helping.

> *"No one can whistle a symphony. It takes a whole orchestra to play it."*
> —H. E. Luccock

Challenging Tasks. The task can be structured so that the sheer volume or difficulty of the task requires the participation and cooperation of all. For example, a giant boulder blocks a car's route. The massive boulder can't be moved unless everyone in the car works together. Adding a time constraint can make the task even more challenging: The passengers are en route to catch a departing plane. In the classroom, we can create tasks that, like the boulder, scream for teamwork. If we tell students their team presentation requires visual aids, music, a skit, and a typed report, students must cooperate to succeed. No single student can do it all alone.

There is strong interdependence. In contrast, if the team's task is to fill out a worksheet, and any single student can do the job alone, we have created only weak interdependence.

Division of Labor. To accomplish difficult tasks, teammates may divide up the labor. We can explicitly structure for division of labor. Instead of allowing students to decide how to split up their workload, the teacher may assign different students to different tasks. Co-op Co-op is a classic division of labor strategy in which each student independently masters a portion of the material: a mini topic. Teammates then meet to exchange and synthesize their knowledge into a team presentation. Co-op Co-op and other division of labor strategies are covered in *Chapter 17: Classic Cooperative Learning*.

Roles. Building a house requires the cooperation of many specialists: contractors, architects, framers, masons, carpenters, and landscapers. Each contributes to the shared goal of building the house. Roles are like jobs. They are assigned specializations. If we assign the role of Recorder, Materials Monitor, Checker, and Measurer for a team project, students depend on each other to fulfill their unique roles to complete the task. In the classroom, when we assign different roles to each teammate that only they can fulfill, we create strong interdependence. In a simple structure like Timed Pair Share, students each have roles to play, so they cannot complete the structure without working together. In the first step, one student is sharing and the other is listening. In the second step, the students switch roles. They cannot complete the structure without each playing their role—the task requires working together.

Resource Access. We can limit each student's access to specific resources to structure for cooperation. If we give a team four crayons and tell them to draw a rainbow, is cooperation required? No. Any single student can draw the rainbow while the others gossip. To create interdependence and cooperation, we limit the access to resources. For example, we assign one color to each student: "You can only touch your color." The result: Teammates work together to draw their rainbow. Resource access is a powerful tool, especially for creating interdependence during cooperative projects.

Ways to Create Positive Interdependence

Creating a Positive Correlation of Outcomes

▶ **Team Goals**
Teammates share the goal of creating an end product (mural, essay, presentation) or teammates share a challenge (raise $100, get an A average).

▶ **Team Rewards**
Recognition, celebration, or praise is based on team performance.

▶ **Pooled Knowledge or Skills**
The knowledge or skills of one student benefits teammates.

▶ **Structures**
Structures often have team goals, celebration or praise, and allow students to pool knowledge or skills.

Creating Task Interdependence

▶ **Pooled Knowledge or Skill**
The knowledge or skills of each teammate helps the team accomplish the task.

▶ **Challenging Tasks**
The task difficulty, size, and/or time limit ensures no single individual can do it alone.

▶ **Division of Labor**
The task is divided, with each teammate taking responsibility for a portion of the task.

▶ **Roles**
Students are assigned unique roles (Recorder, Materials Monitor) that are complementary and necessary for task completion.

▶ **Resource Access**
Each student is given sole access to different resources (scissors, glue, marker, ruler).

▶ **Rules**
Rules promote helping, encouragement, and tutoring. (In multiplication, all teammates must master the 5's before the team can advance to the 6's.)

▶ **Structures**
Different structures have built-in task interdependence in different ways (rules, roles, resource access, division of labor).

Rules. Rules too can increase interdependence. For example, to increase helping and encouragement, we might institute a rule that states the team cannot progress to a new learning center or to a new task until all teammates have completed a task or have displayed mastery. Talking Chips promotes task interdependence with a rule for regulating communication: No student may speak twice before every teammate has spoken.

Structures. Many structures take advantage of these powerful methods for promoting interdependence. The table below lists a sample structure for each method.

Structures Create Interdependence

Method	Sample Structure
Varied Knowledge or Skills	Jigsaw
Challenging Task	Team Projects
Division of Labor	Co-op Co-op
Roles	4S Brainstorming
Resource Access	Team Projects
Rules	Talking Chips

Individual Accountability
The "I" of PIES

The aphorism "There is no 'I' in team" motivates individuals to work as a team and even to make individual sacrifices for the sake of the team. "Taking one for the team" is now a common parlance. In baseball, there's the sacrificial bunt—a tactical team strategy in which a batter bunts the ball and risks getting out to advance teammates around the bases. In the workplace, there's the grunt work—the dirty job that someone on the team has to do. In the military, soldiers put their lives on the line to defend their platoon and the liberty of others.

But in the classroom, team performance is not the barometer for success. The acid test for classroom success is the success of each individual student. Is *each* student learning, growing, and succeeding? In the cooperative classroom, there is an "I" in team—and that "I" stands for Individual Accountability. In the cooperative classroom, students work together as a team to create and to learn, but ultimately every individual student is responsible for his or her own performance.

When individual accountability is violated, individuals can hide behind the efforts of their teammates. They can take a free ride off smarter or more motivated teammates. Lack of individual accountability creates slackers, loafers, logs, and sponges. When individual accountability is in place, no one can hide. Group work that does not make each team member accountable for her/his achievement or contribution does not consistently produce achievement gains.[2]

Individual accountability can take many forms. Students are individually accountable when they take a test, turn in homework, or give a class presentation. What these situations share is a measurable display of an individual student's knowledge or behavior. Did the student know the answers? Did the student complete her/his homework? How did the student perform during her/his presentation? Individual accountability boosts achievement. We try harder when we know someone will hold us responsible by evaluating our performance. We study hard for the test, stay up late to complete homework, and prep extra hard for a speech. We all want to be evaluated well by others. Who wants to fail publicly? Who does not want to succeed in front of others?

> "A chain is only as strong as its weakest link."
> —Proverb

Individual Accountability Boosts Achievement

Individual Accountability increases achievement in athletics, in the workplace, and in everyday life:
- The baseball player tries harder, knowing her/his performance will be witnessed by thousands, and her/his RBI and batting average will be published.
- The author gives extra effort to the book, knowing that once it is published, her/his name will forever be linked to that book.
- The workplace team gives extra effort, knowing their productivity and error rate will be posted.
- A child is more likely to do her homework, knowing her mother will check it for accuracy.

To check for individual accountability, we ask the third PIES question:

Critical Question 3
Is individual, public performance required?

How Do Students Feel?
I am on the hook!

Three Components of Individual Accountability
Individual accountability is created by putting in place three components:
1) **Individual.** The performance is done without help.
2) **Public.** Someone witnesses the performance.
3) **Required.** The performance is required.

Imagine you tell students there will be a test at the end of the week. If you tell students they can ask for and receive help during the test, they will not study as hard. Performance must be *individual* with no help allowed. If you tell students they can grade their own papers, and you will not collect them and no one else will see the test results, they will not study as hard. Performance must be *public*. Finally, if you tell students the test is optional, many will choose not to study or take the test at all. Performance must be *required*. Let's examine these three components a little closer.

Individual. In the classroom, the unit of learning is the individual, not the team. Learning happens between the ears of the learner. Teamwork is the process by which learning is enhanced, but team projects and products are not a yardstick for individual achievement. If we hold the team responsible, but not the individual, an individual may choose to do nothing, and thus learn nothing. But if we hold each student responsible for his/her own learning, if each must demonstrate her/his learning or perform without help of others, there is no diffusion of responsibility. Each student is accountable for his/her *individual* contribution and his/her own learning. Each of us tries harder on a task if we know the success or failure on the task will be attributed to us alone, that we will be held responsible.

Public. Accountability is strengthened by public performance. If students know they will have to display their knowledge or share their personal contribution publicly, they will make a concerted effort. Although we take a test or quiz alone, it is a public performance because the test is viewed by the teacher. When our performance is viewed by a teacher, peer, or someone else, it is a public performance. Tests and quizzes and other public performances are public displays of knowledge and skills. If each student on a team is required to share their best answer with a partner or with teammates, a public performance is required. When we know we will have to perform publicly, we make an extra effort: schoolchildren put in extra effort to do well in the class play; teenagers prepare diligently for their driver's license test; college students cram for midterms and finals; and adults study hard for certification.

Increasing Individual Accountability
Evaluation Tools v. Structures

Tests, quizzes, individual essays, and individual performances, such as reports and term projects, are all powerful ways to structure for individual accountability. However, they are evaluation tools, not instructional strategies. The problem with exclusive use of evaluation tools to structure for individual accountability is that they are one-time events that occur only occasionally and well after instruction. To harness the full power of individual accountability, we need to structure for individual accountability on an ongoing basis—during instruction—as part of every lesson. We can do that through instructional strategies that ensure formative, not just summative, individual accountability.

One of the most important reasons to use established Kagan Structures is that they create individual accountability on an ongoing basis as part of everyday instruction. For example, when the teacher has students do a Timed Pair Share, each student talks for a specified time to a peer. An individual, public performance is required of each student; it is "built into" the structure. No one can hide. When we use structures, instead of a public performance occurring once a week, public performance happens many times each day!

Authentic Assessment
Individual Accountability Increases Authentic Assessment Opportunities

Effective instruction is based on ongoing feedback to the instructor; the effective instructor constantly monitors and adjusts. What do students understand of what I have just taught? What do I need to reteach, or teach a different way? Individual accountability makes public display of student knowledge an integral part of teaching, and therefore increases authentic assessment opportunities on an ongoing basis.

The traditional method of assessing students' knowledge by calling on those students who volunteer by raising a hand is unrepresentative and misleading. After the teacher asks a question of the class, a subset of the class raises their hands, and usually it's the same subset. The teacher calls on one. The student gives the correct answer. The teacher congratulates her/himself: "Great, they're getting it." Wrong! The teacher does not find out that half the students with hands up would have had an only partially correct answer, and that the rest of the class—the majority—likely did not know the answer or were not even thinking about the question! Feeling the class is doing well, the teacher moves deeper, losing more students. Voluntary accountability creates a systematic illusion: The teacher thinks the class is mastering the content far better than it actually is because the teacher is hearing only from the high achievers.

In contrast, structures with individual accountability require regular individual public performances from all students, resulting in frequent authentic assessment opportunities. For example, the teacher is exploring with the class the importance of conflict in literature. The teacher does a Timed Pair Share, "Partner A's please identify for Partner B's the main conflict in the story." The teacher then walks around listening, sampling the class. In this structure, the teacher does not hear only from the high achievers; the teacher takes an authentic, representative sample of the class. If the students cannot identify the conflict, the teacher has the opportunity to reteach. Had the teacher asked for volunteers, she/he would have heard only from those who knew. By using all-students-respond structures that demand an individual, public performance by each student, the teacher obtains authentic assessment on an ongoing basis and continually improves instruction.

Required. The final component of individual accountability is making the individual public performance required. Individual contribution is not voluntary. It is compulsory. If students know they can opt out of the public performance, some will, so there is no individual accountability. If it is required that I must perform, I pay attention and prepare.

Accountable To Whom? For What?
Individual accountability may exist for outcomes other than academic achievement. For example, if the teacher tells students that following a discussion they each will be called on to state ideas they heard from others, then there is individual accountability *to* the teacher *for* listening to a peer.

Ways to Create Individual Accountability

Students may be held individually accountable to the teacher or to peers for many different classroom objectives.

▶ **For Achievement**
• Administer individual quizzes, tests, assignments
• Assign and grade minitopics
• Have each student share her/his answer with a partner, team, or teacher

▶ **For Task Completion**
• Students check to ensure their partner is finished
• Students submit work to be checked by teacher or peers
• Students all simultaneously hold up AnswerBoards for teacher to check work

▶ **For Skill Mastery**
• Students demonstrate mastery to the teacher
• Partners or teammates evaluate individual performance

▶ **For Participation**
• Use turn-taking structures
• Students reflect on and summarize their participation

▶ **For Contributions**
• Color-code individual contributions
• Students summarize individual contributions
• Teammates summarize teammates' contributions

▶ **For Note-Taking**
• Students submit notes to teacher
• Students use their notes to share with a partner
• Students allowed to use notes for test-taking

▶ **For Comprehension**
• Students demonstrate to a partner they understand the teacher's instructions
• Students demonstrate understanding to the teacher

▶ **For Decision-Making**
• Students independently write down their decisions or priorities and their reasoning before teaming up

▶ **For Brainstorming**
• Students independently generate ideas on their own sheets of paper

▶ **For Listening**
• Use paraphrasing (Paraphrase Passport) or listening gambits ("The most important thing I heard….")
• Students share with a partner what they heard from someone else (Three-Step Interview)

Accountability To Whom? Students may be accountable to a partner, a team, the class, and/or the teacher. Reports home create accountability to parents. The greater the accountability, the greater the probability of achievement. In Numbered Heads Together, before students put their heads together, each student independently writes his or her best answer to share with the team. Thus, each is held accountable to teammates. Further, when a student's number is called, that student must share the team's answer, so they are held accountable to the teacher and the class as well. In RallyCoach, each student in turn is accountable to a coach, their partner.

Accountability for What? Depending on the structure and the content, students are held accountable for different things. For example, in Paraphrase Passport, the right to speak is earned by paraphrasing the previous speaker. This structure holds students accountable for empathetic listening. Talking Chips holds students accountable for participating. In a RallyTable of prime numbers, learners are held accountable for listing prime numbers. If the RallyTable were filling in blanks on the periodic table, the learners would be accountable for very different content.

Creating Individual Accountability
How to Make Individual Accountability *"Individual"*

When using cooperative teams, we ensure each individual is held accountable for thinking, contributing, and learning. To do this, we can isolate individual performance before, during and, after teamwork.

Me Before We. If we ask a question and have teammates put their heads together to come up with a team response, one quick student may do all the team's thinking and blurt out an answer. Students are not required to independently process the content and generate their own response. If we want to hold students individually accountable for generating their own response, we have individuals respond independently before they put their heads together as a team. To do this, we simply ask the question, call for think time, then have each student write down his/her own answer. After they have all responded, then they show and read their answers to their teammates. Then, they put their heads together to improve their answers.

If we want to hold students individually accountability for deciding among alternatives, we have them first independently make and write down their decisions. Then, they huddle up to make a team decision. If we miss this *"me before we"* step, students may accept the decision of a persuasive or influential teammate without having given the decision much independent thought. When doing an Estimate Line-Up, we have students write down their estimate before lining up; otherwise they are likely to simply group with friends. Similarly, in Corners, we have students write their corner preference before they go to their corners. We make each student accountable by taking the time to have students respond or perform independently before the team or class interaction. Teamwork is the synergy of individual thinking, not a substitute for it.

Me During We. *"Me during we"* means we

hold each individual accountable during the process of team collaboration. In team products or presentations, it is often difficult to discern who did what. Recognizing this, less motivated students can sponge off their teammates' efforts. There are a number of things we can do to isolate individual performance during team performances. By doing so, we hold each student accountable and get a more accurate picture of each individual's contribution to the team's performance.

Color-Coding. Color-coding contributions makes each individual's contribution easy to see. Each student receives a unique colored crayon or marker and may only use his or her own color. When the team Mind Map is complete, we can determine every student's contribution. When a team worksheet is completed, we can verify that all colors are represented. When a team does a RoundTable, it is easy to see at a glance who has written each response if the students write with different colored markers.

Mini Topics. Assigning mini topics or dividing the labor in a specific way makes individual contributions to team projects easy to determine. If the team topic is transportation, each student can be held accountable for researching, presenting, and turning in a paper on a different mode of transportation. Or if the topic does not divide nicely into mini topics, students can select or each be assigned a different portion of the task. One student assumes responsibility for creating the visuals; another for the music and sound effects; another for working the computer; another for the team summary; and all students play a part in the presentation.

Individual Worksheets. To hold every student accountable for completing a worksheet, we might give each student the worksheet to complete in her/his own words instead of allowing the team to submit a single worksheet with all teammates' names on it. Teammates can still interact and help each other, but each individual is responsible for their individual performance.

Me After We. The final way to make learning "individual" is to structure for individual performance after team interaction—*"me after we."* After the teamwork portion is complete, students independently solve problems and turn in their own worksheets. After the team practice session, students take individual tests and quizzes. After the team reads and discusses the new chapter, students write their own summaries.

Isolating Individual Performance
Before, During, and After Team Performance

▶ **Me Before We**
- Students write own responses prior to teaming up
- Students create own products to share with teammates
- Structures: Showdown, Numbered Heads Together, Placemat Consensus

▶ **Me During We**
- Color-code individual contributions
- Assign mini topics
- Students fill in own worksheets, create own product
- Structures: RallyCoach, Team Mind-Mapping, Talking Chips, Jot Thoughts

▶ **Me After We**
- Students turn in individual worksheets
- Students take tests, quizzes after team interaction
- Structures: Team-Pair-Solo, Numbered Heads Together

How to Make Individual Accountability *"Public"*

We strengthen accountability by making students' knowledge or skills public. Public simply means students must display their knowledge or skills to someone else. The most traditional forms of individual public performance are responding to a teacher's question in front of the class, or turning in homework or a test to the teacher.

Individual accountability is not only for academic achievement. We must ask, accountable to whom, for what? If we want to hold all students accountable to the teacher for responding to an oral question, we can have the class simultaneously hold up their response boards. If we want to hold students accountable to their teammates for coming up with a decision, we can have them write down their decisions and take turns sharing what they wrote with teammates.

If we want to hold students accountable to their partners for attentively listening, we can have them paraphrase their partners after they speak. In a simple RallyRobin, each student is accountable to their partner for adding to the oral list they are generating. In a minute of RallyRobin, each student is accountable for contributing a number of times. Cooperative learning structures make it easy to hold all students accountable for a public performance.

In the traditional classroom without student-to-student interaction, we don't have as many options for individual accountability. Students are accountable only to the teacher. Cooperative learning provides us with a multitude of ways to hold students accountable to their peers for their performance. Students can be accountable to the teacher, to teammates, to a partner, or even to their parents. They can be held accountable for achievement, for mastering a skill, for listening, for participating, or for making a decision. The advantage of peer performance is that it is immediate and simultaneous.

How to Make Individual Accountability "*Required*"

There are a number of ways to make individual public performance *required*: structures, sequence, verification, and consequences.

Structures. Structures sequence student interactions in a way that requires individual public performance. For example, if pairs are asked to RallyRobin (take turns orally stating) different mammals, partners are both individually accountable to each other for naming mammals. After one student names a mammal, the other is required to respond. Individual performance is required.

Sequence. Sequence also can be used as part of lesson design without the use of structures. For example, the class cannot move on to the next topic until all students have turned in their papers on the previous topic. The sequence exerts a social pressure for mandatory public performance.

Verification. We may ensure individuals have done their part by verifying their individual contribution or completion. We can verify completion by having all students hold up their

Structures Create Individual Accountability

Structure	Accountable For What	Accountable To Whom	How
Numbered Heads Together	Independent response and representing the team's answer	Teacher and teammates	Students show and read independent response; teacher simultaneously checks student answers
RallyRobin	Contributing Ideas	Partner	Turn taking
Paraphrase Passport	Active Listening	Teammates	Students must paraphrase teammates before they may share
Jigsaw and Co-op Co-op	Mastering content	Teammates	Students must master own portion to teach it to teammates
Talking Chips	Participating in discussion	Teammates	Each must use their chip before proceeding to next round

answers, or turn in their work. Or partners or teammates can confirm participation by responding to the teacher, "Let me see by a show of hands, who has a partner (or teammate) who still needs to … ." By receiving confirmation, we verify that each student has made their individual contribution.

Consequence. Consequence adds teeth to required individual public performance. Performance can be rewarded with positive consequences such as cheers, celebrations, praise, and recognition. Failure to perform can result in negative consequences. To maintain a positive learning environment, positive consequences are more prevalent than negative consequences.

Potential Pitfalls of Individual Accountability

Individual accountability must be coupled with positive interdependence—otherwise it will backfire. For example, we can create very strong individual accountability simply by asking a question, randomly calling a number, and having the student with that number stand up and answer in front of the whole class. If we do that, some students will fail publicly and will soon dread class, content, and the teacher. Learning and change come about best by a combination of pressure and support. Individual accountability creates the pressure; positive interdependence creates the support. Either without the other is ineffective. If we never quiz or have students perform publicly, they will not achieve as well. However, if we do not provide plenty of instruction, tutoring, guided practice, encouragement, and celebrate student accomplishments, they also will not achieve as well. The Kagan Structures build in pressure and support—a combination of positive

Accountability Requires Support

The No Child Left Behind Act is a national attempt to improve educational outcomes by increasing public accountability. Opponents believe the legislation is condemning students and schools to sure failure, citing many problems including the lack of federal funding and support. In the classroom, we must remember that it is unrealistic and unfair to insist on public accountability without proper support. Doing so can be a recipe for disaster.

interdependence and individual accountability. For example, before doing problems alone in Team-Pair-Solo, the students first do them as a team and then as a pair, receiving plenty of tutoring, encouragement, and support. The positive interdependence precedes the individual accountability, so the student has received the necessary support prior to the individual performance. Similarly, in Numbered Heads Together, the students have the support of their teammates (heads together) prior to being required to perform in front of the class.

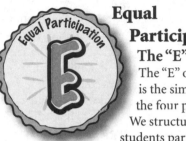

Equal Participation
The "E" of PIES

The "E" of PIES is the simplest of the four principles: We structure so that students participate about equally. Participation is an integral part of the learning process. Students learn by interacting with the content and with fellow students. For equitable educational outcomes, we need participation to be relatively equal.

Participation Produces Achievement

Research has established a strong link between participation and achievement. Research in cognitive psychology demonstrates that mastering a new skill requires practice spread out over time. The first practice sessions produce the greatest gain, but successive sessions with smaller incremental gains are required to achieve competency. Also, long-term, meaningful retention of knowledge and skills is the result of practicing beyond the point of mastery.[3] If students do not participate in the practice sessions, they will not learn as much or score as high on tests.

Research on the internal dynamics of cooperative learning also links different patterns of participation with increases in achievement. Students who ask for and receive adequate help from teammates during team interactions tend to do well on later tests, as opposed to those who did not ask for or did not receive the required help. There are also academic benefits for students who offer elaborate help. Non-participation during group interaction had the most deleterious effect on low-achieving students, especially on tests of long-term retention.[4] Participation has benefits for those who need and receive help, as well as for those who offer help.

Why do some students participate more than others? It is likely an interaction between student characteristics and the structure of learning. Let's look first at student characteristics that explain the disparity of participation in the traditional classroom.

Brain Link

Student Characteristics Affecting Participation

Students are different. Some are outgoing and naturally inclined to participate. Some may require gentle prodding. And some are downright shy. Fearing potential embarrassment, they avoid public participation if at all possible.

Personality Types. Personality theory and research indicates some individuals are extroverts while others are introverts. Extroverts are outgoing and more prone to participating in socially engaging activities. Introverts tend to shrink from social situations and turn inward. Harvard psychologist Jerome Kagan asserts social inhibition is genetic and relatively stable.[5] Recent research by Joseph LeDoux, Ph.D. suggests that shy people have an overactive amygdala. The part of the brain that regulates emotional responses causes some individuals to feel anxiety in everyday social situations.[6]

Another psychological theory divides individuals into two categories, depending on how they cope with stress. There are the "approachers" and the "avoiders." Approachers face stressful situations head on, while avoiders push away. Along the same lines is the shy versus confident individual dimension. Shy or timid students may feel uneasy participating in social situations. Shyness can range from a very mild social discomfort and awkwardness to a totally inhibiting social phobia. The percentage of self-reported shyness has escalated gradually in the last decade to nearly 50%. It is the third most prevalent psychiatric disorder.[7]

Achievement, Success Orientation, and Self-Esteem.
Participation in school is also a function of a number of interrelated constructs: academic achievement, success orientation, and self-esteem. Students who perform well in school often have a high self-esteem. "I'm smart. I'm good at this. I've succeeded in the past, and I'll succeed in the future. Success becomes a self-fulfilling prophecy. The opposite is true for low achievers. Students who perform poorly are much more likely to withdraw. Academic performance is the single greatest contributor to high school drop out rates. Fear of failure or protecting a fragile self-image leads low achievers to choose to avoid participation. They have a different attribution and orientation toward success: "I'm not smart. I'm no good at this. I'll never succeed."

Developmental Appropriateness.
Developmental appropriateness helps explain participation and motivation. If a task is at the appropriate level of difficulty, students will participate; if not, participation will wane. Students withdraw from tasks that are too difficult. They don't see that they will be able to learn the content, or solve the problems. It's just too hard. On the flip side, tasks that are too easy lack challenge. Students perceive them as repetitive and boring, and participation drops off.

Cultural and Language Minorities.
Achievement, participation, and retention is often lower among ethnic and language minority students compared to their majority counterparts. Language minority students often lack the academic language required for success. Many feel uncomfortable participating in intimidating whole-class situations. A broad field of theory and research has posited a cultural mismatch hypothesis, stating there is a mismatch between Hispanic, Black, and Native American cultures and traditional classrooms, resulting in decreased participation and achievement.

Classroom Structural Variables Affecting Participation

In the traditional classroom where participation is not mandatory, who participates and who doesn't? High achievers tune in. Low achievers tune out. Extroverts vie for attention. Introverts shy away from it. Cultural minorities withdraw from instruction that does not respect different styles of learning. Language minorities tune out of learning they can't comprehend. Participation patterns are predictable and opposite of what is needed to produce equitable achievement outcomes for all students: Students who need the least help participate the most while those who need the most help rarely participate. The achievement gap crisis we are facing as a nation is no mystery. It would be reduced dramatically if all students participated about equally.

Research on cooperative learning suggests that not only do all students learn more, the strongest gains are for the traditionally lowest achievers. They play a dramatic game of catch-up when they are included in the learning process. Students who would otherwise slip through the cracks of systemic voluntary nonparticipation become active participants. See *Chapter 3: What Does the Research Say?*

This brings us to our fourth PIES question. We aim to equalize classroom participation, but perfectly equal participation is never possible. Therefore, we ask the fourth PIES question to check for equality of participation among learners:

Critical Question 4
Is participation approximately equal?

How Do Students Feel?
We are all equal status.

With students that differ greatly on so many dimensions, how do we create approximately equal participation? The answer: We structure for it. If we do not structure for equal participation, it does not occur magically. Volunteer participation in the whole class leads to participation dominated by a few high achieving and/or extroverted students. We call on those who least need to practice and least on those who most need the practice. Similarly, volunteer participation in a group leads to very unequal participation—we have all been in a group dominated by a few who took over. The teacher aware of the importance of equalizing participation is constantly asking her/himself, "How equal is the participation in my class at this moment?" The way successful cooperative classroom instruction is designed may not completely overcome individual differences in participation, but it makes participation approximately equal and education far more equitable. Let's see how.

"Creating Equal Participation"

Let's examine six approaches to equalize participation: 1) turn taking, 2) time allocation, 3) think and write time, 4) rules, 5) individual accountability, and 6) roles.

Turn Taking. Turn allocation is the simplest and perhaps most effective way to equalize participation. With turn allocation, everyone gets a turn. In the traditional whole-class structure, turn allocation is too time-consuming and impractical to use. To give every student their turn, we have to come up with thirty questions, one for each student, and allow time for thirty responses! If each question and answer sequence took one minute, it would take half a class period for each student to answer just one question.

With cooperative structures, turn allocation is easy. In a RoundRobin, the teacher can ask one question, and each student on the team of four takes their turn to share their thoughts with teammates. Or with each new question, the next student on the team shares. With RallyRobin, students take turns sharing with a partner. Turn taking includes everyone. Teachers often report with amazement that students who they wrote off as disinterested, too shy, or less capable, surprise them when they are included in the learning. Turn taking is inclusive, not elitist. It ensures every student gets their turn, not just a select few. Turn taking equalizes the status among teammates.

Time Allocation. Time allocation is an extension of turn taking. With time management, we ensure that not only does every student get his or her turn, but he or she also participates for approximately the same amount of time. Timed Pair Share involves turn taking with time allocation: In pairs, Partner A speaks for one minute, then Partner B speaks for one minute. Every student receives the same amount of time to share. Turn taking and time allocation are very strong tools for equalizing participation; they almost guarantee near equal participation. Time allocation may be combined with turn taking in a number of structures, as when the teacher calls for a Team Interview in which each team member in turn is interviewed for one minute, or a Timed RoundRobin in which each student shares for one minute. Equal time allocation equalizes status and alleviates the traditional malady of unequal participation. Every student is looked up to and participates for about the same amount of time.

Think Time. Research on "wait time" reveals that most teachers provide an average of only one second of think time after they ask a question. This is not enough time for all students to formulate their ideas. By expanding this think time to 3–5 seconds, participation increases: students who otherwise would not respond have time to think through their answers and then volunteer to respond. A host of other benefits result from increased think time: students listen better to each other, respond more accurately, feel more confident, offer more varied responses, are more willing to speculate, ask more questions, and behave in a more focused manner.[9]

Is it surprising to learn that simply waiting has such positive effects? When we reflect on it, the explanation seems clear: If we ask a question, and ask for an immediate voluntary response, only the quickest thinkers or most impulsive and outgoing students volunteer to share. Some individuals formulate their thoughts as the words come out of their mouths. Introspective and slower students need time to formulate their ideas *before* they are ready to respond. Think time promotes participation from more reflective students. When we couple think time with turn taking and time allocation, all students have a turn, a time, and content to share. Now everyone participates.

Think time complements the "Me Before We" rule of Individual Accountability. I do something as an individual before I pair or team up. Now I'm ready to participate. This structured "me-time" can take myriad forms: think time, writing time, or filling out a graphic organizer.

Some students will participate regardless if they are given think time. More reflective students will participate only if allowed sufficient time and ways to formulate their ideas. We respect individual differences, encourage equal participation, and promote a host of other benefits by providing students think time.

Promoting Participation
Why Some Students Don't Participate and What to Do About It

▶ **Shyness and Introversion**
- Allow think time and preparation time.
- Promote interaction in pairs, and small groups.
- Create a caring, inclusive classroom to reduce fear of rejection and embarrassment.
- Provide equal time for students to participate.

▶ **Poor Achievement and Low Self-Esteem**
- Break curriculum into small steps to promote success at each step.
- Build esteem through affiliation and belonging.
- Celebrate successes and improvement.
- Hold students accountable for participating.

▶ **Developmentally Inappropriate**
- Provide inherently motivating tasks.
- Provide challenging tasks (not too easy nor too difficult).
- Provide differentiated instruction.

▶ **Cultural and Language Minorities**
- Use culturally-responsive pedagogy.
- Use turn taking and time allocation to equalize participation.

Rules. Rules equalize participation. For example, each student must do two problems on the team worksheet. Everyone must add a sentence to the team story. Everyone must play a part in the team presentation. Many structures have built-in "rules of engagement" to equalize participation. In Talking Chips, the rule is that on each round of discussion, no one can speak twice unless each person has spoken once. The rule is explicitly designed to equalize participation: It guarantees participation by all.

Individual Accountability. Individual accountability equalizes participation when students are held accountable for participation. For example, during Jot Thoughts, each student may be required to write her/his brainstormed items in a unique color. This creates individual accountability for participation. Knowing everyone will see what I have created makes it more likely I will participate.

Role Assignment. The Gatekeeper role is explicitly designed to equalize particiation. It is the job of the Gatekeeper to open the gate for some while gently shutting the gate for others during a discussion. For example, if Bob is doing all the talking and Susan is not participating, the Gatekeeper may say, "Bob, that is very interesting, Susan, what do you think of that idea?" When students learn and practice the Gatekeeper role, participation is equalized.

Another way of using roles to equalize participation is to assign each student a unique and necessary role. During a project, one student may be the only one to use the ruler, another the scissors, the third the protractor, and the fourth the glue. If all four roles are necessary for task completion, participation is equalized. A few Kagan Structures have unique roles or rotating roles that equalize participation. For example, in 4S Brainstorming, each student has a unique role: Speed Captain, Synergy Guru, Sergeant Support, and Sultan of Silly. Because each is given the gambits to use to fulfill her/his role, participation is equalized somewhat, but there is no certainty all students will fulfill their roles or that students will participate equally. Fan-N-Pick uses role assignment to ensure equal participation. In Fan-N-Pick, one student fans the question cards, the next picks and reads, the third

answers, and the fourth paraphrases and praises. After each round, the role cards are rotated so each student gets a new role, Not only does each participate approximately equally, each fills each role approximately equally.

Flexible Use of the Six Approaches. The six approaches to equalizing participation may be used flexibly, as needed. For example, during 4S Brainstorming, a teacher wishing to ensure participation by all may add a rotating role of Recorder. Each student in turn records the next idea generated. Or during a team discussion, a teacher walking by a group, seeing the conversation dominated by one or two students, may ask the group to use Talking Chips. When we are sensitive to the need to equalize participation, we structure for equality using any combination of the six approaches.

Acceptable Unequal Participation. There are times when we do not want equal participation. Overemphasis on equality of participation can be inhibiting and can prevent good ideas from being voiced. For example, the class may be dealing with a controversial issue, and strong feelings about the issue are evoked in some but not others. In that situation, some students have a need to express their opinions;

Six Approaches to Equalizing Participation

Approach	How	Sample Structures
① **Turn Taking**	Every student receives an equal turn.	RoundTable
② **Time Allocation**	Every student receives the same amount of time.	Timed Pair Share
③ **Think Time**	Students are given the opportunity to formulate own ideas.	Think-Pair-Share
④ **Rules**	Rules of engagement establish guidelines for equal participation.	Talking Chips
⑤ **Individual Accountability**	Students are held accountable for participation.	Showdown
⑥ **Role Assignment**	Students participate by filling a unique or rotating role.	4S Brainstorming

Kagan Cooperative Learning • Dr. Spencer Kagan & Miguel Kagan
Kagan Publishing • 1 (800) 933-2667 • www.KaganOnline.com

others do not feel strongly about the issue. In that case, we may well want to allow those who have a need to speak to speak, and allow those without a need to speak to simply listen. In those times, an unstructured Group Discussion might be more appropriate than a RoundRobin or Timed Pair Share. The caution, however, is that whenever an unstructured Group Discussion is used, it is very likely that some students will dominate the discussion, and some will choose to participate little or not at all.

Equal participation is not desirable in some tutoring situations. In RallyCoach, one student may know how to solve a type of problem and the partner may not. Although the students do an equal number of problems, the tutor-tutee roles are very unequal. In this case, it is more meaningful to speak of "equitable" participation, rather than "equal" participation.

Everyone Participates with Equal and Equitable Participation

Emphasis of equal and equitable participation increases the probability that everyone will participate in athletics, in the workplace, and in everyday life:
• In baseball, each player in turn comes to bat. (Equal Participation)
• Because of their unique roles, the author, the editor, the graphic designer, and the publisher must all participate for a book to be published. (Equitable Participation)
• We stand in lines, taking turns to order food, pay for groceries, cash checks, ensuring that we each receive a turn. (Equal Participation)

Simultaneous Interaction
The "S" of PIES
Active engagement increases student learning. If students are off task, they are less likely to learn. If students are only occasionally engaged, they learn less than when they are regularly engaged. Simultaneous interaction is the most powerful tool we have for increasing active engagement. Let's explore the power of simultaneous interaction.

Sequential v. Simultaneous Interaction
Sequential means one at a time. Often, interaction in the traditional classroom is sequential. Many traditional classroom

interactions occur in a serial fashion. In the common Whole-Class Q & A, 1) the teacher asks a question; 2) one student answers; 3) the teacher responds to the answer. This classroom pattern is so predominant, researchers have labeled it IRE—Initiation, Response, Evaluation.[10] The interaction happens in sequence. The teacher is active, then a student is active, then the teacher is active again. What's wrong with this picture?

The problem is the teacher is the most active participant in the classroom. The teacher talks twice for each time a student speaks. And this is during students' primary opportunity for interaction. Imagine that there are thirty students in a class. When the teacher and one student are interacting, what are the other twenty-nine students doing? Listening, hopefully.

Hopefully. But are they actively engaged? No. Passive listening does not qualify as active engagement. By many definitions, it would qualify as disengagement. Many students are looking at the back of the head of a student responding to the teacher. This participation pattern is a prescription for disengagement. Disengagement does not produce learning. In fact, disengagement is one of the leading causes of classroom discipline problems.[11] You know the saying about idle hands. It's no wonder traditional, sequential classrooms are plagued by discipline problems.

Simultaneous interaction actively engages a high percent of students at once. With effective cooperative learning, we dramatically increase the amount of active engagement because effective cooperative learning produces simultaneous, rather than sequential, engagement. Let's see how cooperative learning transforms the IRE pattern into an II discourse pattern—Initiation, Interaction. As in the traditional class, the teacher asks the class a question. But instead of calling on one student to respond, the teacher simply asks students to turn to a partner and give their best answers. Now, half the class is actively engaged, all at the same time. In each pair, one student is talking. When we look at the mathematics of the increased amount of active engagement per student, the difference is staggering. We'll turn to the mathematics in a minute, but let us first overview the tremendous power of interaction. It turns out that interaction is more powerful than solo engagement.

Learning Time v. Time on Task v. Overt Interaction

Having more time for learning is a good thing, spending more time on task during learning time is a better thing, but interacting over the learning content is the best thing! Learning Time refers to amount of time students spend on a lesson. One way to increase Learning Time is to increase the length of the school day or school year. Surprisingly, research reveals extending learning time has only a very small positive impact on achievement. Time on Task refers to the amount of time students are focused on the learning task. For example, during a long, boring lecture the students' minds may drift, so they are disengaged, not focused on the learning task. Research reveals increased time on task has a strong positive impact on achievement.

How to Boost Achievement	
Kind of Time	**Impact on Achievement**
Learning Time	Marginal
Time on Task	Stronger
Overt Interaction	Strongest

Importantly, not all time on task improves achievement equally. There is a difference in the *quality* of time on task. Time on task during interactive activities produces the strongest gains.[12] The research suggests there is a hierarchy of effective use of classroom time. Interaction adds a social component to learning. Interaction is a transaction between two or more individuals. It is this stimulating social interaction that maximally activates the brain and has a positive influence on learning. PET scans reveal there is far greater activation during social interaction than during independent engagement. See *Chapter 4: Why Does Cooperative Learning Work?*

Overt v. Covert Interaction. When evaluating the power of a learning task, we focus on overt interaction. Overt engagement is something we can see or hear; covert engagement is something we can only hope is happening. For example, if we ask a question of the whole class, when one student answers, we hope all the other students are listening, thinking, and learning, but we cannot be certain; they may be daydreaming. Because their engagement is covert, we cannot be certain how much they are truly engaged with the content. If instead of having one student respond, we have every student answer with a thumbs up or down, a Choral Response, or by using an AnswerBoard, their response is something we can see—it is overt. Focusing on overt interaction allows us to be certain of the amount of engagement in our class.

When focusing on simultaneous interaction, we focus on overt interaction. For example, while students are doing a RoundRobin, all the students in each team are interacting. But at any one moment in a team of four, only one is overtly engaged (talking), while the others are covertly engaged (listening). In contrast, during a RallyRobin students are in pairs, so at any one moment, half our class is overtly interacting. Pair work doubles the amount of overt interaction compared to square work (teamwork). Because students are more engaged during overt than covert interaction (they remember much more of what they say than what they hear), we can conclude that all other things being equal, we would rather have the students interacting in pairs than in larger groups.

Putting It Together. What can we conclude from this research? If we want to maximize achievement, we need to structure for overt simultaneous interaction: 1) We want interaction in the classroom to proceed simultaneously rather than sequentially; 2) We want to engage students in interactive activities rather than just keep them engaged in independent tasks; and 3) we prefer tasks that maximize overt rather than covert interaction. This doesn't mean that we should exclusively use interactive activities and abandon individual, engaging activities. Not at all. Engagement is both good and necessary in the classroom. In fact, most Kagan Structures incorporate both individual engagement and cooperative interaction. Regular inclusion of simultaneous interaction dramatically increases engagement, liking for class, and retention of content. To check for simultaneous interaction among students, we ask the simple question:

Critical Question 5
What percent of students are overtly interacting at once?

How Do Students Feel?
Engaged with others.

A simple look at the mathematics reveals the staggering difference in amount of overt active engagement during traditional instruction and cooperative learning structures.

Simultaneous Interaction Increases Active Engagement.

Let's use our critical question to evaluate whole class, team, and pair structures. In Whole Class Q & A, we call on students one at a time. In a class of thirty, a very low percent (3.33%) are engaged at any one moment. If instead, we have students in groups of four and have them do a RoundRobin, we have one in four (25%) overtly active at any one moment, verbalizing their response. Pair work, such as a RallyRobin, doubles the overt active participation to 50%. The percents are impressive. We can go from a little over 3% of the class active at one time to 50%. Even more impressive is what this does to student participation time per each hour of instruction. The results are summarized in the table below.

Simultaneous Interaction Saves Time.

As the table demonstrates, simultaneous interaction saves classroom time. We can engage more students at a time, and thus get more accomplished more quickly. Take the typical book report, current event, or any other student presentation. In a class of 30, if we have each student do a three-minute presentation, it would take at minimum 90 minutes. This does not include the time for feedback from the teacher, the transition time for students to sit down, and the time for the next student come to the front of the class. If we have students do the same report in teams, it would take 12 minutes (3 minutes times 4 students). Presenting to a partner would only take 6 minutes (3 minutes time 2 students). We save well over an hour of classroom time by choosing a simultaneous presentation structure rather than a sequential structure! With simultaneous interaction, we accomplish in six minutes something that takes the traditional teacher 90 minutes!

Time for Three-Minute Student Presentations

Structure	Required Class Time
Student Presentation Student presents to class.	**90** minutes
Timed RoundRobin Student presents to teammates.	**12** minutes
Timed Pair Share Student presents to partner.	**6** minutes

Let's examine another common classroom goal: to give students time to express their ideas or opinions. We know students retain far more of what they say than what they hear because listening is passive and talking is active. So we want to allow students to verbalize their ideas. Let's say we want to give each student one minute of air time—just one minute each to summarize their learning. If we use the traditional structure and call on the students one at time in a class of thirty, it would take over an hour. Why? Because with the traditional structure, the teacher talks twice for each time a student talks. The teacher talks about 60%

Simultaneous Interaction Increases Engagement and Participation

Structure	Percent Actively Engaged at Once	Student Participation Time per Hour
Whole Class Q & A	1 in 30 (3.33%)	**2** minutes per student
RoundRobin	1 in 4 (25%)	**15** minutes per student
RallyRobin	1 in 2 (50%)	**30** minutes per student

of the time because the teacher must first ask a question, then the student answers, then the teacher responds to the answer with a praise, a correction, or a comment. Now we would never spend a straight hour this way. But we do spend many hours this way spread out over time. Today we might spend five minutes near the beginning of class, five minutes in the middle, and five minutes at the end. Tomorrow we might spend only five minutes total of Q&A. Over time, it would take us over an hour to reach our goal of one minute of air time per student. And how have the students spent their time? One minute expressing their ideas and the rest of the hour waiting their turn! This is a prescription for boredom.

Now let's see what happens if we use simultaneous interaction to reach our goal of one minute per student. We ask a question and have students do a Timed Pair Share, each student sharing with a partner for one minute each. In a little over two minutes, we accomplish what would take the traditional teacher over an hour! Simultaneous interaction is a miracle worker. It is more efficient, saving hours of time, plus it is aligned with how the brain learns best—through interaction. Taking a simultaneous approach to teaching allows us to produce dramatically more engagement in less time. As the table above

The Simultaneous Advantage

Teacher's Goal	Sequential Structure	Simultaneous Structure
Distribute Supplies	Teacher or student walks around and hands out materials one at a time.	Materials Monitor from each team distributes materials to teammates.
Discuss Topic	One student at a time states their opinion to the class.	All students discuss their opinions in pairs.
Form Teams	Sequential reading by the teacher of students' names and assignments.	Students simultaneously look for names on cards on team tables.
Share Answers	Teacher calls on one student at a time.	All students engage in Choral Response or display answers on AnswerBoards.
Receive Help	Students raise hands and wait for teacher to come over.	Students ask a teammate and receive immediate help.

illustrates, a simultaneous approach to teaching is more effective for a variety of classroom goals.

Equality v. Quantity

Before we examine how to create simultaneous interaction, let us emphasize the distinction between equal participation and simultaneous interaction. Equal participation deals with the equality of participation. Simultaneous interaction deals with the quantity of participation per student. We can create perfectly equal classroom participation, yet still violate the principle of simultaneous interaction. For example, if we call on students, check off their names on a class list as we call on them, and not call any student a second time before everyone has had a turn, the principle of equal participation is satisfied—students are participating about equally. But student engagement is sequential, not simultaneous. Students are called on one at a time and it will take us an hour to give each one minute of active engagement. Equal participation is not enough, we also need the "S" of PIES—simultaneous interaction.

Creating Simultaneous Interaction

Teams and Pairs. We create simultaneous interaction by breaking down the traditional whole-class unit into smaller learning teams and pairs. Without teams or pairs, learning is necessarily either whole class or independent. When we have teams and pairs, we can make learning simultaneous because interaction is occurring simultaneously in each group.

Simultaneous Interaction Increases Engagement and Saves Time

Emphasis on simultaneous interaction increases the amount of engagement in athletics, in the workplace, and in everyday life:
• A baseball coach increases participation and performance by having the team split into pairs to work on catching and throwing drills.
• Ford revolutionized auto manufacturing and sparked the Industrial Revolution when he abandoned the one-car-at-a-time model in favor of the assembly line in which each worker was doing a different job, all at the same time.
• One family member clears the table, another washes dishes, another dries—all at the same time, cutting the time and labor for each in third.
• A caterer opens four identical buffet lines, serving all the guests in a quarter of the time.

The table below illustrates many ways we can use teams and pairs to create simultaneous interaction, all of which create more active engagement than the traditional one-at-time sequential structure.

pair sharing her/his ideas). Understanding the principle of simultaneous interaction, we more often use pair work than square work in teams, doubling the overt active participation.

Many Forms of Simultaneity

Simultaneous Organization	Example	Percent Overtly Active
Student-to-Student	A student presents to her partner.	1 in 2 (50%)
Student-to-Teammates	A student presents to his teammates.	1 in 4 (25%)
Team-to-Team	A team presents to another team.	4 in 8 (50%) 1 in 8 (13% if one at a time)
Team-to-Class	A team presents to the class.	4 in 30 (13%) 1 in 30 (3% if one at a time)

Simultaneous Response Modes and Sharing.
We can boost simultaneity by using simultaneous response modes. For example, rather than calling on one student to agree or disagree with a statement, we can have every student in the class show a "thumbs up" or "thumbs down." Or if we want students to answer a problem, we have all students simultaneously display their answers on their AnswerBoards. Or each team holds up a team slate with their team answer. Slates, response cards, choral practice, and team representatives all at the board responding simultaneously create greater engagement and greater accountability than calling on one student.

Kagan Structures.
Almost all of the Kagan Structures are designed for simultaneous interaction. Even in the classbuilding structures, there is care to break large groups into small groups for maximum engagement. For example, in Corners, approximately one-fourth of the class is standing in each corner. Rather than saying, "Talk it over in your corners: Why did you go to the corner you did?" the teacher says, "Form pairs in your corner and discuss why you went to the corner you did." With the first way of structuring the interaction, the teacher would have four active participants at any one moment (one student in each corner talking to the group); with the second way, the teacher has half the class actively engaged at any one moment (one per

When Not To Use Simultaneous Interaction
We don't always want simultaneous interaction. If, for example, we know that a student has a unique or important idea we want the whole class to hear, we do not want the student to share the idea only with a partner. To take another example, it can be worthwhile to have one student do a demonstration at the board, or to have a student give a report to the whole class. We need to know, however, that sequential participation, one student at a time sharing with the class, should be used very sparingly and with great caution because it is purchased at the expense of active engagement by the rest of the class. Whenever we have one student at a time talking, we need to focus not on the one student who is actively engaged, but rather on the 29 who are not.

Objections to Simultaneity
A common objection to simultaneous sharing is that the teacher will not hear everything said in the class, so wrong answers may be shared. In a sequential structure, all student answers are reviewed by the teacher. If an incorrect answer is shared, the teacher can correct the answer. When there is simultaneous sharing, the teacher cannot review the many answers all at once. There are three solutions to this potential problem. 1) Students or teams can write their responses on team slates and hold them up so the teacher can quickly review the answers. 2) Put in place a classroom norm for accuracy. It works like this: to avoid the spread of misinformation, if anyone shares with you an answer you are not sure is correct, you need to check with another pair, team, or the teacher. 3) Walk around for authentic assessment. While students are busy working, work the room. Sit down with a team to hear what's going on. Eavesdrop on teams. If

you hear any misinformation that may apply to the whole class, stop the class and announce the correction.

With simultaneous interaction, wrong answers will be shared. Upon analysis, though, buying simultaneous interaction at the cost of some wrong answers being shared is a very good purchase. Let's see why. Those students who share a wrong answer during simultaneous interaction would have had that wrong answer in mind in the traditional classroom, but would have been the very students least likely to verbalize their wrong answer. Thus, they fail to receive a correction opportunity and leave class with the wrong answer uncorrected. The probability of a correction opportunity is far greater if we allow simultaneous interaction. We have set up heterogeneous groups so the highest achievers are spread around, one per team. Further we have set up a norm: If you are ever in doubt about the correctness of an answer, everything stops until we check with a resource (another team, a book, the teacher). Thus, the probability of wrong answers being corrected is far greater given simultaneous interaction than if we choose the traditional sequential approach. In support of this argument is data which shows tremendous achievement gains when teachers switch from traditional to cooperative learning. Data also shows the gains are greatest among the lowest achieving students.

Another objection to simultaneous interaction is that there is so much interaction going on all at once, there is no way for the teacher to ensure all students are on task. This is true. But it is also true that when students are not actively participating, there is no way for the teacher to ensure they are not daydreaming. Many are off task without any obvious behavioral cues. At least when we see a student staring blankly at the front of the class when she/he should be interacting, we know for sure she/he is off task and we can do something about it. Circulating throughout the class while students interact allows us to guide students back on task if they have wandered.

A PIES Analysis

Let's cement the PIES principles by examining three common structures: 1) Whole Class Q & A, 2) Group Discussion, and 3) Timed Pair Share. We will perform a PIES Analysis. That is, we will simply ask the five critical questions of each of these structures. When we analyze these three ways of structuring our classrooms using the PIES critical questions, we find they are radically different, and that PIES is an indispensable evaluative tool.

The Three Structures at a Glance

1. **Whole Class Q & A** is the traditional teacher-led question and answer strategy: The teacher asks the class a question. Students voluntarily raise their hands. The teacher selects a student to answer. The student answers, and the teacher responds to the student's answer.

2. **Group Discussion** is unstructured discussion. The teacher has students sitting in groups and asks a question. Groups discuss the teacher's question. Who speaks and for how long is up to the members of the group.

3. **Timed Pair Share** is structured pair interaction. Students are paired up. The teacher asks a question. Each partner has an equal time to express his/her ideas. For example, one student speaks for one minute while her/his partner listens. The listening partner responds to the partner who shared using response or paraphrasing gambits ("What I found most interesting about what you said was…." "What I heard you say was….") Partners switch roles for one minute, and the listener becomes the speaker. Again, the listening partner responds to the student who shared.

12.24

Kagan Cooperative Learning • Dr. Spencer Kagan & Miguel Kagan
Kagan Publishing • 1 (800) 933-2667 • www.KaganOnline.com

Analyzing for Positive Interdependence

Critical Question 1: *Positive Correlation: Are students on the same side?*

1. **Whole Class Q & A.** The answer is yes and no. When a classmate answers a teacher's question, the other students may hope the student gives a correct answer so they can learn. But students who wanted to answer hope the student called on misses the answer so they have a chance to shine. **Result:** *Mixed.*

2. **Group Discussion.** Information shared by a group mate is a benefit for all members. The students feel they are on the same side trying to come up with the right answer or good ideas. **Result:** *Yes.*

3. **Timed Pair Share.** Information shared by a partner is a benefit for the other. Students feel they are on the same side, sharing their best ideas. **Result:** *Yes.*

Critical Question 2: *Interdependence: Does the task require working together?*

1. **Whole Class Q & A.** Students are expected to respond on their own. They are not expected to interact; they do not need to cooperate. **Result:** *No.*

2. **Group Discussion.** One student can do all the talking. There is nothing in the structure that demands listening or cooperation by all; some students can tune out. **Result:** *No.*

3. **Timed Pair Share.** Students take turns sharing: One is sharing and the other listening. They are dependent on each other to complete the steps of the task; they cannot do a Timed Pair Share without the cooperation of their partner. **Result:** *Yes.*

Analyzing for Individual Accountability

Critical Question 3: *Is individual, public performance required?*

1. **Whole Class Q & A.** There is an individual public performance only for the student called on, but answering is voluntary, not required. Any student can choose not to perform. **Result:** *No.*

2. **Group Discussion.** Contributing to the group discussion is purely voluntary. Some students can choose not to contribute at all. **Result:** *No.*

3. **Timed Pair Share.** Individual public performance is required of each student two times. The first, of course, is during their allotted time to share. The second is as they paraphrase or respond to their partner. Students are held accountable to their partners for sharing and for listening. **Result:** *Yes.*

Analyzing for Equal Participation

Critical Question 4: *Is participation approximately equal?*

1. **Whole Class Q & A.** Participation is very unequal. Some students always have a hand up and are often called upon; others seldom or even never have a hand up. **Result:** Very *Unequal.*

2. **Group Discussion.** Without a mechanism for equalizing participation in a group discussion, in heterogeneous groups, equal participation is rare. Some students do most of the talking. One or two students within the group may dominate the conversation, while others are content to just listen, or to tune out. **Result:** *Unequal.*

3. **Timed Pair Share.** Turn taking and time allocation are both used to equalize participation. All students share and listen for approximately equal time intervals. **Result:** *Equal.*

Analyzing for Simultaneous Interaction

Critical Question 5: *What percent of students are overtly interacting at once?*

1. **Whole Class Q & A.** At any moment, only one student is responding. **Result:** *3.3%.*

2. **Group Discussion.** At any moment, one student per group of four is sharing. **Result:** *25%.*

3. **Timed Pair Share.** At any moment, one student per pair is sharing. **Result:** *50%.*

The table on the next page summarizes the results of our PIES Analysis. As we have seen, these three structures are very different with regard to the PIES principles. They also differ greatly with their capacity to make the classroom more cooperative, engaging, and to equalize and improve the educational outcomes for all students.

PIES Analysis Results

Basic Principles	Traditional Whole Class Q & A	Group Work Group Discussion	Kagan Structure Timed Pair Share
Positive Interdependence	Same Side? **Mixed**	Same Side? **Yes**	Same Side? **Yes**
	Teamwork Required? **No**	Teamwork Required? **No**	Teamwork Required? **Yes**
Individual Accountability	No	No	Yes
Equal Participation	Very Unequal	Unequal	Equal
Simultaneous Interaction	3.3%	25%	50%

Chapter Summary

Cooperative learning consistently produces powerful gains when the research-based and classroom-proven PIES principles are in place. Kagan Structures implement PIES. Any teacher can easily learn some simple structures and be confident he/she is implementing good cooperative learning.

A firm understanding of the basic principles underlying successful cooperative learning empowers us to evaluate our instructional practices and implement effective instructional strategies, replacing less-effective traditional strategies. Instead of creating a hostile, competitive classroom environment, we create a supportive, cooperative class. Instead of assessing students' knowledge using unrepresentative samples and infrequent tests, we authentically assess the entire class on an ongoing basis. Instead of allowing a subset of the classroom to opt out of participating, we promote

approximately equal participation. Instead of calling on one student at a time and creating downtime for the rest of the class, we have all students interact over the content simultaneously.

PIES is more than an evaluative tool. PIES offers insight and points the way to implementing successful cooperative learning. When students are not cooperating, we focus on the "P" of PIES. If they are not achieving well, we focus on both the "P" and the "I" of PIES. If some students are not participating, we focus on the "E" of PIES. If the class is generally disengaged or low energy, we focus on the "S" of PIES. The PIES principles tell us where to look and how to restructure when things are not going well in our class.

Command of the basic principles makes us more effective in implementing cooperative learning. PIES is foundational knowledge; it helps us all become better teachers.

Chapter Questions

► Questions for Review

1. Name the four PIES principles.
2. Why are there four PIES principles, yet five critical questions?
3. What are the five critical questions?
4. What methods can a teacher use to equalize participation?
5. How and when can individual accountability be created in the classroom?

► Questions for Thinking and Discussion

1. Of the four PIES principles, which do you think has the biggest impact on student learning? Which one is least important? Why?
2. Students need to learn to compete. Making them positively interdependent in the classroom is a disservice. Do you agree or disagree? Why?
3. Equal participation could completely eliminate the achievement gap. Do you agree or disagree? Why?
4. According to the PIES principles, should group grades be used? Why or why not?
5. If you performed a PIES analysis on your classroom instruction, what would it reveal?

References

[1] Kagan, S. "In Praise of Praise." *Kagan Online Magazine,* 2007: 10(1).

[2] Slavin, R. *Cooperative Learning.* New York, NY: Longman, Inc., 1983.

[3] Willingham, D. "Practice Makes Perfect—But Only If You Practice Beyond the Point of Perfection." *American Educator,* 2004, Spring.

[4] Webb, N. "Testing a Theoretical Model of Student Interaction and Learning in Small Groups." In Hertz-Lazarowitz, R. & N. Miller (eds.). *Interaction in Cooperative Groups.* New York, NY: Cambridge University Press, 1992.

[5] Kagan, J. *Galen's Prophecy.* Boulder, CO: Westview Press, 1998.

[6] LeDoux, J. *The Emotional Brain: The Mysterious Underpinnings of Emotional Life.* New York, NY: Touchstone, 1998.

[7] Henderson, L. & P. Zimbardo. "Shyness." In Friedman, H. (ed.). *The Encyclopedia of Mental Health.* San Diego, CA: Academic Press, 1998.

[8] Au, K. & J. Mason. "Social Organizational Factors in Learning to Read: The Balance of Rights Hypothesis." *Reading Research Quarterly,* 1981, 17(1): 115–152.

[9] Rowe, M. "Wait Time: Slowing Down May Be a Way of Speeding Up." *American Educator,* 1987, 11: 38–43, 47.

[10] Mehan, H. "Structuring School Structure." *Harvard Educational Review,* 1978, 48(1): 32–64.

[11] Kagan, S., P. Kyle & S. Scott. *Win-Win Discipline.* San Clemente, CA: Kagan Publishing, 2004.

[12] Borg, W. "Time and School Learning." In Denham, C. & A. Lieberman (eds.). *Time to Learn.* Washington, DC: National Institute of Education, 1980.

Quartarola, B. *A Research Paper on Time on Task and the Extended School Day/Year and Their Relationship to Improving Student Achievement.* Sacramento, CA: Research, Evaluation, and Accreditation Committee, Association of California School Administrators, 1984.

Rosenshine, B. "Content, Time, and Direct Instruction." In Peterson, P. & H. Walberg (eds.). *Research on Teaching: Concepts, Findings, and Implications.* Berkeley, CA: McCutchan Publishing Corp., 1979.

Sanford, J. & C. Evertson. "Time Use and Activities in Junior High Classes." *Journal of Educational Research,* 1983, 76: 140–147.

Seifert, E. & J. Beck. "Relationships Between Task Time and Learning Gains in Secondary Schools." *Journal of Educational Research,* 1984, 78: 5–10.

Stallings, J. "Allocated Academic Learning Time Revisited, or Beyond Time on Task." *Educational Researcher,* 1980, 9: 11–16.

Strother, D. "Another Look at Time on Task." *Phi Delta Kappan,* 1984, 65: 714–717.

Resources

AnswerBoards. San Clemente, CA: Kagan Publishing. www.KaganOnline.com

Erickson, F. "Conceptions of School Culture: An Overview." *Educational Administration Quarterly,* 1987, 23(4): 11–24.

Kagan, S. "Group Grades Miss the Mark." *Educational Leadership,* 1995, May: 68–71.

Ogbu, J. "Opportunity Structure, Cultural Boundaries, and Literacy." In Langer, J. (ed.). *Language, Literacy and Culture: Issues of Society and Schooling.* Norwood, NJ: Ablex Press, 1987.

Cooperative Projects & Presentations

• limit the resources
(so team members have to participate
with their resources)
• Assign roles

Far too much of traditional education is aimed at transfusing basic facts and skills into students. Academic standards and benchmarks are established, and much of the teaching profession is focused on instilling in students predefined competencies. High-stakes tests largely dictate what is taught and are barometers of whether educators are successfully "teaching" students. In this transmission model of education, students are viewed as empty vessels into which existing knowledge is incrementally poured. Empty student bottles with their narrow cylindrical necks come marching down the conveyer belt of traditional schooling, and year after year new knowledge is poured in. At graduation, the bottle is capped. This transmission model is so prevalent in its various forms, it is easy to lose sight of another way to teach and learn—the constructivist model of education.

Cooperative projects are perhaps the purest form of constructivist education. As students construct their projects, they are simultaneously constructing meaning and understanding.

In the constructivist model, students are not the passive recipients of known facts. Instead, they are active participants in constructing their own learning. Students have unique minds: products of their nature, their past experiences, and current circumstances. Learners interact with each other and with the world to assimilate new learning into their current cognitive schemes of how things work and how they can work with things.

Cooperative projects are perhaps the purest form of constructivist education. As students construct their projects, they are simultaneously constructing meaning and understanding. Cooperative teams are ideal for social learning, language use, and cognitive development. Students discuss, elaborate, and debate ideas as they work together, each making an important individual

sneak peek

contribution toward a group goal. Not only are students' minds engaged, but so too are their hands and bodies as they build their projects and practice their presentations. Learning is active, communicative, hands-on, and real. And it is intrinsically motivating. Cooperative projects align instruction with students' natural desire to interact, play, experiment, and create.

Behold the Power of the Cooperative Project

Some of the world's greatest ideas, accomplishments, and products are large-scale cooperative projects:

- Democracy
- Internet
- Landing a man on the moon
- Human Genome Project
- Golden Gate Bridge
- Personal Computers
- Exploration of the world
- Exploration of the cosmos

Shouldn't education strive to ignite creativity and cultivate cooperation, at least as much as to transmit knowledge?

Nothing new that is really interesting comes without collaboration.
—James Watson, Co-discoverer of DNA

Projects are more representative of the real world. How many jobs do people have where they receive information, memorize the information, then take a test on what they memorized? In the real world, people work on real projects, and people frequently work in teams. In the 21st century, there has been a massive organizational restructuring toward greater interdependence and teamwork in the workplace. Teamwork in the classroom equips students with life skills students will need to succeed in the workplace.

We parody transmission-based education for the sake of comparison, but of

course there is an important place in education for the transmission of content knowledge. But there is also a place for students to be creative, solve real problems, and construct their own understanding of the world. Cooperative learning in general corrects the imbalance created by an over-emphasis on transmission and an under-emphasis on construction. There is no purer form of true construction and negotiation of meaning in education than in cooperative projects.

Project Principles

As students work on projects, they may need a block of time with no teacher intervention. The extent to which this time is productive depends in part on the amount and kind of structuring put in place before the students go to work.

Under the influence of constructivist theory, the thoughtful educator may ask, "Why then do we need structures and structuring? Why not give teams a task and let them wrestle with how they will accomplish the goal?" Following this line of thinking leads us invariably to unstructured group work. In some cases and with some students, unstructured group work may work just fine. However, in most educational settings, the reality is the pitfalls of unstructured group work outweigh the potential benefits. Unstructured group work usually leads to unequal participation, time off task, power conflicts, and poor learning. Structuring facilitates the construction of knowledge for *all* students. In a democracy where we have an obligation to equity in education, it is not acceptable for a select group of students to reap benefits at the expense of others.

"Education is not the filling of a pail, but the lighting of a fire."
—W. B. Yeats

We can think of team projects as a continuum, with highly structured projects on one side and completely unstructured projects on the other. Young students and students without good teamwork skills need a step-by-step teacher-led project to be successful. As they become more skilled, they require less direction and structuring from the teacher. Ideally, students eventually internalize the principles of effective teamwork—learn to take turns, divide the work fairly, ensure that everyone participates, and make fair decisions. At that point, they need no direction and structuring. In our experience though, if we want good and fair teamwork, at least at first, structuring is helpful even with adult learners. As students acquire teamwork skills, we begin to de-structure our projects, but starting without structure before students possess the requisite skills of effective teamwork can be a recipe for disaster.

With the PIES principles applied to projects, we create conditions to promote active engagement and inclusion for all students in all aspects of cooperative projects. To ensure our cooperative projects are good cooperative learning as opposed to dubious group work, we apply the basic principles of cooperative learning, use structures, and occasionally use processing. Let's look first at the basic principles applied to cooperative projects. For a comprehensive description of the basic PIES principles, see *Chapter 12: Basic Principles (PIES)*. Here, we focus on the principles as they apply to creating successful cooperative projects.

Positive Interdependence
Are students on the same side? Does the task require working together?

Structuring positive interdependence into cooperative projects is useful for a number of reasons. When students work together on a project and the success of one contributes to the success of all, a positive climate is created. Positive interdependence fosters helping, encouraging, and tutoring. There are a number of ways to promote positive interdependence in project work. See box: Structuring Projects for Positive Interdependence.

Individual Accountability
Is individual, public performance required?

Making each student individually accountable for his/her contribution to the team project is another way to ensure all students participate. Students put more effort into a project if they know they are being held individually accountable for their contributions. Individual accountability increases individual participation, aids in equalizing participation, and eliminates the problems of the freeloader and the workhorse. For suggestions to structure for individual accountability in cooperative projects, see box: Structuring Projects for Individual Accountability.

Structuring Projects for
Positive Interdependence

▶ **Goals**
We all have the same goal in doing this project.

▶ **Rewards**
We will receive team recognition for our project.

▶ **Task**
The task is structured so we can't do it alone. Everyone must contribute for our project to be successful.

▶ **Division of Labor**
Everyone is responsible for completing a portion of the task.

▶ **Limited Resource Access**
We depend on Sue for work with the scissors, Jose for gluing, Veronica for writing, and Pete for drawing.

▶ **Roles**
We each have an important role: Joe is the Materials Monitor, Peter the Reporter, Christine the Cheerleader, and Stacy the Recorder.

Structuring Projects for
Individual Accountability

▶ **For Participating**
- Color-code individual contributions.
- Students summarize or reflect on their contributions.
- Divide the labor.
- Break the project into mini-topics.
- Teammates evaluate each other on their contributions.
- Use turn taking structures (RoundTable).

▶ **For Performance and Achievement**
- Grade students on their individual portion of the project.
- Grade students on their part of the team presentation.
- Students turn in an individual paper.
- Students take an individual quiz or test.
- Students give an individual performance.

Equal Participation

Is participation approximately equal?

One of the biggest pitfalls for cooperative projects is unequal participation: One student or some students work extra hard on the projects, while the others do little. As much as possible, we want students to contribute about equally. Students have different abilities and different talents, so not every student needs to do the exact same thing for the exact same amount of time. The point here is that slacking is not an option. There are some basic ways to ensure that students will participate about equally or equitably. See box: Structuring Projects for Equal or Equitable Participation. Later in this chapter there are a number of student processing forms for students to evaluate their own contributions and that of their teammates as a way to reflect on and improve the equality of participation.

Simultaneous Interaction

What percent of students are overtly interacting?

Simultaneous interaction increases engagement and decreases off-task time during cooperative projects. We structure the task so that interaction occurs simultaneously both within and among teams. Downtime decreases learning opportunities and is an open invitation for management problems.

For team projects, interaction is naturally simultaneous among teams. Every team is busy working on their own project. For a class project, every student or every team needs to be assigned a specific part to play so there is little to no downtime.

The same is true within teams. We want each teammate actively working on their team project at the same time. The biggest obstacle to simultaneous engagement is a sequentially designed project. That is, the project must be performed in a series of sequential steps: Something needs to happen before the next step can happen. This can be a recipe for one teammate working while others sit around waiting for the step to be completed.

Most projects do have a logical sequence to completion, so some sequential interaction may be unavoidable. However, there are things to consider when designing cooperative projects to avoid downtime. See box: Structuring Projects for Simultaneous Interaction.

Structuring Projects for Equal or Equitable Participation

▶ **Division of Labor**
Assign each teammate a specific task.

▶ **Turn Taking**
Structure so that everyone has a turn at doing a task necessary for project completion.

▶ **Time Allocation**
Structure so that every student receives the same amount of time for a portion of the project.

▶ **Resources**
Divide the resources. Hold each individual accountable for the way their own resources are used.

▶ **Roles**
Assign each student a different, important role. Roles might be task-specific such as "Gum Drop Holder," "Spaghetti Pusher." Roles such as Gatekeeper, Focus Keeper, and Encourager are effective for encouraging equal participation.

▶ **Teacher as Filter**
Check to see how the task is divided and, if necessary, intervene to make the division more fair or appropriate for students' ability level.

▶ **Student Choice**
Allow students to choose their mini topics or task. Students select what is most fitting for them.

▶ **Student Self-Evaluation**
Schedule a time for students to evaluate their contributions. Have them reflect: Are they working to their capacity and, if not, what could they do to improve?

▶ **Teammate Evaluation & Processing**
Structure time so students give their teammates feedback on their contributions and discuss how to create more equal or equitable participation in the future.

Kagan Cooperative Learning • **Dr. Spencer Kagan & Miguel Kagan**
Kagan Publishing • 1 (800) 933-2667 • www.KaganOnline.com

Structuring Projects for
Simultaneous Interaction

▶ **Simultaneous Interaction**
Can the project be designed for simultaneous interaction rather than sequential steps? Can the project be designed so teammates or pairs can each work on their own parts at the same time, later putting the parts together?

▶ **Teammate Cooperation**
Can pairs or teammates work together on a step to speed completion?

▶ **Sufficient Resources**
Will multiple materials (multiple scissors, multiple black markers) help?

▶ **Forward Progress**
To avoid downtime, make students aware there is always something else teammates can do to move the project forward. Can teammates:
- Begin planning the presentation?
- Refine or improve completed portion?
- Plan the next step?
- Brainstorm ideas?
- Prepare materials for the next step?

▶ **Simultaneous Sharing**
Can projects be shared simultaneously instead of one at a time?

▶ **Challenge Problem or Task**
If the team finishes early, encourage students to extend their projects with additional tasks.

Project Structures

Cooperative projects are among one of the biggest changes in the Kagan approach to cooperative learning over the past decade. A decade ago, when we spoke of team projects, we spoke of big multi-step, cooperative investigation—such as Co-op Co-op, Co-op Jigsaw, Group Investigation, and a handful of other project structures—we called "project designs." They are based on powerful educational theory and produce high levels of cooperation and learning. However, the project designs require considerable teacher planning and a substantial block of classroom time. We'll briefly review these "classic" cooperative learning project designs, but first let's examine what we have found to be easier to implement and more frequently used—Team Projects.

> *"Great discoveries and improvements invariably involve the cooperation of many minds."*
> —Alexander Graham Bell

Team Project

The Team Project structure, developed by Laurie Kagan, is a high utility structure ideal for anytime a team works together to create a product. The product can be a team book, team art project, team science project, team experiment, team model, team collage, even a team performance—anything that can be created or performed by a team. The steps of a Team Project are very simple. The beauty of this structure is its simplicity and ease of use.

Team Project Steps

1. The teacher announces the team project.
2. The teacher assigns roles and resource access.
3. Students work in teams to create the project.

You may have noticed in our discussion of project principles above that roles and resources kept popping up as ways to implement the PIES principles. Notice how they appear here in Step 2: The teacher **assigns roles** and **resource access**. The Team Project incorporates these two powerful techniques as part of the structure. In developing the structure, Laurie Kagan discovered she could almost always guarantee successful cooperative projects if different roles were assigned to each student and each student had sole access to essential resources. Step 2 is what distinguishes Team Projects from group work. The teacher does not just say, "Work on this project in your team." This would violate the principles of good cooperative learning. There is nothing in unstructured group work that guarantees individual accountability or equal participation. Students could all work together in harmony without any structure, each contributing their own fair share. But then again, one student could do most of the work while another chooses to write her boyfriend a note. That's why Laurie introduced two simple structural alterations, Roles and Resources, that transform group work into true cooperative learning.

Kagan Cooperative Learning • Dr. Spencer Kagan & Miguel Kagan
Kagan Publishing • 1 (800) 933-2667 • www.KaganOnline.com

13.5

Role Assignment.
To complete the team project, every student will have his or her own, unique role. The roles can be the generic cooperative learning roles such as Focus Keeper and Gatekeeper (see *Chapter 11: Social Skills*). However, project-specific roles are desirable for many projects. For example, if the team project is creating a collage, the roles might be:

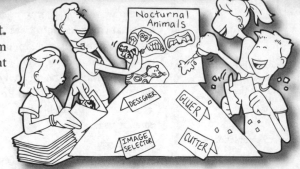

- **Student 1. Image Selector:** *Selects the images to use.*
- **Student 2. Cutter:** *Cuts out the images to use.*
- **Student 3. Designer:** *Determines the arrangement of the images.*
- **Student 4. Gluer:** *Glues the images in place.*

Project-specific roles are, in essence, assigned division of labor. These roles can be rotated on a specific time schedule. If the project is twenty minutes, every student performs each role for five minutes. Roles can also be switched, based on the completion of a certain task. For example, students can switch roles after each image in the collage are pasted down.

Resource Access. Through resource access, we decide who on each team can use which resource. Who will use the scissors? Who can touch the glue? Access to the resources may be dependent on a student's role. For example, the Cutter is the only student who can use the scissors. If the Cutter role is rotated to another student, so are the scissors. But resources are not always dependent on the role. For example, if part of the team project requires the team to draw a picture, then all students should have access to the markers. To equalize participation and create individual accountability, we might say the team picture will be evaluated on the integration of colors and only Student #1 can touch the red marker; only Student #2 can touch the blue marker, and so on. This way, every student is included in the team project.

Introducing a Project. The roles and resources are reviewed with the class prior to starting the project. To clarify the roles and resources for students, you may use T-Charts. For the roles, describe or have students generate ideas for "what to do" and "what to say" to fulfill each role (see graphic below). For the resources, list the materials and who is allowed to use each material (see graphic below).

Assigning Roles T-Chart	
What to Do	**What to Say**

Allocating Resources T-Chart	
Materials	**Who Uses It**

Both the roles and resources are posted somewhere prominently, so each student knows unequivocally what materials he or she is in charge of and what he or she is supposed to do. The T-Charts may be posted on the blackboard, on an overhead projector, or on the project blackline master. Or we can post something indicating the Student, the Role, and the Materials. For the science project example (see box below), the team builds a model of an atom, but each teammate has a specific role and is the only teammate allowed to handle the assigned materials. Mendeleev is in charge of the periodic table; Rydberg is in charge of the protons.

> *"Teamwork divides the task and doubles the success."*
> —Unknown

You may also distribute to each team a filled-in Team Project Task Form (see the following page). If teams are rotating through a series of project centers, a Team Project Task Form is left at each center so the team reads their team goal and individual responsibilities before performing the team project.

Science Project
Building A Model of An Atom

Student	Role	Materials
Student 1	Mendeleev	Periodic Table
Student 2	Rydberg	Protons
Student 3	Moseley	Neutrons
Student 4	Bohr	Electrons

Team Project
Task Form

Instructions. Review your team goal, individual roles, and individual responsibilities before beginning your team project.

> **Team Project Name**

Your Team's Goal

Your Individual Responsibilities...   Rotate Roles ❑ No ❑ Yes   Rotate Every_____

Role 1

Role_____

_____

Responsibility_____

_____

Materials_____

_____

Role 2

Role_____

_____

Responsibility_____

_____

Materials_____

_____

Role 3

Role_____

_____

Responsibility_____

_____

Materials_____

_____

Role 4

Role_____

_____

Responsibility_____

_____

Materials_____

_____

Kagan Cooperative Learning • Dr. Spencer Kagan & Miguel Kagan
Kagan Publishing • 1 (800) 933-2667 • www.KaganOnline.com

Structures for Sharing and Presenting Projects

Teams can learn a lot from each other. Teams can reap benefits from sharing their projects with other teams or the class at various stages of project development: during the planning stage, during the creation stage, and after completion of the final product or presentation.

If, during planning or in the process of creating a team project, students have the opportunity to hear other teams' ideas, or see how other teams have solved a problem, they can synthesize, and synergize, often resulting in much improved products. If teams' only opportunity to view each other's projects is after the projects are completed, it's too late to implement improvements.

Sharing among teams is helpful also if each team is working on a different piece of the class project. Teams can coordinate efforts so their piece fits well in the larger class puzzle.

Sharing among teams furthers the cooperative community norm. It says, "We are in this classroom to learn from each other and to create the best projects we can." In contrast, an interteam competitive atmosphere is created when teams hide their projects from other teams in fear that another team may steal their ideas and create an equal or better project. Interteam competition can be a strong motivator for teams striving to be the best, but in the long run it undermines motivation because only one team is the best and the others become dispirited.

Long-term projects may be worth sharing at all three stages. Quick team challenges may not be worth sharing at all. For example, we would likely forego sharing the team challenge: "How many ways you can build 79¢ with these coins?" Sharing, especially full-fledged presentations, can be time-consuming, so we perform a cost-benefit analysis: How much time will it cost? What are the benefits of sharing?

Let's look at key structures for sharing during the three stages of projects: 1) sharing project plans, 2) sharing project process, and 3) sharing products and presentations.

Sharing Project Plans (Before)

Here are three structures for teams to share their ideas before they launch into their projects:

Teams Post. Teams Post is an easy way for teams to share their plans while taking very little time off task. Each team is designated a place at the whiteboard. After teams generate ideas, a team representative writes or draws the team's ideas on the whiteboard. Students can see at a glance what other teams are planning.

Team Whip. The teacher asks each team to prepare a short statement of their project plans. In turn, one representative from each team stands to share his or her team's plans.

Team Stand-N-Share. If each team generates a list of ideas, they can share their ideas using Team Stand-N-Share. Teams stand with their list in hand. The teacher calls on one student, and he or she shares one item from the team list. The Recorders on the other teams add the item to their list if it is a new idea, or check it off if they also came up with that idea. Teams sit when all ideas have been shared.

Sharing Project Process (During)

Here are some strong structures for teams to share their works in progress:

One Stray. One teammate stands up and "strays" to another team. He or she views the other team's project and reports back to his/her own team. Often for One Stray, each teammate gets a turn "straying" to a different team.

Three Stray. Three teammates stand up and as a group "stray" to another team. One teammate stays behind to answer questions and share his or her team's progress.

Roving Reporter. While working on team projects, the teacher announces, "Roving Reporters, you have three minutes." Every team selects their Roving Reporter. The Roving Reporter visits other teams, and may take notes or make sketches of what he or she learns. When the teacher calls time, Roving Reporters return to their teams and share the information they gathered. Some teachers call the Roving Reporter a "Scout."

Roam-the-Room. Once students have made visible progress on their project, the teacher says, "Everyone, please stop working and stand up. Roam the room." Teammates may go from project to project together, they may break into pairs, or everyone can go their own way. When they return, they discuss what they learned and what they want to integrate into their project.

Sharing Products and Presentations (After)
Once teams have completed their projects, it's time to share with other teams. There are a number of good structures for sharing team projects:

Number Group Presentation. Team projects are displayed on the team's table. Students number off in their team from 1 to 4. All Student 1's go to Team 1; All Student 2's go to Team 2, and so on. In each new group, there is one student whose team created the project. That team rep presents the project to the group. The group rotates to the next project, and the next team rep shares the project. When done, students return to their original teams to discuss what they saw and heard.

Number Group Interview. Number Group Interview is the same as Number Group Presentation except the rep is asked questions by the members of his/her group.

Carousel Feedback. Team projects are placed on the team's desk or posted around the room with a feedback form. Each team stands in front of their project. They rotate clockwise to the next team's project. For a specified time, the team discusses their reaction to the project. Timed RoundRobin works well for this team discussion. When discussion time is up, Student 1 records the team's feedback. The team rotates to the next project, discusses it, and Student 2 records the team's feedback. The process is continued for each team project. The Recorder role is rotated for each project. Teams use the Carousel Feedback Form to record their feedback (see page 13.11). When teams rotate back to their own projects, they read and review the feedback from other teams.

Carousel Discuss. Carousel Discuss works the same as Carousel Feedback except students do not leave written feedback for other teams. They discuss the project, then when time is up, move to discuss the next project.

Roam-the-Room. Like touring an art gallery, students are free to browse other teams' projects for a specified time period. Students may roam the room with teammates, a team partner, solo, or even with a student or students from another team. When they return to their teams, students discuss what they saw as they roamed the room using Team Interview or Timed RoundRobin.

Roam-the-Room and the Carousel structures are designed for viewing visual projects such as illustrations, maps, and models that don't require explanation because no team representative stays behind to present the project.

Team Presentation. Each team makes a timed presentation to the class. An important component of a team presentation is that each teammate plays a role in the presentation, and that the roles students play are equal or equitable. For example, if each team has four minutes for their presentation, each student is responsible for sharing for one minute. Or each student is responsible for a different aspect of the presentation. The disadvantage of team presentations are that they are sequential, violating the simultaneity principle. Four students are actively engaged, while the rest of the class is relatively passive. Team Presentations

Ideas for
Improving Our Team Project

Instructions. Use this form to record what you like about other teams' projects. Record ideas to improve your team's project. Make sketches in the boxes and use the lines to record ideas.

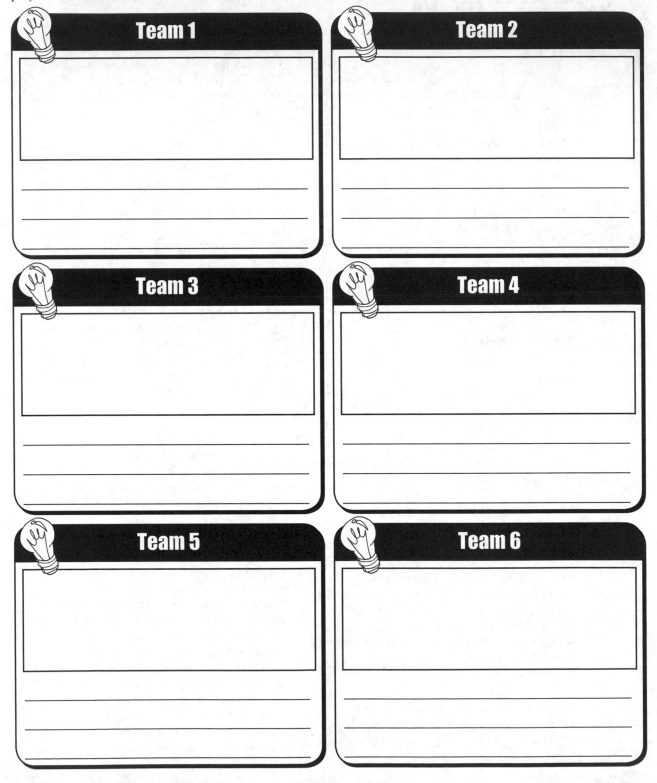

Team 1

Team 2

Team 3

Team 4

Team 5

Team 6

Kagan Cooperative Learning • Dr. Spencer Kagan & Miguel Kagan
Kagan Publishing • 1 (800) 933-2667 • www.KaganOnline.com

Carousel Feedback Form

Instructions. Fill in your team name, project name, and project description.
Post this form next to your team project. One student on each team records his/her team's feedback to your project.

Team Name_____   Project Name_____

Project Description _____

Post Your Team's Feedback

Team 1 Team Name _____

Team Feedback _____

_____

_____

_____

_____

Team 2 Team Name _____

Team Feedback _____

_____

_____

_____

_____

Team 3 Team Name _____

Team Feedback _____

_____

_____

_____

_____

_____

Team 4 Team Name _____

Team Feedback _____

_____

_____

_____

_____

_____

Team 5 Team Name _____

Team Feedback _____

_____

_____

_____

_____

_____

Team 6 Team Name _____

Team Feedback _____

_____

_____

_____

_____

_____

Team 7 Team Name _____

Team Feedback _____

_____

_____

_____

_____

Team 8 Team Name _____

Team Feedback _____

_____

_____

_____

_____

Management Tips for Team Projects

▶ **Use a Timer**

- **Allot Time.** Tell the class in advance how much time they will have for their project, their presentation, their feedback, and their sharing.

- **Break it Down.** Help students manage their time by breaking the project into timed pieces. For example:
  - Project Planning—10 minutes
  - Project Building—30 minutes
  - Presentation Planning—15 minutes

  Feedback can also be broken into time periods:
  - Team Discussion—2 minutes
  - Recording Feedback—1 minute

- **Display Time.** Use a large clock, overhead timer, or projected LCD timer for students so they know how much time they have remaining and can manage their time accordingly.

- **Announce Time's Up.** When there's only five minutes left and when time's up, let everyone know it by announcing it, using an alarm, or appointing the class Town Crier to announce "Oyez, Oyez! Thee time is up." When time's up, everyone needs to be ready to move on.

▶ **Prepare Sponge Activities**

Have an activity ready for teams that finish early. Project-related sponge activities are best such as an enhancement, an additional task, or questions or problems relating to the problem for the team to solve or discuss.

▶ **Teacher Consultation**

Visit with teams as they create their projects. Check in with their progress. We ask questions, answer questions, offer suggestions, but don't tell students how to do their team project!

may be used on an occasional basis to allow students to practice presenting in front of a large audience. One way to increase audience engagement is to require teams to actively engage classmates during the presentation. Students who are familiar with structures use structures such as Timed Pair Share or RallyRobin as they present, and use structures like Numbered Heads Together to check for understanding and cement learnings.

Team-2-Team. Team-2-Team has a number of important advantages over the traditional approach of team presentations—having each team take a turn at the front of the class. Let's analyze the two.

Let's say we have an hour to devote to the team presentations. With the traditional approach, each team would stand in front of the class for about five minutes. Each team would take at least one minute of transition time—to take their place in front of the class before the presentation and then to sit down after the presentation. Further, we would probably want to devote at least two minutes per team for feedback, question and answer time, and/or appreciations. With eight teams, that would be all we could fit into an hour.

Applying the simultaneity principle, we can get a great deal more from our hour. For Team-2-Team presentations, four teams are sent to the corners of the classroom or spread out around the perimeter of the classroom. Then the other four teams are sent out to face one other team, resulting in two teams in each corner of the room—a presentation team and an audience team. The presentation teams present for five minutes followed by a two-minute RoundRobin of specific appreciations and/or feedback by the audience team members. Each student says what he/she liked about the presentation, what he/she learned, and offers constructive criticism. Next, teams reverse roles and the audience team now presents, followed by RoundRobin appreciations.

Using Team-2-Team, so far we have accomplished in 14 minutes what it would have taken 64 minutes with the traditional approach! See box: Sequential v. Simultaneous Presentations (on the following page).

13.12

Kagan Cooperative Learning • Dr. Spencer Kagan & Miguel Kagan
Kagan Publishing • 1 (800) 933-2667 • www.KaganOnline.com

Sequential v. Simultaneous Presentations

Traditional Team Presentations Sequential

Presentation: 8 teams x 5 minutes	=	40 minutes
Transitions: 8 teams x 1 minute	=	8 minutes
Feedback: 8 teams x 2 minutes	=	16 minutes
	Total =	**64 minutes**

Team-2-Team Presentations Simultaneous

Presentations: 8 teams simultaneously for 5 minutes	=	5 minutes
RoundRobin Feedback 8 teams simultaneously for 2 minutes	=	2 minutes
Presentations: 8 teams simultaneously for 5 minutes	=	5 minutes
RoundRobin Feedback: 8 teams simultaneously for 2 minutes	=	2 minutes
	Total =	**14 minutes**

With the time saved using Team-2-Team presentations, we have time for additional learning! There is a second half to the Team-2-Team structure. In the second half, tremendous learning occurs that we would not have time for using the traditional, sequential approach. After teams have presented, we have them pull apart and spend five minutes working on their presentations to improve them. They have just gotten specific feedback and have just experienced giving the presentation, so they are motivated to improve.

Following their improvement session, the teams return to where they gave their presentations. The teacher calls for one team in each pair of teams to rotate clockwise to a new partner team. When the teams have their new partner teams, they each give their presentations again. Students learn that by working on their presentations, they improve them. The second round of presentations takes only an additional fourteen minutes. Applying the simultaneity principle, we have accomplished far more than twice as much in half the time!

Let's examine how students have spent their time. In the traditional approach, they have spent about seven minutes as active participants and the remainder of the hour as passive observers. With Team-2-Team, the students have been active participants for almost the full hour because even when they were not presenting, they were the direct recipients of a presentation following which they were each held accountable for giving specific feedback.

If the teams do not give their best presentation in their first try, they are left in the traditional approach to conclude that they are not very good at team presentations. In contrast, with Team-2-Team, they have an opportunity to improve and are likely to conclude that with practice they can give great presentations. With Team-2-Team presentations, motivation to do future presentations is high. Without exception, teams find their second presentation greatly improved over their initial attempt, leading to enhanced skills and pride.

Team Up! Whereas Team-2-Team is a formal presentation structure that allows reflection and improvement following an initial presentation, sometimes we want teams to quickly share something they have made or ideas they have generated. Team Up!, developed by Laurie Kagan, fills that niche. When it is time to share, we simply say, "Odd numbered teams, stand up!" When half the teams are standing, we have the seated teams beckon for a visiting team to come over. (Alternatively, teams can be pre-assigned partner teams.) The visiting team stands around the seated team, and the seated team shares with the visitors something they have made (e.g., reciting a poem, explaining their model of an atom) or shares ideas they have generated, often using a RoundRobin. The visitors give appreciations to the sharing team, each visitor in turn using specific praise. Rather than saying "Good job!" or offering other generic praise that can follow any presentation, the visitors positively respond to something that is unique about the presentation (e.g., "I like the way your Poem for Two Voices includes movement."). Following the first round of presentations, roles reverse and the visiting team presents. Alternatively, if the teams have something at their desk to share, we have the visitors return to their seats and the teams that have shared stand and travel to a different team to listen to or see and appreciate what they have created.

Structures for Presenting and Sharing Projects

▶ **Sharing Project Plans**
- Teams Post
- Team Stand-N-Share
- Team Whip

▶ **Sharing Project Process**
- One Stray
- Roam-the-Room
- Roving Reporter
- Three Stray

▶ **Sharing Products and Presentations**
- Carousel Feedback
- Carousel Discuss
- Roam-the-Room
- Team-2-Team
- Team Presentation
- Number Group Interview
- Number Group Presentation
- Team Up!

Team Project Planning Form

Teacher Instructions. Use this form to plan your team projects.

Creating the Team Project

Team's Goal _____

_____

Role Assignment & Resource Access
What role will each student have? What will be their responsibility?
Which materials will they be in charge of? Fill in roles, responsibilities,
and materials for each teammate.

Time

Teammate 1
Role _____

Responsibility _____

Materials _____

Teammate 2
Role _____

Responsibility _____

Materials _____

Teammate 3
Role _____

Responsibility _____

Materials _____

Teammate 4
Role _____

Responsibility _____

Materials _____

Rotating Roles
☐ No   **If Rotating:**

☐ Yes   ☐ Time Interval _____ or ☐ Task Interval _____
                     (time)   (task)

Sharing Team Projects

How will teams share their projects?

Sharing Project Plans
☐ Teams Post   ☐ Team Stand-N-Share   ☐ Team Whip

Sharing Project Process
☐ One Stray   ☐ Roam-the-Room   ☐ Roving Reporter   ☐ Three Stray

Sharing Products and Presentations
☐ Carousel Feedback   ☐ Carousel Discuss   ☐ Roam-the-Room   ☐ Team-2-Team
☐ Number Group Interview   ☐ Number Group Presentation   ☐ Team Up!

Notes _____

_____

Kagan Cooperative Learning • Dr. Spencer Kagan & Miguel Kagan
Kagan Publishing • 1 (800) 933-2667 • www.KaganOnline.com

Planning a Team Project. The Team Project Planning Form (on the previous page) is provided to help you plan team projects. It combines the use of roles and resource allocation. For each student, decide which materials they will be in charge of and which role they will play in the project. Decide whether the roles will be rotating or not. If so, decide if they will be based on a time interval or based on the completion of a specific task. The form also includes structures to consider for sharing team projects during their creation, and for presenting projects to other teams.

Classic Approaches to Cooperative Projects

There are a number of excellent classic cooperative learning methods. Among the classics are some true gems for cooperative projects. See box: Classic Cooperative Learning. For more information about these classics, see *Chapter 17: Classic Cooperative Learning*.

Classic Cooperative Learning
Approaches to Projects

▶ **Co-op Co-op**
▶ **Co-op Jigsaw I and II**
▶ **Group Investigation**
▶ **Partners**
▶ **Project Learning Centers**

Project and Presentation Feedback & Processing
Feedback

Feedback helps students improve their projects and presentations. Teams learn what other teams and the teacher think about, and have learned from their project or presentation—what they did well and what they could have improved. Team-2-Team, Carousel Feedback, and Team Up! each have a feedback component built into the structure. For other sharing structures, a feedback component can be tacked on.

For evaluative feedback—feedback that judges students on the good-bad dimension—it is helpful for students to know in advance the criteria by which their projects and presentations will be judged. Often, we involve the students in creating the evaluation matrix or rubric. Teams put in extra effort, knowing that they will be evaluated by their peers.

However, not all feedback needs be evaluative. Beyond the classroom, focus groups are used to provide insight to how others perceive something. Peer feedback can be used for the same purpose within the classroom. The presenters can ask the audience questions such as, "What did you learn?" or "What didn't you understand?" or "What questions were you left with?" Feedback provides teams valuable insight to the audience's perception of the team's project or presentation. For more formal feedback, use the Team Project Feedback Form or the How Did They Do? form for little ones (on the following pages). If using a feedback form, the teacher can also fill out a feedback form, or provide oral feedback.

Processing

After teams complete their project presentations, it is helpful for them to reflect on the process of completing the project and presentation, as well as reflect on the resulting product. How well did the team work together? How well did the project turn out? As a rule of thumb, the shorter and more structured team projects are, the less time required for processing group dynamics.

A number of processing forms are provided following the feedback forms. Students can fill out these forms while the other teams are providing written feedback. After all the presentations are completed and students have received feedback, students RoundRobin read the feedback forms, then each share their own reactions to the feedback via a second RoundRobin.

Project Ideas and Activities

We > I
—Spencer Kagan

There are countless cooperative projects we can create—projects for every subject area, for themes, for thinking, for decision making, and even fun projects for teambuilding. See Cooperative Project Ideas on 13.22–13.23 for a wide variety of terrific projects. Following, there are a number of sample projects to use or examine to get a flavor of the possibilities.

How Did They Do?

Instructions. Circle the face for how you feel about each statement.

1. I could hear them.

   YES   NO

2. They took turns.

   YES   NO

3. I could see the project.

   YES   NO

4. I liked the project.

   YES   NO

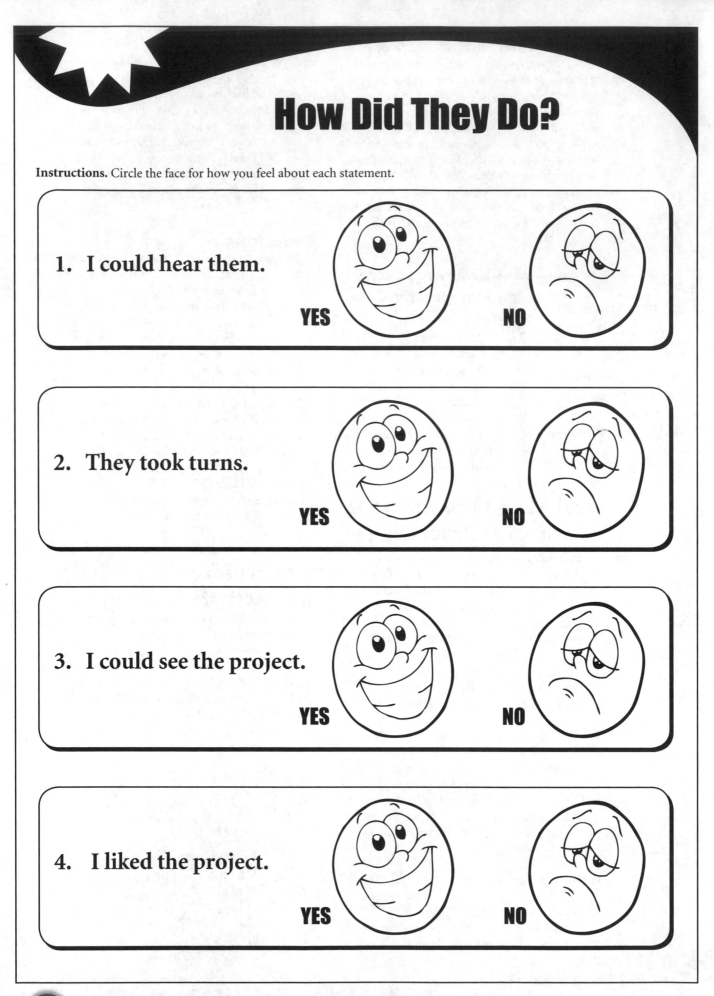

Kagan Cooperative Learning • Dr. Spencer Kagan & Miguel Kagan
Kagan Publishing • 1 (800) 933-2667 • www.KaganOnline.com

Team Project
Feedback Form

Instructions. Provide teams feedback on their projects and presentations.

Team Project

What I liked best about your project is _____
_____
_____
_____

One idea for improvement is _____
_____
_____
_____
_____

Team Presentation

One thing I liked about your presentation is _____
_____
_____
_____

One thing I learned from your presentation_____
_____
_____
_____

A question I have is _____
_____
_____
_____

One idea for improvement is _____
_____
_____
_____

Our Team Project

Instructions. Circle the face for how you feel about each statement.

1. Our team project was good.

   YES   NO

2. My part was good.

   YES   NO

3. I helped my teammates.

   YES   NO

4. My teammates helped me.

   YES   NO

Kagan Cooperative Learning • Dr. Spencer Kagan & Miguel Kagan
Kagan Publishing • 1 (800) 933-2667 • www.KaganOnline.Com

Team Project Processing Form

Instructions. Reflect on how well you and your teammates did as you worked on your team project. Circle the number corresponding to how you feel about each statement.

Student Name _____

Team Name _____ Date _____

① Strongly Disagree ② Disagree ③ Neither Agree nor Disagree ④ Agree ⑤ Strongly Agree

How Did I Do?

I performed my role.	1	2	3	4	5
I completed my task.	1	2	3	4	5
I contributed my ideas.	1	2	3	4	5
I was cooperative.	1	2	3	4	5
I respected my teammates' materials and roles.	1	2	3	4	5

How Did Our Team Do?

We worked together well.	1	2	3	4	5
We stayed focused on completing the project.	1	2	3	4	5
We used only our assigned materials.	1	2	3	4	5
Our project came out well.	1	2	3	4	5
Our presentation went well.	1	2	3	4	5

Reflection Questions

What would you do differently if you did this project again? _____

_____

_____

What did you learn from this project? _____

_____

_____

Team Project
Processing Form

Student Name _____ Team Name _____ Date _____

Instructions. Reflect on how well you and your teammates did as you worked on your team project.

Team Project

How did you contribute to the team project? _____
_____
_____

How did you contribute to the team presentation? _____
_____
_____

How well did your team work together? Were there any problems? _____
_____
_____

Did every teammate play their role? _____
_____

Were you pleased with how the team project came out ? Why or why not? How could it have
been improved? _____
_____
_____

Did any teammate go above and beyond for the team? If yes, who and how? _____
_____
_____

What would you do differently if you did this project again? _____
_____

What would you do differently if your team could present again? _____
_____

What are the most important things you learned from this project? _____
_____
_____

Kagan Cooperative Learning • Dr. Spencer Kagan & Miguel Kagan
Kagan Publishing • 1 (800) 933-2667 • www.KaganOnline.com

How Hard Did We Work?

Instructions. Reflect on how hard you and your teammates worked on the team project. Circle either Working Hard, Working, or Hardly Working for yourself and your teammates. Explain your evaluation in the space provided. Use your evaluation to discuss your contributions and how to improve for next time.

Myself

_____
(Your Name)

Working Hard   **Working**   **Hardly Working**

Explain your evaluation _____
_____
_____
_____
_____

Teammate 1

_____
(Teammate Name)

Working Hard   **Working**   **Hardly Working**

Explain your evaluation _____
_____
_____
_____
_____

Teammate 2

_____
(Teammate Name)

Working Hard   **Working**   **Hardly Working**

Explain your evaluation _____
_____
_____
_____
_____

Teammate 3

_____
(Teammate Name)

Working Hard   **Working**   **Hardly Working**

Explain your evaluation _____
_____
_____
_____
_____

Cooperative Project Ideas

Math

- Create a survey and graph the results
- Measure the area of the classroom
- Create a box with a given volume
- Create items of various lengths
- Solve a challenging problem
- Measure the volume of plastic containers
- Draw a shape with a given perimeter
- Make geometric designs
- Create a poster with analog clock times
- Calculate the probability of an event
- Create funny money and practice making change
- Design a poster illustrating a concept (e.g., symmetry, congruency)
- Create a classification system for numbers
- Build numbers using manipulatives

- Build fraction models
- Graph the number of buttons that classmates are wearing
- Design patterns
- Use beans to represent ratios
- Write a how-to guide for performing an algorithm
- Create a tessellation
- Create a poster, making a symbolic equation concrete
- Design a flowchart for performing long division
- Come up with a real-world application for…
- Write a story about a math problem
- Write a how-to book to tell time
- Create a pie chart of an average day
- Calculate the mode, median, and mean of outcomes you observe

Science

- Assemble a toy or kit
- Perform a science experiment
- Build a model of…
- Design a brochure describing a planet
- Create a safety plan for…
- Map the causes and effects of a natural disaster
- Create a poster of a scientific process (e.g., rain cycle)
- Write a song about an animal
- Dissect a…
- Clone a plant from a cutting
- Draw the stages of… (e.g., cell division)
- Create an illustrated time line for… (e.g., human embryo development)
- Design an experiment

- Generate alternate explanations of an observation
- Debate an ethical scientific issue (e.g., cloning)
- Build a bridge
- Build a catapult
- Build a model of a famous invention
- Invent something
- Take apart and label the parts of an appliance
- Train an animal
- Grow a plant or garden
- Record playground behavior

Kagan Cooperative Learning • Dr. Spencer Kagan & Miguel Kagan
Kagan Publishing • 1 (800) 933-2667 • www.KaganOnline.com

Cooperative Project Ideas

Language Arts

- Write a short story
- Write a poem
- Write a letter
- Write an instruction manual
- Create a persuasive presentation or commercial
- Write a collaborative book
- Create a grammar guide
- Write a book of commonly misspelled words
- Write a brief story with comprehension questions
- Create a 5W or 5 senses chart
- Create a poster illustrating the use of end marks
- Write an argument why adjectives are more important than adverbs and vice versa

- Perform a mock interview of an author
- Create a book report
- Have a party in character roles
- Write a play
- Build a pop-up book
- Write a screenplay for a short movie and film it
- Write an event from multiple points of view

Social Studies

- Create a time line for an event
- Write a biography of a historical character
- Perform a skit of an historical event
- Create a model of a mission
- Create a slide show (using Internet graphics)
- Design a travel brochure for a state
- Draw an annotated map of an area
- Report on a country
- Debate a social issue
- Mind-map an idea or event
- Write an anthem for a country
- Design a new flag for a state
- Record an interview with a historical figure
- Create a video, re-creating an event
- Re-create a famous court case
- Perform the dance of a culture

Halloween Haunt

Team Goal. Your team's goal is to design a Halloween decoration. You may only use shapes cut from construction paper, which are then pasted down on poster paper. Use the roles and materials below. Rotate roles after every two shapes have been pasted.

Role	Your Job	Materials
Designer	Decide which shape to cut next and where it belongs. Draw the shape on the construction paper.	Pencil, Construction paper
Cutter	Cut out the geometric shapes.	Scissors
Gluer	Glue down the geometric shapes.	Glue
Artist	Add details to the shapes.	Black marker

Permitted Shapes

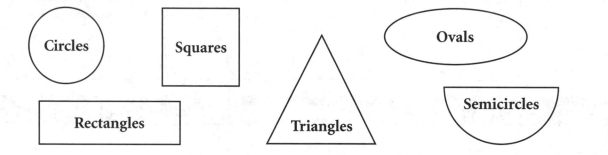

Circles Squares Ovals

Rectangles Triangles Semicircles

Sample Decoration

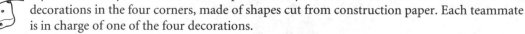

Sponge Activity If you finish early, create a Halloween poster with your team name in the middle and four Halloween decorations in the four corners, made of shapes cut from construction paper. Each teammate is in charge of one of the four decorations.

13.24 **Kagan Cooperative Learning • Dr. Spencer Kagan & Miguel Kagan**
Kagan Publishing • 1 (800) 933-2667 • www.KaganOnline.com

Team Story

Team Goal. As a team, write a 12-page children's story with the moral, "Many heads are better than one." Each teammate is responsible for writing and illustrating the following three pages.

Role	Your Job	Materials
Author #1	Write and illustrate pages 1–3.	Paper, Pen, Crayons
Author #2	Write and illustrate pages 4–6.	Paper, Pen, Crayons
Author #3	Write and illustrate pages 7–9.	Paper, Pen, Crayons
Author #4	Write and illustrate pages 10–12.	Paper, Pen, Crayons

Plan Your Story

As a team, discuss your story and reach consensus on the following story elements. When you all agree, write them down.

Story Title _____

Authors _____

Moral of the Story *Many heads are better than one.* _____

Setting: Where does the story take place? _____

Plot: What happens in the story? _____

Conflict: What is the problem? _____

Resolution: How is the problem solved? _____

Main Character: Who plays the leading role? _____

Supporting Characters: Who else is in the story? _____

Map Out Each Page

As a team, map out and reach consensus on each page of the story using the space below. Once you have your story mapped out, you may begin writing and illustrating the story.

Page 1	Page 2	Page 3	Page 4	Page 5	Page 6

Page 7	Page 8	Page 9	Page 10	Page 11	Page 12

 Sponge Activity If you finish early, work as a team to create a front and back cover for your book. The back cover should have a short summary of your story.

Kagan Cooperative Learning • Dr. Spencer Kagan & Miguel Kagan
Kagan Publishing • 1 (800) 933-2667 • www.KaganOnline.com

Candy Store Math

Team Goal. Your team's job is to create a candy store menu and write 8 word problems, based on your menu, to send to another team to solve.

1. Plan Your Menu

Each teammate is responsible for adding at least two sweet treats to your team menu.
Use the space below to plan which treats you'll have on your menu.

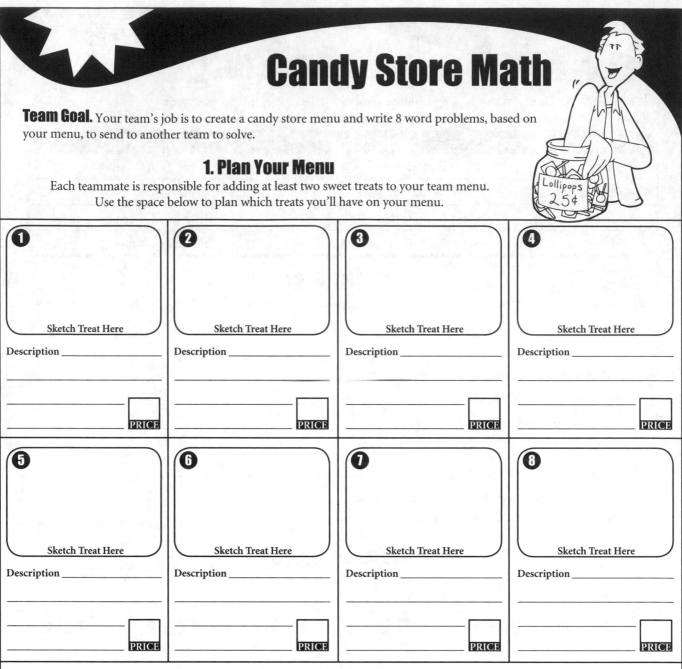

❶

Sketch Treat Here

Description _____

_____

_____ [ ] **PRICE**

❷

Sketch Treat Here

Description _____

_____

_____ [ ] **PRICE**

❸

Sketch Treat Here

Description _____

_____

_____ [ ] **PRICE**

❹

Sketch Treat Here

Description _____

_____

_____ [ ] **PRICE**

❺

Sketch Treat Here

Description _____

_____

_____ [ ] **PRICE**

❻

Sketch Treat Here

Description _____

_____

_____ [ ] **PRICE**

❼

Sketch Treat Here

Description _____

_____

_____ [ ] **PRICE**

❽

Sketch Treat Here

Description _____

_____

_____ [ ] **PRICE**

2. Design Your Menu

On a separate sheet of paper, design your menu. Each teammate is responsible for adding two treats to the menu.

3. Write Word Problems

On a separate sheet of lined paper, write at least 8 word problems about the sweet treats on your menu.

> **Sample Word Problem**
> You buy 3 packs of gum and pay with a dollar bill.
> How much change are you owed?

4. Trade Your Problems

Trade your menu and your word problems with another team.
Solve each other's problems, then trade with another team.

Sponge Activity If you finish early, everyone on the team writes one word problem using your finished menu. Pass the problems one person to your right for your teammate to solve.

13.26

Kagan Cooperative Learning • Dr. Spencer Kagan & Miguel Kagan
Kagan Publishing • 1 (800) 933-2667 • www.KaganOnline.com

Sports Safety

Team Goal. As a team, fill out the form below with questions regarding sports injuries. Use a rotating Recorder for every new line. No writing until the team agrees on the answer!

Rank and Estimate ER Visits

Rank the following sports according to the number of children ages 5 to 14 who were treated in hospital emergency rooms (ER) for an injury related to each sport. Estimate how many children visited the ER for each sport annually.

Sport	ER Ranking					Estimated ER Visits
Baseball and Softball	1	2	3	4	5	
Basketball	1	2	3	4	5	
Football	1	2	3	4	5	
Gymnastics	1	2	3	4	5	
Soccer	1	2	3	4	5	

Sport-Related Deaths

Which sport do you think more children ages 5 to 14 die from each year than any other sport? (circle one)

Baseball　　　Basketball　　　Football　　　Gymnastics　　　Soccer

How many fatalities do you estimate? _____

Why? _____

_____

Sport Injuries

What percent of children ages 5 to 14 report being injured in the following sports:

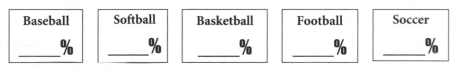

| Baseball ____% | Softball ____% | Basketball ____% | Football ____% | Soccer ____% |

Is your injury percentage in the same order as your ranking above? _____

Why or why not? _____

_____

 If you finish early, pick one sport. Discuss what kind of injuries a player could get and how the injuries can be avoided. Write down your team's ideas to share with the class.

Answers. Cover up answers before copying this form. Share answers with teams after completion.
Ranking: 1) Basketball: 205,400; 2) Football: 185,700; 3) Baseball and Softball: 108,300; 4) Soccer: 75,000; 5) Gymnastics: 22,000
Deaths: Baseball is most deadly: 3 to 4 children die per year. **Percents:** Football: 28%; Baseball: 25%; Soccer: 22%; Basketball: 15%, Softball: 12%
Source: Safe Kids USA, Facts About Childhood Sports Injuries, 2003. http://www.usa.safekids.org

Food Guide Pyramid

The food guide pyramid has been rebuilt! A rainbow of six colored, vertical stripes represent the five food groups, plus fats and oils. And there's even a person running up the stairs. What does it all mean?

Team Goal. As a team, research, plan, and draw a model of the food guide pyramid to share your design and what it means with another team.

Teammate Roles

Each teammate is responsible for at least one vertical stripe on the pyramid. Each stripe needs to be in its correct color, plus have two drawn sample food items. Use the grid below to decide which teammate is responsible for which stripe(s) and what sample foods you will use on your pyramid.

Team Materials

• **Poster Paper.** Draw your model of the pyramid on the poster paper.

• **Pencils.** Use to sketch out your designs.

• **Black Marker.** Use to outline your sketches.

• **Ruler.** Use to measure and make straight lines.

• **Crayons.** Use to color your pyramid. The following colors are required, but more colors may be used.
  • **Orange**   • **Blue**
  • **Purple**   • **Yellow**
  • **Green**   • **Red**

Stripe	Pyramid Food Group	Sample Foods	Which Teammate?
Orange	grains		
Green	vegetables		
Red	fruits		
Yellow	oils		
Blue	milk and dairy products		
Purple	meat, beans, fish, and nuts		

Sponge Activity

If you finish early, create a healthful menu for breakfast, lunch, and dinner using the food guide pyramid. Each teammate is responsible for at least one food item for each meal.

Source: United States Department of Agriculture, 2005. http://www.mypyramid.gov

Kagan Cooperative Learning • Dr. Spencer Kagan & Miguel Kagan
Kagan Publishing • 1 (800) 933-2667 • www.KaganOnline.com

World Population

Team Goal

In July 2008, the world's population was estimated at 6,677,563,921—that's more than 6 billion people! As a team, use a world map and discuss what you know and think about population to rank-order the top 15 countries (or unions) by their population. Use a rotating Recorder to write a rank, from 1 to 15, in every box below. No writing until the team agrees on a ranking!

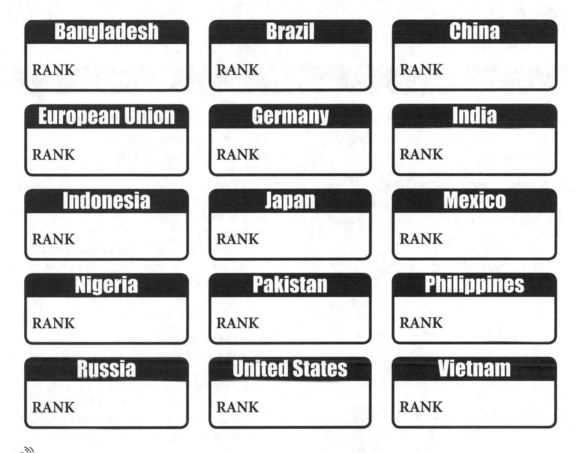

Bangladesh	**Brazil**	**China**
RANK	RANK	RANK

European Union	**Germany**	**India**
RANK	RANK	RANK

Indonesia	**Japan**	**Mexico**
RANK	RANK	RANK

Nigeria	**Pakistan**	**Philippines**
RANK	RANK	RANK

Russia	**United States**	**Vietnam**
RANK	RANK	RANK

Check your ranking against the answers, then take turns answering the following questions:

- How well did your team do?
- Which countries surprised you?
- Did the world map help or hinder your team? Why?
- Was a teammate very persuasive, but turned out to be wrong?
- Was there someone with a correct answer that did not persuade the team?
- What did you learn about team decision making from this process?
- What did you learn about geography from this activity?
- What is the most important thing you learned about world population from this activity?

Answers. Cover up answers before copying this form. Share answers with teams after completion.
1) China: 1,330,044,605; 2) India: 1,147,995,898; 3) European Union: 491,018,677; 4) United States: 303,824,646; 5) Indonesia: 237,512,355; 6) Brazil: 191,908,598; 7) Pakistan: 167,762,040; 8) Bangladesh: 153,546,901; 9) Russia: 140,702,094; 10) Nigeria: 138,283,240; 11) Japan: 127,288,419; 12) Mexico: 109,955,400; 13) Philippines: 92,681,453; 14) Vietnam: 86,116,559; 15) Germany: 82,369,548
Source: Central Intelligence Agency. The World Factbook. July, 2008. http://www.cia.gov

Let's Make Squares
Teacher Guide

Overview

Each teammate receives three unique game strips. Teammates work together to use their game strips to play one of five games to make squares. Use the steps below to lead teams through the game.

Team Materials

Let's Make Squares—Game Strips
Let's Make Squares—Game Rules

Steps

Step 1. Students Prepare Materials

Hand out the team materials. Have students cut out their game strips.

Step 2. Teams Read Game Rules

Have teams RoundRobin read the game rules. Tell them to pay special attention because they will be quizzed on the rules.

Step 3. Check for Understanding

Use Showdown or Numbered Heads Together to check for understanding using these questions:
- How many strips must you use?
- Which strips are you allowed to touch?
- Is stacking allowed? Draw a "Stacker."
- Is touching allowed? Draw "Touching."
- Is crossing allowed? Draw "Crossing."

Step 4. Assign Rotating Social Roles

Have students make role cards and then tell them to pass their role cards one person to the left after each new square or each new game.

1. **Chief Scribe**
   Record all solutions with paper and pencil.

2. **Cheerleader**
   Make sure your team stops to celebrate each time a solution is found.

3. **Focus Keeper**
   Keep the group focused. If someone gets off task, politely get their focus back.

4. **Executive Encourager**
   If the group gets discouraged, find a way to increase optimism and effort.

Step 5. Play Let's Make Squares

There are five games to play, see below. Announce to students which game they are to play.

The 5 Games

1. **Step It Up**
   Have students make one square, then two, then three. "After you make one square from the twelve strips, try making two, then three, and so on. See how high your team can go. Be sure to record each solution."

2. **Roll and Race**
   Roll dice and give your team and another team a time limit, say 10 minutes, and see how many ways you can make the number of squares on the roll of dice Work alone as teams, record your solutions, and when the time limit is up, compare your solutions.

3. **Ways to Make It**
   How many ways can you find to make 5 squares? How many ways can you find to make 11 squares?

4. **Try Eight**
   Once your team has found a way to make every number of squares from 1 to 12 with all 12 strips (this could take several sessions), see what you can do with only 8 strips—two per teammate.

5. **Greatest Number**
   What is the greatest number of squares you can make with all 12 strips? With only 8 strips?

Kagan Cooperative Learning • Dr. Spencer Kagan & Miguel Kagan
Kagan Publishing • 1 (800) 933-2667 • www.KaganOnline.com

Let's Make Squares
Possible Solutions

Teacher Instructions: Here are some of the many possible solutions using 12 game strips. Do not show teams these possible solutions before playing.

1 Square
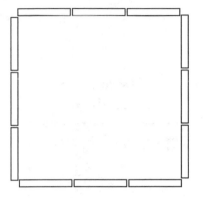

2 Squares
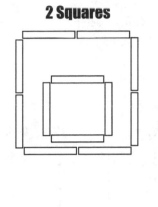

3 Squares
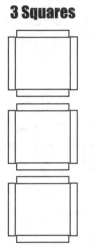

4 Squares
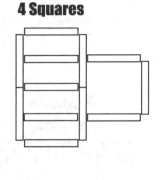

5 Squares
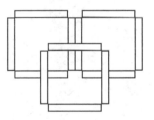

6 Squares
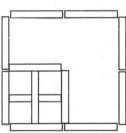

7 Squares
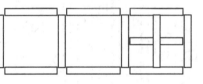

8 Squares
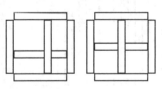

9 Squares
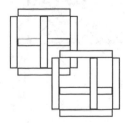

10 Squares
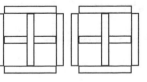

11 Squares
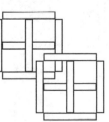

12 Squares
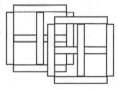

Let's Make Squares
Game Strips

Instructions. Cut out these strips, and divide them so each person in the team of four has three strips with the same pattern.

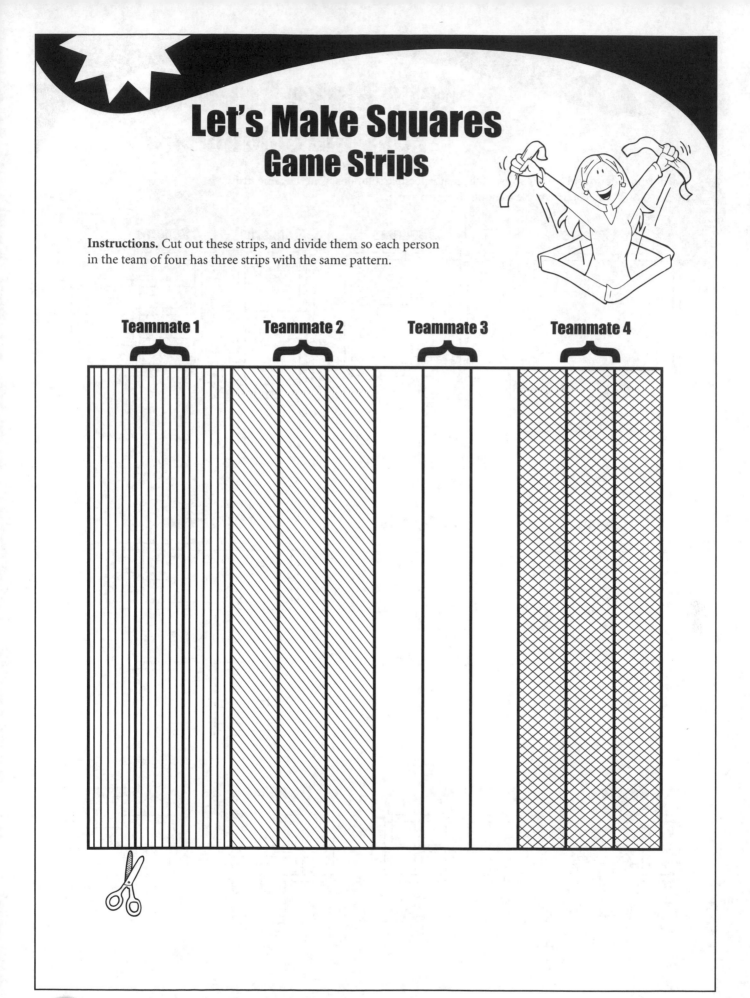

Teammate 1　　Teammate 2　　Teammate 3　　Teammate 4

Kagan Cooperative Learning • Dr. Spencer Kagan & Miguel Kagan
Kagan Publishing • 1 (800) 933-2667 • www.KaganOnline.com

Let's Make Squares
Game Rules

Team's Goal
Use your Game Strips to make squares based on your teacher's instructions. Follow the game rules.

How To Play

1. **Teams of Four.** Work in teams of four.

2. **Own Strips.** Each teammate gets three strips with a unique pattern. Only you may touch your own strips, but your strips can cross the strips of teammates.

3. **12 Only.** Your team must use all twelve strips for each solution.

Game Rules

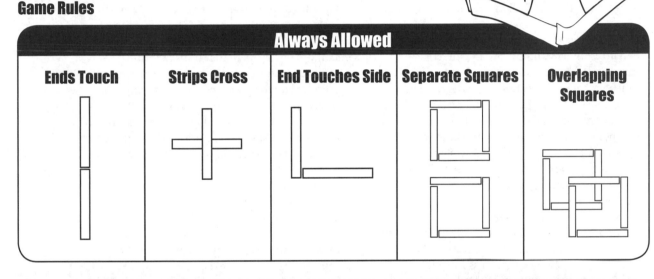

Always Allowed

| Ends Touch | Strips Cross | End Touches Side | Separate Squares | Overlapping Squares |

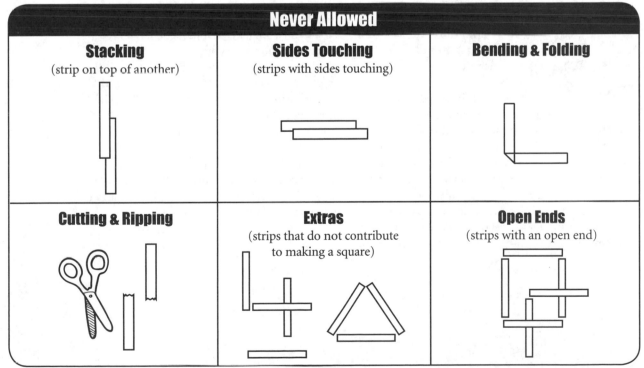

Never Allowed

| **Stacking** (strip on top of another) | **Sides Touching** (strips with sides touching) | **Bending & Folding** |
| **Cutting & Ripping** | **Extras** (strips that do not contribute to making a square) | **Open Ends** (strips with an open end) |

Chapter Summary

Cooperative projects are the epitome of constructivist education. As students cooperate to build their team projects, they build a deeper understanding of the content than they would through traditional transmission models of knowledge. Doing projects and receiving direct instruction is the difference between learning about something and really learning something.

Making projects cooperative accelerates and enhances understanding. Surely, students can and do learn a tremendous amount from independent projects. But to the degree that students are isolated and not interacting, they are missing the ever important social component of learning. They miss out on the opportunity to build deeper understanding by explaining a procedure to a teammate. They miss the opportunity to have a phenomenon explained by a more knowledgeable peer. They miss the opportunity to synergize. They miss the opportunity to wrestle with a team decision, and become an advocate for a position. And of course, they miss learning social skills embedded in social interaction. For learning, there is no substitute for interaction and cooperation.

From a brain-based perspective, there is a marked difference, too. Direct instruction through auditory channels primarily engages the semantic memory pathways (memories of facts). The semantic memory pathway is the most unnatural way the brain learns, and semantic information is the most difficult for the brain to remember. Redundant input and practice is usually required to cement semantic information in the learner's

mind. In contrast, hands-on learning with real-world content engages procedural (memories created through performing procedures) and episodic memory (memories built on experiences); procedural and episodic memories are more natural and easily encoded memories.

Cooperative projects are not group work. When we carefully design our projects to align with the PIES principles, we promote the equal and maximum engagement that translates into accelerated learning for all students. The two most powerful tools we have in structuring projects are simply Roles and Resources. By carefully assigning roles and limiting access to resources, we easily design projects that engage all learners. Feedback and processing allows learners to reflect, plan, and improve. For project presentations, by implementing the simultaneity principle, we accomplish more than twice as much in less than half the time!

Admittedly, not everything can or should be taught through cooperative projects. But a lot can be. To the extent possible, we strive to make learning hands-on and cooperative for students. Students become independent learners: In the process of a cooperative project, we allow students to discover facts and concepts for themselves. We don't spoon-feed them information. Critics may complain, "The knowledge has already been discovered. Why should we have students re-invent the wheel?" Our response is because that's what true learning is. Learning is not merely pumping existing knowledge into students' brains. It is lighting the fire for discovering truth, constructing meaning, and creating beauty.

Chapter Questions

► Questions for Review

1. What distinguishes a cooperative project from group work?
2. Name common roles to assign during project work.
3. Describe ways to limit resources.
4. What is the primary difference between the Carousel family of structures and the Team Rep family of structures?
5. List two structures that work well for sharing projects during the project's creation.

► Questions for Thinking and Discussion

1. Cooperative projects are the best way to implement constructivist educational theory. Do you agree or disagree? Explain.
2. Do you think it is ever OK to assign students a cooperative project, without providing some guidelines as to how they are to work together? Explain.
3. A lot of what students need to learn can be learned through cooperative projects. Do you agree or disagree? Give specific examples to support your stance.
4. When would you have teams share their projects with the entire class, as opposed to teams sharing with teams? Describe the benefits and drawbacks of both.
5. What are some team projects you could do with your class to replace direct instruction? What are some class projects?

References

Resources

Cohen, Elizabeth. *Designing Groupwork*. New York, NY: Teacher College Press, 1986.

Johnson, David, Roger Johnson & Edythe Holubec. *Circles of Learning: Cooperation in the Classroom*. Edina, MN: Interaction Book Company, 1986.

Planning Cooperative Lessons

Structures were developed as an alternative to lesson-based cooperative learning; structures can be sequenced to create powerful lessons.

Planning lessons with structures differs from other approaches to cooperative learning. Classic approaches to cooperative learning are lesson-planning approaches. That is, they instruct teachers how to design cooperative learning lessons using either cooperative learning principles or cooperative learning lesson design frameworks. We review these approaches in *Chapter 17: Classic Cooperative Learning*. Although very powerful, lesson-based approaches to cooperative learning result in sporadic implementation, and students do not reap the full benefits of cooperative learning because it is not integrated into daily instruction across the curriculum. Structures can be implemented without special planning or preparation and are easier to implement, so the structural approach results in daily implementation across the curriculum. Although structures were developed as an alternative to lesson-based cooperative learning, structures can be sequenced to create powerful lessons. In this chapter, we will look at the implementation challenges of classic cooperative learning lessons, and then offer a structure-based alternative for lesson planning.

Early Implementation Challenges

In the decade of the 1980s when cooperative learning first began to be widely implemented in the United States, all of us who were researching, advocating, and training teachers in cooperative learning were adopting lesson-based approaches. That is, we were telling teachers how to design cooperative learning lessons. We had good reason to advocate cooperative learning lessons due to the outpouring of positive research—cooperative learning lessons increased achievement, enhanced empathy and social skills, improved ethnic and social relations, facilitated inclusion, improved self-esteem, and increased liking for class and academic content.

Although the different cooperative learning lesson designs consistently produced improvement, they were not consistently implemented.

Our training approaches were different, and teachers trained in one approach did lessons that little resembled the lessons of teachers trained in other approaches. For example, if teachers went to training by David and Roger Johnson[1] at the Univesota of Minnesota, they were taught the Learning Together model; they learned how to design cooperative learning lessons that each included a social skill, as well as an academic skill. Each lesson needed to be carefully designed to include positive interdependence, individual accountability, face-to-face interaction, and processing of both the social and academic skills. In contrast, if teachers went to a training by Robert Slavin[2] at John Hopkins University, they were taught the Student Team Learning model; they learned how to design cooperative learning lessons that included direct instruction, followed by teamwork to master the content, individual accountability (based on a quiz and improvement scoring, or a competitive tournament), and team recognition based on the sum of individual scores.

If teachers went to one of my trainings at the University of California, they were taught various complex lesson designs, which differed depending on the lesson content. For example, for investigations, teachers learned Co-op Co-op[3]: The class divided a unit into team topics and the teams further divided their team topic into mini-topics so each student researched and reported to the team on their mini-topic. The team then synthesized their information into a report for the class. There was cooperation within the team to further the learning goal of the class. For mastery of discrete facts, teachers learned Color-Coded Co-op Cards: Each student made up flashcards of items they needed to master. The week-long design included three rounds of cooperative practice on each card, a practice test, a final test, and team recognition based on individual improvement.

Although the different cooperative learning lesson designs consistently produced improvement, they were not consistently implemented. For example, I could go into a classroom where teachers had just been trained in one of the methods and find the students sitting in rows, not cooperating. When asked why, a teacher might respond, "You should have been here yesterday; we did our cooperative learning lesson yesterday." Teachers were treating cooperative learning as one more content area to teach. They had math lessons, language arts lessons, social studies lessons, science lessons, and cooperative learning lessons. Cooperative learning was not seen as a better way to teach any content, but rather as additional content to teach! Worse yet, I could return to a school a few years after teachers had been trained and find no cooperative learning being implemented. When asked why, teachers would respond, "Oh it was too hard to spend my night planning cooperative learning lessons and my day teaching." Or "We got new textbooks, and we did not have time to rewrite or redesign our cooperative learning lessons."

A particularly distressing reason cooperative learning lessons were not being implemented was that it had become replaced as just one more crashing wave in the school or district's innovation replacement cycle. For example, when asked why they were not doing cooperative learning, a teacher might reply, "Oh, we moved on, we have a new district-wide thrust, everyone is learning how to design multiple intelligences lessons." (Or brain-based lessons, differentiated instruction lessons, character education lessons, higher-level thinking lessons, or whatever had become that year's new thing.) I realized that lesson-based innovations have a built-in half-life. That is, because educational innovation is inevitable and because a teacher does not have time to plan a cooperative learning lesson and plan a lesson based on whatever the latest innovation of the year happens to be, cooperative learning gets dropped in favor of the next year's innovation.

Observing the problems with lesson-based approaches to cooperative learning, a light went on for me. I realized that although at one level all of us doing cooperative learning training were teaching teachers quite different methods, at another level all of us were doing the same thing! We were all telling teachers how to design different lessons. In essence, we were telling teachers to stop doing what they were already doing and to do cooperative learning lessons instead. And teachers were finding that too difficult to do. They could not spend each night planning new cooperative learning lessons—especially when the school or district had moved on to a new innovation.

"Don't do cooperative learning lessons; make cooperative learning part of every lesson."

At that point, I decided to advocate a different approach. Instead of training complex and time-consuming lesson designs, I began to develop and emphasize smaller units of instruction I called

Structures. Instead of training teachers in how to do a two-week Co-op Co-op project or how to do a two-day Double Expert Group Jigsaw lesson, I began emphasizing how to do a two-minute Timed Pair Share, or a four-minute Team Interview. I began telling teachers, "Don't do cooperative learning lessons; make cooperative learning part of every lesson." I wanted teachers to see cooperative learning not as one more thing to teach, but rather as a powerful, easy-to-use set of tools to teach anything.

What makes a good cooperative learning lesson?

Lesson Planning Options

In this chapter, we present a variety of options and forms for planning cooperative learning lessons. There is no single recipe for a successful cooperative learning lesson. You are welcome to use any approach or all of them. How you plan your lessons is for you to decide, based on your own teaching philosophy or the particular learning objective at hand. While there is no single recipe for success, there is an ingredient central to all the forms of lesson planning you will find herein. That ingredient is structures. When we use structures in our lessons, we can feel confident that we are planning and delivering effective cooperative learning lessons.

Sponge Activities

An important consideration when planning any cooperative learning lesson is what to do with teams or pairs who finish early. If you're not doing timed activities, having a sponge activity ready is a management must. For more on Sponge Activities, see *Chapter 8: Management*.

Transforming Lessons into Cooperative Lessons

Almost any lesson can be improved by replacing an element of the lesson with a cooperative learning structure. You don't have to throw away your current lesson plans and start from scratch. Instead, keep your lesson plans that work well for you and make them better by infusing cooperative learning structures. For example, if we want our students to master a problem-solving algorithm, before students work independently on worksheets, we have them practice with RallyCoach: Students work in pairs and coach each other as they solve the problems. By having students work together to coach each other before they work independently, we dramatically increase the probability of their independent success. Madeline Hunter alerted us to the importance of guided practice before independent practice; RallyCoach provides the guidance. Or, to paraphrase Lev Vygotsky, "What children can do only with the assistance of others, they will later be able to do alone."

In her extensive work with teachers, Laurie Kagan developed a lesson planning process designed to help teachers replace traditional (Teacher A) instruction and group work (Teacher B) instruction with cooperative learning (Teacher C) by inserting structures into their preferred lesson sequences. For a detailed description of Teachers A, B, and C, see *Chapter 6: Structures*.

Using the Teacher ABC Lesson Planning Form

Step 2. Sequence the Lesson

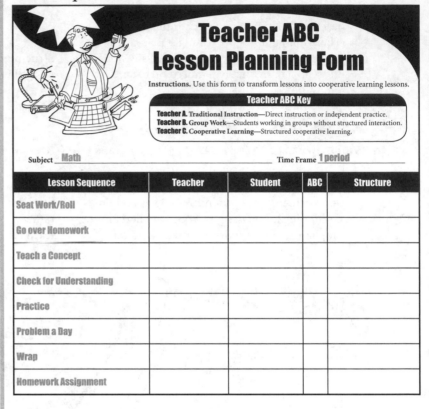

Teacher ABC Lesson Planning Form

Instructions. Use this form to transform lessons into cooperative learning lessons.

Teacher ABC Key
Teacher A. Traditional Instruction—Direct instruction or independent practice.
Teacher B. Group Work—Students working in groups without structured interaction.
Teacher C. Cooperative Learning—Structured cooperative learning.

Subject __Math__   Time Frame __1 period__

Lesson Sequence	Teacher	Student	ABC	Structure
Seat Work/Roll				
Go over Homework				
Teach a Concept				
Check for Understanding				
Practice				
Problem a Day				
Wrap				
Homework Assignment				

Step 3. Fill In Teacher and Student Actions & Step 4. Analyze for ABC

Lesson Sequence	Teacher	Student	ABC	Structure
Seat Work/Roll	Take Roll	Seat Work	A	
Go over Homework	Review Questions	Observe	A	
Teach a Concept	Lecture	Listen, Take Notes	A	
Check for Understanding	Sample Problems	Work Solo	A	
Practice	Assign Book Work	Work Solo	A	
Problem a Day	Assign Problem	Work in Groups	B	
Wrap	Summarize	Listen	A	
Homework Assignment	Assign Homework	Take Notes	A	

Kagan Cooperative Learning • Dr. Spencer Kagan & Miguel Kagan
Kagan Publishing • 1 (800) 933-2667 • www.KaganOnline.com

Using the Teacher ABC Lesson Planning Form

Step 5. Substitute Structures

Lesson Sequence	Teacher	Student	ABC	Structure
Seat Work/Roll	Take Roll	Seat Work	A	
Go over Homework	Review Questions	Observe	✗C	RoundRobin
Teach a Concept	Lecture	Listen, Take Notes	A	
Check for Understanding	Sample Problems	Work Solo	A	
Practice	Assign Book Work	Work Solo	✗C	Sage-N-Scribe
Problem a Day	Assign Problem	Work in Groups	B	
Wrap	Summarize	Listen	✗C	Timed Pair Share
Homework Assignment	Assign Homework	Take Notes	A	

The basic lesson planning process is to fill out a lesson planning form with an existing lesson or lesson pattern, then analyze the lesson to see where in the lesson to substitute one or more cooperative learning structures. See the Teacher ABC Lesson Planning Form on the following page. Let's walk through five steps together to plan a lesson using the form.

Step 1. Pick a Lesson

As a first step, pick a lesson or a typical lesson pattern that you'd like to improve with structures.

Step 2. Sequence the Lesson

Determine the sequence of the lesson. For example, the pattern might be: 1) seat work, 2) review the homework, 3) teach a new concept, and so on. Fill in the first column, "Lesson Sequence," of the form as shown at left.

Step 3. Fill In Teacher and Student Actions

In the second and third columns, fill in what the teacher does and what students do for each step of the lesson. See columns two and three on the sample form on bottom of the previous page.

Step 4. Analyze for ABC

Analyze each step with respect to what the teacher and students are doing and label each step as A, B, or C in the "ABC" column using the following key:
  A) **Traditional Instruction.** Direct instruction or independent practice
  B) **Group Work.** Students working in groups without structured interaction
  C) **Structures.** Structured cooperative learning.
See the "ABC" column on the form on the previous page.

Step 5. Substitute Structures

Finally, examine the lesson or lesson pattern and replace one or more of the Teacher A and B steps with a Teacher C cooperative structure. Write the name of the structure in the last column, "Structure." In our sample lesson planning form above, we've substituted in three structures: RoundRobin, Sage-N-Scribe, and Timed Pair Share.

This lesson planning process is relatively easy because we start with what we're already doing. We're simply looking for opportunities to inject cooperative learning structures into the lesson. With just one substitution, the lesson becomes more engaging and successful. As we become fluent in more structures, additional substitutions are made. A Teacher ABC Lesson Planning Form is provided (on the next page) to help you transform your lessons into more cooperative and engaging lessons.

Teacher ABC
Lesson Planning Form

Instructions. Use this form to transform lessons into cooperative learning lessons.

Teacher ABC Key

Teacher A. Traditional Instruction—Direct instruction or independent practice
Teacher B. Group Work—Students working in groups without structured interaction
Teacher C. Cooperative Learning—Structured cooperative learning

Subject _____ Time Frame _____

Lesson Sequence	Teacher	Student	ABC	Structure

Kagan Cooperative Learning • Dr. Spencer Kagan & Miguel Kagan
Kagan Publishing • 1 (800) 933-2667 • www.KaganOnline.com

Structure Sequences

Each structure accomplishes a distinct objective. For example, Jot Thoughts is a great structure for teams to brainstorm ideas. But brainstorming is just one activity in part of a larger lesson plan. After brainstorming ideas, we probably want students to do something with the ideas. Perhaps we want students to categorize their ideas, so we use the structure Find-A-Frame. Or maybe instead we want teams to vote on their best idea, so we use the structure Sum-the-Ranks. Either way, we are stringing together structures to accomplish a bigger learning objective. As teachers use structures, they often rely on preferred multiple-structure patterns; we call these patterns Structure Sequences. Just as a beginning instrumental music student first learns chords, and then puts the chords together to play increasingly complex sequences, a teacher first learns simple structures and then sequences structures to create increasingly complex, meaningful learning experiences.

Two-Structure Sequences.

Structure sequences allow us to meet broader learning objectives than using just a single structure. In our example, Jot Thoughts met the objective of brainstorming, and Sum-the-Ranks met the objective of voting as a team. Together, they met the larger aim of generating, then settling on the team's best idea. Some other frequent two-part learning objectives include create a team project, then share it with the class; generate ideas as a pair, then share them with teammates; receive input, then process the input; and respond individually, then share with the team. Each of these sequences can be accomplished by different two-structure sequences. A small sample of the almost infinite number of possible two-structure sequences are shown in the box: Structure Sequences.

Longer Structure Sequences.

Naturally, it is possible to create longer sequences of structures. For example, I might have students RallyRead a poem, taking turns reading each

---

Structure Sequences
Common Two-Structure Sequences

Generate Ideas, then Categorize Ideas
• Jot Thoughts ➡ Fill-A-Frame
• 4S Brainstorming ➡ Find-A-Frame

Generate Ideas, then Evaluate Ideas
• Jot Thoughts ➡ RoundTable Consensus
• 4S Brainstorming ➡ Proactive Prioritizing
• AllWrite RoundRobin ➡ RoundRobin Consensus

Generate Possible Solutions, then Vote
• Jot Thoughts ➡ Spend-A-Buck
• 4S Brainstorming ➡ Sum-the-Ranks
• Placemat Consensus ➡ Sum-the-Ranks

Create Project, then Share Project
• Team Statements ➡ Team Up!
• Team Mind-Mapping ➡ Carousel Feedback
• Team Projects ➡ Roam-the-Room
• Team Projects ➡ Three Stray
• Team Projects ➡ Team-2-Team

Generate Individual Ideas, then Share with Team
• Solo ➡ Instant Star
• Solo ➡ Three-Step Interview
• Solo ➡ RoundRobin
• Solo ➡ Timed Pair Share

Generate Team Ideas, then Share with Other Teams
• AllWrite RoundRobin ➡ Traveling Star
• Team Projects ➡ Number Group Presentation
• Team Projects ➡ Roving Reporter
• RoundTable ➡ Carousel Review

Generate Team Ideas, then Share with Classmates
• RoundTable Consensus ➡ GiveOne–GetOne
• RoundTable Consensus ➡ Team Stand-N-Share
• RallyTable ➡ Pair Stand-N-Share
• RallyTable Consensus ➡ Mix-Pair-Share

Receive Input, then Process the Input
• Listen Right! ➡ Timed Pair Share
• Listen-Sketch-Draft ➡ Mix-Pair-Share
• Listen Up! ➡ StandUp–HandUp–PairUp
• Teacher Talk ➡ Numbered Heads Together

---

stanza. Next, they do a Pair Discussion focused on which word in the poem they think is the most important word, and why. Next they do a StandUp–HandUp–PairUp, finding someone in the room with the same number as their own. Finally, they do a Timed Pair Share, sharing with a classmate the thoughts that were expressed in the pair discussion. The possibilities are endless.

Frank Lyman created a very powerful frame for sequencing three structures, called Think-Pair-Share.[4] Since there are many ways to think, many ways to pair up, and many ways to share with the class, Think-Pair-Share is a structure sequence generator. Two of the hundreds of possible examples include:

Think-Pair-Share on Slavery

- **Think** *Point of View: Imagine you are a slave during the time of slavery.*
- **Pair** *Paraphrase: Share with a partner your feeling as a slave. Partners paraphrase your partner.*
- **Share** *Move: Show how you are feeling as a slave using only body language.*

Think-Pair-Share on Chemical Reactions

- **Think** *Think/Write: Write some possible causes for the chemical reaction.*
- **Pair** *RallyRobin: Take turns with your partner naming possible causes.*
- **Share** *Question: Share some questions you have about the possible causes.*

Because Lyman and his associates have defined 17 distinct ways to think, 20 distinct ways to pair, and 20 distinct ways to share, the Think-Pair-Share framework can generate thousands of different three-structure sequences!

Multi-Structural Lessons

Notice, as we sequence more structures together to meet broader learning objectives, what we are really doing is—*voilà*—planning cooperative learning lessons. We call a lesson that consists of multiple structures a multi-structural lesson. Oftentimes, we'll use a structure or structure sequence on the fly with no pre-planning, but longer multi-structural lessons are usually planned in advance. We've developed the Fundamental Formula to illustrate how structures, content,

activities and lessons fit together for multi-structural lessons. The Fundamental Formula states that we make a learning *activity* when we use a *structure* to deliver some *content*. We create a *lesson* when we string multiple activities together to meet the lesson objective.

> ## The Fundamental Formula
> Structure + Content = Activity
> Activity + Activity + Activity = Lesson

How we sequence our structures to meet lesson objectives depends largely on our lesson objectives, but also on our teaching philosophy. We can create freeform lessons, or if we are strong believers in multiple intelligences, we may create lessons that use structures that engage and develop the multiple intelligences. There are a number of different frameworks for designing lessons and various elements of lesson design. We will overview some frameworks and show where structures fit in. We have also provided a blank Lesson Planning Form (on page 14.11) for you to plan your own multi-structural lessons.

> ## Tools & Blueprints
>
> If structures are tools in a teacher's toolbox, then the lesson plan is the blueprint of what we're trying to build. The blueprint illustrates the objective. The effective teacher selects structure after structure to reach the desired objective.

Structure-Based Lessons and Activity Resources

Over the years, educators working with structures have created a wide range of powerful structure-based lesson and activity resources to reach the range of objectives across grade levels and academic content areas. We highly recommend these books as time-saving resources, but also as models for teachers wishing to develop their own cooperative activities and lessons. The box on the following page lists selected books.

Structure-Based Lesson and Activity Books

This table lists books that use structures in lessons and activities across the curriculum. Some books string structures together to create multi-structural lessons, while others use a single structure to accomplish more specific learning objectives.

Mathematics
- Cooperative Learning & Algebra (7–12)
- Cooperative Math: Engaging Structures and Activities (3–5)
- Discovering Decimals through Cooperative Learning (3–8)
- Fraction Fun through Cooperative Learning (2–12)
- Mathematics Lessons for Little Ones (K–2)
- Write! Mathematics: Multiple Intelligences & Cooperative Learning Writing Activities (4–9)

Language Arts
- Balanced Literacy through Cooperative Learning and Activities Engagement (K–5; Series)
- Cooperative Learning & Language Arts (K–8)
- Cooperative Learning Reading Activities (K–8)
- Cooperative Learning Writing Activities (K–8)
- Lessons for Little Ones: Language Arts (K–2)
- Write! Cooperative Learning & the Writing Process (3–8)

Science
- Cooperative Learning & Hands-On Science (3–8)
- Cooperative Learning & Science (8–12)
- Cooperative Learning & Wee Science (K–3)
- Structures for Success in Chemistry (8–12)
- Write! Science: Multiple Intelligences & Cooperative Learning Writing Activities (4–9)

Social Studies
- Cooperative Learning & Social Studies: Toward Excellence and Equity (6–12)
- Write! Social Studies: Multiple Intelligences & Cooperative Learning Writing Activities (4–9)

Classbuilding and Teambuilding
- Communitybuilding in the Classroom (All Grades)
- Cooperative Learning Structures for Classbuilding (All Grades)
- Cooperative Learning Structures for Teambuilding (All Grades)
- Crafting Creative Community (3–8)

ESL & Foreign Language
- Second Language Learning through Cooperative Learning (All Grades)
- Spanish: Cooperative Learning & Multiple Intelligences Activities (Beginning)

Higher-Level Thinking
- Higher-Level Thinking Questions (All Grades; Series)
- Logic Line-Ups: Higher-Level Thinking Activities

Single Structure Books
- Match Mine (Series)
- Mix-N-Match (Series)
- Same-Different (Series)

These books are available from Kagan Publishing: www.KaganOnline.com

Elements of Effective Instruction Design

Madeline Hunter's Elements of Effective Instruction[5] provides a powerful framework for lesson planning. The basic idea is that as we plan lessons, we include a series of elements that result in achieving the stated lesson objective.

The sample cooperative learning lesson plan at right illustrates a lesson on Inventors and Inventions. The lesson is organized using five elements of effective instruction: Set, Input, Guided Practice, Individual Practice, and Closure. Not every lesson requires these five elements. Some may have fewer and some may have more. On page 14.12, a list of possible lesson design elements, along with a short description of each is provided.

For each Design Element, we select a structure. For example, for the Set of the lesson, we have students do a Three-Step Interview: Students break into pairs and take turns asking each other what they know about inventors and inventions, and what they would like to learn. Then pairs pair up and each teammate shares what he/she heard from his/her partner. The Set primes the pump for the lesson.

Not every Design Element need be a cooperative learning structure. We may want to incorporate Individual Practice into the lesson. Or during Input, we may choose to use traditional direct instruction.

A blank Co-op Lesson Planning Form is provided on the following page for you to use to plan your own lessons.

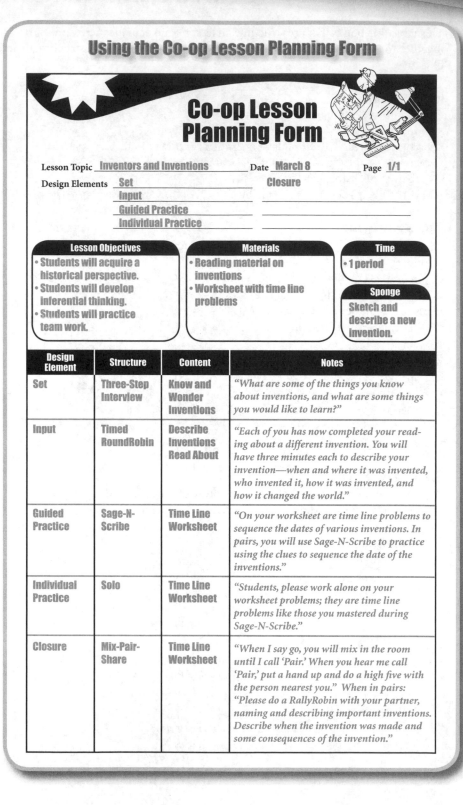

Using the Co-op Lesson Planning Form

Co-op Lesson Planning Form

Lesson Topic __Inventors and Inventions__ Date __March 8__ Page __1/1__

Design Elements Set Closure
Input
Guided Practice
Individual Practice

Lesson Objectives
- Students will acquire a historical perspective.
- Students will develop inferential thinking.
- Students will practice team work.

Materials
- Reading material on inventions
- Worksheet with time line problems

Time
- 1 period

Sponge
Sketch and describe a new invention.

Design Element	Structure	Content	Notes
Set	Three-Step Interview	Know and Wonder Inventions	*"What are some of the things you know about inventions, and what are some things you would like to learn?"*
Input	Timed RoundRobin	Describe Inventions Read About	*"Each of you has now completed your reading about a different invention. You will have three minutes each to describe your invention—when and where it was invented, who invented it, how it was invented, and how it changed the world."*
Guided Practice	Sage-N-Scribe	Time Line Worksheet	*"On your worksheet are time line problems to sequence the dates of various inventions. In pairs, you will use Sage-N-Scribe to practice using the clues to sequence the date of the inventions."*
Individual Practice	Solo	Time Line Worksheet	*"Students, please work alone on your worksheet problems; they are time line problems like those you mastered during Sage-N-Scribe."*
Closure	Mix-Pair-Share	Time Line Worksheet	*"When I say go, you will mix in the room until I call 'Pair.' When you hear me call 'Pair,' put a hand up and do a high five with the person nearest you." When in pairs: "Please do a RallyRobin with your partner, naming and describing important inventions. Describe when the invention was made and some consequences of the invention."*

Co-op Lesson Planning Form

Lesson Topic _____ Date _____ Page _____

Design Elements _____ _____
_____ _____
_____ _____
_____ _____

Lesson Objectives	Materials	Time
		Sponge

Design Element	Structure	Content	Notes

Kagan Cooperative Learning • Dr. Spencer Kagan & Miguel Kagan
Kagan Publishing • 1 (800) 933-2667 • www.KaganOnline.com

14.11

Structures for Design Elements

Different lesson frameworks emphasize different design elements. For example, some lesson designs include social skills, while others don't. Some include teambuilding, classbuilding, assessment, and/or feedback. Regardless of the lesson design chosen, there are many possible structures to use with each design element to make the lesson more engaging and more successful. The box, Structures to Implement Design Elements, lists some sample structures for twelve different lesson design elements.

Structures to Implement Design Elements	
Design Element	**Selected Structures**
1. Anticipatory Set The Anticipatory Set motivates students to learn the content and gets them "set" to learn.	• RoundRobin • Team Interview • RoundTable
2. Closure Closure activities summarize the learning, often making connections for students.	• RallyRobin • Three-Step Interview • Think-Write-Share
3. Reflection Reflection is a time to look back over the lesson, assessing how well a skill has been used.	• Timed Pair Share • Placemat Consensus • RoundTable Consensus
4. Input Input is information presented to students as a lecture, presentation, activity, or through a textbook or video.	• RallyRead • Roam-the-Room • Partners • Jigsaw
5. Guided Practice Guided Practice provides the student the opportunity to practice new skills while teammates or tutors have the opportunity to coach and correct.	• Flashcard Game • Inside-Outside Circle • Match Mine • Numbered Heads Together • Pairs Check • Sage-N-Scribe
6. Independent Practice Independent Practice gives students time to work alone on an activity congruent to the objective.	• Observe-Write-RoundRobin • Team-Pair-Solo • Showdown
7. Assessment Assessment can be formative activities that provide the teacher insight into student understanding, or can be summative to grade student learning.	• Choral Practice • Inside-Outside Circle • Numbered Heads Together • Show Me! • Stand-N-Share
8. Feedback Feedback provides students with specific knowledge of results and recognition of accomplishments.	• Affirmation Chips • Showdown • Pairs Check • Paraphrase Passport
9. Teambuilding Teambuilding creates the will to work together in teams and creates positive and supportive peer relations.	• 4S Brainstorming • RoundTable • Team Interview
10. Classbuilding Classbuilding creates feelings among classmates of belonging, mutual respect, and security.	• Corners • Formations • Line Ups • Mix-Freeze-Group • Who Am I?
11. Social Skills Social skill instruction develops students' ability to understand and work successfully with others.	• Assignment of Roles • Match Mine • Paraphrase Passport • Pass-N-Praise • Talking Chips
12. Transitions Transitions refer to the procedures and directions given during and between the elements of a lesson design.	• Checking for Understanding • Structuring • Sponges • Modeling

Into-Through-Beyond Lesson Design

The Into-Through-Beyond lesson design, developed by Laurie Kagan, is a very simple format for developing multi-structural lessons. It has three main parts:

1. **Into.** We motivate students to learn the content.
2. **Through.** We engage our students throughout the lesson while learning the content.
3. **Beyond.** We cement and extend their learning.

We select structures for each part of the lesson. Into: We select structures to get students excited about the lesson. Through: We select structures to engage students in the learning. Beyond: We select structures to summarize or extend the lesson. An Into-Through-Beyond Lesson Planning Form is provided on page 14.15 for you to plan your own lessons. We'll walk through planning a sample reading lesson.

Sample Reading Lesson

Refer to the form in the box for an illustration of what this sample reading lesson might might look like.

Into. Before reading the story to students, we have students look at the cover of the book and do a Timed Pair Share, sharing their predictions about what the story will be about.

Through. As we read the story, we stop at critical points and ask questions to engage students in critical thinking and to boost their processing and comprehension of the story. For example, after a long dialogue between two characters, we may stop and have students pair up and use RallyRobin to re-create the character dialogue. Or we can ask a question and use a Timed RoundRobin, giving every student a chance to share on the topic. Or we may use an an Instant Star and have just one teammate share an idea with his/her team. On our sample form, we show all three structures.

Beyond. To conclude the lesson, we have teams play Fan-N-Pick using higher-level thinking questions about the story.

More Sample Lessons

On the following page are three more sample Into-Through-Beyond lessons for Math, Social Studies, and Language Arts.

Sample Into-Through-Beyond Reading Lesson

Into-Through-Beyond Lesson Planning Form

Lesson Topic Reading Fiction **Date** April 29

Lesson Objectives	Materials	Time
• Reading for thinking and comprehension	• Book • Higher-Level Thinking Questions	1 period
		Sponge Draw a new cover for the book.

Content	Structure
Into	
Predictions: "What will the story be about?"	Timed Pair Share
Through	
Teacher Reading	Solo: Students Listen
Re-create Character Dialogue	RallyRobin
Teacher Reading	Solo: Students Listen
Summary Question: "What is one important event so far?"	Timed RoundRobin
Teacher Reading	Solo: Students Listen
Prediction Question: "What will happen next?"	Instant Star
Beyond	
Higher-Level Thinking Questions	Fan-N-Pick

Sample Into-Through-Beyond Lessons

Mathematics: Solving Story Problems

Into. The teacher presents a story problem. In pairs, students use RallyRobin to take turns sharing their proposed problem-solving strategy.

Through. This is a typical skill-building lesson:
- The teacher models solving the problem while students watch and listen.
- The teacher shares another story problem and pairs use RallyCoach, with Partner A solving and Partner B coaching.
- The teacher shares another story problem and pairs use RallyCoach, with Partner B solving and Partner A coaching.
- The teacher gives the class problems to solve and students solve them in pairs using RallyCoach or Sage-N-Scribe.
- When done, students come together as a team, and use RoundRobin to share their answers, celebrate their successes or work out discrepancies.

Beyond. The teacher provides a new story problem and every student writes (or draws) their problem-solving strategy and shares it with a partner using RallyRobin.

Social Studies: Slavery

Into. Using Continuous RoundRobin, students take multiple turns in their teams answering the question, "Why were slaves willing to risk their lives for freedom?"

Through. This is a basic lecture punctuated by multiple stopping points for student processing and interaction:
- Students take notes while the teacher lectures about slavery.
- The teacher reads a descriptive script about the Underground Railroad, while students close their eyes using Guided Imagery to picture it.
- Students pair up and do a Timed Pair Share, explaining the emotions they felt during the guided imagery.
- Students take notes while the teacher lectures about Harriet Tubman.
- Students do a Single RoundRobin to share one thing they learned about Harriet Tubman.
- Students take notes while the teacher continues to lecture about slavery.

Beyond. Students pair up to do a RallyRobin, each sharing what they learned or found most interesting from the lecture.

Language Arts: Story Character

Into. Students read or are read a story.

Through. Using Team Interview, each teammate is interviewed in the role of a story character:
- Each teammate is assigned a different story character.
- Students independently research their characters and take notes.
- Use Pair RallyTable to generate a list of interview questions to ask the other story characters, relating to the story.
- Each teammate takes a turn being interviewed by teammates while the interviewers take notes.

Beyond. Each student writes a character sketch about the four featured characters. Then they use Mix-Pair-Share to pair up with a different classmate and share their character sketches, one sketch per each new pairing.

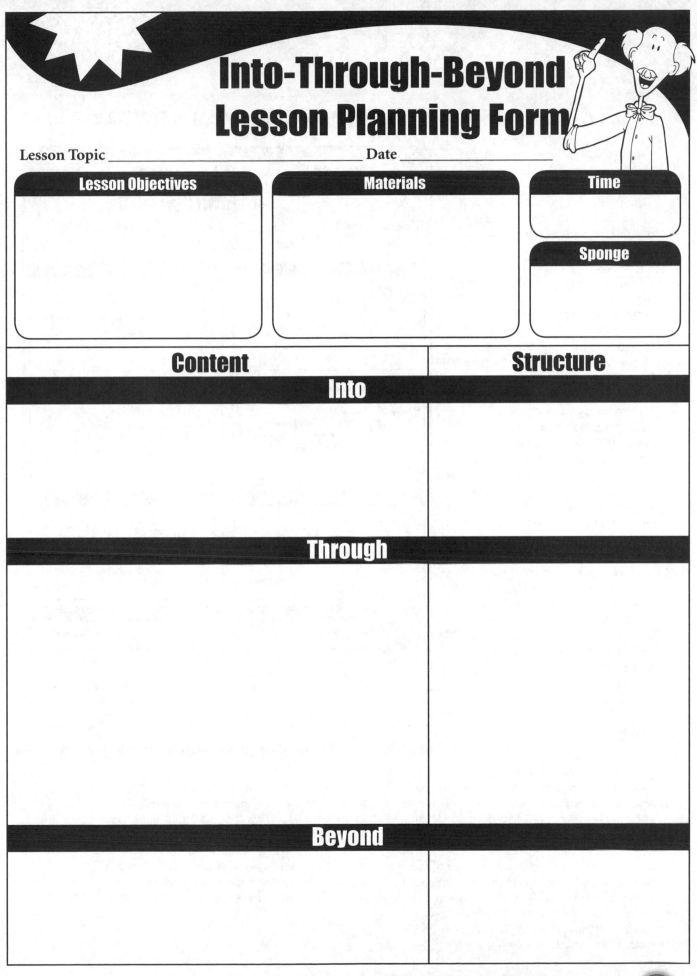

Into-Through-Beyond Lesson Planning Form

Lesson Topic _____ Date _____

Lesson Objectives

Materials

Time

Sponge

Content	Structure
Into	
Through	
Beyond	

Kagan Cooperative Learning • Dr. Spencer Kagan & Miguel Kagan
Kagan Publishing • 1 (800) 933-2667 • www.KaganOnline.com 14.15

Multiple Intelligences Lesson Design

A multiple intelligences lesson aims to teach the lesson content in many ways to match the different ways students best learn. To plan a multiple intelligences lesson, we use the eight intelligences as eight possible elements of our lesson design. We make a concerted effort to regularly engage each of the intelligences, but we don't need to go overboard and try to hit all eight intelligences in every lesson.

Cooperative learning structures are a great asset for multiple intelligences lesson planning. We have developed structures that engage each of the eight intelligences. In our work on Multiple Intelligences,[6] we describe in detail how to plan multiple intelligences lessons using structures and therefore won't go into detail here. In a nutshell, we use a range of structures to address the multiple intelligences. By using a variety of structures that engage the multiple intelligences, at times we match some of our students' strengths, and at other times we stretch students in their weaker intelligences. The sample MI lesson on the Gold Rush (see box) illustrates how structures can be used to address each intelligence. A blank MI Lesson Planning Form is provided on the following page to plan your own MI lessons.

Sample MI Lesson on the Gold Rush

MI Lesson Planning Form

Lesson Topic _Gold Rush_   Date _December 4_
Materials _____

Verbal/Linguistic
RallyRead
Students take turns reading the text about the discovery of gold.

Logical/Mathematical
Sequencing
Teams sequence the events of the gold rush.

Visual/Spatial
Team Mind-Mapping
Teams create a mind map on "Gold Rush."

Musical/Rhythmic
Team Chants
Teams create and perform a chant on a selected topic related to the gold rush.

Bodlily/Kinesthetic
Team-2-Team
Teams prepare a short skit and share it with other teams.

Naturalist
Sum-the-Ranks
Students plan a travel route to California, and select the most favorable route as a team.

Interpersonal
Team Interview
Students are interviewed by their teammates in the role of Sam Brannan, a prospector, James Marshall, or John Sutter.

Intrapersonal
Think-Write-RoundRobin
Students write whether or not they personally would set off in search of gold, then RoundRobin their thoughts with teammates.

The Big Four Design

Many years ago, when first trying to convince teachers and districts that there was merit in cooperative learning, I did demonstration lessons. For a number of years, I would not agree to work at a site unless the principal and teachers saw a cooperative learning lesson. The power of seeing students supporting each other and taking joy in learning together was far more convincing than any words I could provide. The demo lessons created administrator buy-in and desire among teachers to learn the structures.

Because I wanted to demonstrate that lesson planning in the structural approach took little or no special materials or planning, I would give myself a challenge. I would tell schools not to tell me the content of the lesson until one hour before the demo lesson. They would then give me a typical chapter the students were mastering or some other content the students were to learn.

14.16

Kagan Cooperative Learning • Dr. Spencer Kagan & Miguel Kagan
Kagan Publishing • 1 (800) 933-2667 • www.KaganOnline.com

MI Lesson Planning Form

Lesson Topic_____ Date_____

Materials_____

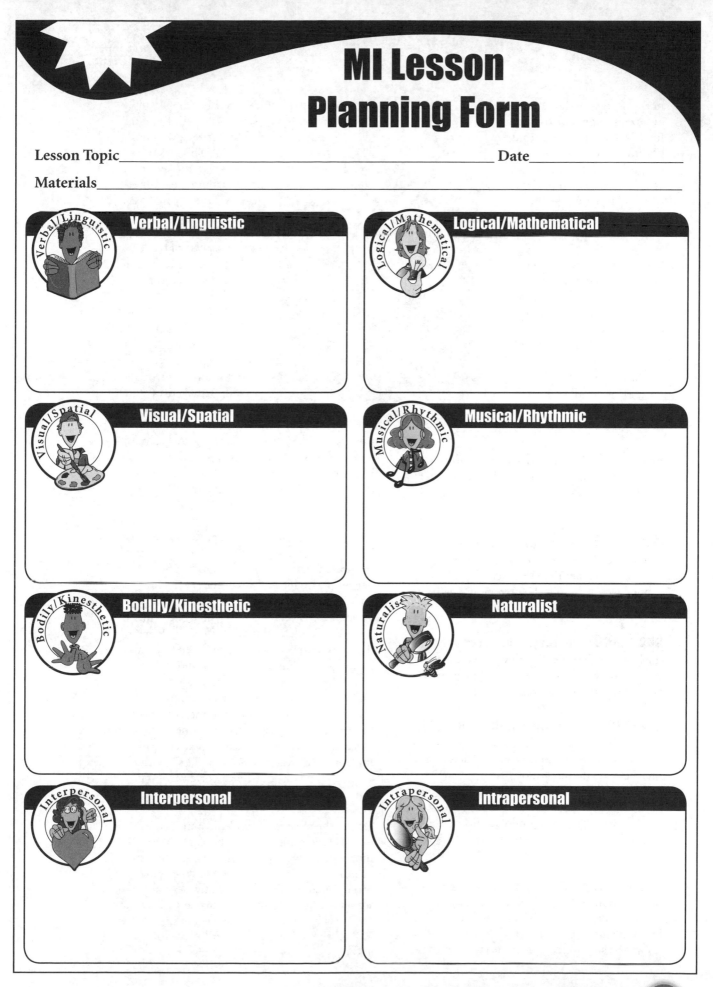

Verbal/Linguistic

Logical/Mathematical

Visual/Spatial

Musical/Rhythmic

Bodlily/Kinesthetic

Naturalist

Interpersonal

Intrapersonal

In the process of designing hundreds of demonstration lessons for kindergarten through twelfth grade, I fell into a simple lesson design. Because I was to teach students who had never worked in teams, the lessons always began with a teambuilding activity. Because I wanted to demonstrate the power of structures for content mastery and thinking skills development, I would look at the curriculum and decide which structures would be exciting to use to produce thinking and mastery. My criteria for deciding if I had planned a good lesson was to ask myself four questions:

The Big Four

1. **Teambuilding**
2. **Classbuilding**
3. **Mastery**
4. **Thinking Skills**

building structure, a classbuilding structure, a mastery structure, and a thinking skills structure. This formula was most often very successful. This was true regardless of the grade level or the curriculum area. For efficiency, I usually made the teambuilding and classbuilding content-related, so all four aspects of the lesson worked together toward the main academic objective.

I called my approach "The Big Four," and began training teachers in the Big Four lesson design. Later, when I had the honor of working with Beth Andrini and Jeanne Stone in developing multi-structural lessons for their books in Math[7] and Language Arts[8], we applied the Big Four Design, including in each lesson some content-related teambuilding and classbuilding, as well as mastery and thinking skills.

Question 1: Teambuilding. When I get done with the lesson, will team members feel better about themselves as a team and about working together?

Question 2: Classbuilding. When I get done with the lesson, will students have interacted with classmates—other than their teammates—in a supportive way, and feel better about being part of this class?

Question 3: Mastery. When I get done with the lesson, will students know something they did not know before, and be able to perform better on a test related to the objective?

Question 4: Thinking Skills. When I get done with the lesson, will students have sharpened their thinking skills, be more likely to ask themselves critical questions, be more analytic, have a clearer evaluative framework, be more likely to apply information to a new context, and/or be better able to put discrete bodies of information together in a meaningful category system?

And that was it. I felt that if during each one-hour demonstration lesson, I made progress toward all four goals, the lesson was a success. And lesson planning became very easy. All I needed to do was be sure I included in the lesson a team-

The Big Four Design allows a great deal of flexibility. While planning a lesson, a teacher may include any lesson design element in any order, depending on the dictates of the curriculum and the needs of the students. When the lesson is planned, however, there is a final check to see if the Big Four questions have been answered in the affirmative: Does the lesson include Teambuilding, Classbuilding, Mastery, and Thinking Skill development? Classbuilding, for example, may come at the end, middle or beginning of the lesson, but when the lesson is done, students will have made some progress toward one of the aims of classbuilding (getting acquainted, creating mutual trust, creating a positive class identity, valuing individual differences, or developing synergy).

One of the most memorable demonstration lessons I did came when a school gave me what they thought would be an impossible challenge. I think they wanted to prove that this young professor could not do cooperative learning with students who had never been in teams. They gave me a class with many students who were limited in English proficiency, I had little time to prepare, and the lesson topic was Greek history!

By including structures, cooperative learning becomes a way to make any lesson more engaging.

I began the lesson with a RoundTable, having students list TV shows they watched. If a student could not write, a teammate recorded for them. They set that paper aside, and did another RoundTable listing sports they played or watched. Next, I had them return to the paper with the TV shows and had them draw three columns to the right of the list, and put a happy face at the top of one column, a sad face at the top of the second column, and a happy and a sad face as the third column header. They then did RoundTable Consensus to label the programs as happy, sad, or both. After the students completed categorizing the TV shows, I told them what they had done had its roots in Greek history—the origins of comedies and tragedies began hundreds of years before Christ was born in the small Greek city-states, which I briefly described. Next, I had the students turn to the list of sports. I told the students that the origins of many of the sports we play and compete in today had their origins in Greek history. I described how the Greeks developed the Olympics, the eleven events that were in the original Olympics, how only men participated, how they all were completely nude except those who had to run in full armor, and how the ancient Olympics were held for about a thousand years. Then, I had students get up

and do a RallyRobin with a classmate to recall original Olympic events. They paired up with two other classmates to form groups of three to do a RoundRobin, naming things they remembered about the Olympics. Finally, they found someone they had not talked with that day to do a Timed Pair Share on what they thought was most interesting in the lesson and why.

The students had never worked together before in teams, but the RoundTable served as a content-related teambuilder. They had never paired up or formed triads with classmates, but the RallyRobin and RoundRobin at the end of the lesson served as a classbuilder—the meta-communication: In this class we all work together. Although relatively simple, there were two thinking skills fostered: categorization (Comedy, Tragedy, Both) and evaluation (What was most interesting?). Finally, for mastery, the students learned some information about Greek history and the original Olympics.

The Big Four Design played out quite differently with different content, grade-level, and ability-level students. It remains my favorite lesson design for creating lessons on the fly.

By including structures, cooperative learning becomes a way to make any lesson more engaging. Unlike the other approaches to cooperative learning, structures are not an alternative lesson design. They can be used to successfully implement any lesson design.

Chapter Summary

Lesson planning using structures is different from other forms of cooperative learning lesson planning. All other approaches to cooperative learning provide either a prefab lesson design, or recommend principles with which to construct lessons. The structural approach allows us to make cooperative learning part of any lesson design. The structures give us freedom to make any lesson a cooperative learning lesson either by substituting or inserting structures, by inserting structure sequences, or by planning multi-structural lessons to meet any lesson objective.

Instead of designing lessons from scratch using abstract principles, or a basic cooperative learning lesson framework, with structures we have tools to easily create engaging activities to reach any goal. If our goal is to promote content mastery, we will be certain to include structure(s) that promote mastery. If our goal is to develop thinking skills, we will include structure(s) that develop thinking skills. If our goal is to develop the multiple intelligences, we will include structures that engage and develop the different intelligences. Lesson planning with structures is the art of selecting the appropriate structures and sequencing them to meet the lesson's objective.

Whether we are just replacing a few elements of our lesson with structures or creating a full-blown multi-structural lesson, with structures we can be confident that our lessons will be successful; structures respect the basic principles of effective cooperative learning.

Chapter Questions

▶ Questions for Review

1. How is lesson planning with structures different from other forms of cooperative learning lesson planning?
2. How do you use the Teacher ABC lesson planning form?
3. What are the four objectives of the Big Four lesson design?
4. What is a structure sequence? Give an example.
5. Why is Think-Pair-Share considered a structure sequence and also a structure?
6. What are the three main objectives of an Into-Through-Beyond lesson design?

▶ Questions for Thinking and Discussion

1. Are there any structure sequences that you use frequently? If yes, pick one and describe how you use it. If no, create a unique sequence and describe how you would use it.
2. In your opinion, which lesson design elements should be included in your everyday lessons and why?
3. Why do you think Kagan focuses on the development and dissemination of cooperative structures instead of ready-made instructional packages?
4. What does it mean to say that the cooperative learning teacher is more of a designer of learning experiences than a transmitter of knowledge?
5. How could you integrate a structure or structures into one lesson that you teach?

References

[1] Johnson, D. & R. Johnson. *The New Circles of Learning: Cooperation in the Classroom and School.* Alexandria, VA: Association for Supervision & Curriculum Development, 1994.

[2] Slavin, R. *Cooperative Learning Theory, Research, and Practice.* Needham Heights, MA: Allyn & Bacon, 1990.

[3] Kagan, S. "Co-op Co-op: A Flexible Cooperative Learning Technique." In Slavin, R., S. Sharan, S. Kagan, R. Hertz-Lazarowitz, C. Webb & R. Schmuck (eds.). *Learning to Cooperate, Cooperating to Learn.* New York, NY: Plenum, 1985.

[4] Lyman, F. *Think-Pair-Share SmartCard.* San Clemente, CA: Kagan Publishing, 2006.

[5] Hunter, M. *Enhancing Teaching.* Upper Saddle River, NJ: Prentice Hall, 1993.

[6] Kagan, S. & M. Kagan. *Multiple Intelligences: The Complete MI Book.* San Clemente, CA: Kagan Publishing, 1998.

[7] Andrini, B. *Cooperative Learning & Mathematics.* San Clemente, CA: Kagan Publishing, 1998.

[8] Stone, J. *Cooperative Learning & Language Arts.* San Clemente, CA: Kagan Publishing, 1994.

Assessment & Grading

Grades are often misused. We have much better ways to give students feedback, to motivate students, and to assess how well students are learning.

Cooperative learning is not only a powerful set of instructional strategies, it is a powerful approach to assessment. Using cooperative learning enables us to easily perform ongoing, authentic assessment that accurately captures students' level of understanding across many dimensions. During our cooperative lessons, projects, and challenges, we can observe our students interact. We can plainly see what they can do and what they can't. We can measure how well they can use their knowledge and creativity to create projects and solutions, rather than merely select the correct answer on a test or complete a worksheet. Cooperative learning promotes verbalization of the content; it enables us to listen in and hear not only what our smartest students know, but what all our students know. In this chapter, we will examine what good assessment is and how cooperative learning helps us perform effective assessment.

We will also examine grading. Grades are misused. They are misused by teachers who use cooperative learning, and they are misused by teachers in general. Well-intended teachers use grades to assess students' knowledge, to provide feedback, and to motivate students and groups, all of which can be done more effectively in other ways. Some teachers who use cooperative learning have adopted the blatantly unfair practice of group grades, giving all students on a team the same grade. The use of group grades is an ill-conceived practice that violates our sense of equity, as well as basic principles of cooperative learning.

Let's turn first to effective assessment via cooperative learning.

Cooperative Learning and Assessment

Tests and grades do give us an indication of how students are doing over time, but do they really help us do what's most important for us to do—help students learn? Are grades the best tools we have to analyze how our students are doing, and help them take the next step? Definitely not! For that we have a powerful range of cooperative learning assessment approaches.

Dimensions of Good Assessment

Good assessment is 1) Formative, 2) Authentic, 3) Representative, and 4) Multi-dimensional. Let's look at each of these dimensions, why they're important, and how cooperative learning helps us improve assessment.

Dimensions of Good Assessment

► **Formative**
► **Authentic**
► **Representative**
► **Multi-dimensional**

Formative v. Summative Assessment

The best way to understand formative assessment is to contrast it with its counterpart, summative assessment. Formative assessment is ongoing—while learning is occurring. We perform observations and activities to monitor students' learning and the effectiveness of the teaching strategies. Are students getting the concept? If students are getting it, we can proceed. If they're not, perhaps we need to prolong practice, or teach the concept another way. Formative assessment is process oriented. The question here is, *What and how are students learning?*

In contrast, summative assessment is not ongoing. It is a one-time, final test to sum things up—to evaluate student proficiency. It is a test after the learning has occurred. Examples include the unit test, or the state exam. The goal is not to improve teaching or learning in the present. The goal is to test what students have learned. Summative assessment is outcome oriented. The question here is, *What did students learn?*

This table illustrates the difference between formative and summative assessment.

Formative v. Summative Assessment		
	Formative Assessment	**Summative Assessment**
When	During Learning	After Learning
Examples	• Teacher Observations • Team Project • Journals	• Unit Test • State or National Tests • Entrance Exams (SAT, ACT)
Goal	Improvement of Instruction	Evaluation of Student

What distinguishes formative and summative assessment is the time frame. The question for formative assessment is present tense: *What and how **are** they learning?* Formative assessment is ongoing. It is done to "form" or modify teaching and learning. The question for summative assessment is past tense: *What **did** they learn?* Summative is final. It is a concluding "summation" of what students learned.

Assessment and the Chili Cook-off

To distinguish between formative and summative assessment, think of the chili cook-off.

Formative Assessment
A cook-off contestant tastes her own chili to see how to improve it.

Summative Assessment
The cook-off judge rates the chili.

Formative Assessment & Cooperative Learning. Cooperative learning facilitates formative assessment. As students interact with one another, the teacher can clearly hear and see students' thoughts, ideas, and even misconceptions. What usually occurs between the ears of the student is now outside the student's head and easy for the teacher to assess. This formative assessment process allows the teacher to adjust input, correct problems, identify gaps, and help students grasp the concept well before the problem is revealed with a test score—when it's too late!

Representative Assessment

In the United States, we have a representative democracy. Citizens vote for the official who they think will best represent them. Involving every citizen in every decision and every aspect of governance would be impractical and unmanageable. Therefore, we have a proxy government. We elect politicians to act on our behalf. The elected politician "represents" his constituents. Representative assessment in the classroom is similar. It would be impractical and unmanageable to hear from every single student every single time, so teachers select students to respond as a representative sample for the class. Good assessment takes a representative sample of the class: the high, the medium, and the low achievers. What do they know? Where do we need to go?

Representative Assessment and Cooperative Learning.

In a traditional classroom, the teacher presents something. Next, she/he checks for understanding by asking a question. The smart students wave their hands and "oohhh" and "aaahh" to be called on. This is not representative assessment. We have another name for this behavior—display behavior. We call it display behavior because students are showing off to the teacher, to the class, and to themselves how smart they are. Often only the brightest or most motivated students raise their hands. The teacher calls on a student with his/her hand up and thus ends up hearing from a very unrepresentative sample of the class. This is more a form of self-deception than an effective assessment

> *"In the end we retain from our studies only that which we practically apply."*
> —Johann Wolfgang von Goethe

technique. We fool ourselves into thinking we have taught our students well because a student has answered correctly, not focusing on the many students who did not raise their hands and did not know the answer. In a traditional class, we have the illusion there is far greater understanding than is actually the case.

In contrast, when teachers use Kagan Structures, they get a very representative sample of the class because, as the students are engaged in the structures, the teacher walks around, listening in to the high achievers as well as the low achievers. A representative sample of the class is sampled, not just those who want to show off. When all students hold up their AnswerBoards at the same time, we see what everyone knows. This allows us to fine-tune our input, to better adjust to the actual level of all our learners.

Authentic Assessment

Proponents of authentic assessment criticize standardized tests, claiming they aren't a true measure of student learning. Instead, standardized tests measure how well students test. Assessments too often target factual knowledge—recall and recognition level thinking. Can a student pick the correct choice on a multiple choice test? Often they fail to capture higher levels of thinking, including application and synthesis. Students may be able to remember isolated facts for the test, but can they really apply the learning to real-world challenges? Can they synthesize what they've learned to solve problems and create products of value? Knowledge that cannot be applied has no practical value.

Traditional assessments don't measure what is important to measure, and therefore students don't learn what's important to learn. Tests are usually paper-and-pencil, right-or-wrong, easy-to-evaluate, out-of-context measurements of knowledge. Science tests measure if students have mastered a body of science knowledge, but fail to measure students' ability to generate hypotheses and carry out valid experiments to test them. They measure the content of science, but not the process of science. Too often standardized language arts tests gauge competence on mechanics, but fail to measure how well a student can polish an essay or delve deeply into the meaning of a poem. Don't we value creativity, collaboration, artistic expression, and oral and written articulation? If assessment dictates instruction and traditional assessments don't measure the full array of desirable outcomes, then instruction is headed in the wrong direction.

Authentic assessment seeks to correct these flaws by directly examining students during "authentic" learning tasks—challenging and meaningful real-world tasks embedded in real-world contexts.

Authentic Assessment and Cooperative Learning.
Cooperative learning provides an ideal context for authentic assessment. First, the products and performances of cooperative learning are particularly well-suited for authentic assessment. See *Chapter 13: Cooperative Projects & Presentations*. Student teams perform skits, present reports, conduct research, share experiments, create literary works, design art projects, build models, and solve challenges. In addition to being conducive to meaningful learning pursuits, cooperative learning adds an important authentic context. As they work together, students debate issues, reach consensus, summarize findings, practice different roles, provide feedback, make decisions, generate ideas, and negotiate. Assessment of students in cooperative learning is completely contextual. It mirrors real-world situations with open and varied intercourse where students' full range of skills and knowledge are on display.

Multi-Dimensional Assessment
Multi-dimensional assessment broadens what we assess. As an educational community, we are moving toward a greater understanding of and respect for individual differences. Learning styles, thinking styles, multiple intelligences, and differentiated instruction all help break the notion that intelligence is a unitary entity. We as educators are becoming more aware that students are different, have different minds, come from different backgrounds and experiences, and learn differently. The world beyond the classroom values more than linguistic and logical skills and products. Therefore, learning tasks need to be varied to engage and develop the various senses, intelligences, and learning and thinking styles. Good assessments seek to understand students along these multiple dimensions. We more accurately understand what students know and what students can do if we assess them under varied learning conditions.

Cooperative Learning and Multi-Dimensional Assessment.
Cooperative learning improves multi-dimensional assessment in two ways. First, and most obviously, is we simply have more windows into student learning when we add cooperative learning activities to our other classroom activities. We see students perform in a broader range of contexts with a broader range of content. We have more ways to assess.

Secondly, cooperative learning can be used to add the cooperative, social, and interpersonal dimensions to just about any type of activity. Take the very independent act of journal writing. We can add a cooperative dimension to the activity by adding a prewriting RoundRobin: Students share with teammates what they will write about. Or we can tack

Multi-Dimensional, Cooperative Assessment Tools

- **Audio or Video Recording.** Teams create a song, story, movie, or presentation.
- **Artwork.** Teams create an art project.
- **Charts/Graphs.** Teams create a chart or graph.
- **Debates.** Pairs or teams take opposite sides of a debatable issue.
- **Group Processing Forms.** Teams process their interaction.
- **Interviews.** Students interview a partner or classmate.
- **Investigations & Experiments.** Teams investigate or conduct an experiment.
- **Journals.** Students share their journals with teammates.
- **Models.** Teams create a model.
- **Open-Ended Questions.** Teams write thinking questions about the content.
- **Presentations.** Teams plan and present a team project, word-web or mural.
- **Papers & Reports.** Students collaborate to submit a team report or paper.

on a publishing-stage RoundRobin: Students read their journal entries to teammates. Both stages enrich the activity, boost engagement, and offer insight to a different dimension of student understanding. Cooperative learning can make any activity multi-dimensional.

The box on the previous page lists some cooperative activities to engage students' many intelligences. Observing students during these multi-dimensional cooperative activities provides clearer insight into students' many ways of knowing and understanding. Observations can range from informally listening in to checklists, inventories, and rubrics.

Cooperative Learning Assessments

Cooperative learning adds a number of valuable assessment approaches to a teacher's repertoire. Cooperative learning offers new and better ways to observe students during teamwork, monitor students, make adjustments during lessons, target individual students without putting them on the spot, and it offers structures for polling the entire class, every team, and every student.

The Walkabout

Often in cooperative learning, we provide direct instruction, then set pairs or teams to work together on problems or on a project. This is the perfect time for the "Walkabout." In the Walkabout, we circulate from team to team, observe students working, and listen in. The Walkabout is also an important management tool. We are available to answer questions, we use our presence to prevent discipline problems, we connect with students, we help keep teams on task, and we can challenge and redirect students with pointed questions. As we walk around the class observing our students, we ask ourselves:

- Did students comprehend the instructions?
- Are students doing the structure correctly?
- Could the task be structured better?
- What do students know?
- What skills do students have?
- What do they need to learn?
- What additional instruction would be helpful?

Assessing for Adjustments

If during the Walkabout we observe a consistent problem or identify a way to improve instruction, we interrupt teamwork, and make the appropriate adjustment. The type of problem dictates the most appropriate response.

Assessing for Adjustments	
Problem	**Solution**
Incorrect Use of Structure	Practice the Structure or Drop Reminder
Students Not Following Instructions	Clarify Instructions or Provide Modeling
Students Lack Academic Skills	Repeat Instructions or Teach in Different Way

For example, during RoundRobin, we noticed that students were talking out of turn. To get students' attention, we say, "High-five please" and raise a hand indicating the quiet signal. All hands go up, and all eyes are on us. Then we might tell the class, "Let's do a quick refresher on taking turns. Student #1s please stand. Please sit. Student #2s please stand. Please sit. Student #3s please stand. Please sit. Student #4s please stand and remain standing. Student #4s will start. When done, Student #4s will sit, and Student #1s will stand. Only the student standing is talking, everyone else is listening. Please begin."

If the problem we identify is a problem with the structure (like the example above), we may have students practice the structure or remind them of the steps. If we find students do not understand our instructions, we clarify the instructions or provide better modeling. If we find students lack the academic skill, we teach the skill again or reteach the skill in a different way. Assessment allows us to identify what it will take to get the class on the right track and make the necessary adjustment.

Targeting Individual Students

Occasionally, we may wish to target a specific student. We're curious to find out what Jaime knows about the subject. Or maybe we're uncertain if Sarah really grasps the concept. In the traditional classroom, the teacher calls on that student. This puts the student on the spot, but also violates the principle of Simultaneous Interaction since the rest of the class is idle during a teacher and student one-on-one.

Cooperative learning gives us a better option. We target an individual student by asking all Student #3s to stand and share. Or if we don't know the student's number, we may ask the person with the shortest hair (or any other attribute that will select that student, but also one student in each team) to stand and share. We have targeted the student we want, and we can casually listen in.

Simultaneous Sharing Structures

Simultaneous sharing structures allow us to assess the whole class at once. For example, we ask a question, tell our students to think, and then have each student write an answer on his/her AnswerBoard. Finally, we say, "Show Me!" As the students hold up their AnswerBoards, we see at a glance what percent of the class has the right answer.

All-Students-Respond Structures

Many structures have every student respond, although not necessarily all at once. For example, in RoundRobin, teammates take turns responding. Some All-Students-Respond structures have more simultaneous interaction than others. During RoundRobin, one student out of four in the class is responding at any one moment; during RallyRobin, we double the active participation because half the class is responding at once.

How Many? v. How Many at Once?

As we select structures for assessment, it is helpful to keep both questions in mind—*How many students am I hearing from?* and *How many am I hearing from at once?* The answers will be different, depending on which structure we choose, and even which variation of a structure we choose. For example, during Numbered Heads Together, I might call on Student 4 from Team 3 to respond. In that case, I will hear from one student in the class, and I will be hearing from only one at a time. In contrast, if I call for all the Student 4's to come to the whiteboard and write their answer at once, I am hearing from one quarter of the class, and I am hearing from all of them at once. Clearly, the choice of structures that let me hear from more students and more students at once allows more representative and quicker assessment. With more students

responding, I get a better picture of how well my whole class is learning. With more students responding at once, I do a quicker, more representative assessment.

Clearly there are some trade-offs. For example, in a Class Whip, each student in the class in turn gives a response. We assess every student, but it takes a long time. In a Team Whip, a representative from each team responds. We don't hear from all students, but we cut the response time by three-fourths and still get a representative sample. If, however, we cut the number of students responding to one volunteer, as we do when we do Whole Class Q&A, we have a very quick sample, but it is totally unrepresentative and tells us next to nothing about what most students have learned. Good assessment depends on creating a representative sample of the class. During RoundRobin, Showdown, or Quiz-Quiz-Trade, for example, because every student is responding as we circulate, we take a representative sample of the class (we hear the thinking of the high, middle, and low students) and do our authentic assessment quickly. Cooperative learning structures allow a more authentic, more representative, and more efficient assessment.

How Many? vs. How Many at Once?

Structure	Students Responding	Students Responding at Once
Traditional Q & A	1 per class	1 per class
Team Whip	1 per team	1 per class
Class Whip	Every student	1 per class
RoundRobin	Every student	¼ of the class
RallyRobin	Every student	½ of the class
Quiz-Quiz-Trade	Every student	½ of the class
Showdown	Every student	Every student
Show Me!	Every student	Every student
Choral Practice	Every student	Every student

Kagan Cooperative Learning • **Dr. Spencer Kagan & Miguel Kagan**
Kagan Publishing • **1 (800) 933-2667** • **www.KaganOnline.com**

Physical Response Structures

Similar to the simultaneous sharing structures, we get a good idea of what students know or where they stand when using structures that require a physical response. With the following structures, we can literally see where students stand.

- **Formations.** Students use bodies to form answer or concept.
- **Estimate Line-Ups.** Students line up in a sequence corresponding to the estimate.
- **Agreement Circles.** Students step into the circle proportionate to the degree they agree with a statement.
- **Corners.** Students go to the corner of the room representing their selection.
- **TakeOff–TouchDown.** Students stand or sit to respond to the teacher's poll.
- **Kinesthetic Symbols.** Students display content or response with physical symbols or movement.

Tips for Cooperative Learning Assessment

Random Sampling. To get a representative sample of the class, avoid calling on the same students who repeatedly volunteer to answer. Use a Student Selector to pick one student on each team to respond. Or use the Name Selector in SelectorTools to randomly pick one student by name.

Recommended Resource

SelectorTools

Kyle

SelectorTools allows you to select students and teams in a variety of ways, including by name for random sampling of the class.

Think Time. After you ask a question, give students 3–5 seconds of silent think time. This gives reflective students time to formulate their answers. Answers following a bit of wait time are more representative of what students know.[1,2]

Write Time. Give students a little time to each write their response before calling on a student to respond. Write Time gets all students engaged in answering every question. It allows students to not only collect their thoughts, but to organize them and record them. Students can read their responses instead of feeling put on the spot.

Space to Walk. Easy access to approach teams and listen in is essential for good cooperative learning assessment. When arranging your team desks or furniture layout make sure there is free and open access to every team from every angle.

See illustration of Interior Loop, *Chapter 8: Management.*

Establish a Sense of Security. In cooperative learning, students are frequently asked to share their ideas and answers with teammates and the classroom. Because of the increased simultaneity, there is much more idea sharing. We establish class norms so that students feel secure to take risks and make mistakes. "Mistakes are OK. If we were all perfect, none of us would need to be here." "The only dumb questions are the questions we don't ask." We do not ridicule or allow other students to ridicule students for incorrect answers or off-the-wall ideas. "All ideas are welcome." Validate student efforts, "It's not what I was looking for, but it was a great effort." Validate almost-right answers: "Correct. The thigh bone is the longest bone in the body. It is also called your femur."

If a student gives a wrong answer, one way we can validate the student is to state the question to which the answer was correct. We ask, "Who was the first president of the United States?" Pilar answers, "Abraham Lincoln." We say, "Pilar, Abraham Lincoln is famous for preserving the union during the Civil War, and it was during his term that that Emancipation Proclamation was issued that freed the slaves. Abe Lincoln was our 16th president. George Washington was our first."

When to Correct. If a team is interacting and they aren't following a procedure, or they share incorrect information, do we interrupt the team then and there? A handy decision rule is to ask if the correction would benefit the whole class, or if it would benefit only the team we are observing. If we think several teams need to hear the correction, we give the quiet signal, and give the correction to the whole class: "Class, during RallyCoach, let's remember there is only one pencil out for the pair." If, however, we think only the team we are observing needs the correction, we make the correction without interrupting the other teams: "Just one small correction, the capital of Texas is Austin, not Dallas."

Teachable Moments. While we are walking the class and making assessments, we are still teachers. We take any appropriate opportunity to help students learn. For example, if we are listening in to a team where a student makes an error and we think the correction might be helpful to the class, we get the class's attention, and create a teachable moment. We begin by

Kagan Cooperative Learning • Dr. Spencer Kagan & Miguel Kagan
Kagan Publishing • 1 (800) 933-2667 • www.KaganOnline.com

15.7

appreciating the student: "Ashley brings up an important point that is easily confused. The difference between radius and circumference is…." If a team gives an incorrect answer, you may use it to teach new information: "Close! *Eureka* is actually California's state motto. It's Greek for 'I have found it.'"

Simultaneous Assessment. We know anytime we ask one student a question, we are creating a poor ratio of student engagement and getting an unrepresentative sample. Only one student in the entire class is actively engaged. So why do we do it so consistently? This practice is so entrenched in our teaching repertoire, it's a tough habit to kick. Anytime we want to hear from a student, we consider having all students respond. We listen in on a Timed Pair Share for elaborated answers. Or we use Show Me for quick answers. Even if we're narrowly focusing on one student, it is better to at the same time engage the rest of the class than to leave the class disengaged.

Differentiated Instruction & Multiple Intelligences. As we assess students, we find that students are at different levels of understanding. Helping students take the next step is not always a one-size fits all proposition. Resources on differentiated instruction and multiple intelligences offer numerous suggestions for how to help all students succeed.[3, 4]

There are many ways to differentiate instruction while using structures. For example, while doing Quiz-Quiz-Trade, students may have different colored cards indicating difficulty level or content. Students with red cards find others with red cards to work with; students with blue cards find others with blue cards. To take another example, during the Flashcard Game, each student may have her/his own set of cards, so each is working on the developmentally appropriate type of problem or difficulty level.

Cooperative Learning and Grading

There is a heated debate in the field of cooperative learning. Do we give group grades or not? We are the most vocal opponents of group grades.[5, 6] We share here why we oppose group grades, and then suggest ways to ensure that grades represent individual achievement.

No Group Grades

Here are a dozen reasons we are unequivocally opposed to group grades. With so many negatives stacked against the use of group grades, we urge all teachers not to use group grades as part of cooperative learning—ever.

1 Group Grades Are Not Good for Cooperative Assessment. The first portion of this chapter was devoted to effective methods of cooperative assessment. Dimensions of good assessment were outlined. Group grades do not make assessment more formative, representative, authentic, or multi-dimensional. There's no need for group grades from an assessment perspective.

2 Group Grades Undermine Motivation. Group grades undermine motivation at both ends of the achievement spectrum. They reward slackers, who have no incentive to work harder, if they are fortunate enough to have a high achiever as a teammate. Conversely, the high achiever may feel there is no use putting in a lot of effort if his/her teammates won't pull their own weight. In the next chapter, we will explore methods far better than group grades to motivate students and teams.

3 Group Grades Are Not Good for Certifying Students. If a student receives an A in a regular class, she may be qualified to take an Advanced Placement or Honors class. If a student receives a D, he may be demoted to a remedial class. If a student fails the class, she may not receive the units and may have to take the class again, or have to make it up in summer school. In college, students can opt to take the course "Pass" or "Fail" and respectively receive credit or no credit. Group grades tell us how a team performed. But they can tell us little to nothing about the individual student. In our present educational system, we certify or fail to certify individual students, not teams. Group grades allow us to certify a student on a successful team who has not performed and not learned anything!

4 Group Grades Are Not Good Feedback.

A defining characteristic of good feedback is that it is specific. The more specific the feedback, the more helpful. An overall grade on a test is less specific than individually corrected questions. If we receive only the grade, we don't know what was correct and what was incorrect. We don't know what to improve. Group grades compound the problem. By definition, the grade becomes more general, not more specific. There is no differentiation. For effective feedback to teams, we recommend differentiated feedback forms and comments on aspects of team presentations, not a single grade.

5 Group Grades Are a Poor Method of Communication.

If group grades are given and are partially a function of who the student happens to have as teammates, report cards are meaningless. How can a parent, scholarship committee, admissions officer, or potential employer interpret grades if they partially reflect the work of other students? Group grades debase the report card and degrade communication.

6 Group Grades Are Not Fair.

Group grades are so blatantly unfair that on this basis alone, they should never be used. Consider these two typical situations.

Situation 1: Equally Good Work, But Different Grades

Two students, Joan and Ed, are each hovering between an A and a B in a science course. The amount of work they've done, what they've learned, and their motivation are comparable. They are on different cooperative learning teams, each working on its final team project, and their team grades will be a factor—albeit a minor one—in determining individual grades in the course. Joan and Ed each do about the same amount and quality of work to support their team projects—both independent work and teamwork. And their presentations to the class are equally competent.

The problem is this: One of Ed's teammates is a brilliant student who has access to a color graphics program. She creates very attractive color banners and graphs for the presentation. As for Joan's teammates, none is brilliant, and one, in fact, is a slacker. Her team receives a grade of C+, while Ed's team receives an A+. As a result, Joan gets a B in the course, and Ed, an A. Two students who have performed equally receive different course grades!

Situation 2: Equally Poor Work, But Different Grades

For years, Susan and Bob have been very poor students. They are both in their senior year of high school, and it is not certain if either of them will graduate. In their history course, they are assigned to two different teams.

Neither Bob nor Susan contribute to their team's project. On Susan's team, two bright and motivated students do all the work, earning the group a grade of B+. Bob's teammates, on the other hand, don't get along well, and aren't motivated. As a result, their final project is given a D-. Fortunately for Susan, her B+ enables her to squeak through the course with a barely passing grade, and she graduates from high school. Bob's D- does nothing for his poor average, and he does not graduate. Again, two students performing equally receive different grades!

7 Group Grades Convey the Wrong Message.

The grading practices we choose affect students' values. They can communicate a healthy message: Whatever your ability, the harder you try, the more you will learn, and, in turn, the better your grade will be. But what if we tell students their grades are partially a function of forces entirely out of their control—namely, what their teammates do? What happens when students perceive a weakened relationship between their own efforts and their ultimate reward? First, they will be less motivated. But they may also become alienated from the entire education process.

⑧ Group Grades Violate Individual Accountability. When students know that they will be held individually accountable for their learning or performance (one of the basic principles of cooperative learning), they are more likely to achieve more. The group grade, however, breaks this one-to-one connection between what one does and the grade one receives. If a team consists of one high-, two middle-, and one low-achieving student, the team's best strategy is for the two middle-achieving students to keep the low achiever occupied while the high achiever completes the project! This is a reasonable, adaptive strategy when all that counts for the grade is the final group product.

⑨ Group Grades Create Resistance to Cooperative Learning. Many teachers attending my workshops relate how their own son or daughter has been victimized by group grades. The stories are usually similar: "My child is very bright and motivated. He or she was put on a team with some low achievers who did no work, so my child worked doubly hard, yet received a lower grade." Among parents, this is one of the greatest sources of resistance to cooperative learning.

⑩ Group Grades Evaluate the Wrong Entity. The unit of evaluation in education is the individual student, not the group. Like it or not, grading is a high-stakes operation. An individual student's grades determine that individual's fate. It is the individual student who receives a grade on his/her report card. It is the individual student who may be held back a year, must retake the class, or must attend summer school. It is the individual student who receives or is denied the diploma or scholarship. It is the individual student who is denied admission to the university. And it is the individual who applies for a job. Unlike team sports, where the whole team wins or loses, there is no group contingency in our present educational system. Therefore, there should not be group grades either.

⑪ Group Grades Miss the Mark. The fundamental purpose of grading an individual is to evaluate the degree to which students have mastered content knowledge or have mastered skills. Interaction with others promotes learning, but the measure of the learning is in the mind and body of the individual. How can we differentiate the degree to which individuals have independently mastered knowledge or skills if we assign collective grades?

⑫ Group Grades Could Be Challenged in Court. Because grades are often the basis for scholarships and admission to colleges and universities, any system that gives different grades to students whose achievement is comparable is not merely unfair, it should not hold up to legal scrutiny.

Group grades are untenable, impractical, and ineffective. If not group grades, then what type of grading should we use for cooperative learning? By now, you have probably guessed our stance. The acceptable alternative is what teachers have been doing for years—assigning individual grades based on individual learning and performance.

Group grades are untenable, impractical, and ineffective. The acceptable alternative is assigning individual grades based on individual learning and performance.

15.10

Kagan Cooperative Learning • Dr. Spencer Kagan & Miguel Kagan
Kagan Publishing • 1 (800) 933-2667 • www.KaganOnline.com

Learning Together, Testing Alone

Teamwork is a terrific tool for practice and learning. But if we want valid, fair grades, they must be based on individual learning and performance.

Cooperative Practice and Learning Structures

Each cooperative learning structure is designed to promote a specific type of learning. There are numerous structures designed to help students master information, skills, and procedures. Other structures promote the development of thinking skills, communication skills, and social skills. All cooperative learning structures are designed to promote learning, not grading. We must make a clear distinction between learning, assessment, and grading. We structure learning cooperatively to promote engagement and enhance under-standing and retention. If we want to know how students and teams are doing—what they know and what they still need to learn—we assess individuals and teams. But we don't assign grades to cooperative processes or products, at least not collective grades that feed into individual report cards.

Team Test-Taking. A chapter on evaluation would be remiss if we did not highlight Team Test-Taking. In Team Test-Taking, teammates take a practice test individually. Then they team up to review their answers. Each teammate has a role that is rotated with each problem. The role of the Leader is to lead the team in sharing their answers. "What did everyone get for problem 1?" The role of the Checker is to check if everyone got the same answer. "It looks like we have different answers; let's do this problem together." The Coach leads the team in coaching the student(s) who need help. And finally, the Cheerleader celebrates correct answers or the teamwork process. "Great tutoring team!"

Notice two things about Team Test-Taking. First, students take the test individually. Why? There needs to be Individual Accountability. Students learn more if they are held individually accountable for their actions. If they took the test as a team, not all students would necessarily need to answer each problem. Students could hide behind teammates who knew the answers.

Second, notice that this is a practice test. For the real test, each student is on his/her own again. Each student receives his/her individual grade, based on his/her individual performance on the test.

Individual Accountability, Individual Grades

How can we assign individual grades if students work so closely together during cooperative learning? If we want to give students fair and accurate grades, but we regularly have them working in teams, are we limited to individual quizzes and tests? Isn't it too difficult to disentangle individual products and performance from team products and performance? Not if we remember the principle of Individual Accountability.

Even during cooperative learning, we require of students individual public performances. We structure learning tasks so that students are responsible for a public exhibit to a partner, to teammates, or to the teacher. Without Individual Accountability, we have group work. In group work, we have no mechanisms in place to ensure that each individual student is participating and learning. In *Chapter 12: Basic Principles (PIES)*, we examined how we can isolate individual performance before teamwork (Me Before We), during teamwork (Me During We), and after teamwork (Me After We). All of these individual performances are candidates for individual evaluation. Take a team project for example:

- Me Before We. ***Students independently research the topic.*** *We can have students turn in their own research papers for a grade.*
- Me During We. ***The teacher divides the labor so each student has a responsibility.*** *We can grade students on their mini-topic or portion of the team project or presentation.*
- Me After We. ***Students solve the problem or re-create part of the project independently.*** *We can use tests, quizzes, performance evaluations, or portfolios to grade each student independently.*

If we use cooperative learning correctly and structure for individual accountability, there are plenty of opportunities for individual evaluations.

Chapter Summary

Cooperative learning facilitates formative, authentic, representative, and multi-dimensional assessment. In cooperative learning, we have students interact frequently, create cooperative projects, and perform team presentations. As we observe students work together, listen in to their team and pair conversations, and use all-student-response structures, we understand not just what our brightest students learned, but where our whole class stands and where each student stands.

Assessing our students and class on an ongoing basis is a powerful ally to improving our instruction, and helping every student take the next step forward. If they aren't getting it, then we really haven't taught it. We don't wait to grade a test to find out what they know—by then, it's too late!

Cooperative learning is a time for, as the name suggests, students to learn together. It's not called "cooperative grading." When it comes time to grade students, the most fair and appropriate way is to grade students based on their individual performance—not on what their teammates know or did. Even the most cooperative projects can and should have individual accountability components (before, during, and after teamwork) that we use to evaluate students' learning. Even though we have students work in teams to learn, we give students individual grades which are a true measure of their performance, and individual feedback to help each student reach his or her full potential.

Chapter Questions

▶ Questions for Review

1. What is the difference between formative assessment and summative assessment?
2. Why is traditional Q & A unrepresentative?
3. What is authentic assessment?
4. Describe what the Walkabout looks like.
5. Describe one structure for each of the following types of response:
   1) Every-Student-Responds, 2) Every-Team-Responds, and 3) Physical Response.
6. Describe several arguments against group grades.

▶ Questions for Thinking and Discussion

1. Are group grades acceptable if they contribute only slightly to students' grades?
2. Do you agree or disagree with the argument against group grades?
   Which argument for or against group grades resonates most with you?
3. What might you learn by listening in to a team?
   What might you do with your newly learned information?
4. What is the difference between a team score on the sports field and a group grade in the classroom?
5. What does it mean to say someone is in favor of team assessment, but against team grading?
6. Have you ever received a group grade? How did it make you feel?
7. Describe a way to ensure representative assessment that is quick and involves no downtime for the class.

References

[1] Rowe, M. "Wait Time: Slowing Down May Be a Way of Speeding Up." *American Educator.* 1987, 11: 38–43, 47.

[2] Rowe, M. *Wait-Time and Rewards as Intructional Variables, Their Influences in Language, Logic, and Fate Control.* Paper presented at the National Association for Research in Science Teaching. Chicago, IL: 1972.

[3] Kagan, S. & M. Kagan. *Multiple Intelligences.* San Clemente, CA: Kagan Publishing, 1998.

[4] Tomlinson, C. *Fulfilling the Promise of the Differentiated Classroom: Strategies and Tools for Responsive Teaching.* Alexandria, VA: Association for Supervision & Curriculum Development, 2003.

[5] Kagan, S. "Group Grades Miss the Mark." *Educational Leadership,* 1995, 52(8): 68–71.

[6] Kagan, S. "Avoiding the Group-Grades Trap." *Learning,* 1996, 24(4): 56–58.

Resources

AnswerBoards. San Clemente, CA: Kagan Publishing. www.KaganOnline.com

SelectorTools™ Software. San Clemente, CA: Kagan Publishing. www.KaganOnline.com

Student Selector Spinners. San Clemente, CA: Kagan Publishing. www.KaganOnline.com

Motivation Without Rewards & Competition

Every teacher dreams of highly motivated students. Cooperative learning neatly sidesteps the many pitfalls in the motivation game, providing an enormous variety of proven, positive motivators.

How do we motivate our student teams? At workshops, teachers frequently ask, "What can I do with the reluctant learner?" "What if my students don't want to work together?" Every teacher dreams of highly motivated students. Creating the will to learn is more than half the battle—once there is a will, there is a way. Motivated students find a way to succeed.

There are common pitfalls in the motivation game—things many teachers try that backfire. Cooperative learning offers a large of array of positive alternatives.

Some early models of cooperative learning were based on competition between teams and rewards for team performance. Years ago, researchers explaining the success of cooperative learning attributed its success to its reward structure. Do we motivate students by pitting teams against one another? Do we offer teams rewards for winning, working well together, completing a task, or creating fabulous work? It is tempting. Competition and rewards arouse student interest and excitement.

However, both rewards and competition are rife with problems. It is now firmly established that certain kinds of rewards erode intrinsic motivation.[1] We defeat our very mission of turning students onto the curriculum and learning. Rewards may motivate students in the moment, but the rewards drive them away from the content once they are removed. Rewards are not the answer.

Competition is not the answer either. In most forms of competition, there is one winner and many losers—not a good ratio. Why would we want to unnecessarily turn our many winners into losers? When students consistently lose, they understandably withdraw from the system that attacks their self worth. Competition in the short term may produce enthusiasm, but in the long run, competition undermines motivation and creates a hostile learning environment.

Our current model of cooperative learning has evolved over the decades; it little resembles its predecessors. Competition and rewards have fallen by the wayside. Yet this new kind of cooperative learning is more motivating than ever. We continue to produce impressive results without the negative side effects of rewards and competition. In this chapter, first we will detail the problems with rewards and competition, and then examine numerous positive alternatives that work to create a high degree of engagement and motivation.

Motivational Pitfalls
The Reward Pitfall

Over thirty-five years ago, controversial research suggested that expected, tangible rewards undermine intrinsic motivation.[2] It was so controversial at the time because psychology as a field was enamored with Skinner's behavior theory that showed reinforcement—rewards following behavior—could be used to increase desired behaviors. If we set up the right reward contingencies, we could get animals to behave differently. The theory was applied to humans. "If you do this, you will get that." In classrooms, the "reinforcement" included points, gold stars, and certificates to improve student discipline and raise performance. But it turns out schoolchildren are not pigeons nor rats. They have complex brains. And they have a strong need for self-determination and autonomy.

Rewards have become a bad word in education, albeit hardly less ubiquitous. Alfie Kohn, perhaps the most recognized name in the battle against inducements, presents an eloquent and provocative indictment of rewards in his book *Punished by Rewards*.[3] For a comprehensive argument against rewards, we recommend his book. Here we'll summarize some key arguments against rewards supported by numerous studies.

Rewards Erode Intrinsic Motivation

The most damaging blow against rewards is that tangible, expected rewards diminish students' intrinsic motivation. Rewards can make a task less pleasurable for its own sake and decrease the likelihood students will continue to perform once the rewards are withheld. For example, let's say we reward students for solving a kind of problem, and they begin to work for the reward. If then we take away the reward, they will be significantly less likely to choose to do more problems on their own. When they are asked if the task for which they were rewarded interests them or not, they report much less interest in the task. Decades of research and hundreds of studies have confirmed the finding that expected tangible rewards undermine intrinsic motivation.[4] We erode students' interest in a task when

Rewards Erode Intrinsic Motivation

Imagine two scenarios:

Scenario 1: No Reward

I give you several interesting puzzles to solve. You enjoy solving the puzzles and feel pleased and proud as you solve each one. I ask you if you would like to solve more. Having found the puzzles intrinsically interesting and rewarding, you say yes.

Scenario 2: Reward

I give you the same puzzles to solve. You enjoy solving the puzzles and feel pleased and proud as you solve each one. Then I tell you I will give you $100 for each puzzle you solve. You continue solving the puzzles and are excited to receive the $100 for each. I ask you if you would like to solve more puzzles but say, "This time I can only give you one cent for each puzzle you solve." You decline the offer.

Why? In Scenario 2, you made an attribution shift. You saw yourself as solving the puzzles for the money, not for the intrinsic rewards of solving the puzzles. When the money was taken away, you saw no reason to solve more puzzles.

The Question: Do we want our students working for tokens, or for the rewards of learning? Do we want to build a love of learning or a love of tokens?

we reward them in a way that they begin working for the reward.

The reason rewards can erode intrinsic motivation is explained by an *attribution shift*. Students switch their attribution from "I'm doing this task because it is enjoyable," to "I am doing this task to get the reward." The implications of these findings are clear. We should not aim to control our students and teams with expected, tangible rewards. We should not set up incentive systems that say, if you work hard on this team project, or if your team finishes your assigned work on time, or if you all get an A on your test, you will get a reward. Although the prize may appear to serve its intended purpose—to get students to work harder, faster, or longer—it is actually counterproductive. It diminishes students' interest in the curriculum. Our mission as educators is to turn students on to the curriculum, not away from it. It is our job to ignite a passion, enthusiasm, and curiosity, not a repulsion.

Rewards Don't Improve Performance

Research on rewards demonstrates that people perform poorly in situations in which they begin working for a reward.[5] In numerous experiments, compared to the reward group, the no-reward control group were more creative, solved problems quicker, continued improving longer, and got more correct answers. If we want our students and student teams to perform well, although it may seem counterintuitive, in the long run, giving rewards will usually hinder performance.

Rewards Don't Sustain Motivation

Expected tangible rewards kill interest. So it may come as no surprise that these types of rewards don't work to effect lasting change. If we give tangible rewards to students, then remove the rewards, we in essence remove the motivation for continuing to do the task. As teachers, our goals are to help our students become more excited about the curriculum, to persist in the face of adversity, to cooperate with teammates, and to better understand the content. Bribing students to perform works against these

goals. Initially, students become excited about the opportunity for a reward. But once the reward becomes the goal, learning is devalued. Learning becomes merely the means to get a token or a gold star; it is not valued for its own sake. When we remove the goodies, goodbye motivation.

Rewards Violate Brain-Based Learning Principles

Based on brain science, we can now say with some certainty that what we need to do to align our instruction with how brains best perceive, process, retain, and recall information. That is, we know how to teach in ways the brain best learns: To produce meaningful, enduring learning, students need to connect new learning with prior knowledge and personal experience. Students need to make curricular links, so new learning can be integrated into their cognitive scheme and not suffer the disappearing fate of disparate facts. We need to make learning more emotionally salient; emotional learning is better remembered. Students should be perceptive, take in peripheral information, and strive to make sense of the different types of input. Students should process the information they take in, seek patterns, and construct meaning. This type of processing increases neuronal connections in the brain and enhances understanding and retention. Learning for the sake of rewards flies in the face of these important brain-based learning principles. Not only do students perform worse on learning tasks, but their focus is more limited.

The following is an adaptation of an experimental study: One pair of students is told that if they master the vocabulary words on their flashcards, they will get a reward. Another pair is given the same deck of flashcards and told to master the words, but not offered an incentive. There also happens to be a small picture on each card. After the practice session, the students are tested not on their mastery of the vocabulary words, but on how many words they can match with the picture on the card. Guess which pair wins? Who is better at incidental learning? The pair not offered the prize. When offered a reward, students focus narrowly on what needs to be done to gain the reward and shut their eyes to what they consider extraneous information. True learning is not a straight line between points A and B. We want to open our students' minds, not shut them down.

The Competitive and Comparative Pitfalls

Using competition between students and between teams is alluring. It appears to create excitement and interest. Teams will work fast and furious to beat other teams. But beware: Competition is a trap. Let's see why.

Competition is the Worst Reward Contingency

Why are we opposed to competitive reward structures? The answer is simple: They are detrimental to our students. Edward Deci and his colleagues who have thoroughly researched rewards and intrinsic motivation conclude:

"Tangible extrinsic rewards reliably undermine intrinsic motivation under most circumstances, and, interestingly the most detrimental reward contingency involves giving rewards as a direct function of people's performance. Those who perform best get the most rewards and those who perform less well get less (or no) rewards. This contingency, which is perhaps the one most often used in life, seems to be the one that is most detrimental to the motivation, performance, and well-being of the individuals subjected to it." [6]

Competition Erodes Motivation

Losing teams become less motivated. One of my favorite examples of this occurred years ago when I was called in to consult with a principal who was having trouble motivating the pupils in her school to increase the number of books they read. She had set up what she thought would be a motivating competitive reward system, but it had backfired. What had she done? She had three classes per grade and had told the classes that the class that read the most books each month would get to have ice cream as a reward. The first month all the classes were highly motivated, and as per plan one class at each grade level won the ice cream treat. The second month, at most grade levels, the same class won again. By the third month, motivation in the non-winning classes at each grade level was markedly down. "Oh we don't care about that stupid ice cream" became the rationale to cover for the reality, "We don't want to try again and feel the disappointment of losing again." It is safer not to play than to play, knowing you probably will experience the pain of another loss.

> *"People have been known to achieve more as a result of working with others than against them."*
> —Dr. Allan Fromme

To solve the problem, we instituted a cooperative group reward alternative. We posted a huge school thermometer in the cafeteria and announced that every book read by every child would be counted toward school rewards. When the thermometer reached certain levels, everyone would get an ice cream treat. Further, when the thermometer reached the top, there would be a "sleep in" with a professional reader. Students, teachers, and the principal would come to school in their pajamas, blanket, and pillow; they would have a late night with the professional reader as the main attraction. All the classes encouraged each other to read lots of books—the students wanted to see the principal in pajamas!

It was a classic case of converting negative interdependence into positive interdependence. When the between-class competition was in place, students actually hoped students from other classes would not read many books; when the cooperative group reward was instituted, students encouraged each other—anyone's gain helped everyone. Competition erodes motivation in two ways: 1) there is less mutual support and encouragement; 2) losers lose interest in playing the game.

Competition Erodes Community

Positive interdependence is one of the basic principles of cooperative learning. We endeavor to create situations in the class where students feel they are on the same side, and that the success of one student contributes to the success of another. Positive interdependence motivates students to work together and to help each other learn. It promotes collaboration and sharing. It creates a sense of community and a feeling that students are in this together.

But when we have students compete, we create a situation of negative interdependence. Students no longer see themselves on the same side. They are opponents. They must beat out classmates to reap rewards. Helping and sharing are replaced with hindering and hoping for the failure of others. Competition erodes the positive sense of community.

Competition Creates Anxiety

Competition has a different effect on different people. Some people are excited about competition and successfully manage their competitive juices to achieve success. For many, however, competition breeds stress and anxiety. Many link performance in competition with the establishment of their personal identity; poor performance diminishes their sense of self-worth. Stress and anxiety have a deleterious effect on learning, memory, performance, and concentration. Situations in which we perceive threat release stress hormones that interfere with perception, cognition, and the establishment of memory for new learning. Competition, for many students, creates a hostile environment and a brain less primed to learn.

Challenging the Gifted

If we compare our students to each other, the academically gifted will come up on top. Often, there is a large enough discrepancy between the gifted students and the rest of the class that the gifted student doesn't really need to exert much effort to outperform peers. The inherent hazard here is that it is easy for the student and the teacher to become complacent. When exceptional students are compared to the rest of the class, it is easy for the teacher to feel they are smart enough. If instead, we compare students to themselves or to a standard of excellence, there is always a next step. No student is ever too smart or too good to improve.

Struggling Students and Success

The opposite is true for struggling students. When we compare our struggling students to the rest of the class, they often come out on the bottom. This breeds negative expectations in the teacher that can perpetuate the problem. This can also create a defeatist attitude. "I'll never be as good as Susie." Or, "I'm just not very smart." When we compare students to their prior performance or their potential, we never write off struggling students as the classroom losers. Through positive attention and encouragement, we can help each student take the next step in their personal development.

Why have we as a democratic society and as a democratic educational system settled so universally on such an elitist reward system?

Competition Creates More Losers than Winners

In the competitive and comparative classroom, there are a scarce number of rewards. Only some students will get the teacher's attention, praise, top prize, or best grades. They will be the winners. The "A" students. The teacher's pets. The rest will fall anywhere between second place and flat-out losers. With fewer rewards for the lowest achievers—the students who most need encouragement—we have created in our classrooms the quintessential hierarchy. Why have we as a democratic society and as a democratic educational system settled so universally on such an elitist reward system? Why do we need to artificially limit the amount of praise, high grades, and recognition? We say it is to motivate and reward students, but we have better alternatives—ways to motivate not just our best students, but all our students.

Motivational Strategies that Work

There are numerous positive ways we can motivate our students without the negative side effects of competition and rewards. We focus here on motivation for a cooperative classroom, but many of these strategies apply to good teaching in any classroom.

In Praise of Praise

There are many reasons we favor a praise-rich classroom:

Intrinsic Motivation. We are advocates of praise in the classroom.[7] We are especially fond of getting our teammates and classmates praising each other. Others, however, equate praise with rewards and admonish against its use. They cite the research that rewards erode intrinsic motivation. Close analysis of the research reveals that verbal praise and tangible, expected rewards are very different and have opposite effects. Unlike expected, tangible rewards, research finds verbal rewards or positive feedback enhances intrinsic motivation as measured by free-choice behavior and self-reported interest.[8]

There are two likely explanations why praise works to increase motivation while tangible, expected rewards erode intrinsic motivation. First is the notion of *attribution shift*. When students are told they will receive a reward if they work on the task, they may shift their attribution so that they feel they are working for the reward. This is very different from a teammate saying, "Great idea, Kyle!" The praise is taken as a compliment, not a payment for doing the task. The second explanation is praise often serves to increase *perceived competence*. We are more internally motivated to do things we feel we can be good at or succeed in. Students who are praised for their efforts feel, "Hey, I'm good at this. I feel proud. I'd like to do more of this!"

Self-Esteem. Everyone has a need to feel competent, important, and loved. When we receive a compliment, it feels good. It makes us feel good about ourselves. Students with a fragile sense of self are often the same students who are academically at risk. If we can help boost students' self-image with some kind and true words, why would we ever withhold praise?

Positive Classroom Atmosphere. Not only do we feel good about ourselves when we receive praise and compliments, we feel good about those who dispense the adulation. When we as teachers praise our students, students like us more and are more

Praise Increases Motivation

Let's contrast two scenarios:

Scenario 1: Praise

A student loves solving geometry problems. As the student is completing a problem, the teacher walks by and says, "You are fully engaged; your proofs are clear and logical!" The student was not expecting the praise, and certainly was not doing the problem in order to get the praise. The student experiences a flush of pride.

Scenario 2: Rewards

A student loves solving geometry problems. The teacher announces that for each problem students solve, they will receive a token. The tokens can later be traded for desired candy and other rewards. The student works hard, solving many problems, and takes pride in earning many tokens.

What's the Difference? Later we assess the intrinsic motivation of the two students. We want to determine how motivated the two students are to solve geometry problems when there are no extrinsic rewards. We test the students in two ways: 1) we give them a choice to do more problems on their own; and 2) we ask them how much they like solving geometry problems, how interested they are in geometry. If the results follow the pattern established by studies on the impact of reward v. praise on intrinsic motivation, we find the student who got the unexpected verbal compliment has increased intrinsic motivation whereas the student who received the expected tokens has decreased intrinsic motivation.

cooperative. They are more eager to learn. When classmates and teammates shell out the goodwill, it helps contribute to a safe and positive learning community conducive to taking risks and learning.

Positive Feedback.
Feedback is important for learning. It can be argued that there is little difference between praise and positive feedback. When we tell a student without emotion, "That's correct, Johnny," we just as well may be saying, "Great job, that's correct, Johnny." Feedback carries a valence, positive and negative. Whether we like it or not, positive feedback is tantamount to praise. Negative feedback, even when we attempt to sugarcoat it, is often equated with criticism. Eliminating praise is in essence eliminating positive feedback. If we go down the route of omitting all positive comments, the feedback we provide our students is lopsided on the negative side.

Pro-Academic Peer Norms.
Students thirst for peer approval. Peer pressure is that social force peers exert on a student to act a certain way or do a certain thing. We blame peer pressure when a good kid gets in with the wrong crowd and begins behaving badly. But, peer pressure is a powerful force we can harness for good. When we structure our classrooms so that teammates praise each other for positive performance, we have created positive peer pressure, which promotes achievement.

Positive Emotion and Retrograde Memory.
Brain research reveals that emotion plays a pivotal role in learning. Emotions influence what we attend to. Emotions make the content memorable. Neurons in the brain actually fire at an increased rate when emotion is involved. At a chemical level, arousal is a bath of norepinepherine, adrenaline, enkephalin, vasopressin, and more. These chemicals act as memory fixatives.[9] The limbic system, our emotional center, signals the brain, "Pay attention. Remember this." Positive emotion enhances attention and retention.

Further, studies on retrograde memory suggest that we can enhance remembrance with positive emotion not only during but even following the learning task.[10] When students receive praise from their peers or from their teacher, the praise triggers reward centers in the brain, releasing positive chemicals that cement learning.

Praise and Kagan Structures.
Many of the Kagan Structures have built-in praise and celebrations to take advantage of the beneficial effects of team-based verbal celebrations. For example, in RallyCoach, one student works on a problem while a partner coaches. When the student solves the problem correctly, his coach offers praise. Like all the other Kagan Structures that have verbal praise as part of the steps of the structures, RallyCoach can be done without praise. Yet, praise is included in many structures to enhance positive emotions and to contribute to the cooperative class tone. Praise is a signal to students that their teammates are on their side, hoping for their success. Students feel support and are more likely to strive for future achievement.

> *"He who praises everybody praises nobody."*
> —Samuel Johnson
>
> *"He who praises nobody has misinterpreted the research on rewards and extrinsic motivation."*
> —Spencer Kagan

Praising Tips

Here are some tips to make the most of praise in the classroom. We share these tips with students so they too can use effective praise.

- **Make it specific.** "I really liked your idea of making the four corners of the house self-supported."
- **Promote self-validation.** "How do you feel about your accomplishment?"
- **Make it public.** "Everyone, look at what the Wiz Kids just did! Isn't it awesome the way they…!"
- **Use genuine appreciation.** Do not use insincere flattery. Praise behavior that deserves it.
- **Avoid praise for overly simple tasks.** Use praise lavishly, but be careful not to make it meaningless.
- **Use surprising and delightful praisers.** Unexpected praise produces emotions that cement learning.

Teambuilding

An important dimension of teambuilding is having fun together. As part of teambuilding, students create team cheers, team handshakes, and team celebrations. They use these celebrations as a regular part of academic learning. Teambuilding has a spill-over effect, boosting academic achievement. The team that just had a great time designing their team tower yesterday is more motivated to work together on some difficult problems today. See *Chapter 10: Teambuilding*.

Classbuilding

Classbuilding is Teambuilding's whole-class counterpart. Students engage in fun and motivating whole-class activities. Classbuilding makes learning fun, creates a sense of belonging and support, and creates a motivational context for learning. For a variety of ideas and activities to enhance the classroom climate and to make learning more fun and motivating, See *Chapter 9: Classbuilding*.

Make the Curriculum Motivating

If the curriculum is boring, we may feel the need to motivate students with bribes. But without a great deal of effort, we can make our curriculum intrinsically fun and intriguing. The anticipatory set is a great way to open lessons with a bang (perhaps literally in science). The set serves as an introduction to the lesson, but is also the lesson's "attention getter." Rote memorization is often dubbed "drill and kill" because it kills meaningful learning and student motivation. There are other ways for students to learn basic facts. A number of Kagan Structures, such as Numbered Heads Together, RallyCoach, Quiz-Quiz-Trade, and the Flashcard Game, add a motivating social component to mastery-oriented learning. Another approach is to embed the basic facts in meaningful experiences or stories. See the box at left for numerous tips to make the curriculum motivating.

> *"Whatever we expect with confidence becomes our own self-fulfilling prophecy."*
> —Brian Tracy

Tips for Making the Curriculum Motivating

- **Promote interaction:** "Share with your partner…."
- **Tell stories:** "Did I ever tell you the story about…?
- **Make it personal:** "How would you have felt if…."
- **Evoke emotion:** Make students laugh. Make them angry at the villain.
- **Pose provocative questions:** "Why don't spiders stick to their own webs?"
- **Share interesting anecdotes:** "Did you know the microwave was invented when a researcher walked by a radar tube and a chocolate bar melted in his pocket?"
- **Role-play characters:** Dress as Abe Lincoln and describe why you opposed secession.
- **Integrate freak incidents:** In England, it actually rained small fish called sprats. How is this possible?
- **Point out interesting phenomena:** Astronauts become taller in space. Their bones are less squashed together by Earth's gravity.
- **Share strange statistics:** Of the total time watching TV and talking with a parent, the average child spends 3% of the time talking with a parent and 97% of the time watching TV!

High Expectations

In the classic Pygmalion studies, teachers were told that students were tested, and some were identified to be on the brink of rapid intellectual growth.[11] In truth, the students were randomly selected. Later, the targeted students showed superior performance on IQ tests, leading researchers to conclude that teachers' expectations for their students became a self-fulfilling prophecy.

If we want our students to be highly motivated, we expect with confidence that our students are motivated, or at least that they can become motivated. See the box below for some expectations Do's and Don'ts.

The Do's and Don'ts of High Expectations

What to Do

- Have high expectations for all students. "I expect good things from this class."
- Suspend initial judgments of students, giving all students an equal chance.
- Monitor students frequently and objectively to keep a real and current understanding of their ability.
- Look for the good in every student.
- Communicate high expectations to students. "I know you can do this if you set your mind to it."
- Give students or the class a good reputation to live up to. "I can't wait to see what this creative team comes up with."

What Not to Do

- Don't hold preconceptions of gender, race, or socioeconomic status.
- Don't form quick and lasting impressions of students.
- Don't make negative comments to yourself or others about students.
- Don't track students in static ability groups.
- Don't label students as "lazy," "unmotivated," or "window watcher."
- Don't give into the "halo effect," witnessing one negative characteristic and making unfounded general assumptions about the student.
- Avoid letting the comments of others jaundice your own observations.
- Don't compare students to each other. "Johnny did it. Can you do it?"

The Interaction Incentive

Students crave social interaction.[12] Cooperative learning empowers us to parlay that need to socialize into engaged interaction over the curriculum. The interaction can be as simple as a quick RoundRobin or a Timed Pair Share to have students discuss, "What do you find most interesting about the subject?" Or the student-to-student interaction can be a fully engaging multi-structural lesson. The opportunity to express one's ideas, hear the ideas of others, and interact in the classroom is a tremendously motivating force. The Kagan Structures offer a full menu of instructional strategies to create interaction and engagement with any curriculum.

Appeal to Virtue

Educators have embraced character education. There is a universal set of virtues worthy of fostering in students. Among the list of virtues are a few germane to student motivation, namely cooperation, creativity, industriousness, fairness, perseverance, and responsibility. We can motivate students by appealing to their sense of virtue, encouraging good character and discouraging poor character. For example, for engendering creativity as students prepare to work on a team project, "You are my creative class. Show me how creative you can be with your projects." For encouraging responsibility, "Everyone has an important part to play. Your teammates are counting on you." We can motivate students to be creative, to be fair, and to be cooperative by appealing to and developing their sense of virtue.

Instill a Sense of Excellence

Some people seem to excel at everything. They may be talented or smart. But it isn't always their smarts or ability that is the secret of their success. They are simply more motivated. What motivates them? For many, it boils down to one simple virtue: Excellence. It is this pursuit of excellence that drives them to try harder and study longer.

This core value pervades the Japanese work ethic, and is cited as the key to Japan's success.[13] The Japanese term, *Kaizen*, means continuous improvement by doing things better and ratcheting standards higher. How do we instill this philosophy into our students? One way is to imbue the value of excellence. We can nurture pride in one's work. Reflection is a powerful method to do this. For example, the teacher can do a quick Timed Pair Share on, "What are you most proud of about your project?" Or students can independently write then RoundRobin share their answers to the question, "If we were to do the project again, how could we improve it?" If we can instill in our students the desire to excel and to improve on past performance, we have gone a long way toward motivating our class.

Team on Team Competition

We outlined the problems with competition. But that is not to say we can never use team competition. Incredible feats, amazing performances, and positive character virtues are forged in the crucible of competition. In a public education system where our goal is to "leave no child behind," we must be weary of an imbalance of competition where the success of a few is bought at the expense of everyone else. A form of team competition that multiplies the number of winners is team-on-team competition. Instead of one team in the class winning, and everyone else losing, we can allow half the class teams to win and the other half to come in second place by using team contests. In team contests, two teams face off. There is a first place and a second place team. There are no losers. Occasional team competition and team contests are probably good for students, but in the cooperative class, there are always more cooperative class goals and within team cooperation.

Create a Challenge

Students respond to a challenge, much in the same way they respond to intergroup competition, with great zeal. Unlike team competition, challenges don't create negative interdependence and don't carry the baggage that comes with winning and losing teams. With challenges, teams can work toward a teacher-defined goal. Or the teams can work cooperatively toward the class goal. They don't have to work against each other.

- **Quantity of responses:** "Let's see how many ideas your team can come up with toward the class goal."
- **Quality of a product:** "Can your team create a toothpick bridge that will hold six science textbooks?"
- **Time limit:** "Let's see if you can solve the problem in five minutes."

To motivate students, we throw down the gauntlet and watch teams take it up.

Take an Interest

Think of a teacher who took a special interest in you. Did you try harder in that class? "Students don't care how much we know until they know how much we care." This commonly quoted educational insight speaks volumes about motivation. Take an interest in your students and watch them become more motivated to learn in your classroom. Ask them about their weekend. Ask them about their hobbies and favorites. Ask them about their classwork. Show a genuine curiosity in what they've done. Listen attentively as students talk about their work. Connect with them. When we are interested in our students, they're motivated to perform well in our class.

Convey a Positive Attitude

Here's a simple truth: We work harder for those who have a positive attitude. Here's another truth: A positive attitude is contagious; and so is a negative attitude. Think of your favorite teacher. Did he or she have a positive or negative attitude? If we can genuinely convey that we like class, school, and the subject matter, it improves student motivation.

Share Your Enthusiasm

It is often said that high school teachers go into teaching for love of the subject. Many teachers have an appreciation for and an affinity toward the curriculum. Ignite students' passion for the curriculum by sharing your own interests in the curriculum. What turns you on about geometry proofs? Why do you find this historical event so fascinating?

Create Relevance

Students turn off to some learning with the un- spoken attitude that, "We're never going to need this in the real world." They cannot see the link between what they are learning and how they will apply it in their own life. The curriculum has no relevance. If there truly is no relevance, then it's time for us to re-examine our curriculum. But if there is, we need to point it out. We need to have students hear or discover why the curriculum is important, how they can use it in their lives, and who uses it often in the real world. When we introduce multiplication to students, we have them interview adults on how they use that skill and do a Team Interview to report back to teammates.

> "If I accept you as you are, I will make you worse; however if I treat you as though you are what you are capable of becoming, I help you become that."
> —Johann Wolfgang von Goethe

The Mission Incentive

Individuals are motivated by a sense of mission. Volunteers work for a charitable cause. Doctors donate time and expertise to provide international medical assistance. Lawyers take on pro bono cases. Teachers enter the profession to make a difference. We work hard for something we believe in. In our classrooms, that something can be a service learning project or a charitable contribu- tion, a class or school beauti- fication project, or simply increasing the number of tardy-free days. If students have a clear vision, they can rally around the cause. Create an emotional commit- ment to performance.

From Status to Prestige

Status is the relative position of individuals in a group. For there to be high-status individuals, there need to be low-status individuals. In most classrooms, the high-status students are the smart, participa- tory students. The low-status students are the daydreamers and dolts. Having students compete for high status is an age-old teaching technique to motivate some students to succeed. High- status students listen attentively, raise their hands, and study to get in the teacher's good graces and to be held in high esteem. But on the flip side, be- ing relegated to low status is a blow to a student's esteem. Who wants to be looked down upon by the teacher and peers? Students who do not win the competition for those coveted high-status positions disengage and seek attention in, shall we say politely, less productive ways.

By definition, we can't give everyone a high status. There would be no relative position. Everyone would have the same, equal status. And that's exactly what we're advocating to motivate more students. Everyone should be equal. But not equal in the sense of average or mediocre. Instead, every student and the class should be held in high esteem. Everyone gets a high stand- ing. Everyone gets prestige. "You are a brilliant class!" Or, "Do I have awesome teams in my class, or what?" Like high expectations, when we give all students an excellent reputation to live up to, many will do just that.

Novel Instructional Strategies

How we teach students can also motivate our unmotivated students. If we always teach the same way, it becomes monotonous. Our brains attend to novel stimuli. If we always rely on the same teaching strategy, or small set of strategies, there is little novelty or excitement. We use a wide range of cooperative structures to keep instruc- tion fresh and interesting. If students are bored, we mix it up. We use a variety of structures and introduce new structures to heighten novelty, interest, and motivation.

A Sense of Accomplishment

There is great joy in learning something new, solving a difficult problem, creating a novel solution, putting on a wonderful perfor- mance, displaying complete mastery of the subject matter. We teach teams cheers and celebrations and encourage teams to take pride in their accomplishments. If it is worth celebrating, it is mean- ingful and motivating.

Emphasize Good Work, Not Good Grades

Grades are a form of reward. They can punish like rewards too. If our students are doing the work for the grade, they are performing for an extrinsic reward, not for the inherent interest in the curriculum. As with rewards, we must be careful not to dangle grades in front of students to motivate them to work harder, faster, longer, or better. We encourage good work and getting smarter, and place far less emphasis on good grades.

Public Sharing and Feedback

As we discussed in detail in *Chapter 12: Basic Principles (PIES)*, individual accountability can be highly motivating. If individual public performance is required, students will work remarkably hard. If they know that they will present something to the class, and/or if the teacher and classmates will give them written or oral feedback on their performance, they are motivated to do a good job.

Team Goal Setting

Have teams set their own goals so they are intrinsically motivated to reach their targets. Here's a generic process for team goal setting that works with a variety of team tasks. First, announce the parameters of the task or project. For example, creating a team book. Before setting teams to work, have teams brainstorm performance goals. The goals should be very specific and measurable. "It should be a good book" is not a measurable goal. "The book should have illustrations on each page" is specific and measurable. Teams review the goals generated, and prioritize them. They pick goals they like and record them on a goal sheet. Next, they record specific jobs or activities they can do to reach each goal. Once the project or task is complete, the team revisits their goals and processes via writing or discussion if they achieved their goals, and why or why not.

Create Buy-In

When students "buy-in," they are motivated to participate. When they're not motivated, they "buy-out," or to put it in their words, they are "over it." How do we create student buy-in?

- Make the task seem do-able.
- Ask students for their suggestions and input.
- Let students state benefits, especially what's in it for them personally.
- Let students take ownership, contributing their own ideas.
- Make the task appear fun. "There will be a surprise when we have worked for ten minutes."
- Link the task to other enjoyable tasks. "Remember how much fun we had…."

Flow

Mihaly Csikszentmihalyi's Flow Theory has a lot to offer us as we seek to promote motivation in the classroom.[14] Mr. Csikszentmihalyi describes flow as:

> *"being completely involved in an activity for its own sake. The ego falls away. Time flies. Every action, movement, and thought follows inevitably from the previous one, like playing jazz. Your whole being is involved, and you're using your skills to the utmost."*

Wouldn't it be wonderful to have students completely engaged in learning, not for a grade, not for approval, not for status, but for its own sake? Flow occurs when we have the optimal match between the challenge of the learning task and the student's ability. If the challenge is too high, the task is too difficult, and the student becomes anxious. If the student is too skilled for the task, the student becomes bored. Flow occurs with developmentally appropriate learning tasks. Anxiety and boredom replace flow and undermine motivation when tasks are too hard or too easy. When we create learning projects that balance task difficulty with each student's skill level, we produce the optimal conditions for learning, enjoyment, and motivation. For more on Flow Theory, see *Chapter 4: Why Does Cooperative Learning Work?*

Bite-Sized Success

If we threw a child in a pool, he or she would likely drown. We wouldn't do that. But we do that in the classroom all too often. We throw students into tasks that exceed their ability. Challenge is good. But too much challenge leads to frustration and failure. Students need support much in the same way a child needs support in learning to swim. We break down the task into smaller pieces that children can master, one step at a time. First we hold the child in the water and develop a sense of aquatic comfort. Then we teach the child to kick. Then we practice blowing bubbles. Then we practice going under water, and so on. Students remain motivated to the extent they can be incrementally successful. When we don't scaffold for success with bite-sized learning tasks, our students are likely to flail, then drown.

Choice, Autonomy, and Internal Locus of Control

The concept of Locus of Control was developed by Julian Rotter in the 1950s.[15] The basic concept is that individuals either have an internal or external locus of control. You have an internal locus of control if you ascribe your successes and failures to your own actions. You have an external locus of control if you feel external agents, such as luck, the environment, or other factors outside your control, are responsible for your fate. Individuals with an internal locus of control feel more like kings than pawns and are more motivated. They attain higher levels than those who feel their destiny is out of their hands.

In the cooperative classroom, we encourage self-determination and autonomy by structuring learning tasks so students are not passive recipients of knowledge, but rather active creators of their own projects and understanding. Structures, such as Team Projects, Team Statements, and Jot Thoughts, empower students as the agents of construction and creativity. They see their outcomes as a product of their own efforts.

To the extent practical, we give our students choices. "What book would you like read?" "What topic would your team like to research?" "Which experiment would you rather do?" Students per-

Internal v. External Locus of Control

Event	Internal Control	External Control
Bad Grade	I am dumb. I didn't study.	Teacher is mean. I was unlucky. Test was too hard.
Good Grade	I am smart. I studied hard.	Teacher is nice. I was lucky. Test was easy.

If I attribute my outcomes to the teacher, luck, or other factors outside my control, I am not motivated to study harder. If I feel my outcomes are due to my efforts and ability, I am more motivated to study.

ceive a greater sense of autonomy when they are free to pursue their choices than when tasks are imposed on them. Decision-making structures, such as Sum-the-Ranks, Spend-A-Buck, and Proactive Prioritizing, allow teams to make their own decisions and foster a sense of internal control.

Another way we as teachers can promote students' internal locus of control is to ask questions and solicit student input instead of giving orders. Students generally resent being told what to do, but perform willingly if we ask questions or drop suggestions. Instead of "You need to…" we elicit student input, "Tell me about…" or "What do you think about…?" The greater sense of agency we give our students, the more they have a sense of autonomy and personal power, and the more motivated they are.

Chapter Summary

We opened this chapter with a difficult question: How do we motivate our student teams? If we take our students' perspective, motivation boils down to simple questions: Does it interest me? Will it benefit me? Am I any good at it?

When we assign tasks with no apparent relevance—with no sense of mission, without student input as to what is to be studied, how it is to be studied, and how it is to be evaluated—motivation plummets.

When we give tangible rewards to our students for completing a learning task, then ask "Does this task interest you?" students are more likely to say, "No." Rewards kill interest. The desire to get the reward supplants the intrinsic interest in the curriculum.

When we use competition, we create more losers than winners. If we then ask our students, "Are you any good at it?" an elite few say, "Yes," but the rest of the class answers, "No." We lower most students' perceived competence when we compare them to their classmates, and then add insult to injury by rewarding others for coming out ahead. Competition and rewards are not the answers for motivating students in the cooperative learning classroom, or in any classroom.

How do we get our students to say, "Yes, this does interest me," "Yes, this has payoff for me in my life," and "Yes, I am good at this."? Praise buoys students' perceived competence. Students feel a sense of pride when they are complimented by the teacher and classmates for their positive performance. When we expect our students to succeed, they live up to our high expectations. When our students help each other and contribute to a winning team, they become winners and feel more competent.

To spark and sustain student interest, we provide students choices allowing them to set learning goals. We use celebrations, teambuilding, class-buildling, and energizers to make the learning environment more fun and inviting. We make the curriculum more appealing to our students when we share our enthusiasm for learning and for the subject matter. And, of course, our best tool for creating student interest is to engage all of our students with interactive instructional strategies, coupled with intrinsically interesting content.

Chapter Questions

▶ Questions for Review

1. How docs the Kagan model of cooperative learning differ from earlier models of cooperative learning with regard to motivation and rewards?
2. What are three problems with expected, tangible rewards?
3. What are the pitfalls of using competition in the classroom?
4. What are three arguments in favor of the use of praise with cooperative learning?
5. What are three ways to motivate students and teams without using rewards?

▶ Questions for Thinking and Discussion

1. How do you handle competition personally? Do you always perform your best?
2. What does it mean to say that many people link their performance in competition with the establishment of their personal identity? What implications does that have for the classroom?
3. Rewards are bad. Do you agree or disagree? Explain.
4. Is there a place for competition in the cooperative learning classroom?
5. Is it a contradiction to be against tangible rewards yet in favor of verbal praise?
6. How can you celebrate the accomplishments of a team without diminishing the accomplishments of other teams?

References

[1] Deci, E., R. Richard & K. Richard. "A Meta-Analytic Review of Experiment Examining the Effects of Extrinsic Rewards on Intrinsic Motivation." *Psychological Bulletin,* 1999, 123(6): 627–668.

[2] Deci, E. "Effects of Externally Mediated Rewards on Intrinsic Motivation." *Journal of Personality and Social Psychology,* 1971, 18: 105–115.

[3] Kohn, A. *Punished by Rewards: The Trouble With Gold Stars, Incentive Plans, A's, Praise and Other Bribes.* New York, NY: Houghton Mifflin Company, 1993.

[4] Deci, E., R. Richard & K. Richard. "A Meta-Analytic Review of Experiment Examining the Effects of Extrinsic Rewards on Intrinsic Motivation." *Psychological Bulletin,* 1999, 123(6): 627–668.

[5] Kohn, A. *Punished by Rewards: The Trouble With Gold Stars, Incentive Plans, A's, Praise and Other Bribes.* New York, NY: Houghton Mifflin Company, 1993.

[6] Kagan, S. *Brain-Based Learning SmartCard.* San Clemente, CA: Kagan Publishing, 2001.

[7] Kagan, S. "In Praise of Praise." *Kagan Online Magazine,* 2007, 10(1).

[8] Deci, E., R. Richard & K. Richard. "A Meta-Analytic Review of Experiment Examining the Effects of Extrinsic Rewards on Intrinsic Motivation." *Psychological Bulletin,* 1999, 123(6): 627–668.

[9] Jensen, E. *Brain-Based Learning.* Del Mar, CA: Turning Point Publishing, 1996.

[10] McGaugh, J. *Memory and Emotion: The Making of Lasting Memories.* New York, NY: Columbia University Press, 2003.

[11] Rosenthal, R. & L. Jacobson. *Pygmalion in the Classroom: Teacher Expectation and Pupils' Intellectual Development.* New York, NY: Holt, Rinehart and Winston, Inc., 1968.

[12] Sylwester, R. *A Biological Brain in a Cultural Classroom.* Thousand Oaks, CA: Corwin Press, Inc., 2003.

[13] Imai, M. *Kaizen: The Key to Japan's Competitive Success.* New York, NY: McGraw Hill/Irwin, 1986.

[14] Csikszenthmihalyi, M. *Flow: The Psychology of Optimal Experience.* New York, NY: HarperPerennial, 1990.

[15] Rotter, J. *Social Learning and Clinical Psychology.* New York, NY: Prentice-Hall, 1954.

Classic Cooperative Learning

The bulk of this book is dedicated to outlining the theory and practical implementation of the Kagan approach to cooperative learning. The Kagan model has been variously called The Structural Approach to Cooperative Learning, Cooperative Structures, Kagan Structures, and most recently Kagan Cooperative Learning. Although the Kagan model has evolved over the past few decades, and has had been identified by a variety of names, one thing has never changed—the central role structures play in the Kagan approach to cooperative learning.

Kagan Structures are the most widely trained and applied approach to Cooperative Learning worldwide. But Kagan Structures are but one approach—there are many ways to release the power of Cooperative Learning.

As of this writing, training in, publications about, and classroom implementation of the Kagan model is at an all-time high. The Kagan approach is the most widely trained and used approach to cooperative learning worldwide. Kagan has conducted trainings in numerous countries including Australia, Canada, China, Cypress, Denmark, Finland, India, Israel, Italy, Japan, Korea, Mexico, Malaysia, Mexico, the Netherlands, Philippines, Scotland, Singapore, the United Kingdom, and Venezuela. Educators from many more countries have traveled to the United States to attend Kagan Summer Academies and workshops over the past decades. Kagan works have been translated into numerous languages. There are hundreds of books, videos, and learning materials all dedicated to supporting teachers in successfully implementing Kagan Structures at the various grade levels and across all subject matters. The success of the Kagan approach to cooperative learning is due to the ease of learning Kagan Structures, the flexibility of the structures, and the dramatic positive effects they produce.

But Kagan Structures is not the sole approach to cooperative learning. In the 1980s, when cooperative learning was "the big new thing" in education, when researchers were finding positive results for cooperative learning in just about every dimension studied, there were numerous approaches to cooperative learning. Many were very popular and successful in the past, but have fallen from favor for one reason or another. The table, Classic Approaches to Coopera-

sneak peek
• Jigsaw Designs **17.2**
• Cooperative Investigations **17.7**
• Mastery Designs **17.17**

tive Learning (see below), lists major cooperative learning models, along with their central developers. We have divided the classic cooperative learning methods into four types: Jigsaw Designs, Cooperative Investigations, Mastery Designs, and Learning Together. In this chapter, we will briefly summarize these four approaches to cooperative learning and provide references for those seeking to learn more.

Jigsaw Designs
Original Jigsaw

The first jigsaw activities were developed at the national training labs as teambuilding activities. Each participant was given some of the information necessary to solve a problem, so they had to cooperate to be successful.

Elliot Aronson and his associates were the first to apply the Jigsaw concept to the classroom. Working in a desegregated school, in an attempt to improve ethnic relations, they created racially integrated teams and then rewrote the curriculum so each student on the team had access to only one part of the curriculum, but each would be tested on the whole. The students had to cooperate to be successful. Working together, the students came to like each other and ethnic relations improved.[1]

Jigsaw II

Although the original Jigsaw worked, it was not practical. Teachers do not have time to rewrite the curriculum into parts to give each student exclusive access. Robert Slavin and his associates overcame this problem by creating Jigsaw II.[2] In Jigsaw II, students were assigned expert topics to read from a regular text or curriculum materials, met in expert groups to master the material, and then returned to their teams to report on their topic. Finally, all students took a quiz on all the material. Improvement points were calculated and teams received recognitions, based on the sum of individual improvement points.

Classic Approaches to Cooperative Learning

Method	Developers	Page
Jigsaw Designs		
Original Jigsaw	Aronson	17.2
Jigsaw II	Slavin	17.2
Kagan Jigsaw Variations • Within-Team Jigsaw • Pairs • Team Jigsaw • Partner Expert Group Jigsaw • Double Expert Group Jigsaw • Workstation Jigsaw • Leapfrog Jigsaw	Kagan	17.3–17.4
Controversy Jigsaw	Coelho & Winn-Bell Olsen	17.5
Jigsaw Problem Solving	Lawrence Hall of Science	17.5
Partners	Kagan	17.7
Cooperative Investigations		
Group Investigation	Thelen, Sharan & Sharan	17.8
Co-op Co-op	Kagan	17.9
Co-op Jigsaw	Kagan	17.13
Complex Instruction	Cohen	17.16
Mastery Designs		
Color-Coded Co-op Cards	Kagan	17.17
STAD	Slavin	17.20
TGT	DeVries & Edwards	17.21
TAI	Slavin, Leavey & Madden	17.21
CIRC	Madden, Slavin & Stevens	17.21
Co-op Centers	Kagan, Olsen & McClay	17.22
Learning Together		
Learning Together	Johnson & Johnson	17.22

Kagan Jigsaw Variations

Spencer Kagan and his associates developed many variations of Jigsaw.[3] Some were quite simple and others complex. Like Jigsaw II, the Kagan variations worked with existing curriculum, but unlike Jigsaw II they did not include extrinsic rewards or points. The Kagan Jigsaw variations relied on highly structuring the interaction among students, both in their teams and in their expert groups, to create interdependence and intrinsically interesting learning tasks.

Jigsaw Designs

- Original Jigsaw
- Jigsaw II
- Within-Team Jigsaw
- Pairs
- Team Jigsaw
- Partner Expert Group Jigsaw
- Double Expert Group Jigsaw
- Workstation Jigsaw
- Leapfrog Jigsaw
- Controversy Jigsaw
- Jigsaw Problem Solving
- Partners

All of the Jigsaw methods have a number of positive outcomes. Because each student has a unique contribution to make, the methods boost status and self-esteem—each student is an expert in turn. Teammates encourage each other to do their best because they need the information that each student can provide. Teammates gain an enhanced sense of interdependence—none can succeed without the help of each of their teammates.

Here's an overview of the Jigsaw variations developed by Spencer Kagan and the teachers he trained:

Within-Team Jigsaw

In the simplest of all the Jigsaw variations, students never leave their teams. Each student on the team is given a different poem or a different section of the text to read and analyze. They then use RoundRobin to each teach the others what they have learned. Within-Team Jigsaw becomes more powerful if the individual work and sharing time is structured. For example, all students receive a four-page worksheet packet, one page for each expert topic. During the individual work, students fill out their own expert topic questions; during the sharing time, the expert teaches from her/his page while the teammates take notes on that page of their packet.

Pairs

The class is divided in half. Half the class is given material to master (a math problem, a story, or a history event to read and analyze). The other half is given different material to master. When they have finished, a person with each topic finds a partner with the other topic, and they take turns teaching each other what they have learned.

In the initial learning time, students with one topic may be seated on one side of the room, and students with the second topic on the other. Students are encouraged to ask for and offer help to same-topic classmates. For management, it is helpful to reproduce worksheets on a different color for each topic, so students can see at a glance who has which topic.

Team Jigsaw

In Team Jigsaw, each team becomes an expert on a topic, and then individuals from that team each teach another team. For example, in a classroom with eight teams, a textbook chapter might be divided into four parts. Teams 1 and 2 are assigned Part 1; Teams 3 and 4 are assigned Part 2, and so on. After the teams have mastered their portion, the teacher calls for students with Part 1 to stand. In our example, Teams 1 and 2 stand up. Each student on these two teams is an "Expert" on Part 1. Next, each Expert from Teams 1 and 2 goes to a different team to teach the expert content. After teaching, Experts return to their seats. The process is repeated so that each expert topic is covered.

One caution: There must be at least as many Experts as teams to teach. For example, you can't have just 3 experts and 5 teams to teach. As you divide the content, make sure you have at least as many Experts on each part as teams. When there are more Experts than teams to teach, some Experts pair up to team teach. For example, with eight Experts and only six teams to teach, four teams will be taught by one Expert and two teams will have Expert pairs.

Jigsaw Puzzle Teambuilder

As a quick and fun teambuilder and review activity, teams create a jigsaw puzzle for another team to solve.

1 Each teammate writes one important fact from the lesson on a single blank piece of paper. They each write their facts in different directions on the paper.

2 The first teammate rips the paper down the middle, turning it as he/she rips, so the two resulting pieces resemble jigsaw puzzle pieces.

3 The two pieces are handed to two other teammates who tear them in half, so there are now four jigsaw puzzle pieces.

4 Each teammate receives one piece and tears it in half, so there are now eight pieces.

5 The pieces are traded with another team. Each team now has a puzzle to solve with four important facts from the lesson.

Partner Expert Group Jigsaw

Partner Expert Group Jigsaw[4] begins like traditional Jigsaw: The curriculum is divided into four parts. Students are in teams of four and each is assigned one expert topic. Each student is assigned a same-topic partner from another team, and the partners work together to master the topic. The pairs then pair up with another pair with the same topic to check for agreement and mastery. The partners prepare and practice their presentations. Finally each Expert returns to his/her team and each in turn presents and tutors his/her teammates on the content.

Advantages of Partner Expert Group Jigsaw:
1. Pair work in the expert groups doubles the active engagement.
2. Students can be assigned to a partner taking into consideration language fluency, ability level, and social skills.
3. Students practice their presentations and receive feedback before presenting to their teammates.

Double Expert Group Jigsaw

In the traditional Jigsaw, students each went to one large expert group. With eight teams in the class, that meant there were eight students in each expert group. Expert groups of eight result in low levels of active engagement. The solution: Double Expert Group Jigsaw. Double Expert Groups means there are two expert groups for each topic. Now, instead of eight students in an expert group, there are only four, doubling the active engagement.

With two expert groups on each topic, there is the added advantage of including a time to have "experts consult." That is, each student pairs up with an Expert from the other same-topic expert group to check for completeness and accuracy before returning to their original teams to teach their teammates.

Workstation Jigsaw

Rather than forming expert groups as in the original Jigsaw, each student on a team may go to a different workstation to learn, returning to their teammates to report on what they have learned.[5] For example, one Expert may view a filmstrip, another may work with instructional cards, a third may do an experiment, and a fourth may go to an Internet link. Or if students all have access to the Internet, each may explore a different informational Web site.

Workstation Jigsaw breaks the traditional set that textbooks should be the primary source of information. Workstations can be integrated into more traditional Jigsaw formats. For example, one or two students may become experts at workstations while others turn to more traditional written materials.

Leapfrog Jigsaw

Many projects are best completed in a sequence of steps. Many of these sequential step projects can be taught with Leapfrog Jigsaw.[6] Student #1 teaches a skill to teammates who are each working on their own version of the project. Then Student #2 teaches a skill, which is applied to the project, and so on until the project is complete.

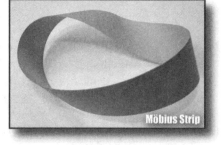

Möbius Strip

For example, in teaching very young students how to make and test a Möbius strip, the first child learns how to rule a straight line on paper and teaches that to teammates. The second expert shows his teammates how to cut along the line. The third student models how to twist and tape the strip. The last student shows teammates how to test the Möbius strip to determine if it really has only one side.

Very young students can be taught one step at a time from the teacher, and then go back to their teams to teach their teammates. For management, the students need a coloring task or some other sponge activity to keep productively occupied while the teacher is teaching each expert. Older students can learn skills in expert groups and then go back and teach them to teammates, one at a time, to lead each other through a project.

Additional Jigsaw Variations

Controversy Jigsaw

Elizabeth Coelho and Judy Winn-Bell Olsen developed a powerful Jigsaw variation to have students view issues from different perspectives. All four Experts are given information representing different sides of an issue. For example, a Developer wants to cut down some trees to build homes in a very picturesque area by a lake. Homebuilders are eager to take advantage of the opportunity. Real Estate agents hope to make the sales. But the representative from the Environmental Protection Agency sees the trees as a forest to protect because of the resident species. In their expert groups the Developer, Homebuilder, Real Estate Agent, and EPA Rep are all given information to make their case. They return to their teams to see if they can formulate a solution to which they can all agree. Powerful topics, along with their resources, are available for Controversy Jigsaw.[7]

Jigsaw Problem Solving

The Lawrence Hall of Science, a public science center on the University of California–Berkeley, developed cooperative logic and math activities published in a series of books.[8] This problem-solving approach is a simple form of Jigsaw for solving problems. Thus, we have dubbed the underlying structure, Jigsaw Problem Solving. Jigsaw Problem Solving works like this: Students work in teams of four, and each student receives one of the four clues to solve the team problem. Everyone must share the information on their clue card because the team can only reach a solution by connecting the information from all clues.

Managing Jigsaw

Dealing with Absences.

If students meet in expert groups one day and report back to their teams on another, there are two types of absences we need to deal with: absences when students become experts, and absences when a member is to share her/his expertise. Both have the same easy solution: If an Expert is absent when it is time to report or if the Expert was absent when the expert group met, when it is time for that Expert to report to her/his team, we simply have the team sit with another team when that Expert topic is presented.

Jigsaw Twins.

If we have a number of very low achieving students or a number of students limited in language ability, Jigsaw Twins offers a powerful solution. We don't want very weak students or students very limited in language ability to be the primary or sole source of a quarter of the information to their teammates. The solution: Create five-person teams and have the highest and lowest ability students go as twins to the expert group and return to team teach their teammates. One caution: We either need to teach the high achiever in the twin pairs ways to include their partner in the teaching process or structure for engagement and participation by both twins by using turn-taking, roles, or the division of labor.

Differentiated Expert Groups.

In some situations, it can be worthwhile to assign a very difficult topic to Expert Group 1, and to assign the highest achiever in each team to that expert topic and/or to assign the least difficult topic to Expert Group 4 and to assign the lowest ability student to that topic. Jigsaw lends itself to four levels of differentiation, if desired. A caution, of course, is in order: Students know when any form of tracking has taken place, and if done too often or in an overt way, the low students begin to internalize lower expectations and a lower self-concept.

Jigsaw Worksheet Packets.

In my experience, the single most important determinant of the success or failure of Jigsaw is the quality of interaction in the expert groups and the quality of the interaction when the Experts return to their teams to teach their teammates. Students are not born teachers, and telling is not teaching. Unstructured interaction in the expert groups and in the teams is a prescription for failure. A powerful antidote is the Jigsaw Worksheet Packet combined with clear steps for interaction during the time Experts share with each other, and later when they tutor their teammates.

A Jigsaw Worksheet Packet contains four different worksheets, one on each of the four Jigsaw topics. Each student is assigned one topic. Before they go to their unique expert groups, they can preview the entire packet to get the big picture of what they will be learning about. Next, team-

Kagan Cooperative Learning • Dr. Spencer Kagan & Miguel Kagan
Kagan Publishing • 1 (800) 933-2667 • www.KaganOnline.com

17.5

mates go to their unique expert groups to master the content and fill in their respective worksheets.

The typical sequence of work in the expert groups is as follows: 1) Experts put their pencils in a pencil cup in the center of the table. 2) One Expert reads the first question. (This is a rotating role.) 3) Experts discuss their answers and/or turn to resources to find an answer. 4) When they have reached consensus on the best answer, they take up their pencils and each write the answer on their own worksheet in their own words. This sequence minimizes the tendency for Expert Group Meetings to degenerate into low level dictation with high achievers telling low achievers word for word what to write.

When the Experts return to their teams, they have a worksheet completed that helps them teach the content to their teammate. The Experts teach and tutor their teammates in a scripted set of steps: 1) Teammates have their pencils down while the Expert explains the answer. 2) Teammates then ask questions for clarification. 3) When all questions have been answered, Teammates pick up their pencils and fill in their own worksheet in their own words. 4) The Expert then teaches the next question. When the worksheet packets have all been filled out, the Expert quizzes the students with their worksheet packets closed, to make sure all students understand and can answer the questions. Depending on the content, the Expert may engage in coaching using sample problems.

The quality of the worksheets in the packets and the structured interaction within the groups determines the quality of learning in expert groups and also the quality of teaching by the Experts. A good worksheet includes the target learning objectives, as well as questions across the levels of thinking.

Team Worksheets. An additional step that can be added to many forms of Jigsaw is the Team Worksheet.[9] After students have completed the expert presentations, they are given a team worksheet. The team worksheet includes questions that demand students integrate and synthesize material from each of the four expert presentations. Well constructed team worksheets push students to integrate their learning with questions like "How does X presented by Expert 1 explain Y presented by Expert 3?" or "Create a

review question that can only be answered using information presented by two or more Experts."

Steps of Partners

1 **Partners are formed within teams.** Often the high and low achievers are partners, as are the two middle achievers.

2 **Class divides: partners sit together.** Topic 1 partners are all on one side of the class; Topic 2 partners on the other. (We have pairs physically move so they can consult with same-topic partners in Step 5.)

3 **Topics are assigned and/or materials distributed.** Topic may be different sides of debate (e.g., pro or con on capital punishment). Materials may consist of reading and a worksheet to stimulate higher-level thinking.

4 **Students master topics.** Students may master materials given, or may do independent research. For example, research the arguments pro or con on an issue.

5 **Partners consult with same-topic partners.** Partners consult with like-topic partners sitting next to them, checking for correctness, and completeness.

6 **Partners prepare to present & tutor.** Partners analyze critical features and decide on a teaching strategy. Students are encouraged to make visuals and other teaching aids. Partners must evaluate what is important to teach and how to determine if learning has occurred in their teammates.

7 **Teams reunite; partners present.** Partners work as a team, dividing the labor as they teach the other pair in their team. For Partners Debate, each side presents their arguments on the issue.

8 **Partners tutor.** After presenting the skill or information, partners check for understanding and tutor their teammates.

9 **Individual assessment.** An individual quiz, essay, or a structure (Showdown) assesses individual mastery.

10 **Team processing.** Teammates reflect back over the process: How did we do as teachers? As learners? How could we do better next time? What social skills did we use? Which should we use more next time?

Partners

Partners is like Jigsaw, but in pairs. Student partners work together to master some content and then to present it to another pair. The box on the previous page summarizes the ten steps of Partners. Partners lessons can be quite elaborate with time for students to do independent research in preparation for their presentation, or Partners lessons can be quite simple as when each pair reads and interprets a different poem. Partners lends itself to a wide range of content: Different sides of a controversial issue, different experiments to conduct, different problems to solve, different inventions to describe, different characters to analyze.

Cooperative Investigations

Magic happens when teams engage in intrinsically interesting investigations. Learning becomes far more relevant and exciting when students work together first to understand a concept, then team up to apply their knowledge to create a project or presentation. With cooperative investigations, the class becomes an investigative community. When we unleash the powers of cooperation and curiosity, sometimes all we have to do is get out of the way!

Partners Content Examples

Literature

The two pairs on each team read different short stories by the same author. When they return to their teams, first they teach each other the content, then they discuss similarities and differences between the two stories and how the author revealed herself/himself in each. Or, assign two authors with different styles, or two poems by the same author.

Social Studies

One pair researches autobiographical information, the other the accomplishments of the person. After sharing the information, they discuss how historical accomplishments have their roots in personal experience. Or, partners simply work on different parts of a chapter, with the emphasis on sharing information and ideas.

Science

Each pair conducts a different experiment on a related topic; they then describe their results and discuss what conclusions the results together support. Or, one pair studies the life of a scientist and the other studies her/his contributions.

Math

Each pair learns how to solve a certain kind of problem. They then teach the other pair. Or, each pair conducts and presents a class survey on a different topic. They present and analyze their data in different ways.

Cooperative Investigations

- Group Investigation
- Co-op Co-op
- Co-op Jigsaw Experts Present
- Co-op Jigsaw Team Projects
- Complex Instruction

Indeed, inquiry coupled with cooperative projects is a powerful force for in-depth learning. We communicate a powerful message to students when the outcome of the inquiry rests in the hands of the investigating students. True inquiry is not a canned exploration, leading to an outcome predetermined by the teacher. When students are unfettered and allowed to follow their own interests, they bring their own strengths to light and there is no limit to their creativity, innovation, and ability to create meaningful projects and learning. Case in point:

Let us explore an example of authentic cooperation.[10] In Lee County, Florida, a mixed group of gifted and at-risk students gathered to work individually and collectively on environmental topics of their choice. They were enrolled in grades 10 through 12 and were given each Monday to meet and attempt to accomplish their chosen inquiry. After several sessions, the students decided to cooperate collectively in a single effort. They chose to try to save a pristine cypress swamp that was destined for destruction by developers and a projected highway. Once the decision was made, they enrolled the assistance of scientists, politicians, conservation groups, the park authority, garden clubs, school officials, the sheriff's department, and dozens of other groups. They created highly accurate maps, conducted a plant and wildlife census, and took their results to present at city council and county commissioners meetings. They led field trips by the dozens into the swamp and spoke before and lobbied developers ceaselessly. Finally, their efforts got the proposal on a referendum ballot. They then canvassed residents of the county and helped convince people to increase their own taxes by voting yes on the swamp. The results were totally unprecedented, as the vote passed by the largest margin in the history of Lee County. Today the Six-Mile Cyprus is a wildlife sanctuary in the midst of one of the fastest growing communities in the nation.[11]

Of course, not all cooperative investigations have such dramatic effects, but almost without exception, they result in important, multifaceted learning. Cooperative investigations embody the democratic, cooperative philosophy of John Dewey:

The way is, first, for the teacher to be intelligently aware of the capacities, needs, and past experiences of those under instruction and, secondly, to allow the suggestion made to develop into a plan and project by means of the further suggestions contributed and organized into a whole by the members of the group. The plan, in other words, is a cooperative enterprise, not a dictation. The teacher's suggestion is not a mold for a cast-iron result but is a starting point to be developed into a plan through contributions from the experience of all engaged in the learning process. The development occurs through reciprocal give-and-take, the teacher taking but not being afraid also to give. The essential point is that the purpose grow and take shape through the process of social intelligence.[12]

Group Investigation
Appreciations to Yael Sharan for providing information for this summary.

Group Investigation is a cooperative learning strategy in which students work in small groups to "investigate" a learning topic. Group Investigation was first developed by Herbert Thelen,[13] based on his deep concern for fostering self-realization for students through meaningful inquiry as members of an inclusive, interdependent society. Writing half a century ago, Thelen's ideas were prescient: He foresaw the need to prepare students to work both independently and interdependently, to follow their curiosity rather than just mastering content spoon-fed by a teacher. His vision of Group Investigation was to stimulate the desire of students to engage in inquiry—inquiry which leads to places neither the teacher nor the students could anticipate.

…what we have been struggling with in the microcosm of the classroom is part and parcel of the struggle for survival of the society of men on earth. We are, whether we like it or not, increasingly interdependent with all other men, and our survival is going to be decided by our ability, together, to develop a sense of common cause that expresses and reflects our common human aspirations. This sense of common cause will have to emerge from our experience in working together, and the quality of these experiences will in turn depend upon our ability to kindle and capture the flame of individual inspiration and insight. Life in these times is a social process of inquiry, of seeking to establish a way of life to which all can contribute, in which all can participate, and through which each may achieve self-realization simultaneously as a member of the emerging common society and of the human species. And the extent to which our boys and girls shall be effective in this quest is being decided right now by the quality of inquiry in the classroom.[14]

Kagan Cooperative Learning • Dr. Spencer Kagan & Miguel Kagan
Kagan Publishing • 1 (800) 933-2667 • www.KaganOnline.com

Thelen outlined stages of inquiry.[15] These stages were adapted and developed by Yael and Shlomo Sharan who trained teachers in Group Investigation and researched the outcomes. They conceptualized Group Investigation as a form of advanced cooperative learning, appropriate for students who have become skilled in working together. "Investigating in groups calls for students to use all the interpersonal and study skills acquired in other cooperative learning methods and to apply them to the planning of specific learning goals."[16]

Group Investigation is designed to provide students with broad and diverse learning experiences—quite in contrast to STAD, TGT, Color-Coded Co-op Cards, and the Jigsaw methods that are oriented toward student acquisition of predetermined facts and skills. Research has revealed that Group Investigation is particularly effective in increasing higher-level cognitive abilities among students.[17]

Basic Features of GI

There are four basic features of Group Investigation:[18]

Feature 1. Investigation. The classroom becomes a "inquiring community," and each student is an investigator of the class topic or problem.

Feature 2. Interaction. Students interact in small groups throughout the stages of investigation.

Feature 3. Interpretation. Students interpret findings from the information they gather from a variety of sources.

Feature 4. Intrinsic Motivation. Students are intrinsically motivated by their active role in the task and their natural curiosity in the subject matter.

Stages of GI

Students in Group Investigation progress through six consecutive stages:

Stage 1. Identifying the Topic and Organizing Pupils into Research Groups. A balance is struck between the need to organize students into heterogeneous groups and the need to allow students choice of inquiry topics.

Stage 2. Planning the Learning Task. Group members or pairs of group members determine subtopics for investigation. Groups decide what and how to study. They set the goals of learning.

Stage 3. Carrying Out the Investigation. Multilateral communication is stressed as students communicate with collaborators, teacher, other groups, and other resource persons. They gather information, analyze and evaluate the data, and reach conclusions.

Stage 4. Preparing the Final Report. Students prepare a report, event or summary. Students organize, abstract, and synthesize information. Groups decide on content and format of their presentation; a steering committee of representatives of the groups coordinates the work of groups.

Stage 5. Presenting the Final Report. Exhibitions, skits, debates, and reports are acceptable formats, as is inclusion of cast members not in the group.

Stage 6. Evaluation. Assessment of higher-level learning is emphasized including applications, synthesis, and inferences. Teachers and students may collaborate on evaluation; the steering committee may work with the teacher in creating the exam.

Co-op Co-op

Co-op Co-op[19] is based on the assumption that following one's curiosity, having new experiences that modify one's conception of oneself and the world, and sharing these experiences—especially with one's peers—are inherently satisfying, and that no extrinsic reward is needed to motivate students to engage in these activities, which are the most important forms of learning.

Kagan Cooperative Learning • Dr. Spencer Kagan & Miguel Kagan
Kagan Publishing • 1 (800) 933-2667 • www.KaganOnline.com

17.9

The Co-op Co-op structure communicates to students that we value their interests and abilities. We prize, release, and nourish their natural intelligence and curiosity. Students become responsible for learning and for sharing what they have learned. The structure prepares students for participation in a democratic society.

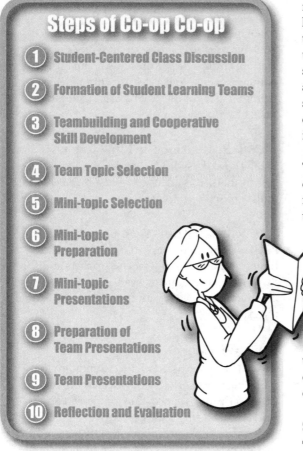

Steps of Co-op Co-op

1 Student-Centered Class Discussion

2 Formation of Student Learning Teams

3 Teambuilding and Cooperative Skill Development

4 Team Topic Selection

5 Mini-topic Selection

6 Mini-topic Preparation

7 Mini-topic Presentations

8 Preparation of Team Presentations

9 Team Presentations

10 Reflection and Evaluation

The essence of Co-op Co-op is to allow students to work together in small groups, first to advance their understanding of themselves and the world, and then to provide them with the opportunity to share that new understanding with their peers. Students each contribute to their team, and each team contributes to the class. They are cooperating within their teams so their team can better cooperate with the other teams to reach a class goal. Thus the name, Co-op Co-op. The method is simple and flexible. We may choose any number of ways to apply the approach in a given classroom. Nevertheless, the inclusion of ten elements or steps increases the probability of success.

Steps of Co-op Co-op

Step 1. Student-Centered Class Discussion. After introducing a topic, an initial set of readings, lectures, demonstrations, or experiences prior to the student-centered class discussion is helpful in stimulating and generating curiosity. The aim of the discussion is not to lead the students to certain topics for study; rather, it is to increase their involvement in the learning unit by uncovering and stimulating their curiosity. The discussion should lead to an understanding among the teacher and all the students about what the students want to learn and experience. In Co-op Co-op, learning is not seen as progress toward a predetermined teacher-defined goal; it is a process that flows out of the interests of the students.

This first step of Co-op Co-op is successful to the degree students see learning as an opportunity to find out more about a topic they wish to explore; the students identify with the learning process. They become more intrinsically motivated and increase their sense of internal control. A second major reason for the initial discussion is to let students see that their own learning can be of use to their classmates. As they listen to other students express what they would like to know, the students discover that they can be instrumental to the goal attainment of others, that knowledge can lead not only to the satisfaction of their own curiosity but also to helping others.

Step 2. Formation of Student Learning Teams. Students may be assigned to teams or may be allowed to select their teams, depending on the goals of the class.

Step 3. Teambuilding and Cooperative Skill Development. If the students have not worked together before, teambuilding activities are necessary so that they bond as a team and gain a sense of mutual trust. The number and type of teambuilding and skill development activities to be used in Co-op Co-op depend on the needs of a particular classroom.

Co-op Co-op cannot proceed successfully until the members of each team feel they are a "we" and have learned basic listening and communication skills. Teambuilding and skill development are not a one-time event but an ongoing process, as needed.

How Did Co-op Co-op Come About?

Co-op Co-op has its roots not in cooperative learning but rather in individual inquiry and information sharing! When I first became a professor in 1972, I wanted to give my students the opportunity to explore a topic of interest in depth. Half their course grade in my upper division Abnormal Psychology course was a term paper on a topic of their choice in abnormal psychology.

As I sat in my little red fishing boat at the end of the first semester reading and writing comments on the term papers, it occurred to me that it was a shame that only I was learning from what the students had written. So, the next term I allowed time for students to present to the class. The individual presentations were terrible. Most students simply read parts of their papers.

In thinking of how to have students share, I decided to have them form groups on similar topics and do team rather than individual presentations. Not only were the presentations far more interesting and informative, the individual papers were at a much higher level! Working in groups led to enhanced motivation and a cross-fertilization of ideas.

For a few semesters, I based students' grades on their exams and on their Co-op Co-op projects, half and half. The grade for the Co-op Co-op project was based half on their write-up of their mini-topic, one quarter on the evaluation of their team presentation by the class; and one quarter on the evaluation of each student by their teammates.

After awhile it dawned on me, evaluation of the team presentation was not a fair grade of an individual because the individual could do nothing and get a good grade if her/his teammates pulled off a good presentation. Teammate evaluation was also unfair: A student liked by teammates would get a better grade.

So, with some trepidation, the next semester I had classmates give students feedback on their team presentations and teammates give them feedback on their individual contribution to the group, but left those ungraded. I thought some undergraduates might put in little effort if they knew the presentation and group work were ungraded. To my surprise, the presentations were better than ever. What I discovered is that students did not need a bribe to work hard on a topic of interest and to do an engaging and informative presentation to their peers. What fuels Co-op Co-op is not a grade, but rather the chance to follow one's interest and to be of value to others!

Step 4. Team Topic Selection. Teams select their topics. Students are reminded (via whiteboard, overhead, or handout) which topics the class as a whole has indicated are of greatest interest. It is pointed out that the team can cooperate most fully in realizing the class goals if they choose a topic related to the interests of the class. The teammates are encouraged to discuss among themselves the various topics so they can settle on the topic of most interest to themselves, which will best serve the interests of the class.

As the teams discuss their interests and begin to settle on a topic, the teacher circulates among the teams and acts as a facilitator. If two teams begin to settle on the same topic, this can be pointed out, and the teams can be encouraged to reach a compromise, either by dividing that topic or by having one of the teams choose some other topic of interest. If no team settles on a topic that the class deems important, this too can be pointed out, and the students are encouraged to respond to the need.

When the fourth step of Co-op Co-op is successfully completed, each team has a topic and feels identified with its topic. The teacher may facilitate a spirit of class unity by pointing out how each of the topics makes an important contribution to the class goal of mastering the learning unit.

Step 5. Mini-topic Selection. Just as the class as a whole divides up the learning unit into sections to create a division of labor among the teams within the class, each team divides its topic to create a division of labor. Individual students select mini-topics, each of which covers one aspect of the team topic. Mini-topics may have some overlap, and the students within teams are encouraged to share references and resources, but each mini-topic must provide a unique contribution to the team effort. As the students settle on mini-topics, the teacher may need to be involved, requiring that mini-topics meet teacher approval because some topics may not be appropriate for the level of a given student (a student might bite off too much or too little), or because sufficient resources may not be available on a given topic.

It is acceptable and natural for some students to make a larger contribution than others to the total team effort because of differences in abilities and interests, but all members need to make an important contribution. If mini-topics are selected properly, each student will make a unique contribution to the total group effort and work at her/his appropriate level of difficulty.

Step 6. Mini-topic Preparation. Students work individually on their particular mini-topics. Students each know that they are responsible for their mini-topics and that the group is depending on them to cover an important aspect of the team effort.

The preparation of mini-topics takes different forms, depending on the nature of the content covered. The preparation may involve library research, data gathering via interviews or experimentation, creation of an individual project, introspection, or an expressive activity such as writing or painting. These activities take on a heightened interest because students know they will be sharing their product with their teammates and that their work will contribute both to the team presentation and to class knowledge.

Step 7. Mini-topic Presentations. After students complete individual work on their mini-topic, each in turn presents his/her mini-topic to teammates. Each team member has a specific time allotted for mini-topic presentation. Each team member stands while presenting his/her mini-topic.

Following mini-topic presentations, teammates are able to discuss the team topic as a panel of experts. The students know that the mini-topics, like the pieces of a jigsaw puzzle, must be put together in a coherent whole for a successful team presentation to the entire class. In the process of interacting with peers over a topic of common concern, some of the most important learning can occur.

During the mini-topic presentations, a division of labor within the teams may be encouraged so that one teammate may take notes, another may play critic, another supporter, and another check for points of convergence and divergence in the information presented in the mini-topics.

Time may be allotted for a feedback loop: Students may report back to the team after they research, redo, or rethink their mini-topics in light of the feedback they receive from the team. Team members are encouraged to let their teammates know what questions remain unanswered regarding the mini-topic.

Step 8. Preparation of Team Presentations. The team discusses and integrates all of the material presented in the mini-topics in order to prepare their team presentation. For the synergy principle to operate, there must be an active synthesis and integration of the mini-topics; in the process of integration, the team presentation becomes far more than the sum of the mini-topic presentations. The whole is equal to more than the sum of its parts.

The form of the team presentation follows the active synthesis and integration of the mini-topic material. Panel presentations, in which each team member reports on his or her mini-topic, are discouraged; they represent a failure to reach high-level cooperative synthesis. The form of the presentation should be determined by the content of the material. For example, if a group cannot come to consensus, the ideal form for their presentation would be to present a debate. Non-lecture formats such as debates, videos, PowerPoint presentations, displays, demonstrations, learning centers, skits, and team-led class discussions are encouraged. The use of whiteboard, overhead, audiovisual media, and handouts are encouraged.

Teams are informed that the classroom is theirs for the time of their presentation; within reason, they can rearrange furniture or make use of available resources if that will contribute to making their presentation interesting and informative. Team-2-Team practice presentations with feedback allow teams to improve before presenting to the whole class. For their presentations, teams may ask for and receive the help of other class members or teams, if that will aid in their presentation.

Step 9. Team Presentations. During their presentation, the team takes control of the classroom. They are responsible for how the time, space, and resources of the class are used; they are encouraged to make full use of the classroom facilities. There may be a need to appoint a class timekeeper who is not a member of the presenting team. The timekeeper can hold up warning cards when there is just five, one, and no minutes remaining.

The team may wish to include a question-answer period and/or time for comments and feedback as part of its presentation. In addition, the teacher may find it useful, following the presentation, to lead a feedback session and/or to interview the team so that other teams can learn what was involved in the process of developing the presentation. Particularly successful aspects of presentations are pointed out for other teams to emulate. During post-presentation interviews, the teacher uncovers useful strategies to use in future Co-op Co-op units.

Step 10. Reflection and Evaluation.

Students reflect on their use of social skills with the aim of improving interpersonal skills and team relations. Reflection can occur with teacher-led reflection questions during the projects ("How well are you taking turns?"), as well as after with reflection and discussion forms. In *Chapter 11: Social Skills*, there are a number of social skills reflection forms across the grade levels. Reflection, evaluation, and planning on use of social skills is not a one-time event at the end of Co-op Co-op. Rather, it occurs at various points as an ongoing process.

In addition to processing their use of social skills, it is helpful for students to reflect on their projects and presentations with an eye toward future improvement. For example, students reflect on how well their projects and presentations turned out, analyzing their own performance or contribution as well as that of their teammates, and the team as a whole. See *Chapter 13: Cooperative Projects & Presentations* for processing forms across the grade levels.

Evaluation and feedback from audience teams and the teacher offers students insight to how their projects and presentations were received by others. Feedback can be in the form of a class discussion following the presentation or through feedback forms filled out by the audience. See *Chapter 13: Cooperative Projects & Presentations* for team project feedback forms. The teacher also offers individual feedback and often a grade to either the individual writeup or presentation of the mini-topic by each student. In the spirit of shared decision making, students can have a say in determining the form of feedback and evaluation.

Scheduling Co-op Co-op

Co-op Co-op projects can be scheduled for as little as a day or as long as an entire course. Short Co-op Co-op lessons can be carried out in one day. In this short format teams take only 10 or 15 minutes to prepare short presentations of 5 minutes or so. An intensive two week Co-op Co-op project for the last two weeks of a long unit becomes a welcome addition for the students and teacher. A Co-op Co-op unit may run as long as ten weeks with the presentations serving as a culminating activity. Co-op Co-op projects at the end of the quarter or semester are particularly attractive because they allow students to extend, reinforce, and integrate the knowledge they have acquired over the course.

The acquisition of knowledge takes on a different tone when students know they will use that information in a presentation to the class. An excellent format in a course is to have two Co-op Co-op lessons. The first lesson may be highly structured by the teacher, with relatively minimal demands on students; the second lesson may be less structured as students take more responsibility for their education.

Co-op Jigsaw

There are two forms of Co-op Jigsaw: Co-op Jigsaw Experts Present and Co-op Jigsaw Team Projects. Both combine elements of Co-op Co-op and Jigsaw, offering the best of both worlds: We inspire creative inquiry and sharing among students via Co-op Co-op, but at the same time via Jigsaw ensure students master predetermined critical information.

Co-op Jigsaw Experts Present

Chris Harrison, a teacher at Chaparral Middle School in Diamond Bar, California, developed Co-op Jigsaw Experts Present. In Co-op Jigsaw, as in Jigsaw, each teammate first becomes an expert on an assigned topic, meeting with Experts on the same topic from other teams. Yet the Experts do not stop at gathering basic information. As a group of experts, they make a presentation to the whole class. Further, often Co-op Jigsaw Experts Present does not stop there. When students return to their teams, they can put their information together to create a novel team product. See box at right for a sample Co-op Jigsaw lesson on forms of government.

Co-op Jigsaw Team Projects

As I began to experiment with Co-op Jigsaw, I created Co-op Jigsaw Team Projects. In this version, each teammate is assigned or selects an expert topic. For example, if the class topic is "Seasons," each teammate goes to a different area of the class to become an expert on one of the four seasons: Fall, Winter, Spring, and Summer. Unlike the Experts Present version of Co-op Jigsaw, Experts do not report to the class; rather, they return to their teams to apply their new expertise to create a unique team project that draws on all teammates' expertise. Continuing with our "Seasons" example, Team 1 may be assigned the team topic "Clothing," Team 2 is assigned "Foods," Team 3 is assigned "Weather", and so on. Each team creates a unique project and/or presentation. For example, the Clothing team presents to the class how clothing changes with the seasons, dressing up in different seasonal clothing. The Weather team creates posters of the weather of each season, and so on.

Co-op Jigsaw Team Projects is very flexible, and can be used in almost any subject. It is best understood by examples, see the box on the following page with sample projects across the grades.

Co-op Jigsaw is powerful at almost any grade level across the range of curriculum. It has the advantage of producing comprehensive coverage of a topic while allowing creative expression. The Team Projects version has the advantage of allowing application-level thinking. Too often, we teach important principles, but do not have

---

Co-op Jigsaw Experts Present
Forms of Government Sample Lesson

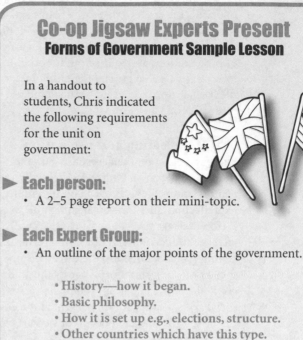

In a handout to students, Chris indicated the following requirements for the unit on government:

▶ **Each person:**
- A 2–5 page report on their mini-topic.

▶ **Each Expert Group:**
- An outline of the major points of the government.

  - History—how it began.
  - Basic philosophy.
  - How it is set up e.g., elections, structure.
  - Other countries which have this type.
  - Your opinion of this type of government.

- A chart showing the organization of the governing body and a list of the strengths and weaknesses.
- An oral presentation for the class covering the basics of the government.

▶ **Each Team:**
- A new and unique constitution for a colony on the moon, incorporating the knowledge the group has gained on government.

How it Played Out: Each student became an expert on one type of government (Communism, Dictatorship, Democracy, Monarchy, and—in the case of five-member groups—Socialism). They met in expert groups with other students assigned the same type of government. The Experts worked together to master and chart the major points of the government and then created a presentation to the class. When they returned to their teams, they combined the best of each government to create a unique constitution for a new colony on the moon.

Results: Expert teams presented the required information on each type of government. Base teams engaged in high-level discussions of ideas and ideals and creatively synthesized elements of various types of governments. Individuals wrote and submitted reports on the type of government they were assigned.

Co-op Jigsaw Team Projects
Sample Projects Across the Grades

Each teammate is assigned a different expert topic. Students go to expert groups in four different areas of the classroom to study their expert topics with same-topic students from other teams. They return to their teams to teach teammates about their topic. Next, the team works together to apply their collective expertise to make a project or presentation on the assigned or selected team topic.

Primary: Seasons

Experts learn about their season. Then they join their teammates to apply their knowledge to make a project or presentation. For example, the Weather team makes four posters illustrating the weather patterns for each of the four seasons.

Expert Topics	Team Topics
• **Student 1:** Fall • **Student 2:** Winter • **Student 3:** Spring • **Student 4:** Summer	• **Team 1:** Weather • **Team 2:** Foods • **Team 3:** Holidays • **Team 4:** Recreation • **Team 5:** Clothing • **Team 6:** Vacation

Elementary: Nutrition

Experts learn about a specific food group and which foods the group includes. Then they join their teammates to apply their knowledge to plan an assigned type of balanced meal, identifying foods from each group.

Expert Topics	Team Topics
• **Student 1:** Grains • **Student 2:** Fruits & Vegetables • **Student 3:** Milk • **Student 4:** Meat & Beans	• **Team 1:** Breakfast • **Team 2:** Lunch • **Team 3:** Dinner • **Team 4:** Thanksgiving Dinner • **Team 5:** Fast Food • **Team 6:** Chinese Food • **Team 7:** Italian Food

Middle School: World History

Experts receive a general overview of the meaning of their expert topic and what it encompasses. Then they join teammates to create a project or presentation on the assigned or selected civilization, with special emphasis on geography, politics, economy, and religion.

Expert Topics	Team Topics
• **Student 1:** Geography • **Student 2:** Politics • **Student 3:** Economy • **Student 4:** Religion	• **Team 1:** Roman Empire • **Team 2:** Islam in Middle Ages • **Team 3:** China in Middle Ages • **Team 4:** Ghana and Mali in Medieval Africa • **Team 5:** Medieval Europe • **Team 6:** Meso-American Civilizations

High School: Literary Responses and Analysis

Experts learn about different structural features of literary analysis. Then they join their teammates to apply their knowledge to create a response and analysis of their assigned or selected short story with respect to the expert topics.

Expert Topics	Team Topics
• **Student 1:** Theme • **Student 2:** Imagery • **Student 3:** Style • **Student 4:** Language	• **Team 1:** *Tales from the Secret Annex* by Anne Frank • **Team 2:** *Dubliners* by James Joyce • **Team 3:** *The Metamorphosis* by Franz Kafka • **Team 4:** *My World and Welcome to It* by James Thurber • **Team 5:** *The Illustrated Man* by Ray Bradbury • **Team 6:** *I, Robot* by Isaac Asimov

Co-op Jigsaw Team Projects
Team Newspaper Sample Project

When the Challenger exploded, Kathy Reider had her students create a Co-op Jigsaw newspaper. Each team was responsible for creating a newspaper. Because Kathy wanted all of the students to deal with their feelings, she required that they all write a letter to the editor about their personal experience that was printed in the newspaper.

▶ **Expert Topics**

Each teammate became an expert on one aspect of a newspaper:
- **News Experts** met together to learn the elements of a good news story, including how to write a "lead" and how to sequence details of an event.
- **Human Interest Columnists** read about reactions to the event.
- **Science Editors** learned about the physics of rockets and space travel.
- **Editorial Writers** wrestled with issues like how to weigh the costs against the benefits of undertaking exploration.

▶ **Team Projects**

When students mastered their new skills, they returned to their teams to make a team newspaper. The newspapers were remarkable products. When we showed the newspapers to teachers who did not know the students' grade level, the teachers consistently overestimated the maturity of the students by several years. When students follow a topic in which they are passionately interested, they are capable of dramatically more than when they are assigned to master the next chapter in the text.

students apply them to new content. Thus, the principles do not become part of the active repertoire of students. If students learn about volume and weight, and then apply them to describing the difference between a golf ball and a ping-pong ball, it is more likely the skills will be retained and applied throughout life. Co-op Jigsaw represents a marriage of mastery and concept development, and theory and practice.

Complex Instruction

Appreciations to Elizabeth Cohen and Rachel Lotan for providing materials[20] and contributions to this summary.

Complex Instruction is a cooperative instructional strategy developed by Elizabeth Cohen and her associates at Stanford University. The primary focus of Complex Instruction was the development of English language skills through the use of demanding group projects that require language-intensive interactions.

Central Components of Complex Instruction

There are a few components central to Complex Instruction:

Component 1. Skill-Builders & Roles. Using specially designed activities and roles, students learn how to work together productively. The social skills component focuses on language-specific skills, including instructions for students how to describe and explain accurately, and how to engage in group discussions. Students also assume cooperative learning roles such as Facilitator, Materials Monitor, and Reporter. The Facilitator's job is to make sure all group members understand the task, and each gets a turn. The Materials Monitor collects the supplies and monitors clean-up. The Reporter is tasked with sharing what the group discovered, or how the group worked together.

Component 2. Group-Worthy Learning Tasks. Groups are assigned intellectually challenging, open-ended learning tasks. The groups must explore complex learning concepts or solve problems that no single student can do independently. The group prepares a culminating product. For many tasks, there is no right nor wrong solution. Instead, they have specific evaluation guidelines for good group products. It is up to the group to demonstrate their understanding of the content and to display their intellectual mastery of the topic and teamwork skills.

Component 3. Cooperative Learning Principles.
Positive interdependence is created by requiring groups to create a product. Students must each make important contributions for the group to succeed in the mastery of the content and creation of the product. Individual accountability is included by requiring each student to complete an individual report after the group task.

Component 4. Equal Status Interactions.
Research indicates the amount of student participation in the group products is significantly positively related to learning gains.[21] Basically stated, the more students participate, the more they learn. To equalize and ensure participation by all, Complex Instruction proposes teacher interventions, including assigning competence to low-status students, and reinforcing the concept that students have different abilities and strengths, each worthy of respect.

Finding Out/*Descubrimiento*
Complex Instruction was originally built around Finding Out/*Descubrimiento*, a discovery-based science and math program designed by Edward DeAvila. The program was based on activities grouped by themes or units such as optics, electricity, or measurement. For example, in the unit on probability, students graph the height of a bouncing ball, the frequency of outcomes on a flipped coin, and the frequency of outcomes of spinning a polysided object.

Students are assigned to linguistically and academically heterogeneous small groups at learning centers. Each learning center has a different activity card and worksheet. Each student must complete the worksheet from each learning center. Students are trained to take responsibility for each other with each person playing a different role. Roles are rotated.

Because these tasks are so varied and challenging, children who do not have basic skills find that they can make intellectual contributions

while accepting help from classmates who have better academic skills. As needed, students receive help reading the activity card and writing on the worksheets. Students develop academic skills, as well as higher-order thinking skills. With regard to language development, students use sophisticated language to express their ideas and translate the ideas into English and Spanish, promoting dual language development.

Mastery Designs

Mastery of basic facts and skills has gotten a bad rap. Those who focus on "higher-level thinking" say they want to educate minds, not memories. As noble as that sounds, the ability to retain information is just as much a part of the mind as is the ability to evaluate or analyze. Brain research reveals distinct memory systems, and we can apply findings from brain science to make memory more efficient. It turns out too, that, we can't do higher level thinking in a vacuum—if we have no information to work with, how can we evaluate, synthesize, or analyze? If we are to test our students on how much they retain the content we teach, then we would do well to provide them with efficient approaches to master and retain that content.

Mastery Designs
- Color-Coded Co-op Cards
- Student Teams Achievement Divisions (STAD)
- Teams-Games-Tournaments (TGT)
- Team Accelerated Instruction (TAI)
- Cooperative Integrated Reading and Composition (CIRC)
- Co-op Centers

Color-Coded Co-op Cards
Color-Coded Co-op Cards is a week-long sequence of activities to help students memorize any content. Almost all curriculum areas have memorization components, see box (on the next page). Typically, memorization is relegated to homework, and some students do well while others, for lack of motivation or lack of knowledge how to memorize, perform poorly. The Color-Coded Co-op Cards sequence provides motivation to memorize while providing students an efficient memorization method.

The method is simple: For each item missed on a pretest, students makeup a flashcard (using their own colored pen or writing on cards that are a different color than that of their teammates). Students then quiz each other in a systematic way, playing the Flashcard Game. Following this practice, they take a practice test, checking on how much improvement they have made (how many cards they answered correctly), practice again using the Flashcard Game, take a final test, and receive individual, team, and class recognition for improvement. The color-coded cards allow students to pool and count their team improvement points. They are a tangible marker of success—a visible, countable, poolable, yet retrievable token of achievement. The cards allow even very young students to calculate their team improvement points—all learned items are placed in the center of the table and counted.

The color coding allows easy retrieval by each student of his or her items for future work. At the heart of the method is how students drill each other—the Flashcard Game. The game is based on well-established principles of learning, including frequent positive feedback following repeated, distributed trials. The method maximizes the time-on-needed task for each individual, and includes multi-modal associative links.

The Ten Steps of Color-Coded Co-op Cards

Step 1. Pretest. All students take a pretest on the week's memory items.

Step 2. Students Create Color-Coded Co-op Cards. Each student on the team, using a different colored marker, makes a set of flashcards on the items missed on the pretest. If students missed no items or just a few items, they make up cards from a pool of bonus or challenge items.

Step 3. Students Play the Flashcard Game. Students win back cards they master through the three rounds of the Flashcard Game (see *Chapter 6: Structures*).

Step 4. Practice Test. Following the Flashcard Game, students take a practice test on all of the items.

Step 5. Initial Color-Coded Improvement Scoring. Teammates place a star on the flashcards they answered correctly on the practice test, then pool and count the starred cards for the team, celebrating their success.

Step 6. Repeated Practice on Missed Items. The Flashcard Game is played again on all items missed on the pretest. For a few students, following the practice test there will be a need to increase their

What Do We Want Our Students to Memorize?

Every subject area we teach has a memory component. Among the many things we want our students to memorize are the following:

1776

- Definitions of key vocabulary words
- Spelling words
- Steps of algorithms
- Math facts and formulas
- Properties of elements
- Laws of physics
- Dates of events
- Steps to make a bill a law
- Steps of lab procedures
- Accomplishments of historical figures
- Size, temperature, and distance of planets
- Parts of a letter
- Bones of the body
- Literary terms
- Rights guaranteed by each amendment of the Bill of Rights

deck of flashcards—they will miss an item or two on the practice test that they did not miss on the pretest. These new items are included for the second round of practice, along with flashcards that have not yet earned a star.

Steps 7 & 8. Final Test and Final Improvement Scoring. Students take the final test, star all cards they answered correctly on the final test, pool the starred cards, and count them to determine the final improvement score for the team.

Step 9. Individual, Team, and Class Recognition.
Recognition may be given at three levels:

• **Individuals.** Individuals may post their improvement scores on individual improvement score graphs. Students with improvement greater than the prior week, or at a certain level, may be asked to stand to be recognized by the class.

• **Teams.** Teams may announce the sum of their improvement scores, and post them on their team improvement graph. Teams that improved more than the prior week, or at a certain level, may be asked to stand, give a team cheer or handshake, and be recognized by the class.

• **Class.** The sum of improvement points of teams may be posted on a class graph. Teams are recognized not for having "beaten" other teams, but rather for having advanced the class toward its next goal. Between-team competition is minimized; teams see themselves as all on the same side, contributing toward a common goal.

Step 10. Reflection. Students are allowed time to discuss how they can best help their partner while playing the Flashcard Game. Some students like fantastic visual images; others prefer mnemonic devices, and so on. If the students are given time to work on their process, they become more efficient helpers. Reflection is the time for students to work out how best to help each other learn.

A Pleasant Surprise

Ken Attebury from the ABC School District always made the Bill of Rights an important part of his American history course. He is a fine teacher, and his students always do well. After a Kagan Cooperative Learning workshop, he decided to use the Color-Coded Co-op Cards to have students memorize the Bill of Rights. The cards had the number of the amendment on one side and the principle feature of the amendment on the other. What followed that semester was quite different from what had happened in the many previous times Ken had taught the course. Always in the past, students had memorized the first ten amendments to the Constitution, taken their test on it, done well, and then moved on to other topics in the course. The students never again mentioned the Bill of Rights.

When Ken used the Co-op Cards, what followed changed dramatically: Students not only did better than any previous class on the quiz, but what followed the quiz was the pleasant surprise. After students had memorized the amendments using the Co-op Cards, as they discussed other topics, they repeatedly referred back to the Bill of Rights with comments like "Wouldn't that violate the first amendment?" By providing a secure information base, the Co-op Cards promote higher-level thinking. Application, Analysis, Synthesis, and Evaluation cannot occur in a vacuum.

Benefits of Color-Coded Co-op Cards

Color-Coded Co-op Cards are a useful addition to cooperative learning because the method:

• Addresses a dimension of the curriculum not efficiently treated by other methods;
• Focuses the attention of each student on his or her own most needed learning tasks;
• Provides immediate and frequent tangible and social feedback to each student regarding improvement;
• Includes a simple improvement scoring system, which even very young students can manage; and, most importantly,
• Converts dull unsuccessful drill into a fun, efficient learning game.

Student Team Learning

Dr. Robert Slavin and his associates from Johns Hopkins University in Baltimore Maryland developed Student Team Learning. Student Team Learning encompasses four methods: Student Teams Achievement Division (STAD), Teams-Games-Tournaments (TGT), Team Accelerated Instruction (TAI), and Cooperative Integrated Reading and Composition (CIRC).

STAD: Student Teams Achievement Divisions

STAD is an extremely well-researched, effective approach to mastery of basic facts and information. Research of STAD has also revealed very positive effects on ethnic relations and various types of prosocial development. The use of STAD includes enduring teams (usually lasting about six weeks) and an improvement point scoring system, which provides high motivation for students across the range of ability levels.

The following is a description of STAD reproduced by permission with only slight modifications from Robert E. Salvin's *Using Student Team Learning*.[22]

STAD is made up of five interlocking components: Class presentations, teams, quizzes, individual improvement scoring, and team recognition. These components are described below:

① Class Presentations. Materials in STAD are initially introduced in a class presentation. This is most often a lecture-discussion conducted by the teacher, but could include audio-visual presentations. Class presentations in STAD differ from usual teaching only in that they must be clearly focused on the STAD unit. In this way, students realize that they must pay careful attention during the class presentation because doing so will help them do well on the quizzes, and their quiz scores determine their team scores.

② Teams. Teams are composed of four or five students who represent a cross-section of the class in academic performance, sex, and race or ethnicity. (See Heterogeneous Teams, *Chapter 7: Teams*.) The major function of the team is to prepare its members to do well on the quizzes. After the teacher presents the material, the team meets to study worksheets or other material. The worksheets may be materials obtained from the Johns Hopkins Team Learning Project, or they may be produced by the teacher. Most often, the study takes the form of students quizzing one another back and forth to be sure that they understand the content, or working problems together and correcting any misconceptions if teammates make mistakes.

The team is the most important feature of STAD. At every point, emphasis is placed on team members doing their best for the team, and on the team doing its best to help its members. The team provides the peer support for academic performance that is important for effects on learning, and the team provides the mutual concern and respect that are important for effects on such outcomes as intergroup relations, self-esteem, and acceptance of mainstreamed students.

③ Quizzes. After approximately one period of teacher presentation and one period of team practice, the students take individual quizzes. The quizzes are composed of course content-relevant questions that students must answer. They are designed to test the knowledge gained by students from class presentations and during team practice. Students are not permitted to help one another during the quizzes. This makes sure that every student is individually responsible for knowing the material.

④ Individual Improvement Scoring. In addition to the quiz score, students receive an improvement score each week, indicating how well they are performing compared to their usual level of performance.

⑤ Team Recognition. Each week, teams receive recognition for the sum of the improvement scores of the team members. A newsletter is the primary means of rewarding teams and individual students for their performance. Each week, the teacher prepares a newsletter to announce team scores. The newsletter also recognizes individuals who showed the greatest improvement or got perfect papers, and reports cumulative team standings. In addition to or instead of the newsletter, many teachers use bulletin boards, special privileges, or small prizes or other rewards to emphasize the idea that doing well as a team is important.

TGT: Teams-Games-Tournaments

TGT was the first of the Johns Hopkins cooperative learning methods, and was created by David DeVries and Keith Edwards. TGT is identical to STAD except it used academic game tournaments instead of quizzes, and a bumping system instead of individual improvement scores.[23] Details of TGT are not included in this book because my own research with the method revealed that cooperative and minority students can suffer negative consequences from the very competitive tournaments. Although students are not told which tournament tables are for the high achievers and which are for the low achievers, many know, and this form of within-class tracking may be responsible for the self-esteem drops we observed for cooperative and minority students.[24] The critical elements that differentiate TGT from STAD are game tournaments and the bumping system.

TAI: Team Accelerated Instruction

In math, it is often the case that different students need to work on quite different skills, and that students can progress at quite different rates. Team Accelerated Instruction (TAI) was designed to allow each student to progress at his or her own rate, working on the skills he or she most needs. At the same time, each student is part of a team, caring about and encouraging the progress of teammates.

TAI was designed by Slavin, Leavey, and Madden[25] to create a happy marriage between cooperative and individualized learning. As students progress at their own pace through carefully designed individualized learning modules, they earn points for their teams. Unlike typical individualized programs, in TAI students do the routine checking and management. TAI uses heterogeneous teams and team recognition, much like in STAD.

There is some peer tutoring in TAI (team members turn to their teammates for help), but because the individual learning modules are designed to be self-explanatory and because team members are usually working at quite different levels, cooperative interaction is minimal. There are some learning modules that students receive as a group, but the groups are of students of similar academic ability.

CIRC: Cooperative Integrated Reading and Composition

CIRC was developed by Madden, Slavin, and Stevens.[26] The program represents a bold attempt to apply the principles of cooperative learning and other research to the areas of reading, writing, spelling, and English language mechanics. In CIRC, all of these skills are integrated so that instruction in each reinforces the others. The approach also incorporates training in metacognitive strategies for comprehension, retention, and thinking skills.

The class is divided into two reading levels: a "code/meaning" group that receives instruction in phonic decoding skills, vocabulary, and comprehension; and a "meaning" group that has adequate decoding skills and receives instruction on vocabulary, comprehension, and inference. Sometimes the "meaning" group is subdivided into two levels.

Students are assigned to 4–5 member teams. They are assigned in pairs to teams so that they have a partner on their reading level to work with during the reading activities. The team, thus, usually has both "code/meaning" and "meaning" ability pairs within it; the work of all members contributes to a team score and team recognition.

Students work in their teams to assess mastery of vocabulary, decoding, and content presented in each basal story. Materials are prepared to accompany specific commercial basals. There are written pretests and final tests for each unit, and an oral reading list for each story.

The study of reading and writing is integrated. For example, when students are studying quotation marks, they write dialogues. A peer editing approach is used to facilitate writing for revision and evaluation of writing.

Co-op Centers

Co-op Centers can be designed to create engaging activities to master any content. I worked with Gertrude McClay and Carol Olson from Vista Unified School District in Vista, California, to design a practical, low cost approach to centers. The initial design was for science, but the concept is applicable to any content. In order to minimize work for the teacher and allow time each week for other activities, three learning centers are created for each unit. The centers are duplicated so that there are three identical centers on each of three topics. This allows teams to rotate through three centers a week. Three teams work at identical centers each day, and then rotate to a new topic the next day. The centers are designed to be independent, so the teams can work at any center in any order. Because three teams are on the same topic each day, there is an opportunity for same-topic teams to consult at the end of the day. Also, with only three days a week at learning centers, there is time for teacher demonstrations, and other teamwork. In a typical week, students are at centers Tuesday, Wednesday, and Thursday.

Science lends itself nicely to teamwork and learning centers because there are so many hands-on instructive projects. The best science centers allow students to generate hypotheses and devise ways of testing them. Too often, students only read about or experience the outcomes of that process, rather than experience it. This is true even when teachers include "experiments" for students to do because the "experiments" are pre-planned by the teacher, with predetermined outcomes. Those experiments are really demonstrations the students perform—they do not involve students in original hypothesis generation and testing.

The most important thing in creating successful Co-op Centers is carefully designing the tasks so that an important contribution by each student is necessary. Otherwise, the high achiever is likely to take over. The projects should "run themselves" with minimal or no input from the teacher.

Most content can be presented via learning centers. In math, hands-on experiments with manipulatives, such as base 10 kits, algebra tiles, and fraction manipulatives, are perfect learning center content. In language arts, students can read and react to a poem or short reading, or respond to an experience via a cooperative writing project. Social studies projects include time lines, creating pro v. con charts on issues, and finding locations on the globe using longitude and latitude. Successful centers deepen the knowledge base of students while promoting critical or creative thinking.

Co-op Centers provide students opportunity for student-directed learning. At the same time, the teacher is able to work with individuals or teams.

Learning Together

The Learning Together model can be applied to have students master facts and skills, or it can be used to have students engage in cooperative investigations. It differs from the other approaches to cooperative learning in that it is a principles-based approach. Teachers are trained in five principles, and then they make specific decisions to design lessons that incorporate those principles.

Learning Together is David and Roger Johnson's cooperative learning model.[27] The Johnsons were Morton Deutsch's students at the University of Minnesota. They refined his teaching and testing, and applied it to the classroom. The focus of the Learning Together model is to teach principles fundamental to cooperative learning so that teachers may create cooperative learning lessons in any subject area and any grade level. The five principles in the Learning Together model are Positive Interdependence, Face-to-Face Interaction, Individual Accountability, Interpersonal Skills, and Group Processing. Each lesson has specified academic and social skills objectives. The Johnsons have emphasized the following principles in establishing cooperative learning: Shared Leadership; Shared Responsibility; Direct Instruction of Task Related and Social Relationship Skills; Teacher Observation and Intervention (including structured observation and feedback on specific academic and social skills); and Group Processing. In Learning Together, teachers follow 18 steps, divided into five main types, as follows:

Specifying Objectives
Specifying Academic and Collaborative Skill Objectives. Both the academic and cooperative skill objectives are specified before each lesson begins.

Making Decisions
Deciding on Group Size. Depending on the objectives and the nature of the learning task, cooperative groups range in size from 2–6 members.

Assigning Students to Groups. Decisions are made regarding homogeneous or heterogeneous ability grouping; separating or grouping non–task-oriented and task-oriented students; allowing student input into grouping; and length of time before reassignment.

Arranging the Room. Members of each group sit in a circle and are close enough to communicate without disrupting the other learning groups.

Planning Materials. Materials are distributed in carefully planned ways to communicate the assignment is a joint effort.

Assigning Roles. Interdependence may be arranged though the assignment of complementary and interconnecting roles to group members. For example, one student may be assigned the role of "the praiser", another "the checker."

Communicating the Task, Goal Structure, and Learning Activity
Explaining the Academic Task. Teachers set the task so that students are clear about the assignment; explain the objectives of the lesson; relate the concepts; define relevant concepts; explain procedures, and give examples; and ask specific questions to check students' understanding of the assignment.

Structuring Positive Goal Interdependence. The group goal is emphasized, and it is made clear that students must work collaboratively to reach the group goal.

Structuring Individual Accountability. There is frequent assessment of the level of performance of each group member. Thus, students know which members need encouragement and help.

Structuring Intergroup Cooperation. Positive outcomes found within cooperative groups are extended throughout the whole class by structuring intergroup cooperation.

Explaining Criteria for Success. Teachers explain at the beginning of the lesson clear criteria by which the students' academic work will be evaluated.

Specifying Desired Behaviors. Teachers also define cooperative work by specifying the behaviors that are appropriate and desirable within the learning groups.

Monitoring and Intervening

Monitoring Students' Behavior. After group work begins, teachers spend most of their time observing group members to determine what problems they are having in completing the assignment and working collaboratively.

Providing Task

Assistance. Teachers clarify instructions, review procedures and strategies for completing the assignment, answer questions, and teach task skills as necessary.

Teaching Collaborative Skills. Teachers also intervene to suggest more effective procedures for working together.

Providing Closure. Teachers summarize the major points of a lesson, ask students to recall ideas, and answer final questions.

Evaluating and Processing

Evaluating Students' Learning. Whatever the product of the lesson, it is always evaluated by a criteria-referenced system. Group members also receive feedback on how effectively they collaborated.

Assessing How Well the Group is

Functioning. Even if class time is limited, some time should be spent talking about how well the groups did, which things were done well, and which could be improved.

Chapter Summary

Kagan Structures, in the perhaps not-so-humble opinion of the authors, is the way to teach cooperative learning to teachers, and the way for teachers to use it successfully every day in the classroom. It is easy to learn. It provides very specific step-by-step cooperative strategies that can be easily incorporated into any classroom. It includes a wide variety of structures to match the many classroom objectives. It has a solid theoretical background. And the step-by-step structures incorporate all the essential elements of cooperative learning, ensuring social and academic success.

Although the classic cooperative learning methods produce proven positive outcomes, they are often complex and involve extensive preparation, lesson designing, scoring, recordkeeping, and/or preparation of specialized materials. In the busy life of a teacher, these complex methods tend to be relegated, at best, to occasional events. No teacher can spend all day teaching and all night preparing tomorrow's lesson. In contrast, structures involve little or no preparation or record-keeping and are easily incorporated every day as part of any lesson. With structures, cooperative learning becomes not one more thing to teach, but rather a more engaging and successful way to teach anything.

We are biased, of course. Being biased is OK. But being blinded by bias is not. We encourage you to try these classic approaches to cooperative learning. Some are extremely powerful, and we lament the fact there hasn't been broader sustained implementation of many of these powerful approaches. These classic approaches to cooperative learning and the researcher-developers responsible for these major cooperative learning methods have all made wonderful contributions to the field of cooperative learning and to education in general.

As researchers, developers, and trainers of cooperative learning, we are a small cooperative community. We have presented, compared, agreed, and agreed to disagree about our different approaches to cooperative learning. But most importantly—just as our students do—we have learned from these open and varied interactions. As a result, collectively we have advanced the theory, research, and practice of cooperative learning. Each approach is very different indeed, but we are more alike than different. All approaches provide an alternative to the traditional competitive and individualistic model of education. Common to all approaches is a welcome transformation. We see students working together as a team to learn instead of competing against classmates for grades, attention, and recognition. Each approach charts a different route, but we're all sailing to the same destination: a better education and a better tomorrow.

Each approach charts a different route, but we're all sailing to the same destination: a better education and a better tomorrow.

Chapter Questions

▶ Questions for Review

1. How could you summarize Group Investigation to a colleague?
2. What are the three main components of Complex Instruction?
3. What is an "expert" in the context of Jigsaw?
4. What does it mean to say Learning Together is a principle-based model?
5. Which models are focused more narrowly on content mastery, and which are focused on developing understanding?
6. Which Jigsaw variations involves students working primarily in pairs?

▶ Questions for Thinking and Discussion

1. Select two major approaches to cooperative learning. What do they have in common? In which ways do they differ?
2. What are the benefits of the Learning Together model? What are the potential drawbacks for implementation?
3. Are the various approaches to cooperative learning more complementary or contradictory? How so?
4. Which of the major models of cooperative learning is most in line with your educational philosophy?
5. If many of these classic models have extensive research that shows positive results on a variety of dimensions, why do you think they are not more widely implemented?
6. Some models of cooperative learning rely heavily on cooperatively structured tasks; others make rewards a prominent feature. What contributes more to student learning, the task or the reward structure? Explain.
7. If you had to make a policy decision and select one of the major approaches to cooperative learning to be taught in every school of education, which one would you select? Defend your selection.

1 Aronson, E. *The Jigsaw Classroom.* Beverly Hills, CA: Sage Publications, 1978.

2 Slavin, R. *Using Student Team Learning.* Baltimore, MD: The Johns Hopkins Team Learning Project, 1986.

3 Kagan, S. *Cooperative Learning.* San Clemente, CA: Kagan Publishing, 1985.

4 Partner Expert Group Jigsaw was created by Billie Telles, Los Angeles, CA: Los Angeles County Office of Education.

5 Workstation Jigsaw was developed by Dolores Sasway, Vista, CA: Lincoln Middle School.

6 Leapfrog Jigsaw was created by Doug Wilkinson, Dana Point, CA: R. H. Dana Elementary School.

7 Coelho, E., L. Winer & J. Winn-Bell Olsen. *All Sides of the Issue: Activities for Cooperative Jigsaw Groups.* Hayward, CA: Alemany Press, 1989.

8 Goodman, J. *Group Solutions: Cooperative Logic Activities for Grades K–4.* Berkeley, CA: Lawrence Hall of Science, 2007.

Goodman, J. & J. Kopp. *Group Solutions, Too! More Cooperative Logic Activities for Grades K–4.* Berkeley, CA: Lawrence Hall of Science, 1997.

Erickson, T. *Get It Together: Math Problems for Groups Grades 4–12.* Berkeley, CA: Lawrence Hall of Science, 1989.

Erickson, T. *United We Solve: 116 Math Problems for Groups Grades 5–10.* Oakland, CA: Eeps Media, 1996.

9 Team Worksheets were created by Doug Wilkinson, Dana Point, CA: R. H. Dana Elementary School.

10 WREEC. *Project WILD Secondary Activity Guide.* Boulder, CO: WREEC, 1986.

11 Samples, R. "Cooperation: Worldview as Methodology." In Davidson, N. & T. Worsham. *Enhancing Thinking Through Cooperative Learning.* New York, NY: Teachers College Press, 1992.

12 Dewey, J. *Experience and Education.* New York, NY: Macmillan, 1957.

13 Thelen, H. *Education and the Human Quest.* New York, NY: Harper & Brothers, 1960.

Joyce, B. & M. Weil. *Group Investigation: Democratic Process as a Source, in Models of Teaching (2nd ed.).* Englewood Cliffs, NJ: Prentice-Hall, Inc., 1980.

14 Thelen, H. *Education and the Human Quest.* New York, NY: Harper & Brothers, 1960.

15 Thelen, H. "The Classroom Society: The Construction of Educational Experience." *American Journal of Education,* 1982, 90(4): 377–381.

16 Sharan, Y. & S. Sharan. "Group Investigation in the Cooperative Classroom." In Sharan, S. *Handbook of Cooperative Learning Methods.* Westport, CT: Greenwood Press, 1994.

17 Sharan, S., P. Kussell, R. Hertz-Lazarowitz, Y. Bejarano, R. Shulamit & Y. Sharan. "Cooperative Learning Effects on Ethnic Relations and Achievement in Israeli Junior High-School." In Slavin, R., S. Sharan, S. Kagan, R. Hertz-Lazarowitz, C. Webb & R. Schmuck (eds.). *Learning to Cooperate, Cooperating to Learn.* New York, NY: Plenum, 1985.

18 Sharan, Y. & S. Sharan. "Group Investigation in the Cooperative Classroom." In Sharan, S. *Handbook of Cooperative Learning Methods.* Westport, CT: Greenwood Press, 1994.

[19] Kagan, S. "Co-op Co-op: A Flexible Cooperative Learning Technique." In Slavin, R., S. Sharan, S. Kagan, R. Hertz-Lazarowitz, C. Webb & R. Schmuck (eds.). *Learning to Cooperate, Cooperating to Learn.* New York, NY: Plenum, 1985.

[20] Lotan, R. "Developing Language and Mastering Content in Heterogeneous Classrooms." In Gillies, R., A. Ashman & J. Terwel (eds.). *The Teacher's Role in Implementing Cooperative Learning in the Classroom.* New York, NY: Springer, 2007.

[21] Cohen, E. & R. Lotan. (eds.). *Working for Equity in Heterogeneous Classrooms: Sociological Theory in Action.* New York, NY: Teachers College Press, 1997.

[22] Slavin, R. *Using Student Team Learning.* Baltimore, MD: The Johns Hopkins Team Learning Project, 1986.

[23] DeVries, D., R. Slavin, G. Fennessey, K. Edwards & M. Lombardo. *Teams-Games-Tournament: The Team Learning Approach.* Englewood Cliffs, NJ: Educational Technology Press, 1980.

[24] Kagan, S. "Cooperation-Competition, Culture, and Structural Bias in Classrooms." In Sharan, S., A. Hare, C. Webb & R. Lazarowitz. (eds.). *Cooperation in Education.* Provo, UT: Brigham Young University Press, 1980.

[25] Slavin, R., M. Leavey & N. Madden. *Team Accelerated Instruction: Mathematics.* Watertown, MA: Charlesbridge, 1986.

[26] Madden, N., R. Slavin & R. Stevens. *Cooperative Integrated Reading and Comparison: Teacher's Manual.* Baltimore, MD: Johns Hopkins University, Center for Research on Elementary and Middle School, 1986.

[27] Johnson, D., R. Johnson & E. Holubec. *Advanced Cooperative Learning.* Edina, MN: Interaction Book Company, 1988.

Resources

Learning Together

For more information on Learning Together, contact David and Roger Johnson, Cooperative Learning Center, 202 Pattee Hall, 150 Pillsbury Dr. SE, Minneapolis, MN, 55455. Phone: (612) 831-7031.

Books

Johnson, D. & R. Johnson. *Learning Together and Alone (5th ed.).* Edina, MN: Interaction Book Company, 1999.

Johnson, D., R. Holubec & E. Holubec. *Circles of Learning (5th ed.).* Edina, MN: Interaction Book Company, 2002.

Johnson, D., R. Johnson & E. Holubec. *Advanced Cooperative Learning.* Edina, MN: Interaction Book Company, 1988.

Videos

University of Minnesota. *Circles of Learning.* Minneapolis, MN: University of Minnesota, 1983.

Web Site

The Cooperative Learning Center at the University of Minnesota http://www.co-operation.org/

Student Team Learning

TAI

Slavin, R. *Using Student Team Learning (revised ed.).* Baltimore, MD: The Center for Social Organization of Schools, The Johns Hopkins University, 1980.

CIRC

For further information about CIRC, contact Dr. Robert Slavin, Center for Research on Elementary and Middle Schools, Johns Hopkins University, Baltimore, MD 21218. Phone: (301) 338-8249.

Slavin, R. *Using Student-Team Learning.* Baltimore, MD: The Johns Hopkins Team Learning Project, 1986.

Slavin, R. *Student Team Learning: A Practical Guide to Cooperative Learning (3rd ed.).* Washington, DC: National Education Association, 1992.

Slavin, R. *Cooperative Learning.* New York, NY: Longman, Inc., 1983.

Videos
The Johns Hopkins University. *Cooperative Integrated Reading and Composition.* Baltimore, MD: The Johns Hopkins University, 1988.

The Johns Hopkins University. *Team Accelerated Instruction.* Baltimore, MD: The Johns Hopkins University, 1984.

Group Investigation
Books & Articles
For more information on Group Investigation Projects (GRIP), contact Yael Sharan, Tel Aviv, Israel. E-mail: yaelshar@zahav.net.il

Sharan, Y. & S. Sharan. "Group Investigation Expands Cooperative Learning." *Educational Leadership,* 1989, 47(4): 17–21.

Sharan, Y. "Group Investigation: Expanding Cooperative Learning." In Brubacher, M., R. Payne & K. Rickett. (eds.). *Perspectives on Small Group Learning: Theory and Practice.* Oakville, Ontario: Rubicon, 1990.

Sharan, Y. & S. Sharan. *Expanding Cooperative Learning Through Group Investigation.* New York, NY: Teachers College Press, 1992.

Sharan, Y. & S. Sharan. *Expanding Cooperative Learning Through Group Investigation (Italian ed.).* Gardolo, Italy: Edizioni Erickson Publisher, 1998.

Sharan, Y. & S. Sharan. *Expanding Cooperative Learning Through Group Investigation (Japanese ed.).* Kyoto, Japan: Shobo Press, 2001.

Sharan, Y. & S. Sharan. "Group Investigation in the Cooperative Classroom." In Sharan, S. (ed.). *Handbook of Cooperative Learning Methods.* New York, NY: Greenwood, 1994.

Sharan, Y. & S. Sharan. "What Do We Want to Study? How Should We Go About It? Group Investigation in the Cooperative Social Studies Classroom." In Stahl, R. (ed.). *Cooperative Learning in the Social Studies: A Handbook.* Menlo Park, CA: Addison Wesley, 1994.

Sharan, Y. "Music of Many Voices: Group Investigation in a Cooperative High School Classroom." In Pederson, J. & A. Digby (eds.). *Cooperative Learning in the Secondary School: Theory and Practice.* New York, NY: Garland, 1995.

Sharan, Y. "Enriching the Group and the Investigation in the Intercultural Classroom." *European Journal of Intercultural Education,* 1998, 9(2) pp 133–140.

Jigsaw
Books
Aronson, E., N. Blane, C. Stephan, J. Sikes & M. Snapp. *The Jigsaw Classroom.* Beverly Hills, CA: Sage Publications, Inc., 1978.

Aronson, E. *Nobody Left to Hate: Teaching Compassion After Columbine.* New York, NY: W. H. Freeman, 2000.

Aronson, E. & S. Patnoe. *The Jigsaw Classroom: Building Cooperation in the Classroom (2nd ed.).* New York, NY: Addison Wesley Longman, 1997.

Coelho, E., L. Winer & J. Winn-Bell Olsen. *All Sides of the Issue: Activities for Cooperative Jigsaw Groups.* Hayward, CA: Alemany Press, 1989.

Goodman, J. *Group Solutions: Cooperative Logic Activities for Grades K–4.* Berkeley, CA: Lawrence Hall of Science, 2007.

Goodman, J. & J. Kopp. *Group Solutions, Too! More Cooperative Logic Activities for Grades K–4.* Berkeley, CA: Lawrence Hall of Science, 1997.

Erickson, T. *Get It Together: Math Problems for Groups Grades 4–12.* Berkeley, CA: Lawrence Hall of Science, 1989.

Erickson, T. *United We Solve: 116 Math Problems for Groups Grades 5–10.* Oakland, CA: Eeps Media, 1996.

Web Site
Jigsaw Classroom
http://www.jigsaw.org

Complex Instruction
Books & Articles
Cohen, E. "Talking and Working Together: Status, Interaction, and Learning." In Peterson, P., L. Wilkinson & M. Hallinan. (eds.). *The Social Context of Instruction: Group Organization and Group Processes.* New York, NY: Academic Press, 1984.

Cohen, E. "Teaching in Multiculturally Heterogeneous Classrooms: Findings From a Model Program." *McGill Journal of Education,* 1990, 26 (1): 7–23.

Cohen, E. *Classroom Management and Complex Instruction.* Paper presented at the Annual Meeting of the American Educational Research Association. Chicago, IL: 1991.

Cohen, E. *Designing Group Work: Strategies for the Heterogeneous Classroom (2nd ed.).* New York, NY: Teachers College Press, 1994.

Cohen, E., R. Lotan & N. Holthuis. "Talking and Working Together: Conditions for Learning in Complex Instruction." In Hallinan, M. (ed.). *Restructuring Schools: Promising Practices and Policies.* New York, NY: Plenum Press, 1995.

DeAvila, E. *Finding Out/Descubrimiento.* Compton, CA: Santillana Publishing, 1989.

Web Site
Program for Complex Instruction
http://cgi.stanford.edu/group/pci/cgi-bin/site.cgi

Subject Index

To locate structures, see Table of Structures on pages ix–xi.

A

About Me Question Cards, 10.6
Absent students, 1.8–9, 7.2
Academics
  classbuilding and, 5.7
  gifted students, 1.11
  teambuilding structures, 10.3
Accountability. See Individual accountability
Achievement
  boosting, 1.2, 1.4–5
  crisis in, 2.2–3
  differentiated instruction, 1.13
  group work, 6.4
  heterogeneity of, 5.4
  higher education, 1.19
  homogeneous teams, 7.19–20
  individual accountability, 12.9
  interdependence, 5.10
  international comparisons, 2.2–3
  learning, 3.4
  participation and, 12.14, 12.15
  positive interdependence, 4.2
  research, 3.2–3, 3.8–15
  self-expectations, 4.21
  structures, 3.8–15, 6.4
  teambuilding, 10.4
  team selection, 7.4, 7.5, 7.8, 7.10
  traditional instruction, 6.3
Achievement gap, 2.3, 3.2, 3.3–4, 3.11, 3.13, 3.14, 6.3
Achievement levels. See High achievers; Low achievers
Achievement-Ranked List Method, 7.8–9
Acquainted, getting, 9.2, 9.3–9, 10.2, 10.4–13
Activities, 9.25
  classbuilding, 9.1–25
  resources for, 14.8–9
  teambuilding, 10.3–37
African-American students, 2.6
  achievement gap, 2.3
  dropouts, 2.4
  Kagan Structures, 3.13
  research on cooperative learning, 3.3–4
Aggression, 2.6, 2.13–14, 11.32–33
Alertness, 1.5, 8.20
All About Me, 9.8, 9.11
All-students-respond structures, 15.6
America, quality of education in, 2.2
Amphitheaters, 8.14
Anchor activities, 1.8
Anderson County schools, 3.10
Animal Sounds, 7.13, 7.15
Answers
  sharing, 8.6
  sharing wrong, 12.23–24
Anxiety, 5.8
  competition creating, 16.5
  motivation, 4.15
  tests and, 4.9
Applause, public, 8.5
Approachers, 12.15
Arrangement. See Classroom, arrangement
Asian-American students, dropouts, 2.4
Asians, population increases of, 2.6
ASK IF I, 4.15–16

B

Banner, class, 9.12
Behavior
  aggressive, 2.6, 2.13–14, 11.32–33
  expectations, 8.11–13
  modeling, 4.6–7
  off-task, 7.19
  procedures, 8.9–11
  rewarding, 4.2–3
  separating students with issues, 1.8
  situation and, 4.21–24
  social skills challenges, 11.27–39
  structuring, 8.8
Behaviorist cooperative learning structures, 1.16–17
Belongingness, 4.13, 5.6
Berkley Elementary School, 3.4, 3.13
Big Four lesson design, 14.18–19
Birthday calendar, 9.5, 9.7
Bite-Sized Bits, 8.6
Black students. See African-American students
Boredom, 6.8, 12.22
Bow, public, 8.5
Brain, 4.9–12
  active engagement, 6.9
  nourishment, 4.10
  praise and, 16.7
  processing functions, 6.16–18
  rewards and, 16.3
  social interaction, 12.20
  stimuli, 4.19
Brain-breaks, function of, 1.5
Brainstorming, 10.21
Bulletin boards, student, 9.21
Bully, 11.32–33
Buy-in, 16.12

C

Calling on students, 4.5, 5.10
Candy Store Math, 13.26
Card Sorting Method, 7.7
Caring, 2.15, 5.6–7, 11.3
Carpet patches, 8.13
Catalina Ventura School, 3.8–9
Categorizing skills, 6.18

Assessment, 15.1–8
  authentic, 15.3–4
  formative v. summative, 15.2–3
  individual accountability and, 12.10
  individuals, 15.11
  multi-dimensional, 15.4–5
  representative, 15.3
  simultaneous, 15.8
  understanding, 8.2
Attendance, 3.7
Attention
  maintaining procedures, 8.11
  managing, 8.14–16
  movement affecting, 8.20
  novelty, 4.12
  positive v. negative, 8.3
  seeking, 11.32, 11.33
Attribution shift, rewards and, 16.3, 16.6
Authentic assessment, 15.3–4
Autonomy, 16.13
Avoiders, 12.15
Awards, 8.4

Celebrations, 1.9–10
  birthday, 9.5
  board for, 8.5
  class goal, 9.21
  motivation and, 16.8
  multiple intelligences and, 1.13
  recognition as, 8.4
  team, 12.6
Chain of Friendship, 9.13
Challenges, motivating, 16.10
Chant, class, 9.12
Character
  decline of, 2.8
  education, 16.9
  social skills and, 5.9
Checker, 11.10–11
Cheerleader, 11.10–11
Cheers, 8.5, 10.14, 10.15
Chemistry, Kagan Structures outcomes and, 3.15
Choice, 16.13
Class bar graphs, 9.5
Classbuilding, 5.6–7, 8.22
  activities, 9.1–25
  aims of, 9.2–3
  creating love of learning through, 1.5
  lesson planning for, 14.18
  motivation and, 16.8
  structures for, 1.8, 6.11–12, 9.1–25
Classic Cooperative Learning, and projects, 13.15
Class identity, 9.3
Classmate BINGO, 9.8, 9.10
Class meetings, 9.17–19
Class name, 9.9
Class projects, 9.17, 9.20
Classroom
  arrangement, 1.7, 5.6, 8.13–14, 9.21
  restructuring, 9.17
  setting up, 8.13–14
  structure in, 5.2–3
  student ownership, 9.21
Classroom management, 1.2, 8.1–25
  heterogeneous teams, 7.4, 7.5
  room setup, 1.7, 5.6, 8.13–14, 9.21
  See also Management
Class tone, positive, 9.20–25
Cliques, 9.2
Clown, 11.33–34
Coach/coaching, 11.10
  learning using, 1.4, 4.9
  mediation as, 4.7
  structures for, 5.3
  student as, 9.25
Cognitive development
  discussion facilitating, 1.17
  social interaction effects, 3.7
  teams of four and, 7.2
Collaboration, 16.5
Collage cubes, 10.14
College graduation, and race, 2.4
Committees, student, 9.21
Communication builders, 6.15
Communication regulators, 6.15
Communication skills
  employability, 1.18, 2.7
  research, 3.6
  structures for, 6.14–15
  TV effects, 2.12
Community, competition eroding, 16.4–5

Kagan Cooperative Learning • Dr. Spencer Kagan & Miguel Kagan
Kagan Publishing • 1 (800) 933-2667 • www.KaganOnline.com

 I.1

Kagan Cooperative Learning • Dr. Spencer Kagan & Miguel Kagan
Kagan Publishing • 1 (800) 933-2667 • www.KaganOnline.com

I.3

P

Pacific Islanders, population increases, 2.6
Pair Up, 1.20
Paired heads together, 6.21
Pairs
  interviews, 6.22
  simultaneous interaction, 12.22–23
  talk time, 4.5
  teams of four and, 7.2
Pairs Selected, 7.17
Participation
  acceptable unequal, 12.18–19
  equal, 4.2, 5.9, 5.11, 6.13, 6.21
  group work, 6.4
  simultaneous interaction, 12.21
  structures, 6.4
  student characteristics affecting, 12.15
  traditional instruction, 6.3
Party, class, 9.13
Peers
  approval from, 4.15
  correction, 4.5
  desire to interact with, 4.16
  low achievers, 3.4
  negative influences, 2.12, 2.14
  pro-academic norms, 16.7
  status among, 4.13, 16.11
  tutoring, 1.4, 4.8–9
Perceived competence, 16.6
Performance, individual accountability and, 12.10, 12.13–14
Personality types, participation and, 12.15
Perspective, other, 1.11, 1.12, 1.15, 1.20, 3.5, 3.7, 6.16, 9.3, 9.16
Physiological stimuli, 4.19
PIES, 5.3, 5.9–12, 12.1–26
  checking for implementation, 8.3
  principles, 4.2
  projects, 13.3–4
  structures and, 6.2
Planning
  reflection, 11.27
  social skills, 5.9, 11.20–27, 11.36
  See also Lesson planning
Points of view, taking other's, 1.11, 1.12, 1.15, 1.20, 3.5, 3.7, 6.16, 9.3, 9.16
Positive correlation
  among outcomes, 12.2–4
  creating, 12.5–6
Positive interdependence, 4.2
  analyzing for, 12.25
  concepts, 5.9–10, 12.2–8
  projects, 13.3
Practice
  guided, 6.3
  procedures, 6.17
Praise, 8.3
  feeling tone, 4.16
  maintaining procedures, 8.11
  reasons for, 1.9–10, 3.6, 16.6–13
  social skills development, 11.4, 11.19
  team, 12.6
  traditional classroom, 4.4
  use of, 11.20
Praiser, 11.10–11
Presentations
  cooperative, 13.1–34
  structures, 6.19

Pride, 9.20, 16.9
Problem solving, 1.12
  class meetings, 9.17–19
  international comparisons, 2.3
  pooled knowledge, 12.6, 12.7
  research, 3.7
Procedures, 6.16–17, 8.9–11
Processing
  after project, 13.15
  information, 6.16, 6.17
  time for, 1.5
Projects
  cooperative, 13.1–34
  sharing, 13.8–15
  social skills, 11.2
  workload distribution, 1.15
Public performance, and accountability, 12.9–10, 12.12–13
Puzzled People, 7.13

Q

Question and Answer, 6.2
Question and answer
  PIES analysis, 12.24–25
  simultaneous management, 8.5
  time for, 6.7–8, 12.17, 12.22
  See also Answers
Question cards, 9.5
Question Commander, 11.10–11
Quiet Captain, 8.17, 11.11–12
Quiet cooperative learning, 1.7
Quiet signal, 8.15

R

Race
  achievement gap, 2.3–4
  college graduation, 2.4
  differential dropouts, 2.4
  heterogeneous teams, 7.4, 7.5
  See also Minorities
Race relations, 2.5–6, 3.4–5, 6.23
Racism, progressive, 3.4–5
Random sampling, 15.7
Random teams, 5.4, 7.11–19
Rap music, 2.13
Reading
  finished signals, 8.9
  international comparisons, 2.3
Reasoning, deductive versus inductive, 5.3
Recorder, 11.10–11
Re-establishing Expectations, 8.23
Reflection, 1.4
  collaborative process, 9.17
  social skills, 5.9, 11.20–27, 11.36
Reflector, 11.10–11
Refusenik, 1.10, 8.21, 8.22, 8.23, 11.10–11, 11.28–29
Reinforcement
  infrequent, 4.3
  social skills, 5.9, 11.5, 11.18–20
Relationship skills, 2.6
Replacement cycle, 6.5–7
Representative assessment, 15.3
Required performance, individual accountability and, 12.10, 12.13–14
Research
  cooperative learning, 3.1–16, 6.5
  four crises, 3.2–6

Resistance
  group grades, 15.10
  team participation, 1.10, 8.21, 8.22, 8.23, 11.10, 11.28–29
  teambuilding overcoming, 11.1
Resource access
  interdependence and, 12.7
  for projects, 13.6
Retention, 1.5
  active engagement, 6.9
  novelty and, 4.12
  See also Memory
Review
  ideas, 1.4
  reflection, 11.27
Rewards, 1.2, 1.9–10
  accountability and, 12.14
  class, 8.5
  class goal, 9.20, 9.21
  competition and, 16.4
  desirability of, 4.2–3
  elitist, 16.5
  extrinsic, 16.4
  frequency of, 4.2–3, 11.19
  helplessness and, 4.15
  immediacy of, 4.2–3, 11.19
  intangible, 1.9, 1.11
  intrinsic, 8.4
  motivation effects, 1.9, 1.11
  peer approval, 4.15
  power of, 4.2–3
  process-based, 4.3
  tangible, 1.9, 1.11, 16.2–5
  team, 8.5, 12.5
Role cards, 11.12
Roles
  assigning for team project, 13.5, 13.6
  interdependence and, 12.7
  keeping students on task, 11.35
  participation, 12.18
  power of, 4.22
  social skills, 5.9, 11.9–13
Rules
  classroom, 9.13
  interdependence and, 12.8
  participation and, 12.17

S

Saboteur, 11.35–36
Safety
  brain-based learning and, 4.9–10, 5.8
  need for, 4.13, 11.32, 12.3
Science, international comparisons, 2.2–3
Scrapbooks, 9.12, 10.14
Seating arrangement, 5.6, 5.8, 7.3, 8.13–14
Security, sense of, 15.7
Segregation, voluntary, 3.4–5
SelectorTools, 8.7
Self-actualization, 4.13
Self-esteem, 16.6
  employability, 2.7
  learning, 3.4
  life success, 2.15
  participation, 12.15
  praise effects on, 1.10
  research, 3.6
  special education students, 1.12
  status and, 16.11
  success boosting, 1.13

Kagan Cooperative Learning • Dr. Spencer Kagan & Miguel Kagan
Kagan Publishing • 1 (800) 933-2667 • www.KaganOnline.com

Author Index

Kagan Cooperative Learning • Dr. Spencer Kagan & Miguel Kagan
Kagan Publishing • 1 (800) 933-2667 • www.KaganOnline.com